The Early Shortwave S

The Early Shortwave Stations

A Broadcasting History Through 1945

JEROME S. BERG

McFarland & Company, Inc., Publishers

Jefferson, North Carolina, and London

LIBRARY OF CONGRESS CATALOGUING-IN-PUBLICATION DATA

Berg, Jerome S., 1943–
The early shortwave stations : a broadcasting history
through 1945 / Jerome S. Berg.
p. cm.
Includes bibliographical references and index.

ISBN 978-0-7864-7411-0
softcover : acid free paper ♾

1. Shortwave radio stations—History.   2. International
broadcasting—History.   I. Title.
TK6557.B47 2013   384.54—dc23   2013025615

BRITISH LIBRARY CATALOGUING DATA ARE AVAILABLE

On the cover: QSL cards (courtesy Committee to Preserve Radio
Verifications and author's collection)

Manufactured in the United States of America

*McFarland & Company, Inc., Publishers
Box 611, Jefferson, North Carolina 28640
www.mcfarlandpub.com*

To Dr. Adrian M. Peterson,
keen explorer of long-forgotten corners
of the shortwave world,
and to P.V.

Contents

Preface

This is the fourth, and final, volume in the series on the history of shortwave listening and shortwave broadcasting that I have written and that has been published by McFarland.

The first book, *On the Short Waves, 1923–1945: Broadcast Listening in the Pioneer Days of Radio,* covered shortwave listening and shortwave broadcasting during the early years of the medium, and included some basic information about the stations. The story was brought up to mid–2008 in the second and third books, *Listening on the Short Waves, 1945 to Today,* which was about the shortwave listening culture, and *Broadcasting on the Short Waves, 1945 to Today,* a year-by-year account of the stations that were on the air from World War II to the time of publication.

The station information in *Broadcasting* was much more comprehensive than that in *On the Short Waves.* In this new volume I have returned to the years 1923 to 1945 and applied the year-by-year approach of *Broadcasting* to that early period. Together, the two volumes present as full an account as there is of the shortwave broadcasting stations that were heard in the United States for nearly the entire period of the medium's existence. All the books have been written from an American perspective.

As with my earlier books, this one presupposes an understanding of the basics of shortwave. Although it touches on a few tangential topics where necessary—mediumwave, FM, commercial shortwave, amateur radio, radio regulation, etc.—the focus is on the stations. For a fuller discussion of the clubs, literature, QSL practices, etc. of the period, the reader should consult *On the Short Waves.* Much has been written on the important topic of international radio propaganda during World War II, and the content of the various propaganda broadcasts. Although the provenance and the transmission activities of the propaganda stations, official and "clandestine," is addressed in this volume, and the content of their broadcasts covered in a general way, a detailed examination of wartime propaganda techniques must be left to others.

I have been generous with notes, in large part for the benefit of those who would like to do further research. I have relied principally on the popular and professional literature of the time, including books, magazines and journals, plus some later works. The considerable coverage of shortwave in *The New York Times* was helpful, as were some web materials (links were correct as of August 6, 2013). However, it is mainly print materials on shortwave broadcasting, of which I have been a collector for more than 25 years, on which I rely. In addition, I hope that more than a half century of shortwave listening has contributed to my understanding of the medium at ground level, and to a correct telling of the story.

In this volume, as in the others, I use the technical conventions of the day — kc., mc. and kw. instead of kHz., MHz. and kW. Time is shown in Eastern Standard Time (Eastern War Time for the war years), rather than Greenwich Mean Time (today's UTC), because that was the uniform practice in early American radio publications, which were hesitant to embrace GMT and risk inconveniencing readers. I have however, adopted the 24-hour clock in place of the 12-hour, A.M.-P.M. system that was in common usage in early radio literature. Place names and spellings also follow the conventions of the time. Where good authorship demanded I have changed some abbreviations, made occasional small changes in punctuation, case and spelling, and converted megacycles to kilocycles or vice versa, with no change in meaning or emphasis. And references to "commercial" stations should be read in context. They usually mean point-to-point transmissions for hire, not broadcasting supported by advertisements.

Precision on some details of shortwave history is complicated by sometimes-conflicting accounts, even in reportage close to the events. I have tried to reconcile facts where possible, or else note the inconsistencies. As to wavelength vs. frequency, generally I have used kilocycles rather than meters when referring to specific channels, even where the source material uses the latter (which was common in the twenties). However, where historic references to meters appear to have been approximations only — often the case in early reports from listeners, who lacked the equipment for precise measurement — I have retained the wavelength references.

During the years in question, stations changed hours and frequency constantly, and while I have reported some of the changes to help illustrate the state of the bands at the time, these make up but a tiny portion of the ebb and flow of shortwave frequency changes that occurred over the years. Capturing all or even most of them would be impossible.

In the preparation of my books about shortwave's post-war years I was assisted by a legion of friends and correspondents who were able to fill in blanks and lend perspective on many issues. This volume was a more solitary affair, since most of those with first-hand knowledge have themselves become part of history. Happily, the fruits of many DX careers have survived in the QSL collections gathered over the last quarter century by the Committee to Preserve Radio Verifications, which I chair, and whose home is the Library of American Broadcasting at the University of Maryland. Many of the graphics are from these collections. My thanks to the LAB's key men, Chuck Howell and Michael Henry, for their usual cooperation in making this material available.

Special thanks are again due the staff of the Interlibrary Loan Department of Cary Memorial Library in Lexington, Massachusetts, whose patience and attentiveness to my requests has been indispensable to my research. I could not have written this book without them. I extend appreciation as well to the rights owners who have agreed to the use of their works. If I have overlooked any, it is entirely inadvertent.

And once again I say thanks to my wife, Ruth, who has accepted my pronouncement that this is the last of my big shortwave projects with knowing skepticism, and who I know will understand if it turns out I was wrong.

Glossary

AIR . . . . All India Radio
ARRL . . . . American Radio Relay League
AT&T . . . . American Telephone & Telegraph Co.
AWA . . . . Amalgamated Wireless (Australasia) Ltd.
BBC . . . . British Broadcasting Company, British Broadcasting Corporation
C&W . . . . Cable & Wireless Ltd.
CBC . . . . Canadian Broadcasting Corporation
CIAA . . . . Coordinator of Inter-American Affairs
COI . . . . Coordinator of Information
DX, DXing . . . . distance, listening to distant stations
EST, EWT . . . . Eastern Standard Time, Eastern War Time
FIS . . . . Foreign Information Service
FRC . . . . Federal Radio Commission
HF . . . . high frequency (3–30 MHz.)
IDA . . . . International DXers Alliance
ISWC . . . . International Short Wave Club
kc. . . . . kilocycle(s)
kw. . . . . kilowatt(s)
m. . . . . meters
mc. . . . . megacycle(s)
NHK . . . . Nippon Hoso Kyokai [Japan]
NNRC . . . . Newark News Radio Club
OWI . . . . Office of War Information
PTT . . . . Post, Telephone & Telegraph
QRM . . . . interference
QSL . . . . verification of reception
QST . . . . Journal of the American Radio Relay League
RADEX . . . . Radio Index magazine
SWL . . . . shortwave listener
TRF . . . . tuned radio frequency
VOA . . . . Voice of America
"Zeesen" . . . . Deutscher Kurzwellensender

1

Prelude to Shortwave

Two years ago the only interpretation of the word "receiver" would have been a man appointed by the courts to take over a bankrupt firm. —*Radio Broadcast, May 1922*[1]

It was a short 17 years between the Christmas and New Year's season of 1906, when Reginald Fessenden, operating on a frequency probably around 50–80 kc., sent the first voice transmission over a continuous wave radio transmitter,[2] and 1923, when Frank Conrad commenced shortwave broadcasting over KDKA. Much had happened in the interim, and it is illustrative of the rapid advance of radio that Conrad's vacuum tube technology was bottomed on principles entirely different from Fessenden's historic alternator-based transmissions.

There were two events that overshadowed all others in the technological development of radio. One was Marconi's historic "S" transmission from Poldhu, England, to St. John's, Newfoundland, on December 12, 1901. Although doubts have been expressed as to whether the event actually occurred (in daylight on a spark-generated "broadband" frequency probably centered around 800 kc.),[3] Marconi's work clearly established "Hertzian waves," rather than induction or light, as the conceptual anchor for the future development of wireless.[4]

The other event was Lee De Forest's 1906 modification of the two-element Fleming Valve. Adding a grid to control the flow of electrons, he produced a vacuum tube whose properties of amplification and oscillation, when fully understood in later years, would greatly simplify both the production of the continuous waves needed for voice transmission and the quality of the resulting signal. He called the three-element tube the audion.

These events fundamentally shaped the development of the three branches of radio that were their lucky beneficiaries— amateur radio, two-way, or "point-to-point," transmission (commonly referred to later as utility stations), and broadcasting. It was the last, called "radiophone," which, for a while, made every man a DXer.

The Amateurs

Radio's early development is the story of experimenters who were fascinated by the science, or enthralled at the magic of hearing sounds through the ether from places to which they were otherwise unconnected, or both. It included all the founding fathers of radio, most of whom hoped as well to profit from their work. For the larger group, however, the reward was mainly in the fun of it.

There was no "first" amateur.[5] The amateurs as an identifiable group date back to around 1906. Their numbers started to grow in 1908 when crystal detectors came into use. Clubs began forming in 1909. The experimenters were motivated in part by the sheer freedom, and the challenge, of the radio art. Although rummaging through the stock of the growing number of parts stores, such as Hugo Gernsback's Electro-Importing Company in New York City, was the dream of every experimenter, rudimentary equipment could be constructed from commonly available materials if necessary. Some amateurs built impressive stations. For many years there were no laws to constrain either their imagination or their operation. An early amateur radio historian, Clinton B. DeSoto, offered this paean:

> The story of amateur radio is the story of an adventurous band of free spirits, in present times [1936] more than 60,000 strong, scattered over the entire globe in every continent and every country, who hold communication far up in the empyrean spaces over roaring ocean and untracked land. It is the story of men and boys, eminent scientists and young lads in school — and women and girls as well — who at the touch of a key or soft word spoken into a microphone can leap around the world; who have wiped out for all time the age-old barriers of race and language and distance. ¶It is the story of a band of good fellows, happy, convivial, carefree, playing the game for the very love of it; but underneath all that carrying on with the deep earnestness of those who have successfully pierced the veil of the unknown and garnered the secrets of science.[6]

Sentimentalism aside, there is no doubt that much of shortwave's germination took place in the amateur ranks.

The amateurs' success was largely an accident of history. Although the primitive nature of early equipment meant that frequency was usually more a matter of chance than design, in general the amateurs operated around 300–1200 kc., believing, as did everyone in those days, that the low frequencies (high wavelengths) were the prime channels for radio communication.

The Radio Act of 1912 was America's first general-purpose radio law. Although its licensing provisions were notoriously weak, for the first time all non-governmental stations, including the amateurs, needed an operating license from the Secretary of Commerce and Labor.[7] The amateurs had been transmitting at will, dominating the airwaves, and not always respecting the needs of the commercial and military stations whose signals they sometimes outclassed. There was little leadership in their ranks, and they had few friends in Congress. Although they managed to avoid a proposed requirement for the licensing of receiving stations — something that would become common in many other countries — the 1912 act dealt them what was at the time thought a near-fatal blow. It prohibited them from operating on any wavelength above 200 meters without special authorization,[8] and it limited their power to 1 kw. or less. This meant that most amateurs could operate only on a frequency of 1500 kc. or higher.

Nor were the amateurs free to roam from frequency to frequency above 1500 kc. A Department of Commerce license authorized the holder to operate on the specified channel of exactly 1500 kc., and sometimes on one or more other specified channels up to 2.0 mc. This practice was relaxed in 1923 when the 1.5–2 mc. range was opened to general amateur use without specification of frequency on the license.[9] Special authorization was still needed to go above 2.0 mc. In the parlance of the day, the range from 1.5 to 2.0 mc., or 150–200 meters, was referred to as "shortwave." Although the radio spectrum above 1.5 mc., including all of what we think of today as shortwave (up to 30 mc.), would eventually be found to be huge, in 1912 it was almost totally unknown and widely believed of little use. The near universal view was that the longer the wavelength, i.e. the lower the frequency, the better. To the hams of 1912, it looked like they had survived extinction but been moved to the desert.

Compliance with the 1912 law was grudging, and enforcement lax. One observer noted that in reality, as late as 1920, 90 percent of the hams were still operating between 800 and 1200 kc.[10] By mid–1914, some 5,000 licenses had been issued, representing probably half the number of transmitting amateurs. It was a period of technical advancement, and growing amateur interest in the possibilities of long-distance communication. The many new magazines devoted to radio highlighted the amateurs and gave recognition to their operations and accomplishments. With the commitment to good practice made by the newly-formed American Radio Relay League (so named in recognition of the inter-station message relaying that had become popular), the amateurs slowly fell into line.

Amateur operators, along with most other non-governmental stations, were ordered off the air during World War I. But their operating skills were vitally needed in the war effort, and many joined the military, where the amateur fraternity gained new respectability. When they returned to the air at the end of 1919, radio was advancing. Vacuum tubes were slowly becoming available, the move from spark to continuous wave was underway, and new receiver circuitry was just around the corner. Returning radio doughboys were anxious to put their military radio experience to work at home.

Soon broadcasting would take off, exposing ordinary, non-technical people to the thrill of radio, and also producing clashes between ordinary listeners and hams, who were always viewed as the source of interference to broadcast signals, whether true in individual cases or not.[11] In 1922, the ARRL urged that, in places where the airwaves were congested, hams voluntarily adopt "quiet hours," staying off the air from 7:00 to 10:30 P.M. (the hours varied) and on Sunday mornings in order to facilitate better broadcast reception.[12] This was the ARRL's so-called "Rochester plan."[13] Many hams adhered to it, but others did not until the Department of Commerce made quiet hours mandatory in June 1923. (In 1928, the Federal Radio Commission limited quiet hours to cases where there was actual interference.)

By mid–1921 there were nearly 11,000 licensed amateur radio operators in the United States, and they were setting distance records in one-way transmission and reception — coast to coast, transatlantic (1921)[14] and transpacific (1922).[15] The first two-way transatlantic amateur contacts took place in November 1923, and during the following year international contacts became more frequent. New transcontinental relay records were also achieved.

A point worth noting is the definitive turn of amateur radio in favor of the transmitting amateur to the exclusion of fellow radio travelers who had been considered part of the amateur fraternity even though their main interest was in listening rather than transmitting. This change played out on the pages of the ARRL monthly journal, *QST*. Broadcasting was in full flower, and had attracted new listening fans as moths to a flame. Many were interested in radio's DX aspects, a bent they shared with the amateurs, and some of these would gravitate toward shortwave broadcast DXing as broadcasters started using shortwave. Their interest did not extend to two-way communication, however, nor, for the most part, to the finer technical points of radio.

The hams did not know what to do with these "BCLs," or broadcast listeners, as they were called. With the goal of accommodating them, or better educating them about ham radio, or perhaps co-opting them (BCL complaints about amateur interference were on the increase), *QST* inaugurated a column called "With Our Radiophone Listeners" (at first called "With the Radiophone Folks"). It began in December 1921 and it covered broadcasting and other types of voice transmissions, as opposed to amateur radio. But it never amounted to more than a few pages, and the September 1922 column was the last, a victim of the ARRL's decision to define its mission as support of the transmitting amateur rather than the larger body of radio enthusiasts. This turn also manifested itself in the cover design of *QST*. For most months starting in May 1921 the cover expressed the magazine's devotion to "Citizen Radio" in addition to the usual reference to the "Wireless Amateur" or "Amateur Radio." References to "Citizen Radio" were dropped after the August 1922 issue.

"With the Radiophone Folks"

This is the humble beginning of a department which will be devoted to the interests of that constantly-increasing army of Citizen Wireless amateurs who are primarily interested in the reception of radiophone broadcasts.

First and foremost we will endeavor to present here the schedules of the better class of broadcasting stations. The few we list this month by no means cover the field. Suggestions from readers as to where more information on such broadcasts can be obtained will be appreciated.

And then we want to tell in this department of the novel and interesting features of coming affairs and of those of the past month as well, and to present non-technical articles that will be of help in this line of work. Suggestions and ideas will be welcomed.

(A word to the brass-pounding old A.R.R.L. gang: You must know a dozen friends who are interested in receiving radiophones. This is a department for them. Please tell them about it; they will need QST and we want them as members.)

QST
December 1921[16]

For decades, hams would view the listening DXer as a ham in waiting. The situation would change in later years as hams expanded their own horizons beyond the amateur bands.

Utility Stations

Radio telegraphy — the ability to communicate by wireless between two points using Morse code — long preceded voice transmission. The "wireless telegraph" was thought of as just that: a telegraph without wires. Later, when voice became practical, it too was seen as a branch of an existing technology, the telephone, hence the common reference to the "radiotelephone." The concept of broadcasting, or transmitting voice and music to be picked up and enjoyed by anyone, had hardly been thought of.

Before broadcasting, early wireless found two homes besides the amateurs and the experimenters: commercial firms, and the U.S. Navy.

THE NAVY

The U.S. Navy was an essential part of the early development of radio. Marconi had demonstrated wireless to the navy off the coast of New Jersey immediately after his famous coverage of the 1899 America's Cup Race (and before the "S" transmission). Notwithstanding the interference that resulted when two stations were transmitting at the same time, the navy sought to buy Marconi's equipment. However, consistent with what would become company policy, Marconi was willing only to lease it. The navy declined, and continued its investigation of the new technology. In 1903 and 1904 it established the first naval ship and shore installations. The equipment was mostly of German manufacture (Slaby-Arco). In later years the navy would use the equipment of numerous manufacturers. By 1906, 57 ships and 39 shore stations, including stations in the Caribbean and the Pacific, had been equipped. By 1916 the numbers had grown to 315 and 119 respectively.

During this period early spark transmitters were gradually replaced by better-performing arc units, which produced less interference. De Forest equipped the U.S. Navy's "Great

White Fleet" with arc equipment for its 1907–08 cruise around the world, giving the ships a rudimentary capability for voice transmission. (In an interesting historical footnote, the USS *Ohio* on many occasions played phonograph music to other ships of the fleet and to port receivers.) The time allotted for the installation of the arc transmitters had been short, however, and deficient construction and truncated training yielded poor results and slowed the navy's interest in early voice transmission.

The navy first tested vacuum tube equipment in 1913. It came into broader use during World War I when the government, having closed nearly all private stations and assumed liability for patent infringements in equipment sold to the United States, was the main force in radio development. It was the vacuum tube that made relatively reliable voice communication possible.

At first all navy stations operated around 938 kc., but soon the ships were in the 300–500 kc. band and the shore stations were assigned various channels down to 111 kc. Frequencies dropped even further as arc transmitters became more prevalent, with the ships operating at 75–150 kc. and the shore stations at 17.5–75 kc. Power was generally between 500 watts and 10 kw. aboard ship, 35 kw. on shore. In 1912 the navy set up a high power (100 kw.) "headquarters" spark transmitter, the U.S. Naval Radio Station in Arlington, Virginia known as NAA. Widely heard, it usually operated on 120 kc. A better-performing 30 kw. arc unit followed, and tests with tube-type transmitters were conducted from Arlington starting in 1915.

It was the war that proved the indispensability of radio to the military, and the technological advancements that were possible if resources could be marshaled and patent conflicts overcome. Although efforts to give the government a monopoly over all commercial radio operations after the war ultimately failed, in the post-war years the navy became de facto the voice of the United States government on matters pertaining to radio, a role it relished for the stated reason of more effectively mitigating interference from amateur and commercial stations. The required wartime closure of nearly all amateur stations, and the government takeover of commercial ones, helped the navy in this regard. Its credibility was enhanced when it set up its own radio research department, which was established because of dissatisfaction with available commercial equipment and the navy's limited capability to modify it. Two naval radio laboratories, together with a manufacturing capability to complement that of the commercial companies, were set up between 1908 and 1918. In 1923 they became the Radio Division of the new U.S. Naval Research Laboratory.

One of the Laboratory's early missions was to explore the frequency spectrum between 1500 kc. and 3 mc. In this there was much organized cooperation between the navy and the amateurs. The use of HF in the navy progressed throughout the decade of the twenties.

An early navy flirtation with broadcasting were the transmissions of the Naval Aircraft Radio Laboratory, Washington, D.C. The Laboratory began carrying broadcast programming in 1920 using the call letters NSF and NOF. The frequency was 858 kc., and within a year the station had listeners in 28 states. The primary purpose of the effort was to attract amateurs and listeners for the study of propagation and signal reflection that would eventually lead to radar. The programs consisted of music, coverage of important events, talks by national leaders (including the President), lectures by various experts, and even the "re-radiation," as it was called, of various kinds of signals received from Europe over the air or by wire.[17] By the end of 1922 this popular service had become a distraction from the Laboratory's main work and the broadcasts were transferred to NAA, which subsequently became the first station to provide regular weather reports in voice (on 423 kc.).

During the first few years of the 1920s there was much criticism of the navy for interference with the public's reception of the then-new broadcasting stations. The interference was caused mainly by legacy arc transmitters which were still in service. It soon became academic, however, as the outmoded arcs were retired and the development of shortwave led to the military's withdrawal from the lower frequencies.

COMMERCIAL WIRELESS

The business of commercial wireless consisted of sending messages in Morse code between two points. Because users paid for the service, it offered inventors and experimenters the possibility of financial reward, although this was more illusory than real until 1912 when more ships were required to carry wireless equipment. With the proliferation of wireless operating companies came frauds and swindles, usually by unscrupulous financiers, occasionally with the approbation of the experimenters themselves who were, however, sometimes victimized as much as the investors. Government indictments in 1911 and 1912 brought an end to most of the unsavory practices.

Wireless Towers at Naval Radio Station, Radio, Va., near Washington. D. C.

The heart of commercial wireless was ship-to-shore traffic. In the early years this usually took place around 500 kc., below today's standard broadcast band (which, of course, did not exist as such at the time). There were about 130 commercial land stations in 1910, a number that dropped by more than half as transmission range improved and fewer shore stations were needed. The number of ships equipped with wireless, around 300 at the start of 1912, grew rapidly thereafter as a result of the sinking of the *Titanic,* where radio was instrumental in saving lives, and the passage of the Radio Act of 1912, which expanded the number of ships required to have wireless and also mandated a 24-hour radio watch. By 1920 over 2,000 ships were equipped.

When it was commissioned, NAA, the U.S. Naval Radio Station at Fort Myer (Arlington), Virginia, had three massive towers, one 600 feet tall, the others 450 feet. NAA cost approximately $250,000. Later the towers were deemed a danger to civilian aircraft and were removed in 1941.

Untuned spark gap transmitters were the rule during the first few years of the century, giving way to "tuned" sparks by 1908, followed by the much better performing arc transmitters, which were capable of producing continuous waves. The situation remained largely unchanged through the war years. Receivers, designed around a succession of different kinds of detectors, were primitive, and De Forest's audion remained largely undeveloped until around 1913, in large part because of patent conflicts between De Forest and Fleming.

Many of the commercial wireless companies' transmitters were short range, or had been built mainly as an excuse to sell stock. By 1919 there were only a handful of companies left. The Marconi Wireless Telegraph Company of America was by far the largest, its status having been enhanced as a result of the takeover in 1912, following a patent infringement suit, of the considerable facilities of the United Wireless Telegraph Company. The navy had taken over most of Marconi's operating business during the war.

After the war, with Marconi expecting the return of its stations, concern developed in the United States over the foreign ownership of most of the American commercial wireless system, American Marconi being mostly owned by its British parent, Marconi's Wireless Telegraph Company Ltd. That Britain was also the leader in worldwide telegraph systems did not help, as America saw it, nor did Marconi's negotiations with General Electric for an exclusive agreement to purchase Alexanderson alternators, by then a strategic asset in international communications. The situation was exacerbated by an anti-competitive, confrontational style that had long typified American Marconi's dealings on the patent and regulatory fronts.

These fires were stoked by the navy, which had its eye on control of all radio in the country. Wiser heads ultimately prevailed, but America's nationalistic interests, pushed hard albeit seemingly unofficially by the navy, were served when in 1920 the British interest in American Marconi was purchased by General Electric, American Marconi was dissolved, and all its business was transferred to the Radio Corporation of America, a new company created expressly for the purpose of establishing a national, American–owned capability in commercial communications. British Marconi could then procure its alternators like anyone else. American Marconi senior staff transferred to RCA, and this included David Sarnoff, who became RCA's commercial manager and eventually it's president. The navy turned over to RCA the Marconi facilities whose control it had assumed during the war. These included the stations at New Brunswick and Tuckerton, New Jersey; Marion, Massachusetts; Bolinas, California; and Kahuku and Koko Head, Hawaii, together with associated receiving sites.

During the war, radio research had benefitted from the government-induced patent pooling among patent holders. Patent rights reverted to their owners after the war, but many of the developmental constraints that were sure to follow were averted through cross-licensing agreements among RCA, GE, AT&T, Westinghouse and several other companies. Under these agreements, the way would now be open for General Electric and Westinghouse to manufacture radio receivers; for RCA to sell them, and also operate the communications business previously run by American Marconi; and for AT&T to manufacture transmitters. In many ways the arrangement would mirror the efficiencies of radio development during the wartime years, when radio was under the control of the navy. With the introduction of corporate control, and the road to profits cleared, big business replaced the inventor-entrepreneur as the dominant force in the development of radio.

RCA soon replaced the Marconi spark transmitters with units powered by GE-manufactured Alexanderson alternators. It was the behemoth Alexanderson alternator that would permit the establishment of reliable long distance communication from the RCA stations. Most were 200 kw. transmitters operating at very low frequencies such as 18–25 kc. The alternator era was relatively short-lived, however; virtually all the low frequency alternators would be replaced by vacuum tube transmitters operating on shortwave. (Some of the alternators were recommissioned for VLF communication with submarines during World War II.)

Although seemingly unconnected except by way of the technology shared by all branches of radio, the development of commercial wireless impacted early shortwave broadcasting in two important ways. First, although the heart of shortwave broadcasting was the transmission of broadcast programming, for many years the primary use of the short waves was not to reach listeners directly but to carry program material over long distances for pickup and rebroadcast by a local non-shortwave station in the listener's locale. This was not unlike commercial point-to-point transmission. When, in 1929, the Federal Radio Commission recognized shortwave broadcasting as a distinct service, with dedicated frequencies, it called it experimental relay broadcasting and required licensees to have arranged for the rebroadcast of their signals by other stations on standard, non-shortwave frequencies.

Second, RCA's commercial station on Long Island, known as Radio Central from its inauguration on November 5, 1921, played an important part in early shortwave broadcasting. It came into service just as the exploration of the long-distance properties of shortwave was beginning. The 6,400-acre Radio Central transmitter site was at Rocky Point, the 2,000-acre receiver site at Riverhead. The original plan called for twelve 200 kw. longwave transmitters powered by Alexanderson alternators, each transmitter connected to a 1½ mile long, 400-foot tall antenna, the antennas arranged in a hub-and-spoke pattern.[18] Alternator technology was soon to become obsolete, however, and had RCA lacked the foresight to forgo all but two of the transmitters, the project might have turned into a gigantic white elephant instead of the jewel in the crown of RCA's worldwide communication system.

While not as well known as RCA's manufacturing and broadcasting divisions (the latter being NBC), Radio Central, with its extensive laboratory facilities, became home to a host of technological advancements in propagation, transmitters and antennas, and high speed communication experiments of all sorts, including single sideband and Harold H. Beverage's development of diversity reception and the famous antenna that bears his name.[19] Because RCA routinely leased its telecommunication services to others, Radio Central also provided an early profit center when the company needed one. More importantly, it made the United States the leader in international communications.

Radio Central began experimenting with shortwave in 1923. Regular use of the new medium started the following year and RCA made a lucky bet by investing in it heavily. By 1928, the two original Rocky Point longwave transmitters, WQK and WSS, were still in operation. However, the original plan for ten more longwave transmitters had been dropped. Now there were six shortwave transmitters, two of 40 kw. — 2XT and WTT — and four of 20 kw. — WBU, WIK, WQO and WLL. Other transmitters would come in and out of service over the years. At Riverhead there were 17 longwave receivers and 24 shortwave receivers, all of 13-tube design.[20]

The results in terms of cost, range, number of channels, and reduced interference gave shortwave communication the kind of commercial credibility it could not gain from the amateurs alone, and an edge over commercial cable traffic, which had declined in volume and become expensive. In addition to its commercial work, Radio Central became the relay vehicle for much of the international broadcast programming received by, or sent from, broadcast stations in the United States. Although to listeners it may have seemed that local broadcast stations relaying programs of overseas stations were receiving the programs direct by shortwave, in fact many of the broadcasts were received through Radio Central, which served as the essential link between the originating transmitter and the intended rebroadcaster.[21]

Shortwave remained king at Radio Central until the 1960s and 1970s, when new tech-

Construction of RCA's Radio Central transmitting facility at Rocky Point, Long Island, began in 1920. Occupying ten square miles — big enough for longwave antennas — the installation was soon reprogrammed for shortwave. The receiving station was in Riverhead.

nologies made the Radio Central personnel feel, as one observer put it, "like blacksmiths watching the first automobiles coming down the road."[22]

Broadcasting[23]

The broadcasting of news and entertainment to a general, non-technical audience was not something that appeared full blown one day. It developed over time. Its kernel was to be found among those experimenters who discovered that a common device close at hand, the phonograph, could serve as a convenient, hands-free source of modulation while they were fiddling with their transmitters. Add some talking and you had broadcasting.

KDKA, which began operating on November 2, 1920, with its famous 8:00 P.M. broadcast of the Harding-Cox presidential election results, is generally accepted as the oldest broadcasting station still on the air, that is, the one that has been in longest continuous operation with regularly scheduled programming. It is generally reported that its predecessor station, Frank Conrad's 8XK, commenced some voice and music broadcasts in October 1919, although there is evidence that they began even earlier.[24] However, there were many other experimental stations, mostly short-lived, that carried voice and music "programs" with varying degrees of regularity, some well before Frank Conrad and KDKA.

Lee De Forest made occasional experimental transmissions of opera music as early as 1907,[25] and these became more regular over his Bronx station, 2XG, starting in 1916. He moved to San Francisco in April 1920 and operated from there as 6XC (later KZY).[26] Charles "Doc" Herrold in San Jose, California conducted voice and music tests daily starting in 1909, and he was broadcasting scheduled programs as early as 1912. As with all but the few stations that were allowed to operate for various experimental purposes, Herrold was off the air during the war years. He resumed broadcasting as 6XF early in 1920, and the station became KQW in December 1921 (KCBS in 1949).

University of Wisconsin station 9XM was on the air with intermittent voice broadcasts and extensive Morse transmissions to farm communities as early as 1917. The voice transmissions were stepped up in 1919, and regularly scheduled voice broadcasts began on January 3, 1921. (The station was permitted to operate during the war, albeit for non-broadcast purposes.) 9XM became WHA in 1922. Scripps bought amateur station 8MK and put it on the air to carry *Detroit News* reports of the Michigan primaries on August 20, 1920. The station was licensed to a subsidiary of Lee De Forest's company until 1921, when the newspaper received a license in its own name. The call letters, WBL, were changed to WWJ the following year. Western Electric ran experimental stations 2XB in New York City and 2XJ in Deal Beach, New Jersey, and part of their fare in 1920 was speech and music.

Similar events were occurring in other countries. PCGG in Holland began test broadcasts in August 1919. Canadian Marconi station XWA in Montreal, predecessor to CFCF, commenced experimental operation in December of the same year, and regular broadcasts began in May 1920. The well-promoted half-hour broadcast of Australian opera prima donna Dame Nellie Melba, originating from the Marconi station in Chelmsford, England on June 15, 1920, was heard as far distant as 1,500 miles.

There were many other "broadcasters." Often they were ham operators transmitting voice and music programming, sometimes impromptu, but sometimes on a scheduled basis. These practices continued until they were prohibited at the start of 1922.[27] By mid–1920, the Bureau of Standards of the Department of Commerce was offering Friday evening concerts on frequencies variously reported as 500 or 600 kc., and there was also some experimental military broadcasting during the war. David Sarnoff had promoted the concept of the home radio receiver, or "radio music box," within American Marconi as early as 1915 or 1916.[28]

The ragged start to the broadcasting era was reflected in the licensing practices of the day. The Radio Division of the Bureau of Navigation of the Department of Commerce had many license classifications, but none for broadcasting, an activity which had not been thought of when the Radio Act of 1912 was passed. Broadcasting was just another function of radio that developed over time. Because it was not specifically prohibited under the various license categories, stations "broadcast" under whatever license they had — experimental (signified by "X" calls, e.g. 8XK), limited commercial, technical and training school, amateur, etc. Broadcasting as a distinct, licensable activity was first recognized at the end of 1921, but even then it was not given its own license classification; it was lumped into the limited commercial group. Broadcaster licensees were authorized to operate on the broadcasting wavelength assigned to them (see below) and given the W or K call letters of a commercial station. The KDKA license was a limited commercial license. The call letters were simply the next ones on the list.

Operators could hold more than one license, and thus a ham might be heard contacting other hams under his amateur license, and at other times broadcasting music under a limited commercial license. The Department of Commerce took a narrow view of what constituted broadcasting, and in 1923 reminded broadcasters that acknowledging letters from individual listeners over the air as part of a broadcast station "club" was point-to-point transmission and not broadcasting, and that violators were subject to license suspension or revocation.[29] Broadcasters finally received their own license classification in 1927 when the Federal Radio Commission was established.

With a few temporary exceptions, all stations were assigned to operate on the general "entertainment" channel of 360 meters (833 kc.), or a second wavelength, 485 meters (619

JOS. J. PFAFFENZELLER
53 FIELDING STREET
NEW BEDFORD, MASS.
U. S. A.

May 13, 1924

Gentlemen: *Sta. I-XAL*

Your Radio Program of _Midnight - Saturday_

was received and greatly enjoyed.

The Orchestra, Vocalists and particularly the duet of Accordian & Banjo - not omitting Capt. Sistare - all of the N.B Yacht Club

were exceptionally pleasing.

Come again

Sincerely yours,

Jos. J. Pfaffenzeller

Received on a Paragon RD-5 and Magnavox Loud Speaker.

Reception - exceptionally good - Loud Speaker worked fine on Detector tube alone.

W. B. B. G.
"The Voice from Cape Cod"

Mattapoisett, Mass.

This is to acknowledge receipt of your communication and to express our sincere thanks for same.

This station transmits on 240 meters. Its power is now 250 watts. The antenna meter reads 5 amperes. The antenna is a steel tower 120 feet high, with six wires.

The station is entirely operated on 2,400 volts of Jenness Willard Storage Batteries.

The owner and operator of this station is the manager of the Radio Department of Slocum and Kilburn in New Bedford, Mass.

Very truly yours,

Irving Vermilya

Sometimes referred to as the nation's "No. 1 Ham," Irving Vermilya operated from Massachusetts under multiple licenses. His ham call was 1ZE. *Top:* A card from a listener who, in 1923, heard Vermilya's test transmission to Europe using his "special land station" call letters, 1XAL (no relation to WRUL–predecessor W1XAL). *Bottom:* Vermilya's broadcast station was WBBG. This card is from 1924.

kc.), which was more carefully regulated and restricted to market and weather reports. Notwithstanding that most stations operated for but a few hours a day and a few days a week, there was major interference among stations in many locales, outright bedlam in some. In metropolitan areas, stations reluctantly agreed to time sharing. A third channel, 400 meters (750 kc.), which was reserved for "larger" or "better" stations, was added in 1922. Interference got worse as receivers improved and became more sensitive to signals received by way of nighttime skywave propagation. As a result, in 1923 a general broadcast band extending from 550 to 1350 kc. was established, with stations assigned to one of the many channels within it, with 10 kc. spacing, as is the case today. It was extended to 1500 kc. in 1924.

---

360 vs. 485 meters

That license [WHAS], dated July 13, 1922, specified "360 meters for broadcasting music and like matter; 485 meters for broadcasting weather reports...." ¶What logic gave rise to that mandate to tune a transmitter suddenly from its normal operation of 360 meters to 485 for the weather reports, and then quickly back to 360 for the continuance of a program, has never been explained and it still remains one of the most profound [Department of Commerce] enigmas. Practically none but farmers yearned passionately for news of tomorrow's weather, and crystal sets were incapable of serving distant areas. There were a few, though quite exceptional, instances of longer range receivers—using earphones, of course. These were homemade affairs built from published diagrams and strung out from mother's parlor table to the kitchen, but so imperfect and confusing to tune that usually we had sent the forecast on 485, and were back again on 360, before the tyro had emerged from his wilderness of tangled wires, knobs, rheostats and other gadgets. [F]or fifteen years I have tried to discover the father of [the 360/485 rule]. None will confess.

Credo Fitch Harris
Microphone Memoirs, 1937[30]

During the first two decades of the century, listening to stations of any kind was an activity that was largely reserved to the experimenters. They were the audience, for until the twenties there were no receivers for an ordinary person to buy. This was due in part to the state of the technology, and in part to ongoing patent disputes that made manufacturing difficult. So equipment had to be home constructed. However, even when straightforward crystal detectors became known and radio "hookup" diagrams began appearing in newspapers, receiver construction was not for everyone. Also, most of what could be heard on the air was in Morse code, and one had to be motivated to learn the code. The wartime ban on transmitting and receiving also served to retard public enthusiasm for radio. But there were always some who would do whatever it took to capture whatever was waiting in the ether.[31]

After a slow start in 1921, the broadcasting boom took off. There were over 500 stations licensed by the end of 1922, although many licensees never made it to the air, or quickly exhausted their finances and were never heard from again. Self-contained consumer broadcast receivers began appearing (Hugo Gernsback suggested calling them "radiotrolas," after Victrolas[32]). The number of American homes with radio receivers, home-built or commercial, was estimated to have increased from 60,000 at the start of 1922 to a million and a half a year later, and this notwithstanding the need for headsets and external antennas, the inadequacy of instructions that accompanied commercial sets, and the inconvenience of charging batteries and cleaning up after battery acid spills (A.C. radios did not arrive until the mid–1920s). As *Radio Broadcast* observed in its first issue (May 1922):

The rate of increase in the number of people who spend at least a part of their evening in listening is almost incomprehensible. To those who have recently tried to purchase receiving equipment, some idea of this increase has undoubtedly occurred, as they stood perhaps in the fourth or fifth row at the radio counter waiting their turn only to be told when they finally reached the counter that they might place an order and it would be filled when possible.... In the ferry boat and in the subway trains we hear of wavelengths, frequencies, capacities, tubes, amplifiers, etc. in connection with strange combinations of letters — KYY, KDKA, and what not.[33]

Broadcast radio was indeed the talk of the town. Some of the discussion was theoretical, having to do with radio's potential to impact society and affect international relations. Other subjects, such as how radio was to be financed, and how money could be made in radio sales and service, were more practical. Programming was under constant scrutiny, with every category — sports, news, religion, politics, music, women's programs, farm broadcasts, etc. — part of a search for the best broadcasting technique. At first stations were owned by companies involved in radio manufacturing and sales, but soon everyone had gotten into the act — colleges, newspapers, department stores, hotels, churches, banks, municipalities, organizations of every kind, and just about anyone with either a big ego or something to sell. And at least for a few years, radio exhibited a unique culture. Announcers were known by initials rather than by name. Advertising, as well as recorded music, were frowned upon. And artists performed live, for free, with many worth the price.

Radio also developed its own body of popular literature. Numerous books and magazines, both technical and non-technical, were published about radio, and non-radio publications had radio columns. The radio "call book," a station listing typically arranged in multiple ways (location, frequency, call letters) so as to facilitate station finding and station identification, made its debut. All sorts of companies, both radio-related and not, put their names on call books, which were either sold or given away as promotions. Although later years would witness the fierce "radio-press wars" over the right to present news, in the early days newspapers gladly carried station schedules, information on how to build or obtain equipment, radio-related advertising, etc. Many papers had daily columns devoted to radio, and sometimes issued weekly sections or special publications on the subject. Some of the newspaper coverage was surprisingly technical.

Questions & Answers in The New York Times

Q: What should the resistance of an "A" battery rheostat be? — J.R. **A:** Three ohms.

Q: I am using a loose coupler which is rated to cover from 200 to 1,500 meters. The complete circuit is a two-stage amplifier used in conjunction with an outdoor antenna, one wire 100 feet long. I get fine results with code signals and also hear Arlington, Va., time signals very strong, but have had little success in picking up the radio concerts of Newark or Pittsburgh. What can I do to hear the music as clear as the code? — M.J.M. **A:** The size of the loose coupler which you are using generally gives best results on the higher wave lengths and has a tendency to work inefficiently on the low waves. Try a variable condenser in series with the antenna lead-in or with the ground wire. If that does not show an improvement a smaller loose coupler or a vario-coupler will solve your problem.

Q: You state that the secondary coil of the vario-coupler in the Armstrong circuit should have double the number of turns. Can I wind it in layers? — W.E.G. **A:** The coil can be wound in layers, but bank winding will render better results.

Q: What should be the size of a tickler coil? — L.L.D. **A:** The tickler coil should have about one-third of the maximum number of turns as used on the secondary coil of the coupler.

The New York Times
July 23, 1922[34]

The growth of popular radio reception tracked the development of radio receivers. First there was the exhilaration of being able to snatch sounds out of the air, then the excitement of reception over greater and greater distances, and then the replacement of headphones with loudspeakers that boasted improved volume (1923). This was followed by the introduction

A RADIO FIEND'S DREAM

of high-performance amplifying tubes, the availability of early battery eliminators (1924), the improved fidelity of cone speakers over horn speakers (1925), and finally the development of full A.C. operation, with tubes specifically designed for A.C. use (1927).[35]

In her exposition of radio and the American psyche,[36] Susan J. Douglas called the early 1920s years of exploratory listening. She described it as a time when stations were more important than programs, our first encounter with the magic and romance that radio could bring. There was something deep about hearing, something more primal than seeing. Radio listening

As illustrated by this 1922 *Radio News* cover, radio could be a happy obsession.

was an experience that occurred inside our heads. It released the imagination. It was direct and intimate. It created a private, personal bond to live events happening somewhere else, connecting us to a world of sound never before experienced.

Although most listeners would graduate to the world of improved fidelity, easier tuning and better, recurring programming, for hard core DXers it was surprise, not predictability, that was radio's greatest attraction. The vagaries of how radio waves propagated through an unknown and mysterious "ether," sharing space with all manner of noises of unknown origin, were just being learned.

> The sounds from the farthest points were the most fascinating, irrespective of how clear or how interesting they might be with regard to subject matter. And so radio entered the "DX" age and developed, incidentally, greater liars than the fish story. The number of fish caught in one day was changed to the number of stations picked up in one night. And the distance of the stations was substituted for the size of the fish. It became a matter of common conversation, during 1922 and 1923, to talk about distant or "DX" reception. Fortunately, there were a limited number of radio stations in those days, and whatever they might lack in power was more than compensated for by the relative freedom which their signals enjoyed in the virgin ether. Good old WOC, at Davenport, Ia., for instance, filtered into New York City with little difficulty. Stations as far as Fort Worth, Texas, were by no means rare. The radio devotee would stay up half the night tuning in one signal after another from distant points. The ideal station of those days was one which did little more than repeat its call letters over and over again. Its programs were of secondary interest.[37]

There were silent nights, where stations in one area would stay off the air so that distant stations not ordinarily audible might be heard. (Silent nights disappeared by 1928.) In 1923, 1924 and 1926, *Radio Broadcast* and some other magazines organized the week-long International Radio Week Tests, a kind of international DX contest where participating broadcast band stations in America and Europe transmitted at hours conducive to reception on the other side of the Atlantic, while nearby stations shut down. Some stations from Canada and Latin America participated as well. Although widespread public interest in these events could not be sustained beyond a few years, during the tests it seemed like everyone was a DXer.[38] And whether you were searching intensely for distant signals, or casually eavesdropping, escape through the airwaves was always accomplished from the safety and comfort of your own home. Except in those areas that lacked reliable radio service, by 1923 the "itch for distance" of most listeners had been scratched.[39] But for still-hearty DX souls— the etheric obsessives, as Douglas called them — a new radio universe, where appetites whetted on the broadcast band would find a world of listening hitherto unimaginable, was about to be discovered.

2

1923–1929

We may be on the threshold of a day when broadcasting, that application of radio which interests the whole of the civilized world, will have its range enormously increased. Within a year or two, the voice of the King of England, for example, may be easily and clearly heard by millions of his subjects in places as far apart as India, Australia, Canada, and South Africa.... ¶Perhaps the voice of the short wave will be able to accomplish for human brotherhood and our common civilization what has not yet been done by the better-known long wave, although radio is already one of the most powerful agents in the linking of mankind into one great whole.—*Guglielmo Marconi, July 1925*[1]

1923

It was shortwave's anchor year.

KDKA

Westinghouse Assistant Chief Engineer Frank Conrad had been engaged in some impromptu voice and music transmissions for at least a year before the November 2, 1920, start of KDKA. It is said that his first contact with wireless was circa 1915 when, in connection with a $5 bet with a co-worker about the accuracy of a watch, he built a receiver capable of receiving the Arlington time signals and his interest took off from there.

Conrad received an experimental license, 8XK, in 1916. He had the advantage of being one of the limited number of persons authorized to conduct radio transmission work during the war in connection with the country's military needs. This he did by way of station 2WE at the Westinghouse plant in East Pittsburgh and 2WM at his home in nearby Wilkinsburg. He resumed operation as 8XK in 1919. His setup was modest, basically a table full of equipment and a six-wire inverted-L antenna, 105 feet long and 50 feet off the ground.[2]

In the course of his work, Conrad began broadcasting phonograph records so as to avoid the need to constantly talk during transmissions. These "programs" eventually gained a following among both listening and transmitting amateurs, and Conrad adopted a schedule: 7:30–9:30 P.M. on Wednesdays and Saturdays. At the end of September 1920, Joseph Horne's, a local department store, placed an advertisement in the *Pittsburgh Sun*, advising customers

When Westinghouse shortwave transmissions over 8XS became regular in 1923, the programming was a simulcast of the company's historic broadcast band station, KDKA.

that it was selling radio receivers (not of Westinghouse manufacture) capable of picking up the Conrad broadcasts. Broadcasting was entering the final stage of its gestation.

The exact circumstances of the licensing for the historic November 2 transmission are unclear even to this day. Construction of the station had begun only a month before the broadcast, and the Department of Commerce issued telephonic authorization to operate under special amateur callsign 8ZZ. The accepted story is that this was intended as a backup in case the KDKA license did not arrive in time. Another view is that the KDKA license had been sought as part of a Westinghouse plan to set up a point-to-point code service among company facilities in several cities, and it was feared that such a license would not encompass the planned November 2 broadcast, hence the need for special authorization. Whatever the truth, the station was licensed and the broadcast went forward over the station's 100-watt transmitter.[3]

Conrad was not present at the Westinghouse plant's rooftop station on November 2. He was standing by at his home station, 8XK, prepared to substitute its signal for the plant's transmitter should the latter fail for some reason. But all went well. After that first broadcast, KDKA went on to score a variety of "firsts" in broadcasting various kinds of programs, and Westinghouse soon replicated KDKA's success by the establishment of WJZ in Newark, New Jersey, WBZ in Springfield, Massachusetts, and KYW in Chicago, all in 1921. (WJZ was taken over by RCA in 1923.)

Although most of the credit for the creation of KDKA has inured to Conrad because of the pioneering experimental work of 8XK which preceded it, the idea for the station appears to have been that of Conrad's close friend, Westinghouse Vice-President Harry P. Davis. Doubtless his imagination, and his interest in potential profit from supplying radio receivers, were sparked by the Horne's advertisement. Perhaps he had also read the editorial in the September 1920 issue of *Radio News* where Hugo Gernsback took note of the Nellie Melba broadcast in Europe in June, bemoaned the sad state of radiophone experimentation in the United States, and urged someone to help popularize radio by broadcasting band concerts, the speeches of presidential candidates, etc.[4] At the time, as Conrad's fellow engineer and KDKA technical collaborator Donald G. Little has observed, Westinghouse had been doing relatively little in the radio field.[5]

KDKA Shortwave

It was widely, if mistakenly, "known" that radio waves above approximately 1500 kc. were of little value, this belief being based on the so-called Austin-Cohen formula, a mathematical theory holding that as frequency increased, so did ethereal absorption. There had been little experimentation on these higher frequencies, and what there was had been little noticed, and unyielding of the clues that were critical to unlocking its mysteries. Even students of shortwave clung to the belief that the "longer" the short waves — the lower the frequency — the better, hence the focus on the 3 mc. area, the "shortwave" real estate closest to the "good" frequencies that ended around 1500 kc. Huge investments, both cerebral and financial, had been made in what we think of today as the mediumwave and longwave bands, and intellectual inertia was great. Soon this was all to change.

Both the amateurs and Marconi have legitimate claims as "discoverers" of shortwave. From the standpoint of shortwave broadcasting, however, Frank Conrad was the key man.

EARLY SHORTWAVE EXPERIMENTS

Conrad's interest in shortwave was prompted by a concern over deficiencies in the KDKA broadcast band signal which he believed resulted from a loss of power in connection with the radiation of harmonics, a common problem in those days. He built a receiver capable of receiving the harmonic signals and discovered that many broadcast station harmonics were stronger than their fundamentals.

With the advent of vacuum tubes, the generation of radio signals at short wavelengths, using modest power and antennas of manageable size, became possible, as it had not been with alternator technology. This facilitated experimentation. Conrad was one of a number of amateurs who began trying out the higher frequencies as early as the winter of 1920–21.[6] The group consisted of a half dozen hams in the Maryland-Washington, D.C. area who were experimenting relatively close to traditional ham frequencies, circa 1.8 mc., or 170 meters, where their signals proved strong.

Early in 1921, Conrad, operating from his home station 8XK, together with Boston hams J. C. Ramsey, 1XA, and R. D. Decker, 1RD, and the MIT station, 1XM, began experiments in the range of 2.2–3.0 mc. This produced surprisingly good results. In January 1922, Boyd Phelps, operating amateur station 9ZT in Minneapolis, managed to transmit on 35 meters, but there was no one to hear his signal. His tests expanded over the next few months after he moved to Connecticut and joined the staff of *QST* (as 1HX), and soon he became part of the Conrad effort. At some point Conrad arranged for a direct telephone line from KDKA to his home so that he could use the station's programs as a signal source during tests.

Conrad also belonged to a group of hams that had cooperated with the Bureau of Standards in tests on fading, not on short wave but on 250 meters (1200 kc.), during 1920–21.[7] In May and June of 1922, Conrad and the Bureau renewed their collaboration, this time in the 3 mc. region. Reception was found to be almost as good during the day as at night, and the fading that was typical on lower frequencies was largely absent.[8]

In January and February 1923, tests in the 1.5–3.0 mc. range continued between Phelps and well-known Chicago amateur Ralph H. G. Matthews, 9ZN.[9] Soon a half-dozen other stations joined in, either transmitting or listening or both. (With the equipment of the day, receiving signals on 3 mc. was no simple matter.) The results prompted the ARRL to sponsor, in March, a 100-minute "CQ Party" on each of two days for hams wishing to try their luck on 3 mc. Whether all those participating had the necessary authority to use this frequency is open to question, but the results weren't. The event was a great success, even while many stations wound up on frequencies at variance from 3 mc. and many of the signals heard were harmonics of non-participating stations. Later the same year the Bureau of Standards conducted tests on 10 meters.[10] Around the same time, reports surfaced of hams in New Zealand trying their luck on 2.3 mc.[11] and of military transmissions in France on 45 meters (6.6 mc.).[12]

As Conrad later observed, the "short waves are the long distance carriers of radio. We began to realize this fact as early as 1922. We felt even then that there were wonderful possibilities which were being overlooked in the then unused and rather despised short-wave bands."[13] That year — the exact month is variously reported as either August or October — Conrad advanced his experiments by having a 1 kw. shortwave transmitter installed at KDKA so that its programs could be transmitted directly from the station both on its regular channel and on shortwave. This transmitter was licensed as 8XS. At first a vertical transmitting antenna was used, but this was replaced with an inverted-L, 40 feet long and 35 feet high. Transmissions were intermittent until July 19, 1923 when KDKA began simulcasting every night for 4½ hours on 3 mc. with a 10 kw. transmitter. Soon the station was being heard around the world, and it became clear, as reports of reception arrived, that something new was at hand.

As notable a milestone as it was, it would be a mistake to consider the post–July 19 KDKA shortwave broadcasts as much more than an advanced stage of experimentation, for it was only the most dedicated and knowledgeable experimenters who could fashion equipment capable of receiving the KDKA shortwave signals. Consumer shortwave receivers were still a long way off. Even if reception could have been made to depend more on the inherent long distance properties of the signal itself than on the sophistication of the receiver or the experience of the listener, at this time only the most prescient could have foreseen worldwide, direct-to-listener shortwave communications.

Conrad was not alone in his interest in shortwave for broadcasting purposes. Over the next few years industry leaders would wonder if shortwave could provide solutions to a number of problems that had developed in the standard broadcast band.

OVERCROWDING

Although shortwave never provided a practical answer to the problem of overcrowding in the broadcast band, hopes to the contrary provided an early rationale for experimentation in shortwave broadcasting. To a large extent, early regulators had themselves to blame for overcrowding when they made all broadcast stations share but a few frequencies. The situation improved greatly when a general broadcasting band with 10 kc. spacing was established in 1923. (Narrower spacing, with room for more stations but also more interference, was rejected.) Problems continued to develop, however, and sorting out the broadcast band, and delicensing some stations, was the first job the Federal Radio Commission tackled when it was established in 1927. But regulation alone would never completely solve the problem of putting ten pounds of stations in a five pound bag of frequencies. Overcrowding has always been an element of broadcast regulation. In the mid–1920s, shortwave, with its huge range of available channels, was seen as a possible solution.

National Broadcasting

The theme of national broadcasting is one that recurs in the history of early American radio. Although many stations came on the air during broadcasting's first few years, most were small, low power affairs, and many survived but a short time. This, and the hugeness of the nation's territory, meant that there were many parts of the country, particularly rural areas, that were unserved by radio. Hugo Gernsback suggested solving the problem by licensing amateurs to relay broadcast stations.[14] More popular was the notion of a comparatively small number of high power, non-interfering stations which, together, could serve all parts of the country, either directly or by way of networking with local stations. Eventually the concept would become the basis for high power, clear channel AM broadcasting. In broadcasting's early days, however, shortwave's potential as a means of tying together a small number of "super" stations seemed a possibility.[15]

Network Problems

Shortwave was also seen as a possible solution to the technical and corporate problems that had materialized during early efforts to network broadcasting stations for purposes not necessarily as grandiose as the accomplishment of national broadcasting.

Major conflicts had arisen among RCA's founding companies during the first half of the 1920s. One concerned advertising. When AT&T, whose principle business interest was the telephone and who owned many patents underlying the manufacture of transmitters, joined in the cross-licensing ("patent pool") agreements of 1919–21, it granted to the other companies certain rights with regard to wireless telephony in connection with the use of transmitters manufactured by AT&T. However, this did not include wireless telephony for hire, which AT&T conceived as a branch of the telephone business and thus within AT&T's exclusive domain. Broadcasting, while a form of wireless telephony, was not within the contemplation of the parties when the agreements were brought into effect (the first cross-licensing agreement was signed well before the inauguration of KDKA). When broadcasting became a reality, AT&T concluded that the selling of air time to others over AT&T-manufactured transmitters, i.e. advertising, as opposed to presenting non-commercial news and entertainment, or advertising the business of the station's owner, constituted wireless telephony for hire, an activity reserved to itself under the cross-licensing agreements except as AT&T might grant licenses to others for the purpose, which it normally did in connection with a transmitter purchase, or otherwise upon application. Notwithstanding widespread doubts among the other RCA companies and within the infant broadcasting industry generally about the legal correctness of AT&T's position, many stations paid royalties to AT&T for this purpose, but others did not, and AT&T considered their operation outside the law.

The company's perceived primacy in the field of broadcasting for hire led it to establish its own station, WEAF, in New York City on July 25, 1922,[16] and to make the station the nation's first "toll broadcaster." Its purpose was to lease time over its airwaves, just as AT&T charged its customers tolls for the use of its long distance lines for ordinary telephone purposes. AT&T's stated purpose was to permit broadcasting without the need for every broadcaster to operate its own station and thus make the new art more widely available (a concept that echoes in today's leased-time shortwave broadcasting arrangements). WEAF would soon become a leader in both the technological and programming aspects of broadcasting, and notwithstanding the opposition to radio advertising that prevailed among the general public at the time, the station was a success.

A related conflict arose when, in the course of AT&T's operation of WEAF, the company discovered that the linking of points via telephone lines would be a vital element in the development and expansion of radio broadcasting. It was wire connections between field and studio that made remote broadcasts possible. More importantly, at the time, wires would also be the essential element in the networking of the stations themselves. The first experiments in the use of wires to connect stations were in 1922. The first bona fide network connection took place on January 4, 1923 when the programming of WEAF was broadcast simultaneously over WNAC in Boston. Thus was born the notion of "chain" broadcasting, a concept with far reaching potential on several fronts—the delivery of better quality radio programs to outlying areas, the development of a truly national radio system, the enhancement of national culture, and the inauguration of meaningful paydays for artists. It was networking that led to the creation of radio programs as we know them today. Before networks, radio broadcasts mainly featured individual performers.

With its ownership of the long distance telephone lines and its experience and technical know-how in the field of long-distance wire communication, AT&T was in a position of strength on the issue of networking. During 1923 and 1924, WEAF and a variety of cooperating stations set up temporary networks for various broadcasts, followed by a permanent network (with WEAF as network headquarters), which, by 1925, comprised 13 stations in 12 cities.

AT&T's self-proclaimed control over broadcasting for hire was widely resented. When RCA established a network based at WJZ, by then headquartered in New York City, it turned to Western Union for wire lines. Other stations did likewise, often using Western Union lines or the lines of other telephone and telegraph companies.[17] Results were mediocre, however. The AT&T monopoly over high performance telephone lines was one reason underlying the early research into shortwave, which was viewed as a possible alternative.

WEAF had become involved in broadcasting mainly as a means of perfecting the technology used in connection with AT&T's traditional telephone business. As the radio art became more complicated and as various non-technical aspects of broadcasting, such as producing programs and dealing with artists, took the company farther afield of its core activities, broadcasting became a distraction. As a result, in 1926, following the settlement of various claims among RCA's founding companies (and doubtless motivated by a referee's earlier finding against AT&T as to its monopoly on toll broadcasting), AT&T left the business of broadcasting station operation altogether, selling WEAF and leasing permanent network wires to RCA, which turned the network into NBC.[18] NBC would have a significant involvement in shortwave broadcasting from 1927 through World War II.

With the wire line availability problem solved, and with the better fidelity and greater reliability of wires versus shortwave, which was still in its infancy, the search for a shortwave alternative for networking stations lost much of its immediacy.

SARNOFF AND MARCONI

In 1922, early in the RCA inter-company conflicts, many fundamental aspects of broadcasting were yet to be worked out. The government's policy of authorizing all broadcasting to take place on only a few channels was causing widespread interference in many areas, and the adoption of time sharing was an inadequate solution. In other parts of the country, particularly rural areas, there were few stations and reception was poor. The question of how to pay for broadcasting was also very much an issue. The economics of running a station, including the growing demands of artists to be paid for their performances, whether live or recorded, were daunting when every station had to rise or fall on its own. These and other considerations were feeding the discussion of the need for "national" stations.

David Sarnoff had his eye on shortwave early — January and February of 1920 — albeit for commercial wireless telegraphy, which was still in its experimental phase.[19] But soon his attention turned to shortwave for broadcasting.

Although Sarnoff had but limited first-hand experience with shortwave at the time, on August 2, 1922, he wrote to RCA's then-president, Edward J. Nally, in support of shortwave as one alternative for connecting broadcasting stations. He posited that the entire country could be covered with just a few stations connected either by wire or by high power shortwave operating at around 100 meters (3 mc.). Sarnoff recognized that he was on untested ground, and that no one knew how far a high power shortwave signal would travel.

> Although its is purely a speculative statement and necessarily based on incomplete knowledge and information, yet it would not surprise me if in the next few years we find that a radio signal sent out on 100 meters with 100 or 200 kw. of power will travel around the world and be received through the highly sensitive and delicate receiving instruments which are rapidly projecting themselves into the radio art, for example, the super-regenerative [receiver]. ¶It may well be that some day in the future we will signal and talk across the Atlantic and Pacific with short instead of long waves and if this should come true, the problems of static elimination and high-speed operation would take on a new appearance for it is well known one can signal on short waves at a rate of speed many times that possible on the longer waves and static at the shorter wave lengths is not comparable to that on the long waves.[20]

National broadcasting would eventually be achieved through wired networking and the authorization of a limited number of high power standard broadcast stations. Sarnoff's plan conceived of shortwave as a means of relaying signals from one transmitter to another, not as a vehicle for direct reception by listeners (who could not have purchased a shortwave receiver in 1922 in any event). In fact, relaying would be the stated purpose of shortwave broadcasting in the United States until 1936.

Among those who shaped Sarnoff's views was Marconi himself. While he was no longer the commanding influence of earlier years, he was universally respected, and he was probably the world's earliest student of the short waves. His use of frequencies in the range of 75 to 150 meters during the years 1896–1901 had been forgotten under the tidal wave favoring longwave, and neglected even by himself. He turned his attention to shortwave again during the war years, whereupon he continued his experiments aboard his yacht *Elettra*. Marconi's reports on the propagational and directional characteristics of short waves, and on their ability to travel long distances with relatively low power, fueled Sarnoff's interest in the medium.

In 1916, in response to the Italian navy's need for short-range tactical radio communications at sea, Marconi and his fellow engineer and inventor, C. S. Franklin, developed a system operating on 2 meters. At the end of the war, an experimental 15 meter voice link set up by Franklin over the 97-mile route between London and Birmingham was found successful using 700 watts. At the same time, one of Franklin's colleagues, Captain H. J. Round, was carrying out wireless telephony tests between England and Holland on 3 mc., and discovering that the signals often reached much farther afield.

In tests after departing England aboard the *Elettra* in April 1923, Marconi achieved a range of more than 2,500 miles over water on 3 mc. with 12 kw., and more than 1,400 miles during daylight. When reduced to 1 kw., the nighttime signals were still stronger than would have been possible on longwave with 200–300 kw.[21]

The shortwave receiving setup at KDPM, the Westinghouse relay station in Cleveland, was notably spare. The station picked up the KDKA shortwave signal and relayed it on the broadcast band. The experiment lasted just a few months (***Radio Broadcast,*** 1923).

KDPM

Westinghouse engineers picked up on Conrad's shortwave experiments and decided to set up a relay station in Cleveland, where reception of the KDKA broadcast band signal was poor. In those days, relays were how distance was achieved. In its early experiments with radio, the military relayed messages from ship to ship. "Relay messaging" had become the *raison d'être* of ham radio prior to the discovery of the distance potential of shortwave, and the ship-to-ship relaying of commercial messages was standard practice among non-military vessels through the 1920s.

It appears that the Cleveland relay station, KDPM, began testing in September 1922 or sometime soon thereafter.[22] The call letters were those of a Westinghouse telegraph transmitter located at the company's Cleveland plant, part of an inter-plant telegraph system that had been operating on 600 kc. and various longwave frequencies since May 1921. The shortwave receiving setup was rather primitive. Signals were received on an eight-foot, one-turn indoor loop rather than an outdoor wire antenna because, with the small tolerances built into the shortwave receiver, an antenna swinging in the wind could cause it to detune. Instability was a major problem with early shortwave transmitters as well. Every effort was made to eliminate vibrations, and the literature of the time often referred to placing transmitters on springs to absorb vibration, and stretching wire antennas taut to avoid even the slightest movement.

Above: Short wave or high frequency receiver at Hastings, Nebraska, used to receive the high frequency broadcasts from Westinghouse Station, KDKA, at East Pittsburgh, Pa. From there it is passed through a power amplifier, then into the transmitter and rebroadcast.

Above: View of the extremely short antenna used to receive the high frequency broadcasts at Westinghouse Station, KFKX, at Hastings, Nebraska. Left: View of transmitting apparatus at Westinghouse Station, KFKX, at Hastings, Nebraska, the first radio repeating station in the world.

Westinghouse "repeating station" KFKX in Hastings, Nebraska, picked up the KDKA shortwave signal and retransmitted it on 1050 kc., and sometimes on shortwave as well (*Radio News,* 1924).

KDPM's 360 meter (833 kc.) broadcast band transmitter was of 250 watts, and its antenna the same as KDKA's— 200 feet long and 105 feet high. KDPM rebroadcast the KDKA shortwave signal on this channel, thus making KDKA programming available in Cleveland and environs. A major advantage of the relay arrangement was that reception of the KDKA shortwave signal on 3 mc. (alternately 3300 and 3750 kc.) was possible even during daylight, when broadcast band reception was degraded.

KFKX

The KDPM project was novel, but just an experiment, and it was discontinued within a few months. However, Westinghouse saw value in shortwave and went about setting up a more substantial relay station, KFKX, in Hastings, Nebraska. The venue was chosen for several reasons. It was central to the nation, roughly midway between Pittsburgh and Los Angeles; it was thought to be at about the maximum feasible distance from Pittsburgh for rebroadcast work; the surrounding area was flat; and the necessary power facilities were available. Although intended mainly as a KDKA repeater station, KFKX could also originate programs from its own studios, which it did on Mondays and Thursdays at 9:30–11:00 P.M.

The station opened on November 21 or 22, 1923. According to Conrad, what "possibly marks the first regularly scheduled long distance relay transmission" took place on November 22 when a talk in Pittsburgh was received at a meeting of the National Electric Light Association in Salt Lake City, the signal having been sent from KDKA to KFKX on 3 mc. and then rebroadcast over the KFKX 5 kw. transmitter on 1050 kc., from whence it was picked up in Salt Lake City.[23] In addition to picking up KDKA shortwave and relaying it over the broadcast band, KFKX also had its own 10 kw. shortwave transmitter, 9XW, which was sometimes used to further relay the KDKA signal to west coast station KGO. This was the first interconnection of more than two broadcasting stations by radio. The 9XW frequency has been variously put at either 2730 kc., or the same frequency used by 8XS (see below). The relay schedule of KDKA was not fixed.

Experiments as to the best shortwave frequency from Pittsburgh confirmed findings previously made in Cleveland, namely, that reception varied significantly depending on which frequency between 3000 and 3448 kc. was chosen. Given the rather narrow frequency range, this was an odd result, perhaps related to some defect in the Pittsburgh transmitting setup. In any event, the frequency settled upon was 3200 kc.

Although the Hastings area had been thought interference free, once operations got underway it was found that a combination of leaky power lines and radiations from street lights, elevator motors, diathermy and x-ray equipment, etc. were producing serious interference up to at least 3750 kc. As a result, the KFKX shortwave receiver was set up in a farmhouse about a mile from the transmitter building, which was itself located on the outskirts of Hastings, and a second receiving site constructed as well, thus permitting early diversity reception. During the station's sojourn in Hastings it occupied studio and office space in several different locations. All points were connected by telephone circuits.[24]

Westinghouse also installed shortwave receiving equipment at WBZ in Springfield, Massachusetts and KYW, Chicago, both of which picked up some KDKA programs on shortwave and rebroadcast them on their local channels. It appears that the Westinghouse facility in Springfield also had a shortwave transmitter.[25] Whether at this time it was used for relay purposes, in addition to general experimentation, is not known.

THE FIRST OVERSEAS BROADCASTS

The KDKA shortwave experiments soon became known overseas, and starting in the summer of 1922 Westinghouse had discussions with A. P. M. Fleming, manager of the research department at Metropolitan-Vickers Electrical Company of Manchester, England, who was then in the United States, about a plan for Metropolitan-Vickers to attempt to pick up the KDKA shortwave signals and relay them to its listeners. Metropolitan-Vickers was the parent of British Westinghouse, and one of two private broadcasters operating prior to November 1922 when the then-new BBC took over all broadcasting in Britain. It was one of the consortium of companies that had formed the BBC, and it continued to be engaged in many facets of radio and electronics even after leaving the broadcasting business.

Success was achieved in September 1923 when KDKA shortwave was received at the Metropolitan-Vickers facility at Altrincham, Cheshire, where a special receiver and a six-foot loop antenna had been constructed for the purpose. KDKA increased its power to 30 kw. to facilitate further experiments.

In England, the KDKA shortwave signal on 3200 kc. was, of course, much stronger than the KDKA mediumwave signal on 920 kc. (326 m.), which was, reportedly, also heard, no small achievement considering that the broadcast band transmitter operated at 1 kw., the maximum power allowed at the time. Shortwave avoided much of the fading inherent in long distance mediumwave reception. It was largely free of interference, and signals could be received at an earlier hour than mediumwave (although much of the early testing was conducted after midnight EST). There was a good deal of difficulty maintaining stability of the transmitter, however, and the resulting distortion required the stations to be in constant contact by cable until the problems were solved.

The first rebroadcasts took place on December 29, 1923, with the KDKA shortwave signal, by then on about 3410 kc., being sent by landline from Altrincham to station 2AC at the Metropolitan-Vickers research laboratory at Trafford Park, where it was rebroadcast over 400 meters (910 kc.) and also fed by land line to seven other BBC stations which rebroadcast it further. The rebroadcasts lasted for a week and comprised 18 hours in toto, the best results being obtained during the hours 0400–0700 GMT. *The New York Times* reported the New Year's eve program:

> Up to midnight the transmission was badly interfered with, but at 12 o'clock, British time, "God Save the King" came through clearly.... ¶About 1 o'clock there was a long address by a woman, and a second woman was clearest heard of all the speakers in a children's fairy tale. ¶Then the band played "Rule Brittania," and S. J. Nightingale, a member of the staff at Trafford Park, who had been in Pittsburgh several months, sang three songs, each of which was distinctly recognized by his mother and sister, who were among the listeners....[26]

These were the first internationally rebroadcast programs that were made possible by a shortwave link. They occurred one month after the conclusion of the first of the International Radio Week transatlantic medium wave tests, which caused one commentator to observe: "These [the mediumwave tests] had hardly been completed to the satisfaction of the world when this new scientific feat was accomplished and the latter was so much more satisfactory that there was hardly a comparison between the old method [direct transatlantic mediumwave reception —'at best a haphazard arrangement'] and this new method started by the Westinghouse Company [rebroadcast of a shortwave signal]. * * * Developments of the last few months seem to indicate that this may be the ultimate in broadcasting and with events moving so swiftly, the new year may give the answer."[27] *Radio News* said, "It was the greatest triumph that radio had made in the past year and has actually changed the whole future of broadcasting."[28]

Conrad was no less enthusiastic about the possibilities for shortwave. "It seems almost a flight of fancy to state that signals from East Pittsburgh are picked up in England on the two-tube dry cell detector used with an antenna from 10 to 15 feet ... long and the whole inside of a building," he said, "but it is a fact."[29]

Metropolitan-Vickers requested listener reports and over 1,000 were received, some from as far away as Italy and Switzerland, a considerable feat considering that the power of the 2AC mediumwave transmitter was only 1,500 watts. In an early example of a frustration that would forever plague DXers, a company article published in the American radio magazine *Radio Broadcast* thanked all the listeners to the KDKA relays but noted that "only a very small percentage" of the reports could be acknowledged by mail.[30]

REMOTE PICKUPS

An important aspect of Conrad's early shortwave experimentation was the use of low power shortwave transmitters for purposes of connecting field activities with the studio in order to present programming that originated outside the station. Originally this function was accomplished by wires.[31] Although it appears that radio had been used for newspaper reporting from remote locations by at least the London *Daily Mail* and the Los Angeles *Examiner* even before the start of KDKA,[32] the station developed it further.

KDKA is generally credited with broadcasting the first religious service. This was on January 2, 1921, and involved a remote pickup, probably by wire, from Pittsburgh's Calvary Episcopal Church. Soon the station was using shortwave for remote broadcasting purposes, although just when this occurred is unclear. Donald G. Little tells the story of KDKA's installation of a 200-watt shortwave transmitter in the steeple of the Point Breeze Presbyterian Church in the East Liberty section of Pittsburgh. A telephone line was also installed for comparison purposes and so that technicians could communicate with the studio on one link while the other was in use.

> I was talking on the radio link while the service was going out via the wire. The operator at the station, however, got his switches mixed and put both the service and my test talking on the broadcast transmitter at the same time. The result was that in the middle of the Lord's Prayer, my saying "One, two, three, four, testing" was superimposed. Luckily for me, Mr. Davis was not listening that Sunday, but I went to work Monday morning with quaking knees, wondering what was going to happen. Dr. Conrad thought that it was a good joke.[33]

Field shortwave transmitters may also have been in use at Westinghouse stations WBZ in Springfield, Massachusetts and KYW in Chicago. Since the use of shortwave obviated the need to arrange for telephone hookups, the development of small, transportable shortwave transmitters was important. General Electric station WGY in Schenectady was using a portable shortwave transmitting set for remote pickups by late 1923,[34] and the following year 2LO in London was doing the same.

Other Developments in 1923

THE NAVY

The navy began using shortwave in 1923, in part because it had been importuned to relinquish some of its other frequencies so that a broadcast band could be established for the rapidly increasing number of standard broadcast stations. As with almost everyone who was experimenting with shortwave, the navy's first shortwave activities took place in the range of 2 to 3 mc. However, by 1924 it was making use of higher frequencies, reaching across the country and as far as Rio de Janeiro on 54 meters from NKF, the navy's main experimental station located at the Naval Research Laboratory near Washington, D.C. The navy set up four-hour tests on 54 and 100 meters, three nights a week, for the benefit of amateurs.[35] In 1925 it would invite ARRL Traffic Manager F. H. Schnell to join its Pacific cruise for the purpose of communicating with amateurs and demonstrating the effectiveness of shortwave communication. Schnell's station, NRRL, aboard the USS *Seattle,* worked amateurs in many countries and was heard worldwide.[36] The same year, in tests between Washington and the Canal Zone, the navy showed the superiority of a 50-watt shortwave transmitter operating on 15 mc. to a longwave transmitter of 250 kw.

But navy shortwave utilization would remain experimental for several years. Regular operational use of shortwave followed the installation of the first high power shortwave equipment at the navy's headquarters station, NAA, in 1926–27. It operated in four bands— 4000–4525, 8000–9050, 12000–13500 and 16000–18100 kc.— and it provided continuous shore coverage of the entire North Atlantic for the first time.

Although shortwave had proven its merit, it would take most of the rest of the decade for the navy to replace all of its arc equipment with suitable shortwave gear.

THE AMATEURS

While there are traces of shortwave spark activity even before World War I, the exploration of shortwave by the hams did not begin in earnest until 1922–23, and elicited only limited interest until the first two-way transatlantic ham contacts were made on November 27, 1923. These were between F8AB in France and 1MO and 1XAM in the United States, the latter specially authorized to operate on frequencies around — not unexpectedly — 3.0 mc. ARRL station 1MO was operated by F. H. Schnell, who would go on to the navy's NRRL project (see above). 1XAM was John L. Reinartz, who would join the 1925 MacMillan Arctic expedition. Other transatlantic contacts soon followed — sometimes with the required special permission, sometimes not — with operators always staying close to 3 mc.

Spark fell into disuse quickly once transatlantic communication on shortwave was shown to be reliable.

The amateurs deserve a good deal of credit for their work in developing shortwave. The early transatlantic contacts spurred the study of shortwave propagation and the development of shortwave transmitters, receivers and antennas. It is worth noting, however, that KDKA was already broadcasting regularly on shortwave by the time the first transatlantic amateur contact occurred, and was even the source of some interference during French-American QSOs two days after the initial contact.[37]

WWV

Although not a broadcasting station as such, WWV is well known to present-day short-wave broadcast listeners. One of the main activities of the Bureau of Standards was scientific measurement. WWV, then located in Washington, D.C., was the Bureau's laboratory station. It first came on the air in May 1920 with 50 watts, and in its earliest incarnation it broadcast music concerts that pre-dated KDKA. Market reports (in code) for the Department of Agriculture followed later that year via a 2 kw. spark transmitter.

On January 29, 1923, then using a 1 kw. transmitter, WWV began transmitting precise frequency standards, addressing a longstanding problem among stations of all types: staying on channel. Now a station could compare its signal to WWV, which transmitted on one frequency at a time, then moved on to another, on a pre-announced schedule. The frequency range covered was 125 kc. to 2 mc. (soon increased to 6 mc.). Voice announcements were included initially, but were dropped in favor of code.[38]

The Bureau also carefully measured the frequencies of a limited number of broadcast and commercial stations, and certified them for use as frequency standards (in 1925 the ARRL adopted a similar system for amateur stations). It also authorized the transmission of WWV-like standard frequency transmissions by 6XBM at Stanford University, Palo Alto, California (these ended in 1926). Time announcements (in code) would not be added to WWV transmissions until 1945. Time signals over various naval longwave stations were a fact of life as early as 1915, and, together with daily weather bulletins, became a regular service of NAA, Arlington, Virginia.

RECEIVERS

It was Lee De Forest's three-element vacuum tube, or triode, that took receivers beyond the crystal set stage. One of the longest running patent litigations of the day was between De

Forest and Edwin H. Armstrong, both of whom laid claim to having invented the regenerative circuit in 1912. This circuit amplified a signal by repeatedly feeding its output back through the tube. It was regeneration that made consumer-grade receivers for broadcast band frequencies possible. The litigation continued for over 20 years, with the courts finally deciding in favor of De Forest but the radio industry universally recognizing Armstrong as the inventor.

Self-contained regenerative receivers for broadcast use began appearing in 1921. (Regenerative "receivers" for amateurs had been available since at least 1916, but were typically tuners only, requiring the addition of detector and amplifier.) They required careful tuning within small tolerances, and they produced oscillations that turned them into mini transmitters and a common source of interference to other listeners. However, they were the receiver of choice until 1923 when the TRF, or tuned radio frequency, receiver made its appearance. Hams had been experimenting with TRF since 1922. TRF receivers amplified the signal before it reached the detector. By 1924, TRF models had graduated to multi-stage units, typically sporting two or three dials, one for each of the tuned RF stages. The TRF receiver was easier to operate, more sensitive and more stable, and had the added advantage of skirting the Westinghouse regenerative patents. The TRF receiver also lent itself to the eventual incorporation of single-dial tuning and improved neutrodyne circuitry. The performance of early TRF circuitry declined as frequency increased, however, and so TRF receivers were not optimal for the shortwave work then on the horizon.

During the war, Armstrong had invented the superheterodyne receiver, which, while still dependent on batteries— until 1924 all receivers were operated on batteries—far exceeded other receivers in both selectivity and sensitivity.[39] Advanced experimenters might construct their own "superhet" receivers from parts or kits, and a few ready-built superhets fulfilled specialty needs. It was not until 1923, however, that Armstrong, together with his friend and colleague Harry Houck, had improved the design to the point where a consumer grade superhet could be contemplated. The first such units were manufactured by General Electric and marketed by RCA. They were the Radiola Super-Heterodyne (desktop)[40] and the Radiola Super VIII (console), both of which came to market in March 1924.

Superheterodyne receivers were known as the Rolls-Royce of radios. Because superhets were expensive, regeneratives and TRFs continued to be manufactured for years. A survey of the participants in the International Radio Week mediumwave tests conducted in November 1924 revealed that half used regenerative receivers, 55 percent built their own radios, three-quarters used outdoor antennas rather than loops, and the greatest source of interference was the radiation of other people's receivers.[41]

Battery eliminators, which got their power from the home light socket, arrived in 1924. Although they gained popularity in 1925, their use in radio receivers, all of which had tubes designed for battery operation, produced mediocre results. Full A.C. operation had to await the arrival of tubes designed for that purpose. The first radio with tubes specifically designed for A.C. operation was RCA's Radiola 17, a TRF receiver introduced in 1927.

From the standpoint of shortwave history, it is important to remember that all consumer receivers were designed for the standard broadcast band, whose stations were fueling the national interest in radio. There were no receivers available that covered 3 to 30 mc. Some receivers were advertised as including "shortwave," but invariably this was defined as 200 meters (1500 kc.), or at the very most 150 meters (2.0 mc.). So if you were looking for a ready made receiver to capture the shortwave signals of KDKA or KFKX, you were out of luck.

The first true shortwave receivers which were at least nominally of consumer design were of the regenerative type and came on the market in 1926. It would be five more years before they would achieve real visibility. While this was mainly because of patent fights and the state of technology, conceptualizing shortwave as a relay vehicle rather than a means of direct broadcasting contributed to the delay. To the extent that ordinary listeners could benefit from shortwave, it was by listening to a standard broadcast station rebroadcasting a short-wave signal from another standard broadcast station — experiencing the use of shortwave as a point-to-point medium — not by receiving the shortwave signal directly.

METERS VS. KILOCYCLES

The Second National Radio Conference, held in March 1923, recommended that the Department of Commerce use frequency (kilocycles) as the proper reference in radio work, with wavelength (meters) expressed in parentheses thereafter. The government adopted the recommendation and soon the movement toward frequency was underway, although the use of wavelength would continue for many years. Frequency made much more sense, especially in connection with signal bandwidth, which could now be expressed in uniform terms.

1924

Marconi

Marconi continued his shortwave tests in 1924 from Poldhu, site of the famous 1901 "S" transmission. Early in the year, using 17 kw. on 3260 kc. and a non-directional antenna, he found that very strong nighttime reception was reported from aboard the White Star liner *Cedric* in New York. The daytime range was 1,600 miles. From Australia, Amalgamated Wireless (Australasia) Ltd. reported hearing the signals at good strength in both morning and afternoon. They were heard in Canada for 16 hours a day. In May, a non-directional test transmission intended for Sydney, Australia, also on 3260 kc., was well received there.

Further tests between Poldhu and the *Elettra* on approximately 3260, 5000, 6380 and 9375 kc. revealed that the daylight range increased as the frequency increased. Daytime success with Madeira on 3260 kc. was limited, but Beirut, some 2,100 miles distant, could be reached all day on 9375. In October it was found that daylight communication with Montreal, New York, Rio de Janeiro, Buenos Aires and Sydney was possible on 9375 with 12 kw. High frequency communication with Sydney was possible for virtually the entire day.[42]

The concept of "beamed," or directional, transmissions was of particular interest to Marconi. He learned that by using arrays of vertical wires, with a second set of wires behind them serving as a reflector, together with changes in the angle of elevation, signals could be concentrated and focused in a particular direction. Marconi's colleague, C. S. Franklin, solved the problem of feeding so many antenna wires by developing a system of concentric copper tubes, the forerunner of today's coaxial cable. Directionality was also studied by the Bureau of Standards.[43] In the years to come the feasibility of directional transmissions would underlay an immense interest in shortwave for commercial purposes.

Marconi's work had an early practical consequence. The Imperial Wireless Chain was an ambitious albeit unimplemented plan to connect Britain to her dependencies and to foreign countries for commercial traffic. Conceived in 1912, it had been designed around the high power longwave transmitters of the time. Relations over the scheme between the British government and the system's godfather, Marconi's Wireless Telegraph Company Ltd., were tumultuous—a combination of differing views and plans among Canada, India, South Africa and

Australia on the question of large, central stations vs. smaller relay stations; differing concepts of ownership (a Marconi monopoly was feared); and personality clashes. Planning had been interrupted by the war, and drifted thereafter. In July 1924, at Marconi's urging, the government, after much vacillation, scrapped the longwave plan in favor of more economical, lower power shortwave transmitters. This was the "beam" system.[44] With this monumental decision, Britain dodged the same bullet as had RCA when the latter abandoned the huge longwave installation slated for Radio Central in favor of shortwave.

KDKA

There were many instances of rebroadcasts of KDKA in 1924. The BBC set up a special facility on Biggin Hill, Kent to receive the KDKA signals and send them on their way to London by wire. They planned to do such relays once every two weeks. Reception varied.[45]

A significant relay experiment occurred on March 7, 1924 when the MIT annual alumni dinner at the Waldorf Astoria Hotel, which was broadcast by RCA station WJZ in New York City on its regular broadcast band frequency, was also sent out by wire to General Electric station WGY in Schenectady, which broadcast it on both its regular frequency and on 2803 kc. shortwave (by then WGY was experimenting with shortwave).

Form 10396

RADIO STATION KDKA
Westinghouse Electric & Manufacturing Company
East Pittsburgh, Pa.

Thank you so much for your commendation of our concert. Hearing from you and many others is our greatest incentive to arrange concerts and other features that will bring enjoyment into your home. We shall welcome any suggestions you may have.

Advance programs are published by the Pittsburgh Post, Pittsburgh, Pa., as a supplement to the Wednesday edition. The subscription price is $1.00 per year.

WESTINGHOUSE RADIO STATION KDKA
"The Pioneer Radio Broadcasting Station of the World"

In the early days of broadcasting, letters from listeners were the only way of knowing who was listening. Stations were pleased to receive "applause cards," where listeners expressed their opinion of the program. The larger stations replied with a thank-you.

The shortwave signal was picked up by KDKA and rebroadcast on KDKA's standard broadcast channel and on 3060 kc. shortwave. KFKX picked up the shortwave signal and further relayed it on its standard broadcast channel and on 2885 kc. shortwave, where it was picked up by KGO in Oakland which rebroadcast it on its regular frequency. 2AC in Manchester, England also picked up KDKA shortwave and rebroadcast it on its broadcast band frequency, at the same time feeding it to several other stations to which 2AC was connected by wire. *Radio News* called it "the most magnificent example of radio's advance and of its practicability that has yet been shown."[46] The same arrangement (sans 2AC) was used for a speech by an American general in May.

In March, some foreign-language programming from KDKA was reported. During the summer, both national political conventions were carried on shortwave, as were the election returns in November.[47] The conventions were a major event even on domestic American radio. They were heard over station LOZ near Buenos Aires, and Argentine amateurs with shortwave sets reported hearing both KDKA and WGY direct on shortwave "practically any night in the year."[48] The Argentine newspaper *La Nación* arranged for local rebroadcast of the KDKA coverage of the heavyweight championship match between Harry Wills and Luis Angel Firpo, the "Wild Bull of the Pampas," in Jersey City on September 11, 1924 (Wills won on points).[49] This was reported to be a long-distance broadcast record at the time.

On October 11, 1924, the H. J. Heinz Company Founders Day banquet at the Hotel Pennsylvania in Pittsburgh was transmitted on shortwave (3 mc.) by KDKA, relayed on the broadcast band by WBZ and KYW and on shortwave by KFKX, and heard at 62 different sites around the country, where parallel banquets were being held. Some sites received the broadcast from KDKA or KFKX shortwave, others enjoyed the festivities by way of wired transmission from one of the shortwave or broadcast band receiving sites. President Coolidge spoke from the White House, which was connected to KDKA by wire. There were 53 sites in the United States, four in Canada, four in England and one in Scotland.[50] Two months later KDKA was received in South Africa. Reports on the event differed. One said that a newspaper reporter in South Africa was listening to a noteworthy address from the station, took it down in shorthand, and read it over the telephone to his employer, the *Johannesburg Star*, which reported it in the newspaper. Others say that the KDKA program was actually retransmitted in South Africa.[51]

In July 1924, the KDKA shortwave transmitters were upgraded to 20 kw. and moved about a mile from the Westinghouse plant in East Pittsburgh to a new facility in Forest Hills. The broadcast band transmitters followed later. Now KDKA had directional aerials at its disposal.[52] Around the same time, KDKA began experimenting with frequencies in the vicinity of 60–70 meters. And the government authorized the transfer of Frank Conrad's historic call letters, 8XK, to the KDKA shortwave transmitter, which thereafter operated as 8XK.[53]

THE FAR NORTH SERVICE

One of the most interesting early uses of KDKA shortwave was for transmissions to Canada's far north. These programs consisted of news and music, and, more importantly, letters and messages from friends, relatives and fellow employees of persons located above the Arctic Circle — the Royal Canadian Mounted Police (RCMP), the Oblate Fathers, employees of trading posts such as the Hudson's Bay Company and Revillon Frères, ships' crews, surveyors, explorers, etc.

The genesis of these broadcasts appears to have been in January 1924,[54] when friends of the wife of a Hudson's Bay Company trader asked KDKA to broadcast news of the wife's surgery to her husband. The message was included in a KDKA farm program, and its value was acknowledged several months later by the grateful husband. During the summer of the same year, the Canadian government requested KDKA's help in maintaining contact with the three-masted schooner CGS *Arctic*. The *Arctic* was to make its annual trek from Quebec to Greenland, this time destined to reach the 1923–24 MacMillan Arctic Expedition, which lasted from June 1923 to September 1924, as well as other outposts. Westinghouse placed aboard the *Arctic* one shortwave receiver for delivery to Commander Donald B. MacMillan, and another for use aboard ship. MacMillan already had radio transmitting equipment, albeit not shortwave; the *Arctic* had several transmitters, including a new one operating on 120 meters (call letters VDM) with which, for this trip, Canadian hams were authorized to communicate. In order to facilitate one-way, and hopefully two-way, contact between KDKA and the *Arctic*, suitable receivers and transmitters were also placed aboard the Hudson's Bay Company boats *Bayeskime* and *Nascopie* in order to relay the transmissions of each side if necessary. Specially arranged code transmissions from KDKA were heard direct by MacMillan, and aboard the *Arctic*, during weekly shortwave broadcasts on Mondays at 10:30–11:00 P.M. EST on 4760 kc. Regular

KDKA shortwave programming was also heard. KDKA was heard aboard the *Arctic* even when the vessel had sailed well north of MacMillan's encampment.[55]

The Far North Service followed upon these events, and became increasingly popular as specially-built Westinghouse receivers were delivered by the company's Canadian branch to the RCMP and others.[56] It appears that the service began as an identifiable component of KDKA programming in 1925. The Saturday night programs were broadcast four times each year during the Arctic winter over the KDKA and KFKX standard broadcast and shortwave frequencies. They were also broadcast on other dates over WBZ, Springfield, Massachusetts, WBZA, Boston, and KYW, Chicago, on their regular broadcast band frequencies. There is some evidence that they were also carried over the WBZ-WBZA shortwave affiliate, W1XAZ, from the time it opened in 1930, and that the same year saw the inauguration of similar KDKA broadcasts to United Presbyterian missionaries in India, Ethiopia and other countries.[57]

Monsignor Arsene Turquetil, the famed "Arctic Bishop," observed that "[r]adio broadcasting to the north from KDKA is a real Godsend to us, and if it were abandoned, our life over there would be a real misery, a true despair, after we enjoyed so much that only way of communicating with our country, our home and with the one[s] we love so dear."[58] The Far North broadcasts served as a model for the Canadian "Northern Messenger" broadcasts which commenced in 1933.

SARNOFF'S SUPPORT

David Sarnoff received an important lesson about the power of shortwave in the summer of 1924. He and Frank Conrad were among the delegates to a London meeting of American, British, French and German commercial radio interests planning the establishment of a commercial radio link between Europe and South America. The transmissions would be in code. Most attendees had supported using longwave, the traditional means of long distance communication. Conrad was only an observer, and utilized the better-known Sarnoff, head of the RCA delegation, as his proxy in support of shortwave.

Conrad had brought with him a shortwave receiver, and had established a schedule whereby 8XS would transmit to him special daily voice broadcasts, which he found he could receive in his hotel room using a two-tube receiver and a wire-and-curtain rod antenna. Conrad invited some delegates to hear the broadcasts. Among them was Sarnoff, who, while a supporter of shortwave in earlier years of shortwave experimentation, had had relatively little direct experience with it. Sarnoff listened to the 8XS transmissions for an hour and was so impressed that he turned the tide of the skeptical attendees in favor of shortwave. More importantly, he became a strong supporter of the change from longwave to shortwave at RCA's Radio Central. One has to wonder how aware he was of the successful Metropolitan-Vickers relay that had occurred months before. In any case, the London event, together with Marconi's shortwave experiments, spelled the end of longwave for commercial transmission. Sarnoff told a meeting of electrical dealers that international broadcasting was closer at hand than the public knew, and that rebroadcasting would facilitate simultaneous broadcasting of programs worldwide.[59]

WGY

On January 1, 1924, General Electric began relaying its broadcast band station, WGY, over a 10 kw. shortwave transmitter located at the company's Schenectady plant. This was

2XI. The antenna was 80 feet high and 60 feet long. 2XI was heard in South Africa almost immediately. It had begun in 1923 as a shortwave experiment on a frequency around 3 mc. The 2XI radiations disrupted other work in the Schenectady facility, and so the transmitter was relocated to a small island in the Mohawk River. 2XI was widely heard by amateurs possessing the right equipment, and would eventually lead to the creation of GE shortwave stations 2XAD and 2XAF.[60]

As noted earlier, there was some early shortwave collaboration between WGY and KDKA, e.g. the March MIT banquet broadcast. However, WGY would make its own mark. On April 5, the BBC began relaying some WGY programs. A concert at the Wanamaker auditorium in New York City was sent by wire to WJZ, then by wire to WGY, which sent it out on the stations's regular frequency (790 kc.) and on 2803 kc. shortwave. The shortwave signal was picked up by 2LO and fed by wire to other BBC stations.[61] "It is said that the music is as loud and clear across the Atlantic as it is in the cities from which the waves begin their flight through the ether."[62] Good reception in Los Angeles was also reported.

By mid–1924, WGY was transmitting its programs on 15.85 meters, or 18.9 mc., a very high frequency in those days and one with great potential for long-distance reception during the daytime, though this was not fully appreciated at the time.[63] The use of parallel shortwave frequencies would become standard practice in years to come, and the GE station would surpass KDKA in its national and international reach and fame.

WLW

The year 1924 also saw the birth of a station that would be known to generations of shortwave listeners. WLWO began life as 8XAL, an experimental station of the Crosley Radio Corporation.

The Crosley company was owned by Powel Crosley, who was known as the Henry Ford of the radio industry for his use of assembly-line manufacturing techniques and his interest in producing basic, affordable receivers. Powel Crosley had bounced around various branches of the automobile business and the advertising business with limited success. He developed an interest in radio in 1921 while shopping for a radio for his nine year old son, and became hooked. He began making radio cabinets, then parts, and finally full receivers in a group of small factories which he called the Crosley Manufacturing Company. In 1923 he bought the Precision Equipment Company of Cincinnati, a parts and receiver manufacturer, and by the end of the year the two companies were turning out large numbers of sets each day.[64]

In mid–1921, Crosley obtained a license for an experimental station, 8XAA, and began broadcasting records over the air. In March of the following year he obtained a license to broadcast as WLW. For the first six months he operated the 20-watt station out of his home, then moved it to the factory. Soon he increased power to 50 watts, then 500, and, in 1925, 5 kw., by which time Precision had been renamed the Crosley Radio Corporation and had absorbed the Crosley Manufacturing Company. (Crosley Radio Corporation became Crosley Corporation in 1938, Crosley Broadcasting Corp. in 1947.) Powel Crosley also inherited the broadcasting license of the Precision Equipment station WMH and was able to parlay it into longer operating hours for WLW.

8XAL was located in Harrison, Ohio, locus of the WLW standard broadcast transmitter. It operated around 6 mc. with 100 watts, simulcasting WLW programming. It was also used for non-broadcast purposes, including government-sponsored experiments in aircraft communication. Although the station would become well known to shortwave listeners in later years, it appears that in 1924 it was even more of an experimental affair than KDKA and WGY shortwave. There are few traces of the WLW shortwave history of those early years, save that the station simulcasted WLW.[65]

Other Developments in 1924

COMMERCIAL SHORTWAVE

Shortwave tests for commercial message traffic were now well under way in many countries, it having been discovered that the operating speeds possible on shortwave were much higher than on longwave. On the other hand, shortwave was thought to be more useful at night than during the day, the daylight properties of the higher frequencies having not yet been fully explored. The RCA station in Tuckerton, New Jersey was experimenting with a 20 kw. transmitter on 103, 97, 93 and 10 meters. Germany, France and Argentina were in contact on 77 and 88 meters, with Germany using 3 kw. on shortwave in place of its usual 200–1000 kw. longwave senders. Paris and Nice were in communication on 56 meters. Rome was operating on 106 and 117 meters. The U.S. Navy had experimented on 54 meters.[66]

Also in 1924, the National Physical Laboratory in England, taking a cue from WWV, commenced standard frequency transmissions.

THE AMATEURS

The first transpacific amateur contact, between California and New Zealand, took place on September 21. It set an amateur world's record for distance — 6,900 miles— and was all the more notable because it was accomplished on 2 mc. rather than the usual shortwave haunt of 3 mc.

Of even greater significance to shortwave radio was the opening in July of four new ham bands— 80, 40, 20 and 5 meters.[67] These were for code only, and for the first time hams were not bound to operate on designated frequencies. (Quiet hours did not apply in the new bands, the hope being that they were sufficiently distant from the broadcast band to minimize interference.) These were true long distance bands and they gave amateur radio a big boost. Extensive amateur study of these frequencies followed quickly, and international ham radio contacts became almost routine.

One consequence of the expansion of the ham bands was the integration of amateur radio into geographical expeditions of all kinds. There was still a good deal of exploration occurring, and loss of contact with the outside world for long periods was a major problem. Shortwave radio solved it, and there would be countless instances of amateur radio serving as a vital link in adventures to exotic places.[68]

An early example was the year-long expedition of Dr. Alexander Hamilton Rice to the Amazon, his seventh trip to the region. It began in mid–1924 and was said to be the first time shortwave radio was used by an expedition in the field, at least in the tropics. Rice had received longwave signals during Brazilian expeditions in 1916–17 and 1919–20, and one of his goals this time was to test the newly available two-way shortwave technology. He took much radio equipment with him, including a 25- to 50-watt field transmitter and a 500-watt base transmitter ("WJS") which was set up in Boa Vista and which usually operated with 150–200 watts. (The WJS call letters were designated by the Department of Commerce and approved by the Brazilian government.)

The shortwave transmitter was designed for 3 mc., but when the ham bands were expanded it was reconfigured in the field for 40 and 80 meters. Thereafter, numerous hams were worked. As one of the expedition's radio operators put it, "[o]n a whole, while transmission on high frequencies proved to a certain extent freaky, communication was established over such long distances, with so little power that the conclusion seems unescapable that short waves will come to be used extensively in long-range work."[69] *QST* said that many hams in the U.S. and Europe were hearing and working WJS.[70] And the expeditioners were among the earliest shortwave broadcast listeners. "Hearing KDKA and WGY with regularity on high frequency was ... a distinct contribution to the expedition's entertainment...."[71]

When the 200-foot, four-masted schooner *Kaimiloa* sailed the Pacific in 1924–26, researchers from Honolulu's famed Bishop Museum were aboard. Licensed as a commercial ship station, it was also authorized to contact amateurs in the 20, 40 and 80 meter ham bands. Many hams and SWLs were happy to hear signals from the vessel, which boasted the first two-way shortwave radio set installed on a ship in the Pacific.[72]

Shortwavers were also excited by the October 1924 cross-continental journey of the U.S. Navy airship USS *Shenandoah,* which was equipped with HF equipment. Its call letters, NERK, became widely known in the amateur community. The *Shenandoah* was in regular contact with amateurs during the trip, and was heard by many others as well. It met a tragic end the following year when it crashed in an Ohio thunderstorm, killing 14 of the 43 persons aboard.[73]

By the end of the year the use of shortwave for long distance domestic and international amateur communication was firmly established, and exploration beyond 3 mc. was well underway. The amateurs then turned their attention to propagation, applying practice to theory and paralleling Marconi's own work on an essential aspect of the successful use of shortwave: the long distance properties of the various bands at different times of the day.

Relay Broadcasting

Since 1922, Secretary of Commerce Herbert Hoover had sought to regulate civilian radio through a series of informal conferences of industry leaders. The Third National Radio Conference was held from October 6 to 10, 1924.[74] It noted with approval the progress that had been made in both wired and shortwave networking. It recognized shortwave for its ability to reach both international and domestic rebroadcasters at the same time, often in combination with wire links at the ends of the circuit.

The conference also gave the concept of "relay broadcasting" its first semi-official recognition. In April, KDKA's Harry P. Davis spoke of the need for a shortwave relay system with booster stations, and a program development component similar to a news agency but with a broader purview, one that would stay on the lookout for interesting programs from all over the world. He predicted that such a system would be "the 'open sesame' to worldwide wireless."[75] The conference recommended that "relay broadcasting" be assigned exclusive use of the bands 2750–2850, 4500–5000, 5500–5700, 9000–1000 and 11000–11400 kc. "Beam transmissions" were allocated 18.0–56.0 mc. It was the first time that frequencies above 2300 kc. had been recognized as worthy of allocation. The recommended bands were narrowed slightly at the fourth (and last) conference held the following year (and "beamed transmissions" broadened in scope to "experimental"). The third conference also urged that "the use of receivers capable of radiating [regenerative receivers] be discouraged for use on the short wave relay broadcast bands."

Although it does not appear that the recommendations of the third conference as to relay bands were affirmatively adopted by the Department of Commerce, they were used as a guide. Optimism about shortwave's future was in the air. As Hugo Gernsback editorialized soon after the conclusion of the conference, "[T]he chances are that in the distant future all the broadcast stations will be operated on waves far below 100 meters."[76] Others were more guarded. "Despite optimistic reports of the proponents of this plan of [national relay] broadcasting," said a *Radio News* observer, "the records do not show it to be successful as yet. There still remains considerable work to be done in this field, before it can be practically utilized for national broadcasting, as it is altogether too uncertain in performance for reliable communication on a large scale."[77]

1925

KDKA

The year started off busy at KDKA. In late January, special test broadcasts arranged between the station and *The Melbourne Herald* were received in Sydney, Australia and Rabaul, British New Guinea, and these were followed by the retransmission of KDKA in Australia. This set a new record for long-distance broadcasting.[78] A few days later the first relay of KDKA by a station in continental Europe took place at the same time that the BBC was also relaying KDKA. The continental station was in Stuttgart, Germany, and there were further relays from Stuttgart in March. KDKA was operating on about 4760 kc. at the time of these broadcasts.[79]

Soon KDKA was heard in Kenya, India and Iraq.[80] In May, *La Nación,* in Buenos Aires, again set up a rebroadcast of a KDKA boxing event, this time an international amateur boxing tournament taking place at the Boston Arena. The program originated at WBZ and was sent by wire to KDKA, which added Spanish-language commentary and sent it forth on shortwave.

While the success of the venture is unknown, in June KDKA planned to radio birthday greetings to the Prince of Wales during his visit to South Africa.

> KDKA's program will start at 10:30 P.M., Eastern Standard Time, on the 63 and 309 meter wavelengths. The Prince will reply about 11:30 o'clock if the affair is a success. KDKA's 63-meter wave is expected to reach Africa. The 309-meter broadcast will be for the benefit of American listeners.
> ¶The program as proposed follows: KDKA will start transmitting at 10:30 P.M., Eastern Standard Time. Station JB [Johannesburg] will start transmitting [at 11:00], with the broadcasting officials at KDKA listening for the signals. If by 11:30 P.M. the signals from Johannesburg have been received, KDKA will so announce the fact as part of the program, and, following this, the Prince of Wales will go on the air.

Since JB operated on 437.5 meters, or 686 kc. mediumwave, it was certainly a longshot.[81]

Another KDKA South African connection occurred at year's end when an amateur in South Africa heard KFKX and, on an impromptu basis, sent the signal over the telephone line to the local broadcaster who put it on the air. "[T]hose who heard the re-broadcast program declared that it was nearly as clear and understandable as if the artists had been in the local studio, instead of in America, nine thousand miles away."[82]

WBZ

As explained later, in 1930 Westinghouse would inaugurate regular shortwave broadcasting from Springfield, Massachusetts by way of simulcasts of WBZ and WBZA over West-

Referencing the few shortwave broadcasting stations on the air, and headlining the medium's achievements to date, this October 1925 ad in *Radio* magazine is one of the earliest designed to attract listeners with superhet receivers specifically to short wave broadcasting, as opposed to shortwave in general (courtesy Eric Wenaas).

inghouse station W1XAZ. Before that, it appears that WBZ was equipped with a shortwave transmitter, but used it only on a standby basis, if at all. (In those days, WBZ was located in Springfield, and its sister station, WBZA, was in Boston. The stations exchanged call letters in 1931.)

In July 1925, Westinghouse announced that, as part of the development of its Far North broadcasts, it would once again be communicating by shortwave with the CGS *Arctic*.[83] The *Arctic* had been part of the KDKA shortwave experiments in connection with the 1923–24 MacMillan Arctic expedition, and KDKA's shortwave signals had been received successfully aboard ship. The experience was one of the foundations of KDKA's Far North Service. In 1925 the *Arctic* again made her annual trip north, this time equipped to receive and transmit, mainly with hams, on the 20, 40 and 80 meter bands, as well as the special "transcanadian" 120 meter band, plus longwave.

The radio operator on the *Arctic* was an employee of Canadian Westinghouse, and Westinghouse announced that it would conduct tests with the vessel while it was in the north. These were to be on Monday and Friday nights at 10:30–11:00 P.M. EST on the same KDKA frequency used in 1924, 4760 kc. KDKA was also expected to make special transmissions to the *Arctic* on frequencies in the 6 and 12 mc. bands (49 and 24.5 meters). In addition, Westinghouse announced that it had recently installed a shortwave transmitter at WBZ and that WBZ would likewise be testing with the *Arctic* on 49 meters at the same hour, but on Wednesday nights.

It is not known whether the broadcasts from either KDKA or WBZ actually took place. In January 1926, WBZ was added to a list of non-amateur shortwave stations that was published from time to time in *QST*. It was shown as a 20 kw. station on 5996 kc. (49 meters). A station list published in *The New York Times* in April showed the same information. Soon, however, WBZ shortwave disappeared from published lists. It reappeared in 1928, when it was listed on 50 and 70 meters, and, in one source (BBC *World-Radio*), on 4285 kc. But there were no published reports of reception. The following year, a story about KDKA shortwave observed that WBZ and KYW were equipped with standby shortwave equipment.[84] Whether it included a shortwave transmitter is unclear.

There were good reasons in 1925, both before and after the *Arctic*, for WBZ to have had a shortwave capability and thus been able to participate in the expansion of the nascent Westinghouse shortwave "network," which at the time consisted of KDKA and KFKX.

It had been reported in May that during that month's shortwave relay by KDKA of a Boston boxing tournament (see above), an Argentine station had tuned in to the Spanish-language commentary that KDKA added from its studio, and that it had also tuned in to WBZ for the English version. WBZ operated on 900 kc., and the implication was that it was that frequency that the Argentines would try. While such a feat would not have been completely impossible, the use of shortwave by WBZ would have made reception infinitely more likely.

The WBZ broadcasts to the *Arctic* would have contributed to Westinghouse work on the use of shortwave for domestic relay purposes. So would another experiment which took place in November 1925. There, three stations that were equipped with shortwave receiving equipment — WBZ, KYW and KFKX — took a number of concert broadcasts from KDKA shortwave and rebroadcast them on their standard broadcast frequencies. Westinghouse made much of the event, and said it would put the concert broadcasts on a regular schedule. It was reported that, using this method, the stations would be able to network, without wires, for the simultaneous broadcast of programs that originated in any one of the cities where the stations were located.[85] This would have been possible only if each of the stations, including WBZ, had its own shortwave transmission capability. (KFKX was already so equipped.)

History has yet to tell us definitively just what the shortwave capability of WBZ (or KYW) was in 1925. However, WBZ was not among the stations reported by shortwave listeners of the time, suggesting that any shortwave operation was at best intermittent. As late as 1928, when the KDKA Far North broadcasts were radiated over KDKA, WBZ, WBZA (Boston) and KFKX-KYW (Chicago), only KDKA carried them on shortwave; the others used their standard broadcast channels, as had been the case with earlier Far North broadcasts.

WGY

Shortwave transmissions of WGY had been interrupted when the transmitter was reassigned to commercial work at RCA, but resumed when GE brought two experimental transmitters, 2XAF and 2XAD, on line. These were 1 kw. units, with 2XAF later upgraded to 10–20 kw.

With two transmitters, GE was now able to operate on two shortwave frequencies simultaneously. 2XAF and 2XAD were among the first crystal-controlled shortwave broadcast transmitters in use. At this time, 2XAD operated at twice 2XAF's frequency. When 2XAF broadcast on 7160 kc., 2XAD was on 14320. (2XAF used other frequencies as well, including 7895 kc.)

A major WGY event in 1925 involved a December cross-country relay of American broadcast band signals. While the exact route of the signal among the seven cooperating stations is unclear, a concert originating at KFI, Los Angeles, was rebroadcast by KOA in Denver, WHAZ in Troy, New York, WOC in Davenport, Iowa, KMA in Shenandoah, Iowa, and KFKX in Hastings, Nebraska. WGY reportedly picked up the WOC standard broadcast signal and relayed it on 41 meters shortwave (although it would have been easier to pick it up on KFKX shortwave). The WGY shortwave signal was reportedly heard in various places throughout the United States, as well as in Europe and Australia.

WJZ

RCA's 54-acre transmission site at Bound Brook, New Jersey, about 35 miles from New York City, was destined to become known to generations of shortwave listeners. Two new RCA "super power" transmitters were co-located there, one the standard broadcast sender of WJZ, the other for shortwave work. The shortwave transmitter served two purposes: it was used to relay WJZ programs to South America as part of an RCA plan to bolster sales there, and it also handled some RCA domestic and international commercial transmissions. Preliminary testing under the call letters 2XAR began in November.

March 14, 1925, saw an international relaying experiment involving WJZ that was unusual in its combination of shortwave and longwave signals. Unlike most relays, which picked up American stations and retransmitted them in other countries, this relay originated in England, specifically at the BBC's experimental station 5XX, then in Chelmsford, and was rebroadcast in the United States. What made the event unusual was that 5XX operated on longwave only,

Opposite page top: The Marconi Company's 2LO was not the first broadcasting station in Britain. That was 2MT. But 2LO became the BBC anchor station, and it was involved in many shortwave tests between the United States and England. *Opposite page bottom:* In 1925, a longwave transmission originating in London, picked up in Belfast, Maine, relayed on shortwave to New York where it was fed by telephone lines to several broadcast band stations, was memorable less for its audibility than its novelty (*Radio News,* 1925).

RECEIVING
EQUIPMENT.
Right: The high-
powered station at
Belfast, Maine, is
here shown. The
1600 - meter waves
were received here
and re-broadcast on
a short wave-length.
The short waves
were then received
at the experimental
station of the R.C.A.
in New York City.
© Kadel & Herbert.

➤➤➤

SHORT-WAVE RE-
CEIVER. Left:
Where the short waves
broadcast from Bel-
fast, Maine, were re-
ceived and sent on
land wires to stations
WJZ and KDKA for
re - transmission on
their normal wave-
length. © Kadel &
Herbert.

CONTROLS AT
STATION WJZ.
Right: The amplifier
panel. © K. & H.

➤➤➤

1600 meters, or 187.5 kc. Music from London's Savoy Hotel was sent to that city's BBC mediumwave station, 2LO, whence it was dispatched to 5XX by land line. The 5XX longwave signal was picked up by an RCA commercial station, 1XAO, in Belfast, Maine, a facility which RCA had bought from the International Radio Telegraph Company in 1921 and subsequently expanded. The 1XAO antenna was ten miles long. In 1923, Belfast had been equipped with a 6 kw. shortwave transmitter, which was now used to send the 5XX signal to the RCA technical and testing laboratory at Van Cortlandt Park, the Bronx, on approximately 2680 kc. It was then sent by wire to WJZ in New York City, and to KDKA, where it was broadcast on the stations' regular frequencies. WJZ also sent the program, again by wire, to WRC in Washington, D.C., while WGY in Schenectady picked up the Belfast shortwave signal and rebroadcast it on the WGY standard broadcast frequency.

This was the third attempt at a 5XX relay in a week. The first had been unsuccessful. Reception was poor on the second attempt, but it had been put on the air over WJZ anyway. 5XX was operating with 25 kw., and the voice of the British announcer was said to have been "as distinct as if he had been in the New York studio, instead of 3,000 miles away."[86] However, *Radio Broadcast* said that reception of the 5XX programs "was so poor that the encounter must be recorded as a victory for static...."[87] Judging from a recording of the March 14 rebroadcast, it was an event that only a DXer could love.[88] The greater significance of these early transmissions was that they were the start of an ongoing cooperative arrangement between RCA and the BBC.

OTHER EVENTS IN 1925

Commercial stations continued the march to shortwave. In addition to Radio Central and 1XAO, RCA had equipped its commercial stations in Tuckerton and New Brunswick, New Jersey and Bolinas, California with shortwave, along with its stations in Hawaii, Colombia and the Philippines. Transmitter power was typically 3 to 20 kw.[89] By September, in addition to American commercial and government stations on shortwave, there were commercial shortwave stations operating in Nauen, Germany; Poldhu, England; Buenos Aires, Paris, Norway, Sweden, the Netherlands, Moscow, and the Dutch East Indies (Java). They operated on various shortwave frequencies from 3 to 15 mc., mostly in the range below 7500 kc.[90] (The well-known Nauen station, POZ, was used for commercial and military purposes until 1945 when much of it was destroyed by Soviet troops. Commercial operation resumed in 1952. In 1959, Nauen began transmitting the programs of East Germany's Radio Berlin International.[91])

On the amateur front, 1925 was the year of Donald B. MacMillan's most famous expedition to the Arctic. Sponsored by the navy and the National Geographic Society, it lasted from June to October.[92] MacMillan's 1923–24 trip had been big news in the radio world because his 89-foot schooner *Bowdoin* was equipped with radio transmitters. Unfortunately, 100-watt WNP operated on approximately 185, 220 and 300 meters (1620, 1365 and 1000 kc.), not shortwave, whose development was still in its earliest stages when the expedition was being planned. Radio proved important in lessening the expeditioners' solitude, however. The regular Wednesday night broadcasts for the benefit of the expedition sent from Zenith station WJAZ in Chicago on 670 kc. were usually heard by the expedition and were a special treat. Other broadcast stations were heard as well.[93] And while many amateur and professional radiomen heard WNP, or had contact with it, communication was often difficult. WNP operator Donald H. Mix later observed that they had picked up occasional messages about shortwave experiments that were taking place while the expedition was in progress, but they did not realize how successful these had been.[94]

On the 1925 trip, the *Bowdoin* was joined by a second ship, the SS *Peary.* WNP's power this time was 250 watts, and it was able to operate in the 20, 40 and 80 meter ham bands, as well as other shortwave frequencies. (The *Peary,* whose call letters were WAP, also had a spark transmitter for 500 kc. and a vacuum tube unit for 600 kc.) WNP's operator was John L. Reinartz, a world famous amateur and one of the best shortwave men of his time. As 1XAM, he had been on the American end of the first-ever transatlantic amateur contacts in 1923. Along as well was Eugene F. McDonald, Jr., President of Zenith Radio Corporation, whose person-nel had designed and supplied the radio equipment on both trips (in 1925–26 using material donated by various manufacturers). MacMillan and McDonald had become friends in 1923, and McDonald had accompanied the 1923–24 expedition as far as Battle Harbor, Labrador. This time he stayed aboard for the entire trip, effectively serving as commander of the *Peary.*

The expedition had extensive communication with commercial and naval stations, and, in particular, hams, whose interest in the newly-developing shortwave field must have been enhanced by these amateur transmissions from a place synonymous with adventure. The shortwave performance was not unexpected, for in pre-departure tests the transmitter had been heard in New Zealand, and on the USS *Seattle,* located 1,600 miles west of San Fran-cisco. Also among MacMillan's transmissions during the expedition were several rudimen-tary voice-and-music programs sent on 40 meters to Zenith's experimental station near Chicago, 9XN. These occurred in August 1925.

Although both Conrad and Marconi had noted the shortwave "dead" zone in their early shortwave work, it was in 1924 and 1925 that study of this phenomenon deepened. The prin-ciples of how shortwave signals travel between earth and the ionosphere to reach their tar-gets were already understood in general, if not in every detail. But the dead zone within the signal's first hop, and how the zone varied based on frequency, season, time of day, etc., was largely a mystery. Failure to understand the dead zone and recognize it as an exception to the long-distance properties of shortwave had contributed to the early view that shortwave held little promise. Much of the credit for the pioneering work in this area is due the Naval Research Laboratory and John Reinartz, together with other hams who participated in tests that explored the phenomenon.[95]

At year's end, industry prognosticators were high on the potential of the short waves. Orrin E. Dunlap, Jr., Radio Editor of *The New York Times,* opined that "[t]he outstanding radio development in 1925 was the advancement in transmission and reception of waves under 75 meters in length." But radio in general was losing some of its romance. Said J. H. Dellinger, Chief of the Radio Laboratory at the Bureau of Standards, "this was the year in which radio became grown-up.... The whole atmosphere of wonder and mystery was replaced during this year by the definite engineering evaluation of radio's possibilities and achievements."[96]

On the short waves, however, the love affair was just beginning.

1926

The year 1926 was one of consolidation in U.S. shortwave broadcasting. The broadcast-ers continued their experimentation, but no new stations came on the air. Overseas, there were the first glimmers of shortwave broadcasting on a direct-to-listener basis.

KDKA

In October, the 1925 KDKA-Australia rebroadcasting event was reprised when KDKA's shortwave transmission was picked up in Australia and rebroadcast over mediumwave station 2BL in Sydney. This was the third night of a three-day test schedule. The broadcasts were made at 8:00–9:00 P.M. Sydney time and were promoted by *The Sydney Sun* and *The Melbourne Herald* (which had also been involved in the 1925 broadcast). Reception was very good on the first night, a Monday. It was poor on Tuesday, when Henry Ford was to speak, but improved on Wednesday. The broadcast was also heard, but not rebroadcast, in New Zealand and Fiji.[97]

The connection between Zenith and MacMillan dated to a 1923 dinner, attended by Zenith's president, Eugene F. McDonald, Jr., where MacMillan observed that the greatest hardship of arctic exploration was not physical stress, but isolation. McDonald replied that radio was the answer (*Radio News*, 1925).

WJZ

David Sarnoff was a promoter of "super power" broadcasting in the United States, whereby radio broadcasting would be done mainly by a small number of broadcasters that would produce quality programs and make broadcasting pay. The stations would use "super power" (which at the time meant 50 kw.). In anticipation of such an enhanced broadcasting capability, Sarnoff had established an agreement with the BBC for the exchange of programs.

The first such exchange, which took place on the evening of January 1, 1926, was an ambitious undertaking involving many standard broadcast stations on both sides of the Atlantic and the exchange of programs in both directions. The American programming originated at WJZ. Shortwave was part of the plan, and the involvement of KDKA, WGY, KFKX and WJZ, all with shortwave facilities, suggests that their shortwave relaying capabilities were put to good use. (WGY was known to be operating on 7160 kc.)[98] England had no shortwave broadcasting capability at this time, and so it is likely that, as with the March 1925 RCA-BBC experiment, signals from England came on longwave via 5XX, which by then had moved from Chelmsford to a new facility in Daventry.[99]

WGY

It was an active year at WGY and it's shortwave station, 2XAF. In January, a 1:00–4:00 A.M. relay of Davenport, Iowa station WOC was conducted on 7160 kc. (with announcements made in 15 languages). In April, a special transmission was made for rebroadcast in South Africa. In May, 2XAF sent greetings to Commander Richard E. Byrd upon his claim to have been the first person to fly over the North Pole. (The transmitter power was increased to 50 kw. for this transmission.) The first Dempsey-Tunney fight (September 1926), a major national sports event, was also broadcast on 2XAF (and possibly KFKX shortwave as well). Reports of reception of 2XAF were received from Australia and New Zealand.

There was also much experimental shortwave work under way at WGY. The 5 kw. WGY standard broadcast facility was located at the GE plant in Schenectady. However, the bulk of the company's broadcast research was now conducted at a separate, 52-acre "laboratory" site in South Schenectady. Here were located many transmitters—including 2XAF and 2XAD, the two units used for shortwave broadcasting—and a variety of antennas.

Sometimes signals were evaluated by sending GE engineers with shortwave receiving equipment to various cities in New York state, as well as to Boston and Florida (and once to Panama). General Electric also received occasional reports from outside individuals, and decided to enlist amateurs in a special test. This major, multi-day event took place in April and involved reception of five of the facility's seven transmitters. They operated on 2750 and 4580 kc. (2XK, 10 kw.), 5970 (2XAC, 10 kw.), 9150 (2XAF, 10 kw.) and 11370 kc. (2XAD, 1 kw.), as well as 20 mc. (2XAW, 600 watts).[100] Programming from WGY was used on all frequencies except 11370 kc. and 20 mc., which were Morse channels. The ARRL solicited 2,000 of its members to take part, and hundreds did. (WGY would run a special program for the ARRL and the International Amateur Radio Union over 2XAF in November.) Some 9,500 of the reports received were good enough to be coded and key-punched onto cards, which were then sorted and tabulated by machine for analysis.

The study assessed many factors, including range, skip distance, daytime vs. night time audibility, and fading. About half the reports were for 2XAF, which had increased power in February from 1 kw. to 10–20 kw. and changed frequency to 9150 kc. after experimenting on 109, 65, 41 and 35 meters. 2XAF had been relaying WGY for some time, and was already known in the shortwave community.[101] The appearance of 2XAF on an antenna field dominated by 300 foot towers was modest, "an insignificant looking wire just 50 feet long and 60 feet above the earth, with a lead-in running into a wooden shack 25 feet square."[102]

STATION LISTS AND SHORTWAVE RECEIVERS IN THE UNITED STATES

The call books and other popular station lists of the day necessarily were limited to standard broadcast stations before the inauguration of shortwave broadcasting. Even after shortwave arrived, however, for the stations that also transmitted on shortwave, such as KDKA, KFKX and WGY, there was little mention of their shortwave operations. What may have been the first list of international shortwave stations was published in August 1925 in *QST*, where it was seen mainly by amateurs. Soon it was republished in *The New York Times*. It showed a mix of commercial, military and broadcasting stations on 48 shortwave frequencies, three-quarters of them above 3 mc.

In 1926, more radio magazines, including *Radio* and *Radio Broadcast*, carried one-page lists of shortwave stations. The focus was on shortwave as a distinct medium, rather than on particular types of stations, and thus commercial, military and broadcast stations were lumped together, with nothing to distinguish one type from another.

Unlike broadcast band receivers, where there was a model for every taste and pocketbook, there were no consumer shortwave receivers, although there were some shortwave receivers designed mainly for amateurs. J. Gross & Company, Radio Engineering Laboratories, Barawik Company, and Silver-Marshall sold shortwave receivers in kit form. The A. H. Grebe CR-18 "Special" was ready built, and the closest thing to a consumer set at the time.[103] (Grebe reprinted the *Radio Broadcast* shortwave station list in the CR-18 manual.) All these receivers were "bloopers," or regeneratives, which radiated when in use and thus interfered with the reception of other listeners. (Broad adoption of superheterodyne circuitry was retarded by the refusal of RCA, which owned the patents, to license the technology to others until a 1930 anti-trust settlement required it.) *Radio Broadcast* said that, due to radiation, there was no shortwave receiver on the market that it could recommend. Even the best entries in the magazine's contest for the design of a non-radiating shortwave receiver produced some radiation, and the more sensitive the receiver, the greater the radiation.[104]

HOLLAND

Voice and music broadcasting began early in Holland. Private experimental station PCGG operated from 1919 to 1924, first on approximately 445 kc., later on 260. It had many listeners outside Holland, in particular the U.K. (*The Daily Mail* sponsored an English-language concert series over the station). A commercial shortwave wireless telephony link between the Netherlands and its colony, the Dutch East Indies (today's Indonesia), was established in 1925. In 1926, researchers at N. V. Philips Gloeilampenfabriek, a lightbulb maker turned major radio parts manufacturer and reseller, located in Eindhoven, began shortwave broadcasting experiments with a 300-watt transmitter on 3313 kc. PCJJ, as it was called, was heard throughout Europe. Philips was aware of the long distance experiments then taking place in America. Soon they rebuilt the transmitter, increased power to 25 kw. and moved to 30 meters, or 9930 kc., where the full potential of the transmitter soon became apparent.

The main objective of American shortwave broadcasting had been the transmission of programs for rebroadcast by domestic stations in the United States or other countries. PCJJ's goal was to provide a regular shortwave service directly to listeners in the Dutch East Indies, and to be heard as well in the Dutch colonies of the western hemisphere, the Dutch West Indies (the Netherlands Antilles) and Dutch Guiana (Surinam). With the imperatives of empire had come a new mission for shortwave.

1927

HOLLAND

Regular broadcasting from **PCJJ** began on March 11, 1927.[105] It was the first bona fide international shortwave service. (*"Hallo, hallo, hier ist PCJJ. Allo, allo, ici le poste PCJJ. Achtung, achtung, hier ist PCJJ. Hello, hello, this is station PC double-J, Philips Radio at Eindhoven, Holland, operating on 30.2 meters."*)

Philips took a broad view of its legal authorization. Its interest was not entirely technological, but extended as well to things like programming and listener research. With its commercial parentage, PCJJ was operating well outside Holland's interest-group dominated broadcasting structure, and certainly at the far edge of its temporary experimental license. However, on-air addresses over PCJJ in May, first by the Minister of the Colonies and then by Queen Wilhelmina herself, while nominally unofficial, suggested strong official backing.

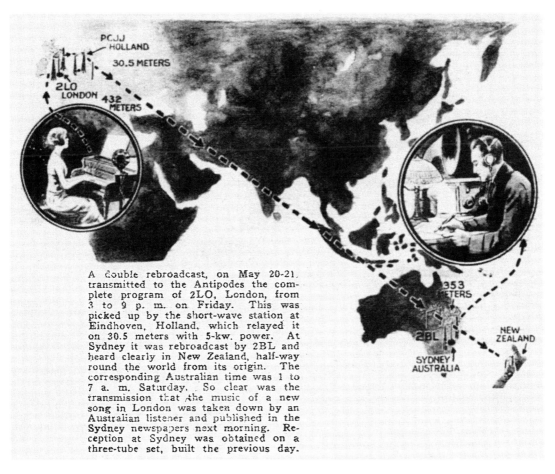

A double rebroadcast, on May 20-21, transmitted to the Antipodes the complete program of 2LO, London, from 3 to 9 p. m. on Friday. This was picked up by the short-wave station at Eindhoven, Holland, which relayed it on 30.5 meters with 5-kw. power. At Sydney it was rebroadcast by 2BL and heard clearly in New Zealand, half-way round the world from its origin. The corresponding Australian time was 1 to 7 a. m. Saturday. So clear was the transmission that the music of a new song in London was taken down by an Australian listener and published in the Sydney newspapers next morning. Reception at Sydney was obtained on a three-tube set, built the previous day.

It was less than three months after PCJJ in Holland came on shortwave that this relay of 2LO, London, to 2BL, Sydney, Australia, via PCJJ, took place. Other relays followed. That British subjects worldwide had to rely on Holland to hear England was one factor behind the creation of 5SW, and, later, the BBC Empire Service (*Radio News,* 1927).

The details of PCJJ's provenance were unimportant to Dutchmen in the country's far flung empire. To them, the station was a voice from home. However, Philips felt it necessary to put its international broadcasting venture on a firmer foundation, and so in June the company, together with a half-dozen firms with commercial interests in the Dutch East Indies, formed a colonial broadcasting company, Philips Omroep Holland-Indie, or PHOHI. Politics and propaganda would not be permitted on air; the government authorization limited it to music and talks of an educational, entertainment, "practical," and religious nature. Although station announcements were multi-lingual, programming was in Dutch, the target audience being Dutch expatriates rather than the indigenous people of the colonies.

At home, powerful private domestic broadcasting interests harbored the same concerns about PHOHI as would, years later, precede the formation of the Voice of America — that government involvement in foreign broadcasting would eventually increase its involvement on the domestic side. However, international broadcasting was seen as sufficiently different, especially in its lack of potential for the kind of membership-supported funding that was typical among Dutch domestic broadcasting organizations, that PHOHI was able to avert any fatal clashes with the domestic broadcasters, at least at this time.

In Holland, PCJJ was the experimental side of the Philips shortwave broadcasting effort, while PHOHI offered a more regularized shortwave service. However, most of the programming was produced in common. The stations were located in Huizen.

Late in the year, PCJJ moved from Eindhoven to Huizen. Studios and office space were set up in nearby Hilversum. Soon thereafter, PHOHI began test broadcasts over its own transmitter, **PHI**, a 40 kw. unit, which was also located at Huizen and which would come into full service at the start of 1929. PHI and PCJJ constituted twin branches of the Philips broadcasting effort. While PCJJ was run by the Philips lab and had a more experimental purpose than PHI, which was run by PHOHI as a quasi-official colonial service, the stations were two peas in a pod.

ENGLAND

Although PCJJ transmitted only in Dutch, it helped spur shortwave broadcasting in the United Kingdom through its informal rebroadcasts of **BBC** longwave station 5XX. These rebroadcasts were solicited by English-speaking listeners who, able to receive the **PCJJ** signal, urged the station to relay the BBC so that they could hear it. 5XX was now heard in the farthest reaches of the British Empire, and stations in South Africa, Australia and New Zealand were known to pick up 5XX programs over PCJJ and rebroadcast them on their local frequencies. (A formal BBC request that PCJJ carry the British Empire Day program on shortwave was, however, turned down.) Englishmen throughout the world wondered why they had to rely on the small nation of Holland to hear voices from the mother country.

In its early stages, broadcasting in England paralleled that in the United States, but on a much smaller scale — informal voice experiments, followed in 1922 by the Postmaster General's licensing of four private broadcasting stations. Two of these — 2MT, Writtle, which operated for about a year, and 2LO, London — were run by the Marconi Company. In addition, Metropolitan-Vickers operated 2ZY in Manchester (along with several sister transmitters), and the Western Electric Company set up 2WP in London.

That was as far as private broadcasting progressed, however. Seeking to establish a market for the sale of radio receiving equipment, and avoid the confusion that was perceived to have engulfed radio broadcasting in America, in May 1922 the Postmaster General convened a meeting of representatives of companies interested in radio, including the companies then engaged in broadcasting. The eventual result was the formation of a cooperative venture, the British Broadcasting Company Ltd., most of whose initial funding came from the participating firms. For continuing support the BBC would rely on a portion of the proceeds of broadcast receiver licenses to be issued by the Post Office, and on royalties on receiver sales by the companies. The receiving license required the use of a receiver carrying a special stamp of approval of the Post Office, an attempt to both preserve a high quality of receiving equipment, and thus a good listening experience, and facilitate sales of equipment. This requirement could not be sustained, however, and the royalties provision was soon dropped.

The BBC commenced operation on November 15, 1922, assuming responsibility for the four existing stations. Within two years a regional broadcasting structure had emerged, complete with low-power satellite stations in hard-to-reach places. In addition, in 1924 an experimental "national" longwave station, 5XX, was set up in Chelmsford. On July 27, 1925, 5XX was relocated to Daventry where the 25 kw. station operated on 187.5 kc.

Creation of an "empire" service had been the subject of some discussion but was a low priority. In May 1926 the Post Office had authorized the establishment of an experimental shortwave station at Daventry. Financial problems and technical uncertainties reflected the same kind of slow progress that had plagued development of the Imperial Wireless Chain up until 1924. Mediocre early test results had been sobering, and there was concern over the signal quality that might be expected. Said the BBC: "[A]t isolated moments it is possible in almost any part of the world to pick up somewhat distorted music and speech transmitted by a short-wave station. On only some of these occasions is reception reasonably good." Together with questions of reception, the BBC was concerned with issues pertaining to the control of BBC programming on rebroadcasting stations, domestic audibility of external broadcasts and the resulting competition with other BBC services, ownership of "rights" to BBC material that might be broadcast in foreign countries, and the propriety of BBC news being broadcast to or rebroadcast in other countries.[106]

Doubts were finally overcome, however, and a shortwave transmitter was rented from Marconi and put on the air from the company's plant in Chelmsford in November, the first major transmission taking place on November 11. This was 5SW, and the start of shortwave broadcasting by what had become by Royal Charter, on January 1, 1927, a government monopoly — the British Broadcasting Corporation. ("*This is the 5SW station of the British Broadcasting Corporation calling you from Chelmsford, England on a wavelength of 24 meters. That concludes the program for tonight. Goodnight, everybody.*")

5SW was a modest affair, a strictly experimental 8–10 kw. "beam" shortwave telegraph transmitter that had been quickly modified for use on 12500 kc. and put in service with a non-directional antenna. Unlike PCJJ, which had mainly direct-to-listener shortwave broadcasting in mind, the BBC, while not dismissing the potential for direct broadcasting, was more interested in the use of shortwave to support the rebroadcasting of the BBC in other countries of the empire, many of which now had local broadcasting stations of their own operating at varying levels of sophistication. Almost a year before 5SW had come on the air, the BBC had considered building an array of shortwave relay stations in Moncton, New

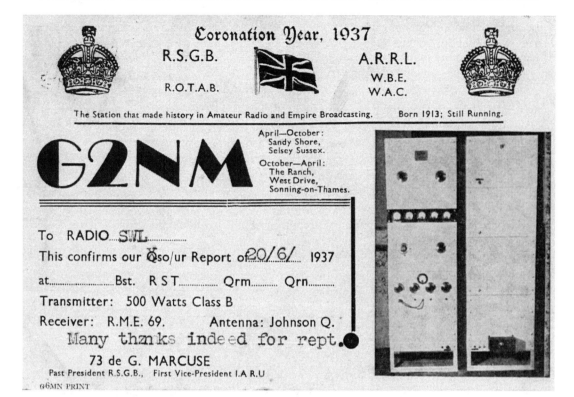

As noted on this 1937 QSL-card, G2NM made history. Its owner, Gerald Marcuse, was conducting licensed shortwave broadcasting from England two months before 5SW came on the air, further highlighting the absence of a British shortwave service.

Brunswick; Fanning Island (Gilbert & Ellice Islands); Sydney and Perth in Australia; Cape Town; Columbo; and Malta.[107] Although that particular plan never came to fruition, rebroadcast of its programs in practically every corner of the world, together with direct-to-listener shortwave broadcasting, would become a hallmark of the BBC for generations.

With 5SW now in operation, a gentleman's agreement formulated in 1925 between Britain and RCA (acting through NBC) to jointly pursue a broader system of program exchange took on greater importance. An example was the BBC shortwave broadcast of Armistice Day celebrations in London in November. Although reception was not very good, it was picked up on shortwave and rebroadcast on WGY, as well as stations in other countries. In the meantime, RCA had had a 30 kw. transmitter, 3XL, installed at Bound Brook, New Jersey, and sought approval to use 11020 and 16020 kc. to send programs to England for rebroadcast.[108]

An interesting event occurred between the authorization and the inauguration of the 5SW service: the commencement of shortwave broadcasts by Gerald Marcuse, 2NM (later G2NM), of Caterham, Surrey. Marcuse was a well-known British amateur (he would serve as President of the Radio Society of Great Britain in 1929–30). These broadcasts, which were authorized by the Postmaster General, lasted for almost a year. Marcuse was an early experimenter with both voice and shortwave, and had been a regular contact of the Hamilton Rice expedition in 1924–25. His shortwave broadcasts began on September 11, 1927, exactly two months before 5SW came on the air. They were fairly elaborate in their cost and organization; studio and transmitter were located in separate houses. And they were eclectic in content; the Marcuse programs ranged from talks to concerts to relays of 2LO to bird calls. The frequency was 9230 kc., and the programs were on the air four days a week at 0600–0700 GMT, plus Sundays at 1600–1800. They were subject to a multitude of restrictions that reflected some reluctance on the part of the Postmaster General — no more than two hours per broadcast, no news, no more than 50 records to be used, no record company advertising, etc.— and some of the terms were honored mainly in the breach. Although the exact impact of 2NM on the development of 5SW is unknown, Marcuse made no secret of his promotion of an official empire shortwave service. "[T]he British Empire is a large one," said he, "and I consider that it is England's duty to provide her scattered subjects with Empire programs."[109] Marcuse reported that his 1.5 kw. signals were often better received than those of his official competitor, the BBC, and were rebroadcast in Australia and Ceylon.[110] Occasional broadcasts from G2NM (on 14320 kc.) were reported even after the station's purported close in August 1928.

The start of BBC shortwave transmissions had followed by a year the inauguration of the Marconi beam system with the opening of the Marconi station in Drummondville, Quebec, in November 1926. The obvious advantages of the beam system, proven during the years of its development, and the speed with which it was implemented once the decision to go ahead was made, no doubt influenced BBC thinking about a shortwave service, notwithstanding its somewhat plodding start along the road that would eventually make it the world's premier shortwave broadcaster.

AUSTRALIA

Australian broadcasting dates back to 1921, when many radio amateurs were transmitting broadcast programming on what are today standard broadcast frequencies.[111] Licensed commercial broadcasting began in November 1923 with 2SB, Sydney (which became 2BL within a few months). Soon it was joined by another Sydney commercial station, 2FC. These stations, together with 3AR in Melbourne and 6WF in Perth, became the Australian Broadcasting Company, predecessor to the Australian Broadcasting Commission, the government-run branch of the country's bifurcated public-private broadcasting structure. (2FC and 6WF, together with 3LO in Melbourne, transmitted on longwave before moving to the mediumwave band.)

Early in 1926, 2BL had conducted some intermittent shortwave broadcasts by way of 2YG, the amateur station of 2BL's engineer. These were taken over by Amalgamated Wireless (Australasia) Ltd. (AWA), a company formed in 1913 to purchase the existing Marconi and Telefunken patents and develop radio communication in Australia. The Sydney shortwave broadcasts went out from the AWA station in Pennant Hills, 14 miles from Sydney, under the call sign 2ME (later VK2ME). Soon the programming of 2FC replaced that of 2BL.

Although Australia would not formalize its shortwave broadcasting efforts until 1931, it began experimental "international" shortwave broadcasting in 1927 by way of a series of AWA "empire broadcasts," which started on September 5 over 2ME on 10525 kc. *("2ME, the experimental station of the Amalgamated Wireless Company of Sydney, Australia, operating on 28.5 meters.")* These programs originated in the 2FC studios and were carried by 2ME over a new 20 kw. transmitter, the most powerful in the country. Consisting of speeches and live music, they were intended for reception as far away as England, and the station was indeed heard there and rebroadcast over 2LO, an event which received wide attention in the British press. It illustrated how shortwave could link the empire, and it reminded Britons that the country's official shortwave voice was still mute (5SW did not commence operation until November). In October there were two like broadcasts from 2ME (also carried domestically over 2FC), by which time the station was also being heard in North America, where it was picked

3LO, Melbourne, Australia, was launched in October 1924 and became the country's most popular and influential station. Its innovative shortwave experiments via 3ME, the AWA transmitter in Braybrook, commenced in 1927 and are reflected in the center photo of this card and the notation, "Short Wave 32 Metres."

up and rebroadcast by WGY on both shortwave and mediumwave. Two further 2ME broadcasts followed before year's end.

The Australian broadcasts were in part a product of the nationalism engendered by the visit of the Duke of York (later King George VI) and the Duchess of York in March and May of 1927, which turned out to be a major radio event in Australia. The shortwave broadcasts were also a return of the courtesy of several transmissions made to Australia and New Zealand over **2XAF** and **2XAD** for rebroadcast by local stations down under. Gerald Marcuse, who was at this time transmitting his programs on shortwave, also rebroadcast 2ME. His rebroadcasts were heard in Australia.

Save for a few earlier experimental shortwave broadcasting efforts by amateur stations, shortwave transmissions from another Australian city, Melbourne, commenced on September 7, 1927, two days after the first empire broadcasts from Sydney.

Also AWA broadcasts, these were by way of a 2 kw. shortwave transmitter located in Braybrook, six miles west of town. This was **3ME**, later **VK3ME**, relaying Melbourne station 3LO (which rented the AWA facilities in Braybrook). The call letters 3ME had originally been used by AWA for a series of experimental longwave and mediumwave concert broadcasts in 1921. It is believed that it was the new 3ME that first introduced the call of the Kookaburra, already well-known to domestic radio listeners, to shortwave (it was later adopted by 2ME and Radio Australia).

CANADA

While not shortwave broadcasting in the usual sense, a shortwave event worth noting was the special Diamond Jubilee Broadcast celebrating the 60th anniversary of Canadian confederation. It took place on July 1, 1927. Born of the Prime Minister's idea that the first sounds of the new carillon in the Peace Tower on Parliament Hill should be heard "from sea to sea," it was a major event from the standpoint of both Canadian history and Canadian broadcasting, for it was the first time that a program had been networked coast to coast.

> "A million hearers, forward-leaning"—on the far shores of the Pacific, the rolling foot-hills of Alberta, the wheat lands of Saskatchewan and Manitoba, in the cities, towns and hamlets of Old Ontario and Quebec, the forests of New Brunswick, the fishing villages of Nova Scotia and the sea-girt Prince Edward Island. Such quickening of national feeling, such impulse of brotherhood has never been known at any one moment before in the history of Canada.[112]

The broadcast connected 19 Canadian mediumwave stations (plus WWJ in Detroit). It involved 11 telephone companies, almost 20,000 miles of telephone and telegraph wires, innumerable amplifiers, repeaters and other equipment, and considerable technical know-how. It was also carried on 11460 kc. shortwave over "CF," the Canadian Marconi Company station in Drummondville, Quebec, the first of the Marconi "beam" stations operative outside the United Kingdom. Test broadcasts on mediumwave were made on June 19, and on June 26 the first shortwave tests were conducted. These, and the July 1 broadcast, were received at many places throughout the world. Some foreign stations, including the BBC, rebroadcast the celebrations.[113]

OTHER COUNTRIES

There were reports that stations in Johannesburg and Durban, South Africa were simulcasting on shortwave, primarily as a means of linking with one another. These transmissions were experimental, as were those from Königs-Wusterhausen, Germany, which was well heard in Europe on 5175 kc.[114] Experimental spark transmissions from Königs-Wusterhausen had begun as long ago as 1908, voice transmissions in 1920.[115]

UNITED STATES

KDKA

KDKA shortwave (**8XK**) could be heard most nights after 6:00 P.M., still on approximately 4760 kc. Starting in February, special broadcasts were made to the SS *Franconia* so that its passengers could listen to KDKA programs during the ship's round-the-world voyage. A shortwave receiver was installed by Westinghouse engineer C. W. Horn, who remained aboard the ship until it reached Cuba. KDKA was also rebroadcast from 6KW in Tuinucu, Cuba, with loudspeakers sometimes set up in public parks for general consumption of the broadcasts. In June, KDKA carried the National Open Golf Championship from Oakmont, Pennsylvania. And the Westinghouse plant in Mexico City picked up the KDKA shortwave signal and made it available to local stations for rebroadcast.

The year 1927 saw the end of **KFKX** in Hastings, Nebraska. Late in 1926 control of the station passed to NBC, which proceeded to convert it into a farm station. An increasing amount of the programming now originated locally, although some was still picked up from KDKA shortwave. By year's end, the farm experiment ended and the KFKX equipment was moved to Chicago where KFKX operated jointly with Westinghouse station KYW, sans short-wave.

WGY

The WGY shortwave schedule included broadcasts on Tuesday, Thursday and Saturday evenings over **2XAF** on 9150 kc., and on other evenings over **2XAD**, 13625 kc. WGY contin-ued an ambitious testing program on shortwave, and its programs were increasingly rebroad-cast by stations in other countries, including England, Germany, Spain, France, Australia, New Zealand, South Africa, Cuba, and various countries of South America. In England, where Tuesday night relays of WGY were frequent, the transatlantic reception point was the BBC receiving site at Keston, Kent, which was set up in 1925. For the WGY rebroadcasts it was equipped with a superheterodyne receiver. (Keston also engaged in high technology frequency measurement. It was replaced by the Tatsfield receiving site in September 1929.[116] Tatsfield would serve as the reception center for shortwave programs to be relayed by the BBC until 1974.) WGY, on behalf of RCA, was also active in testing with the Marconi company in England, which was exploring diversity reception for the BBC.

Foreign stations, as well as American military men, would request that WGY shortwave carry sports events so that they could be rebroadcast and heard overseas. The station believed that programs with an international flavor were especially suitable for shortwave (e.g. the ded-ication of the U.S.-Canadian Peace Bridge in Buffalo in August 1927), as were programs of music. Sometimes WGY would broadcast special programs for particular destinations. "We heard the WGY announcer greeting the passengers, wishing us a good time and a safe return," reported a listener aboard the *Asturias* while in port in Durban, South Africa, where a local station rebroadcast WGY.[117]

An English listener summed up direct reception of WGY shortwave in Europe this way: "The most reliable of the short-wave stations, on the whole, are 2XAD and 2XAF, the relays of WGY.... So completely certain is one of being able to receive them that I have never the slightest hesitation about saying to a friend who is spending the evening with me, 'Would you like to hear some music from America?' This is tempting Providence with a vengeance, but so far I have never been let down once."[118] The next best reception was from KDKA.

Reception reports were important to WGY. Following a series of 2XAF tests, *The New York Times* reported that "[t]hrough a careful analysis of the mail the engineers hope to learn what wave length, what hour and what power are best to reach a definite objective during a particular season."[119]

CROSLEY

In 1925, Crosley had purchased the American Radio and Research Corporation (AMRAD) in Medford Hillside, Massachusetts. The following year, Crosley obtained a license to oper-ate on the shortwave frequencies of 11405 and 14020 kc. between the AMRAD plant in Mas-sachusetts and the Crosley plant in Cincinnati for internal company purposes. However, Crosley announced at the time that it might also use the shortwave connection to relay WLW programs via WARC, the AMRAD station in Medford Hillside that had ceased operating in April 1925.[120]

It is not known if such broadcasts actually took place. What is known is that by April 1927, the WLW shortwave transmitter, **8XAL**, had increased power to 250 watts and was rebroadcasting all WLW programming on 5760 kc. Crosley, by now well ensconced in the receiver manufacturing business, was also marketing a three-tube, plug-in coil shortwave converter, the "Lowave," which connected to a standard broadcast receiver and permitted reception of frequencies from 3750 to 15000 kc. It sold for $40 (without tubes).

OTHER STATIONS

With the experience of KDKA, WGY and others, the practice of simulcasting on short-wave, while still largely a technical diversion, attracted the attention of engineers at some smaller stations, a number of whom made short-lived attempts at shortwave rebroadcasting. These included **KFI**, Los Angeles; **WJR**, Detroit, which used the call letters **8XAO** and oper-ated around 9375 kc.; and **WAAM**, Newark, New Jersey, which operated **2XBA** on 4600 kc. Others included **KOIL**, the station of the Mona Motor Oil Company in Council Bluffs, Iowa, which operated **9XU** on 4910 kc. (later 6060); and **WOWO**, Fort Wayne, Indiana, which was on 13160 kc. Some of these, like WJR and WAAM, were tiny operations, using but 50–75 watts.[121] KOIL used 500 watts, and both KOIL and WOWO shortwave carried the network programs of CBS, which was formed in 1927. By 1928 almost three dozen others were licensed for shortwave broadcasting but seemingly never got on the air or were never widely-enough heard to be reported. Most disappeared within a year or two. Still other stations, like **WHK** in Cleveland, Ohio and **WRAH** in Providence, Rhode Island, experimented with shortwave for remote broadcasts, with unfulfilled intentions to broadcast on shortwave.

While none of these shortwave efforts had any long term impact, it is clear that short-wave did have a niche attraction within the wider broadcasting community.

Although not heard as well as WGY and KDKA, a small station that would have a famous descendant—WRUL—was 2XAL, the shortwave sibling of broadcast band station WRNY. WRNY was owned by Experimenter Publishing Company, then the parent of *Radio News* magazine. It started operation in 1925, and late in 1927 it began sending its programs on short-wave as well. 2XAL operated with 500 watts on 9700 kc. (WRNY's broadcast band frequency was 970 kc.). It was on the air most nights after 1900 EST and Sundays at 1600–1800. Morn-ing and afternoon broadcasts were added in 1928. Both the shortwave and the mediumwave transmitters were located in Coytesville, New Jersey, with studios at the Hotel Roosevelt in New York City.

OTHER ACTIVITIES IN 1927

The first international telephone service utilizing wireless was inaugurated between America and London on January 7. It operated on longwave at first, but moved to shortwave in 1928.[122] A huge expansion of international telephone service followed. (There was no way to keep these calls private. Save for the fact that the voices of the speakers were carried on different channels, the knowledgeable shortwave listener could tune in at will.)

There were two important regulatory events in 1927: the formation of the FCC's pred-ecessor agency, the Federal Radio Commission, and the convening of the 1927 International Radiotelegraph Conference in Washington, D.C.

The Federal Radio Commission had its first meeting on March 15, 1927. It shared cer-tain of its regulatory functions with the Secretary of Commerce before assuming plenary authority over radio regulation five years later (and absorbing the Radio Division of the Department of Commerce). The last regulatory actions with regard to shortwave had been at the third and fourth national radio conferences, held in 1924 and 1925. The conferences had recommended five shortwave bands for relay broadcasting. The Commission defined relay broadcasting as an experimental service. It would be authorized only in cases of broadcasting to a foreign country where there was a pre-arrangement with a corresponding station for reception of the American signal. Beyond that, shortwave broadcasting regulation would have to await the pleasure of the Commission, whose priority was sorting out the interference mess on the broadcast band.

The Washington conference was held from October 4 to November 25, 1927. It was attended by some 79 nations and many non-voting organizations. One of its major accomplishments was the adoption of a table of frequency allocations for most of the known broadcasting spectrum. While international broadcasting was a small part of the work of the conference, for the first time specific bands for international broadcasting were established. These were: 6000–6150 kc. (49 meters), 9500–9600 (31 m.), 11700–11900 (25 m.), 15100–15350 (19 m.), 17750–17800 (16 m.), and 21450–21550 (13 m.). Countries were free to allow shortwave broadcasting outside these ranges on a non-interference basis, and many did. However, these designations, which were expanded over the years, established the basic band allocations for 6 mc. and above that are in force today. The conference made no provision for shortwave broadcasting below 6 mc. The FRC considered these frequencies the "continental band," wherein assignments were basically a domestic matter, with coordination to be worked out with other western hemisphere countries as necessary.

The Washington conference also established a requirement that call letters of amateur and experimental stations reflect the agreed-upon international prefixes. In the United States this meant that the call letters of relay broadcasting stations, all of which held experimental "X" calls, would now reflect a "W" prefix. Thus 8XK became W8XK, 2XAL became W2XAL, etc. The terms of the convention that resulted from the Washington conference became effective on January 1, 1929. However, many countries implemented various of the provisions earlier. In the United States, the call letter provision became effective on October 1, 1928.

On the listening front, broadcast band listener groups began forming in various cities, and December saw the organizational meeting of the club that would become the premier all-wave club in America — the Newark News Radio Club, known for several years as the Newark News DX Club. At first devoted exclusively to broadcast band DXing, it would start covering shortwave in 1935.

The popular radio press began discovering shortwave. Readers who had heretofore encountered little mention of shortwave broadcasting found enticing such articles as "The New Short Wave Field Is Opening" *(RADEX)* and "Why Not Try the Short Waves?" *(Radio Broadcast).*[123] Discussion of the pros and cons of shortwave began appearing. On the pro side: shortwave would open more spectrum space to broadcasting; greater range could be achieved with relatively low power; the cost of erecting broadcasting stations would be reduced; wider channel separation meant less interference; shortwave would promote international goodwill and understanding. The other side of the argument was that there were already too many broadcasters and too much marginal programming; the quality of shortwave reception was not particularly good; the dead zone made shortwave unsuitable for local service; complicated new receivers would be needed; shortwave transmitters were more difficult to keep on frequency than standard broadcast transmitters; spectrum space should be conserved, and devoted to more important uses.[124]

Aero Products, Inc. of Chicago started selling its "Aero Short Wave Receiver" kit. More important on the receiver front, although not shortwave related, was the introduction in September of the RCA Radiola 17, the first light socket-powered receiver utilizing tubes designed specifically for A.C. operation. A TRF circuit, it was not without its flaws, and in April 1928 it was replaced by the Radiola 18. Other A.C. models filled out the RCA line for 1927–28. Full A.C. operation was an important milestone in the development of consumer receivers, and within a few years the use of batteries and battery eliminators in standard broadcast receivers disappeared. Shortwave receivers were more sensitive to line noise and A.C. hum than ordinary radios, however, and thus effective A.C. operation on shortwave lagged behind even as shortwave receivers began appearing in greater numbers.

1928

On January 1, **5SW** changed frequency from 12500 kc. to 11750 in order to conform to the terms of the Washington convention. Within a few days it was picked up by WGY, which fed a 5SW dinner music concert by wire to three other New York stations for rebroadcast. 5SW usually operated at 0730–0830 and 1400–1900 EST, sometimes later, daily except Saturdays and Sundays. WGY and KDKA joined the RCA-NBC plan for more regularized rebroadcasts of the BBC.

The **BBC's** view of shortwave was somewhat crabbed. While not characterizing it as hopeless, the BBC considered the medium strictly experimental. Its goal on shortwave was programming and signal of the same quality as enjoyed by home audiences. The corporation was quick to point out that neither was possible on shortwave as it had developed thus far. It treated shortwave as a stepchild, pursued largely to pacify those who had been seduced by novelty, sentimentality, and the perceived technical possibilities of the medium rather than what it viewed as the more sober goal of a high quality (and high brow) radio service.

In November, the ebullient Edward Startz, who would be known to generations of listeners to shortwave broadcasts from the Netherlands, joined **PCJJ** and became the chief announcer for both PCJJ and PHOHI. Fluent in several languages, including English, and an irrepressible promoter, Startz's "Happy Station" programming on PCJJ (*"This is the Happy Station of a Happy Nation"*) soon gave the station a distinctive international flavor. Announcements were in Dutch, English, French, German, Spanish and Portuguese.

PCJJ was on the air on Tuesdays and Thursdays at 1100–1500 EST, Fridays at 1800–2100 and Saturdays at 1000–1300, on 9555 kc. (*"This concludes the program of the broadcast from PCJJ. We are closing down. Goodnight, everyone. Goodnight."*) PCJJ also broadcast a weekly Spanish program. At the same time, the PHOHI station, **PHI**, provided a Dutch-language service for Dutch citizens in the colonies.

Shortwave broadcasting did not originate exclusively from stations whose primary audience was the general public. Unlike the United States, where message handling and similar commercial radio functions were in the hands of private companies like RCA, Mackay and AT&T, in most countries these functions were performed by post, telephone and telegraph (PTT) departments owned or controlled by the government, sometimes in partnership with private interests. As PTTs made increasing use of shortwave for long distance communication, they sometimes broadcast voice and music programming as well. Often this was just a convenient way to hold open a circuit. In some cases, however, programming was more substantial, with the PTT either originating its own content or making its facilities available for the use of broadcasters wishing to reach the general public.

An early example of PTT broadcasting was **PCLL**, a channel of the major transmitter center of the Dutch PTT in Kootwijk, Holland. **Kootwijk Radio** had gone into service in 1923 for the purpose of maintaining contact with the Dutch East Indies. It operated solely on longwave until 1925, when shortwave was added. In 1928, PCLL started transmitting programs

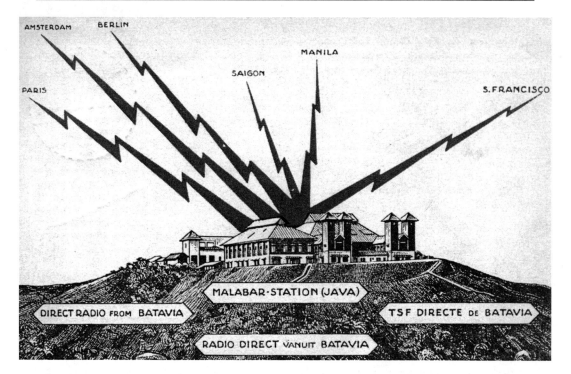

Indonesia, then known as the Dutch East Indies, was the target of early shortwave broadcasts from Holland. Although not a shortwave broadcaster as such, the PTT installation at Malabar, which communicated with similar stations worldwide, sometimes carried broadcast programming.

of general interest. News in Dutch, English, French and German was broadcast on Wednesdays. Programming over the 32 kw. transmitter expanded to include music, and while transmissions were beamed to Java, soon the station was being widely heard, usually on frequencies in the vicinity of 16 mc. (The Kootwijk site is now a national monument.)

On Java, in the Dutch East Indies, there were two 25 kw. transmitters in operation, government telegraph and telephone station **ANH** in Malabar on 17645 kc., and **ANE** in Bandoeng on various frequencies including 9375, 18830 and 19060 kc. As with PCLL, these stations usually carried telephone traffic (often with PCLL), but at times they carried broadcast programming. A shortwave broadcaster was also reported operating from **Medan**, Sumatra, on 8000 kc.

Station **RFM**, in Khabarovsk, Russia, was likewise a PTT station that also broadcast news and music. It operated on 4273 kc. and around 8600 kc. with 10–12 kw., and came on the air most days around 0400 EST (some listeners felt that the higher channel was a harmonic). It could be heard on the west coast with announcements in Russian, Chinese and English.

3LO was widely heard over **3ME**, Melbourne, Australia, on 9510 kc. "Every mail is said to bring sheaves of letters to 3LO from the four corners of the earth, reporting favorable reception. * * * One family tucked away in the Kenya Colony District, Africa, invited guests at Christmas time to listen in to the Australian station. The hostess wrote immediately to thank the station for contributing to their Yuletide party. Every word of a long program was heard clearly, with no fading, and the striking of the clock in Melbourne was a reminder that though distance separated the two countries and time divided them, there was a common bond made more emphatic and understandable by broadcasting."[125]

In nearby Lyndhurst, Post Office engineers built a 600-watt experimental shortwave

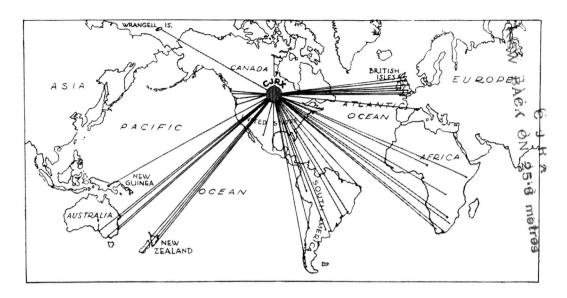

"I was listening to your programme on Wednesday, February 27 [1929], and every word was heard distinctly on loud speaker," reported a New Zealand listener to CJRX, one of Canada's earliest shortwave broadcasters *(CJRX Radio Bulletin)*.

transmitter, **3LR**. The frequency was one that would be familiar to generations of listeners to Australian shortwave: 9580 kc. It too carried programming from 3LO, and also from 3AR. And at Pennant Hills near Sydney, a second 20 kw. shortwave transmitter was installed. Later, Pennant Hills would transmit as **VLQ**.

CJRX in Winnipeg, Manitoba came on the air. Owned and operated by James Richardson & Sons Ltd., a large grain and financial house, it transmitted the programs of CJRW and CJRM in, respectively, Fleming and Moose Jaw, Saskatchewan. Its 2 kw. experimental transmitter operated first on 11720 kc., then 6150, as **VE9CL**. The station invited reception reports and was well heard. *("This is CJRW and CJRX. CJRW, the broadcasting station of Fleming, Saskatchewan; CJRX, 25.6 meters, shortwave station of James Richardson & Sons, Winnipeg, Manitoba, continuing its program.")*

Also in Canada, standard broadcast station CFCA in Toronto began rebroadcasting some foreign programs from the BBC, PCJJ and 2ME. And the **Canadian National Railways**, expressing difficulty in finding good afternoon radio entertainment for its passengers, added **8XK, 2XAF** and **2XAD, 5SW** and **CJRX** to the radio fare to which observation car patrons could listen (with headphones). The railroad was an early user of radio in its passenger cars.[126]

While less well known than the stations in England, Holland, the U.S., etc., other countries were also coming on shortwave. But information about their broadcasts was spotty. In May, the first widely known shortwave broadcasting station in Latin America came on the air. It was **NRH**, a 7½ watt station in Heredia, Costa Rica operated by Amando Céspedes Marín. NRH was on the air most nights at 2230–2330 EST on 9835 kc., and despite its low power it would become one of the best known (and friendliest) of all the shortwave voices.[127] Japan's first radio station, JOAK, Tokyo, had begun broadcasting on mediumwave late in 1924. In 1926, JOAK and its two sister stations in Nagoya and Osaka joined the new government-run national network, **Nippon Hoso Kyokai (NHK)**, or **Broadcasting Corporation of Japan**. Soon, using a new shortwave transmitter at Atagoyama, the station was broadcasting monthly shortwave tests to Australia and the American west coast, and by 1928 it was being heard each day using one of its four shortwave channels, which were on 30, 35, 60 and 70 meters. And **7LO,** the **British East African Broadcasting Company Ltd.,** Nairobi, Kenya, had been testing on 2 mc. for some time. In October 1928, the station moved to 9555 kc., then 9640, and was on the air at 1100–1400 EST. Power was about 500 watts.

Compagnie Française de Radiophonie, often referred to as CFR, was a subsidiary of **Compagnie Générale de Télégrafie Sans Fil** (CSF), a private company roughly paralleling RCA and operating commercially as **Radio France. Société Française Radio-Électrique** (SFR) was part of CFR. Operating as **Radio Paris,** it began broadcasting on longwave in 1922 and had been conducting some experimental shortwave transmissions since 1925. Other French commercial stations, including **Radio "LL"** (F8GC), **Radio Vitus,** and others were also using shortwave. The signals of **"Paris Radio Experimental"** were reported heard in the United States, first on 9480 kc., then on 10345. The 1 kw. transmitter operated at various times for about an hour a day, four days a week.

Two shortwave stations were reported on the air from Denmark. One, **OZ7RL,** Copenhagen, on 3560, 7120 and 9500 kc., was operated by *Radiolytteren* and *Populær Radio,* two Danish radio magazines. The other was **OZ7MK,** "The Midnight Sun," Skamlebaek, relaying the local mediumwave station on around 9375 kc. It would eventually become the well-known **OZF. Saigon** was reportedly operating on 49 meters; **Radio Maroc,** Rabat, Morocco, on 23 meters; and **VRY,** Georgetown, British Guiana, two nights a week on 6850 kc.

A new shortwave station in the United States was being heard. WABC, with studios in New York City and transmitter in Richmond Hill, Long Island, was the standard broadcast station of A. H. Grebe, doing business as the Atlantic Broadcasting Company. It began life in 1924 with the call letters WAHG, which were changed to WABC in 1926. As one of the premier radio manufacturers of the day, and one with a shortwave receiver to sell (the CR-18), it was no surprise that Grebe would be interested in shortwave. The WABC shortwaver, **2XE,** one of a number of Grebe experimental stations, had gone into operation in 1927 and operated on a variety of frequencies, including those around 2830 and 4700 kc. At times it rebroadcast the programs of WABC.

In 1928, Atlantic Broadcasting Company and WABC were sold to the fledgling Columbia Broadcasting System, which had been formed the year before. Until then, CBS had been only a program provider; WABC was the first station it owned. With it came 2XE, which now began simulcasting WABC all day on 5130 kc. Power was increased from 250 watts to 1 kw.

The Crosley broadcasting organization also underwent some changes that would eventually affect its shortwave outlet, **8XAL.** In May, Crosley purchased WSAI, a standard broadcast station in Mason, Ohio. In October, Crosley increased power at its main station, WLW, and moved it from Harrison, Ohio to an expanded Mason facility. Now operating on a clear channel with 50 kw., WLW began promoting itself as "The Nation's Station." For the time being, 8XAL remained at Harrison, but was off the air for a time in anticipation of a move.

Some shortwave broadcasting was just for fun. In February, GE station **2XAD** held a two-way conversation with **5SW** in England and put it all out over its standard broadcast channel. In the course of the program, music was sent by 2XAD to 5SW, which transmitted it back to 2XAD on shortwave. 2XAD then put the 5SW rebroadcast of the 2XAD signal on the air. "It will be a decided novelty for broadcast listeners," said GE before the event. "We have had great success with the stunt thus far and we are hopeful that [this time] will be no exception." Reception was so-so. (*"'Hello, 5SW....' 'Are you there, 2XAD?' 'I hear you, 5SW ... but your signals are not coming clearly.'"*[128])

There were other 2XAD-5SW conversations that went out as well. These were heard as far away as India and New Zealand, and in the latter case a listener heard the conversation carried over both stations simultaneously. There were several two-way programs between **2XAF** and **2ME** in Australia, one of which was heard in Peru. A three-way conversation among 2XAF, 2ME and **ANE** in Bandoeng took place in October 1928, and a later one featured greetings by prominent persons. And there were relays of relays. A listener in England reported hearing a German station relaying 2XAF at the same time that 2XAF was relaying the BBC.

The shortwave broadcast of the Gene Tunney-Tom Heeney championship fight in Yankee Stadium in July 1928 over 2XAF and 2XAD was a big shortwave event. Fight coverage, which originated at WEAF and was broadcast over many American domestic stations, was rebroadcast by the BBC on mediumwave and on longwave, as well as by stations in Sweden, Australia and New Zealand (Heeney's home). An American missionary in the Belgian Congo wrote to WGY to thank the station for carrying the presidential election returns on shortwave. "*When I tell you that it takes the ordinary mail three months to reach this interior post you will appreciate what this means to us loyal Americans.*"[129]

There were other noteworthy broadcasts over WGY shortwave in 1928. Commander Donald B. MacMillan, icebound in northern Labrador at mid-year while on one of his many trips to the Arctic, relied on WGY for news. The expedition's radio operator reported that **2XAD** on 13660 kc. was "very loud" all afternoon, and that **2XAF** on 9555 kc. was usually good from 6:00 P.M. to 9:00 P.M. (when WGY's standard broadcast signal was also often heard). And in December, a special broadcast sponsored by the Indian Foundation in the United States and intended for the 3,000 delegates to the Indian National Congress in Calcutta was broadcast, and picked up and rebroadcast on mediumwave in Bombay and Calcutta.

The power that shortwave could have on isolated peoples in faraway places was demonstrated by explorer Francis Gow Smith, who regularly received WGY shortwave during a 1928 expedition into the Brazilian wilderness. While at a hotel stop in Corumba, on the upper Paraguay River, he invited the proprietor to bring a few friends in to listen to his two-tube radio.

> My guests were thrilled as they had never been in their lives. They were almost incoherent in their enthusiasm. The news spread like wildfire through the town. The leading citizens flocked into my room, uninvited; the crowd jammed the corridor outside. Men waited hours for their few minutes' turn with the phones; many went away disappointed and came back night after night until they had heard for themselves this miracle.... Soon I had become the personal friend of the most important businessmen and politicians in Corumba.... I translated the news every night for the local newspaper. Corumba had never been so intimately in touch with the outside world. The community became pro-American. Nobody could do enough for me.

Smith encountered much the same in the isolated town of São Luiz. "I was welcomed into the center of the town's social life, invited to all the most elite weddings, birthdays, and funerals, and offered banquets in every home." The icing on the cake was the three special programs broadcast to Smith over WGY shortwave. A local dentist translated them from the English for those in attendance. "The old suspicions of the United States vanished, and the town became a focal point of boosting for Uncle Sam."[130]

KDKA's shortwave station, **8XK**, was also active. (It was aided by the establishment of a new shortwave receiving station at a place near Wilkinsburg, Pennsylvania known as Duff's Farm.) In September, Commander Byrd departed for his first trip to the Antarctic, where he would make the first flight over the South Pole. In honor of the trip, the KDKA Far North broadcasts were expanded to cover the South Pole explorers as well. At 2300 EST on various Saturdays from November 1928 through February 1929, 8XK sent a special program to Little America, as well as to the Arctic. There were speeches and performances of various kinds, but it was the messages from family back home that were the highlight of the broadcasts. The Byrd expedition made no broadcasts of its own (it would in 1934). However, in accordance with the by-then standard practice for such journeys, it was outfitted with considerable non-phone shortwave equipment — 22 transmitters and 34 receivers — enabling Byrd to thank KDKA for the broadcasts and to maintain direct contact with the station. Sometimes KDKA rebroadcast the Morse code communication with Byrd over the air. Accompanying Byrd on his trip was a *New York Times* reporter, who radioed his stories from the Antarctic.[131] In 1929, Byrd named his main station the Adolph Ochs Radio Station, in honor of *Times* publisher Adolph S. Ochs. Thanks to shortwave, it was but 45 minutes after the event on November 29, 1929 that the *Times* was on the street with the story of Byrd's historic first flight over the South Pole.

KDKA also used its shortwave facilities in emergency situations, as in August when it alerted officials and others in northern Canada to be on the lookout for two fliers who were overdue at their destination in Greenland.

There was a good deal of joint shortwave broadcasting by KDKA and WGY, usually under the umbrella of the NBC network, of which both were early affiliates. Both carried speeches by the American and Cuban presidents at the Sixth Pan American Congress in Havana in January. 2XAF and 2XAD carried the Cuban president's speech in Spanish, while 8XK presented an English translation. In October, both stations carried the arrival of the *Graf Zeppelin* in Lakehurst, New Jersey after its first intercontinental flight. Other events covered by both stations on shortwave included the welcome of the first east-west transatlantic flyers (also covered by **WOWO** and **KOIL** shortwave), and the notification ceremonies in connection with Herbert Hoover's nomination as Republican presidential candidate (also covered by WOWO, KOIL and WLW).

Commercial shortwave made news in May when the Federal Radio Commission assigned shortwave frequencies in the 6–23 mc. range (called the "transoceanic band") to commercial companies. The exercise was repeated in December for frequencies below 6 mc. A host of business and industrial applicants — telephone and telegraph companies, department stores, newspapers, mining, oil and lumber companies, bus services, public utilities, brokerage houses, and numerous others — had requested many more channels than were available, largely in hopes of reducing their reliance on expensive wire communication. The "unlimited" shortwave spectrum was already becoming a scarce resource.

Lack of information about stations was a universal problem. Although by now there were lists of shortwave stations in many radio publications, seldom did they offer more than call letters and frequency. Slightly more expansive in content (it included the name of the station's owner) was the 30-page megalist, "Radio Stations of the World on Frequencies Above 1500 Kilocycles," prepared by the Federal Radio Commission and published in November in the *Proceedings of the Institute of Radio Engineers.*[132] Shortwave broadcasting stations were included, but were dwarfed in number by the plethora of commercial and maritime stations that were by then using shortwave; and IRE *Proceedings* was not widely-read by shortwave consumers. Of greater value to them was the *Radio News* column, "On the Short Waves," that first appeared in June. It printed readers' letters about their success with various receiver designs that had been featured in the magazine, plus reader comments about shortwave stations they had heard. This was one of the first, if not the first, organized columns about shortwave listening in America. Its focus was shortwave broadcasting stations.

Ready-made receiver development moved forward, if haltingly. A number of shortwave adapters and converters were on the market.[133] Aero offered its "Aero International Four," and Silver-Marshall its "Round-the-World Four," one of the first shortwave units to use a screen-grid tube.[134] Both were kits. Kits had taken different forms over the years. The most complete kits consisted of basic components manufactured by the kit's seller or by other manufacturers, plus front panel, base, and instructions, all in one box. Tubes were not included. However, sometimes the kit included only the manufacturer's core components, instructions, and a list of other parts to be bought separately. These, and the many receiver plans that were featured in radio magazines, often listed parts right down to the manufacturer and part number. And there were other variations. The "Round-the-World Four," for example, could be bought as a complete receiver kit, as an adapter kit for use with a standard broadcast receiver, or as a plan with the basic parts only. Some kits could also be purchased in assembled form.

Two receivers of special note were on the market in 1928. The

The Pilot "Wasp" receivers were among the hottest shortwave radios around. Pilot was one of the first companies to fully explore the technical challenges of shortwave reception (*Radio Design,* 1928).

National Company of Malden, Massachusetts came out with the popular two-tube "National Screen-Grid Shortwave Tuner" kit (also offered in a fully wired version). Known as the "Thrill Box," by 1932 it had been offered in versions having up to five tubes (the most famous "Thrill Box" was the three-tube SW-3, which came to market in 1931).[135] Also available in 1928 was the three-tube "Wasp" shortwave receiver kit of the Pilot Electric Manufacturing Company, then located in Brooklyn (it became the Pilot Radio & Tube Corp. in 1929). Several more-advanced "Wasps"—the "Super-Wasp," the "A.C. Super-Wasp" and the "Universal Super-Wasp" (which featured band switching in place of plug-in coils)—along with the Pilot "All-Wave" superheterodyne appeared between 1929 and 1931.[136]

The National and Wasp receivers were the first serious attempts at shortwave receivers that would appeal to the general listener. They were popular. To underscore the availability of shortwave to everyman, Pilot sold some of their models not just in radio stores but also at S. S. Kresge Company (the "Super-Wasp" price was $29.50). Many were sold overseas. Pilot emphasized that the "Wasp" owner could receive foreign stations direct, "without dependence on local re-broadcasting."

Listeners were often reminded that tuning the short waves was "tricky" compared with operating a broadcast band receiver.[137] *World-Radio,* the BBC publication founded in 1925 to cover foreign broadcasting (mostly mediumwave), put it this way:

> [T]he frequency changes effected by the rotation of the dial will take place far more rapidly. It is for this reason that searching on the short waves demands from the operator a greater delicacy of touch and a higher degree of patience, at least until familiarity with its own special technique is acquired. Even such aids as geared controls need careful handling, if the aim of the searcher is ... to miss no sound that makes itself audible in the telephones or loud speaker.[138]

The advice from *Radio News* was similar.

> Short-wave signals, unlike broadcast signals, are exceedingly sharp. The slightest movement of the tuning dial causes distant signals to come in or pass out. For this reason, it requires no end of patience and care and skill to tune in real distance on the usual short-wave set. Many short-wave set owners have been disappointed in being unable to receive more than just a few American short-wave stations, and have begun to wonder whether it is all the bunk about others receiving Siberia, Java, England, Holland, Germany and so on. Bunk nothing. However, the usual black-smith methods of the present high-power broadcast reception do not make a go of it in the short-wave band. To tune in G5SW ... requires the greatest care. The signals on this side of the water are exceedingly sharp, and may be missed time and again even with careful search. The main consideration is accurately controlled regeneration.[139]

Listeners liked to tell about their reception. Raymond M. Bell, a *Radio Broadcast* reader in Carlisle, Pennsylvania, summarized his experience as follows:

United States
2XAF: Very fine in daylight; hardly audible at night.
2XAO [shipboard transmitter]: Always poor, especially at night.
8XP: Fine in daytime.
8XK: Excellent on some nights.
8XAL: Excellent on some nights.
2XAL: Good only in daytime.
Australia
2ME: Excellent with loud speaker strength 5:30–8:30 A.M. EST....
Java
ANH: Good volume, 7–8 A.M.
Holland
PCJJ and PCLL: Always received with a strong signal, almost any hour.
England
5SW on 24 meters relaying 5XX.... 5SW as received in this part of America is simply phenome-nal.... [E]very evening I can easily run the loud speaker 5–7 P.M. EST. 5SW at 5 P.M. is as strong a signal as WEAF.... 5SW 7:30–8:30 A.M. is received with good headphone strength. But from 2–7 P.M. (when England is in darkness and America in daylight) 5SW is as regular and dependable as many of our U.S. stations. One would think we were in the British Isles.

Whereupon *Radio Broadcast* observed, "Mr. Bell either has a magnificent DX receiver or a grand location."[140] Earlier, the *Radio Broadcast* editors had declared themselves not enthu-siastic about what they had heard of **5SW** and **PCJJ** on shortwave. "The quality is invariably poor, the fading severe, and the whole affair strongly reminiscent of the early days of broad-casting, when any signal was worth getting, so long as it was from a long distance."[141]

A listener in the Yukon said: "I have been listening in for more than two years and find the following stations to have arrived here with loud-speaker volume regularly: 2XAF and 2XAD wonderful; 5SW, London, very good; PCJJ good at times; 3XM (WJZ) just found, but good; CF, Canadian Marconi, very good last year; KDKA generally mushy; 2XAL heard once so that with much strain could get announcement, very weak."[142]

Then, as now, reception quality was often in the eye, or the ear, of the beholder.

As year end approached, Hugo Gernsback, while decrying the long-distance performance of most short-wave receivers, repeated a prediction he had made four years earlier. "It would not surprise me at all," he said, "if, during the next five years, the broadcasting of both sound and sight will be done completely on short waves; and the [standard broadcast band] gradually abandoned, as fast as we learn more about the short waves."[143] Meanwhile, KDKA, WGY and WRNY were among a small number of stations that had begun

Although KDKA can lay claim to being the first shortwave broadcaster, it was eclipsed by General Electric stations W2XAF and W2XAD, which were better heard and had a broader range of programs.

experimenting with another medium that would eventually gain a big following. It was called television.

1929

Thanks to the Washington convention, stations were now adding the country prefix to their call letters. 8XK became **W8XK**, 5SW became **G5SW**, 2ME became **VK2ME**, etc. In other call letter changes in 1929, PCJJ became **PCJ**, Dutch East Indies stations ANH and ANE became **PLF** and **PLE**, and RFM in Khabarovsk became **RA97**.

The center of foreign shortwave broadcasting was Europe, with the Netherlands playing a leading role. In January, the tests of PHOHI station **PHI** concluded and the transmitter went into regular service. The Geneva office of the **League of Nations** had made several broadcasts over **PCLL** in 1928. The power was 25 kw., and announcements were in English, French, Dutch and Japanese. These broadcasts expanded in 1929, and the broadcasts were now targeted to particular areas. The first were made in March, with a series of one-hour transmissions over three days to the Americas on 7730 kc., and half-hour broadcasts to Japan and Australia over three days on 16305 kc. Reports to the Information Section of the League of Nations were requested.

In Germany, **Reichs-Rundfunk Gesellschaft**, Berlin, was now on shortwave, 9410 kc.,

The Zeesen shortwave antennas dominated the landscape of Königs-Wusterhausen.

for 11 hours a day, via the German PTT station at **Zeesen**, near Königs-Wusterhausen. Soon it was on 9560 kc., 8 kw., using the call letters **DJA** and identifying as the **Deutscher Kurzwellensender**. **EAR**, Madrid, Spain was on a frequency around 6870 kc., Monday and Friday at 1730–1900 EST. Sweden had begun using shortwave from its transmitter site in **Motala**. It was on 6012 kc. at first, then 6065. And **OXY**, the Danish PTT station located at Lyngby, began relaying the Copenhagen mediumwave station on shortwave for the benefit of Danish subjects living abroad. The frequency was one that would be associated with Denmark for decades: 9520 kc.

The reliance of Australia's **VK3ME** on 3LO programming ended when the latter merged with 3AR. All VK3ME programming was now produced by Amalgamated Wireless itself. A few shortwave stations started appearing in Asia. The Royal Siamese Post and Telegraph Department in Bangkok, Thailand (then called Siam), which was principally a commercial station, did some broadcasting as well, usually for an hour or two in the morning. The channels were **HS1PJ** on 17750 kc., **HS2PJ** on 10170, and **HS4PJ** on 7980 kc., and the power was believed to be several hundred watts. Announcements were in English, French, German and "Siamese" (now Thai). The King of Siam would turn out to be an avid shortwave listener. In 1931 it was reported that he used an 11-tube Pilot "All-Wave" and a 14-tube Norden-Hauck.[144]

KZRM, Radio Manila, a station of the Radio Corporation of the Philippines, which was an RCA subsidiary, was on shortwave from that country via **KA1XR**, 6150 kc. The power was 1 kw. The station was also reported on a variety of 31 meter channels. *("This is KZRM, Radio Manila, transmitting simultaneously from Manila and Cebu from their studios atop the Manila Hotel.")*

In the United States, the Federal Radio Commission finally addressed the matter of international shortwave broadcasting. In March it assigned 27 channels to "experimental relay broadcasting," which it defined as shortwave transmissions to another station strictly for rebroadcast by the latter on its regular frequency for the general public. "The large number of applicants for the very small number of channels available requires that these channels be put to maximum use," said the FRC.[145] Thus the frequencies were to be assigned to stations on a non-exclusive basis. The channels were:

49 m.	*31 m.*	*25 m.*	*19 m.*	*16 m.*	*13 m.*
6020	9510	11720	15130	17780	21460
6040	9530	11760	15170		21500
6060	9550	11800	15210		21540
6080	9570	11840	15250		
6100	9590	11880	15290		
6120			15340		
6140					

The experimental nature of relay broadcasting was stressed. Applicants had to be qualified to operate a shortwave station over long distances from the standpoint of power and programs and the ability to provide adequate and regular reception, and had to agree to arrange for rebroadcasting of their signal. The FRC did not want to derogate in any way from the provision of programming by landline, or the primacy of the standard broadcast band for domestic broadcasting, and thus domestic shortwave broadcasting of programs for rebroadcast by another domestic station would be approved only where landline service was unavailable. And the receiving station could not rebroadcast on shortwave without FRC consent.[146]

Soon stations started moving to the new frequencies. WABC shortwave station **W2XE**, recently relocated to Jamaica, Long Island, was now operating on 6120 kc. with 5 kw. (*"These are stations WABC and W2XE."*) **W2XAL**, the shortwave station of WRNY, moved to 6040 kc., with authority to also use 11800, 15250 and 21460. The old WRNY had gone bankrupt, and the station, including W2XAL, had been purchased by Aviation Broadcasting Corporation (AVCO). WRNY engineer Walter S. Lemmon had become the station's general manager. On May 7, 1929, the dedication ceremonies for the new station were carried on W2XAL shortwave in hopes of reaching Admiral Byrd in Little America. In its new life as Aviation Radio Station, Inc., W2XAL planned to serve the aviation industry by promoting aviation to the public and providing pilots with needed information, such as aviation weather reports. In addition, the station wanted to serve "worldwide goodwill," and "sell America to the world." Tentative arrangements were said to have been made with stations in Latin America, with Europe, Asia and Australia to follow. Broadcasting to passengers on ships and planes, and the rebroadcasting within the United States of programs originating in other countries, also featured in WRNY's vision.[147]

In June, after being off the air for some months, the transmitter of **W8XAL**, shortwave sibling of WLW, was rebuilt and moved to the latter's facility in Mason, Ohio. Still using 250 watts, it was now on 6060 kc. At the time, W8XAL was not as well heard as some of the other American stations. Its best years lay ahead. Mason would be home to 8XAL and its shortwave progeny, WLWO, for 25 years.

Three new American stations took to the air. **W9XF**, Downers Grove, Illinois, was on 6020 kc. The 5 kw. station, owned by Great Lakes Broadcasting Company, was on the air most of the day, simulcasting all the programs of the company's standard broadcast station in Chicago, WENR, whose announcements included the call letters of both stations.[148]

Starting in August, General Electric station KGO in Oakland, California was heard on shortwave by way of **W6XN**, 12850 kc. The initial purpose of the 5 kw. commercial station was to relay the activities of San Francisco's Sixth Pacific Radio Show to WGY for east coast broadcasting on AM and shortwave. However, soon W6XN was carrying NBC chain programs three days a week, afternoons and evenings. The station was heard very well throughout the country, particularly after it increased power to 10 kw. in 1930. It closed down later that year.

In November, testing began from 500-watt **W9XAA**, the shortwave simulcast of Chicago Federation of Labor station WCFL, which had come on the air in 1926. The station was an effort to spread labor's message internationally. However, the interest of WCFL chief engineer Maynard Marquardt in long distance broadcasting was an important factor in the station's shortwave effort. Known as "the shortwave voice of labor and farmer," W9XAA operated on 6080 kc. It was on the air for an hour in the morning and three hours in the evening. Within 45 days it had

Although now long forgotten, the roots of world famous shortwave broadcaster WRUL go back to 2XAL (W2XAL from 1939). Originally the shortwave outlet of *Radio News* magazine, a later plan to use the station to serve the aviation community was unsuccessful.

reports from all states, four Canadian provinces, plus Mexico, Brazil and New Zealand.[149]

W8XK, which had been operating every day on 4800 and 11815 kc., moved to 6140, 11880 and 15210 kc. and adopted a four-day schedule. Although it—like many other early stations—seldom replied to information requests, it promoted its international activities. At the bottom of its stationery was a line that read, "By means of the Westinghouse international short wave relay system programs are transmitted from KDKA to Europe, South America, South Africa, Australia, New Zealand, and other distant points, where they are rebroadcast through local stations." KDKA often picked up the Big Ben time signal from **G5SW** at midnight London time and rebroadcast it on the KDKA standard broadcast channel. In November, KDKA broadcast a 40-hour program commemorating the station's nine years of broadcasting (and its move to new studios in the William Penn Hotel in Pittsburgh). The program was carried on W8XK as well as the KDKA domestic channel.

General Electric stations **W2XAF** and **W2XAD** were now on 9530 and 15340 kc. respectively, and one or both were broadcasting afternoons and evenings most days, usually with regular WGY programming but sometimes with special features for overseas audiences. (Programming was translated into Spanish on Monday nights at 2000–2130 EST.) GE had many other experimental shortwave transmitters in operation, including television and facsimile. In 1929 it built the 44-acre "Sacandaga" receiving site in Glenville, New York, northwest of its main laboratory in South Schenectady. WGY shortwave also invited Latin American ambassadors to participate in special programs broadcast on their national holidays. During November and December it beamed a series of one-hour broadcasts to Australia and New Zealand every day of the week except Sunday.

When it was proposed that WGY reduce its hours on shortwave, an English listener wrote: "I work late at night, which means I have to cross 'the pond' for most of my radio entertainment. If 2XAD and 2XAF are taken away from me, my life is deprived of its greatest joy. I use two valves (tubes) and the volume from the loudspeaker is just sufficient for an ordinary room.... The quality is all that could be desired. Hands off WGY, please." And from

Panama City: "The many listeners in foreign lands look forward to only two stations in [the] United States to furnish them programs, namely, WGY and KDKA, and if these are removed it will cause any number of hardships for all those who have radio equipment. WGY is considered by us as a household word and a necessary part of our daily life." A Virginia listener reported that in his town of 4,000, where daytime radio reception on the

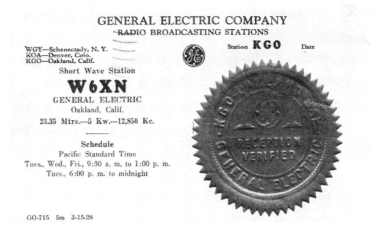

GENERAL ELECTRIC COMPANY
RADIO BROADCASTING STATIONS

WGY—Schenectady, N. Y.
KOA—Denver, Colo.
KGO—Oakland, Calif.

Station **KGO**   Date

Short Wave Station

W6XN

GENERAL ELECTRIC
Oakland, Calif.
23.35 Mtrs.—5 Kw.—12,850 Kc.

Schedule
Pacific Standard Time
Tues., Wed., Fri., 9:30 a. m. to 1:00 p. m.
Tues., 6:00 p. m. to midnight

GO-715 5m 3-15-28

Not a shortwave broadcaster as such, the principal purpose of W6XN was to carry programs from KGO to WGY for rebroadcast. The station was on the air for about a year.

standard broadcast band was poor, "the homes that have short-wave receivers are generally crowded" whenever there were important daytime political or sports events.[150]

WGY and KDKA continued their joint broadcasting of certain programs, including, in March, President Hoover's inaugural address. It was also picked up on shortwave by KGO (and rebroadcast on shortwave to KGU in Hawaii), and by the BBC (which rebroadcast it for home audiences in England). At the time of the Hoover address, Westinghouse officials observed that foreign shortwave broadcasting reception "had come to be accepted as a matter of course."[151]

For several years, the periodic goodwill concerts of the 21-nation Pan American Union in Washington, D.C. had been carried by **NAA** in Arlington, Virginia, operating on the standard broadcast band. In April, NAA was joined by the Columbia network, plus WGY and KDKA shortwave, the latter two using two "Pan American Union wavelengths" that had been designated by the FRC, 6120 and 9550 kc. The plan was for other stations in the Americas to also transmit programs about themselves on the two channels.

Also in March, WGY joined KDKA in broadcasting to the Byrd expedition. The stations broadcast on alternate Saturday nights, KDKA one week, WGY the next. Said C. W. Horn, head of radio operations at Westinghouse, "[t]here is no spot on this earth where [KDKA] cannot lay down a signal and furnish news and entertainment."[152]

Included in the KDKA schedule were rebroadcasts of programs for the Byrd expedition that were shortwaved in to **W8XK** from the powerful German commercial station in Nauen, Germany, from **VK2ME** in Australia, and from **CJRX** in Canada. The programs also included such things as greetings from a class of school children studying the Antarctic, and a "Harvard Night" where the five Harvard graduates who were on the Byrd trip were honored. Both KDKA and WGY turned their Byrd programs into mini-extravaganzas.

WGY had a new, directional antenna which was said to produce the equivalent of a 200 kw. signal from a 20 kw. transmitter. It was used in conjunction with **W2XAF**, which broadcast on 9530 kc., while **W2XAD** carried the Byrd program on 15340 kc. and WGY sent it out on 790 kc. The first Byrd broadcast using the new antenna was at 2300–2400 EST on April 6 and featured a message from President Hoover, the voices of various *New York Times* and Associated Press luminaries, New York City Mayor James Walker, and other speakers, plus a soprano from the Metropolitan Opera and the *New York Times* "Colored Glee Club." The Byrd broadcasts were exciting, even romantic, affairs.

> Static behaved itself despite the fact that the waves from Schenectady shot across the home of static — the Equator and the Tropics. How far the invisible waves were above the Equator when they passed on their southern flight, no one knows. They may have skirted the surface of the sea; they may have traveled along the "radio mirror," believed to exist 100 miles above the earth; they may have gone directly south, or they may have flown up to the North Pole and then down the other side of the globe to find Byrd's camp at the Antarctic foothold on the Great Ice Barrier on Ross Sea. But the direction radio travels matters very little, because with its speed of sunlight the human ear could not detect whether the waves loitered on a trip across the top of the world before reaching the bottom, or whether they went direct as the crow flies to their destination. What is 11,000 miles or 25,000 miles to a musical note or a word that speeds 186,000 miles in a second? This is sufficient speed to girdle the globe seven and one-half times in a second.[153]

The agreement between NBC and the **BBC** for two-way program exchanges took further shape in 1929. In February, a symphony concert from Queen's Hall in London over **G5SW** was picked up at Riverhead and rebroadcast coast-to-coast over NBC. The event was not announced in advance, however. Further discussions between the principals focused on talk and sports, rather than music, the latter being more susceptible to the deleterious effects of shortwave propagation. Problems of signal quality on shortwave were of constant concern to the BBC. In summarizing its participation in rebroadcasting efforts during the year, it observed that it had taken the opportunity "again and again to relay to the world events of national or international significance in which the listener's interest (psychological, sporting or other) is so far secured in advance that the still inevitable technical shortcomings are of minor importance."[154]

In July, a special "thanksgiving" broadcast celebrating the recovery of King George V from an illness was picked up at Radio Central in Riverhead and fed to the NBC Red and Blue networks. **VK2ME** in Australia rebroadcast the London program for Canada, while **W8XK** picked up some related VK2ME traffic and sent it to Riverhead, which then carried it over the network. A December 12 address by Guglielmo Marconi, celebrating the 28th anniversary of the famous "S" transmission from Poldu, was broadcast over G5SW, picked up at Riverhead and rebroadcast over 59 NBC stations.[155]

A special NBC Christmas Day broadcast carried on many stations in the United States was also broadcast by KDKA and WGY shortwave, as well as various commercial, non-broadcast stations in the United States and elsewhere. The event included the rebroadcast of shortwave transmissions from Holland, Germany and England that were picked up at Riverhead and fed to the NBC network. Programs originating at the Westinghouse and GE shortwave stations were likewise rebroadcast in Europe. Eddie Startz was announcing for the Dutch over **PHI** and **PCJ**. (*"Hello, everybody in the United States; hello, everybody throughout the entire English-speaking world."*)[156] It presented an early opportunity to juxtapose the programming of the old world and the new. One American observer commented: "The music received from [Europe] was all of excellent quality, well-presented and interesting to hear. Our program consisted, for the most part, merely of saxophone brayings and other typical evidences of our night-club hilarity."[157] Said another: "Christmas Day, 1929, marked the beginning of a new epoch in international exchange of radio programs."[158]

In other NBC-related shortwave events, the August return of the *Graf Zeppelin* to the United States was covered by the domestic network and by shortwavers WGY, KDKA, WLW and KGO (**W6XN**). In October, a noontime transmission from **PHI** in Holland on 17775 kc. was picked up at Riverhead and carried over the NBC Blue network.

Two other shortwave events of 1929 are worth noting. One was the formation of **Press Wireless, Inc.**, a commercial company organized by a group of American newspapers to handle domestic and international news dispatches, which it did at a fraction of ordinary commercial rates. At its height, the company would operate worldwide with over 100 transmitters, many of its own manufacture (during the war it built hundreds of transmitters and receivers for the Signal Corps). The main Press Wireless transmitter bases in the United States were in **Hicksville**, Long Island (relocated to **Centereach** in 1957) and **Belmont**, California. They were heard often by SWLs. Press Wireless also provided many collateral HF services, including air to ground communications, military communications, weather facsimile transmissions, etc. Much of the field reporting by the famous correspondents of the war years went through Press Wireless. (The company was acquired by ITT in 1965.)[159]

The other event was the birth, in the U.K., of two sister companies: Cables & Wireless Ltd., which would hold the shares of the Eastern Telegraph Company and associated companies, and the traffic business of Marconi's Wireless Telegraph Company Ltd.; and Imperial and International Communications Ltd., which was owned by Eastern, Marconi and the others and actually operated the Marconi and Eastern stations, as well as government stations. The two companies assumed control of all private and governmental cable and commercial wireless communication within the United Kingdom and between Britain and the empire and beyond. Nominally a private company, C&W was a government-created and government-regulated monopoly. The two companies combined into **Cable & Wireless Ltd.** in 1934.

While Cable & Wireless was not a broadcaster, thrills galore accompanied the occasional special news and entertainment broadcasts which would be heard decades later from C&W transmitters in such out-of-the-way places as Kenya, Barbados, Gambia, and Turks & Caicos Islands.[160] It was in commercial applications, however, that the effectiveness of shortwave was most evident. Even before the creation of C&W, shortwave messaging had supplanted some half of the business of the major British cable companies. France was able to install shortwave transmitters of 1 to 5 kw. in many of its colonies, thus bringing communications to numerous places previously beyond reach. All this was accomplished at a fraction of the cost of pre-shortwave technology.

For DXers, the availability of shortwave station information was still a problem, with developments both positive and negative. Gernsback publishing went bankrupt, and *Radio News* came under new management after May. The "On the Short Waves" column, begun in 1928, was dropped after the June 1929 issue, replaced by a brief shortwave subsection of a broader technical column. Most of the station information, and letters from DXers, were gone. In October, two former "On the Short Waves" readers and contributors, Arthur J. Green, then of Klondyke, Ohio, and Charles E. Schroeder of Philadelphia, together with J. R. McAllister of Struthers, Ohio, formed the International Short Wave Club. Headquartered in Klondyke (later East Liverpool), it was the first major listening club in America devoted exclusively to shortwave. Green was the editor and publisher of the club's monthly bulletin, *International Short Wave Radio,* and the club's key man, until it closed its doors in 1942 (it was reborn in England after the war).

A good source of shortwave station data was *Radio Design,* house organ of the Pilot Radio & Tube Corporation. It first appeared in 1928. During the years 1929–1931, as part of the company's promotion of its "Wasp" receivers, *Radio Design* offered authoritative compilations of shortwave station data. *Radio Design's* effort to develop this information was considerable, involving hundreds of letters, telegrams and telephone calls, scanning radio magazines from all over the world and cross-checking the data, gathering individual listener reports, eliminating unverified claims, etc. Unfortunately, *Radio Design* ceased publishing in 1931 when a series of misfortunes befell the company. In October, the New York Stock Exchange collapsed. A decade of worldwide economic depression was to follow.

3

1930–1939

The growth of interest in short-wave broadcasting is nothing short of phenomenal.—*Radio News, June 1930*[1]

1930

In the United States, two new stations took to the air. In January, Westinghouse opened **W1XAZ** in Springfield, Massachusetts. It utilized the same frequency as **W8XK**, 9570 kc., and it relayed WBZ, Springfield and WBZA, Boston all day, with 4 kw. of power. The same month, CBS station **W3XAU** opened in Philadelphia. Its 1 kw. transmitter, located in the suburb of Newton Square, was on the air from 0800 to 2400 EST. Like the other CBS station, **W2XE**, which relayed station WABC, W3XAU relayed the CBS programming of its standard broadcast sibling, WCAU, on one of two authorized channels, 6060 or 9590 kc.

RCA installed a new 12 kw. shortwave transmitter at the WJZ transmitter site in Bound Brook, New Jersey. The new station, **W3XAL**, was operated by NBC and began relaying WJZ on 6100 kc. at 1600–1700 and 2200–2400 EST. It was widely heard and it made frequent announcements.

Canadian shortwave broadcasting expanded. VE9GW in Bowmanville, Ontario, came on the air, relaying standard broadcast station CKGW, first on 6095 kc., then (in 1931) on 11810. The station was owned by Gooderham and Worts Ltd., a well-known Canadian distiller. It was very friendly to DXers, and was soon broadcasting a regular program for the International Short Wave Club. In Nova Scotia, the Maritime Broadcasting Company owned broadcast band station CHNS, Halifax. Seeking broader coverage of the maritimes, it added a 50-watt shortwave outlet on 6050 kc. Eventually to be known as **CHNX**, its call letters at the time were **VE9CF**, which were changed to **VE9HX** in 1933 when the station moved to 6110 kc. Both the standard broadcast and shortwave transmitters were located in Bedford, about ten miles from Halifax. The facility also boasted a receiver setup with a directional receiving antenna used to pick up the BBC for rebroadcast.

W8XK was now on the air Tuesday, Thursday, Saturday and Sunday on three frequencies: 6140 kc. at 1700–2400 EST, 11880 at 1200–1700, and 15210 at 0800–1200. It relayed KDKA, and carried many NBC programs. W8XK had received reception reports from 59 countries. The station experimented with a new shortwave transmitting antenna that could focus signals either locally or at a distance.[2]

𝔚ℭ𝔄𝔘   PHILADELPHIA, PA.   𝔚3𝔛𝔄𝔘

We wish to acknowledge your communication regarding the reception of our short wave transmitter, W3XAU.

This transmitter is operated on two frequencies 6060 and 9590 kilocycles, corresponding to a wave length of 49.5 and 31.28 meters. The power, at the present time, is 500 watts, operating from 8.00 A. M. until midnight daily, using either of the two above frequencies.

We would appreciate very much any further comments you may care to make on the signal strength on the two frequencies.

Sincerely yours,

UNIVERSAL BROADCASTING CO.

W3XAU was the shortwave simulcast of Philadelphia's WCAU. Later called WCAB, it came into operation in 1930 and remained in service until the end of 1941, when CBS opened a new Brentwood, Long Island, facility.

W2XAF, W2XAD, W9XF, W8XK and G5SW were among the broadcast stations whose frequencies were the most accurate, according to measurements made by RCA at Riverhead.[3]

W2XAL (relaying WRNY) increased power from 500 watts to 15 kw. Crosley station W8XAL was off the air during the summer due to licensing problems. NBC was said to be operating station W9XA in Denver, relaying its standard broadcast parent, KOA, on 9530 kc. And WCFL offshoot W9XAA was testing on 11840 and 17785 kc. In October it carried a special program in celebration of the first anniversary of the International Short Wave Club, which publicized the event widely. Receivers and other valuable prizes were awarded for the best reports.[4]

American stations made numerous special broadcasts during the year and also participated in specials of other stations. On New Year's day, W2XE broadcast a musical program, with greetings in 13 languages. Later in the month it carried a meeting at the Metropolitan Opera House in New York City to commemorate the tenth anniversary of the founding of the League of Nations. In the same month it broadcast an international goodwill program dedicated to Peru. W2XE made other special broadcasts during the year, including one to New Zealand which featured music and a greeting from the British ambassador to the United States.

In April, W8XK broadcast an Easter service "directed to explorers in the icy north, in the tropics of South America and in the vast expanse of the Pacific Ocean. This marked the first time that the Westinghouse station has transmitted a religious program especially for groups in such widely separated regions."[5] W8XK also carried weekly messages to the crew of the schooner *Morrissey* on the Northeast Greenland Expedition, and to the Dickey Orinoco expedition in Venezuela. The old Far North Service had by now become a Saturday night program of messages to missionaries and explorers all over the world.

The London Naval Arms Conference in January was the occasion of much shortwave activity, made all the more historic because it was the first time the voice of King George was heard around the world. It was transmitted over **G5SW** as well as a number of radiotelephone circuits. In America the 6:00 A.M. broadcast was carried over the WABC, WEAF and WJZ networks, including **W8XK** and **W2XAF**, and was said to be "extraordinarily clear." The broadcasts were picked up and rebroadcast by **PHI**, **Zeesen**, **VK2ME** and stations in Canada, India and New Zealand. Numerous other stations rebroadcast one of the transmissions further, or received it by landline. Japanese listeners fared poorly on one transmission. "The air seemed to be clearing momentarily, but then a stalwart pianist believed to have been broadcasting from the Russian station at Khabarovsk crashed through with crescendo chords, drowning out the London voice."[6] Another transmission was received, however, and in fact was further shortwaved by **NHK** to KGO. The total worldwide audience was estimated at 100 million. "Never before have such extensive facilities been mustered to insure the success of a broadcast." The affair was touted as "radio's greatest broadcast."[7]

The King's voice was heard again in special broadcasts in July and November. The Prince of Wales was heard on shortwave in July and in October. All of these broadcasts originated at **G5SW** and were picked up by RCA at Riverhead for rebroadcast over NBC, and by several AT&T radiotelephone stations for rebroadcast by CBS.

In February, **PHI** in Holland broadcast a one-hour talk and musical program to the United States, where it was carried over the WEAF, WJZ and WOR networks. These rebroadcast arrangements did not always work out well, however. A March opera broadcast originating in Dresden and transmitted from **Zeesen** to Riverhead, and on to WEAF, was received with only marginal clarity.

The Byrd expedition, begun in 1928, remained one of exploration's biggest events. On March 1, while Byrd was on the way to Dunedin, New Zealand en route back to the United States, **W8XK** transmitted messages from family members to loved ones on the expedition's ships. On March 11, after Byrd had reached Dunedin, a special hookup was arranged from local station 4YA by landline and cable to 2YA in Wellington, then on mediumwave where it was picked up by **VK2ME** in Sydney, Australia and retransmitted on shortwave for pickup by **W2XAF**. Dunedin picked up the American side of the event direct from W2XAF, which broadcast both sides of the transmission on the air (as did VK2ME) while also feeding it to the WEAF and WJZ domestic networks. The conversation among Byrd, Adolph S. Ochs and Arthur Hays Sulzberger, publisher and vice-president respectively of *The New York Times*, and others at both ends, was recounted in detail on page one of the *Times*.[8]

Byrd expeditioners took note of something that would become widely known throughout the DX community in later years— the superb radio reception on both mediumwave and shortwave in New Zealand. One of them referred to New Zealand as "a listeners' paradise, a vast ethereal whispering gallery."[9]

In May, Senator Guglielmo Marconi carried on a transatlantic conversation with New York from his yacht *Elettra* anchored some 36 miles from Rome. He was transmitting with 750 watts on 11235 kc. The New York end of the hookup was at NBC headquarters, and was transmitted on 15385 kc. via one of the GE Schenectady transmitters. NBC President M. H. Aylesworth and others in the NBC studio chatted with Marconi, who expressed his optimism for international broadcasting and for television. However, the Grand Old Man of radio observed that the practical uses for television were likely to be limited, and expressed doubt that it would ever be in as wide use as radio.

In June, GE stations **W2XAF** and **W2XAD** carried the Jack Sharkey–Max Schmeling world heavyweight championship fight, which was heard worldwide and rebroadcast over the

Zeesen station in Germany. Some months later, turning the DX search for Falkland Islands signals—still far in the future[10]—on its head, listeners in the remote British outpost were thrilled to be able to report reception of W2XAF, as well as the BBC. W2XAF would broadcast a special program for the Falklands in 1931 in honor of the success of the country's shooting team in a British rifle contest.

Riverhead was the reception point in July when the King of Norway spoke in a broadcast routed from Oslo to Stockholm to Berlin by wire and cable, then by shortwave from **Zeesen.** Riverhead sent it on to the WJZ network.

The depositing of certain naval treaties was the occasion for a special shortwave transmission from Japan. It was October

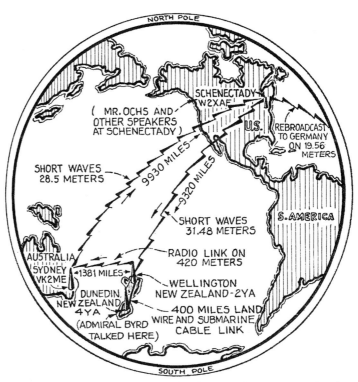

This map shows the wave lengths used and also the distances covered in the famous Byrd broadcast between Schenectady, New Zealand and Australia.

This diagram shows the connections for a special 1930 transmission between W2XAF and VK2ME carrying a conversation between Byrd, in Dunedin, New Zealand, and officials of *The New York Times,* in New York (*Short Wave Craft,* 1930).

when the voice of the Japanese premier originated from a shortwave transmitter associated with JOAK in Tokyo. It was picked up by RCA in California, sent by wire to NBC headquarters in New York, and then to the NBC domestic network as well as **W8XK** and **W2XAF,** from which the signal was picked up by **G5SW** in Britain and rebroadcast there. Meanwhile, a complementary broadcast by the British prime minister was sent out from G5SW, picked up and relayed by W8XK and W2XAF, and also picked up at Riverhead and relayed cross country by wire to the RCA station at Bolinas, California, which beamed it to Tokyo. President Hoover participated in this broadcast. CBS received the same broadcast by wire from the new Department of Commerce monitoring station in Grand Island, Nebraska, the primary task of which was to check the accuracy of the frequencies of all manner of transmitting stations.[11] Other exchange broadcasts with Japan followed.

On Christmas day, voice and music from the Philippines, Japan, Hawaii, England and Germany were shortwaved to the United States mainland for rebroadcast over WEAF and WJZ, which reciprocated with a broadcast to Germany. A London broadcast was carried over WABC. The navy did some relay broadcasting in 1930, pressing **NAA** in Arlington, Virginia and **NSS,** Annapolis, Maryland into service for the December Army-Navy football game. Land stations and ships at sea received the broadcast, which was retransmitted by naval stations in San Francisco, Honolulu and the Philippines (where some 900 guests listened at the Army-Navy club).

Transradio International, Buenos Aires, was not a shortwave broadcaster but a radiotelephone station handling mainly commercial traffic. It would serve as a relay point for transmissions between the Byrd Antarctic Expedition of 1933–35 and RCA's Radio Central on Long Island.

Although the United States held the lead in shortwave broadcasting, other countries were getting more involved in the new medium. Most shortwave broadcasters in other countries, including even local stations that simulcasted on shortwave, were usually on the air only a few days a week, and then for no more than a few hours at a time. Broadcast programming was sometimes heard over non-shortwave broadcasting transmitters. In many countries, commercial (radiotelephone) stations used music for test purposes, or performed relay services for broadcasters, or carried broadcast programs on special occasions. For example, while at this time Argentina had no shortwave broadcasters as such, 10 kw. radiotelephone station **LSX, Transradio Internacional,** Monte Grande (near Buenos Aires), on 10380 kc., often transmitted test programs of music between 2000 and 2200 EST. Japanese station J1AA, a 3–5 kw. commercial station operating from outside Tokyo on 7880, 13085 and 15765 kc., carried some special broadcast programs, such as one on November 11 that commemorated the birth of the late Japanese Emperor Meiji. American commercial stations often relayed network programming, and some standard broadcast stations used portable shortwave transmitters for sending field programming back to the studio. Among shortwave enthusiasts, the line between such stations and regular shortwave broadcasters was unclear and often ignored. To DXers, shortwave was shortwave.

I2RO, Rome, was testing in the afternoons on 11810 kc. with 12 kw., identifying as *Radio Roma Napoli.* Czechoslovakia had plans to begin broadcasting from a station under construction at **Podebrady.** However, it was commercial transmissions that were soon reported from the site on various channels up to 21 mc. The **Electro-Technical Institute of the University** of Bucharest was testing on 13955 kc. on Wednesday and Saturday afternoons (EST), playing music or relaying programming from a Bucharest mediumwave station. Austria was on shortwave as well. **Radio Wien**, Vienna, was operating on 6072 kc., Tuesday and Thursday at 0700–0800 EST and Wednesday at 0600 on 11800. Power was 250 watts.

In October, PHOHI station **PHI** left the air temporarily. One reason was economic. It was the depression, and the broadcasts had produced no tangible benefits to the PHOHI-member companies, which wished to reduce their expenditures. Another was the government's decision to mirror the domestic broadcasting structure on shortwave by dividing up shortwave transmitter time among various Dutch broadcasting associations. This was unacceptable to Philips. PHI would not be heard again until 1932.

More Asian stations could be heard. In India, Madras, Bombay and Calcutta all had been home to some shortwave broadcast experimentation in the twenties and early thirties, with calls like **2GR, 7BY** and **7CA**. These stations eventually became **VUM, VUB** and **VUC** respectively. VUB was now on 6110 kc. VUC broadcast in English and Hindi at 0800–1000 EST on 11870 kc. The stations, which relayed their sister mediumwave channels, were run by the private **Indian Broadcasting Company** until April 1 when the company failed and was continued by the government in the form of the **Indian Broadcasting Service**. RA97 in Khabarovsk became **RV15**. It was a regular on the west coast, and inland as well, on 4273 kc., where it was heard in English. KA1XR, the Philippines, now on 6130 and 11440 kc., was carrying the programs of KZRM. It was heard quite regularly in western parts of the United States before closing in 1931 (and reopening in 1933). From Saigon, in what was then known as French Indochina, another 12 kw. shortwave broadcaster, **FZS**, also called **Radio Saigon** and the "Voice of France in Indochina," opened on July 14. Operated by the Compagnie Franco-Indochinoise de Radiophonie, it was heard quite well on the west coast. Broadcasts were on approximately 6115 kc. in the 0630–1000 EST time frame. Saigon had one of the finest record collections in the Far East, and shortwave listeners recognized the station by the gong that was sounded between selections. (*"Allo. Allo. Ici Radio Saigon."*)

On January 18 and 25, 1930, in what was one of the first, if not the first, special broadcasts for a shortwave club, **HRB**, "Voice of the Tropics," the station of Tropical Radio Telegraph Company in Tegucigalpa, Honduras, put on two special English-language programs for members of the International Short Wave Club. The frequency was 6006 kc., but the advertised power, 25 watts, was questionable, since, as one SWL put it, the station "comes through like the proverbial ton of bricks." (A 350-watt transmitter was said to be in the offing and may already have been on line.) Soon the program became a regular hour-long Saturday night feature. The names of ISWC members were read, and those reporting the time and date when their name was read received a souvenir from the station. (HRB's QSL was reportedly 12×16" in size.) Tropical Radio Telegraph was a subsidiary of United Fruit Company which had been using spark transmitters as early as 1904. Tropical Radio was set up in 1913 to handle the company's radio activities, which were principally commercial. It began using shortwave in 1928.

The widely-heard station in Georgetown, British Guiana, **VRY**, closed down due to financial circumstances. Little **NRH** in Costa Rica increased power from 7½ watts to 75 watts. Ecuador began shortwave broadcasting in May by way of **HC1DR**, Quito, an experimental station owned by a number of amateurs. It operated from 2000 to 2200 EST, daily except Sundays, on 48 meters. Lively programs and announcements in both Spanish and English made it a favorite of listeners. A similar operation was **HKT, Universal Broadcasting Company**, Manizales, Colombia, on 7790 kc. In the Spanish-speaking Americas, shortwave broadcasting was often a product of amateur initiative.

From the land down under, on January 10, 1930, **VK2ME**, Sydney, Australia, took the music and voice from the Paramount film *The Love Parade*, then playing at the Prince Edward Theatre in Sydney, and transmitted it to Commander Byrd in the Antarctic. In December, AWA began regular shortwave broadcasting from 2 kw. **VK3ME** in Melbourne. The programs were heard on 9525 kc.

The shortwave receiver scene was improving. "Until quite recently," noted Hugo Gernsback at mid-year, "it was not possible for the untrained layman to buy a short-wave set and operate it himself; and, indeed, until a few months ago it was not possible to buy an A.C. short-wave set. These conditions, however, are being overcome very rapidly; and the time is now here when the public at large is beginning to ask questions about the possibility of listening in to short-wave stations thousands of miles away."[12]

Among the new receivers to appear were the four-tube CS5 by the De Forest Radio Company of Passaic, New Jersey, the Insuline "Conqueror" kit with five tubes, the Silver-Marshall S-M 737 "Bearcat" with five tubes and the S-M 735 "Round the World Six" with six tubes, along with the ready-built Mercury "Short-Wave Scout," a superheterodyne with ten tubes. The "Conqueror," the S-M 735 and the "Short-Wave Scout" were available in either A.C. or battery configurations, as was a new National "Thrill Box." Silver-Marshall brought out its S-M 738 shortwave converter. Norden-Hauck put out its "Super DX-5," and Lafayette its "Wide World Short-Wave Receiver" ("Pulls in stations all over the world — Java, Australia, Holland, England, etc."). Hammarlund, already a name in broadcast receivers and later to set a new standard in shortwave sets, entered the field modestly with the Hammarlund Short-wave Adapter.

An important step was taken by Aero Products, Inc. of Chicago, which already had a self-contained shortwave receiver on the market, the A.C. "Overseas Four." It introduced the Aero Products Automatic Tuning Unit. One of the problems with general coverage shortwave receivers (defined at the time as 3–20 mc.) was that, when switching bands, a cumbersome process of changing coils and readjusting front panel controls was required in order to sufficiently spread out the desired band and avoid overly sharp tuning. With some special components and some belts and pulleys, the Aero Automatic Tuning Unit solved the problem, covering, on all bands, about 1,500 kc. in 180 degrees of tuning.[13] Although not adopted immediately in all receivers, eliminating coil switching and achieving bandspread would prove to be major advancements in the practicalities of shortwave listening.

Shortwave-only publications started appearing. *Radio News* published its 1930 "Short Wave Manual." Hugo Gernsback returned to the publishing business, and one of the first publications of his new Popular Book Corporation was the bi-monthly *Short Wave Craft*, the first issue of which appeared in June.[14] It covered all aspects of shortwave radio, plus shortwave relating to health, aircraft, TV, facsimile, etc., and "ultra short waves." The magazine's shortwave station list would become one of the best available.

At year's end, both NBC's engineering manager and the radio editor of *The New York Times* opined that the growth of international broadcasting and the general advancement of the short waves were among the most significant events of the year in radio.[15]

1931

Technical advancements within the radio industry in 1931 produced better receivers with better tubes, and improved selectivity, easier, more accurate tuning, automatic volume control and better audio overall. To this was added better frequency management by stations. Programming also improved. Experimentation with television was growing, and, while still a novelty better suited to the laboratory than the home, its eventual success as a consumer medium was now widely predicted. In Chicago there were already some 3,000 sets and seven hours of rudimentary daily programming.

On the short waves, overseas activity increased noticeably, while in America it was a year of modest forward movement.

W9XAA on 6080 kc., and sometimes on 11840, was usually on for three hours in the afternoon. **W8XAL** inaugurated a special 24-hour international program starting at noon EST on the last day of the month. And RCA gave its experimental shortwave station, **W3XL**, to NBC, which used it in conjunction with **W3XAL**. Both were in Bound Brook, New Jersey. W3XAL was on 6100 kc., W3XL on 6415 (W3XL was operating in experimental mode). They usually simulcast WJZ and were often used to relay network programming overseas.[16] Both stations carried Lowell Thomas at 1745–1800 EST.

The **W2XAL** aviation venture had gone poorly. With the proceeds of several patents that he owned, W2XAL general manager Walter S. Lemmon bought the by-then 15 kw. station and moved it from New Jersey to Boston, where it operated as the Shortwave Broadcasting Corporation under new call letters **W1XAL**. The authorized power in Boston was 5 kw. The station was on the air infrequently, mainly conducting tests and intermittently relaying standard broadcast station WEEI and W1XAU, the sound channel (1550 kc.) for experimental TV station W1XAV. (One of the directors of the new corporation was V. S. Morgan, president of W1XAL's sister company, Shortwave & Television Corporation, which was experimenting with TV.)

New issues in shortwave broadcasting were surfacing. The now-35 kw. signal of GE shortwave twins **W2XAF** and **W2XAD**, equipped with multiple antennas,[17] were the best-heard American shortwave stations. W2XAF was on the air mainly at night, and its largest audience was in Latin America. Foreign listeners were seeking programming in their own languages rather than the simulcasting of American standard broadcast stations. As a result, W2XAF treated Latin America as a distinct target audience, and often utilized a Spanish-speaking announcer. There were Spanish-language market quotations, which were often reprinted in Latin American newspapers, sports events (especially boxing) featuring Latin American contenders, and special programs on the occasion of Latin American national holidays. W2XAF also had the ability to record programs and repeat them later, as it did in the case of Pope Pius XI when he opened the Vatican shortwave station in February (see below).

Success in its broadcasts to South America had led **KDKA**, in 1930, to urge the Federal Radio Commission to change the rule prohibiting advertisements in shortwave broadcasts (except in the case of advertising that was built in to the scripts or the program titles of domestic programs). It argued that advertising revenue would help defray expenses and level the playing field with foreign stations, which were often supported by their governments. **WGY** joined the application, urging that advertising be allowed on an experimental basis and pointing out that shortwave broadcasting had progressed beyond the stage where the stations should be expected to bear all the costs. But their efforts were to no avail. In 1931 the FRC ruled against commercials on shortwave. The medium was still experimental, it said, and not yet ready to move to on-air commercials. The chief examiner of the FRC had advised that advertising would discourage further experimentation, and encourage direct-to-listener shortwave broadcasting, which would not be as economical a use of the limited number of channels available as relay broadcasting.[18] The decision discouraged American shortwave stations from producing special programming for particular target audiences.

American stations participated in many broadcasts of note in 1931. The first shortwave rebroadcast of a program from Italy was held on New Year's Day, with a speech by Benito

Mussolini carried over the NBC shortwave stations. The dictator spoke of Italian-American friendship and his country's peaceful intentions. A program from **PCJ** was rebroadcast the same day. Later in January an exchange between **W2XAF** and **VK2ME** in Sydney, Australia featured Australian polar explorer Sir George Hubert Wilkins and Lady Wilkins talking about how Sir Hubert planned to reach the North Pole on the submarine *Nautilus.* The program was rebroadcast on the WGY standard broadcast channel and various Australian stations networked with VK2ME. (The *Nautilus* expedition, which planned to report its progress on shortwave, was largely unsuccessful.)

An April address by the President of Spain, speaking from Madrid, was carried over WJZ and sent via **W8XK** and **W2XAF** to South America, where it was picked up and rebroadcast. The same month, in commemoration of the birthday of the Emperor of Japan, W2XAF participated in a shortwave exchange of programs with that country. Memorial Day saw another shortwave exchange with Japan, although reception on that occasion was not good.

In June, RCA shortwaved to India the Gandhi testimonial dinner of the Indian National Congress of America so that Mahatma Gandhi himself could tune in. The same month, an on-air conversation took place between Australian aviators Harold Gatty and Wiley Post, speaking on site at **W2XAF**, and British flyer Sir Keith Smith, located at **VK2ME** in Sydney. Post and Gatty had just set a round-the-world flight record. Gatty's parents were listening in to 7BL, Hobart, Tasmania, and it was the first time they had heard his voice since he had left Australia in 1925.[19]

The opening game of the world series was carried over **W8XK** and **W2XAF**, and various west coast commercial transmitters. On December 12, the thirtieth anniversary of Marconi's famous "S" transmission, NBC organized a shortwave exchange among 15 countries, with Marconi himself speaking from Italy. NBC engineers called it "the greatest hook-up ever arranged for broadcasting."[20] And on Christmas Day, the RCA-NBC and CBS shortwave broadcast stations in the United States, and their counterparts in Germany, England and Italy, exchanged special transmissions.

Shortwave was now in wide use on expeditions. **W2XAF** carried a number of special programs, with messages from home, to the Dickey Orinoco Expedition in Venezuela. Dr. Herbert Spencer Dickey was on his fifth trip to the country to locate the source of the Orinoco River, and the shortwave equipment he carried with him permitted him to stay in contact with the world. He radioed reports to *The New York Times,* and shortwave time signals permitted him to set his clocks, a necessary precedent to establishing precise latitude and longitude measurements. The programs of **W8XK** and **W2XAF** provided the expeditioners with some much-needed entertainment.[21]

WWV went suburban, moving from Washington, D.C. to College Park, Maryland. Although still a standard frequency station rather than a time signal station, at least three other stations were actively broadcasting time signals in the United States, all operating at specific times rather than continuously. **NAA**, the naval station in Arlington, Virginia, broadcast for three minutes, three times daily (0257–0300, 1157–1200 and 2157–2200 EST) on 4015, 8870 and 12045 kc. There were tones each second, and the final dash at the end of the three minutes represented the exact hour. **NSS** in Annapolis, Maryland followed a complementary schedule on 12045 and 16060 kc. And the Elgin National Watch Company used a similar format on its 500-watt time station, **W9XAM**, 4797.5 kc.

Canadian shortwave broadcasting expanded. To the CJRX shortwave outlet on 6150 kc., **VE9CL**, was added a second shortwave channel, **VE9JR**, on 11765. At times both frequencies (and call letters) were heard. VE9CL was now 3.5 kw., VE9JR 2 kw. New 50-watt **VE9CS**, Vancouver, British Columbia, was owned by the United Church of Canada. It operated on

CANADIAN **MARCONI** COMPANY

SHORT WAVE TRANSMITTERS
DRUMMONDVILLE, QUE.,
CANADA

BROADCAST RELAY

VE9DR

AND

"BEAM"
TELEGRAPH
CGA-CJA-VE9AP-CFA

Although Drummondville was mainly a commercial messaging ("beam") station, starting late in 1931 it also relayed Montreal station CFCF, which eventually operated its own shortwave transmitter (CFCX).

Thursdays at 0000–0130 EST and Sundays at 1345–1930 and 2230–0100 EST on 6070 kc. And the University of Western Ontario, London, Ontario, began broadcasting via 25-watt **VE9BY**. The station was on the air experimentally in the afternoons and evenings on one of several assigned frequencies, including 4795, 6425 and 8650 kc. On December 5 it broadcast a special program for the International Short wave Club. At various times during the year, special programs dedicated to the ISWC were broadcast by HRB in Honduras, X26A in Mexico, VE9BY, VE9CL, VE9GW, W9XAA, and HKA and HKD in Colombia.

On Christmas Day, Canadian Marconi Company station **VE9DR**, 6005 kc., 4 kw., commenced regular relays of CFCF in Montreal. The station was part of the Marconi beam station at Drummondville, Quebec. It later became **CFCX**, which would remain active on the channel for over 65 years.

PCJ was the most widely heard of all the shortwave stations, largely because of its superior antenna system. The station used one non-directional antenna, a second targeted on the Dutch East Indies, and a third beamed to South America. It was now on the air on Wednesdays at 1100–1500, Thursdays at 1300–1500 and 1800–2200, and Fridays at 1300–1500 and 1900–0100 EST. All broadcasts were on 9590 kc. However, in October, PCJ left the air. The Dutch PTT station in **Kootwijk** on 17835 kc. was now carrying English-language news and press dispatches on Saturdays at 0940 EST. It called itself the Voice of Holland.

The first shortwave station dedicated to religious programming was founded. It was **HVJ, Vatican Radio**, in Vatican City. The 12 kw. station was inaugurated on February 12, 1931, the ninth anniversary of the coronation of Pope Pius XI. A special 90-minute inaugural broadcast was picked up by NBC at Riverhead and by CBS at the AT&T commercial shortwave receiving facility in Netcong, New Jersey at 1030 EST and rebroadcast over the WABC, WJZ and WEAF networks, as well as over **W8XK** and **W2XAF** shortwave (test broadcasts had been received during the previous week). Many other countries also picked up the HVJ broadcast, or one of the shortwave relays, and rebroadcast it locally. It was the first time the Pope's voice was heard worldwide. Marconi himself had supervised the construction of the station and spoke at the event. HVJ operated on 5970 and 15120 kc. (the latter channel was used for the inaugural broadcast) and put in a strong signal in the United States with a multi-lingual opening that would become familiar in the decades ahead: "*Laudetur Jesus Christus.*"[22]

France constructed a major shortwave transmitter plant at Pontoise, site of the French Colonial Exposition outside Paris. The power of the two shortwave broadcast transmitters was 12 kw. Broadcasting to the French colonies began in May with the inauguration of **FYA, Radio Coloniale**. Frequencies included 11720, 11925 and 15245 kc., with programs beamed to Asia, Africa, North and South America and Oceania. Soon the Paris post of the Veterans of Foreign Wars was broadcasting a special program over Radio Coloniale on Mondays at 1830–1900 EST. In North America the Paris station was reported heard almost all day long on one or another frequency.

The BBC was still operating **G5SW** on a single frequency, 11750 kc. (*"G5SW, the British Broadcasting Corporation station to the British colonies, is now closing down. Good night everybody, good night."*) The times of operation were weekdays at 0730–0830 and 1400–1900 EST — Saturday transmissions were added in 1932 — with the chimes of "Big Ben" heard at sign off. **Zeesen** in Germany was heard on 15230 kc. The large Telefunken site at **Nauen** was also widely heard but with experimental and commercial rather than broadcast transmissions. And **OXY**, the 500-watt Danish station at Lyngby, was moved to **Skamlebaek**, where it continued operating on 6060 kc., and sometimes 9520, at 1400–1830 EST, signing off with the chimes of the town hall clock.

Another "Radio Colonial" took to the air. **CT1AA, Radio Colonial**, Lisbon, Portugal, was heard occasionally on Fridays at 1700–1900 EST on 6995 kc. **EAQ, Transradio Española**, Madrid, Spain, a private radiotelegraph station, was heard broadcasting music on 9870 kc. **EAN**, owned by the same company, was heard on 10525 kc. And at year's end, **Polskie Radio** in Poland opened a 14 kw. shortwave station to supplement its powerful 150 kw. mediumwave channel. Soon it would be known as **SRI**, and would be heard on 9570 kc.

Shortwave was new in Africa. Best heard from that continent was a French-language service, **CNR, Radio Maroc**, Morocco, on the air via the Rabat PTT facility on Sundays at 1500–1700 EST on 9300 kc., 6 kw. ("This station is easy to get," reported one listener.) Shortwave from South Africa began in January over **ZRJ**, a 250-watt station of the **African Broadcasting Company Ltd.** at Maraisburg (power would be increased to 1 kw. in 1932). At the end of the year, the company opened a 500-watt shortwave station, **ZTJ**, to relay Johannesburg mediumwave station "JB" on 6122 kc. Not heard in the United States but reported active most days at 0930–1130 EST and weekends at 1300–1500 was 400-watt **Radio Tananarive**, Madagascar, on 5692 kc. (later 6000).

In the Dutch East Indies, numerous amateurs took to the shortwaves with broadcast programming, presaging the free form broadcasting scene of later decades. Many of the government radiotelephone stations also broadcast music during periods of transmitter adjustment. **Malabar** was now operating on four channels, two at 40 kw. (**PLR**, 10415 kc., and **PLF**, 17855), two at 80 kw. (**PLW**, 8130 kc., **PMB**, 20605). As in other parts of the world, commercial establishments also got into broadcasting. As *Radio Design* noted, "Java truly is the 'isle of the short waves.'"[23]

XDA in Mexico City, owned by the Trans-Mexican News Agency and principally a telegraph station, began broadcasting a half-hour English news dispatch in voice at 2100 EST on 5870 kc. The station advised that "[t]he report is a good will report pure and simple and its primary purpose is to carry into the homes of foreign people and especially of the people of the United States of America a picture of the Mexico of today, from the political, economic, financial, commercial and business points of view, to the end that the listeners-in may be brought to a better and more sympathetic understanding of Mexico, the people who inhabit it, and what they are doing in the world of affairs."[24] The power was 20 kw. Also reported operating from Mexico was **X26A**, Nuevo Laredo, 7370 kc., relaying mediumwave station XEP, whose programs originated at the Hamilton Hotel in Laredo, Texas, just across the Rio Grande. This was likely an amateur operation, an early shortwave version of what would come to be known as "border radio." And a shortwave station that would become one of Mexico's most famous, **XEW, La Voz de la America Latina**, opened shortwave operations on 6025 kc.

CMCI, Havana, Cuba could be heard evenings on 6060 kc. It operated as the International Broadcasting Company of Cuba. Listeners wondered why promised postcards were not received in exchange for the requested listener letters.

Government station **TGW, Radiodifusora Nacional**, Guatemala City, was on the air on 6675 kc., 100 watts, at 2100–2330 EST. It relayed the mediumwave outlet, TGW. Other Guatemalan stations included 80-watt **TGCA** at the Hotel Rex, Guatemala City, on the air at 2200–2400 EST on 13040 kc., and 25-watt **TGX**, heard on 9373 kc. around the same time. Soon TGX moved to 8955 kc., and then 5937, and increased power to 100 watts.

Shortwave activity was rapidly increasing in Colombia. Experimental Colombian broadcasters heard in the evenings included **HKA**, Barranquilla, on 6160 kc.; 7-watt **HKD**, "the Voice of Barranquilla," on 6993 kc. (later 6000); **HKE**, Medellin, on 5940; **HKF**, Bogota, which was on the air at 1800–2000 EST on 7555 kc.; **HKM**, Bogota, on 6630 kc.; and **HKO**, Colombian Radio & Electric Company, Medellin, on 5930. Many of the emerging Latin American stations were small ventures undertaken by individual amateurs or groups of amateurs.

In Venezuela, **YV1BC, Broadcasting Caracas**, had come on mediumwave at the end of 1930. Soon the 5 kw. station began transmitting on shortwave as well under the callsign **YV2BC**, first on 6080 kc., then 6112. Power was 200 watts, soon increased to 250, and the call letters were changed to **YV1RC** (mediumwave) and **YV2RC** (shortwave). (*"This is station YV1BC broadcasting on a frequency of 960 kc. and also on 6112 kc. We are located in Caracas, Venezuela and welcome reports from listeners, which are all acknowledged."*) The station QSLed with a 16-page booklet printed in Spanish and English.[25]

Also heard from Venezuela was **YV8BC, Broadcasting Nacional**, on 9550 kc. And in Ecuador, "El PRADO" in Riobamba took to the air on approximately 7530 kc. It was on Thursday nights for two hours. Soon it was also testing on 6620 kc., the channel to which it moved in 1932. The station was owned by well-known amateur operator Carlos Cordovez, and was widely heard in North America.

While the Vatican had begun religious shortwave broadcasting in February, **HCJB** would be the first independent shortwave station devoted exclusively to religious programming.[26] Its founding in Quito, Ecuador, was hardly noticed at the time, but would prove to be a major event in shortwave broadcasting. The first broadcast was on Christmas Day, 1931. The frequency was 5986 kc. (soon changed to 4107), and the power was 250 watts. (Soon another Quito shortwave station, **HC1SC**, was picking up HCJB and relaying it over its 15-watt transmitter on 37 meters.) It could hardly have been imagined that, 70 years later, HCJB would be broadcasting worldwide in 10 languages over transmitters of 100 and 500 kw. (or that a decade after that the station would have but a small shortwave presence).

In 1931, the 20 kw. AWA station in Pennant Hills, near Sydney, Australia began paralleling the **VK3ME** shortwave broadcasts from Melbourne. (*"This is VK2ME, the Australian National Empire shortwave broadcasting station on 31.28 meters."*) On July 5, the AWA formalized the Sydney shortwave broadcasts under the name the **Voice of Australia**. Pennant Hills had become AWA "Radio Centre" and boasted many transmitters, used mostly for point-to-point purposes. The Voice of Australia was a Sunday-only service, with separate two-hour broadcasts to the Americas, the Pacific, East Asia, and Europe and Africa, all on 9590 kc. Many of the programs were prepared by the Australian National Travel Association. On the American east coast, three of the four services could be heard. VK3ME in Melbourne broadcast a limited shortwave service, 90 minutes on Wednesday mornings and two hours on Saturday mornings. It was on 9510 kc., and was heard in the United States despite its low power, 2 kw.[27]

Although it was the hope of many that shortwave would attract ordinary radio listeners, the shortwave listening community was still small and composed mainly of those who were attracted either by the technology of the medium or the novelty of distance. Manufacturers began responding to their needs, and the shortwave receiver came of age. Regenerative sets became passé and all-wave superheterodynes took over. Although not fundamentally different from ordinary broadcast sets, they were designed with the shortwave listener in mind.

Many ordinary household radios sported shortwave bands, but the shortwave performance of these receivers was poor. Better shortwave receivers sold in the $100 to $150 range. (Comparison of receivers by price is difficult because radios were often available in varying configurations-with or without tubes, speakers, power supplies, and cabinets.)

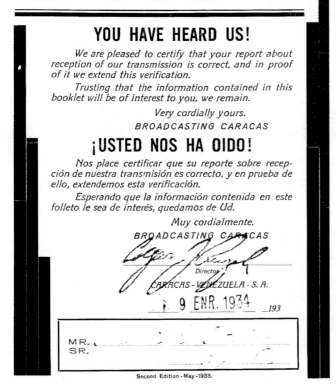

Y V 1 B C

YOU HAVE HEARD US!

We are pleased to certify that your report about reception of our transmission is correct, and in proof of it we extend this verification.

Trusting that the information contained in this booklet will be of interest to you, we remain.

Very cordially yours.

BROADCASTING CARACAS

¡USTED NOS HA OIDO!

Nos place certificar que su reporte sobre recepción de nuestra transmisión es correcto, y en prueba de ello, extendemos esta verificación.

Esperando que la información contenida en este folleto le sea de interés, quedamos de Ud.

Muy cordialmente.

BROADCASTING CARACAS

Director

CARACAS - VENEZUELA - S. A.

9 ENR. 1934 ____193

MR.
SR.

Second Edition - May-1933.

Located 4,000 feet above sea level and five miles from the coast, the shortwave transmitter of Broadcasting Caracas put out an imposing signal. Within Venezuela the station was known for its professionalism and its stable of radio personalities. Letters from foreign countries numbered 1,500 a month, 80 percent from North America.

Among the better performers were the nine-tube SWS-9 superhet kit by Wireless Egert Engineering Inc.; the 10-tube, nickel-plated "Lincoln Deluxe SW32" (A.C.) and "Deluxe DC-SW-10" (battery operated); the 11-tube Pilot "All-Wave" superhet; and the 11-tube Silver-Marshall

"All-Wave 726SW" superhet. At year's end, Hammarlund brought out its entry into the short-wave receiver market, the eight-tube "Comet." It was the start of a line of receivers that would be regarded highly by generations of shortwave listeners.

The 12-tube Scott "All-Wave Superheterodyne," covering 500 kc. to 20 mc. and selling for $212, was, according to Scott, the gold standard of the day. It was the first chrome-plated Scott, and the first of many Scott receivers that would be featured in the company's expansive shortwave advertising campaign. "Precision, hand-building." "A new era in short wave reception." "The new Scott All-Wave brings in London, Rome and many other foreign stations between 15 and 200 meters—just as clearly—just as cleanly—and with just as much volume as a 50,000 watt local in the 200 to 550 meter band! And every short wave station—once logged—is subsequently found at the same, exact dial setting." Satisfied Scott short-wave customers were quoted by name.[28] In 1932, E. H. Scott ran a contest for Scott owners who submitted monthly logs of confirmed reception over a six month period. First prize was a trip around the world or $2,000 cash.

For those seeking a less expensive alternative, shortwave converters, generally selling for $30–$60, enjoyed wide popularity. Among the units available were the Lafayette "Super-heterodyne Short Wave Converter," the Silver-Marshall S-M 739, and the National NC-5. Converters were sometimes paired with standard broadcast receivers and sold in combination.

Pilot Radio's *Radio Design* ceased publishing, but its excellent station coverage was picked up by *Short Wave Craft*, which supplemented its regular listing of shortwave stations with a new (albeit abbreviated) column called "When to 'Listen In,'" which was authored by Robert Hertzberg, who had been *Radio Design's* editor.

1932

The year was an important one for the **BBC**. It moved from Savoy Hill—its locus almost from its birth—to its new home in Broadcasting House. More important to the shortwave world, testing for the new **Empire Service** began on November 14, almost five years to the day after G5SW had come on the air. Formal inauguration was on December 19.[29] It would be more than 30 years before Britain's international broadcasting effort would become known as the World Service, much less for it to earn recognition as the gold standard of shortwave broadcasting.

As of 1932, however, the track record of **G5SW** was distinctly mediocre. In many places the quality of reception of the **Chelmsford** station was only fair. As one commentator had put it in 1931, the "single, inflexible wave of 25.53 meters length [11750 kc.] has failed utterly to reach the very places where it is wanted most. Other stations operate on a sliding schedule of frequencies to meet different transmission requirements, but not G5SW."[30] The transmitter was suffering long breakdowns as early as a year after it had come into service.

Many parts of the empire were served by their own domestic broadcasting stations, but they still benefitted from the added credibility that the rebroadcast of BBC programming provided, and England was clearly behind in getting it to them. Notwithstanding the economic dislocations of the depression, and the BBC's continuing concerns over the quality of shortwave reception generally, it agreed to fund the Empire Service—an estimated $200,000 in development costs and an annual budget of $250,000—out of its existing budget.

Two new transmitters, located at **Daventry**, were dedicated to the new service.[31] Their power was in the neighborhood of 10–20 kw., not hugely more than G5SW (8–10 kw.). Each could operate on any of the eight frequencies assigned to the Empire Service: 6050 kc. (**GSA**),

EMPIRE STATION WAVELENGTHS

The two transmitters at the Empire Broadcasting Station at Daventry may be operated on any of the following waves: GSA, 6,050 kc/s (49.59 metres); GSB, 9,510 kc/s (31.55 metres); GSC, 9,585 kc/s (31.30 metres); GSD, 11,750 kc/s (25.53 metres); GSE, 11,865 kc/s (25.28 metres); GSF, 15,140 kc/s (19.82 metres); GSG, 17,770 kc/s (16.88 metres); GSH, 21,470 kc/s (13.97 metres).

The alternative frequencies in the 25 and 31 metre bands may be used at short notice.

GSD may be used in place of GSE and vice versa.
GSB may be used in place of GSC and vice versa.

It should be noted that the call sign signifies the frequency which is in use; e.g., GSC relates to 9,585 kc/s (31.30 metres).

The present transmission schedule is as follows, but it must necessarily be altered from time to time, consequent upon changing seasonal conditions and reception reports which are received from Empire Station listeners overseas.

Zone	Name	Call Sign	Frequency kc/s	Wavelength metres	Times of Transmission
1.	Australasia	GSD	11,750	25.53	09.30 - 11.30 G.M.T.
		GSF	15,140	19.82	
2.	India	GSB	9,510	31.55	13.30 - 17.30 G.M.T.
		GSE	11,865	25.28	
3.	South Africa	GSB	9,510	31.55	
		GSD	11,750	25.53	18.00 - 22.30 G.M.T.
4.	West Africa	GSB	9,510	31.55	
		GSD	11,750	25.53	
5.	Canada	GSA	6,050	49.59	23.00 - 01.00 G.M.T.
		GSB	9,510	31.55	

ALWAYS LISTEN FOR ANNOUNCEMENTS, BECAUSE WAVELENGTHS,

PROGRAMMES AND TIMES ARE LIABLE TO CHANGE

The British Broadcasting Corporation,
Broadcasting House,
London, W.1.

April 1933.

By 1945, when the BBC was broadcasting in more than 40 languages from multiple high-power transmitter sites, this letter from 12 years earlier, when all BBC shortwave was in English and sent out over two transmitters, seemed quaint.

9510 (**GSB**), 9585 (**GSC**), 11750 (**GSD**), 11865 (**GSE**), 15140 (**GSF**), 17790 (**GSG**), and 21470 (**GSH**). Seventeen directional antennas served five general target areas: Australasia, India, South Africa, West Africa, and Canada. Two hours of programming daily, all in English, were beamed to each target area on two frequencies. It was a mix of home service programs and material specially prepared for the Empire Service. The Christmas Day greeting by the King, long heard on domestic stations, was for the first time broadcast to places far beyond England (the king was said to be pleased when presented with a bound volume of listener letters from around the world). A sixth omni-directional "lunch time" transmission, relaying home service programming at 1100–1300 GMT, was added in 1933.

In its first seven months, listeners to the Empire Service sent the BBC 6,000 letters and 500 cables, and 1,200 Empire Service questionnaires were returned. A number of regular listeners in each target area were supplied with special forms to report reception — the start of the kind of listener monitoring networks that would be adopted by many other stations in the future.[32] Before the Empire Service took over from G5SW, the BBC became the reluctant verifier that listeners would know for decades. The station announced that, due to the large number of reception reports received and the fact that the BBC was supported by listener fees, it would reply to reports only via the "What Station Was That" section of the official BBC publication, *World-Radio,* wherein the BBC advised listeners as to what station (not just the BBC) it believed they were hearing based on their descriptions. Listeners had to submit their QSL requests on a coupon clipped from *World-Radio,* and enclose a stamped, self-addressed envelope, an International Reply Coupon, and sixpence. (The *World-Radio* coupon requirement was dropped for overseas listeners.)

Other European stations were also expanding their shortwave transmissions. **Deutscher Kurzwellensender ("Zeesen"),** until now on 9560 kc. only **(DJA),** was heard on many new channels — 6020 kc. **(DJC),** 11760 **(DJD),** 15110 **(DJL),** 15200 **(DJB),** and 17760 **(DJE).** A 5 kw. transmitter now supplemented the existing 8 kw. unit, with both usually operating in parallel. **EAQ,** Madrid, Spain was now transmitting a regular Spanish-language program for America at 1930–2100 EST on 9868 kc. A directional antenna was used, and the power was 20 kw. A program for Europe was broadcast on Saturdays. Still part of Transradio Española, EAQ now identified as **Radiodifusion Ibero-Americana.**[33] Soon it was sending out a glossy, 40-page monthly program guide to listeners.

At least two months before the opening of the Empire Service, EAQ began carrying an hour-long English-language program of the IBC, the International Broadcasting Company Ltd. The program was on the air at midnight British time on 10000 kc. *("This is the IBC Empire Short Wave programme, radiated by EAQ Madrid.")* Brainchild of the entrepreneurial and larger-than-life Capt. Leonard F. Plugge, the IBC had been established in 1930 for the sole purpose of providing to Britain a lighter, less high-brow domestic programming than the BBC. Unlike the BBC, IBC programs were commercially sponsored, by English firms. Programs were prepared in England and transmitted to the country through leased-time arrangements over various powerful, continental mediumwave and longwave stations (in particular Radio Normandy). EAQ gave IBC a presence on shortwave as well. Plugge, who was elected to parliament in 1935, was more influential in early efforts toward the development of commercial radio in England than is usually acknowledged. And he was no stranger to the BBC. Since 1927 he had been under contract to supply and edit many of the foreign station listings in *World-Radio.*[34]

Elsewhere in Europe, **CT1AA,** Lisbon, Portugal, became more widely heard when it changed frequency to 9600 kc. *("Lisbon calling, Radio Colonial, station CT1AA on 31.25 meters.")* **Rome** added another channel, 3750 kc. **(I3RO),** at 1500–2200 EST. And on Christmas eve, PHOHI station **PHI,** off the air since mid–1930, resumed broadcasting. The frequencies were 11750 and 17770 kc. and the announcer and studio manager was Eddie Startz.[35] **PCJ** was still unheard but not forgotten. *RADEX* observed that **VK3ME's** "efforts to please by transmitting interesting and instructive programs are earning for them the reputation once held by PCJ, that of being the station with the largest audience in the world."[36]

The Swiss PTT, identifying as **Radio-Suisse**, was operating on a variety of shortwave channels from its facility in Prangins, near Geneva. At the expense of the League of Nations, two new 20 kw. shortwave transmitters and associated aerials were installed, and in September **Radio Nations**, the station of the League of Nations, inaugurated a series of multi-lingual broadcasts (English, French, Spanish) over 7744, 7799 and 9585 kc. (**HBQ, HBP, HBL;** HBQ was soon dropped). The transmissions were on Sundays at 1700–1745 EST (changed to Saturdays in 1933), and were the start of broadcasts by the League and later by the United Nations that would continue on and off for decades. The League also had access to the Prangins facility for diplomatic and news purposes, and for emergency international broadcasts if the Secretary General certified the need.[37]

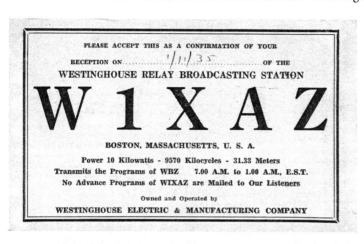

Westinghouse station W1XAZ operated from 1930 to 1934 from Springfield, in western Massachusetts. It moved to Boston in 1934, becoming W1XK the next year, WBOS in 1939. Boston became Westinghouse shortwave headquarters in 1940 when WBOS absorbed the company's Pittsburgh shortwave operations.

In the United States, KDKA moved its shortwave operation, **W8XK**, to Saxonburg, the same 118-acre site, 22 miles north of Pittsburgh, to which the 50 kw. KDKA broadcast band transmitter had been resited in 1931. Four shortwave transmitters were installed in Saxonburg. WWV also moved, to the Experimental Farm of the Department of Agriculture in Beltsville, Maryland. Westinghouse station W1XAZ in Springfield, Massachusetts, and Crosley station W8XAL in Mason, Ohio, increased power to 10 kw. NBC assumed ownership of Downers Grove, Illinois station **W9XF**. And, as a cost-cutting measure, the transmitter of CBS shortwave station **W2XE** on Long Island was moved to Wayne, New Jersey, where the station's 50 kw. broadcast band parent, WABC, was located. The frequencies 11830 and 15270 kc. were now added to the old channel of 6120 kc.[38]

GE shortwave in Schenectady was targeting Europe on 15330 kc. (**W2XAD**) at 1500–1800 daily (from 1300 on weekends), and South America on 9530 kc. (**W2XAF**) at 1700–2300 daily. W2XAF broadcast in Spanish on Mondays at 2000–2200 and Fridays at 2000–2100. **W8XK**, which was on the air for the entire broadcast day on one or another frequency, offered a similar service. And CBS began program exchanges with the BBC and with several South American countries.

There were numerous special broadcasts over U.S. shortwave stations. Domestic stations transmitted news bulletins about the Lindbergh kidnapping over their shortwave affiliates. Both the Democratic and Republican national conventions were shortwaved overseas, as were the returns on the night of the presidential election. W2XAF carried a speech by the President of Rotary International, comments by Amelia Earhart in London, President Hoover's speech on the acceptance of his renomination, and a series of Panamerican programs. There were many similar events on other stations. The "shot heard round the world" was reenacted on the event's 157th anniversary when a musket was fired before the W2XAF microphone.

And April 5 was the occasion of the bark heard round the world. "Short," a wire-haired terrier belonging to a GE engineer, barked into the microphone during a W2XAD test and kept it up as the bark was transmitted from Schenectady to Holland, Java and Sydney and returned in an instantaneous rebroadcast. "Short" was not the station's first on-air pet. In October 1930 the meow of "Kilowatt," the WGY cat, was picked up by **VK2ME** during a W2XAF broadcast.[39]

Two new shortwave stations opened in North America. **W4XB**, Miami Beach, Florida, relayed the programs of "Wonderful Isle of Dreams" station WIOD, part of the NBC network. W4XB operated on 6040 kc. at 1700–2300 EST. A new Canadian was 100-watt **VE9BJ**, Saint John, New Brunswick, on 6090 kc. Owned and operated by C. A. Munro, Ltd., it relayed the company's mediumwave station, CFBO. Also in Canada, **VE9GW** was now using one or both of 6095 and 11810 kc. at different times, and increased power to 500 watts (although sometimes operating at less than half that).

Listeners were learning more about the status of shortwave broadcasting in Russia. **RV15**, Khabarovsk, operated by what was called the **Far East Broadcasting Company**, was on 4273 kc. and was one of the best known shortwave stations in the country. Its power was 20 kw. **RV59**, Moscow, on 6000 kc., also with 20 kw., was heard as well, operating at 0500–0600 and 1400–1900 EST with programs in English, Czechoslovak, Dutch, French, German, Hungarian, Spanish and Swedish (different languages on different days). Kremlin chimes were used as a tuning signal, and the station was a good verifier. *("Hello, this is Moscow calling.")* Other stations reported operating were **RV38**, Moscow, on 5515 kc; **RV72**, a 10 kw. **Red Army** station in Moscow on 6610 kc.; **RV62**, Minsk, on 6420; and **Leningrad** on 9645. And Germany complained that Russia was intentionally jamming its broadcasts.

There were few African shortwave stations, even fewer that could be heard in the United States. **VQ7LO**, Nairobi, Kenya *("7LO, Nairobi, calling")* was now on 6060 kc., 2 kw., but at hours that made U.S. reception difficult: 1100 to 1530 or 1630 EST most days, 0300–0400 on Tuesday and 0800–0900 on Thursday.

Japanese radiotelephone station **JIAA** was relaying standard broadcaster JOAK to Japanese troops in Manchuria at 0500–0745 EST on 9870 kc. The signal was picked up in Dairen, a Manchurian port that had been ceded to Japan in 1905 after the Russo-Japanese War, and relayed on the standard broadcast band. **Radio Bangkok**, Thailand was down to one frequency for its regular broadcast, which was now on the air daily at 0900–1130 EST over **HSP2**, 9495 kc., 2.5 kw. It was also testing in the 41 meter band. However, the station closed down at mid-year. In May, heavy expenses caused **FZS** in Saigon to also close.

Shortwave broadcasting was coming alive in Colombia and Venezuela. There were a dozen stations operating in Colombia, mainly between 4 and 7 mc. They were now using "HJ" calls rather than their former three-letter calls—**HJ3ABB, Colombia Broadcasting**, Bogota (formerly HKU), **HJ4ABB, Radio Manizales** (HKT), etc. A new station was **HJ3ABG, Estación del Barrio Noreste de Bogota**, on 8220 kc. The official list of the Department of Communications in Venezuela showed stations, mostly in Caracas, on 15 shortwave channels in the 25, 31 and 49 meter bands. One of the best heard was 250-watt **YV11BMO, La Voz del Lago**, Maracaibo, on 6130 kc.

HCJB was on the air nightly except Mondays at 1930–2200 EST. And Ecuador had another shortwaver —**HC2JSB, Ecuador Radio**, Guayaquil, on 8000 kc.

In Costa Rica, **TI4NRH** increased power on 31 meters to 150 watts, and experimented for a time on the high frequency of 15075 kc. Costa Rica was also heard on shortwave by way of **TITR**, the **Costa Rica Radio and Broadcasting Station**, San Jose, on 6315 kc. The station was on at 1000–1200 and 1600–2130 EST.

More new receivers designed for the serious shortwave devotee came to market. Coil switching was by way of a band switch (rather than plug-in coils), and tuning, whether broadcast band or shortwave, was typically accomplished with a single knob. These receivers usually covered the broadcast band and shortwave up to 15 or 20 meters and sold for widely varying prices from around $60 to over $200. Among the new crop of sets for the serious SWL were Pilot's six-tube all-wave "Dragon"; National's five-tube SW-58, plus the company's nine-tube "AGS"; and the Scott "Deluxe All-Wave 12." Silver-Marshall had several offerings: the 10-tube 727SW,[40] the 12-tube 728SW, and the company's "custom built" 728SW sibling, the brass-plated 13-tube CB-1 (soon upgraded to 16 tubes). Lincoln offered the 12-tube "Deluxe SW-33," and Norden-Hauck the 16-tube "Admiralty Super-15." Midwest Radio Corp. also had a 16-tube receiver, the "All-Wave Superhet." Midwest was the cut rate brand, but its receivers generally got good reviews.

Things could get informal at W2XAF. "Short" barked into the shortwave microphone and was heard around the world.

Hammarlund brought out the Comet "Pro" ($88.20, less tubes). It featured bandspread (calibration charts included) and a BFO (then called a "station finder"). The "Pro" underwent several iterations over the next few years, adding a crystal filter, automatic volume control, better shielding, a metal cabinet, and other features. It lacked an RF stage, however.

Converters were still a popular way to get into shortwave. Among the new offerings were the Sparton Model 60, Midwest's Model Z-4 four-tube "Super-Het Short-Wave Converter," the three-tube "Majestic Short Wave Converter," and the three-tube "Crosley Short Wave Adapter."

The availability of ordinary home radios with shortwave capability expanded as well. Typically these receivers had four to seven tubes and sold for $20 to $40. Some were advertised as "dual wave" rather than all wave, with some of the dual wave units covering only up to 60–75 meters, others ranging up to 10 or 20 meters.

The popular radio weekly, *Radio Guide,* began carrying some shortwave information. International DXers Alliance president Charles A. Morrison would become the magazine's shortwave editor in 1935. *Short Wave Craft* went from bi-monthly to monthly publication. The magazine founded the Short Wave League, whose stated goals were to popularize shortwave among the public and bring together shortwave enthusiasts; use short wave radio to apprehend criminals (shortwave, just above the standard broadcast band, was in wide use by the police); oppose code requirements for amateur phone licensing; and eliminate static. The International Short Wave Club and others published rudimentary foreign-language reception report forms in Spanish, German, French and Italian. Special ISWC programs were broadcast over **EAQ, CMCI, TGX** and **VE9GW.** And the Madrid Telegraph and Radiotelegraph Conferences established a new 11 meter band for shortwave broadcasting: 25600–26600 kc.

1933

The expansion of shortwave continued. As the radio editor of *The New York Times* put it, "[m]ore countries have been added to the radio map by the use of the magic short waves that rush around the 25,000-mile globe quicker than a fly can crawl around a golf ball."[41]

Shortwave events were making news. In February, Moscow was picked up on 6000 kc. and for the first time rebroadcast in the U.S. (over WEAF). It was said that this was the 54th country whose stations had been relayed in the United States.[42] In June the voice of King George V was heard in many parts of the world as he opened the London World Economic Conference. Other parts of the conference were also broadcast on shortwave. The King's Christmas greetings were again heard worldwide over the BBC, and a roll-call of ten countries participated in a broadcast of Christmas Day greetings.

Hitler came to power in Germany, whereupon the Broadcasting Division of the Ministry for Propaganda, together with the **Zeesen** station, soon took the lead in international propaganda. A North American beam was established on April 1, and the now-20 kw. signals were strong.[43] "Radio wars," on shortwave, mediumwave and longwave, would become commonplace, as would jamming, already standard in many European cities on signals from Moscow. An October speech by Hitler, withdrawing Germany from the League of Nations, was shortwaved to America. But Zeesen also broadcast Christmas programs and much other benign content. Exchange broadcasts with Japan — mostly music — were begun in November.

The network lineup (and power output) of the North American shortwave stations was as follows: **Columbia Broadcasting System, W2XE,** Wayne, New Jersey (5 kw.), and **W3XAU,** Philadelphia (1 kw.); **NBC Red Network, W1XAL,** Boston (5 kw.), **W2XAD** (25 kw.) and **W2XAF** (40 kw.), Schenectady, and **W9XAA,** Chicago (500 watts); **NBC Blue Network, W1XAZ,** Springfield, Mass., (10 kw.), **W3XAL** (25 kw.) and **W3XL** (20 kw.), Bound Brook, New Jersey, and **W8XK,** Pittsburgh (40 kw.); and the **NBC Red and Blue Networks, W4XB,** Miami Beach (2.5 kw.), **W8XAL,** Mason, Ohio (10 kw.), **W9XF,** Downers Grove, Illinois (5 kw.), and Canadian stations **VE9DR** in Drummondville, Quebec (4 kw.) and **VE9GW** in Bowmanville, Ontario (500 watts). (VE9DR sometimes operated as VE9DN. Both calls were assigned to the Canadian Marconi Company.) Most U.S. stations were now on regular (if variable) schedules, which were often given in the DX press.

On March 4, nearly all these stations were networked in order to shortwave an all-day broadcast of President Roosevelt's inauguration. It was picked up and rebroadcast by the BBC and stations in many other countries. German-language commentary was added in a special relay to Germany. Observer aircraft, radio equipped cars and announcers with backpack transmitters also made use of shortwave during the occasion. It was said to be the largest group of technicians and announcers ever devoted to a single radio event.[44] Not all the relays were effective, however. Atmospherics and interference often degraded the quality of received signals and the resulting rebroadcasts.

The fall saw the start of Canada's new "Northern Messenger" program, which was heard Saturday nights at 2330 EST over a network of mediumwave stations as well as shortwavers **VE9DN,** 6005 kc., **VE9GW,** 6095, **VE9CL,** 6150, and **VE9JR,** now on 11720. The program was on the air between the months of November and May, and was usually one and one-half or two hours in length. During the first year the "Northern Messenger" handled some 1,754 messages, a number that would multiply by six over the next four years.[45]

The **BBC** sent a representative around the world to study reception conditions and meet with broadcasters and listeners. To convey shortwave program information to overseas listeners, the BBC inaugurated the Empire Edition of *World-Radio*. Although listeners to the Empire Service learned that reception varied considerably from season to season, their enjoyment of the programs from home was near universal.

> (India) "I, for one, must express my appreciation for your programmes. I think they are very good. They most certainly cheer up the lives of many who are living alone in the Colonies and in various parts of India. I would now be lost if you were to shut down. I have no suggestion to make regarding your programme. You are doing very well indeed."
>
> (India) "[L]et me state at once that your programmes are perfectly priceless—*but,* could you not lessen some of the classics and give us some more of Sydney Baines's light music?"
>
> (Newfoundland) "You ask about our feelings when Big Ben chimes out the hours. Personally, the sound makes me wholesomely homesick. I believe many scorn a person who feels homesick, but I hope I shall never outlive it. 'England' means so much to the average 'exile,' that the link with Big Ben just sends a thrill down one's spine, and Westminster Bridge and its surroundings come into our minds as the hours sound out. Oh, to be there!..."
>
> (Singapore) "I think you will be interested in the following extracts from a letter from my sister in Singapore, written on September 15, in which she says that on Sunday, September 3, she and her husband and son 'motored 46 miles up in the jungle to Johore, to see some wonderful waterfalls. Coming back, we stopped to get some stag's horn moss in a rubber plantation, when suddenly an organ pealed forth — then came a clergyman's voice, followed by a big choir singing 'All people that on earth do dwell.' Not a house in sight, just rubber and jungle. A planter somewhere was getting the morning service from Daventry. It was a most uncanny feeling, sitting in the car listening. We could hear the words, 15 miles up in Johore! Very marvelous and beautiful.' What a wonderful thing wireless is!"[46]

Although the more powerful shortwave stations were the meat and potatoes of shortwave listening, the reach of shortwave gave incentive to many hams and local mediumwave stations to experiment with transmitting on the still-new medium. These often low-power stations provided a growing number of shortwave targets for the serious DXer.

Among the sought-after Iberian-based stations were **EAJ25, Barcelona Radio Club,** Spain, on 6000 kc., and **EAR110,** Madrid, on 6976; **EAR58** (later **EA8AB**), **Radio Club Tenerife,** Santa Cruz de Tenerife, Canary Islands, on 7211; and **CT3AQ,** Funchal, Madeira, which was on the air on Thursdays and Saturdays at 1700–2000 EST, 11181 kc., with multi-lingual announcements. The International DXers Alliance arranged for special November programs from both the Canaries and the Madeira station.

To the many east coast listeners, the hard-to-hear signals from the Far East were always of interest. One station for which they would often try was **ZGE,** the station of the **Malayan Amateur Radio Society** in Kuala Lumpur, Federated Malay States. *("This is the Malayan Amateur Radio Society, Kuala Lumpur.")* ZGE broadcast a program of music, news and stock quotations three days a week at 0640–0840 EST over its 180-watt transmitter on 6130 kc. It had begun regular broadcasting on mediumwave in 1930, and moved to shortwave in 1931.

The greatest expansion of shortwave was in Latin America. DXing these stations was a special challenge. Aside from the language problem, they usually operated on highly variable schedules and on equally variable frequencies, usually out of band.

New from Mexico City was **XETE, Empresa de Teléfones Ericsson,** a radiotelephone station that sometimes transmitted broadcast programming, usually simulcasting mediumwave station XEAL. The station invited reports on its two frequencies, 6130 and 9600 kc., and it also carried special programs for radio clubs. XETE left the air in 1934 after the parent company went bankrupt (and unpaid staff staged a hunger strike).

XETE, Empresa de Teléfones Ericsson, was one of many stations with a dual identity. Mainly a commercial radiotelephone station, it also dabbled in shortwave broadcasting by relaying the signal of Mexico City mediumwaver XEAL.

The Dominican Republic was represented on shortwave by 50-watt **HI1A, La Voz del Yaque**, Santiago, on 6272 kc., **HIZ**, Santo Domingo, on 6315, and **HIX**, also in Santo Domingo, on 5952, with 200 watts. HIX, founded in 1928, was the country's first radio station.

As would be true for decades, Colombia was home to an increasing number of shortwave stations. **HJ1ABB, La Voz de Barranquilla**, operated with 300 watts on 6447 kc. (later 9560), and seemed to be heard by almost everyone. **HJ2ABA, La Voz del Pais**, operated from Tunja, on 5952 kc. (it became **Ecos de Boyaca**, 6150); **HJ3ABB, Colombia Broadcasting**, Bogota, was on 7407; **HJ3ABF, La Voz de Bogota**, 6185; and **HJ4ABE, Radiodifusora de Medellin**, Colombia, 5879. **HJ4ABB**, 7210 kc., formerly **Radio Manizales**, was now announcing as **La Voz de Caldas**. The power of these stations was typically a few hundred watts at most.

In Venezuela, **YV3BC, Radiodifusora Venezuela**, Caracas, was active in the morning and evening on 6135 (later 6160) and 9510 kc. It carried special *RADEX* programs in December (and in January and February 1934). Later it became **YV3RC**. December also saw the presentation of special *RADEX* broadcasts over **HIX** and **HCJB**. HCJB was on the air every day except Monday at 2000–2130 EST on 4107 kc. An International Reply Coupon was requested for a QSL.

A new station in Ecuador, **HC2RL**, "**Quinta Piedad**," Guayaquil, was heard on 6605 kc. calling "Hello America." Although power was only about 200 watts, it was one of the most widely reported South American stations. Bolivia was on the air by way of **CP5, Compañia Radio Boliviana**, La Paz, heard in the evening on 6080 kc. Daytime channels were **CP6**, 9120 kc., and **CP7**, 15300, and power was 1 kw. The station identified as **Radio Illimani**, and claimed that, at over 12,000 feet above sea level, it was the highest broadcasting station in the world. **PRA3, Radio Club do Brasil**, Rio de Janeiro, was relayed by **Companhia Radio Internacional do Brazil**, Rio de Janeiro, a Brazilian commercial station, via **PSK** on 8185 kc. and

Mediumwave station PRA3, Radio Club do Brasil, broadcast from Rio de Janeiro on 860 kc. Its signal was also heard on shortwave via Brazilian commercial station Companhia Radio Internacional do Brazil. This card is for reception on 8185 kc.

PSH on 10220. One of the two frequencies could usually be heard in the evenings around 1900 EST.

The biggest practical challenge to the shortwave listener was knowing just what frequency he was tuned to. Without knowledge of the exact frequency, reception of new stations was often described as "just above" or "just below" a well-known station, or between two known stations. To identify themselves, stations started using interval, or tuning, signals. A cuckoo identified **CT1AA**, Portugal. **TI4NRH** used bugle calls and telegraph dashes, **HCJB** a two-tone chime, **VE9HX** four gongs. A metronome signaled **CNR**, Morocco. And the call of Jacko, the Kookaburra, on **VK2ME** was already well known.

The shortwave receiver industry was now growing rapidly. People were buying new radios, and there were many shortwave models to choose from. About 85 percent of radio manufacturers offered at least one all-wave model, and roughly two-thirds of all new receivers sold had some shortwave coverage. On many, shortwave was just an afterthought. These sets generally offered limited performance, a factor that discouraged acceptance of shortwave among the general public.

An important development was the introduction of all-wave receivers by big consumer manufacturers like RCA and GE. RCA Victor introduced six-tube and eight-tube sets in both console and table models. ("No tapped coils are used — each frequency range is a complete circuit in itself, with separate coils — each with independent trimming adjustment.... A new full-vision airplane type dial [50:1 vernier] provides quick and easy tuning, and gives a distinctive and attractive appearance to the instrument.")[47] General Electric offered the eight-tube K-80 tombstone-style superhet with coil switching, RF stage, AVC, vernier tuning and airplane tuning dial for under $100 ("a good broadcast set and a swell short-wave receiver as well.... It brings short-wave reception up to date — this job has all the refinements you expect in the very best broadcast receiver").[48]

Among lesser-known manufacturers there were countless choices, many at low prices (and matching performance). Among the ready-builts, Insuline Corporation offered its "Short-Wave Scout" at $16.50. Also available was the three-tube "Eagle." The Doerle line of two- and three-tube receivers (wired, $10 to $15) were sold by such firms as Harrison Radio and Radio Trading Company in New York City.

Kits were still popular. Federated Purchaser, Inc. offered the "Discoverer Five," and Lafayette the "Short Wave Master 6" ($19.75 for the kit, plus $2.25 per pair of coils and $9.75 for the power pack).

There was the seven-tube "Air-Marshall," the Postal Radio Corporation "International Nine," and Harrison Radio's line of "Royal" receivers ($15 to $30, less tubes). Some receivers could be obtained in either wired or kit form, including several Powertone brand receivers in the two- to five-tube range.

There were also many options for those who wanted

GENERAL ELECTRIC ALL-WAVE RADIO

MODEL K-80. With this distinctive G-E All-wave superheterodyne table model, the whole world of radio entertainment is yours. Using one of its four wave-bands, you can bring in your favorite American broadcasts; with the other three, all foreign and domestic short-wave stations as well as police calls, amateur and aircraft transmissions. A new airplane type, four-band illuminated tuning dial, operated by a double reduction vernier tuning control, insures easy station selection. Other features: automatic volume control; twin-push amplification; continuously variable tone control; full-size electrodynamic speaker; two-tone walnut cabinet.

Although never outstanding performers, popular-brand consumer shortwave radios like this one introduced the medium to a broader world of non-technical listeners. The relative difficulty of tuning the shortwave bands would always be an impediment to acceptance of shortwave by the general public.

more from a shortwave receiver. National introduced the seven-tube National FB-7 ($55) ("no frequency drift") and, with crystal filter installed, the FBX. Lincoln's successor to the SW-33, the 11-tube R-9, was advertised as "a super powered receiver designed for strictly short-wave reception" — "band spread on all frequencies," "CW beat oscillator," "perfect automatic volume control," "visual signal indicator," "instantaneous band selection." In the super receiver category was the 15-tube McMurdo Silver "Masterpiece" ("unmeasurable sensitivity," "one channel selectivity," "positively no cross modulation under any circumstances,"

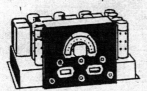

For over 30 years, no receiver manufacturer offered more models at all levels of performance than Hallicrafters. The comparatively expensive H-13 ($139.50) was one of the company's early offerings (*Radio News,* 1933).

"single accurately calibrated dial," "meter tuning," "automatically silent tuning between stations," "lowest signal-to-noise ratio ever achieved in a radio receiver").[50] Said the company: "Admiral Richard E. Byrd, U.S.N., asked Dr. McCaleb of Harvard University which radio receiver would be best for his next Antarctic expedition. In substance, Dr. McCaleb replied, 'McMurdo Silver's Masterpiece, with certain additions.'" Thus the Masterpiece II.[51] A series of Masterpiece receivers followed, ending with the Masterpiece VI in 1937.

A new company was heard from. Hallicrafters' first shortwave offerings, the "H" and "Z" series of "Round the World" receivers, were marketed through the Silver-Marshall Manufacturing Company, Chicago. The H-13 all-wave superheterodyne was promoted with a 32-page booklet ("engineer built," "guaranteed greater selectivity," "automatic tone control," "frequency-index tuning dial").[52] Hallicrafters had purchased Silver-Marshall Manufacturing Co., a shell corporation associated with the by then-bankrupt Silver-Marshall, Inc., and did business under the Silver-Marshall name until 1935. For decades Hallicrafters would be the best-known company in the shortwave receiver business. (Silver-Marshall, Inc. reinvented itself as McMurdo Silver, Inc. and stayed in business until 1938.)

Also released in 1933 was the Hallicrafters S-1 "Skyrider," the first in a long line of "Skyrider" and "Super Skyrider" receivers that culminated in 1946 with the final production runs of the classic SX-28A.

Late in the year, Radio Manufacturing Engineers of Peoria, Illinois, began advertising what has been called the first true communications receiver, the RME-9 "Super." Covering 540 kc. to 22 mc., it was advertised as incorporating "every known feature desired by present operators"[53] — single control tuning, bandspread, bandswitch in lieu of plug-in coils, variable BFO, AVC, tone control, signal strength meter, and, most importantly, high selectivity RF circuitry.[54] This made it a "single signal receiver," a phrase used by manufacturers to indicate good selectivity.

Radio clubs were becoming more popular. Membership in the NNRC reached 1,800. Numerous other DX clubs had formed in 1932 and 1933. The International DXers Alliance, Bloomington, Illinois, publisher of *The Globe Circler* monthly bulletin, would become one of the best known. It started out in 1933 with 12 members, but soon it had many local chapters (the Hollywood–Beverly Hills chapter published its own monthly 24-page bulletin called *The Listening Post*). Another well-known club was the Universal Radio DX Club, founded in San Francisco in 1933 and home to the *Universalite* bulletin. Other DX groups included the Buffalo Evening News DX Club and the Short Wave Club of New York City; the Chicago Short Wave Radio Club; the Central DX Club, La Grange, Illinois; the Globe Circlers Radio DX Club, Hackensack, New Jersey, and the North American Radio Club, also in Hackensack; the Universal DX Club, Oradell, New Jersey; the Interstate Radio Association, Summit, New Jersey; the New England Radio Club, Worcester, Massachusetts (founded in 1930 as the Radio Listeners Club of Central New England); the Quixote Radio Club, Hendersonville, North Carolina; and the Transcontinental Radio DX Club, Hawthorne, New Jersey. The club scene was very fluid. Clubs came and went, with consolidations common.

The International Short Wave Club began offering its bulletin at some radio stores and at S. S. Kresge. The club also announced its Denton Trophy Contest for obtaining the greatest number of shortwave broadcast QSLs for reception during the period August 1, 1933 to February 1, 1934. The winner was H. S. Bradley of Hamilton, New York, using a four-tube receiver. (Subsequently Bradley authored a number of articles on DXing.)

The availability of shortwave station information in the radio press was improving, although often it was tentative and not very authoritative. For several months in 1932, *Radio News* had carried a mini-column called "DXers Corner" which featured club news, techni-

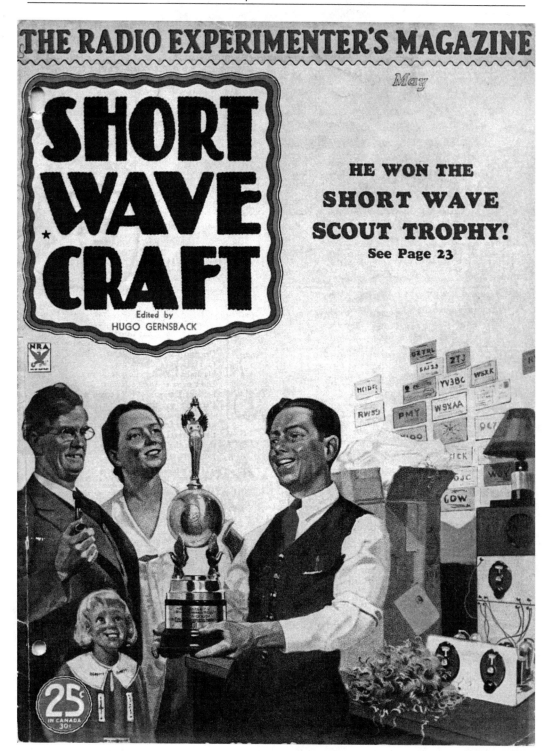

Founded by *Short Wave Craft* in 1933, the Short Wave Scouts offered a trophy for the reader who logged the greatest number of stations in a month, with at least half QSLed. The rules were later changed so that only verified loggings could be counted, with no more than 50 percent from the entrant's own country (*Short Wave Craft*, 1934).

cal tips, and a bit of broadcast band DX information. It supplemented the station lists which the magazine had been publishing for several years. A more substantial shortwave column, "The DX Corner," was begun in April. It featured shortwave station news, mainly submitted by readers, and a list of "best bets" for all hours of the day. In October, to emphasize a new shortwave orientation, *Radio News* changed its cover name to *Radio News and the Short-Waves.*

In February *Short Wave Craft* inaugurated a column called "When to Listen In" wherein Robert Hertzberg presented news of shortwave stations. In April, the magazine began presenting a monthly by-frequency list, "Short Wave Stations of the World," which contained frequency and schedule information for all stations, both shortwave broadcast and "experimental and commercial." Later lists covered police, airport, and even TV stations. In August, the magazine's parent, Gernsback's Popular Book Corp., began publishing *Official Short Wave Log and Call Book,* a magazine containing various station lists. Only a few issues were published, however. To generate up-to-date information for its shortwave efforts, *Short Wave Craft* inaugurated the Short Wave Scouts, awarding a two-foot tall trophy to the listener with the greatest number of verified loggings each month.

In March, *RADEX* appointed a shortwave editor, Page Taylor of Detroit. Although still mainly a broadcast band publication, *RADEX* now covered shortwave in every issue. And in November a new shortwave magazine appeared. *Short Wave Radio* carried extensive station and technical information for shortwave listeners, and although it lasted only a year, it gave a start to two editors who would become well-known shortwave figures of the day, Captain Horace L. Hall (who also wrote for the *The Sun* newspaper in New York) and J. B. L. Hinds.[55] The magazine sponsored the informal "Before Breakfast Short Wave Club" to spread the joys of listening between 5:00 and 9:00 A.M.

The year ended with the publication of two technically-oriented shortwave "handbooks." *Short Wave Radio* published the 128-page *Short Wave Radio Handbook,* authored by engineer Clifford E. Denton. A 136-page introduction to shortwave, *Short-Wave Handbook,* was edited by Laurence M. Cockaday and Walter H. Holze and published by *Radio News.* More important for the general listening public, shortwave gained new credibility in November when *The New York Times* began featuring news of shortwave broadcasting stations worldwide, and their programs, in a column called "Along Short-Wave Trails." It, or similar columns with other names (e.g. "Radio's Short Waves," "Short-Wave Pick-Ups," "Listening-In to Distance," "From the Far Places"), appeared often from 1934 through the war years, together with much other coverage of shortwave activity. The stations in Australia, Spain, Germany, Italy, England, France and other major shortwave broadcast countries were covered, but so were stations like Radio Maroc, ZGE in Malaya, VUC in Calcutta, the numerous Latin American stations, etc. Schedules of Axis stations appeared often.

1934

The shortwave event of the year was the Byrd Antarctic Expedition.[56] The return to Little America had begun in September 1933 with the departure of the expedition's two ships, the SS *Jacob Ruppert* and the SS *Bear of Oakland,* from Boston en route to Antarctica by way of the Panama Canal and New Zealand. For shipboard transmissions, the *Jacob Rubert* was assigned the call letters **KJTY,** the *Bear* **WHEW.** The ships carried almost three tons of radio equipment, including ten transmitters and 14 receivers of various kinds. Most of the radio equipment was for local use on the ice and on expedition aircraft. However, the chronicling of Byrd's activities to the outside world was a major element of the trip. The expedition made many day-to-day contacts with commercial coastal stations and amateurs, and listeners started hearing it immediately after its departure.

Unlike Byrd's 1928 expedition, which used code only, this time there was voice as well, and the main transmitter, a 1 kw. Collins, when transferred from the *Jacob Rubert* to land and coupled to a directional antenna, was used for regular weekly shortwave broadcasts to New York (as well as relays to New York of some of the expedition's intramural activities). The land call for the main base was **KFZ**, the forward base **KFY**. These broadcasts began in February and were on the air Saturday nights at 2200 EST (later moved to Wednesday). Sponsored by General Foods, they were carried over the CBS network, including CBS shortwave station W2XE (a CBS announcer and technical supervisor accompanied Byrd).

The transmissions were picked up by **LSX** in Buenos Aires. LSX, which by then was using a power of 20 kw., relayed them to the RCA receiving facility at Riverhead, Long Island,[57] from whence they were sent by wire to CBS headquarters in New York and then on to WABC, Wayne, New Jersey and the rest of the CBS national network. It was typically the LSX signal, rather than the direct signal from Antarctica, on which CBS relied. When conditions to Buenos Aires were disturbed, Riverhead would sometimes take relays from the RCA stations at **Point Reyes**, California or **Kahuku**, Hawaii, which also monitored the signals. Riverhead also wired the signals to **Rocky Point**, which rebroadcast them so they could be heard in the Antarctic. Careful shortwave listeners thus might hear the Byrd signals from several sources, and often there was confusion over just what the origin of the signal was. The best frequencies for hearing the program direct from KFZ were 11830 and 13200 kc. LSX was usually on 10350.

Many broadcast programs were sent to Byrd, in particular a special series that was broadcast over **W2XAF** on alternate Sundays at 2300 EST. The first half-hour, which was entertainment, was carried on the broadcast band and shortwave. The second half-hour was a radio mailbag program transmitted on shortwave only, usually 9530 kc.

The Byrd Broadcasts

For sheer dramatic interest, the regular 10 o'clock Saturday night programs ... have few equals in the history of radio broadcasting. They reached what is probably a grand climax on March 17th, when Joseph Pelter, the expedition's aerial surveyor, addressed the microphone after successfully going through an emergency appendectomy, which was performed right in the radio shack.

"Byrd Antarctic Programs Successful"
Short Wave Radio, June 1934[58]

During the expedition, the Federal Radio Commission licensed a temporary station in northwestern Alaska so that CBS could link the Arctic and the Antarctic by radio and present the resulting programs over the CBS network. **KILS** operated on 13250 kc. as well as other channels, with 1 kw. When it could not contact the Byrd Expedition directly it was assisted by the RCA transmitters in **Rocky Point** or **Point Reyes**.

Advertisers made the most of the Byrd expedition, announcing that their equipment had been taken along on the trip or promising that their receivers would pick up the Byrd broadcasts. Admiral Byrd was the recipient of the 1934 CBS medal for "Distinguished Contribution to Radio." Unfortunately for DXers, most of the transmissions surrounding the expedition were considered point-to-point and their legal confidentiality made them poor candidates for QSLing.

Several other shortwave excursions caught the attention of listeners during the year. One was that of the *Seth Parker,* the four-masted schooner of Phillips H. Lord, who played the character Seth Parker on radio. Lord and his 25-man crew undertook the round-the-world trip largely to satisfy Lord's wanderlust, and no doubt to enhance his celebrity as well. The call letters of the ship, which was equipped with an RCA 1 kw. transmitter, were **KNRA**, and among the frequencies that were heard were 6160, 9160 and 12345 kc. Listeners heard tests of the equipment even before the ship's March 1 departure. A Tuesday night program from the ship was broadcast nationwide over the NBC network.[59] The voyage of the *Seth Parker* came to an end in February 1935 when the ship was damaged in a typhoon off Pago Pago.

The schooner *Morrissey* had left New York for the Arctic in June 1933. It was well equipped, and its station, **W10XDA**, was a frequent target of radio amateurs and SWLs during its multiple Arctic trips in the 1930s.[60] And amateur station **W9USA** was set up in the Travel and Transport building at the Chicago World's Fair. It operated on 14165 and 14200 kc. and it was often heard around 1600–1800 EST.

In the United States, Westinghouse broadcast band stations WBZ, Springfield, Massachusetts, and WBZA, Boston, exchanged calls. WBZ, now in Boston, moved its transmitter to Millis, about 20 miles from downtown, and its studios to Boston's Hotel Bradford. The Springfield shortwave transmitter, **W1XAZ**, also moved to Millis, from whence it simulcast WBZ at 0730–0100 EST with 10 kw. power.

CBS broadcast many educational programs during the year. Its station, **W2XE**, now identified in German, French, Spanish and Italian, in addition to English. (*"This is station W2XE, the experimental station of the Columbia Broadcasting System in the City of New York, United States of America."*) However, the biggest news in the use of shortwave for educational purposes was the establishment by Walter Lemmon, head of **W1XAL**, of a non-profit educational organization, the World Wide Broadcasting Foundation, to produce educational programming for his station. This was accomplished after a meeting with Massachusetts educational and cultural leaders at the University Club in Boston, which soon became headquarters for the station's studios and offices. Much of the Foundation's programming was produced under the name "World Radio University" or "World University of the Air." "Dedicated to Enlightenment" became the station's motto. Listeners who joined the World Wide Listener's League received *The World Wide Listener* each month. It contained 24 pages of schedule information and news of educational and cultural events. These moneys, together with income from an important collaborator, the Christian Science church, and from the Rockefeller Foundation and others, supported Lemmon.[61]

W1XAL was on the air about two hours a night. It was the first station to focus on program development specifically for a shortwave audience. However, while broadcast band simulcasts were still the main fare of the other American shortwave stations, they continued to tailor some programs for the shortwave audience. On March 16, **W2XAF** and **W2XAD** had a one-hour program in which they sought to reach all parts of the world without relays. It was broadcast at 1800 EST on 9530 and 15330 kc. and was hosted by Robert L. Ripley of "Believe It or Not" fame (who produced a special cartoon for the occasion).[62] In June, the Primo Carnera–Max Baer title fight in Long Island City, New York was carried to the world by shortwave. Foreign-language coverage was provided by special ringside newspaper announcers. An Italian version was sent forth by way of **W8XK**, and a Spanish version from Radio Central in **Rocky Point** for rebroadcast in Argentina and beyond.

In November, W2XAF and LSX in Argentina facilitated a "joint radio meeting" of the

Rotary International clubs in Schenectady and Buenos Aires. The Schenectady end of the link was broadcast at 2100 EST, and was followed by the Buenos Aires transmission. Rotary clubs throughout North and South America were encouraged to listen in, and General Electric dealers obliged by installing two shortwave receivers at each club wishing to participate. Radio's effectiveness was showcased when the Schenectady-bound train carrying Walter D. Head, Vice President of Rotary International, was late, and he was able to address the gathering by way of an ultra high frequency transmitter in a police car sent to pick him up. And shortwave featured in the crash of an American Airlines plane in the woods of the Adirondacks in New York on December 28. The harrowing rescue of the four occupants took several days, during which W2XAD and W2XAF rebroadcast transmissions from the search party's portable transmitter.

May 8, 1934

We wish to verify reception of station W1XAL operating on a frequency of 6040 kilocycles, with power of 3500 watts on___FEB. 11, 1934___. We hope you will listen in often and let us have your comments.

Cordially yours,

for World Wide Broadcasting Corporation

SHORTWAVE AND TELEVISION CORPORATION

70 Brookline Ave., Boston, Mass.

In 1931, Walter S. Lemmon bought New York shortwave station W2XAL and moved it to Boston. In its early years, Lemmon's company, the Shortwave Broadcasting Corporation, was located near Fenway Park.

VE9JR, Winnipeg, Manitoba officially became CJRX, whose call letters now tracked those of its standard broadcast parent, CJRC. It operated on 11720 kc., and transmitted in parallel with its sister station, CJRO (formerly VE9CL), 6150 kc. Both frequencies were 2 kw. These stations carried some programming in French.

"A Listening Tour of Europe"

Music predominates on the Italian waves. The melodies are rarely interrupted by announcers as in this country, so the American with a short-wave outfit can listen to Puccini music for a long stretch without interruption.... Americans will find many recordings on the air from the British Broadcasting House. Following the announcer's talk a recorded playlet was heard so clearly that the needle-scratch came across the Atlantic as a background to the actors' voices.... Dutch announcers are good linguists and often revert to excellent English for American auditors. Music seems of secondary importance in the PHI programs, but occasionally a singer or orchestra is heard.... [In Berlin] [t]he foreign announcers seem never to be in a hurry. Several minutes may pass between the introductory talk and the actual program.... When the atmospherics over the Atlantic are especially favorable, the concerts [from France] sound as clear as local broadcasts.

The New York Times
March 25, 1934[63]

The major shortwave broadcasters were located in Europe. Shifts in programming, from international program exchanges to home grown propaganda, were starting to appear, particularly from Germany. An address by Hitler to the German Reichstag was shortwaved to the NBC network in January. **Zeesen** now had shortwave broadcasts beamed to North and South America, Africa, Asia and Australia. *("Hello America. Hello Africa. This is DJD of the Reich Gesellschaft at Berlin.")*

The **BBC** was sending forth two hours daily to Australasia, three to Malaya and the Far East, three and one-half to India and environs, four and three-quarters to Africa, and two to Canada and the Americas. When shortwave transmission hours were compatible with the broadcast day in England, the transmissions often carried Home Service programming. Otherwise recorded programs were featured, and were always identified as such in BBC program schedules. (The BBC and the German broadcasting authority were early experimenters with reel-to-reel recording, which in the early days used steel tape.) During the overhaul of the clock, the sound of Big Ben was temporarily replaced with the sound of "Big Tom," which was located in the tower of St. Paul's Cathedral in London.

On April 22, the BBC changed the format of its announcements, adopting the 24-hour clock in place of the 12-hour "AM-PM" system. And the BBC's *World-Radio* became headquarters to the World Radio Research League. The League focused on studying scientific aspects of radio, the first being "echoes of long delay," the effect sometimes noted on a signal received via both short path and long path.[64]

Radio Coloniale in France, which usually carried domestic French-language programming, began presenting English news each evening. The station emphasized music rather than talks.[65] And it sent a questionnaire to its listeners. "At what time of the year and at what hour is reception best? What receiving equipment do you use? What other shortwave stations do you hear regularly? What do you think of our programs? How much time do you spend listening to them?"

I2RO of the **Ente Italiano Audizioni Radiofoniche**, or **EIAR**, Rome, which had often been heard on 11810 kc. announcing as Radio Roma Napoli, was off the air during much of the year while the transmitter plant was upgraded to 20 kw. Occasionally EIAR programs were also heard on **Italo Radio** PTT channels such as 9830 and 19520 kc. In October, EIAR returned to the air with an international service from its new transmitter plant at **Prato Smeraldo** in the Rome suburbs. Programs were beamed to North America, South America and the Far East. The frequencies were 6075, 9550, 11800 and 15225 kc., and either a 5 kw. or a 20 kw. transmitter could be used. The North American beam featured the "American Hour" three nights a week at 1830–2000 EST. The station often presented Italian operas.

The new Italian shortwave transmitters also relayed the programs of **Radio Bari**, a mediumwave station (1059 kc.) whose popular Arabic-language broadcasts presented a significant challenge to British policy in Egypt and Palestine. Radio Bari programming featured both entertainment and propaganda, and its carefully crafted news covered Italian and Axis political developments. It was largely the success of Radio Bari that would lead to the inauguration of Arabic broadcasting by the BBC in 1938. It was the first foreign-language broadcasting ever undertaken by Britain.[66]

Radio Centre, Moscow, 12000 kc., carried English at 1600–1700 EST on Sunday, Monday, Wednesday and Friday, plus Saturday night at 2200–2300 EST and Sunday morning at 0500–0700 and 1000–1100 EST. Talks on political, economic, industrial and sports subjects predominated. The power was 20 kw. (the same as RV59, 6000 kc.), and the station operated in the radiotelephone service when not broadcasting. (It appears that RV59 was also the call used on 12000 kc., while RNE was technically the call during periods of commercial traffic.) On December 21, venerable Dutch station **PCJ** returned to the air. Soon it was relaying **PHI** on Sunday mornings circa 0830–1030 on 15220 kc. It was also heard on 9590 kc. Transmissions soon expanded to various times on other days as well.

Hungary came on shortwave by way of stations **HAS** and **HAT**, operated by the **Research Laboratories for Electrical Communication of the Royal Hungarian Post**. The 5 kw. senders, located in Székesfehérvár, southwest of Budapest, transmitted on 6840 and 13685 kc. (later 9125 and 15370). Operations were intermittent within the general period 0045–1800 EST, but the station was often reported in the North American afternoon. QSLs bore small pasted-on photos of various Hungarian scenes.

Radio Wien in Austria, still on 6072 kc., now used the call letters **OER2**. It transmitted at 0300–1900 EST. **CT1AA**, Lisbon, Portugal, experimented on 15345 kc. And in December, **CT1GO, Radio Club Português**, Parede, Portugal, on mediumwave since 1931, opened a short-wave service. It broadcast most days on 6198 kc. at 1920–2030 EST and on 12396 on Tuesday, Thursday and Friday at 1300–1415 EST (plus Sundays at 1000–1130 on 12396 and 1130–1300 on 6198). The power was 350 watts, and the target zone was the Portuguese colonies of Africa.

At Christmas time, special broadcasts emanated from Spain, Italy and London, the last featuring greetings from many locations around the world. On New Year's Eve, the **BBC** sent a special program, "Hail and Farewell to 1934," to the U.S. at 1800 EST (2300 GMT), followed by a service at Winchester Cathedral, the sounds of Big Ben at midnight, the singing of "Auld Lang Syne," and expressions of "Happy New Year." Frequencies were 6050 and 9580 kc. On 6020 at 1735 EST, **Zeesen** offered a review of the year, followed at 2000 by expressions of good luck, and news and music at 2030–2230 EST. **EIAR** played the "Star-Spangled Banner" at 1830 on 6097 kc., followed by a special concert and the voices of American students in Rome.[67]

If Europe was headquarters for "big shortwave," Latin America was the home of the shortwave experimenters. The prevailing culture of private rather than state-owned radio spawned a plethora of small shortwave broadcasters. Most operated in the range of 5 to 7 mc., with low power and frequencies chosen more or less at will. Many were offshoots of existing standard broadcast stations, or amateur stations which, in the lax regulatory environment, decided to try their hand at broadcasting.

The inexactness of the available shortwave information was nowhere more evident than in the case of the Latin American stations. Although slogans ("La Voz de …") were becoming more common, many stations used call letters only. These were frequently misheard by listeners, few of whom had much knowledge of Spanish. Add to this the presence of numerous harmonics, and the difficulty in knowing one's exact frequency, and you had a delightful DX chaos.

South of the border, **XEBT, El Buen Tono**, Mexico City, was on 6075 kc. with 500 watts (later 1 kw.). It relayed its broadcast band sister station, XEB, at 2100–2400 EST, and it sounded an old rubber bulb-type auto horn during identifications. **TIEP, La Voz del Tropico**, San Jose, Costa Rica broadcast a special program for the Chicago Short Wave Club on November 30 at 2000 EST on 6710 kc. Although the power of the station was said to be 30 watts, it was one of the stronger signals on the band. It also worked amateurs under the call **TI1EP**. **TIX** (later **TIXGP3**), **La Reina del Aire**, San Jose, was on 5790.

A new shortwave country came on the air from Central America. **YNLF, La Voz de Nicaragua**, operated on 6950 kc. (later 5960, 6670, 9650) at 1900–2000. The power was 100 watts, soon increased to 1 kw. Its sister mediumwave station had been the first broadcasting station in the country. And **TI4NRH** returned to the Costa Rican airwaves after an absence caused by Sr. Céspedes Marín's trip to Nicaragua to help the Granada Radio Club build a station there (which was reported testing around 6720 kc.).

In the Caribbean, **COC**, Havana, Cuba, 6010 kc., which had been on the air for some time, suffered a fire. It returned in September, broadcasting at 0930–1100 and 1600–1800 EST

Although Central American stations were somewhat better verifiers than the South Americans, Latin American stations were among the hardest to QSL, mainly because of language difficulties and limited resources. Persistence would often yield a very nice reply, however, as this QSL from La Voz del Tropico in San Jose, Costa Rica, attests.

with 250 watts. Soon after, **COH**, also in Havana, came on the air. It broadcast daily at 1000–1100, 1700–1800 and 2000–2100 EST on 9430 kc. with 150 watts, and was one of the best heard stations. Sometimes it relayed mediumwave station CMCY.

Mediumwave station **HIH, La Voz del Higuamo**, San Pedro de Macoris, the Dominican Republic, was now on 6800 kc. shortwave with 75 watts, Thursday and Sunday. Also new from this Caribbean island country were **HI4D, La Voz de Quisqueya**, transmitting from the small town of the same name on 6480 kc., and a 50-watt station in La Romana, **HI3C, La Voz de la Feria,** which was on 6670.

But nowhere was shortwave booming more than in Colombia. New stations that could be identified by their slogans included **HJ1ABE, La Voz de los Laboratorios Fuentes**, Cartagena, 7000 kc. (later 9500); **HJ3ABH, La Voz de la Victor**, Bogota, 6200; **HJ5ABD, La Voz del Valle**, Cali, 6480 kc. (100 watts); and **HJ5ABC, La Voz de Colombia**, Cali, which was on a frequency around 5770 kc. (later 6150) and operated with 15 watts (later 150). Stations using callsigns only included **HJ1ABD**, Cartagena, 6100 kc.; **HJ2ABG**, Cúcuta, 5975; **HJ3ABI**, Bogota, 6050; and **HJ5ABH**, Palmira, 9370.

Although the Colombians offered great DX possibilities, they also caused great confusion. Opined one DX editor: "It would be a great treat to most every short wave listener if the stations in Colombia would arrange new call-signs that would not cause so much confu-

YNLF was the first station in Nicaragua to use shortwave. The country would have an outsized presence on the shortwave broadcast bands in the 1930s and 1940s.

sion and if they would stay on one wavelength for at least one month."[68] "We almost dread the task of trying to straighten out the information received each month on the stations in Colombia, as they all have similar calls and many of them just drift from one wavelength to another."[69] By year's end the situation had not improved. "Boy, how these Colombians get us. We pray for the day when they will decide to use a different call-sign system, for it takes more than an expert to distinguish calls like Colombia uses."[70]

Right behind Colombia in shortwave activity was Venezuela. At 2030–2100 EST on Thursday and Saturday, **YV2BC, Broadcasting Caracas,** carried the "Silvertone Program" sponsored by Sears Roebuck of Chicago. The station had much English-language programming, making it a favorite with American listeners. **YV5BMO** (soon **YV5RMO**), **Ecos del Caribe,** Maracaibo, Venezuela, was new to the air but was soon widely reported on 6070 kc. Also new was **YV6RV,** Valencia, with a station name that would be familiar to DXers for many decades — **La Voz de Carabobo.** The frequency was 6030 kc. (later 6520), and the power was 500 watts. Another new Venezuelan, **YV4BSG** (soon **YV4RC**), **Sociedad Anónima de Radio,** Caracas, was heard in the evenings on 6000 kc. Its power was 150 watts.

In Ecuador, **HCJB,** was now identifying as **Voice of the Andes.** It's address, Casilla 691, Quito, would be well known to generations of shortwave listeners. **PRADO** in Riobamba, Ecuador was now on 6620 kc., and broadcast a special program for the Ecuadorean colony in Paris on various 19 meter channels, including 15300 and 15440 kc. Soon it also had a Thursday night program where the names of people who had sent in reception reports were read. The information on Peruvian shortwave was still very tentative. However, it appeared that a mediumwave station, **La Voz del Peru,** 1360 kc., was now on 5770 kc. "onda corta" at 2000–2230 EST. Known on shortwave as **Radio Dusa, Difusora Universal,** it gave its call let-

LA VOZ DE "LOS LABORATORIOS FUENTES"
Cartagena, Colombia, S. A. - P. O. Box 31
ONDA 31,58 Mts. 9.500 Klc.

PARA LAS ENFERMEDADES DEL PECHO TOME
"JARABE ANTI - TISICO"

The early 1930s was a period of rapid shortwave development in Colombia, which soon boasted more shortwave broadcasters than any other Latin American country. This card verifies a second anniversary program of HJ1ABE, which was founded in 1934. The station was known by its sign off melody, "Aloha 'Oe."

ters, **OAX4D**, in Morse code when it signed off. The shortwave transmissions were made over the transmitters of All America Cables, Inc., a commercial company by then owned by International Telephone & Telegraph Company.

A second shortwave station was activated in Brazil. It was **PRF5,** 9505 kc., another channel of radiotelephone station **Companhia Radio Internacional do Brazil**, Rio de Janeiro. It was on the air at 1730–1815 EST and had segments in English, German, French, Spanish and Portuguese (and later Italian and Esperanto). The English program, called "The Brazilian Hour," was produced by the Brazilian Publicity Service. Soon PRF5 became one of the best-heard of the South American stations. And in addition to LSX, another commercial station, **Compañia Internacional de Radio**, was often heard with broadcast programming from Argentina. CIR station **LSN**, 9890 kc., located in Hurlingham, near Buenos Aires, usually carried the program of 50 kw. mediumwave station LR1, Radio El Mundo, which was said to be South America's most powerful station.

There was still little activity in Africa. In Rabat, Morocco, the PTT station, which was typically referred to by its call letters, **CNR,** transmitted broadcast programming as **Radio Maroc** on Sundays at 1430–1700 EST on 9300 kc. and 0730–0900 on 12830 kc. The power was now 10 kw. But the Rabat broadcast service left the air in 1935 (the station continued operating in radiotelephone mode). **ZTJ** in Johannesburg was still on 6122 kc., now with 5 kw. Two Portuguese colonies, Angola and Mozambique, were reported to now be on short-

YV6RV

RADIODIFUSORA	1350 y 6520 Kc.	HORAS DE TRASMISION:
LA VOZ DE CARABOBO	o sean	DIARIAMENTE
	222,2 y 46,01 Mts.	DE 11 A 2 P. M. Y DE 5 A 10 P. M.

V A L E N C I A - VENEZUELA

Valencia: ....13.!.. *de* ....Abril.................... *de 193* 6

Acusamos recibo de su amable reportaje del ....19. *de* ...Marzo..........
hecha la verificación, certificamos que Ud. oyó nuestro programa del
....19.. *de* ......Marzo............. *de 193* ...6.. *en* ......6520............ *Kc.*

Le damos nuestras expresivas gracias por su fina atención

Por Radiodifusora LA VOZ DE CARABOBO

Few Latin American stations remained on shortwave as long as La Voz de Carabobo, Valencia, Venezuela, a familiar presence on the 60 meter band for over a half century.

wave. The station of amateur Alvaro Nunes de Carvalho, **Estação Radio Difusora CR6AA**, Lobito, Angola, was on 7177 kc., 500 watts, at 1430–1630 EST. **Grêmio dos Radiofilos da Colonia de Mozambique**, Lourenço Marques, used a 150-watt transmitter, CR7AA, 3543 kc., and was on the air Mondays, Thursdays and Saturdays at 1330–1530 EST. Neither of these stations was heard in North America at this time, however.

Asian stations were difficult to hear in the United States—especially on the east coast— and when they were heard they were difficult to identify. **VUB** in Bombay was now on 9565 kc. with 4.5 kw. (soon increased to 10 kw.). Broadcasting from Malaya was expanding from **ZGE** in Kuala Lumpur to stations in both Penang and Singapore in what was called the Straits Settlements, a group of small territories on the Malay peninsula. A British Crown Colony, the Straits Settlements, together with the Federated Malay States and the unfederated Malay states, comprised what is present day Malaysia (Singapore is now independent). In Penang, 49-watt **ZHJ**, the station of the **Penang Wireless Society**, operated on 6080 kc. (soon 7630), Monday, Wednesday and Friday at 0800–1000 EST.

Broadcasting from Singapore had begun in 1931. **VS1AB**, an amateur operator, had started broadcast operations on 7195 kc. on Sunday and Wednesday at 1030–1200 EST, and was followed by another amateur, **VS1AD**, who conducted scheduled broadcasts for two hours daily, four days a week. In 1933 these stations were supplanted by **ZHI, Radio Service Company**, on 6025 kc. The station, whose power was variously put at 90 and 180 watts, was on the air Monday, Wednesday and Thursday at 0540–0810 EST and Saturday at 2240–0110 EST (*"ZHI, Singapore, Straits Settlement"*). Radio Service Co. operated a store that sold radios and other electronic gear. ZHI programming, which included news, music, stock market reports, and Sunday morning church services, was more varied and professional than that of the Singapore amateur operations or, for that matter, either ZGE or ZHJ.

Eddie Startz was sent on a tour of the Dutch East Indies. The decision may have been influenced in part by the creation, in 1934, of **Nederlands-Indische Radio Omroep Maatschappij**, or NIROM, a domestic broadcasting system in the Dutch East Indies. Reliance on international shortwave by the Dutch living in colonial Indonesia would decline as more NIROM stations came into service.[71] Although the PHI broadcasts were still intended for the Dutch East Indies, PHI adopted a distinctive international character, identifying in Dutch, Malay, German, French, English, Spanish and Portuguese.

NIROM was quick to make use of shortwave in order to maximize its reach. On the island of Java, the most powerful shortwave station was **YDA, Bandoeng**, on 6040 and 6120 kc. It was soon moved to the Tanjung Priok district of Batavia (Jakarta)

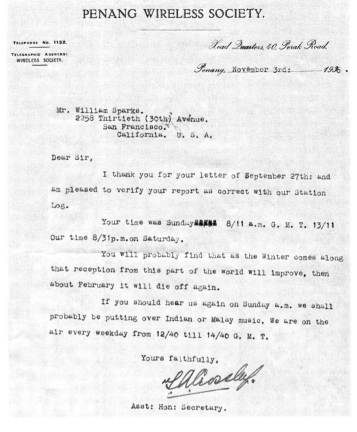

PENANG WIRELESS SOCIETY.

TELEPHONE No. 1132.
TELEGRAPHIC ADDRESS:
WIRELESS SOCIETY.

Head Quarters, 40. Perak Road.

Penang, November 3rd: _____ 19__ .

Mr. William Sparks.
    2258 Thirtieth (30th) Avenue.
    San Francisco.
        California. U. S. A.

Dear Sir,

        I thank you for your letter of September 27th: and am pleased to verify your report as correct with our Station Log.

        Your time was Sunday 8/11 a.m. G. M. T. 13/11 Our time 8/31p.m. on Saturday.

        You will probably find that as the Winter comes along that reception from this part of the world will improve, then about February it will die off again.

        If you should hear us again on Sunday a.m. we shall probably be putting over Indian or Malay music. We are on the air every weekday from 12/40 till 14/40 G. M. T.

        Yours faithfully,

        Asst: Hon: Secretary.

Penang was one of the four territories that made up the original Straits Settlements, later called Malaya. Radio first reached the public through the efforts of amateur radio operators, sometimes broadcasting alone, sometimes through their clubs, of which the Penang Wireless Society was one. There were other amateur-led broadcasting efforts in Singapore and Kuala Lumpur.

and upgraded to 10 kw. There were also 200-watt stations in **Batavia** (4330 kc.) and **Semarang** (4370). In addition, commercial radiotelegraph stations often carried broadcast programming. These were **Bandoeng** (PLV with 80 kw. one of the best-heard stations; PLE, PMA and PMC with 40 kw.; PLP and PMN with 3 kw.), plus **Medan** (YBG, 10425 kc.), **Makassar** (PNI, 8775), and **Menado** (YBZ, 7680), all three of which were believed to be operating with 3 kw.

The existence of NIROM did not prevent the continuation of broadcasting by other entities. Some Indonesian amateur radio operators continued to use their stations for informal broadcasting, a condition that would continue for generations and add to the complexity of the Indonesian shortwave scene. A well-known amateur in this era was **PK1WK**, Bandoeng, who was active on 6120 kc. (and later 3490).

Local governmental authorities (e.g. Technische Bureau Lammeree, Malang), private radio societies (Radio Vereeniging Midden-Java in Semarang and Soerakarta; Solosche Radio Vereeniging, Soerakarta; Batavasche Radio Vereeniging, Batavia), stores of various kinds (Handel Mij, Batavia; Lindeteves Storvis, Batavia), all got on the broadcasting bandwagon, often with shortwave. However, these were generally very low-powered affairs (10–150 watts), operating in the 2 and 3 mc. range, and thus were rarely heard at a distance.

South of the Dutch East Indies, **VK3LR**, Lyndhurst (near Melbourne), Australia, which had been transmitting experimentally since 1928, was upgraded to 1 kw. and began scheduled broadcasting, daily except Sunday at 0330–0730 EST. It was run by the Wireless Branch of the Postmaster General's Department and relayed Melbourne broadcast band stations 3AR and 3LO. The frequency was still 9580 kc. (When the station operated in experimental mode, it used the call **VK3XX**.) And beginning on October 20, all three Australian shortwave stations— **VK2ME, VK3ME** and **VK3LR**— departed from their regular schedules to provide extended coverage of the MacRobertson Centenary London-Melbourne Air Race. It was in celebration of the 100th anniversary of Victoria's capital city, and was sponsored by Australian philanthropist Sir MacPherson Robertson, owner of the MacRobertson candy company.

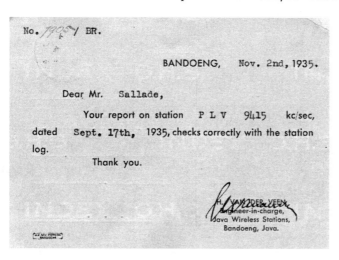

Both before and after the formation of NIROM in 1934, much of the shortwave broadcasting in what is today Indonesia was conducted by commercial radiotelegraph stations. Bandoeng was one of the most often heard.

Commercial stations worldwide continued to be popular DX targets, especially when they were carrying broadcast programming as filler, or in a point-to-point broadcast relay, or for occasional direct-to-listener reception. Listening to ship-to-shore traffic was also popular. Among the frequently reported commercial stations, which typically had three-letter calls, were the numerous "G" calls of **Rugby Radio** in England (**GBB, GCB, GDB**, the widely reported **G6RX** on 4972 kc., etc.). Rugby was a rough equivalent of Radio Central on Long island, albeit owned and operated by the government (the British Post Office). It was inaugurated in 1926 as a longwave station. Shortwave service started in 1928 and, as with Radio Central, it soon replaced longwave as the heart of the Rugby operation. By 1938, ten of the 13 Rugby senders would be shortwave, including two single sideband transmitters. Although the meat and potatoes of Rugby was originally telegraphic messages (plus news and time signals), and then international telephone service, the station was also used for other purposes, including transmission of broadcast programming to other countries for rebroadcast on local wavelengths. The longwave transmitters were of 30, 80 and 500 kw. On shortwave the power was 50–70 kw.[72]

Other regular commercial stations from Europe included the "D" calls of the German PTT station at **Nauen** (which sometimes relayed **Zeesen**); the "F" stations—FRE, FRO, FTN, etc.—from St. Assisse, France; PTT stations **ORG** (19205 kc.) and **ORK** (10330), **Radio Ruysselede**, Ruysselede, Belgium, which regularly carried Belgian broadcast programs for the Belgian Congo; and Norwegian PTT transmitter **LKJ1**, 1 kw., located on the island of Jeløy, south of Oslo, relaying the Oslo mediumwave station to Vadso in the northernmost part of the country on 4100, 4930, 6130 and 9550 kc.

The Russian "R" stations were heard often. These included **RKI** in Moscow, **RTD**, Alma Ata, **RAU**, Tashkent, and others. Harder to catch was **XGW**, Shanghai, China, on 10420 kc. Activity burst forth from Japan in the form of the station of the **International Wireless Tele-**

phone Company of Japan, Ltd. (Kokusai-Denwa Kaisha, Ltd.) in Nazaki, Japan. The station had been established in 1933. Mainly a commercial station using numerous channels and "J" callsigns, it was also used for broadcasting, relaying the programs of **NHK** station JOAK. Often-reported channels included JVN, 10660 kc., JVM, 10740, JVL, 11660, and JVF, 15620 kc. English was heard at 0500–0515 EST.

Latin American commercial stations that were heard included XDC, Mexico City; LSG,

LSL, LSN and other "L's" from Buenos Aires (radiotelephone station LSX carried broadcast programming from LS4, Radio Splendid); PSK, Rio de Janeiro; and YVQ, Maracay, Venezuela. From St. George, Bermuda, ZFS (telephone) and VPN (marine) were heard. And many transmissions were reported from the AT&T commercial stations at **Lawrenceville** and **Ocean Gate**, New Jersey, Hia-

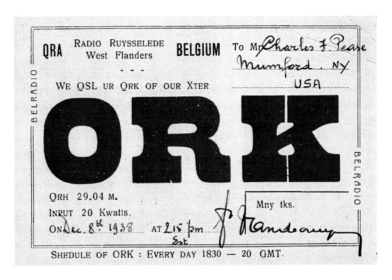

Early shortwave broadcasting from Belgium was by way of ORK, the country's radiotelephone station, which was easily heard in the United States. *Top:* The station's QSL. ORK was a good verifier. *Bottom:* The transmitting facility in Ruysselede.

leah, Florida, and **Dixon**, California, and the RCA stations in **Rocky Point**, Long Island, **New Brunswick**, New Jersey, **Bolinas**, California, and **Kahuku**, Hawaii.

Broadcasting stations large and small sometimes acted like commercial or amateur stations and communicated directly with each other, and listeners would often hear these "QSO's," and informal tests, after hours.

About 4.5 million radio receivers were sold in the U.S. in 1934. All-wave receivers were very popular, and 75 percent of all receivers manufactured had some shortwave coverage. Radios without shortwave were considered obsolete, and the sale of higher-priced sets was increasing. Manufacturers looked for ways to simplify shortwave tuning. The "airplane dial" became popular, with colors or illumination often used to distinguish the different bands. Some sets featured "shadow tuning," whereby color displaced a black bar as a station was tuned in. Bandspread or fast-slow tuning was available on the better receivers, and "noise reducing" antennas with shielded lead-ins were promoted.

The radio editor of *The New York Times* was enthusiastic about shortwave.

> Short waves are rekindling the fascination of picking up distant stations. That was the lifeblood of broadcasting in 1920–23. Tonal quality was secondary. Distance lent enchantment then and it still does, according to the interest now manifest in short-wave broadcasting. Few if any manufacturers will fail to include a short-wave outfit in their 1934–35 line; in fact, they are likely to present several models designed to cover the globe.[73]

But the editor of *International Short Wave Radio*, the bulletin of the International Short Wave Club, wondered why, with so many all-wave radios being sold, so few listeners developed any long term interest in shortwave. He concluded that most did not realize the need for time and frequency information to get the most out of shortwave. "You do not have much success on short waves just roaming over the dials."[74] And many shortwave stations were devoted to purposes other than entertainment (e.g. police and marine stations); frequency was not always easy to judge; and language was a problem. And, of course, reception quality was less predictable, and receiver controls required more of the listener's attention.

"Tossed Across the Atlantic"

Foreign programs were so reliable in general that short wave enthusiasts in the eastern part of the United States learned a new game with their all-wave outfits. When European presentations were being rebroadcast in this country over nation-wide networks, the all-wave set owners quickly switched to the short-waves and succeeded in picking up the same programs directly from the transmitting stations across the sea.

The New York Times
April 1, 1934[75]

For the experienced shortwaver, National introduced the highly regarded HRO, a receiver which would undergo innumerable upgrades over its 30-year life as a vacuum tube receiver (followed by a decade of solid state). Despite various loveable anachronisms that would stubbornly survive obsolescence (coil drawers, separate power supply, etc.), it set a high standard for workmanship and performance.

The availability of information about stations was improving. Both the reader-supplied and "official" information in shortwave magazines was becoming more reliable, although listener-supplied information on new stations was usually tentative and incomplete, particularly with regard to Latin American stations, where the accurate identification of call letters and station slogans often had to await receipt of information from the station by mail. QSLing was becoming more popular, and lists of station addresses appeared in the DX press.

Many of the standalone station "logs" and lists now included shortwave stations. A big step forward was taken in August when *World Short-Wave Radiophone Transmitters* was published by the Bureau of Foreign and Domestic Commerce of the U.S. Department of Commerce. The 96-page book was the first authoritative list of shortwave stations, both broadcast and commercial, that was widely available.

KDKA carried one of the earliest DX programs. The hour-long KDKA DX Club, with shortwave and broadcast band DXing tips supplied mostly by the radio clubs, was on the air early Monday morning at 0030 EST over both KDKA (980 kc.) and **W8XK** (6140). KFI in Los Angeles soon followed suit with a similar program called "Around the World."

During the year, numerous stations dedicated programs to particular clubs. Some were specially transmitted in off hours, others were part of the regular broadcast day or segments of existing programs. Among the stations dedicating programs during 1934 were **VQ7LO**, with a program dedicated to *RADEX*; **Radio Prague, Radio Nations, Radio Illimani, Radio Club Tenerife, XEBT** and others, for the International DXers Alliance; and **EAQ, HCJB, COC, HC2RL** and **TIEP**, for the International Short Wave Club. Other specials honored particular countries (e.g. **EAQ** programs for Peru and Guatemala, **VK2ME** for the provinces of Canada) or particular events (**YV2RC** and **YVQ**, Pan-American Day; **La Voz de Barranquilla**, their fifth anniversary). There were many others.

The Communications Act of 1934 replaced the Federal Radio Commission with the Federal Communications Commission. Two FCC-assisted experimental developments would have significant impacts on shortwave listening: "high fidelity" broadcasting, and exploration of the "ultra high" frequency bands.

There were two aspects to high-fidelity experimentation. One was the establishment of several "high fidelity" AM experimental broadcast stations on channels just above 1500 kc., the high edge of the standard broadcast band. These were 1 kw. stations, and enjoyed bandwidths of 20 kc. rather than the standard 10 kc. The stations were **W1XBS**, Waterbury, Connecticut and **W9XBY**, Kansas City, Missouri, both on 1530 kc., and **W2XR**, Long Island City, New York and **W6XAI**, Bakersfield, California, both on 1550. These stations could be heard on the popular all-wave receivers of the day, as well as many older sets whose tuning overshot the 1500 kc. end point of the AM dial. Although the experiment produced little in the way of concrete results, and the stations adopted 10 kc. separation upon their integration into the regular AM band when it was extended to 1600 kc. in 1941, it illustrated the desire to improve the fidelity of broadcast signals. In its "Touring the World With Radio" program, W9XBY carried shortwave tips daily except Sundays at 1945 EST. (W1XBS, W2XR, W6XAI and W9XBY changed their call letters to **WBRY, WQXR, KPMC** and **KXBY** respectively in 1936.)

Of greater impact on the future of high fidelity broadcasting was the birth of wideband FM. It was in May 1934 that Edwin Armstrong, no stranger to shortwave, began testing his new FM broadcasting technique for RCA at an experimental station, **W2XF**, located in the Empire State Building.[76] These tests ended in 1935 (RCA was more interested in television), whereupon Armstrong turned his attention to developing FM at another experimental station, amateur station **W2AG**, in Yonkers, New York, and, in 1938, his own station, the historic **W2XMN**, in Alpine, New Jersey (regular broadcasting from W2XMN started in 1939). Although the progress of FM would be slow, its eventual impact on broadcasting would be profound.

The FCC also wished to step up experimentation at "ultra high" frequencies, usually taken to mean the area above 25 mc. (The highest frequency in actual broadcast use at the time was 21550 kc.)[77] The properties of radio waves in this range were little understood. The range of the signals was believed to be small, suitable mainly for local broadcasting. The FCC licensed stations of different types (broadcast, amateur, and various utilities) to operate experimentally in these realms. W2XF was licensed to operate on 41 mc., W2XMN on 43.7 mc. (it moved to 42.8 in 1939), W2AG on 110 mc. **W8XH**, an AM offshoot of WBEN in Buffalo, had been operating experimentally circa 43 mc. since 1932. Over the next few years the FCC authorized experimental AM broadcasting on various frequencies in the general ranges of 25–27 and 31–44 mc., plus a few channels much higher. Broadcast stations operating in these bands were known as "apex" stations. Their main purpose was supposed to be research; commercial content was secondary.[78]

The "apex band" was relatively short lived. Once FM broadcasting was assigned its own frequency range, the apex stations either went FM or left the air; the last apex station closed down in 1941. In the interim, however, these high frequency stations made tempting DX targets. It was believed that the apex stations would be audible only within a radius of 25 to 50 miles. However, it was soon learned that, especially around 25–31 mc., worldwide reception was possible. Apex broadcasting also had the effect of putting the largely-empty 11 meter shortwave broadcast band to use, albeit for domestic rather than international broadcasting. The efficacy of 11 meters was heavily dependent on the sunspot cycle.

The development of FM would be long and slow. Its would take decades to gain a foothold. Even at the start, however, it would have been plain to radio prognosticators that, whatever might be the feasibility of shortwave broadcasting in other countries, or its proven capabilities for worldwide transmission, its significance to the average American radio listener would be small. Like AM, FM was easy to tune. It avoided all the complications of shortwave reception, and shortwave audio was no match for FM. Add to this the often-unimaginative quality of foreign shortwave programming, and shortwave was up against formidable competition. It would remain important to those entranced by foreign broadcasts generally, or by DX, or by the special thrill of wartime listening. Increasingly, however, for most people it would be a technological curiosity.

While not a high fidelity or ultra high experiment, 1934 also saw the inauguration of the super power transmitter of Crosley station WLW, Cincinnati, Ohio. WLW was permitted to operate with a 500 kw. transmitter (**W8XO**) on its standard broadcast band channel of 700 kc. This was ten times the maximum broadcast band power otherwise authorized in the United States. The experiment would last only five years, but it illustrated at least one method besides shortwave for achieving nationwide broadcast reception. During the W8XO experiment, WLW continued to simulcast its programs over Crosley shortwave, **W8XAL**, now on 6060 kc.[79]

One of the more insightful observations about shortwave broadcasting in 1934 was made in connection with the October assassination in Marseilles of the French Foreign Minister and King Alexander of Yugoslavia.

[W]hile the London voice [BBC] was declaring, "The assassination of King Alexander is spreading consternation throughout the world tonight," it needed but a slight turn of the dial to realize the world was simultaneously hearing waltzes and any number of other things…. ¶Those who listened in are wondering now whether the radio's greatest contribution to peace is the spreading of news quickly or to give one a sense of proportion by showing how much life around the world is still going on as usual.[80]

Shortwave helped keep things in perspective.

1935

Although it approved of point-to-point shortwave for the relay of program material for local rebroadcast in other countries, early in the year the American Radio Relay League journal *QST* editorialized against direct international broadcasting. There were not enough channels, reception quality would not meet consumer expectations, it would facilitate the growth of propaganda, and it would lead to advertising on foreign stations by American commercial interests. The ARRL had been encouraged in these views by the observation of a receiver manufacturer's spokesman that the amateurs enjoyed too much spectrum space and the broadcasters not enough.[81]

The ARRL's views had little effect, however, as shortwave broadcasting continued to grow. Although published schedules were ever changing and often honored in the breach, the American stations were now transmitting roughly as follows:

American Shortwave Broadcasting Stations, 1935

Station	*Frequency*	*Days and Times*
W1XAL, Boston, MA	6040 11790	Tuesday & Thursday, 1915-2115 Sunday, 1615-1900
W1XAZ, Boston, MA	9570	0600-2300
W2XE, Wayne, NJ	6120 15270	1700-2200 1000-1700
W2XAD, Schenectady, NY W2XAF, Schenectady, NY	15340 9530	1030-1600 1630-2400
W3XAL, Bound Brook, NJ W3XL, Bound Brook, NJ	6100 17780 6425	Monday, Wednesday & Saturday, 1700-1800 Daily except Sunday, 0900-1000; Tuesday, Thursday & Friday, 1500-1600 Operated on an unscheduled, experimental basis
W3XAU, Philadelphia, PA	6060 9590	2000-2300 1200-1950
W4XB, Miami Beach, FL	6040	1200-1400, 2000-2400
W8XAL, Cincinnati, OH	6060	Monday-Friday 1830-2000 & 2300-0200; Sunday 0800-2000 & 2300-0300
W8XK, Pittsburgh, PA	6140 11780 15210 21540	2100-0100 1700-2100 0900-1900 0700-0900
W9XAA, Chicago, IL	6080	1100-1900
W9XF, Downers Grove, IL	6100	Daily except Saturday, 0100-0200 & 0900-1000; Saturday 0100-0230

W1XAZ became **W1XK**. W1XAL went to 10 kw. W2XGB, one of the calls of the **Press Wireless** station in Hicksville, New York, was often reported on 4795.5 kc., 6425 and other channels. Sometimes it broadcast music, NBC programs, or the programming of WOR, which

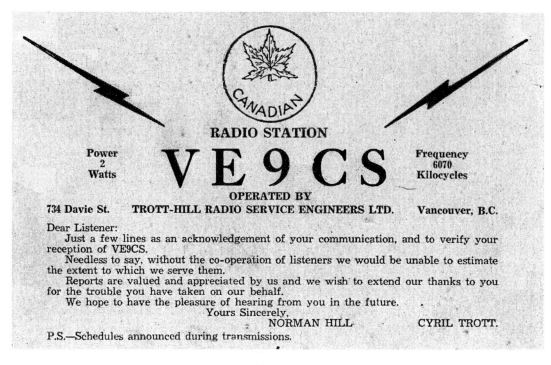

RADIO STATION

Power
2
Watts

VE9CS

Frequency
6070
Kilocycles

OPERATED BY

734 Davie St.   **TROTT-HILL RADIO SERVICE ENGINEERS LTD.**   Vancouver, B.C.

Dear Listener:

Just a few lines as an acknowledgement of your communication, and to verify your reception of VE9CS.

Needless to say, without the co-operation of listeners we would be unable to estimate the extent to which we serve them.

Reports are valued and appreciated by us and we wish to extend our thanks to you for the trouble you have taken on our behalf.

We hope to have the pleasure of hearing from you in the future.

Yours Sincerely,
NORMAN HILL   CYRIL TROTT.

P.S.—Schedules announced during transmissions.

Originally 50 watts and later just two watts, VE9CS was good DX in either case. Its frequency, 6070 kc., would eventually be occupied by CFRX in Toronto.

had dropped plans for its own shortwave simulcast station, **W2XHI**. And NBC began operating an experimental shortwave station in Chicago, **W9XBS**, which carried broadcast programming on Thursdays and Sundays at 1145–1645 EST on 6425 kc.

W1XK broadcast stock market news twice a day. **W2XAF** carried President Roosevelt's address to the Boy Scouts of America in August, as well as numerous other special broadcasts. W2XAF now used three man-made lightning crashes in its identification. (*"This is the Voice of Electricity, and you have just listened to the report of three 10 million-volt discharges of electricity produced in the high frequency labs of the General Electric Company. W2XAF is on the air."*)

In Canada, two new shortwave stations opened. **VE9AS**, operated by the Electrical Department of the University of New Brunswick, Fredericton, was on 6425 kc. at 1000–1200, 1600–1700 and 1900–2200 EST. And **VE9CA**, **"Voice of the Prairie,"** Calgary, Alberta, came on the air on 6030 kc. The 100-watt station relayed mediumwave CFCN at 0900–1500 and 1900–2400. In addition, **VE9GW**, Bowmanville, Ontario, now on 6090 kc., became **CRCX**. And **VE9CS**, 6070 kc., now operated by Trott-Hill Radio Service Engineers Ltd. of Vancouver, was down to two watts of power. It relayed CKFC.

On February 1, **WWV**, the Beltsville, Maryland, station of the National Bureau of Standards (the "National" had been added in 1934), expanded operations. It now operated two days a week rather than one, and on 10000 and 15000 kc. in addition to the usual channel of 5000 kc. WWV transmitted a continuous tone for one hour on each channel, with call letters and frequency given in Morse during the first five minutes and every ten minutes thereafter. On October 1 a third day, with a voice announcement, was added. Reception reports were sought. The WWV transmissions continued to evolve through the years. Seconds pulses were added in 1937.

The broadcasts from Little America ended in February when Admiral Byrd packed up and departed the Antarctic. Now only intramural transmissions were heard (once again using the old

KJTY call sign rather than the land call of **KFZ**). DXers followed the first trips of the transatlantic liner SS *Normandie*. Telephone calls from the ship were heard at all hours, and two special broadcasts from the ship were carried over the CBS and NBC networks, including their shortwave stations. The ship's call letters were FNSK. Additional broadcast programs would be transmitted from the ship in later years, and would sometimes be relayed by the French station at Pontoise.

VERIFICATION CARD
SHORT WAVE STATION W9XAZ
Milwaukee, Wisconsin, U. S. A.

W9XAZ operates on a frequency of 26,400 Kilocycles with 500 watts power. It is low level modulated and has high fidelity standards. The radiating system consists of a one-half wave vertical antenna suspended above the roof of the Schroeder Hotel at a height of 275 feet above the street.

W9XAZ is owned and operated by The Milwaukee Journal, which also owns and operates Station WTMJ (620 Kilocycles).

W9XAZ broadcasts daily from noon to 11:00 P. M., C. S. T.

(If your communication asked for any information not given above, you will receive a special letter shortly)

W9XAZ was one of many "apex" stations that operated in AM mode at the top of the shortwave range during the late 1930s, usually simulcasting a standard broadcast parent. The apex experiment ended in 1941, and most of the stations converted to FM.

Of interest to shortwavers was the stratospheric balloon flight of Explorer II from Rapid City, South Dakota on November 11. Sponsored by the National Geographic Society and the U.S. Army Air Corps, Capt. Orville A. Anderson and Capt. Albert W. Stevens transmitted from the gondola via an 8-watt transmitter, **W10XFH**, on 13050 kc. Their words were retransmitted from the ground station, **W10XFN**, on 6350 kc. and picked up by **W3XL** and **W3XAL** and rebroadcast over the NBC network, including the shortwave affiliates. It was reported that "[r]adio listeners could hear instruments clicking in the gondola."[82] QSLs were signed by the captains Anderson and Stevens. A like flight of the craft's predecessor, Explorer I, had ended in a crash (with no loss of life) in 1934; a second attempt earlier in 1935 also failed.

Ultra-high station **W9XAZ**, experimental sister station of WTMJ, was being operated by *The Milwaukee Journal* on 31.6 mc. (later 26.4). The power was 500 watts. Hams used W9XAZ as a frequency standard and established a close relationship with the station, which hosted a ham radio program on Saturday nights. On October 30, KSD, the station of *The St. Louis Post,* began operating as **W9XPD** on the same apex band frequency, 31.6 mc. The power was 100 watts. **W2XDV**, in New York City, came on 31.6 mc. in November with 450 watts. It simulcast WABC.

The **BBC** added a new beam to its daily transmissions. This one was to Western Canada at 2200–2300 EST on 6100 and 9585 kc. It was widely heard throughout the U.S., and also in India, where it was picked up in the morning. The BBC antenna system was also upgraded, and the old **G5SW Chelmsford** transmitter, redesigned to operate at 20 kw. (it would be increased to 60 kw. in 1937), was returned to service at **Daventry**, mainly for experimental work and special transmissions.

On May 6, the Silver Jubilee of the reign of King George V was the subject of special BBC programs, many of which were rebroadcast by stations throughout the world, including the United States. The BBC closed the year with a nighttime service from St. Paul's Cathedral, followed by two specials, "Chimes at Midnight" and "A Good Year to One and All." Throughout the British empire there was extensive rebroadcasting of BBC programs over local frequencies or on local wired networks, which were popular in various places, e.g. the Falklands, Sierra Leone, Ghana, Nigeria, Gibraltar, etc.

To improve the availability of information about BBC shortwave, the *World-Radio*

Empire Edition was replaced with a weekly program schedule, the *Empire Programme Pamphlet* (later *BBC Empire Broadcasting*), which was distributed to individual subscribers and to various British press offices around the world. By year's end the total number of reception reports and letters that had reached London from overseas since the start of the Empire Service in 1932 was 53,000. In the early days about 60 percent were from the U.S. As more people began tuning in from other countries, that figure dropped to under 40 percent. To standardize reception reporting, the BBC's team of regular monitors were sent a recording of typical reception under various conditions at the Tatsfield receiving station, with written descriptions corresponding to those on the BBC logging forms ("good," "excellent," etc.) .

Germany's **Reichs-Rundfunk Gesellschaft ("Zeesen")** was now on the air to North America at 1730–2230 EST on 6020 and 9570 kc. In 1934, Zeesen was operating on a total of six frequencies, with power of either 5 or 8 kw. In 1935 there were 13 frequencies in use, six of which were on 40 kw. senders. These were soon upgraded to 50 kw. In addition to its usual foreign service broadcasts, Zeesen sent many programs to the U.S. specifically for rebroadcast. These were usually transmitted over **DJB**, 15200 kc. Zeesen acknowledged reception reports over the air in the Wednesday night "Letter Box" program and rewarded listeners with a small phonograph record containing the station's tuning signal, a short greeting, and a song. One side was in German, the other in English, and the English-language label urged, "Let's make Shortwave Broadcasting Stand for Good Fellowship." **VK3ME**, Melbourne, acknowledged reports in its mailbag program, which was also on the air on Wednesdays, 0700 EST on 9510 kc.; and Holland responded to listener letters in "The PHOHI Club" program, Monday nights on 17775 kc.

A new station was heard from Poland. **Polskie Radio Warsaw** was on 13653 kc., 10 kw., at 1130–1230, using the country's PTT transmitter, **SPW**, located at Babice, near Warsaw. And testing from Portugal was a government station, **CSW, Emissora Nacional**, heard on 6140 kc. It announced its call letters phonetically — "C, Canada, S, Spain, W, Washington." **CT1AA, Radio Colonial**, Lisbon was still on the air, now with 2 kw.

OXY in Denmark was operating on three channels — 6060, 9495 and 15300 kc., carrying either the Copenhagen or Kalundborg mediumwave programs over its 500-watt transmitter. **Ríkisútvarpid**, Iceland was mainly a commercial station, transmitting radiotelephone messages over **TFK**, 9060 kc. and **TFJ**, 12240 kc., both with 7.5 kw. However, it also carried some broadcasting, which soon became regularized on Sundays at 1335–1400 on TFJ. It operated as the **Iceland State Broadcasting Service** (*"Icelandic Broadcast calling"*).

Radio Nations in Switzerland supplemented its Saturday broadcasts with a new Monday service at 0315 EST on 18560 kc. In another Swiss development, on August 1, Swiss National Day, **Schweizerische Rundspruch-Gesellschaft**, the **Swiss Broadcasting Corporation** in Berne, which had been making occasional limited-range mediumwave broadcasts for Swiss expatriates in Europe, utilized the Prangins transmitter to beam a special program to the Americas for the benefit of Swiss citizens living there. Monthly Prangins shortwave relays of home service programs in German, French and Italian for countrymen abroad followed. These were on the first Monday of the month at 1800–1900 over **HBL** (9595 kc.) and **HBP** (7797). Cooperating with the SBC was the Swiss Shortwave Association, an amateur radio society. Some amateur transmitters utilizing directional antennas also carried the monthly program in the 20 and 40 meter ham bands.

RV15 was still broadcasting from Khabarovsk, U.S.S.R., on 4273 kc. Soon it would move to 5720, where its programs, often of classical music, were better heard, but later it returned to 4273. Harmonics on 8 and 12 mc. were sometimes better than the fundamental. All the Russian broadcasting stations were consolidated under one body, the Comité de Radiodiffusion et Radiofication, Moscow, which verified reports on all stations. Moscow would soon be broadcasting in eight languages on shortwave. The main frequencies used were 9600 and 12000 kc., with occasional transmissions on 6000 (**RV59**), 15145 (**RKI**), and 15183 (**RW96**). The broadcast day typically was 4½ or 5 hours, 11 hours on Sunday.[83]

Although there was as yet no shortwave broadcast station as such in the Belgian Congo, the 6 kw. transmitters, **OPM** and **OPL**, Leopoldville, on 10140 and 20040 kc. respectively, were often heard with commercial traffic, OPM circa 0000–0230 EST, OPL around noon. And OPM sometimes broadcast music on Saturdays at 1500–1630 EST.

The Ethiopian PTT station in Addis Ababa was heard with commercial traffic, and as tensions that would lead to the Second Italo-Abyssinian

ENTE ITALIANO **E.I.A.R.** AUDIZIONI RADIOFONICHE
(ITALIAN BROADCASTING COMPANY)
5 Via Montello, Rome (Italy)

SHORT WAVE STATION 2 RO PRATO-SMERALDO, ROME

31.13 meters, 9.635 megacycles

"AMERICAN HOUR" PROGRAMS FOR DECEMBER 1935

6 - 7,30 p. m. E.S.T.

MONDAY, DECEMBER 2nd.

6 p.m. News.
Royal March and « Giovinezza ».
Transmission from the Rome Studios of the opera « NAMICO SAN »
 by Aldo Franchetti. Conductor, Giuseppe Morelli.
« The Treasures of the Vatican », a talk by BARTOLOMEO NOGARA,
 curator of the Vatican Museums.
Piano Recital by Giuseppina Teofani Zannoni.
Close with Royal March and « Giovinezza ».

WEDNESDAY, DECEMBER 4th.

6 p.m. News.
Royal March and « Giovinezza ».
Symphonic Concert from Rome's « Augusteo ». Conductor Bernar-
 dino Molinari.
« The italian question in East Africa », first of a series of four talks
 by Prof. A. DE MASI, in which the reasons for Italy's direct action
 in Africa in favour of civilization will be explained.
Concert of light music by the CETRA orchestra.
Close with Royal March and « Giovinezza ».

FRIDAY, DECEMBER 6th.

6 p.m. News.
Royal March and « Giovinezza ».
Transmission from the Rome Studios of selections from the opera
 « FEDORA » by Umberto Giordano.
« Rome's Midnight voice », a series of talks to be given every Friday by
 Miss AMY BERNARDY, on various topics of general interest.
 Some of these talks will have musical comments.
Concert of Classical Duets by soprano Quaranta and mezzo-soprano
 Marice.
Close with Royal March and « Giovinezza ».

MONDAY, DECEMBER 9th.

6 p.m. News.
Royal March and « Giovinezza ».
Transmission from the Rome Studios of the opera « GOYESCAS » by
 «Granados. Conductor: Mario Rossi.
« The Tourist Organization in Italy, and American Travellers », a talk
 by Senator CARLO BONARDI, President of the Italian Touring
 Club.
Concert for Violin and Piano: Violinist Tina Bari and pianista Gina
 Schelini.
Close with Royal March and « Giovinezza ».

Even well into the war, Italy's 2RO was the least strident of the Axis stations.

War in October increased, so did radio activity. Now the station began carrying some broadcast programming under the name **Imperial Ethiopian Broadcasting Station**. Meanwhile, on October 11, in an early example of the convergence of politics and shortwave, Britain refused to shortwave to the United States the remarks of the Italian envoy to the League of Nations, made in Geneva and set for relay from England, because it felt it would violate the League's sanctions against Italy.[84]

Two stations were being operated by the Post Office in Southern Rhodesia: **ZEA**, Salisbury on 5882 kc., and **ZEB**, Bulawayo on 6147. But their broadcast times—Tuesday at 1315–1515 and Friday at 1100–1200 EST — made them near impossible catches in the U.S., as did their power, which was 325 watts. The chances of hearing the Azores increased; on Wednesdays and Saturdays an amateur station in Ponta Delgada, **CT2AJ**, carried broadcast programming between 1700 and 1900 EST on 4000 kc.

On June 1, Japan began a regular if modest foreign broadcasting effort through a newly-established **NHK** Overseas Service that would later become known as **Radio Tokyo**. A nightly program in Japanese and English for North America was heard at 0000–0100 EST over the facilities of the **International Wireless Telephone Company of Japan**, Nazaki, on 14600 kc. (**JVH**), 20 kw. NHK rented the facilities for this purpose. Sometimes other frequencies were used in parallel. (*"Good evening neighbors. You are listening to Tokyo."*) Another English hour for North America was added on Monday and Thursday at 1600–1700 (later daily), and a daily hour for Europe on Wednesday and Friday at 1400–1500 EST. The transmitters at Nazaki also carried JOAK programming at 0400–0800 EST. Government censorship of the NHK overseas broadcasts was very heavy, as it would continue to be through the war.

Shortwave broadcasts from Hong Kong were now being heard by a great many DXers. Mediumwaver **ZBW**, **Radio Hong Kong**, used one of two shortwave channels, 5410 and 8750 kc., with a power of 250 watts. It was heard in the United States circa 0500–0700 EST, and was a good verifier. The shortwave call letters were ZCK, but the ZBW call is what was usually heard. (*"This is station ZCK at Hong Kong, relaying a program from ZBW... . This is ZBW, the Hong Kong broadcasting station, calling you."*)

New **NIROM** shortwave transmitters were coming on the air from many places, including Solo (also known as Surakarta; **YDL2**, 4810 kc.; **YDL3**, 3335), Semarang (**YDK2**, 3190), Jogjakarta (**YDL4**, 3410), Jember (**YDQ2**, 3390), Malang (**YDQ3**, 3388), Banjermasin, Borneo (**YDV2**, 3330), and numerous others.

Khabarovsk, USSR
February 8, 1936

Dear listener,
This is to inform you that English programs are given over the radio from the Frunze station in the Far Eastern region of the USSR — wavelength 70.2 metres — call letters RV15.

These English broadcasts take place every odd day at 1 PM Khabarovsk time. We would be glad if you listen in and send us any criticism or suggestions regarding the programs.

With warm radio greetings
Yours fraternally
Rowena Meyer
(Editor)

Radio Committee
Khabarovsk, USSR.

In the 1930s, Khabarovsk shortwave station RV15 was regularly reported in the United States, particularly on the west coast. The frequency was 4273 kc. Classical music was the station's mainstay.

Latin America was shortwaving with a vengeance, and already manifesting the characteristics that would always make "LA" DXing a specialty. Said Captain Hall:

South American stations are everywhere but although their programs are sometimes very pleasing from an entertainment standpoint, they lose many listeners' interest because they talk so rapidly and rarely if ever identify themselves in any other language but their own. I doubt very much if even the thousands of Spanish-speaking short-wave fans here in the United States can "make them out." I doff my hat to the fan who can distinguish the various call letters, especially the ones of six variations. Is it a good old Spanish custom to send hours of musical selections and then go off the air without giving call letters? Time and again I have written page after page of a South American

ZBW   HONG KONG

The Hongkong Broadcasting Station thank you for your communication dated *8ᵗʰ October 1935* and take pleasure in confirming your reception of ZBW on *8ᵗʰ October 1935*.

VERIFIED

Secretary, *[signature]*
Hong Kong Broadcasting Committee.
Post Office Box No. 200

ZBW, Hong Kong, was heard throughout the world and was inundated with reception reports when it moved to higher frequencies in 1936. The station's plan to stop verifying never came to fruition. During the war years, Radio Hong Kong was known as JPHA.

program into my log book, only to have the announcer sign off with "Good night everybody."[85]

There was growth in Mexican shortwave broadcasting on both the governmental and private sides. **XECR**, Mexico City, was a 20 kw. station operated by the government's Secretaria de Relaciones Exteriores. It was on 7380 kc. and operated Sundays only, 1800–1900 EST. **XBJQ**, owned by Banco Nacional, Mexico City, was on 11000 kc. and was widely heard. It mainly relayed XEW, and it identified in English. (*"XBJQ, broadcasting from the City of Mexico on 11 megacycles."*)

Other new Mexicans also provided good reception, including **XECW**, Mexico City, on 5980 kc.; **XEDQ, Radiodifusora del Pueblo**, Guadalajara, 9520 kc. (it relayed XED); and **XEFT, La Voz de Veracruz**. XEFT relayed its mediumwave parent, XETF, on 6120 kc. The power was said to be 20 watts. Also in Veracruz was **XEUW, El Eco de Sotavento**, on 6020 kc. It relayed XEU. And **XEVI, Estación Radio Cultural**, Mexico City, was on 5970 kc. and also produced a strong harmonic in the 25 meter band. The power was 250 watts.

More shortwave stations came on the air from Cuba. **CO9GC, Laboratorio Radio-eléctrico Grau y Caminero**, Santiago, was on 6185 kc. The new **COCD, La Voz del Aire**, Havana on 6130, relayed mediumwave station CMCD. COCD used 250 watts. Also new were **CO9JQ**, Camaguey, on 8665 kc., and **CO9WR**, Sancti Spiritus, 6280 kc. Both operated with 100 watts. CO9WR relayed CMHB. At year's end Cuba adopted the uniform use of four-letter calls. COH was now COCH, COC became COCO, CO9GC became COKG, etc.

On the island of Hispaniola, **HH2R**, Port-au-Prince, Haiti, was on 9545 kc. It was operated by Société Haitienne de Automobile. Port-au-Prince had three other shortwave stations.

Panama became active on shortwave in 1935, and over the years a dozen stations were heard. Most were still on the air after the war, but by 1960 nearly all were gone. This QSL is from 1946.

HH2S on 6040 kc. (later 5915), 100 watts, was operated by Société Haitienne de Radiodiffusion. It usually carried the programs of mediumwave station HHK. **HH2W** was on 9595 kc. with 30 watts, and **HH3W** was on 9615, also with 30 watts. (Many years later HH3W would become **Radio Haiti.**) Still on Hispaniola, **HIH, La Voz del Higuamo,** San Pedro de Macoris, Dominican Republic, had a DX program on Sundays at 0300–0500 EST on 6810 kc. And **HIZ,** Santo Domingo, long on 6315 kc., now identified as **La Voz de los Muchachos**. The power was 100 watts.

Elsewhere in the Caribbean, some lucky listeners who were tuning early in the year heard Barbados by way of an amateur station doing some cricket broadcasts when the British team was in town. The station, **VP6YB,** owned by Thomas A. Archer and operating on behalf of the Barbados Radio Association in Bridgetown, made the broadcasts on 7070 kc. with the approval of the island's government (presaging by many years the special cricket transmissions from **Cable & Wireless,** Barbados from the late 1940s to the 1960s). Soon VP6YB returned to regular amateur operation on the 20 meter band. And Port-of-Spain, Trinidad was heard by way of broadcasts from another mainly-amateur station, **VP4TC,** 7500 kc.

Central America was also well represented on shortwave. New from Honduras were **HRP1, El Eco de Honduras,** San Pedro Sula, on 7085 kc. (later 6045), and **HRN, La Voz de Honduras,** on 5890 kc. HRN relayed the station's mediumwave channel. New from Panama City were **HP5A, Radio-Teatro Estrella de Panama,** on 6010 kc. and **HP5J, La Voz de Panama,** on 9590. From Miramar, 100-watt **HP5B, Estación Radiodifusora Miramar,** was on 6030 kc., and in Colón there was **HP5F, La Voz de Colón,** on 6080.

New from Costa Rica was **TIGPH, "Alma Tica,"** San Jose, on 5820 kc. It identified in English. There was confusion on 6550 kc., where two stations were operating. One was **TIPG,**

La Voz de la Victor, in San Jose (it used the call **TI2PG** when working amateur stations), and the other was **TIRCC, Radioemisora Católica Costarricense**, a new 500-watt station of the Catholic church in San Jose. TIRCC was operated by Amando Céspedes Marín of TI4NRH fame, and its harmonic on 13100 kc. was sometimes better than the fundamental. To remedy the interference, TIPG moved to 6400 kc.

Three new stations came to air in Managua, Nicaragua. **YN1GG, La Voz de los Lagos,** was on 6450 kc. with 100 watts; **YNOP, Radiodifusora "Bayer,"** was on 3480 (later 5760) with 1 kw.; and **YNLG, Radioemisora Rubén Dario**, operated on 8600 kc. with 150 watts. (Rubén Dario was a well-known Nicaraguan poet, diplomat and literary figure.)

TGWA, Radiodifusora Nacional, in Guatemala City, was now on 6000 kc., broadcasting daily except Sundays with 300 watts at 1200–1300, 1830–1930 and 2100–2300 EST. On Saturday night the station stayed on until 0600 EST. (TGWA sent samples of Guatemalan coffee with its QSL.) **TG1X**, an experimental station of the Ministerio de Fomento [Public Works], was on 9450 kc. irregularly, relaying TGWA with 200 watts. DXers were also hearing another station from Guatemala City — 200-watt (soon 500) **TG2X**, operated by **Dirección de la Policía Nacional**. It was on 5940 kc. at 2100–2300 EST.

There was also shortwave news from the Guianas, situated on the north coast of South America. British Guiana returned to the air in the form of **VP3MR**, the **British Guiana Broadcasting Company**, on 7080 kc. The 150-watt station operated for an hour or two most days around 1700–1900 and Sundays at 0745–1015. And from Surinam (Dutch Guiana), a new station, **PZH**, Paramaribo, was on the air mornings and evenings on 7140 kc. (later 6996 and 11515). It was owned by **Algemeene Vereeniging Radio Omroep Surinam (AVROS)**, and the power was 30 watts.

The blossoming of shortwave broadcasting in Colombia continued. Most of the stations operated with 50–100 watts, some less, a few more. Among the new ones heard were **HJ1ABC, La Voz del Choco**, Quibdo, on 6006 kc. (100 watts); **HJ1ABG, Emisora Atlantico**, Barranquilla, 6040; **HJ1ABH, La Voz de Ciénaga**, Ciénaga, 6230; **HJ1ABJ, La Voz de Santa Marta,** 6025; and **HJ2ABD, Radio Bucaramanga**, 5980. Also new were **HJ4ABA, Ecos de la Montana**, Medellin, 11710 kc.; **HJ4ABC, La Voz de Pereira**, Pereira, 6250 kc.; **HJ4ABD, La Voz de Catia**, the 300-watt municipal station of Medellin, 6460; **HJ4ABJ** (later **HJ6ABC**), **Ecos del Combeima**, Ibague, 6460; and **HJ4ABL, Ecos de Occidente**, Manizales, 6100 kc. **HJ1ABD**, Cartagena, 6100 kc., had adopted the slogan **Ondas de la Heroica**, and HJ4ABE, formerly **Radiodifusora de Medellin**, was now **La Voz de Antioquia**.

Next door, in Venezuela, several new stations began operating. **YV8RB, La Voz de Lara**, Barquisimeto, was on 5880 kc. with 400 watts. **YV9RC, Ondas Populares**, Caracas, operated on 6400 kc. (later 7830). Also new was a Venezuelan whose name if not its call letters would be known to generations of DXers, **YV10RSC, La Voz del Tachira**, San Cristóbal, broadcasting on 5720 kc. **YV4RC**, Caracas, now on 6370 kc., adopted the slogan **Ecos del Avila**. And **YV2RC, Broadcasting Caracas**, became **Radio Caracas**, increased power to 1 kw., and began dedicating special programs to various radio clubs on Tuesday nights at 2100 EST. The first club so honored was the Short Wave Club of New York City. (In October, the club's president, Harry C. Lange, was in Moscow and spoke over **RNE**.)

Although it did not reach the Colombia-Venezuela level, activity in other parts of South America was on the increase as well. **HC2AT**, Guayaquil, Ecuador, owned by the American Trading Company, Ecuador's largest radio importer, was operating on 8400 kc. with only 15 watts. Its "monkey" QSL-card became well known in DX circles. The station was short-lived, however. It was sold to **HC2CW, Ondas del Pacifico**, Guayaquil, which operated on the nearby channel of 8630 kc. (later 9130). Other shortwave stations operating in Ecuador included

HC2ET, El Telégrafo, Guayaquil, on 4600 kc., and **HCETC** (later **HC1ETC**), **Teatro Bolivar** (**"Empresa de Teatros Cinemas"**), Quito, on 6976 kc. with 90 watts.

For $10, HC2AT would send you "a first class Panama hat."

A new Peruvian was **OAX4J, Radio Internacional**, Lima, a 100-watt station on 6000 kc. (later 9520). **OAX4G**, Lima, was on 6230 kc. nightly at 1900–2200 EST, relaying mediumwave station OAX4B. **PRA8, Radio Clube de Pernambuco**, Recife, Brazil, already on mediumwave for a decade, added shortwave, and its 1 kw. transmitter got out well. (The station would increase power to 5 kw. circa 1937.) PRA8 tried a multitude of channels between 6020 and 6090 kc. before settling on 6040, and it was anxious to get reports from listeners.

In 1935, **LR1, Radio El Mundo**, Buenos Aires, Argentina, established its own shortwave plant, carrying the LR1 mediumwave programming from 0700 to 2300 EST daily over **LRX**, 9580 kc. and **LRU**, 15290, both 5 kw. As would be true for decades, the main commercial station in Argentina, **Transradio Internacional, LSX**, still relayed broadcast programming from various of the country's mediumwave stations on shortwave frequencies such as 7460, 7980, 9900, 10300, 14530, 15810, 18120 and 19130 kc. In November, teams at **LSX** and **W2XAF** played a game of bridge over the air. An exotic Pacific DX locale, the Fiji Islands, "Garden of the Pacific," became a routine log with the inauguration of shortwave broadcasts from radiotelephone station **VPD**, Suva, station of **Amalgamated Wireless (Australasia) Ltd.** *("VPD, Radio Suva, Fiji").* The 2 kw. station put forth a surprising signal on 13070 kc. at 0020–0130 EST. ("Anyone in the United States with a fair receiver and a fair location should be able to get this station now." "The VPD signal often is as clear as that of DJD, Berlin.") Programming was from local mediumwave station **ZJV, Fiji Broadcasting Company**, an AWA subsidiary.

"Distance Lends Enchantment"

The fascinating pastime of tuning in foreign stations has attracted men and women of all ages from every walk of life. It has been said that "Distance lends enchantment, except when you're out of gas." The motorist and the aviator must prepare for such emergencies, but the short-wave fan can travel without a care to many countries of the world over the shortest possible distances in fractions of a second, hear the native music of far-off Java and Japan, the English accents of Great Britain, the delightful Spanish language of Central and South America, weird mountain folk-songs from Spain, symphonies from Germany, operas from Rome, and even the laughing notes of the kookaburra, or laughing jackass, from distant Australia, "The Noah's Ark of the Pacific."

The Enchanting Short Waves
Chicago Short Wave Radio Club, 1935[86]

QRA:—RADIO CLUB PORTUGUÊS

PAREDE—PORTUGAL

| SIGS
TO   YR FONE RCVD HR *1-31-35* at   GMT - QSA   QRK r   T   QRG
| CARD *17 - 3 - 35*

CT1GO

Transmitter — 350 watts crystal controlled 100 % modulated on 48.40 metres (6198 kc) and 24.20 metres (12396 kc). DX All Continents.

Remarks — *Very interesting your reports. And many thanks dear O.M. We confirm your reception, verified with our station log, of CT1GG*

Best 73's es DX *on 24.12 metres.*

Yours faithfully   Director

The most westerly station in Europe, CT1GO, Radio Club Português, Parede, Portugal, was the country's second shortwave broadcaster. Built and run by amateur radio operators, it signed on in 1934.

Listeners worldwide began hearing "**Hawaii Calls**," a new weekly program originating at the Moana Hotel in Honolulu and shortwaved to the United States by way of the RCA commercial transmitting facility in **Kahuku**. At the outset the program's founder, Webley Edwards, paid for the transmitter time himself ($22.50, $37.50 or $47.50, depending on which story you believe). Soon "Hawaii Calls" would be funded by a grant from the Hawaiian government to the Hawaiian Tourist Bureau. At its peak it was carried over 750 local stations around the world. When it closed in 1975, however, that number was down to nine.[87]

There were numerous broadcasts dedicated to various radio entities—for the KDKA DX Club, **HIH, La Voz del Higuamo**, Dominican Republic; for *RADEX*, **TIRCC** (Costa Rica); for the ARRL, **CT1GO** (Portugal); and for the International Short Wave Club, **HJ1ABD, Ondas de la Heroica**, and **HJ1ABE, La Voz de los Laboratorios Fuentes**, both in Cartagena, Colombia, and **HJ1ABJ, La Voz de Santa Marta**, also in Colombia; **HP5B**, Panama; **EAQ**, Spain; **RNE**, Moscow; **CT1GO; XEVI**, Mexico; **TIRCC**; and **W2XAF**. In addition, the ISWC arranged for special broadcasts from 35 different stations in connection with a DX contest celebrating the club's seventh anniversary. And a phonograph recording made by the London chapter of the ISWC was broadcast over W2XAF.

The flood of all-wave receivers continued. (The ISWC arranged with a number of receiver manufacturers to recommend the club in the literature that accompanied their products.) Virtually every radio in the 1935 Allied Radio catalog included some shortwave coverage. Hugo Gernsback pointed out that many all-wave sets were still in need of bandspread, larger, illuminated tuning scales, antenna trimmers, and better automatic volume control.[88] But technology was marching on. The "magic eye"—a small cathode ray tube whose "retina" thinned to a narrow line when the listener was tuned exactly on frequency—was introduced.

In recognition of the potential of, and the popular interest in, shortwave, the Waldorf Astoria Hotel in New York City installed high-performance shortwave receivers in its radio room and erected a shortwave antenna between its two towers, 660 feet above ground. With this installation the hotel could distribute up to six shortwave programs throughout the establishment's 2,000 rooms.

New shortwave-related magazines appeared, including *All-Wave Radio* (it would be absorbed by *Radio News* in 1938) and *Official Short Wave Listener* magazine (only seven issues were published). *Radio News* again changed its name, from *Radio News and the Short-Waves* to *Radio News and Short-Wave Radio*. (The reference to shortwave in the title would be dropped in June 1938.) And the Department of Commerce published a revised edition of *World Short-Wave Radiophone Transmitters*.

Two heretofore broadcast band-only clubs started carrying shortwave news. The NNRC's column, one page at first, was called "High Frequencies" and was written by Earl R. Roberts. The National Radio Club (NRC) also began coverage of shortwave, and soon there were as many members interested in HF as in the broadcast band. NNRC coverage of shortwave would last throughout the club's life. The NRC dropped shortwave in 1944.

At year's end, 53-year old Oswald F. Schuette formed the Short Wave Institute of America. Its purpose was to promote shortwave, both domestic and foreign, among the general public, and to serve as a clearinghouse for the schedules of stations. Schuette was a newspaperman who interested himself in a wide variety of public matters. In 1935 he was consulting for RCA, which supported the Institute, presumably in an effort to improve the commercial potential of shortwave broadcasting. The project lasted only about six months, however, and appears not to have gotten much beyond press releases and some other public relations initiatives. Schuette had been a European war correspondent during World War I and had experience and contacts in Germany. He was affiliated with the National Association of Broadcasters, and the National Press Club (where he suffered a fatal heart attack in 1953).[89]

1936

Shortwave was praised by the industry for its contributions to world peace. "[N]o other accomplishment of man has done more to bring about a better understanding among peoples of the earth than shortwave radio," said E. H. Scott, father of the Scott receivers. McMurdo Silver observed that "the avoidance of European war is in large measure the first evidence of the tremendous human effects of world-wide short-wave radio…. [T]he era of peace on earth and goodwill to men is not inconceivably distant."[90] But the years ahead would show that the relationship of shortwave to peace was hardly simple.

In January, Westinghouse celebrated its fiftieth anniversary with a special golden jubilee program that was shortwaved to company workers in 100 American cities and 80 countries where the company had offices. In April, **W2XAD** and **W2XAF** transmitted to 37 countries a "worldwide reunion" of graduates of Rensselaer Polytechnic Institute in Troy, New York. Each alumnus received a postcard with information about the planned broadcast. In November, a similar broadcast celebrated Alumni Night at Massachusetts State College, Springfield, through the facilities of WBZ shortwave station **W1XK**. Attendees at meetings in 20 American cities listened in. And W2XAD and W2XAF ended the year with a broadcast lasting from 1000 EST on December 31 to 2400 on January 1. The frequencies were 9530 and 15340 kc.

W2XAD increased its on-air time by three hours a day. Often it carried boxing or football games outside its regular broadcast hours. **W9XAA** in Chicago moved its transmitter to Downers Grove, Illinois, the same location as W9XF. RCA's **Rocky Point** facility had been upgraded. The power of its most potent shortwave transmitter, **WEF**, which was often used to relay broadcasts overseas on 10620 kc., went from 40 kw. to 200 kw. One of the frequently heard **Rocky Point** calls was **W2XBJ**, which was used for general experimental purposes. And the *Queen Mary* was launched. Many listeners heard its radiotelephone transmitter, call letters **GBTT**.

How were the U.S. stations being heard overseas? The radio editor of *The West Australian* in Perth reported as follows:

> W2XAF, Schenectady, is best both in regard to strength and quality; W8XK, Pittsburgh (25 meters) is loud enough but a signal of poor quality; W3XAU, Philadelphia, good quality, fair strength; W1XK, Boston, is okay; W3XAL, Bound Brook, N.J., very strong for an hour (9 A.M. to 10 A.M., E.S.T.); W2XAD, Schenectady, fair at times; W8XK, Pittsburgh (19 meters), fair at times; W2XE, Wayne Township, N.J., clear but weak; W9XAA, Chicago, fair considering its low power. W8XAL, Cincinnati, was regular in our Summer, but is a rare visitor at present [May]. W8XK, Pittsburgh (on 49), is heard sometimes at 4 P.M., E.S.T.[91]

At Boston's **W1XAL**, predecessor station to **WRUL**, new antennas were built and the power was increased from 10 kw. to 20 kw. With its focus on international education, W1XAL sounded very different from the other American stations. Much distinct programming was produced, usually with the international audience in mind, as the station enhanced its connections with colleges and universities, including Harvard. But financing problems would always dog the station's effort to become a national leader in education by radio.

New FCC rules for shortwave broadcasting went into effect in September. Acknowledging that direct-to-listener broadcasting had replaced rebroadcasting as the medium's *raison d'être* and that shortwave had moved beyond the strictly experimental, shortwave broadcasting was now referred to as "international broadcasting" rather than "experimental relay broadcasting." ("Relay broadcasting" was now used to describe what had been called "broadcast pickup stations," or mobile field transmitters.) A new requirement that stations have a minimum power of 5 kw. impacted several broadcasters. **W4XB** would soon increase power to 5 kw., **W3XAU** to 10 kw., while a planned increase for **W9XAA** did not take place and the station soon left the air. And while stations could be licensed for up to eight frequencies, they could use only one channel at a time.

The new rules requiring that stations render an "international broadcast service" emphasized the international character of shortwave broadcasting. Station identifications and announcements were to be made with the international nature of the service in mind, and rebroadcasts of domestic material had to be identified as such. Commercials were not allowed unless they were part of a rebroadcast of standard broadcast programming, nor could stations advertise their shortwave services domestically or use their shortwave call letters on domestic stations. And while the production of special international programming would grow, the dictate that domestic programs could be rebroadcast on shortwave "only when they are of special international service or when programs for international service are not available" had little impact on the widespread presentation of standard broadcast programming on shortwave.[92]

Apex stations started coming on the air in greater numbers. Among them were **W3XEY**, Baltimore (its parent was WFBR); **W4XCA**, Memphis, Tennessee (WMC); **W6XKG**, Los Angeles (KGFJ); **W8XAI**, Rochester, New York (WHAM); and *Detroit News* station **W8XWJ** (WWJ). Most operated on 31.6 mc., but some used other frequencies, and stations sometimes changed frequency or operated on more than one. **W9XOK**, St. Louis (WEW), was on 35.5 mc.; **W1XKA**, Boston (WBZ), **W3XKA**, Philadelphia (KYW), and **W8XKA**, Pittsburgh (KDKA), were all on 55.5 mc.; and **W1XEH**, Hartford, Connecticut, rebroadcast WTIC on 63.5 mc.

THE ULTRA - HIGH - FREQUENCY - CLUB
OF PHILADELPHIA
Broadcasts every Tuesday Night at 8:30 P. M.
through the courtesy of the
WESTINGHOUSE ELECTRIC AND MFG. COMPANY
over their special experimental station

W 3 X K A

This Confirms:- ......receipt..of..your..communication.... ....
frequency is: 55.5 mc not 50.710 thanks for writing.

President W3AUY - Vice-President W3AFQ - Secretary W3AYG

Westinghouse apex station W3XKA in Philadelphia usually simulcast the programs of KYW. The frequency was circa 55 mc.

The power of most of the apex stations was between 50 and 150 watts (W6XKG operated with 1 kw., the highest power allowed), and they were usually on the air for less than the entire broadcast day. Many of the apex stations were beyond the frequency range of many shortwave sets, but some weren't. For those with the right equipment they were a great novelty. And as reports to W8XWJ from England, to W2XDV from Ireland, and to W6XKG from Australia and New Zealand proved, under the right conditions the range of apex signals was far greater than expected, particularly during these years when the sunspot cycle was approaching its maximum.[93]

In Canada, VE9DR, Drummondville, Quebec became CFCX, Montreal, which now operated its own 750-watt transmitter on 6005 kc. VE9CS had been leased to the Standard Broadcasting System Ltd. True to its United Church of Canada origins it still carried church services, but other time was sold to sponsors. It was around this time that its call letters were changed to CKFX.

PHI in Holland began broadcasting a Sunday program to North America at 1900–2000 EST on 11730 kc. Eddie Startz was already being referred to (in *RADEX*) as "the best-known man among DXers."[94] CSW, Emissora Nacional, Lisbon, Portugal had now adopted a regular schedule on 9940 kc. It was on the air from 1600 with announcements in Portuguese and English and clock strikes at 1900, followed by English news until 1905 sign off. The power was 5 kw. And the French station at Pontoise, often referred to as FYA, now used new call letters—TPA2, TPA3, TPA4, etc. It broadcast in French, Spanish, English, Arabic, Portuguese, German and Italian.

The BBC Empire Service was broadcasting more than 17 hours a day. On the technical side, improvements to the antenna system at Daventry led to better reception of BBC shortwave. Programmatically the year began and ended with events whose worldwide significance was reinforced by shortwave. London carried regular bulletins on the failing health of King George V. The funeral that followed his death on January 20 was the Empire Service's most momentous broadcast of the year. *The New York Times* reported:

> A few seconds before 10 o'clock the whistle stopped; there was a sound like wind and then chimes, quickly ending as the bellowing gong of Big Ben struck three times. It was 3 o'clock in the morning along the Thames.
> There was a pause, then an ominous voice. If anyone now in tune with England had not heard the news earlier in the evening, he need not hear the announcer say more than, "This is London calling," to realize that solemn tidings were about to be electrified. Again, across the empire echoed, "Death came peacefully to the King at 11:55 P.M."[95]

On December 10, George V's successor, King Edward VIII, abdicated the throne in order to marry the twice-divorced Wallis Simpson. It was the shortest reign of an English monarch in almost 400 years. Shortwave contributed to the story on this side of the Atlantic.

> Briefly ... the London announcer would report calmly on the situation. There were no excited voices; no sudden activity or colorful commentaries ... . In the middle of the night the British Broadcasting Corporation's main broadcast transmitters have been silent, while from the BBC studios American radio representatives have gone on the air in special broadcasts, which reached out to the Dominions, too, because of the globe-encircling short waves.[96]

There were numerous special broadcasts from Germany during the August Summer Olympics in Berlin. Unlike many of the international stations, **Zeesen** broadcast for extended periods to each target area, making it one of the most ubiquitous signals on the bands. The schedule was as follows: to North America at 1650–2245 on 11770 kc., and 1930–2130 on 6079; to South Asia at 0030–0300 on 9560, 0130–0330 on 15340, 0350–1100 on 15200, 0805–1100 on 9560, and 0545–0730 on 15110; to East Asia at 0030–0350 on 9540 and 15280, 0805–1100 on 9540 and 17760, and 0350–0700 on 15280; to Africa at 1135–1620 on 6020 and 11770, 1200–1400 on 11855, and 1500–1620 on 11795; and to South and Central America at 1650–2245 on 9540 (to South America) and 9560 (to Central America). Germany ended the year with a shortwaved Christmas greeting from Rudolf Hess in which he reviewed Nazi accomplishments and thanked God for giving Herr Hitler to Germany.[97]

LZA, **Radio Sofia**, Bulgaria came on the air. The station operated daily at 0400–0530 and 1100–1345 EST, Sundays at 2300–1530, on 14970 kc., 1.5 kw. It was difficult to hear in the United States. And from Yugoslavia, the 1 kw. **Belgrade Short-Wave Station** transmitted over YUA and YUB, both on 6100 kc., and YUC, 9505. Soon it would be presenting 10-minute news bulletins in Turkish, Albanian, Greek, Rumanian, German, Hungarian, Italian, French and English.

In July, longtime plans for shortwave broadcasting in Czechoslovakia came to fruition with a new 35 kw. transmitter in Podebrady which began testing on 6115, 11760 and 15230 kc. Regular broadcasting from the **Czechoslovak Shortwave Station**, which announced as **Radio Podebrady** but soon became known as **OLR**, or **Radiojournal** (the name of the PTT-owned transmission company founded in 1923), commenced the following month, and before long the station was on the air more than six hours a day in Czech, Slovak, English, German, French and Ruthenian. A program for North America was broadcast on Mondays and Thursdays at 2100–2300 EST on 15230 kc. The mission of the station was to provide information and propaganda and maintain contact with Czechs living abroad. It was very well heard, and by year's end it had received over 4,000 letters from around the world, a number that would triple in 1937.[98] For six International Reply Coupons listeners could receive the monthly program guide for a year. (*"Hello! Hello! Hello! Radio Podebrady, Czechoslovakia. I'll spell it for*

GERMAN SHORTWAVE STATION
BROADCASTING HOUSE, BERLIN

Zone V
North-America Program

June 1937

Call	Wavelength	Kcs	Time Schedule: Berlin		B. S. T.	
DJL	19.85 m	15110	14.00—15.00		8.00 a.m.— 9.00 a.m.	
DJB	19.74 m	15200	} 22.50— 4.45		4.50 p.m.—10.45 p.m.	
DJD	25.49 m	11770				
DJB*	19.74 m	15200	17.10—18.25		11.10 a.m.—12.25 p.m.	

*) only on Sunday   14.00—15.00 M.E.Z. Musical Entertainment

Announcements of program changes and supplements will
be made daily after the news

Other Transmissions
of the German Shortwave Station
(Berlin time)

SOUTH ASIA

DJA	31.38 m	9 560 kc	} 6.05—11.15
DJB	19.74 m	15 200 kc	
DJB	19.74 m	15 200 kc	11.55—17.00

EAST ASIA

DJQ	19.63 m	15 280 kc	
DJN	31.45 m	9 540 kc	} 6.05—11.15
DJE	16.89 m	17 760 kc	
DJE	16.89 m	17 760 kc	} 11.55—17.00
DJN	31.45 m	9 540 kc	
DJQ	19.63 m	15 280 kc	14.15—17.00

AFRICA

DJL	19.85 m	15 110 kc	6.00— 8.00
DJD	25.49 m	11 770 kc	
DJL	19.85 m	15 110 kc	} 17.35—22.30
DJC	49.83 m	6 020 kc	
DJL	19.85 m	15 110 kc	12.00—14.00 (only on Sunday)

SOUTH AMERICA

DJQ	19.63 m	15 280 kc	12.00—14.00
DJN	31.45 m	9 540 kc	
DJQ	19.63 m	15 280 kc	} 22.50— 4.45
DJQ	19.63 m	15 280 kc	
DJE	16.89 m	17 760 kr	} 17.10—18.25 (only on Sunday)

CENTRAL AMERICA

DJR	19.56 m	15 340 kc	14.00—15.00
DJA	31.38 m	9 560 kc	
DJR	19.56 m	15 340 kc	} 22.50— 4.45

Please note the German-English vocabulary on the back of the programsheet

Printed in Germany

This foot-high monthly schedule from the German shortwave station unfolded into a yard-long, two-sided, German-English listing of the programs for each day of the month.

you, P-O-D-E-B-R-A-D-Y, testing on a wavelength of 25.51 metres, or 11760 kc. Our test transmissions started at 2000 British Summer Time and will continue until 0800 BST today on three wavelengths as follows: 19.69 meters, 15230 kc.; 25.51 metres, 11760 kc.; and on 49.05 metres, 6115 kc., changing wavelengths every hour and a half. Reports are welcome relative to signal strength and tone quality. Address: Radio Podebrady, Czechoslovakia.")

From Scandinavia, SM5SX, the part-amateur, part-broadcasting station of the Royal Technical University in Stockholm, was on 11710 kc. relaying the Motala mediumwave station. Some special Wednesday tests to North America at 1600–1700 EST were heard here, and on other days the station could be heard in the 1100–1700 EST period. It was reported to be operating with 400 watts.

The Spanish Civil War began on July 17. Fighting would last almost three years, during which General Francisco Franco and the conservative "Nationalist" insurgents, supported by Nazi Germany and Fascist Italy, battled the Loyalist forces of the Second Republic, which were supported by the Soviet Union and various non-governmental brigades from many countries. The fighting, in which Franco was eventually victorious, was city-by-city, very bloody, and very divisive of the Spanish populace.

Broadcasting played a major part in the conflict. Even before the great radio propaganda wars of World War II, Spain was a laboratory for the use of broadcasting by the combatants. As one observer on the ground put it, the war brought about "a complete radio metamorphosis throughout Spain."[99]

When the war began, Spain had eight regional transmitters, plus some sixty 200-watt stations, most of them privately owned. All stations were mediumwave, and within a week all were in the hands of one side or the other. The Loyalists controlled the most powerful outlets, usually through unions, political parties or local governments, as national organs had quickly broken down. Stations changed hands

SM5SX was a combination ham-broadcast station, the first one to offer broadcast programming on shortwave from Sweden.

as Nationalist territory expanded, and propaganda displaced nearly all other programming. Slight changes in frequency were made daily by many stations in order to avoid pervasive open-carrier jamming.

The insurgents controlled all the stations in their territory, the main one being the **Union Radio** station in Seville. They also controlled three important Spanish dependencies—the Canary Islands, the Balearic Islands, and the Spanish zone of Morocco—all of which had valuable radio assets. Over the air it was common to hear the Nationalist greeting, "Viva Franco! Arriba España!" from these stations.

On the shortwave side, **EAQ**, with studios in Madrid and transmitters some 35 miles distant at Aranjuez, was in Loyalist hands. Its foreign broadcasts were expanded. Many foreign journalists, most of whom supported the Loyalists, were heard over EAQ, as were participants in the international brigades. The station broadcast in 15 foreign languages. (Its Welsh broadcasts were even relayed by the BBC Welsh Home Service until a very disapproving Lord Reith, head of the BBC, put a stop to it.) In addition to foreign broadcasting, EAQ transmitted Loyalist propaganda to the Nationalists, in particular the rebel military.

The insurgents controlled **Radio Guardia Civil**, sometimes called **Radio Tetuan**, a shortwave station in Tetuan, Spanish Morocco, that operated on various channels circa 6590 kc., and **EAJ43, Radio Club Tenerife**, in the Canaries. EAJ43 traces its history back to an amateur station, **EAR58**, that operated in 1925. EAR58 became **EA8AB** in 1934 when Spanish callsigns were changed. Although these were amateur stations, they did some broadcasting as well under the name Radio Club Tenerife. It was through the initiative of EA8AB and its supporters that a mediumwave broadcasting license was obtained, permitting Radio Club Tenerife, with call letters EAJ43, to begin operating in 1934 on 1492 kc., 201.1 meters, with 200 watts. EA8AB carried the broadcast programming of EAJ43 on various 40 meter ham frequencies.

Amateur stations played an important role in the war. Although both sides nominally prohibited amateur activity and made traditional ham contacts a criminal offense, many amateur operators continued making ham contacts during the war. A goodly number relayed the programming of the broadcast stations of one side or the other, and many were put to use for military purposes or for part-time propaganda broadcasts on behalf of political parties and other interest groups (including dissident factions within the Nationalist movement). The insurgents controlled the **Radio Requeté** broadcast network, which had been set up by the Carlists, an ultra-traditional monarchist political party. Radio Requeté was composed largely of amateur stations, some of which continued to operate also as amateurs in addition to broadcasters. Most of the amateurs, whether operating in ham or broadcast mode, transmitted on 40 meters; some were on 20 meters. There were also clandestine stations on both sides ("radios fantasmas," or "ghost radios," as they were called), and commercial radiotelephone stations were pressed into broadcasting service as well.

A London newspaper writer observed in 1937:

> At first [amateur gear] was used for what the operators termed (in Spanish) "Succour Service." A ham in rebel HQ, Tetuan, would call government Madrid. "Attención Madrid, Attención Madrid … Aquí Tetuan, aquí Tetuan." He would then state that he was part of the amateur succour service, and would, for example, read out the name of a man a dozen times. Then he would say, "Please tell his wife X, in Y street, Madrid, that he is safe at B hotel Tetuan." He would read through a long list of names in this fashion, sometimes stating that they were dead or wounded. ¶Notices would be given out about food rationing, train services, hospitals, the calling up of certain sections of the militia, etc. The great feature of the "Succour Service" was that government and rebel situated hams used to contact each other.
>
> * * *
>
> Gradually the hams have been taken over for pure propaganda use. At the present time the entire 7-Mc. band is filled with them. Their power has obviously been increased, speeches are broadcast in Spanish, news in English, French and German, while the intervals are filled with broadcast music. ¶At one swing of the dial I have counted 42 different Spanish stations on the 7-Mc. band, all S9 max. After dark it is absolutely impossible to contact any but very local stations owing to the terrific QRM. Such is the present state of the 7-Mc. band in Europe.[100]

Soon after the war began, EA8AB could be heard with EAJ43 programming on Monday, Wednesday and Friday at 1515–1615 EST. However, EAJ43 had an even better signal on 10370 kc., for the station was now transmitting by way of the 20 kw. transmitter of Canaries commercial radiotelephone station **EHZ** at El Tablero, Gran Canaria. It was this connection that gave EAJ43 and the insurgents the capability of reliable overseas broadcasting. In the United States the station was heard during the period 1800–2000 EST. *("This is EAJ43, Radio Club Tenerife, on 201 and 28 meters.")* And it was a good verifier.

Amateur station **EA9AH** in Spanish Morocco, first located in Ceuta and then in Tetuan, was another important link in Franco's broadcasting network. It was heard daily with war news in various languages, and sometimes music, from around 1600 EST on about 7030 kc. It was also heard during later evening hours, sometime on frequencies in the 20 meter ham band. EA9AH said it was operating with 200 watts (believed later increased to 500 watts). Another famous Nationalist "amateur broadcaster" was Bartolome Pinia, **EA6AF**, in the Balearic Islands.

At the end of 1936 the Nationalists established a nacent national broadcasting service called **Radio Nacional de España**. The Germans provided it with 20 and 30 kw. mediumwave transmitters for Salamanca and Zaragoza respectively, and while the local Loyalist stations provided good local coverage, the German transmitters were more powerful than even the strongest Loyalistas. These were the first Spanish mediumwave transmitters that could provide nationwide coverage. Local stations under rebel control often relayed the Radio Nacional news. When the Nationalists consolidated the power of their constituent groups in May 1937, they formed the **FET** network (**Falange Española Tradicional**), which would survive the war and become the voice of the Falange during Franco's rule.

Though strident in its approach, Radio Nacional gained a following on both sides for

During the Spanish Civil War, Dr. Angel Mora operated amateur station EA9AI, Melilla, Spanish Morocco, as a broadcast station. It supported Franco, and was on the air Saturday and Sunday nights from 2200 to 2300 EST on 7180 kc.

the broadcasting of names of those wounded, killed or captured, and for presenting a Saturday night midnight mass, which appealed to the Catholic faithful in secular Loyalist areas.

Other countries barraged Spain with propaganda broadcasts on behalf of one side or the other, with Germany and Italy in support of the Nationalists, France and the Soviet Union on the side of the Loyalists. Both shortwave and mediumwave were used. **Radio Club Português** in Lisbon, whose mediumwave signal could be heard in Spain, supported the rebels. And the war's conclusion in 1939 did not end war-related foreign broadcasting to Spain. The anti-Franco **Radio España Independiente** began broadcasting on shortwave from the Soviet Union in 1946. It would be heard worldwide until its close in 1977.

It is important to remember that while Spanish shortwave provided fascinating DX opportunities, shortwave was not in wide use among the general population in Spain. As a result, domestic political events there were influenced much more by events on the mediumwaves.

In Africa, the **Imperial Ethiopian Broadcasting Station** (the country's PTT) carried broadcast programming on Wednesdays at 1645–1715 EST over the commercial station at Akaki, near Addis Ababa. The channels generally used were **ETA** on 18270 kc., **ETB**, 11955, and **ETD**, 7620. Power had recently been increased from 3.5 to 12 kw. In May the Italians occupied Addis Ababa and the station came under Italian control.

Thailand was heard once again. **HSP** was mainly a commercial station, but sometimes it broadcast music on 17740 kc. In addition, **Experimental Radio Broadcasting Station HS8PJ**, Bangkok, with 5 kw., broadcast on Mondays at 0800–1000 EST on 10995 kc. and Thursdays at 0730–1000 on 9350. IDs were in English, French and Siamese, and English news was heard at times. A 300-watt sister amateur station, **HS1PJ**, broadcast intermittently on 14200 kc.

Until now, China had been heard mainly by way of commercial stations. Now mediumwave station XGOA, operated by the Central Broadcasting Administration in Nanking, China's capital, had an English broadcast on its new shortwave outlet in that city, 500-watt **XGOX**, at 0500 EST. At first it used various 31 meter band frequencies, e.g. 9470 and 9545 kc., before moving to 6820.

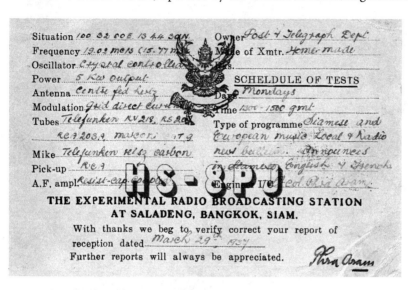

On Taiwan (which had been ruled by Japan since 1895), the mediumwave programs from Taihoku (Taipei) were being carried over 10 kw. radiotelephone senders JIA, 15400 kc., JIB, 10535, and JIC, 5890.

In February, an unsuccessful coup attempt in Japan took the country's shortwave transmitters off the air briefly. Thereafter, NHK expanded its broadcasts and developed a regular overseas schedule, which was as follows: to Europe on Tuesdays and Fridays at 1400–1500 on 9535 and 15160 kc.; to South America and Eastern North America on Mondays and Thursdays at 1600–1700 on 9535 and 15160 kc.; and to Western North America and Hawaii daily at 0000–0100 on 14600 kc., and sometimes on 9535 or 15160 as well. There was also a broadcast to Malaya and Java at 0900–1000 on 10660, 14600 or 18910 kc. All transmitters were **International Wireless Telephone Company** senders of 20 kw., located in Nazaki. Each frequency had its own call letters, which denoted whether the senders were

Top: The shortwave station in Siam was recognizable by its three ascending chimes. At sign off, it wished listeners "good health, good luck and a very good night from Siam." *Bottom:* When the Japanese seized Nanking in December 1937, the government, and its broadcasting station, moved to Chungking, which became the wartime capital. This QSL dates from before the move.

those assigned principally to the broadcasting service ("JZ," e.g. **JZI, JZK, JZL**), or commercial transmitters temporarily assigned to broadcasting ("JV," e.g. **JVH, JVN, JVT**). NHK sent its listeners a special form for submitting reception reports. In addition to scheduled broadcasts, Japanese commercial stations often transmitted broadcast programming while waiting for telephone calls to be put through.

Hearing a signal from Saigon on 11710 kc., DXers thought it was **FZS**, which had been off the air for several years. It turned out to be a new station, **Philco Radio**, which was testing with Asian music at 0630–0730 EST, European music at 0730–0930, and news in French at 0900–0910. Soon it took the name of the local Philco agency, becoming **Station Boy-Landry**. The chief engineer described

This shortwave station bearing the Philco name was in Saigon. There were others in Cuba, Colombia, Venezuela and the Dominican Republic.

the 250-watt transmitter as being "built up from ordinary Philco receiver parts, augmented by some copper tubing, a few high voltage condensers and transmitting tubes."[101] By 1938 it was on three frequencies— 6200, 9760 and 11690 kc.

Two other stations started operating from what would become Vietnam. One was in Saigon. Named after its owner, **Radio "Michel Robert"** was on 9524 kc. and used 10 watts. From Hanoi there was **Radio-Club de l'Indochine du Nord**, a 5 kw. station on 13953 kc. Neither was reported heard in the U.S.

Mediumwave station **KZRM** in Manila was being heard again by way of commercial stations **KAZ** on 9970 kc. and **KBD** on 8710. However, the broadcasts were discontinued by year's end. **CQN**, Macao, was on 9665 kc. with 300 watts. The **Colombo Broadcasting Service** in Colombo, Ceylon, a mediumwave station, was also transmitting experimentally on shortwave as **ZOI**, 6065 kc., at 0800–1000 EST. With only 300 watts, *"Colombo Calling"* was a longshot in North America. The ZOI shortwave broadcasts ended in 1938.[102] On the positive side of the ledger, **ZBW**, Hong Kong, moved to 9525 and 15190 kc., and was now heard world wide.

The broadcasting scene in the Dutch East Indies was chaotic and ever changing. **NIROM's** main shortwave transmitters were on Java. They were, in Batavia, 10 kw. **YDA**, now on 3040 and 7250 kc.; **YDB**, Soerabaya, 9550 kc., 1 kw.; and three 1.5 kw. stations in Bandoeng — YDC, 15150 kc., **PLP**, 11000, and **PMN**, 10260. They were on the air weekdays at 2230–0200, 0430–1030 and 1800–1930 EST, Sundays at 1900–0200 and 0430–1030. A locally oriented station, **PMH**, was on 6720 kc. with 1.5 kw. Nine other regional and local short-wave stations, operating in the 2 and 3 mc. bands with powers ranging from 15 to 150 watts, were located through-out Java, together with 11 mediumwave stations. On Sumatra, **YDX** in Medan operated on 4945 and 7220 kc. with 500 watts. From a receiving site near Batavia, NIROM could pick up broad-casts from **PHI** or **Kootwijk** in Holland for rebroadcast over the NIROM network.

In the U.S., a nice Pacific catch was **9MI**, a broadcast-ing station situated aboard the M/V *Kanimbla*, a large passenger vessel which plied the waters between Mel-bourne and Sydney. It tested at first on 6075 and 11740 kc., but soon moved to 6010 and 11710, and was sometimes heard on the west coast. Broadcasts were a half-hour in length, and power, according to the QSL, was 50 watts (other sources said 200, 250 or 1,500). Owned by McIlwraith McEacharn Ltd. in Australia, the ship was said to be the first passen-ger vessel equipped with a permanent broadcasting studio. Its voice went silent in 1939 when it was taken into Australian naval service.

VPD, Fiji moved to 9540 kc. (**VPD2**) and expanded its transmission hours. The signal was of good strength, but overmodulated. **FO8AA, R. Océania**, Papeete, Tahiti, operated by Radio Club Océanien, was reported on the air on 10070 kc., Tuesdays and Fridays at 2310–0100 EST. The 25-watt station soon increased power to 200 watts and moved to 7100 kc., but usu-ally suffered intense QRM from amateur code stations. The broadcasts began with "La Mar-seillaise" and ended with "Aloha 'Oe." FO8AA would stay on the air until 1949 when it was replaced by **FZP8**, predecessor to the **Radio Tahiti** of later years.

M/V "KANIMBLA" 11,000 TONS.

MARINE BROADCASTING STATION.

Call Sign—9.M1. Wave Length, 6010 K.C. — 49.917 metres.

McILWRAITH McEACHARN LTD.
MELBOURNE.

Owners and Operators.

PROGRAMME OF BROADCASTS.
(Subject to alterations and additional Relays from time to time).

Date.	To Station:	Time (E.S.T.)	Position of Vessel Between :
Fri., May 6th	3BO, Bendigo ..	10.00 to 10.30 p.m.	Fremantle and Adelaide.
Sat., May 7th	2GN, Goulburn ..	10.00 to 10.30 p.m.	Fremantle and Adelaide.
Tues., May 10th	3HA, Hamilton .	5.15 to 5.45 p.m.	Adelaide and Melbourne.
		(Children's Session).	
Tues., May 10th	2AY, Albury ..	10.00 to 10.30 p.m.	Adelaide and Melbourne.
Sun., May 15th	2GF, Grafton ..	10.00 to 10.30 p.m.	Melbourne and Sydney.
Wed., May 18th	4WK, Warwick ..	10.00 to 10.30 p.m.	Sydney and Brisbane.
Sun., May 22nd	4TO, Townsville	10.00 to 10.30 p.m.	Brisbane and Mackay
Fri., June 2nd	4CA, Cairns ...	10.00 to 10.30 p.m.	Mackay and Brisbane
Sun., June 5th	2GN, Goulburn .	10.00 to 10.30 p.m.	Brisbane and Sydney.
Wed., June 8th	3HA, Hamilton .	5.15 to 5.45 p.m.	Sydney and Melbourne
		(Children's Session).	
Wed., June 8th	2AY, Albury ..	10.00 to 10.30 p.m.	Sydney and Melbourne.
Sun., June 12th	3BO, Bendigo ..	10.00 to 10.30 p.m.	Melbourne and Sydney.
Wed., June 15th	2GF, Grafton ..	10.00 to 10.30 p.m.	Sydney and Brisbane.
Sun., June 19th	4WK, Warwick .	10.00 to 10.30 p.m.	Brisbane and Mackay
Thurs., June 30th	4TO, Townsville	10.00 to 10.30 p.m.	Mackay and Brisbane
Sun., July 3rd	4CA, Cairns ...	10.00 to 10.30 p.m.	Brisbane and Sydney.
Wed., July 6th	3HA, Hamilton .	5.15 to 5.45 p.m.	Sydney and Melbourne
		(Children's Session).	
Wed., July 6th	2GN, Goulburn .	10.00 to 10.30 p.m.	Sydney and Melbourne.
Sun., July 10th	2AY, Albury ...	10.00 to 10.30 p.m.	Melbourne and Sydney.
Wed., July 13th	3BO, Bendigo ..	10.00 to 10.30 p.m.	Sydney and Brisbane.
Sun., July 17th	2GF, Grafton ..	10.00 to 10.30 p.m.	Brisbane and Mackay
Thurs., July 28th	4WK, Warwick .	10.00 to 10.30 p.m.	Mackay and Brisbane
Sun., July 31st	4TO, Townsville	10.00 to 10.30 p.m.	Brisbane and Sydney.
Wed., Aug. 3rd	3HA, Hamilton .	5.15 to 5.45 p.m.	Sydney and Melbourne
		(Children's Session).	

The passenger ship *Kanimbla,* with its ship-borne station 9MI, operated in Australian waters from 1936 to 1939, when it was com-missioned as a troop transport. The local Australian stations shown on this 1938 schedule picked up the 9MI shortwave signal and rebroadcast it to their local audiences.

Nowhere was there more shortwave activity than in Latin America. Following the American model of private broadcasting, amateurs and all manner of businesses took to the air with abandon, filling the shortwave bands with signals. The 49 meter band, to which many of these stations were attracted, was the most popular (and most crowded) of the international shortwave broadcasting bands, and the free-form frequency usage that marked Latin American shortwave led many stations to utilize out-of-band channels. Frequency moves inevitably proved temporary, however.

A number of stations were heard from Mexico, and it was hard to tell the "broadcasting amateurs" from the solo broadcasters. In the latter category were **XEME, La Voz de Yucatan**, Merida, 8190 kc., which relayed XEFC, and 100-watt **XEXA, Cadena Radiodifusora "DAPP,"** operated by the Mexican Departamento Autonomo de Prensa y Publicidad, Mexico City, which was reported on various frequencies in the 6130–6160 kc. range (later 6175). XEVI changed its call letters to **XEWI** and began carrying some programming in English, French, German and Esperanto. It used the slogan, "My Voice to the World from Mexico." Its programs reflected the transcendental teachings of its parent, the Impersonal Life Institute in Mexico City.

In Cuba, a new Havana shortwave station heard by many was **COCQ**. It was part of the CMQ network, which was founded three years earlier and would become one of the two major Cuban radio networks of the decade (the other was Radio Havana Cuba-Cadena Azul).[103] COCQ's frequency was highly variable at first, but soon the 400-watt station settled down on 9750 kc. It was known for the multitude of sound effects that accompanied its advertisements — laughter, babies crying, trains chuffing, etc. Also new in Cuba was **COCX, La Voz del Radio Philco**, Havana, which was heard testing on various 25 meter band channels including 11795 and 12250 kc. The station relayed mediumwave CMX, and the power was 2 kw.

Whether the change of the name of the capital, Santo Domingo, to Ciudad Trujillo by the country's like-named president had anything to do with it or not, shortwave broadcasting in the Dominican Republic exploded. In the capital, 50-watt **Radiodifusora HIL** was on various frequencies around 6500 kc., while another 50 watter, **HIG** (later HI1G), **Radio "La Opinión,"** was on 6280. Widely heard was **HIN, La Voz del Partido Dominicano**, broadcasting with 750 watts on 6243 and 11280 kc., and identifying in Spanish, French and English. **HIT, La Voz de la RCA Victor**, also in the capital, was on 6630 kc. with 200 watts.

Still in Ciudad Trujillo, **Estación Perifonica HI3U–La Voz del Comercio**, was on 6383 kc.; **HI5N, La Voz del Almacén Dominicano**, was on 6130; **HI8A, "FA-DOC" (Fabrica Dominicana de Calzado)**, was on 6600 with 100 watts; **HI8Q, La Voz de la Philco**, was on 6240 (300 watts); and **HI2D, La Voz de la Asociación Católica**, was on 6900 (signing off with "Ave Maria"). Dominican shortwavers in other towns included **Radiodifusora HI1J**, San Pedro de Macorís, on 5860 kc.; **HI1S, La Voz de la Hispaniola**, in Santiago, on 6420 (it featured English on Tuesday and Friday nights); **HI4V, La Voz de la Marina**, San Francisco de Macorís, on 6560; and **HI9B, "Broadcasting Hotel Mercedes,"** 6045 kc., operating, as the name implies, from the roof garden of the Hotel Mercedes in Santiago.

Activity was also increasing in Central America. New from Honduras was **HRD, Voz de Atlantida**, La Ceiba, on 6235 kc. The 250-watt station announced its call letters in English at the end of the broadcast: "*H for Happiness, R for Radio, D for Delight.*" A new Panamanian station was heard, **HP5K, La Voz de la Victor**, in Colón, on 6005 kc.; and in Nicaragua, 200-watt **TGS, Radiotransmisora de la Casa Presidencial**, Managua, came on the air on 5740 kc., while **YNAM, La Voz del Pacifico**, also in Managua, was on 7200. Many other stations, mainly "broadcasting hams," were active from Nicaragua.

New in Costa Rica were **TI5HH, La Voz de San Ramon**, on 5480 kc.; 120-watt **TI8WS**

The first program of the Saturday night English hour of Radiodifusora Cartagena was said to have brought 135 reception reports.

(later **TIWS**), **Ecos del Pacifico**, Puntarenas, on 7600; and 400-watter **TIOW, Ondas del Caribe**, Puerto Limon, 6560 kc. (later 6850). TI4NRH had been off the air while Sr. Céspedes Marín was getting **TIRCC** off the ground. Now the venerable Costa Rican station returned in the evenings, this time on various 31 meter channels, finally settling on 9670 kc. The now-200 watt station broadcast at 2100–2400 EST.

Colombia continued as a hotbed of shortwave broadcast activity. New to the air in 1936 were **HJ2ABC, La Voz de Cúcuta**, 9576 kc.; **HJ4ABH, La Voz de Armenia**, Armenia, 9533; and **HJ4ABP, Emisora Philco** (later **Emisora Claridad**), Medellin, on 6030. The 750-watt **HJ1ABP, Radiodifusora Cartagena**, was new, and put out a strong signal on 9600 kc. It had an English program on Saturday nights at 2200 EST, and the station said it received about 800 reception reports a month. Also new was **HJU, La Voz del Pacifico**, in Buenaventura. It was owned by the National Railroads of Colombia, and transmitted around 9020 kc. And Cali station **HJ5ABC, La Voz de Colombia**, moved to Bogota and got new call letters, **HJ3ABX**, as well as a new frequency, 6122 kc.

The number of shortwave stations in Venezuela was also growing. New were **YV1RG, Radio Valera**, on 6230 kc.; 250-watt **YV1RH, Ondas del Lago**, Maracaibo, on 6350; **YV5AM, Ecos del Llano**, San Juan de los Morros, on 6600; **YV5RP, La Voz de la Philco**, Caracas, 6270; **YV11RB, Ecos del Orinoco**, Ciudad Bolivar, on 6545 kc. with 30 watts; and **YV15RV, Radio Valencia**, 5910. **YV12RM, Emisora 24 de Julio** (later **La Voz de Aragua**), broadcast from Maracay on 6300 kc. Radiotelephone station **YVQ**, also in Maracay, carried music on Saturday nights with announcements in English between selections. The frequency was 6670 kc. **YV5RMO, Ecos del Caribe**, in Maracaibo, got a new slogan — **Ecos del Zulia**. The station moved to 5850 kc., and its old channel, 6070, was now occupied by **YV7RMO, Radiodifusora Maracaibo.**

A second station came on the air from British Guiana. It was VP3BG, "the Voice of Georgetown," on 7220 kc. It was owned by the **Crystal Broadcasting Company**, and could also be heard in amateur operation on 20 meters. And a second station was heard

Amateur station VP3BG also operated in broadcast mode, where it called itself the Voice of Georgetown. In 1938, after two years of operation, it merged with VP3MR, and the joint venture became the British Guiana United Broadcasting Company Ltd.

from next-door Surinam. Thought an amateur station at first because it was operating in the ham bands, 25-watt **PZ1AA**, Paramaribo, turned out to be an experimental government station.

HCJB, Quito, Ecuador was now operating on mediumwave ("La Voz de Quito") and on two shortwave channels, 4107 kc. ("**Broadcasting Provincial**") and 8948 ("**La Voz de los Andes**"). Station Director Clarence W. Jones, who was from Chicago, was the only non-Ecuadorean at the station. The development of shortwave in Ecuador was comparatively slow, however. New stations included **HC1PM, Estación El Palomar**, Quito, on 5725 kc.; **HC1VT, La Voz del Tungurahua, "Radio Ambato,"** on 6550; and 250-watt government station **HCK, Radiodifusora del Estado**, Quito, on 5885. Well-known **HC2JSB, Ecuador Radio**, Guayaquil, was now on 7854 kc. with 500 watts.

Several new stations were said to be operating from Peru, although their origins were not known and they had not yet been reported in North America. They were **OAX4K, Radio Colcochea**, Lima, 6425 kc.; **OAX4P, Radio Huancayo**, 5975 kc., 200 watts; **OAX5A, Radio Universal**, Ica, 11796 kc., 100 watts; **OAX6A, Radio Arequipa**, 6122 kc., 100 watts; and **OAX7A, Radio Cuzco**, 6128 kc., 100 watts.

And Chile was now on shortwave. Although hearing its 500-watt transmitter was a challenge, **CB960, Radio Difusora "Pilot,"** Santiago, was on the air at night on 9600 kc.

Particular songs became trademarks of certain stations. XEWI used "Ah! Sweet Mystery of Life"; HI1J, "Indian Love Call"; EAJ43, "Lady of Spain"; YV5RMO, "Strike Up the Band"; CB960, "Rhapsody in Blue"; and TIPG, "Parade of the Wooden Soldiers." W1XK played "Stars and Stripes Forever," and the Java stations closed with "End of A Perfect Day." There were many other examples.

Some articles introducing program personalities from shortwave stations around the world began appearing in radio publications. And for those wishing to enjoy high fidelity reception, 23- and 24-tube receivers made their appearance. (The Scott Philharmonic had 30 tubes.) Said the Stromberg-Carlson Company, a receiver manufacturer of the day: "The listener is no longer content to put up with squeals and howls, the poor tone quality and noise which marked the earlier efforts in [shortwave reception]. Today we have radio receivers which, under normal conditions, bring in programs from across the seas with the tone quality and fidelity of local broadcast stations."[104]

For the died-in-the-wool DXer, the year's biggest news was that the well-regarded eight-tube Hammarlund Comet "Pro" of 1933 had been succeeded by the 16-tube "Super-Pro," a five-band dream receiver covering up to 20 mc. It had two RF stages, bandspread (calibrated for the ham bands), crystal filter, AVC, "tuning meter," a shutter dial that displayed only the band you were tuned to, and other desirable features, the most important of which for SWLs was an early example of continuously variable selectivity—a bandwidth control that was adjustable from 3 to 16 kc. Either a 10-inch or a 12-inch speaker was available. Hammarlund was a manufacturer of precision radio parts, many of which were used in the company's receivers and contributed to the line's strong reputation. Allied and Lafayette sold the original "Super-Pro" (SP-10) for $241. It was followed by many other models, and the "Super-Pro" line would go on for decades.

Also introduced in 1936 by RME was the DB-20 preselector. Often used with the nine-tube RME-69 receiver that was introduced in 1935, but useable with any receiver, the DB-20 added two RF stages, improving both sensitivity and image rejection. The DB-20 and its three successor models were popular accessories with hams and SWLs for many years.

To promote U.S.-based shortwave broadcasting, the Bureau of Foreign and Domestic Commerce of the Department of Commerce began providing a weekly list of U.S. shortwave broadcasts to the bureau's foreign offices, which in turn distributed them to newspapers, trade papers, etc. for republication. The Bureau also published *A Guide to Reception of Short Wave Broadcasting Stations,* which covered the operation of shortwave receivers and various subjects relating to shortwave listening. And New York City broadcast band station WNYC carried a series of weekly programs about shortwave listening. It was arranged by the New York chapter of the International Short Wave Club.

Domestically, in an effort to promote shortwave, the Radio Manufacturers Association operated a Short-Wave Program Service which collected shortwave schedules of American and foreign shortwave stations and distributed them weekly to newspapers. According to the Association, 479 newspapers in the United States and 39 in Canada carried shortwave schedule information on a regular basis, although the scope of coverage varied widely from one paper to another.

It was another year of numerous special club programs. No club was more active than the NNRC, which arranged for specials from **CFCX** (Canada), **XECR** (Mexico), **COCH** and **COCQ** (Cuba), **HP5F** (Panama), **HRD** (Honduras), **HJ1ABP** (Colombia), **HC2CW** and **HC2RL** (Ecuador), **HIZ** (Dominican Republic), **TI4NRH** (Costa Rica), **YV5RMO, YV8RB** and **YV10RSC** (Venezuela), **Zeesen** (Germany), **2RO** (Italy), **ZHI** (Singapore), and **ZHJ** (Penang), as well as **W3XAL,** and **W2XAD** and **W2XAF.** With its experience in setting up special programs on the broadcast band, the NNRC was easily able to transfer the skill to shortwave.

1937

The end of shortwave as an experimental medium was symbolized by Marconi's death from a heart attack on July 20. In the United States, the evolution of shortwave broadcasting was exemplified by new services, and new programs specifically intended for foreign audiences, a pattern already underway in Europe.

General Electric stations **W2XAD** and **W2XAF** were now beaming some programs specifically to South America and Europe. W2XAD on 15330 kc. operated at 1100–1800 EST to Europe and 1800–2100 to South America. W2XAF on 9530 kc. was non-directional at 1600–1800 and directional to South America at 1800–2400. Although not sharing the same educational mission as **W1XAL**, the GE stations did carry some programs produced by Cornell University and Union College. They also carried a ten-week travelogue series, with separate presentations in English, French and Spanish. It was so popular that it was extended for another 20 weeks. A 15-minute English news bulletin, "American News Tower," covering domestic U.S. news and intended specifically for Americans abroad, was on the air at 1700 EST weekdays on the usual W2XAD and W2XAF frequencies.

In July NBC set up an international division to support the **W3XAL** transmitter at Bound Brook, New Jersey. It appointed international journalist and news commentator Percy Winner as director. Four directional antennas were set up. Together with new non-directional aerials, they occupied 25 acres, or nearly half the WJZ site. Although much of the programming still consisted of material from the NBC domestic network, some was specially produced for target audiences. The news as well as some other programs for the South American beam were in Spanish and Portuguese, and French, German and Italian were used in some of the European transmissions.

The South American aerials went into service in January, and the antennas for Europe followed. These greatly improved signal strength in the target areas. Most of the broadcasts were on 17780 kc. The European program was transmitted on a directional antenna at 0800–1400 EST and a non-directional antenna for four hours thereafter. This was followed by a directional transmission to South America at 1800–2000 EST, and a non-directional transmission on 6100 kc. at 2015–2400. W3XAL also beamed the 1400 EST Saturday matinee performances of New York's Metropolitan Opera Company to South America (where they were rebroadcast by Radio Splendid in Buenos Aires and Radio Bras in Rio de Janeiro). The opera broadcasts were also carried on W2XAD and W2XAF. W3XAL sent advance program schedules in Spanish to some 500 publications throughout Central and South America.

Letter from the Belgian Congo to W3XAL

"This day, the 6th of December, I have got reception of your broadcast in the Belgian Congo on the short-wave band … you are heard very clearly and the broadcast in French is understood perfectly. You have a very good announcer.

"I am an official in the Colony and am located in the wilds at about 100 kilometers to the North-East of Leopoldville, the capital of the Belgian Congo. I get reception on an American radio set, with 6-volt battery. I shift places every week and the set is carried on the back of a man. Upon arrival of the caravan in a village two policemen put up the antenna on two sticks and in ten minutes the set is operating … .

"On February 14, 1938, I shall be at 300 kms. (180 miles) from Leopoldville, right in the heart of the equatorial forest, and I shall hear your broadcast at 9:00 o'clock in the evening Central European Time."

"W3XAL's Short-Wave Voice Reaches Every Clime"
Short Wave & Television, June 1938[105]

Like NBC, CBS increased production of special programming for shortwave, including programs in foreign languages, particularly Spanish. Elizabeth-Ann Tucker was named Director of Programs at **W2XE**, where she had worked for over six years as secretary to the chief engineer. On May 12, CBS dedicated a new 10 kw. transmitter at W2XE.[106] Programs were now beamed to Europe at 0630–0900 on 21520 kc., and 1400–1630 and 1730–1800 on 15270; and to South America at 0900–0930 on 21520, 1630- 1700 on 15270, and 1800–2300 on 11830. W2XE was getting about 100 reception reports a week. Starting in November, 2230 EST on Mondays was reserved for "Brave New World," a series of 26 half-hour programs designed "to further the friendship between the United States and Latin America." The program was sponsored by the Office of Education of the U.S. Department of the Interior, and it covered Latin American history, culture and contemporary problems. Also carried on the CBS domestic network, it was heavily promoted by both CBS and the government.

Westinghouse also improved its plant at **W8XK**, modernizing the antennas for its four shortwave transmitters. Now two directional antennas were available for broadcasts to South America, with a third directed toward Europe. The frequencies used were 6140, 11870 and 15210 kc. The 21540 kc. channel continued to use one of the old antennas.

Consistent with its educational mission, **W1XAL** began carrying "URSI-grams," five-minute scientific voice bulletins of solar, magnetic and ionospheric activity prepared by the Union Radio-Scientifique Internationale and heretofore available only in Morse code over naval station NAA in Arlington, Virginia and two stations in France. The W1XAL broadcasts used simplified English in order to make them useful to a wide international audience. The URSI-grams were on 11790 kc. at 1655–1700 EST. A 15-minute weekly summary was broadcast on Mondays at 2030 on 6040 kc.[107]

President Roosevelt's inauguration in January was a major shortwave event. All the major American shortwave stations carried it, including **W2XE, W3XAU, W3XAL, W8XK,** and **W2XAD** and **W2XAF**, and there was much foreign-language coverage. W2XAD and W2XAF were on the air for over 60 hours non-stop.

The internationalist actions of the private broadcasters were in part a response to the Roosevelt administration's support of the proposed construction of a government shortwave broadcasting station that would more effectively counter the growing volume of propaganda broadcasts from overseas. Private American shortwave broadcasting was no match for the government-sponsored efforts of Germany, Italy and Japan. The government was especially concerned about Axis broadcasts to South America, where Germany had the economic capability to harm American economic interests. In addition, pockets of ethnic Germans in Argentina, Brazil and Chile were thought to represent a possible source of political influence and subversion. German-language broadcasts in particular were well heard and widely promoted in the local press, which sometimes used the German news broadcasts as an alternative to expensive wire services. In Brazil, both Germany and Italy provided Portuguese-language programs for occasional use during the daily hour during which all Brazilian stations carried the same government-produced program. A significant broadcasting capability to Central and South America would also serve Roosevelt's good neighbor policy. Combating Axis broadcasting to Latin America would remain a major American goal until Pearl Harbor changed the nation's priorities.[108]

Between 1937 and 1939, several bills to establish a government shortwave station were introduced in Congress. Among the proposed transmitter sites were California, Florida, Texas, and the Canal Zone. None of the bills was successful, due in large part to the opposition of the private broadcasters, and the press (otherwise no friend of radio in those days). Both were intent on keeping the government out of the information-dissemination business, as were many members of Congress.[109] However, the bills did result in greater government interest in shortwave broadcasting and increased scrutiny of the private shortwave broadcasters, as did Roosevelt's appointment in February 1938 of an Interdepartmental Committee to Study International Broadcasting. These activities heightened broadcaster sensitivity about program content and about better serving a broader public interest in the shortwave arena. There was a step up in their efforts to transform what had largely been a collection of experimental appendages to the domestic broadcasting business into a more coherent international service — in short, to match results with the industry's public service rhetoric.[110]

This more focused international broadcasting effort by the major American shortwave stations provided a vehicle for addressing some of their acknowledged weaknesses. At a time when England, Germany, Italy and Japan were increasing transmitter power and honing their international broadcasting skills, the United States had a shortwave service of limited capability. As one observer noted, in comparison to these other stations "the American efforts in international broadcasting seem puny indeed."[111] Rather than an integrated service, it was a collection of private efforts, each grounded in a culture of experimentation rather than content development. Equipment was not always well maintained, leading to transmissions of poor technical quality — carrier hums, undermodulation, overmodulation, etc. Scheduling and frequency usage was often haphazard, and because stations could not carry advertising they had little commercial incentive. Station operators were reluctant to admit this, however, out of fear of the introduction of government broadcasting and its potential to spill over into domestic radio. The result was a new commitment to showing that, whatever the problems of the past, the private shortwave broadcasters were now "up to the job." As GE's Assistant Manager of Broadcasting put it, in addition to the opportunity for scientific development,

> we consider [operating shortwave stations] to be a medium of good will between the various people of the world, and we feel that if the various peoples of the world understand each other better they should be able to live more peaceably, and further, that if our country has peaceful and friendly relations with other nations it will prosper, and that if it prospers and our company carries out its functions properly it also will prosper.[112]

On the plus side, one of the strongest arrows in the private broadcasting quiver was the news. Whether broadcast in English or other languages, American stations were respected for their unbiased news.

On the apex broadcasting front, new apex stations included, on 26.1 mc., **W9XJL**, Superior, Wisconsin (relaying WEBC); on 31.6, **W4XBW**, Chattanooga, Tennessee (relaying WDOD), and **W5XAU**, Oklahoma City (relaying WKY); on 35.6, **W3XES**, Baltimore (WCAO); and alternatively on both 35.6 and 41.0, **W9XOK**, St. Louis. W6XKG in Los Angeles on 25950 kc. went to 24 hour operation. And **W9XAZ**, Milwaukee, on 26.4 mc., separated its programming from parent station WTMJ. It was the first ultra-high station to do so. **W8XWJ**, Detroit, now on 41.0 mc., soon followed suit.[113]

On February 11, CFRB, the Toronto mediumwave station of the Rogers Radio Broadcasting Company, opened a shortwave outlet, **CFRX**, "The Rogers Short-Wave Station," on 6070 kc. It simulcast the programming of CFRB (including a five-minute program of NNRC DX tips at Friday midnight). In October a new station of the Canadian Marconi Company in Sydney, Nova Scotia began testing on 6010 kc. It was 1 kw. **CJCX**, simulcasting CJCB.

Besides CFRX and CJCX, the Canadian shortwave lineup was now as follows: **CFCX**, Montreal, 6005 kc.; **VE9DN**, Drummondville, also on 6005 (it was used for the Saturday night "Northern Messenger" program, together with CJRO, CJRX, CRCX and W8XK); **VE9CA**, Calgary, 6030; **VE9CS**, Vancouver, 6070; **CRCX**, Bowmanville, 6090; **VE9HX**, Halifax, 6130; **CJRO**, Winnipeg, 6150; and **CJRX**, Winnipeg, 11720 kc.

Readying the Northern Messenger

[Communications] for transmission are first attacked with a blue-pencil, all superfluous remarks being deleted, until the message has been pared down to the allowed four lines, or as near to it as possible. As time is short, and "the show must go on," many are the split second decisions to be made, such as: which should be left in — a breathless announcement that "Baby John is sprouting a new tooth"? or the news that "Sister Mary has the Mumps"? However, the heavy volume of letters to be handled does demand that messages be ruthlessly edited.

* * *

After the letters have been sorted and edited they are whisked to the stenography department where the flying fingers of a battery of typists neatly transfer each message on a separate sheet of paper. The typing is double spaced and letters are capitalized so that the announcer may read with a minimum of difficulty.

The messages, thus prepared, are then filed alphabetically and on Saturday afternoon they are delivered to CBO, the [CBC] studios in Ottawa, where they are counted off in batches of thirty. They are studied by the announcers who familiarize themselves with the contents and with the sometimes difficult place names, of which "Kugaryuak" is a sample. Three announcers, besides Mr. [Sydney S.] Brown [director of the service], participate in the broadcast, each one reading thirty messages before being relieved.

"The Northern Messenger"
February 1938[114]

In March, the Loyalist government of Spain opened a sister station to **EAQ**. At first called **EAQ No. 2**, it was renamed **EAR**, **Voice of Republican Spain** (also announcing as **La Voz de Libertad**, **La Voz de Madrid**, and **La Voz de España**). EAQ's main channel was 9860 kc., while EAR's was 9480. Among other things, EAR was used for external broadcasting in English, transmitting to Britain at 1350 EST on 7130 kc. and 1640 on 9480, and to North America at 1930 and 2040 on 9480. It carried accounts of the civil war by American and Canadian press correspondents, and programs such as "Union Today, Freedom Tomorrow." Questions were answered over the air on Tuesday night. *("Write and tell us how you have been receiving our program. Write and ask us questions about any aspect of the Spanish situation. Address your questions and your letters to Broadcasting Service, Station EAR, Madrid, Spain.")* EAR's 20 kw. signal was very strong in the United States.

The radio scene in Spain continued to change almost daily. Additional Loyalist stations utilizing shortwave included **EAJ1, Union Radio**, Barcelona, 7194 kc., operated by the socialist-communist trade union, Unión General de Trabajadores; **ECN1**, 6990, operated by the anarchist union, Confederación Nacional del Trabajo, Barcelona; **ECP2, "Radio POUM,"** 7143, station of Partido Obrero de Unificación Marxista, or the United Marxist Workers Party; and **PSU1**, 7128, operated by Partit Socialista Unifacat de Cataluña, or the Catalan United Socialist Party, Barcelona. There were many others on mediumwave. Call letters of both Loyalist and rebel stations were often unofficial, reflecting the name of the group that was operating the station. Happily for DXers, it was not unusual for stations on both sides of the war to QSL listener reports.[115]

The main insurgent, or Nationalist, shortwave voice, **EAJ43** in the Canary Islands, now had four daily transmissions on 10370 kc.: 1400–1600 EST, 1745–1900, 1920–1955 (English for North America), and 2000–2145 (Spanish for Central and South America). The first two programs included news in Spanish, Russian, Italian, German, English, French and Portuguese.

«LA VOZ DE ESPAÑA REPUBLICANA»

THE VOICE OF REPUBLICAIN SPAIN — FOREIGN BROADCASTING SERVICE

MADRID — CALLE MEDINACELI, 2

QSL   28th of March 1938.

We confirm your reception of «The Voice of Republicain Spain», Madrid.

Call letters E. A. R. Broadcasting on February 7th 1938
at 7:30p.m. DST 9:30 a.m. WL 31.65 m KHZ 9.480 Power 20Kw

Many thanks for your report. We hope you continue to listen in to our programmes and that you find them interesting. We would be glad to hear from you again.

Yours sincerely,

F. Alberg

(OVER)

Loyalist station EAR broadcast special English-language programs to the United Kingdom and North America.

Many other stations operated on behalf of the insurgents. **Radio Requeté** was the major rebel domestic network. Among its outlets were **EAJ8, Radio Requeté**, Bilboa, 7260 kc.; **Radio Requeté de Guipuzcoa**, San Sebastian, 7203; **Radio Requeté**, Malaga, 7099; and **Radio Requeté**, Santander, on 14060. Also reported were **EARR**, an "official" rebel station near Madrid on 14500 kc.; **EDR4**, Majorca, Balearic Islands, 6480; **FET1**, Valladolid, 7025; and many other "FET" outlets. (Some rebel stations that claimed to be in Spain were believed to be broadcasting from Italy.) War news was also broadcast by insurgent ham stations that made no secret of their amateur status. **EA8AE, EA8AK, EA8AS** and **EA8AT**, all in the Canaries, broadcast news on 20 and 40 meters, as did **EA9BJ** in Spanish Morocco.

As time went on, the number of insurgent stations identifying as "Radio Nacional" increased. By the end of 1937, the existence of **Radio Nacional de España (RNE)** was formalized and the broadcasting situation stabilized somewhat for the balance of the war. At the time, RNE headquarters was in Salamanca.

One of the year's great shortwave mysteries was an anti–Fascist clandestine station, seemingly belonging to the German Communist Party and broadcasting hour-long programs in various languages, including German, Italian and French, on many frequencies, e.g. 7320, 9450, 9830, 10070 kc. It began operation in January. Frequencies changed often to avoid the relatively unagile jamming. (*"Listeners of the Freedom Station, take notice. In two minutes time this station will shift from the present broadcasting wave to one of 30.1 meters; five minutes later we go to 30.8, then to 29.8. Follow us."*)

The station carried news from a communist perspective, mainly about Spain but also about conditions in Germany and Germany's support of the Fascist rebels. It opened and closed with the playing of the Internationale. In the U.S. it put in a good signal in German

English translation of an address read at the microphone by the chairman of Radio Club Tenerife to listeners abroad who have written to us since we began our short wave broadcasts.

If we are grateful in normal times for all expressions of sympathy with our country or for praise of its institutions and organisations, how much more grateful and touched shall we not be when such marks of affection and admiration reach us in history-making days of patriotic enthusiasm and expectancy such as we are living now.

We have recently received nearly a thousand letters from listeners in England, Ireland, Germany, Italy, Portugal, France, Belgium, Austria, Morocco, South Africa, the Philipines, Japan, China, the Continent of America and Australasia. All these letters are full of sympaty with our dear Spain and of admiration for our great chief, General Franco, as well as for our valiant army. They encourage us in our fright for the nation's cause against sovietic terror and barbarity. They contain enthusiastic commendation of the intense and all-important work which this Radio Club Tenerife is carrying on. They are written in terms of such sincerity, such genuine feelingi that I frankly confess to you, dear listeners abroad, that many of your letters have profoundly touched us; our hearts have beaten faster with gratitude and our aspiratiens have been fulfilled. We are proud to know and to feel that, over five continents, there are thousands—nay, millons of right—minded people of all nationalties, of conscientious citizens. of men of honour, who understand the meaning of the word "country" and who are in intimate spiritual union with us, the true Spaniards, and who, from their far-way homes, stretch out their hands to greet us while they send us words of affection, encouragement and high—minded patriotism.

Top: This is part of a message sent to listeners of EAJ43, Radio Club Tenerife, in 1937. A key part of Franco's international broadcasting effort, the Canary Islands station was well heard in the United States. *Bottom:* EA9AH, a combined amateur-broadcast operation located in Spanish Morocco, was one of the best-heard Nationalist (Franco) stations during the Spanish Civil War. It was also a good verifier.

at 1600–1700 on 10065 kc. Reports addressed to "any communist party in the world" were invited.[116] *("Here speaks an illegal broadcasting station in Germany of the German Communist Party.... We will broadcast again tomorrow night punctually at 10 despite the Gestapo, and if this station should be traced and ourselves captured all arrangements have been made for a broadcast to be made from another station.")*

Eventually the station was found to be announcing as **Deutscher Freiheitsender** ("German Freedom Station"). There was wide speculation as to its location; France, Germany, Holland, Italy, Czechoslovakia, Spain and Russia all were candidates. In fact it appears that the programs were prepared by German communist members of the international brigades supporting the Loyalists, and by the exiled Italian Communist Party, and transmitted over the high power radiotelephone facilities of the Loyalist Spanish government (including the transmitters at Aranjuez, which also carried the **EAQ** programs).[117] The Deutscher Freiheitsender operated for at least two years. However, "Deutscher Freiheitsender" was a name that would attach to various clandestine stations well into World War II, and as time went on the exact provenance of whichever "Freiheitsender" was being heard was less and less determinable.

In nearby Portugal, the government station, **CSW, Emissora Nacional**, was expanding and was now operating on three frequencies: 22000 kc. at 1100–1600 EST, 11050 at 1600–1800 (beamed to the Portuguese colonies in Africa), and 9940 at 1800–2100 (to Brazil). The programming was taken from the station's 629 kc. mediumwave outlet. By year's end the power was increased from 5 to 10 kw. Emissora Nacional would be underfunded for decades; the power increase was made possible by the station itself through savings from within its budget. **CT1AA, Radio Colonial**, also in Portugal, became **CS2WA. Radio Club Português** left shortwave. And in January a new station was heard from Portugal. It was **CS2WD, Radio Renascença,** "Emissora Catolica Portuguesa," a 200-watt Catholic station on 5997 kc. It operated daily on both mediumwave and shortwave at 1430–1630 and Thursday and Sunday at 0600–0700. Later it increased power and moved to 9690 kc.

In December, **Vatican Radio** increased power to 50 kw. The **BBC** station at **Daventry** was also upgraded. A new transmitter building was opened and two new 50 kw. transmitters were brought into service. More would be added. During this period the aerial system at Daventry was also expanded to include some 25 new antennas.

The coronation of King George VI, who succeeded his brother Edward VIII, took place on May 12. In addition to the **Daventry** senders, many of the radiotelephone transmitters at **Rugby** were put into service for this very big radio event. It was estimated that, with rebroadcasts and with the help of the excellent atmospheric conditions that prevailed at the time, the worldwide audience for the seven-hour broadcast was 300 million. "The King's broadcast message to his people at 3 P.M., New York time, was preceded by a dramatic radio roll-call of the British Empire, with London calling far across the world to invite representatives of the colonies to broadcast greetings of loyalty and devotion to the crown. From London the Ministers of the various dominions pledged their allegiance."[118]

2RO, the **EIAR** station at Prato Smeraldo, Italy, was now broadcasting as follows: to the Mediterranean area at 0820–0900 EST; to the Near and Far East at 0900–1030; to North America at 1800–1820; to Latin America at 1820–1845; to Italian East Africa at 2320–0020; and to Turkey at 0050–0100. News in Italian was included in most transmissions, together with news in other languages appropriate to the target area. The "Arabian Hour" was presented at 0030–0050. The "American Hour" in English was also still on the air, at 1700 EST. 2RO also carried relays of Italian domestic stations at 0643–0820 and 1405–1730, and an hour of 20-minute foreign-language news bulletins (German, English, French) at 1300–1400. An abbreviated schedule was used on Sundays. 2RO utilized 11810 kc. until 1230 EST, 9635 thereafter.

Some of the programs, including the hour of foreign-language news, the Mediterranean broadcast and the "Arabian Hour," were also carried on Italian mediumwave stations.

Radio Prague commenced broadcasts in Spanish, Portuguese, Italian and Serbian, with occasional programs in other languages as well. Its broadcasts were now beamed to Europe, the Americas, and the Far East. "OLR" operated on just one channel at a time. Frequencies changed from day to day, and there were many to choose from: 6010 kc. (**OLR2A**), 6030 (**OLR2B**), 6115 (**OLR2C**), 9500 (**OLR3B**), 9550 (**OLR3A**), 11760 (**OLR4B**), 11840 (**OLR4A**), 11875 (**OLR4C**), 11900 (**OLR4D**), 15160 (**OLR5C**), 15230 (**OLR5A**), 15320 (**OLR5B**), and 21450 (**OLR6A**). Reception in the United States was very good.

Denmark was now broadcasting from a new transmitter at Skamlebaek. After some initial tests on both 9520 and 11805 kc., **Statsradiofonien**, using the call letters **OZF**, adopted 9520 as its regular channel. The power was 6 kw. (*"This is the Danish shortwave transmitter operating on 11805 kc. This is a test transmission to North America."*) Usually the station carried the programs of the Copenhagen or Kalundborg mediumwave stations. However, special broadcasts were also beamed to South America and the Far East at 2000–2130 EST, and to North America and Greenland (a Danish possession) at 2130–2300. Soon tests were also heard on 15160 kc. (**OZH**) and 17750 (**OZI**).

Sweden's **SM5SX** was joined by a new government shortwave transmitter, **Motala Rundsradiostation**, at Motala. It was on 11705 kc. (**SBP**) until 1330 EST, then 6060 (**SBO**). Later, SBT on SM5SX's channel, 15155 kc., was also heard, although the two stations were separate. The power of this PTT-operated station (which was usually referred to generically as **SBG**) was 12 kw., and it relayed the Stockholm broadcast band program.

PCJ began regular shortwave broadcasting in 1927, one of the first stations on shortwave. Philips innovation in shortwave broadcasting continued for years. This QSL depicts the one-of-a-kind rotatable antenna system installed at Huizen in 1937.

PCJ was often heard on 9590 and 15220 kc., and Eddie Startz was still the station's main personality.[119] During the year a new antenna system was erected that consisted of two unique 60 meter-tall wooden towers that were placed on tracks so they could be rotated and the signals beamed in any direction.[120] PCJ also established a system of regular signal monitors in various countries.

Starting in January, the monthly program of **Schweizerische Rundspruch-Gesellschaft** in Switzerland became weekly. It was transmitted on Saturday night at 1900–2040 EST over the same two frequencies as before, 7797 and 9595 kc., with one channel beamed to North America, the other to South America. In two European low-power developments, **Radio Wien**, Austria, long on 6072 kc., moved to 25 meters, 11801 kc. The power was now 1.5 kw., and the tuning signal was a fast-ticking metronome. And **SPW**, Poland, was now using an additional

QRA: POLSKIE RADIO · WARSAW · 5 MAZOWIECKA St

SPW

POLAND

THIS CONFIRMS YOUR REPORT RECEIVED ON..........193.

SCHEDULES

QRG: 13635 KC   POWER 10 KW

TNX   QSL   73's

Although it would soon become part of the Reich broadcasting network, in 1938 Polskie Radio was a reliable, independent shortwave voice, its modest 10 kw. signal heard regularly in the United States.

transmitter—**SPD** on 11535 kc. The power was only 2 kw., but the signal reached America during the North American beam at 1800–1900 EST (Sundays to 2000), parallel to **SPW** (10 kw.) on 13635 kc. Two further channels were opened in 1938, **SP19**, 15175 kc., and **SP25**, 11775; and two more 5 kw. transmitters were added in 1939, **SP31**, 9525, and **SP48**, 6140.

Africa was grudging in yielding intelligible signals to North American DXers, but things were improving. As the year began, **VQ7LO**, Nairobi, Kenya, made some mid-afternoon appearances on its frequency of 6085 kc. Closedown was early, generally at 1500 EST, but in time to give east coast listeners a small opening for reception. In North Africa, **TPZ, Poste Algerien**, the Algerian PTT station, carried some French-language news and music programming on 12120 kc. around 1530–1630 EST (the channel was more often used for scrambled radiotelephone transmissions).

CR7AA in Mozambique had put a higher frequency channel in use, **CR7BH**, 11718 kc., to supplement its main 6137 kc. frequency. The schedule was weekdays at 2345–0045 EST, 0930–1100 and 1245–1545, Sundays 0530–0700, 1030–1230 and 1330–1530. CR7AA used 600 watts. CR7BH, with 250 watts, was now being heard in North America. *("This is Lourenço Marques, CR7AA, calling on 6137 kc., 48.88 meters, and CR7BH, testing on 25.60 meters, 11718 kc.")* CR6AA in Lobito, Angola, which had increased power from 500 to 750 watts (and would soon increase again to 2 kw.), was still on 7177 kc., with occasional tests on 9660. Soon it would add 7614 kc.; but it was rarely heard. (CR6AA would become **Radio Clube de Lobito.**) Likewise **FIQA, Radio Tananarive**, Madagascar. Its frequency varied between 5980 and 6020 kc. The station was also searching for a higher band frequency and tried various 25 and 31 meter band channels. Eventually it settled on 6010 and 9530 kc.

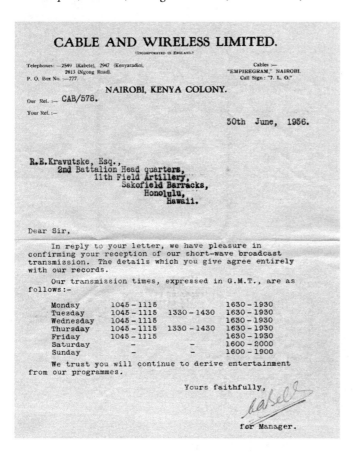

Rarely heard in the United States, Kenya, which was active from the early 1930s, boasted one of the first shortwave stations on the air in Africa. A lion's roar identified VQ7LO.

South Africa expanded its shortwave operations. The African Broadcasting Company Ltd. had given way to the **South African Broadcasting Corporation.** The SABC operated from four different locations as follows: ZRH, Roberts Heights (near Pretoria), was on 6007 kc. at 1000–1600 EST and 9523 kc. at 2345–0730 with 5 kw.; ZRK, Klipheuvel (near Capetown) was on 6097.5 kc. at 1200–1600 and 9606 at 2345–1145, also with 5 kw.; ZRJ, Maraisburg (near Johannesburg), was also on 6097.5 kc., at 2345–1130 EST with 200 watts; and ZRD, Durban, was on 6150 kc. at 2345–0730 and 0900–1545 EST with 10 watts. ZRK, Klipheuvel on 9606 kc. at 2345 was the best heard in the U.S. Bugle blasts were sounded at sign on and sign off, and were followed until midnight by physical exercises directed by a man accompanied on the piano. As one observer noted, "[h]itherto only a 'rare catch,' South Africa is now definitely on the short-wave 'map' and soon the bells of Cape Town or Johannesburg should ring out familiarly for the midnight short-wave listener in America."[121]

Serving the nearby British protectorate of Bechuanaland, ZNB, at Mafeking, was operating on 5900 kc., 250 watts, at 0200–0300, 0900–1000 and 1300–1400 EST. Mainly a police radiotelephone station, it was a tempting DX target when operating in broadcast mode. The station became very popular, and soon the SABC was providing programming for it. *("This is ZNB, Mafeking.")* Although Mafeking was located across the border in South Africa, it was

The SABC, based in Johannesburg, used a single QSL-card for all reports, but gave the call letters and specific location of the particular station being verified.

Bechuanaland's capital until replaced by Gaborone, located inside Bechuanaland, in 1965, the year before the territory gained independence as Botswana.[122]

Radio activity in Asia paralleled the increasingly dangerous military situation there. Following the Mukden Incident in 1931, where a section of Japanese railway in Manchuria was destroyed (with the connivance of Japanese militarists), Japan had occupied south and central Manchuria. The following year it installed a puppet government, and soon thereafter it declared the area the "independent" state of Manchukuo. There had been numerous skirmishes between China and Japan on the Chinese mainland in the years since, leading to full scale war in 1937. By year's end, the Japanese controlled both Shanghai and Nanking, and Chiang Kai-shek and the Nationalist government, to which most of the Chinese warlords had pledged allegiance, had retreated to the country's interior. The ether was full of the ubiquitous Chinese radiotelephone "X" stations, e.g. **XTR, XBX, XTF, XTJ**, etc., and often they carried broadcast programming. The Nanking shortwave relay of broadcaster **XGOA** switched from **XGOX** on 6820 kc. to **XGRX** on 9590, but then disappeared altogether.[123] XGOA moved to the new Nationalist capital, Chungking, but Japan continued to use the call letters for the Nanking station in hopes of keeping its listeners.

In July, **JDY**, the radiotelephone station of the **Manchurian Telephone & Telegraph Company** in Dairen, the main port of the Kwantung Leased Territory in Manchukuo, began carrying broadcast programming. It transmitted in Japanese, Manchu, and English daily at 0700–0800 EST on 9925 kc. *("Hello, dear friends, this is Dairen calling.")* At first JDY relayed the programming of mediumwave station JQAK, but soon it was producing its own programs, identifying as the **Voice of Manchukuo.** JDY operated with 10 kw. Its stated purpose

Mediumwave station JQAK, Dairen, Manchuria, was the source of the early programming for JDY, the Manchurian Telephone and Telegraph Company, which soon took the name Voice of Manchukuo.

was "to inform the whole world of the righteous standpoint of Japan and the progress of the China incident, against the incorrect and malignant 'propaganda' broadcast by China."[124]

In Japan proper, the **International Wireless Telephone Company** increased the power of its "JZ" (broadcast) shortwave frequencies to 50 kw. (*"This is the International Wireless Company of Japan calling."*) With improved reception from Japan, listeners in the United States were advised that they could send their reports to the Consul General of Japan, 500 Fifth Avenue, which would cable them to Japan. In Japanese-ruled Taiwan, the programming of mediumwave station **JFAK** in Taihoku (Taipei) was being heard on 6640 and 9625 kc. at 0400–1030 EST. English news was presented during the final 20 minutes. Around 0900, Taihoku radiotelephone channel **JIB**, 10535 kc., joined the relay.

In India, **VU7MC**, originally an amateur station, was said to be transmitting broadcast material on 6085 kc. from the Mysore Palace in Mysore, southern India. Broadcasting was also underway in "Indian" Burma. Burma had been a province of India since 1886. While it would not gain independence from Britain until 1948, in April 1937 it became a separately administered territory. In May, some lucky DXers began hearing broadcast signals from **Mingaladon Radio**. This was a government radiotelegraph station in the town of the same name, used for communication with India. As an experiment, the 1.5 kw. transmitter was put to work broadcasting news and music on 6010 kc. when it was available.

Elsewhere in the Far East, **KZRM**, **Radio Manila**, the Philippines, was back on shortwave. The frequencies were 9570 and 11840 kc., used alternately, and the power was 1 kw. KZRM operated at 1650–1800 and 0500–0900 EST (Sundays 0400–1000). It was owned by a well-known department store, Erlanger & Galinger, Inc. In the Dutch East Indies, **YDB**, Soerabaya, 9550 kc., and Bandoeng channels **YDC**, 15150, **PLP**, 11000, and **PMN**, 10260, all carried the same program at 0530–1000 (weekends to 1100 or 1130). And **RV15** in Khabarovsk, 4273 kc., broadcast in English at 0400 EST on even days of the month. (*"Hello everybody! Station RV15 on the air, broadcasting from Khabarovsk in the Far Eastern region of the U.S.S.R."*)

Shortwave broadcasting continued to be at its most expansive in Central and South America. It was estimated that there were some 150 shortwave stations in Latin America, a figure that was, if anything, low. The quality of programming seemed inversely proportional to the level of shortwave activity. The highest quality programming was from Argentina and Brazil, large countries with big populations but doing limited shortwave

```
                                          Engineer In-charge,
                              Office of the ████████████.
                              Mingaladon Radio,
                                          11th October, 1937.

Mr. William Sparks,
2258 Thirtieth (30th) Avenue,
San Francisco, Calif., U.S.A.

Dear Mr. Sparks,
          Many thanks for your letter of the 31.8.1937. I
confirm (from your report) that you heard this station on the
morning of the 31st August 1937.
          We are merely experimenting at present, using in
its free moments our very up-to-date 1½ K.W. Beam Telephony /
Telegraphy Marconi Transmitter which is installed for commercial
speech between Burma and India.  It is difficult, if not imposs-
-ible, to determine a wavelength that will give satisfactory
broadcast reception in all parts of Burma, and it is unlikely that
any official broadcasting will be established in Burma until this
and other requirements are met.

                              Yours faithfully,

                              William J. Byrne.
                              Engineer-in-charge,
                              Government Radio Station
                              Mingaladon (Burma).
```

Mingaladon Radio was a small station in Burma that operated for a brief time in 1937. The substitution of "Burma" for "India" in the embossed seal at the top reflects the division of the two territories which had occurred six months earlier.

broadcasting. Elsewhere, shortwave programming necessarily followed whatever was the standard on mediumwave, for shortwave stations usually simulcast a parent mediumwave station with the goal of extending its reach to larger swaths of territory, often mountainous and not susceptible of optimal mediumwave coverage. In addition, vanity, both national and personal, played no small part in the growth of Latin American shortwave broadcasting.

To those more oriented to the culture of the large European shortwave broadcasters, it was a damnable state of affairs.

[T]he great majority of the programs now being broadcast are of such low intrinsic worth that they would better not be heard at all. And even when the program is of some interest, the advertising is so voluminous and so rapidly and apathetically read that the listener is overwhelmingly tempted to turn to another station. No broadcaster should be permitted to interrupt a presentation of, say, Tschaikowsky's "Caprice Italien" every three minutes with 5 to 10 announcements of patent medicines. Yet this "custom" is all too religiously followed.[125]

That was the view of the professionals. To DXers, it was all part of the novelty and excitement of shortwave.

The increase of Latin American shortwave broadcasting was breathtaking. Stations increased their power, and countless new voices took to the air. In Mexico, **XEWW, La Voz de la America Latina**, on shortwave since 1931 (6025 kc.), began using two 10 kw. HF channels, 9500 and 15150 kc. New stations included, in Mexico City, **XEJW, La Voz del Aguila**

Azteca, 6110 kc. (relaying XEPW); **XEUZ, Cadena Radio Nacional**, 6120 kc., 5 kw., relaying mediumwave XEFO; and **XEYU, Universidad Nacional**, 9600 kc. with 500 watts.

Mexican stations were hardly confined to the capital, however. In Vera Cruz there was **XEAW** on 8630 kc.; in Guadalajara, **XEBF**, 6090, **XECU**, 6075 (45 watts), and **XEWB, Radio Cultural**, on 11710 kc. Shortwave from Mazatlan included **XEBM, El Pregonero del Pacifico**, relaying XEBL on Sundays on 15440 kc. with 50 watts, and **XEBQ, La Voz del Pacifico**, a 50-watt station on 6030 kc. Hermosillo had **XEBR**, owned by the newspaper Heraldo de Sonora and relaying mediumwave XEBH with a 150-watt signal on 11820 kc. In Monterey there was **XETA** on 11760, 1 kw., relaying XET; **XETW, La Voz de Tampico**, 11730 kc., was in Tampico; and Villahermosa had **XETM** on 11525.

There was no less activity farther south. El Salvador came on shortwave in the form of a government relay of its mediumwave station YSS. YSD operated on 7894 kc., YSH on 9520, and YSM on 11710. The frequencies were used at different hours, and all were 500 watts. New in Panama City were **HP5H, Radiodifusora Panamericana**, on 6050 kc., and **HP5I, La Voz del Interior**, which commenced broadcasting on 11895. Following soon from the town of David was **HP5L, Las Ondas del Baru**, 350 watts on 11740. And in Costa Rica, **TI2RS, Radioemisora Athenea**, San Jose, came on the air on 6880 kc. (later 7445).

In Guatemala, **TGWA**, the "Voice of Guatemala," increased power to 5 kw. and began using international frequencies—9685, 11760, 15170 and 17800 kc. A special program in Spanish and English for North America was broadcast twice a week at 2100–2300 EST. Also in Guatemala, **TG2, Radio Morse**, a station of the government's Dirección General de Comunicaciones Eléctricas, Guatemala City, was heard. It was on 6300 kc. with 300 watts, relaying mediumwave TG1 (1510). And new in Nicaragua was **YNPR, Radioemisora Pilot**, Managua, 500 watts on 8650 kc. (the owner was a Pilot Radio dealer), and 50-watt **YNGU, "Alma Nica,"** Managua, on 9300 kc.

If you were diligent you used the 15-minute window between 1930 and 1945 EST on Monday, Tuesday, Thursday or Saturday to log **ZIK2**, the new government broadcast station in Belize, British Honduras. It was on 10600 kc. and used 250 watts.

In Cuba, **CO9WR**, 6280 kc., became **COHB**, relaying CMHB. There were many new stations now on the air, nearly all from Havana. These included **COBC, El Progreso Cubano**, 9310 kc. (relaying CMBC); **COBZ, Radio Salas**, 1.5 kw. on 9030 (relaying CMBZ); **COBX, Radio Alvarez**, 9200 kc., 500 watts (relaying CMBX); **COCA**, 9100 kc. ("We Would Like to C-U-B-A Constant Listener of Ours"), relaying CMCA and signing off with "Indian Love Call"; **COCM, Transradio Columbia**, 1 kw. on 9775 kc. and other 31 meter channels (relaying CMCM); and **COCW, La Voz de las Antillas**, 6324 kc. From Matanzas there was 1 kw. **COGF, Ecos del Valle del Yumuri**, 11790 kc., relaying mediumwave CMGF; and from Camaguey, 2 kw. **COJK, Radio Zenith**, 8665 kc., relaying CMJK. Frank H. Jones, owner of historic Cuban mediumwave station 6KW in Tuinucu, did some government-sponsored testing on shortwave under the call **CO9XX**. The frequency was 15550 kc. and the power 2 kw. And an oft-heard weather station in Cuba was **CLX, Observatorio Nacional**, Havana, on 6990. It broadcast weather reports daily at 1900.

There were now 20 shortwave broadcast stations in the Dominican Republic. A new one in Ciudad Trujillo was **HI7P, Emisora "Diario del Comercio"** (a newspaper), on 6800 kc. **HI5G** was in Concepción de la Vega and broadcast on 9500 kc. **HI5N** on 6160 kc. was now **La Voz de Moca**, in Moca. And HIX, the mediumwave station on 800 kc., had expanded to three shortwave outlets: **HI1X**, 6340 kc., 900 watts; **HI2X**, 11960, 300 watts; and **HI3X**, 15260, also 300 watts.

Elsewhere in the Caribbean, **Radio CUROM**, operated by **Curaçaosche Radio Vereenig-**

ing, Willemstad, Curacao, took to the air on March 1 over **PJC1**, 5930 kc., 150 watts. It broadcast daily at 1830–2030 and on Sundays at 1030–1230, and soon added a second channel, **PJC2**, on 9090 kc. Also new on shortwave was the French island of Martinique. There were two 31 meter band stations there — a short-lived **Radio Fort-de-France** on 9450 kc., which soon went to mediumwave only, and the longer-lasting **Radio Martinique**, also in Fort-de-France, on various 31 meter channels, eventually settling around 9680 kc. It was heard at 1900–2100 in French, with English announcements at sign off. The power was 200 watts.

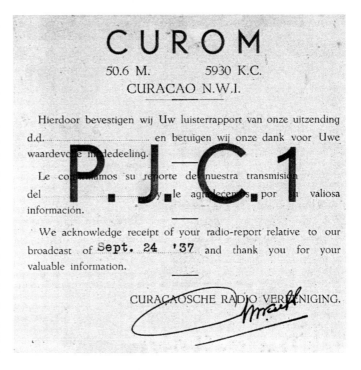

By the time Radio CUROM made a few appearances on shortwave in 1960 and 1970 as a program source for a utility station, it had been long forgotten that the station was on the air via its own shortwave transmitter in the late 1930s and early 1940s.

Things were finally slowing down in Colombia. **HJ2ABD**, **Radio Bucaramanga**, was now **HJ7ABD**, on 9630 kc. **HJ3ABD**, by then known as **Emisora Nueva Granada**, Bogota, moved its 1 kw. transmitter from 6050 to 4841 kc.; and **HJ3ABH, La Voz de la Victor**, also in Bogota, moved from 6012 to 4980. There was little new activity in the country in 1937. However, with roughly 22 shortwave stations already on the air, Colombia remained the leader in South American shortwave broadcasting. Its stations were the first to abandon the hugely overcrowded 49 meter band for frequencies in what would eventually be the home of countless Latin American stations, the then-empty 60 meter tropical band. (The tropical bands would be formally recognized at the 1938 Cairo International Telecommunication Conferences.)

The big, and confusing, news from Venezuela was that the government had created new radio districts and all shortwave stations got new call signs. The known changes were as follows:

New Call	Old Call	
YV1RB	YV5RMO	Ecos del Zulia, Maracaibo
YV1RD	YV7RMO	Radiodifusora Maracaibo
YV1RG	YV4RG	Radio Valera
YV1RH	YV1RH	Ondas del Lago, Maracaibo
YV2RN	YV10RSC	La Voz del Tachira, San Cristóbal
YV3RB	YV8RB	La Voz de Lara, Barquisimeto
YV4RB	YV6RV	La Voz de Carabobo, Valencia
YV4RD	YV12RM	La Voz de Aragua, Maracay
YV4RH	YV15RV	Radio Valencia
YV5RC	YV2RC	Radio Caracas
YV5RM	YV3BC	Radiodifusora Venezuela, Caracas

New Call	Old Call	
YV5RF	YV4RC	Ecos del Avila, Caracas
YV5RH	YV9RC	Ondas Populares, Caracas
YV5RP	YV5RP	La Voz de la Philco, Caracas
YV6RB	YV11RB	Ecos del Orinoco, Ciudad Bolivar

In addition, four new stations were heard: **YV1RI, Radio Coro**, 150 watts on 6210 kc.; **YV1RL, Radio Popular**, Maracaibo, on 5930; **YV5RJ, La Voz de la Esfera**, Caracas, 6255, owned by the newspaper Diario de Esfera and operating with 1 kw.; and **YV6RC, Radio Bolivar**, Ciudad Bolivar, on 6320 kc.

In November and December, DXers were able to hear signals from **VP3THE** (*"Two Homesick Explorers"*), the Terry-Holden Expedition to British Guiana, which was sponsored by the American Museum of Natural History. The station usually operated around 13470 kc. using a 200-watt base camp transmitter (it also had a 50-watt mobile unit). In addition to ham contacts, VP3THE could be heard communicating with British Guiana broadcasters **VP3MR** and **VP3BG** and sending occasional broadcast programs to NBC via the RCA receiving station in Riverhead, Long Island. VP3THE was in operation until January 15, 1938.[126] It was reported that, "[a]s the other members of the expedition are already far afield, the [base camp] radio operator is left to find his own company, which, aside from the Indians, he says, consists of two monkeys and a parrot, while bats, lizards and rattlesnakes abound just outside his door."[127]

Except for Peru, the Andean countries were slower to board the shortwave bandwagon. In Bolivia, a new 400-watt station, **CP1, Radio Chuquisaca**, Sucre, was said to be operating, first on 6220 kc., then on 9895, but it was not heard in North America. Ecuador brought forth **HC1CE, Emisora "El Condor,"** Quito, which operated Thursday evenings only on 7411 kc., and **HC2ODA, La Voz del Alma**, Guayaquil, on 9445. HCJB was expanding. On shortwave it was operating as follows: on 4107 kc. at 0745–0830, 1130–1430 and 1700–1900 EST, and on a varying frequency around 8948 kc. at 1900–2200. The power was 250 watts on 4107 kc., 1 kw. on 8948. The station was often heard contacting amateurs under the call **HC1JB**.

The shortwave situation in Peru was becoming clearer, and the number of stations was growing. The main station was the Peruvian government station, **Radio Nacional del Peru**, Lima, which transmitted on two channels, **OAX4T**, 9562 kc., and **OAX4Z**, 6082 kc., both 10 kw. Broadcasting was inaugurated at Radio Nacional on January 30, 1937. The other shortwave stations in Lima were: **OAX4D, La Voz del Peru** (relaying **Radio Dusa, Difusora Universal**), 5780 kc., 3.5 kw.; **OAX4G, Radio Grellaud** (the owner's name), 6230 kc., 400 watts; **OAX4J, Radio Internacional**, announcing 9520 kc. but actually heard on 9340 (200 watts); **OAX4K, Radio Colcochea** (the owner's name), 6425 (later 9715), 200 watts; and **OAX5C, Radio Universal**, 9580 kc., 100 watts.

Shortwave was also being introduced outside the capital. On the air from other Peruvian towns were **OAX1B, Radio Delcar**, "La Voz de Chiclayo" (relaying OAX1A mediumwave), 6150 kc., 200 watts; and **OAX4M, Radio Record**, Huacho, on approximately 10345 kc., 150 watts. Unlike the Brazilian shortwave scene of future decades, that country was slow to embrace shortwave broadcasting. However, channels of the Rio de Janeiro commercial station **Companhia Radio Internacional do Brazil**, now known as **Radio Bras**, were still heard with broadcast programming, now often from mediumwaver PRF4, Radio Jornal do Brasil, Rio. The frequencies included **PSH** on 10220 kc.; **PPM**, 10310; **PPQ**, 11670; **PSE**, 14935; and **PPU**, 19960. An English program was presented at 1900 EST. (*"Nobody should ignore that Brazil's coffee is the world's best coffee? ... Why not spend your vacation in Rio de Janeiro?"*)

The number of stations in Chile was also small. A new station, owned by a ham who operated a radio shop, was **CB615, Radio Service**. It was located in Santiago and used 1 kw. Although the call letters reflected a frequency of 6150 kc., the channel commonly heard was 12300 kc., seemingly an intentionally-generated harmonic. Also operating in Chile were **CB1170, Emisoras Otto Becker**, Santiago, on 11710 kc., relaying the station's mediumwave channel over a 1 kw. shortwave transmitter; and **CB1190, Radio Sur**,

CHILE

C B 960 RADIO "LA AMERICANA"
CIA. DE SEGUROS DE VIDA (ORGANIZACION KAPPES)
SALUDA ATENTAMENTE AL SEÑOR
R. F. Young
Y AGRADECE SU COMUNICADO DE RECEPCIÓN DE FECHA
22 de mayo de 1939.

Frecuencia: 9,600 KC. 31.25 metros.
Potencia: 1,250 Watts.
Transmite: Diariamente 12.30 - 14.00.
Noche: 19.30 - 23.30 (Hora chilena).
CASILLA 13155 - SANTIAGO DE CHILE.

Radio "La Americana" in Chile signed off nightly at 2300 EST, "until the next experimental program." The station had taken over the 9600 kc. channel of Radio Difusora "Pilot" in December 1938 and was testing a new antenna with a north-south beam.

Valdivia, "Voz de Valdivia para todo Chile y America," 11900 kc., which carried the station's mediumwave program (CD69). Reception of Radio Sur was best on Sundays when code QRM was not too heavy.

In Uruguay, the shortwave stations took their programming from nearby Argentine broadcasters. **CXA2, Radio Continental**, Montevideo, on 6005 kc., had a power of 5 kw. and mainly relayed Argentine station LS2, Radio Prieto, in Buenos Aires. Another station, **CXA8, Radio Real de San Carlos**, 9640 kc., in Colonia (soon changed to **CXA14**, 15170), took its programming from LR3, Radio Belgrano, also in Buenos Aires. The power of CXA8 was 2.5 kw. In nearby Paraguay there was but one shortwave station operating, **ZP14, Radio Cultura**, "La Voz del Corazón en Sudamérica," Villarica, on 6040 kc. Later the station would be moved to Asuncion where it operated on 11721 as **ZPA2, Radiodifusora de la Teleco Paraguaya**. It relayed mediumwave station ZP4, Radio Nacional, and was well received in the evening.

Shortwave listeners were used to hearing Australia. The three broadcast stations in operation were: **VK2ME**, Sydney, on the air Sundays at 0000–0200, 0430–0930 and 1130–1330 on 9590 kc.; **VK3ME**, Melbourne, 9510 kc., weekdays at 0400–0700; and **VK3LR**, Lyndhurst (near Melbourne), now operated by the Australian Broadcasting Commission, transmitting at 0300–0800 EST Sunday through Friday, and from 2200 on Friday to 0830 on Saturday, on 9580. (*"3LR, the Australian national shortwave station."*)

Now there was a new AWA "ME" station. Commencement of planned broadcasts from Western Australia over **VK6ME**, Perth, had been delayed when the planned new transmitter was diverted to the AWA station in Fiji. Broadcasts from VK6ME finally began on March 22, 1937. The station was on 9590 kc. (the same frequency as VK2ME) using a 5 kw. transmitter that usually operated at 2 kw. It was heard Monday, Wednesday and Friday at 0600–0730 EST. (*"Good morning, good afternoon, good evening. This is station VK6ME, the Perth shortwave station of Amalgamated Wireless [Australasia] Ltd., operating on a wavelength of 31.28 meters, corresponding to 9590 kc. The time is … . VK6ME will be pleased to receive reports on its transmission from listeners in all parts of the world. When reporting, please mention some of the pro-*

gram items heard. Comments on signal strength and fading would also be appreciated. Kindly address your reports to station VK6ME, Amalgamated Wireless [Australasia] Ltd., Perth, Western Australia.")

Two non-broadcast stations could also be heard from down under. The Flying Doctor Service, then known as the **Australian Aerial Medical Service**, was on the air via its Port Hedland transmitter, **VK8SC**, on 6960 kc., 200 watts. (*"VK8SC, the broadcasting station of the Australian Aerial Medical Service in Port Hedland, Australia. Please let us know how reception is."*) And many DXers heard the stately liner TSS [Turbine Steam Ship] *Awatea*, owned by New Zealand's Union Steamship Company. It sailed between Australia and New Zealand and up the North American west coast. Though the ship's transmitter, **ZMBJ**, was mainly a communications setup, it did some broadcasting as well, calling itself "The Ears and Voice of the Tasman Sea." The best-heard frequency was 8840 kc. and the power was 400 watts. (*"Good morning, good night, and aloha"*). The broadcasting ended when the *Awatea* went into military service in 1941.

Another interesting shortwave event was the U.S. Navy-National Geographic Society Solar Eclipse Expedition which set sail for Enderbury Island, 1,800 miles south of Honolulu, to monitor the solar eclipse which took place on June 8. It was the longest total eclipse of the sun in 1,200 years. Transmissions originated from a 25-watt transmitter on the island, **W10XEP**, whose antenna was kept aloft with kites. Its signal, which was in the 30–40 mc. range, was picked up by the navy minesweeper USS *Avocet*, anchored off shore, and the ship's 1 kw. transmitter, **WMEF**, relayed the signal to the RCA stations at Kahuku, Hawaii and Bolinas, California and on to the NBC radio network. Eight NBC broadcasts were scheduled to originate from the expedition. WMEF used 8655, 12862.5 and 17310 kc.

Radio featured in the July 2 disappearance of Amelia Earhart on the near-final leg of her round-the-world flight. Her signal on 3105 kc. was heard loud and clear aboard the USCGC *Itasca* which was standing by, awaiting her arrival at speck-in-the-ocean Howland Island. She was unable to receive essential navigation instructions from the *Itasca*, however, for, unbeknownst to her, the main receiving aerial on her plane had been lost on takeoff at Lae in Papua New Guinea. While the exact circumstances surrounding her disappearance have never been established, a recent near-forensic examination of the relevant radio traffic and the last leg of the flight suggests that confusion over times, frequencies and equipment capabilities on the plane and aboard the *Itasca*, plus Amelia's limited experience with radio, were major contributing factors.[128]

During the search there were many reports of transmissions possibly originating from the plane. Some were from those involved in the search, others from people far afield, but all proved inconclusive (some were clearly hoaxes). Almost 35 years after the event, Betty Klenck, who was 15-years old and living in St. Petersburg, Florida in 1937, produced a notebook containing what she said were handwritten notes she had made while listening to a purported distress call from Amelia on the family's shortwave console (believed to be a Zenith 1000Z "Stratosphere").[129]

Clubs continued to arrange special broadcasts. The NNRC had six shortwave specials, the International Shortwave Club about a dozen. The ISWC celebrated its eighth anniversary with a contest that offered a world globe for the best report on each of eight specified transmissions from various stations. The International DXers Alliance also arranged about a dozen special programs, plus special transmissions from hams in Holland, Morocco and Reunion. The Reunion broadcast was from Nguyen Vinh San, **FR8VX**, the former Emperor of Vietnam, who had been exiled to Reunion in 1916. (The broadcast was repeated in 1938.) An IDA ham member also arranged a special "Trip Through Algeria" program that was broadcast on mediumwave over **Radio Alger** and on shortwave via the Algerian PTT and the French broadcasting plant at Pontoise, France.

More stations, both large and small, had programs where they greeted listeners, read letters and answered questions. **W2XAD** and **W2XAF** presented "Short Wave Mailbag" on Tuesdays at 1835 EST. **W1XAL** had "Listeners Mailbag" on Friday at 1815 EST and "European Post Box" at 1545 EST on Saturday. The **BBC** featured "Empire Mailbag" on Wednesday at 2100 EST. A few DX programs were appearing as well, including "Radio Round the Clock" on Monday at 1530 EST over **W1XK**. It covered times and frequencies of foreign stations, broadcasts of interest, SWL literature, etc.

All-wave receivers were becoming easier to use. Some manufacturers equipped their receivers with "automatic tuning," a rotary telephone dial or a push-button arrangement that permitted the user to return directly to frequencies that he had pre-set (or that the dealer had pre-set for him). On some high-end units, a few companies (Philco, Sparton, Stromberg-Carlson) coupled this mechanical approach with "automatic frequency control" (AFC), which locked onto the signal electronically and fine tuned it without operator intervention. (Philco called this "Magnetic Tuning.") But serious shortwave listeners still preferred the communications receiver.[130]

The year ended with another marathon shortwave broadcast from **W2XAD** and **W2XAF**, which celebrated the New Year by staying on the air for 40 hours straight.

1938

Shortwave broadcasting was an important topic at the 1938 Cairo International Telecommunications Conferences. Effective September 1, 1939, four of the seven shortwave broadcast bands were expanded, and a new band, 7200–7300 kc., was added for broadcasting outside the Americas.

Old band	New band	Change
6000–6150	6000–6200	added 50 kc.
none	7200–7300	new band (outside N. & S. America only)
9500–9600	9500–9700	added 100 kc.
11700–11900	11700–11900	no change
15100–15350	15100–15350	no change
17750–17800	17750–17850	added 50 kc.
21450–21550	21450–21750	added 200 kc.
25600–26600	25600–26600	no change

Cairo also created special bands for the use, concurrently with fixed and mobile services, of stations located in the tropical regions of Asia, the Pacific, Africa and the Americas. The new bands were: 60 meters, 4770–4965 kc.; 90 meters, 3300–3500 kc.; and 120 meters, 2300–2500 kc. These channels became known as the tropical bands.[131]

Following Cairo, the FCC authorized ten new frequencies for U.S. international broadcasting: 6170, 6190, 9650, 9670, 17830, 21570, 21590, 21610, 21630 and 21650 kc. That five of the 10 channels were in the underused 13 meter band reflected at least in part the FCC's continued interest in higher frequency broadcasting.

The expansion of targeted foreign-language broadcasting among the U.S. shortwave broadcasters continued. NBC daily fare for Europe over stations **W3XAL** and **W3XL** consisted of five hours of English and an hour each of French, German and Italian. The broadcasts to South America were in Spanish and Portuguese. Times devoted to each language continued to expand. Programming consisted mainly of news bulletins in the relevant languages and rebroadcasts of American network programs with foreign-language announcements replacing English. However, there were also some special programs intended only for foreign listeners. A huge jump in listener response was reported, from 157 letters in May 1938 to 3,425 in March 1939.[132]

This same general pattern was followed in the European and South American beams of General Electric stations **W2XAD** and **W2XAF** and CBS stations **W2XE** and **W3XAU**. At GE, the 10-person international staff produced Spanish and Portuguese programs that were transmitted to South America simultaneously on different frequencies. At CBS, in addition to its expanded European and South American broadcasting, W2XE experimented with directional transmissions to Egypt for the rebroadcast of CBS programs there. Like W2XE, sister CBS station W3XAU installed directional antennas for Europe and South America. Expansion of the CBS international staff to nine persons meant more shortwave-specific programming, particularly for South America.

W9XF, the NBC station in Downers Grove, Illinois, closed down. **W4XB** moved from Miami Beach to Miami, and while it was not one of the major shortwavers, it also added some Spanish programming—news at 1345 EST. Although W4XB was supposed to broadcast at 1300–1500 and 2100–2400 EST, frequently it was off the air.

Starting in May, NBC, GE, CBS and Westinghouse adopted a joint plan of operation in order to maximize their impact in their target areas. With its superior content-development capability, NBC became an important program provider for the other three companies. The staff of the NBC international division, located in New York City, grew quickly. In addition to announcers, translators and secretarial staff, there were section chiefs for each language, plus separate directors for music, talks, and production, plus a traffic supervisor — 38 employees altogether.[133]

Speeches by various dignitaries were translated into other languages and broadcast worldwide on the four international networks, with the RCA and AT&T point-to-point shortwave facilities often pressed into service as well. (They were also used to bring foreign programs to the U.S.)[134] Although one might think that the heightened tensions in Europe would have made it the prime target for U.S. shortwave broadcasting, Latin America remained the higher priority.[135]

Notwithstanding these efforts at improved programming by the big corporate shortwavers, World Wide Broadcasting Foundation station **W1XAL**, with its educational and cultural orientation, offered the best on-air material. It transmitted daily programs in Spanish, French, Portuguese and Greek, plus newscasts in several other languages. Classroom lectures were regular fare. They were recorded in order to allow retransmission at times convenient for listeners, and transcriptions of many programs intended for Latin America were sent direct to local stations for rebroadcast. Full courses were offered on many topics, including basic English. W1XAL also broadcast a popular weekly course on radio theory and repair. Written materials were made available,[136] and a course on television was added in 1939. As one observer noted, "[t]he type of material sent out [from W1XAL] is of a much higher caliber than that which the average commercial broadcast station would send out."[137]

An event worth noting in connection with shortwave broadcasting to Latin America was the inauguration of the so-called Pan American frequencies. Five shortwave channels had been registered by the navy with the International Telecommunication Union during the years after 1929. These were 6120, 9550, 11730, 15130 and 21500 kc. Although the United States placed the channels at the disposal of the Pan American Union, which nominally encouraged countries to make use of them for the purpose of broadcasting inter-American programs, they went almost entirely unused. In 1936 the Pan American Union revisited the issue and voted to begin a Pan American Radio Hour. The FCC assigned the 6120 kc. channel to CBS (**W2XE**), 9550 and 21500 to GE (**W2XAD**), and 11730 and 15130 to the World Wide Broadcasting Foundation (**W1XAL**), which had already been broadcasting some Pan American Union recorded programs. No channels were assigned to NBC for the stated reason that its programming would have largely duplicated that of CBS. The first broadcast took place on February 15, 1938 over W1XAL. W2XAD also put the channels to early use (1930–2400 on 9550, 0800–1200 on 21550).[138]

All of these shortwave efforts were noted approvingly by the Interdepartmental Committee to Study International Broadcasting, which was established by President Roosevelt in 1938 and reported to him the following year. Overall, however, the Committee concluded that while commercial American shortwave broadcasting was less propaganda-oriented than that of the other major countries, it was well behind them both in targeted program content and transmission capability.[139] Early in 1938, *The New York Times,* which often listed the schedules of major shortwave stations audible in the United States, showed the European and Asian transmissions as follows (times in EST):[140]

Berlin:		
DJL	15.11 MC.	8:00–9:00 A.M.
DJB	15.20	4:50–10:45 P.M.
DJD	11.77	4:50–10:45 P.M.
DJC	6.20	4:50–10:45 P.M.
London:		
GSD	11.75	3:00–5:25 A.M.
GSD	11.75	9:12 A.M.–6:00 P.M.
GSD	11.75	8:57–11:00 P.M.
GSC	9.58	4:15–8:30 P.M.
GSC	9.58	8:57–11:00 P.M.
GSB	9.51	3:00–5:25 A.M.
GSB	9.51	12:17–8:30 P.M.
GSB	9.51	8:57–11:00 P.M.
GSL	6.11	6:17–8:30 P.M.
GSL	6.11	8:57–11:00 P.M.
Paris:		
TPA-2	15.24	6:00–11:00 A.M.
TPA-3	11.88	2:00–5:00 A.M.
TPA-3	11.88	12:15–6:00 P.M.
TPA-4	11.72	6:15–8:15 P.M.
TPA-4	11.72	10:00 P.M.–1:00 A.M.
Rome:		
2RO	11.80	6:00 A.M.–12:20 P.M.
2RO	9.63	12:30–9:00 P.M.
Tokyo:		
JZJ	11.8	12:30–1:30 A.M.
JZJ	11.8	3:00–4:00 P.M.
JZJ	11.8	4:30–5:30 P.M.
JZI	9.53	3:00–4:00 P.M.
JZI	9.53	4:30–5:30 P.M.

On the apex scene, there were now over 40 stations in operation. Most used 100 watts, but some more. Among the more powerful of the newcomers were, at 1 kw., **W9XUP**, St. Paul,

Minnesota, on 25950 kc. (relaying KSTP); at 500 watts, W1XER, Boston (WNAC), and W1XKB, Springfield, Massachusetts (WBZA), both licensed to operate on 31.6, 35.6, 38.6 or 41.0 mc.; and, with 200 watts (later 1 kw.), W8XNU, Cincinnati (WLW), on 25950 kc. W6XRE, Los Angeles, was a 1 kw. station relaying KGFJ, but on channels far beyond the common definition of shortwave — 88, 120, 240 and 500 mc. A Thursday-night program of DX tips, "The SWL Chatterbox," was presented over Detroit apex station W8XWJ. Starting in November, W2XJI, ultra-high sister station of WOR in New York City, began carrying a special 15-minute program for the NNRC on Tuesdays at 2000 and Fridays at midnight. It was arranged by WOR chief engineer and longtime NNRC patron Jack R. Poppele. The frequency was 26.3 mc., the power 100 watts. The high frequencies were getting more industry attention. *All-Wave Radio* started a column called "Ultra-High," and RME came out with its 510X "Frequency Expander," which could extend the range of most superhet receivers up to 70 mc.

In Canada, VE9HX, Halifax, Nova Scotia, which relayed CHNS, officially became CHNX. The frequency was 6130 kc., where the station would remain for over 60 years. And CRCX, 6090 kc., originally on the air as VE9GW, closed down.

In March, Hitler annexed Austria and occupied the country. Soon the Austrian station became Reichssender Wien, and the call letters of the Austrian frequencies 6072 and 11801 kc., which had been OER2 and OER3, were changed to DJY and DJZ. Austrian broadcasts now consisted of relays from German mediumwave stations, and transmissions closed with the playing of "Deutschland Über Alles." In October, Hitler moved into the Sudetenland, thereafter occupying the rest of Czechoslovakia (with Hungary and Poland sharing in the spoils). Radio Prague would now have a reduced presence on the shortwave bands. (A two-hour North American Service survived — ten minutes of news and the rest music, on 11840 kc., 15230 in the summer.) At some times its programs would originate from Prague, at others the Prague frequencies would join the German network. In March 1939, as Germany expanded its takeover of Czechoslovakia, a knowledgeable observer noted: "After the German occupation of Bohemia, Prague continued its short-wave broadcasts. But they are not the same now. One misses the informal talks about toys and dollmaking and the folk tunes and dances. Heavy music and stilted talk are substituted."[141]

The BBC foray into foreign-language broadcasting began modestly on January 3 with a daily news broadcast in Arabic at 1715–1820 GMT over GSC, 9580 kc. This was followed on March 14 by back-to-back 15-minute news bulletins in Spanish and Portuguese for the Americas at 0130–0200 GMT over GSB, 9510. There were announcements in the three languages during some other programs as well. The immediate cause of the decision to begin transmitting in some foreign languages was pressure from the Foreign Office to counter Italy's increasingly strident Arabic broadcasts over the Bari mediumwave transmitters, which were relayed on shortwave, and the considerable scope of the foreign-language service already on the air from Germany. The Spanish and Portuguese broadcasts were mainly a fig leaf to create the impression that the Arabic transmissions were part of a larger undertaking.

The Arabic service expanded fairly quickly, Spanish and Portuguese more slowly, although local stations in Latin America picked up and rebroadcast the Spanish and Portuguese news bulletins, giving them added reach. On September 27, with the Munich Conference two days away and the European conflict on the verge of expansion, the BBC was asked to broadcast French, German and Italian translations of a speech that Prime Minister Chamberlain was to give to the nation that very night. The BBC scrambled to find the translators. This was the crash start of BBC news bulletins in these three languages, which thereafter were put on the air at 1400–1500 EST (Sundays 1300–1345). Additional English news broadcasts in the Empire Service were also added as political and military circumstances dictated.

Reprising its ambivalence over getting into shortwave in the first place, the BBC (and to some extent the British government itself) was conflicted over the matter of foreign-language broadcasting. All who were involved were feeling their way. There were questions of resources, and the seemingly inevitable conflict with the BBC's until-then principal mission of serving the English-speaking empire. In addition, there was the concern that "propaganda" broadcasting would tarnish the BBC's reputation for truth and objectivity. Said one official: "We will not deviate from impartial reports. We believe the best propaganda, if one wishes to call it that, will result only if listeners in South America feel they can tune in London for accurate, impartial news. Once news is suspected of being tampered with or modified, it loses at least half of its effect."[142] The BBC was also fearful of losing its operational independence. On the other hand, foreign-language broadcasting could lead to an expansion of the BBC's role, and it would eliminate the possibility of the government undertaking a separate short-wave broadcasting effort outside the BBC's control.

Consideration had been given to using mediumwave stations in Jerusalem or Cyprus for the BBC Arabic transmissions, but there were shortcomings to both locations, and shortwave from **Daventry** would be more cost effective and cover the largest area. The wisdom of this decision in the short term seems open to question, for it was mediumwave to which **Radio Bari's** listeners tuned most often, shortwave being used mainly by the elite. From a long-term perspective, however, shortwave provided the foundation for a worldwide foreign-language service, a concept which the BBC soon embraced, and which was probably inevitable. By the time war broke out in September 1939, the BBC was broadcasting in nine languages. Two and a half years later the number was 45.[143]

An early if small entry in what would become a fierce clandestine radio war between the Allies and the Axis was the anti–German **Sender der Deutschen Feiheitspartei**, or German Freedom Party Radio. The party was founded in England and France by a group of German exiles of various stripes, and for three months in early 1938 transmitted two daily half-hour programs from a 1913-vintage, British-registered fishing boat, the *Faithful Friend*, which was located outside French territorial waters circa the northern ports of Dieppe and Cherbourg. The frequency was 7843 kc. (the station was also reported heard around 10070). It appears that the funding for the station came from Britain.[144]

Meanwhile, **Zeesen** was using a variety of methods to attract listeners. It offered prizes to listeners who sent in the best photos of themselves listening to the German broadcasts. It also offered a German-language course built around the subject of broadcasting. A text, *Kleines Deutsches Rundfunk — ABC of Broadcasting for Listeners of the German Shortwave Station*, was available by mail. The station also offered an informative monthly program booklet for listeners (replaced by a single sheet in 1939). One on-air Zeesen tactic that was used to capture listeners was to broadcast a powerful signal near the channel of another station using the same language, so the listener might inadvertently find himself listening to Germany's transmission rather than, say, the BBC.[145]

2RO at Prato Smeraldo, Italy, upgraded its transmitters. As of October 31, senders of both 50 and 100 kw. were available, together with a variety of directional antennas, giving Italy one of Europe's most powerful shortwave capabilities.[146] 2RO transmissions, including the "American Hour," now at 1815–1945 EST, were also increasingly being relayed over Italian commercial transmitters, e.g. **IRF**, 9830 kc., **IQY**, 11676, etc.

In April, to supplement its shortwave station at **Pontoise**, France opened a second transmitter base, this one at **Essarts-le-Roi**.[147] Its power was 25 kw. and its call letters were **TPB** (**TPB1**, **TPB2**, etc.). Transmissions from both sites thereafter identified first as **Paris Ondes Courtes**, then as **Paris Mondial**, rather than **Radio Coloniale**. The schedule was: 0100–0300

EST to the East Mediterranean and North Africa on 9570 (Essarts) and to Africa, the Near East and Australasia on 11885 (Pontoise); 0830–1000 to Indochina on 17780 (Essarts) and at 0500–1000 on 15243 (Pontoise); 1015–1700 to the East Mediterranean and North Africa on 9570 (Essarts) and to Africa and South America on 11885 (Pointoise); 1800–2015 to South America on 15130 (Essarts) and to the Americas on 11714 (Pontoise); and 2030–2300 to North America on 11885 (Essarts) and to North and Central America on 11714 (Pontoise). On the North American beam there was English news at 2200 and German news at 2245. As one DX editor put it, "The new French station is making quite a name for itself with the phenomenally strong signals it is putting across the Atlantic."

In June, the Grand Duchy of Luxembourg, a country of 1,000 square miles located at the intersection of Belgium, France and Germany, came on shortwave. French-controlled, commercial **Radio Luxembourg**, already on longwave with 200 kw., would now be heard in English, French, German and Spanish on 11782 kc. in the late afternoon and evening in America, also announcing 6090, 9527 and 15350 kc. The British government arranged for the station to carry German translations of important official statements surrounding the Munich Crisis in September 1938, with the aim of giving local radio listeners in Germany the truth (and contributing to increased unrest).[148] It is not known if these broadcasts were carried on shortwave. (The BBC was historically opposed to commercial broadcasting. However, its active opposition to Radio Luxembourg had been dropped, at least officially, at the start of 1938.)

In February 1938, the headquarters of the Spanish insurgent **Radio Nacional de España** was transferred from Salamanca to Burgos. Its programs were relayed by EAJ43 in the Canary Islands on 10370 kc.—the main shortwave frequency on which RNE was heard in North America—and later on 7500. The station was in operation practically all day, with relays to Europe at 1500–1630 and 1700–1900, to South America at 1945–2045, and to North America (in English) at 2100–2200. (*"Hello United States, Canada and all English speaking people. This is Radio Club Tenerife, EAJ43. We broadcast every day from 1 to 2 A.M. GMT on 40 meters, 7500 kc."*)

The other shortwave stations that comprised the heart of the RNE network were: **Radio Nacional "AZ,"** 6750 kc., and **Radio España**, 7060 kc., operating at 0500–1900 EST; FET1, Valladolid, 7006 kc., 0700–1800; **EAJ8, Radio Requeté** (later **Radio España**), San Sebastian, 7203, 0330–1700; **Radio España**, Bilbao, 7246, 0300–1800; FET5, Burgos, 7350, 0845–1600; **RR6, Radio Requeté**, Vitoria, 11991 kc.; and **Radio Malaga**, which operated on 7220 and 14440 kc. While broadcasting mainly in Spanish, at various times these stations also carried news in English, French, German, Italian and Portuguese. Numerous other Spanish stations came and went.

Radio Nations in Geneva was now broadcasting Sundays at 1045–1130 EST on 18480 kc. (**HBH**), 1345–1430 on 6675 (**HBQ**) and 14535 (**HBJ**), 1900–1945 on 11402 (**HBO**), 0200–0215 on 11402, and 0230–0245 on 14535. A North American program was also broadcast on Mondays at 1845–2030 on 14535. Also on the air from Switzerland was **Schweizerische Telegraph Verwaltung**, Berne, operated by the Director General of Posts and Telegraph. It was heard testing at 1300–1400 EST on 9535 kc., 1845–1945 on 15365, and 2000–2100 on 11865 kc. The power was 300 watts. Multi-lingual IDs were heard every 15 minutes, and reports were requested.

Norway was still broadcasting from **LKJ1**, Jeløy, usually heard on 9530 kc. at 0500–0800 and 6130 at 1130–1700. Both were 1 kw. Following some testing at the end of 1937, Finland officially came on shortwave. The 1 kw. transmitter of the **Finnish Broadcasting Corp. (Oy Suomen Yleisradio Ab)** at Lahti was carrying home service programs on one of three fre-

This station in Malaga, Spain, broadcast in support of Franco from 0900 to 1000 and from 1530 to 1740 EST on 7220, and from 1745 to 1930 on 14440 kc. The power was 700 watts.

quencies: 9500 kc. (**OFD**), 11780 (**OFE**), and 15190 (**OFB**). The times were 0100–0145, 0500–0630 and 1000–1700 EST (0145–1700 Sundays). The Finnish programs were also carried over a 200-watt transmitter in Helsinki on 6120 kc. By the end of the year the power of the Lahti station had been increased to 10 kw. Soon the call on 15190 was changed to **OIE**, and two new channels added, **OIH**, 17800 kc., and **OII**, 21550. (*"This is Finland, land of 1,000 lakes."*)

CSW, **Emissora Nacional**, Lisbon, Portugal was now broadcasting in Portuguese to North and South America nightly at 1800–2100 on 9735 kc., plus English on Fridays at 2000–2100. One of the station's most popular programs was the half-hour "Meia Hora da Saudade," where those with relatives in other countries were invited to come to the studio and send them greetings over the air.

Several new stations opened in Africa. In Angola, **CR6RC, Radio Clube de Angola**, a 100-watt station in Luanda, operated four to six hours daily on 11790 kc. Soon it increased power to 250 watts and also opened transmission on 14630 kc. (**CR6RS**). There had been occasional music broadcasts from the radiotelegraph station in Leopoldville, the Belgian Congo. However, it was not until 1938 that the first dedicated shortwave broadcaster commenced operation. It was **OQ2AA, Radio Leo**, also in Leopoldville, a station operated by two Jesuit priests. It had 25 watts of power (increased to 250 watts in 1939) and was on the air Sundays and holidays only, and at times not compatible with propagation to the U.S.— 0535–0700 EST on 6140 kc. In later years Radio Leo would be home to Belgium's **OTC**.

Starting in May, there was a new voice from Ethiopia. **Radio Addis Ababa**, operated by the Office of Press and Propaganda of Italian East Africa, presented news in several languages at 1300–1400 EST on 9000 and 9525 kc. Ethiopia was still under Italian rule (and would

The Finnish Short Wave Broadcasting Transmitter at Lahti, Suomi (Finland)

Geogr. loc. 25° 39′ E, 60° 59′ N

Mr. August Balbi

We acknowledge with thanks Your report on our short wave transmissions. It checks well with our own log and we would be pleased to receive further reports from You of the audibility of our other wavelengths. They are:

31,58 m — 9500 kc
25,47 m — 11780 kc
19,75 m — 15190 kc

Our short wave transmitter is daily on the air and usually relays the regular Finnish Broadcasting Programmes.

Lahti 20.9.38

sign.

Oy. Suomen Yleisradio Ab.
Lahden Yleisradioasema
Lahti, Suomi (Finland)

The 1 kW transmitter You have heard. The two crystal controlled exciters corresponding to two wavelengths are on both sides of the high level modulated power amplifier.

Soon after this QSL was issued late in 1938, the Lahti, Finland, station increased power from 1 kw. to 10 kw.

remain so until 1941). From the same neighborhood, **Radio Mogadiscio** in Italian Somaliland was said to be broadcasting on Sundays at 0830–0930 EST on 8875 kc. And from Tripoli, Libya, also an Italian colony, radiotelegraph station **IQN** occasionally relayed the EIAR programs from Rome over a 5 kw. transmitter on 9460 kc.

Another country that commenced shortwave broadcasting at this time was Turkey. The 20 kw. shortwave station of the **Turkish Broadcasting System** in Ankara began experimental transmissions on 9465 kc. (**TAP**) at 2330–0500 EST and 15195 (**TAQ**) at 0530–0700. Programs were in Turkish, English, French and German. A mailbag program was presented on Saturdays at 0320. (*"This is Ankara calling, transmitting the Turkish National Program."*)

In Southeast Asia, Hanoi was back on the air in the form of **Radio Hanoi**, which was operated by Radio Club d'Indochine, Hanoi. It started on 7440 kc., then moved to 9510 and 11900, and broadcast at 0000–0200 and 0600–1000 EST. The transmitters were of 15 and 100 watts. Also on the air was 15-watt **Radio Hai Phong**. The Hai Phong station closed in 1938, the Hanoi channels in 1939. Neither of these stations was heard in the U.S.

ZHI, Singapore, had left the air on December 31, 1936. The next month, mediumwave tests on 1333 kc. commenced from **ZHL**, the station of the newly-licensed **British Malaya Broadcasting Corporation Ltd.** (**BMBC**), Singapore. Regular broadcasting from this 2 kw. station was inaugurated in March 1937. Notwithstanding the expense of receiver license fees, radio was very popular in the Malayan states. ZHL greatly expanded its coverage area when it began operating on shortwave in July 1938. The frequencies were 6012 kc. (**ZHO**) and 9530 (**ZHP**, later 9690), and the power was 400 watts. (*"This is the Singapore station broadcasting on 31.48 meters, 9.53 mc. per second."*) Soon thereafter, **ZGE** in Kuala Lumpur closed down.

The Penang station, **ZHJ**, remained on the air. The BMBC's Thomson Road address would appear on the QSLs of British Malayan stations (British Far Eastern Broadcasting Service, BBC Far Eastern Station) for decades.

The **Indian Broadcasting Service** had become **All India Radio** in 1936. (*"This is All India Radio calling you from Delhi."*) Except for the English-language and external service broadcasts, it would be known as *Akashvani*, "the voice from the sky." In 1938 it adopted a plan for the use of shortwave in order to supplement mediumwave with a nationwide service. During the year, in addition to mediumwave transmitters, 10 kw. shortwave stations were built in Bombay (**VUB**), Calcutta (**VUC**), and Madras (**VUM**), while 5 and 10 kw. units were installed in Delhi (**VUD**).[149] India, together with Colombia, was an early user of the new 60 meter band for nighttime transmissions: VUC, 4880 kc.; VUB, 4905; VUM, 4950; and VUD, 4995. Daytime transmissions were in the 31 meter band, and there was a Delhi channel on 15160 kc. In the U.S., one of the best-heard AIR transmissions was

This 1936 QSL verifies reception in England of CSW, Emissora Nacional, Lisbon, Portugal, on 9550 kc., 5 kw.

VUD, Delhi, opening on 9590 kc. at 2030 EST with eight clock chimes.

Commercial station **XTJ**, Hankow, on 11691 kc., in addition to its radiotelegraph transmissions, carried some broadcast programming, including news in English at 0000–0030 EST and in French, German, Japanese and Chinese at 0700–0730. It was well heard on the west coast. Another radiotelephone channel, **XGX**, operating around 9290 kc., relayed **XGOW**, a powerful Hankow government mediumwave station. The XTJ transmissions continued to be heard even after the Japanese entered the city on October 25, so its exact location, at least at that time, was uncertain. Later it moved to the interior, and the Hankow station came under Japanese control as **XOJD**.

Also newly heard, and under Chinese control, was **XPSA**, the **Kweichow Broadcasting Station** in Kweiyang, China. It operated on 6970 kc. at 1800–1930, 0100–0200 and 0800–1010 EST. English news was at 0900. (*"This is XPSA, the Kweiyang Broadcasting Station, Kweichow Province, China, operating on 43 meters."*)

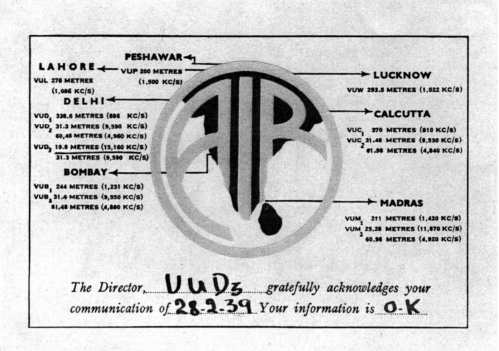

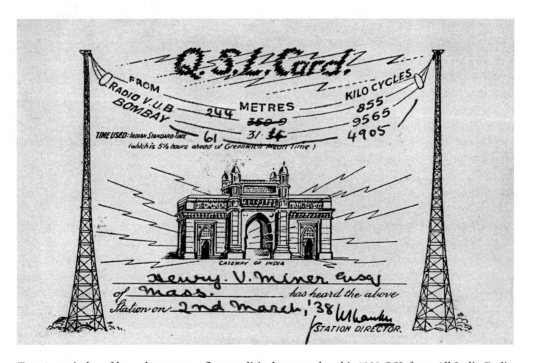

Top: A reminder of how shortwave reflects political geography, this 1939 QSL from All India Radio shows stations in Lahore and Peshawar, cities that would become part of Pakistan when it separated from India in 1947. *Bottom:* The call letters of the Indian stations reflected their locations. VUB was Bombay, VUC Calcutta, VUD Delhi, VUM Madras.

From Java, the best-heard channels, in roughly the order of signal quality, were: **PLP**, Bando-eng, 11000; **PMH**, Bandoeng, 6720; **YDB**, Soerabaya, 9610 and 15300; **PMN**, Bandoeng, 10260; and **YDC**, Bandoeng, 15150, all 1.5 kw. except YDB, which was 1 kw. Some stations in the Dutch East Indies were also appearing on lower frequencies. **YDX**, Medan, Sumatra, was on 5170 kc. with the same program as on the high frequency channels. And from Java, **YDA**, Bandoeng, was on 3990, and **YDE2**, Solo, was on 4820.

It was the year that Pitcairn Island, of Fletcher Christian and "Mutiny on the Bounty" fame, entered the shortwave conscious-ness. The existence of tiny station "**PITC**," first discovered in 1930, was confirmed by ham operator Alan Eurich, W8IGQ, who met Pitcairn operator Andrew Young when Eurich went ashore in January 1937 during a world cruise of the *Yankee* schooner. Young was found to be operating intermit-tently on 500 kc. using a low

CHINA INFORMATION COMMITTEE

Hankow, China
October 17, 1938

Mr. Roger Legge, Jr.
20 Beethoven Street
Binghamton, N. Y.
U. S. A.

Dear Mr. Legge:

This is to confirm your reception of our radio programme brought to you through the short-wave transmitter XTJ in the city of Hankow, operating on 25.66 meters or 11691 kilocycles.

Our programme, "The Voice of China," comes on the air twice daily — 1 o'clock in the afternoon and 8 o'clock in the evening (Central China Time). We give you war news and feature stories in different languages.

XTJ is the only Chinese broadcasting station which can be heard by listeners abroad. We sincerely hope that you will again tune in our programme and give us further report on your reception conditions.

With regards,

Very truly yours,

H. P. Tseng
Chairman

The date on this QSL from XTJ, Hankow, a radiotelephone sta-tion that operated as the "Voice of China," was eight days before the Japanese entered the city.

power, battery-powered spark transmitter which had been brought to the island years before, and a crystal receiver (with which Young was able to hear KFI, Los Angeles). The absence of a steady supply of gasoline made generator charging of the battery impossible, and the sta-tion was off the air for long periods while the battery was sent to New Zealand for recharg-ing.

Eurich's description of the Pitcairn setup in *QST* captivated the ham world, and a move-ment to replace Young's ancient equipment with new gear ensued. Soon, thanks to the con-tribution of parts and equipment from numerous manufacturers, a new 60-watt station, including a wind-driven generator, was on its way to the island in the custody of two engi-neers, Granville Lindley and Lew Bellem of Coto-Coil, Inc., the Providence, Rhode Island, electronics firm that built the station. **VR6A** went on the air on March 5, 1938, but then went silent for lack of a license, which was finally received in April, whereupon the station resumed operation as **VR6AY**. Numerous hams worked the station at night, usually on 14346 kc., and additional equipment enabled several NBC broadcasts to originate from the island while the engineers were still in residence. These broadcasts were sent through the RCA commercial facility in **Bolinas**, California and relayed nationwide. Bellem and Lindley left Pitcairn on May 5. Although equipment faults put the station off the air at times, Young persevered and Pitcairn would remain on the amateur radio map, and on DXers' want lists.[150]

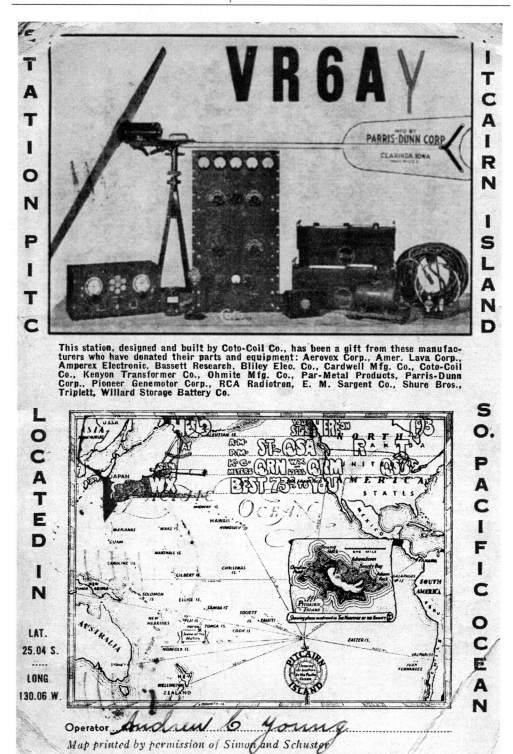

The QSL cards that were brought to Pitcairn with the donated equipment in 1938 reflected the call letters VR6A. The "Y" was added by hand after a proper New Zealand license with that designation was finally obtained.

Elsewhere in the Pacific, the Mutual Broadcasting System's "Hawaii Calls" was heard on Sunday nights at 2030 EST over various RCA radiotelephone channels in **Kahuku,** e.g. **KQH** on 14950 kc., **KKP** on 16040, **KHE** on 17950. A similar program from NBC, "**The Voice of Hawaii,**" was also heard. In Australia, **VK3LR** in Lyndhurst had become simply **VLR** on December 1, 1937. It called itself the **Australian National Short Wave Station,** and the

By the 1930s, shortwave had become a standard part of expeditions to out-of-the-way places. Richard Archbold's groundbreaking trip to Dutch New Guinea was greatly aided by the Catalina flying boat pictured on this QSL.

frequency was still 9580 kc. In 1938 the power was increased to 2 kw., and a second frequency, 11880, was brought into service. It operated at 0000–0200 EST, switching to the old channel, 9580, soon thereafter. VLR was among the best heard of the Australian stations. And a new country was on the air — New Caledonia. Amateur operator Charles Gaveau, FK8AA, was broadcasting as **Radio Noumea** on 6120 kc. at 0230–0430 EST, opening and closing with La Marseillaise. The power was 50 watts.

An interesting non-broadcast station which for a time was heard almost nightly on the 20 meter ham band was amateur station **PK6XX** in Dutch New Guinea (today the Indonesian province of West Irian). It was the station of the Richard Archbold Expedition, sponsored by the American Museum of Natural History. The expedition's headquarters was Hollandia (known today as Jayapura). Although PK6XX was the station's best-known call, it also operated as **PO6ZA** for intramural expedition communications and for relaying some expedition-based broadcast programing back to the United States. It was on the air for about a year, closing down in September 1939. Devoted today to long-term ecological research, "Archbold Expeditions" is still in existence.[151]

A Broadcast from Pitcairn, 1938[152]

Granville Lindley: *Good evening, ladies and gentlemen. We greet you from lonely Pitcairn Island in the middle of the South Pacific. It was to this remote, rock-bound island 149 years ago that the nine mutineers of His Majesty's Ship Bounty came in search of refuge after rebelling under the command of Captain Bligh. Today on this same island is to be found 200 odd natives and embracing but seven family names, nearly all of whom are direct descendants of the original Englishmen and their Tahitian wives. Those familiar with the history of Pitcairn will recall the names of Fletcher Christian, Edward Young, Adams, Moody, and so on.*

Ladies and gentlemen, it is indeed an honor to present to the world for the first time Mr.

Richard Edgar Christian, chief magistrate of Pitcairn Island, representative of His Majesty, the King of England, and great grandson of Fletcher Christian, First Officer of the H.M.S. Bounty. Mr Christian:
  Richard Christian: *Good evening. We on the island appreciate more than words can express this modern radio station which has been given to us. Only those who have known the isolation such as we have endured on Pitcairn can realize what it means to us to be able to talk to the outside world. Thank you.*
  Lindley: *Thank you, Mr. Christian. And now may we present a typical island melody song in the Tahitian tongue.*

                                    * * *

  In the few remaining minutes we would like to have Mr. Andrew Young say a few words to you. Mr. Young:
  Andrew Young: *Hello America. I can only say that I am very grateful for the chance to thank all our friends for the many kindnesses they have shown us. Good night.*
  Lindley: *We conclude with a native melody, a heritage of the early days on Pitcairn.*

                                    * * *

  You have been listening to a program originating at Pitcairn Island and sent you through the facilities of the National Broadcasting Company. This is Lew Bellem speaking and returning you to San Francisco.

The inauguration of new stations in Central America, the Caribbean and South America slowed but did not stop.

St. Kitts, in the British West Indies, was heard on shortwave by way of **VP2LO**. The station was operated by **ICA Radio Sales & Service Laboratories** in conjunction with the **Caribbean Broadcasting Service**. The frequency was 6380 kc., and the power 500 watts. The call letters were changed to **ZIZ** in 1939, and the schedule was 1900–1930 EST on Wednesdays.

In February, Guatemalan mediumwave station **TGQ, La Voz de Quetzaltenango**, began simulcasting its programs over 200-watt **TGQA** on 6440 kc. **TGWA, Radiodifusora Nacional**, usually on 9685 kc. (and now with 10 kw.), was joined by a second, 1 kw. transmitter, **TGWB**, on 6040 kc. TGWA had a special program for European listeners on weekdays at 1245–1345 EST, Sundays 1245–1715, on 15170 kc. It was heard in the United States as well.

New from Nicaragua was ham broadcaster **Radiodifusora YN3DG** (later just **YNDG**), "**Station 'Gilfillan,'**" Leon, on 7128 kc. (later 7660), 200 watts. During special DX broadcasts it operated on 13900 kc. **YSP, La Voz de Cuscatlan**, San Salvador, El Salvador, 10400 kc., was a new one from that country. A new station was heard from Panama City on the high frequency of 11780 kc.—**HP5G, Emisora Ron Dalley**, using 1.5 kw. And several new stations were operating from the Dominican Republic: **HI1L, Radioemisora Nacional "El Diario,"** Santiago, on 6180 kc., 200 watts; **HI5P, Ecos de Isabel de Torres,** Puerto Plata, on 6560; and **HI8J, La Voz de la Provincia**, La Vega, widely heard in the evenings on 6380 kc.

Shortwave broadcasting was also expanding in Costa Rica. Now heard, all from San Jose, were **TILS, Broadcasting Station "Para Ti,"** on 5905 kc.; **TIMC, Estación Cultura**, 5230; **TIEM, Radio El Mundo**, 10050 (later 6150), relaying its 970 kc. mediumwave transmitter; and **TI2XD**, announcing as **Voz Radio Pilot** or **La Voz de la Republica**, on 11920 kc., 600 watts. And in May, to celebrate its tenth anniversary — its first broadcast had been on May 4, 1928 — pioneer shortwaver **TI4NRH**, the "Voice of Costa Rica," now operating with 500 watts, broadcast a series of 31 special programs, each one dedicated to a particular station, club, publication or person with a connection to TI4NRH. The programs were presented at 2100–2200 EST over 9670 kc. A special three-color 14 × 18" diploma was offered for reports.[153] Although reception of the pioneer broadcaster was becoming increasingly unpredictable, the varied sound effects that colored its programs—bells ringing, trains chuffing, etc.—made its presence unmistakable.

In Honduras, old faithful **HRN, La Voz de Honduras**, had long been a non-verifier. In 1938, the Quixote Radio Club published an explanation from the station's manager:

> Little did [HRN] dream that the collection of verification cards was like the stamp craze. In a short time they received thousands of letters, chiefly from the United States and Canada, most of them containing reply coupons and requesting verification cards. Although costing the purchaser nine cents, these coupons are of no value whatsoever in Honduras, their acceptance by the postal authorities being optional and, in this case, refused. In order to grant these requests the station would also have been confronted by the necessity of employing an English speaking clerk whose salary would have been a serious burden to a station just making its start in business. Although a minor item, printing costs had also to be considered. [The station manager's] partner, Mr. Paul John, suggested the acknowledgment of reports by means of an "Appreciation Hour" Sunday evenings and for a time this was done, but later was abandoned due to causes beyond the station's control.[154]

Farther south, in British Guiana, broadcasters **VP3MR** and **VP3BG** merged and became the **British Guiana United Broadcasting Company Ltd.**, retaining the call letters VP3BG. The frequency was 6130 kc., and the station operated at 0900–1000 and 1415–1830 EST. Soon it would be called ZFY. (*"This is the British Guiana United Broadcasting Company, VP3BG, in Georgetown, transmitting on 48.94 meters."*)

W2XAF sent messages from home to the Theodore Waldeck Expedition which was searching in British Guiana for American pilot Paul Redfern, who in 1927 had been unsuccessful in his attempt to fly from Brunswick, Georgia to Rio de Janeiro, a distance a thousand miles greater than Charles Lindbergh's famous flight. Persistent reports of Redfern's jungle survival fueled a dozen rescue attempts in the 1930s, this being the last. He was never found.

A new station in Colombia was **HJ4ABU, Emisora Universidad de Antioquia**, Medellin, on 8650 kc., 1 kw. The big news from Colombia, however, was the movement of many stations to the new 60 meter band. With the exception of a few Venezuelans and some stations in India and the Dutch East Indies, Colombia had the band almost to itself.

Venezuelan shortwave broadcasting had stabilized, but there were several new stations: **YV1RN, Radio Maracaibo**, 6500 kc.; **Radio Barquisimeto**, on both 4820 kc. (**YV3RN**) and 6450 (**YV3RD**); **YV4RQ, Radio Puerto Cabello**, on 5020, 2 kw.; and **YV5RU, Estudios Universo**, Caracas, on 5830 kc. Venezuelan stations also started migrating to the 60 meter band, although most were by now operating mainly in the ranges 5700–5970 and 6210–6700 kc.

At year's end the newly authorized 60 meter band looked as follows. (True to longstanding habits of out-of-band usage, some stations were already choosing channels beyond the band's edges.)

4600	HC2ET	El Telégrafo, Guayaquil, Ecuador
4775	HJ7EAB	Radio Bucaramanga, Colombia
4780	HJ1ABB	La Voz de Barranquilla, Colombia
4795	HJ6FBC	Ecos del Combeima, Ibague, Colombia
4815	HJ2BAC	La Voz de Cúcuta, Colombia
4820	HJ7ABB	Radio Santander, Bucaramanga, Colombia
4820	YDE2	NIROM, Solo, Java
4820	YV3RN	Radio Barquisimeto, Venezuela
4825	HJ5ABD	La Voz del Valle, Cali, Colombia
4835	HJ1ABE	La Voz de los Laboratorios Fuentes, Cartagena, Colombia
4840	HJ3CAB	Emisora Nueva Granada, Bogota, Colombia
4850	HJ3CAF	La Voz de Bogota, Colombia
4860	HJ1ABG	Emisora Atlantico, Barranquilla, Colombia

4865	HJ2BAJ	La Voz de Santa Marta, Colombia
4870	YV2RN	La Voz del Tachira, San Cristóbal, Venezuela
4875	HJ6FAH	La Voz de Armenia, Colombia
4880	VUC	AIR, Calcutta, India
4880	YV6RB	Ecos del Orinoco, Ciudad Bolivar, Venezuela
4885	HJ4ABP	Emisora Claridad, Medellin, Colombia
4895	HJ3CAH	La Voz de la Victor, Bogota, Colombia
4905	VUB	AIR, Bombay, India
4950	VUM	AIR, Madras, India
4990	YV3RB	La Voz de Lara, Barquisimeto, Venezuela
4995	VUD	AIR, Delhi, India
5010	YV5RM	Radiodifusora Venezuela, Caracas, Venezuela
5020	YV4RQ	Radio Puerto Cabello, Venezuela

In Ecuador, new stations on the air included **HC1GQ, La Voz del Diablo**, Quito, 4585 kc. (but usually heard on its harmonic of 9170); **HC1RB, Diario Hablado**, Quito, 7870; and **HC4JB, La Voz de Manabí**, Portoviejo, a low-power HCJB-affiliate on 7410 kc. that was intended to cover an area not reached by HCJB. And Peru now had **OAX2A, Radio Rancho Grande de la Hacienda Chiclin**. The 250-watt station, located in Trujillo, announced 11970 kc. but was heard closer to 11835.

TI4NRH was famous for its elaborate certificate QSLs. This one was designed to commemorate the station's tenth anniversary in 1938.

Still farther south, **LRA, Radio del Estado**, in Buenos Aires, Argentina was being heard nightly on 6180 and 9690 kc., relaying the LRA mediumwave program. The daytime channel was 11730, and the power was 500 watts. Two new stations were operating from Santiago, Chile. They were **CB1178, Radio Sociedad Nacional de Agricultura**, on 11780 kc. with 2.5 kw., simulcasting mediumwave CB57; and **CB1185, Radio El Mercurio**, on 11850 with 2.5 kw. From Valparaiso, **CB970, Radio**

Cooperativa Vitalicia, came on the air. The frequency was 9720 kc. and the power 5 kw. It was heard in the evenings, and the station's tuning signal was "Anchors Aweigh."

A new station was heard from Asuncion, Paraguay. It was **ZP8, Radio Nacional**, 9260 kc., audible at 1700–2030 EST. As yet unheard in the United States but reported on air in Uruguay were **CXA4**, a government station operated by **SODRE, Servicio Oficial de Difusión Radio Eléctrica**, in Montevideo, on 6125 kc., relaying mediumwave CX6, 650 kc.; and two 5 kw. stations owned by El Espectador, Ltda.—**CXA9** on 9440 kc. and **CXA19** on 11695. CXA9 and CXA19 relayed mediumwavers CX14, El Espectador, and CX18, Radio Sport.

Most DXers were unfamiliar with Spanish and thus found Latin American DXing a particular challenge. To increase listenership, a few stations offered some English programming. **TIPG**, San Jose, presented the "Hour of Costa Rica" on Saturdays at 2000 EST on 6410 kc. **HP5A, Radio-Teatro Estrella de Panama**, had English news daily at 1830–1900 EST. It was sponsored by a local Chevrolet-Buick dealer. English announcements were also heard during a tourist program at 1700–1800. And at 2230–2300 on 9630 kc., **HJ7ABD, Radio Bucaramanga**, presented the "Bucaramanga Mild Coffee Hour." It included news, letters, and information about Colombia.

Some English was also available from two French-speaking stations. In Haiti, **HH2S**, identifying in English as the **West Indian Broadcasting Company**, carried an English program for Jamaica nightly at 2030–2100 EST. The frequency was 5915 kc. And **Radio Martinique**, whose latest channel was 9705 kc., had English on Mondays and Wednesdays at 1830–1900 EST. The station also relayed some French-language programs of **Paris Mondial**.

As usual, many special broadcasts were arranged by clubs and other radio organizations. *Short Wave & Television* magazine arranged for a special broadcast from ham station **HS1BJ**, Siam. The operator was the assistant engineer of shortwave broadcaster **HS8PJ**.

Shortwave was growing up. *The New York Times* described the situation at the time of the Sudeten crisis as follows:

> With Europe on the brink of war, short-wave news from London, Czecho-Slovakia, Berlin and Rome suddenly became an important factor in the daily home life. Short waves stepped into the household spotlight as never before; and since that time short-wave listening in many homes has jumped from a young-boy hobby to a grown up necessity.[155]

1939

During 1939, shortwave broadcasting underwent a continual albeit slow expansion in Europe. However, events in September would accelerate development of the medium and define its future path.

On April 1, the Spanish Civil War came to an end with the victory of General Franco and the Nationalist forces. After a brief time off the air, **Radio Nacional de España** became Spain's official radio voice. The conclusion of hostilities meant that the amateur broadcasting of the previous three years would soon come to a halt. For a time, however, many amateurs continued to broadcast under the RNE umbrella. These included operators in **Alcazarquivir**, on 7125 kc.; **Ceuta** (Morocco), 7134; **Córdoba**, 7117; **Huelva**, 7037; **Jaca**, 7117 and 14115; **Las Palmas** (Canary Islands), 7931 and 14115; **Malaga**, 7220 and 14440; **Melilla** (Morocco), 7151, 7184 and 7190; **Oviedo**, 7135; **San Sebastian**, 7299; **Santander**, 7160; **Tenerife** (Canary Islands), 7500; **Tetuan** (Spanish Morocco), 6990, 7194 and 13992; **Valladolid**, 7006; **Villa Sanjuro**, 7147; and **Vitoria**, 11991.

France began using a third transmitter site for shortwave broadcasting. The new 100 kw.

transmitters, co-sited with the powerful longwave transmitter at **Allouis**, greatly improved reception of the **Paris Mondial** broadcasts. As Pontoise was **TPA** and Essarts-le-Roi **TPB**, Allouis was known as TPC. **Zeesen** opened an Arabic service for the Middle East, where Germany's political influence historically had been less than that of France and England.[156] **Radio Centre**, Moscow, was by now broadcasting in Czech, Dutch, English, French, German, Hungarian, Italian, Portuguese and Spanish, usually utilizing one or more of five stations, which still retained separate call signs: **RAN** (9600 kc.), **RNE** (11710, 12000), **RKI** (7520 and 15083),

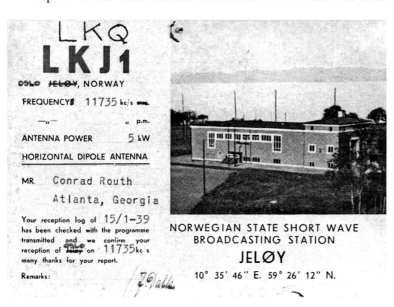

NORWEGIAN STATE SHORT WAVE
BROADCASTING STATION
JELØY
10° 35' 46" E. 59° 26' 12" N.

Designed for the Jeløy station, this QSL was pressed into use for the new shortwave service from Oslo. The station relayed the Norwegian national program.

RV59 (6000), and **RW96** (6030, 9520, 15180 and 15210). A station in Kaunas, Lithuania, **LYR**, was being heard on 9285 kc., relaying the Kaunas longwave station. It was said to be operating with 500 watts at 1200–1400 and 0000–0100. And **RV15**, Khabarovsk, moved from 4273 to 6045 kc. where it continued to be widely heard, particularly on the west coast. It operated at 0200–1100 EST.

Norway was now on shortwave by way of the state broadcaster, **Norsk Rikskringkasting**. The power of the new shortwave plant was 5 kw., and numerous frequencies were available, including 6999 kc. (**LKL**), 9530 (**LKC**), 9550 (**LKD**), 9573 (**LKE**), 11735 (**LKQ**), 11830 (**LKU**), 15170 (**LKV**), 17755 (**LKW**), 17785 (**LKX**), 21460 (**LKY**), and 21500 (**LKZ**), plus 6185 (**LLI**), 6195 (**LLJ**), 9550 (**LLD**), 9610 (**LLG**), 11850 (**LLK**), 15175 (**LLM**), 25900 (**LLA**), and 26350 (**LLC**). The best-heard channels in the U.S. were 9530, 9610, 11735 and 15170 kc. Also on line was a new Norsk Rikskringkasting transmitter in **Trømso**, callsign **LLS**, which operated with 5 kw. on 7210 kc. And the 1 kw. station in **Jeløy** on 6130 was also still on the air.

In 1938 the Swiss Parliament had approved the construction of a major transmitter base at **Schwarzenburg**. On July 1, 1939, following low power tests on 6055, 9535, 11865 and 15305 kc., the **Swiss Broadcasting Corporation** began transmitting via the new 25 kw. transmitters. Beams were to North America, South America, Africa, Asia and Australia. Five days after startup, however, the facility was completely destroyed by fire. It would return to the air the next year. In the meantime, the SBC transmissions were moved to the **Radio-Suisse** PTT station at Prangins. The Prangins frequencies were 11402kc. (**HBO**), 14538 (**HBJ**), and 18450 (**HBF**).

The **Belgrade Short-Wave Station** in Yugoslavia added new transmitters and directional antennas. Now operating with 10 kw., the new channels were **YUC** and **YUD** on 9505 kc. for North and South America, **YUE** on 11735 for North America, and **YUF** and **YUG** on 15240 for North and South America. The 9505 kc. channel was the best heard. Another 10 kw. transmitter, **YUB**, operated on 6100 kc., the same channel that was still used at times by 1 kw. **YUA**. Twice a month the station's program was relayed to Yugoslavs abroad via **Zeesen, DJP**, 11850 kc.

A nice catch was the testing to the Americas conducted by the **Royal Hungarian Post** station in Budapest, Hungary (sometimes called **Radiolabor**) over a 200-watt experimental transmitter, **HAAQ2** (the call was later changed to **HAD**). Frequencies varied — 7220, 9625, 11850 and 21680 kc. — and times were, to North America, 1700–2300, to South America, 2130–2300. The programming consisted mostly of orchestra and military music, with announcements in English, Spanish and Hungarian. At times when HAAQ2 was on the air, a second station, amateur transmitter **HA1K**, was also put in operation on the ham bands in order to obtain immediate reception feedback from amateurs.

Two new experimental outlets were heard from Rumania, relaying Bucharest mediumwave stations. One was run by the **Bucharest Polytechnic School** and was on 12160 kc. at 1400–1500 EST. (*"This is the short wave of the Polytechnic School in Bucharest."*) The other, known as **Radio Experimental**, was on 9230 kc., with news in different languages on different days at 1645 EST, closing down at 1700. The power was variously put at 250 watts and 2 kw. This station soon became **Radio Bucharest**, operating on 15410 kc. and heard at 2100–2215 EST.

Smaller countries were making their voices heard. Situated between France and Spain, Andorra, under 200 square miles in size, came on the air. **Radio Andorra** was reported heard in England on 8570 and 11830 kc. And **ZAA, Radio Tirana**, Albania was now broadcasting on shortwave. It was another example of broadcast programming sent over an otherwise commercial station. ZAA was heard on 7850 kc. until closedown at 1400 EST and on 6084 from 1500 to 1800. (*"Hello everybody. Radio Tirana, Albania, is on the air, 3 kw. in the antenna, transmitting on 49.30 meters."*)

Another new country on shortwave was Ireland. **Radio Éireann**, an experimental station at Athlone operated by the Department of Posts and Telegraph in Dublin, was testing on a variety of channels — 6190, 9595, 11740, 15120 and 17840 kc. — and asking for reports. The best-heard frequency in the U.S. was 17840, where they were on at 0830–1000 and 1230–1630 EST. The power was 1.5 kw. (*"This is the Irish shortwave station on 17.84 mc., closing down until tomorrow."*)

The Fascist ascendancy in Europe eventually spawned the great world conflict. Germany and Italy announced a formal alliance in May, and a Soviet-German nonaggression pact was signed in August. World War II began when Germany invaded Poland on September 1, and two days later England and France declared war on Germany. In two weeks the Soviet Union entered Poland, and by the end of the month Germany and the Soviet Union had partitioned the country. In November the Soviets invaded Finland, where they encountered significant ongoing resistance. They gained some Finnish territory in an armistice reached in March 1940.

On September 3, King George VI and the British Prime Minister spoke to the nation and the world on the **BBC**. Noted *The New York Times* later, "[e]very wave was hot that day with declarations of action. It marked the end of the bluff-talk radio era. The war was on, and guns began to speak."[157]

The BBC moved to a war footing. News bulletins were tripled in number. Seven new languages were added, so that less than two years after its cautious entry into foreign-language broadcasting, England was broadcasting in Afrikaans, Arabic, Czech, French, German, Greek, Italian, Hungarian, Polish, Portuguese, Rumanian, Serbo-Croat, Spanish and Turkish. As one commentator put it: "There was once a time when an American all-wave listener knew what country he was in tune with by the tongue. Now he must wait to hear the identification. Language is no longer a clue. The German is heard talking perfect Italian, English and Spanish. London announcers are expert in French, Polish and Arabic. And any of them may be speaking Greek, Portuguese, Rumanian, Magyar or Croatian. Tongues of all nations are mixed up in the war on the wave lengths."[158]

The BBC external services developed into two main blocks: the European Service, serving a wide, European foreign-language audience; and the Overseas Services, composed of the Empire Service (all English), some news bulletins in major European languages, and a catchall group of other foreign-language services (Afrikaans, Arabic, Turkish and Greek, plus Spanish and Portuguese to Latin America). By year's end there were 51 news bulletins daily in the Overseas Services. BBC broadcasts of all types, but especially news, were rebroadcast in many places throughout the world. (BBC Portuguese-language news broadcasts aimed at Portugal rather than Brazil were inaugurated in May, and for the first seven months were rebroadcast by Emissora Nacional.)[159] English broadcasts ended with: "*And now we shall say goodnight. Sleep well. Wherever you may be in the colonies, this is a very good night from home.*"[160] *World-Radio* ceased publication, and *BBC Empire Broadcasting* became *London Calling*.

Radio Luxembourg's shortwave signal was silenced when the station closed down on September 21 as fighting broke out along the border. Following the German invasion of the country in May 1940 the station would come under German jurisdiction and would join the extensive network of European longwave and mediumwave outlets that served the considerable German propaganda machine targeted on continental Europe and Britain. A widely-heard German clandestine beaming to England, **Worker's Challenge**, transmitted on mediumwave for almost five years.

In America, stations expanded their international staffs, increased both the volume and the variety of their foreign-language output, and improved their transmitters and antennas. The principal target areas were Latin America and Europe. This pattern would continue in the years 1940 and 1941.

Westinghouse stations **W2XE** and **W3XAU** better coordinated their schedules so that when one was broadcasting to Latin America the other was transmitting to Europe. **W1XAL** moved its transmitters to a 32-acre site in Scituate, Massachusetts, 22 miles from Boston. (The site had been used to test heavy guns in World War I.) The station began using a second 20 kw. transmitter, **W1XAR**, on February 27. Soon thereafter, *Christian Science Monitor* headquarters in Boston started helping the station prepare news broadcasts.

The New York World's Fair opened. Noted the International Short Wave Club: "A dazzling array of Emperors, Kings, Queens and diplomats of 17 nations will be heard in a series of weekly broadcasts throughout the U.S.A., saluting the opening of the New York World's fair, beginning January 1st. [The fair opened on April 30.] The programs will be carried by three networks and will include W2XAD, W2XAF, W2XE, W3XAU, W8XK and W8XAL. The programs will come via RCA stations at Rocky Point and Bolinas, and many overseas stations will be heard. The programs will take place each Sunday from 2:30 to 3:00 P.M. Famous orchestras will introduce each program."[161] The fair also boasted a rather elaborate amateur station, **W2USA**, which got extensive use. Starting at 0645 EST on New Year's Day, 1940, and repeated every hour, W2USA transmitted a 15-minute recorded greeting from the fair's president. It was relayed by other amateur stations throughout the day.[162]

From a DXer's point of view, the New York World's Fair was eclipsed by the shortwave doings on the west coast. In 1937, General Electric had started work on a shortwave station in California to service mainly Asian audiences, as Far East reception of signals from the east coast of the United States was not very reliable. Although the station, **W6XBE**, soon to become **KGEI**, was destined for eventual operation from Belmont, California, it began testing on February 18, 1939, from a temporary home in the "Palace of Electricity" at the specially-constructed Treasure Island site of the 1939 San Francisco World's Fair (also known as the Golden Gate International Exposition). Tests included many repetitions of "Anchors Aweigh," and official inauguration was on March 2. Operating every day on 9530 and 15330 kc. at hours complementary to W2XAD and W2XAF (which used the same frequencies), it put General Electric engineering on display. The power was 20 kw.[163]

W6XBE was the first major shortwave broadcast station west of the Mississippi. Broadcasts were directed to Asia at 0700–1000 EST, and to South America at 1830–2200. Alternate frequencies included 6190 and 21590 kc. Programming was sometimes live, but often taken from **KPO** or **KGO**.[164]

The construction of the station had the strong support of Addie Viola Smith, U.S. Trade Commissioner in Shanghai, who had been promoting the idea enthusiastically since 1935. Although improved cultural and economic relations, and increased Chinese-American friendship, were articulated goals of the station, the main audience of its Asian beam was always Americans living in China (12,000 in Shanghai alone), and its principal accomplishment was helping them stay in contact with home. Indeed, by unreservedly serving the American community in China, it may well have exacerbated the historic Chinese antipathy to foreign influence.

Smith had demonstrated the problematic nature of east coast signals through the compilation of reception data which she submitted to Washington, and once transmissions began she solicited listeners for feedback on the broadcasts. She also cited pledges from local station owners to rebroadcast American west coast shortwave signals over local channels. Reception of W6XBE in China was good at the outset, although it soon suffered from jamming. Programming was somewhat wanting at first, especially in comparison with the station's Latin American lineup, and NBC, which was the source of most of the material, improved its offerings in response to her complaints. The Sunday mailbag program, in which messages from Americans in the U.S. to friends and relatives in China — sometimes presented live over the air by their authors— became a special favorite of many listeners.[165] The story of Chinese dramatic soprano Louise Kwan, temporarily in the U.S., successfully appealing in June 1939 over KGEI (then still W6XBE) for help in locating her four-year old son who had been in the care of her parents when Nanking fell, became part of the station's lore.[166]

W6XBE programs were often relayed by Asian stations, including U.S.-owned **XMHA** in Shanghai. XMHA had a colorful history, much of it tied to its larger-than-life newscaster, Carroll Alcott. Operating as the Continental Broadcasting Company, the station was owned by Ulysses Severlin "U.S." Harkson, President of the Henningsen Produce Company, which was in the ice cream and candy business. (XMHA was also a dealer in RCA Victor equipment.) The 1 kw. station on 600 kc. mediumwave had come on the air in the early thirties, and by now was simulcasting on shortwave for the interior. Identifying as "the Call of the Orient" and opening and closing with the "Under the Double Eagle" march, it operated on various 25 meter channels, e.g. 11860, 11910, 11940 kc. Most programs were in English, but there were some in Chinese and German, the latter mainly for the considerable Jewish refugee community in Shanghai.

The extensive English-language news programs were produced in cooperation with the *Shanghai Evening Post & Mercury.* The station served mainly an American and expatriate audience and was something of a model for W6XBE. XMHA programs were strongly anti–Japanese in tone and content, and, notwithstanding Japanese jamming, served as a lifeline for many when fighting spread to Shanghai in 1937. It transmitted over 15,000 personal messages over the air. "XMHA will long be remembered in the hearts of these people during these stirring times," wrote Addie Viola Smith.[167] *("You are listening to station XMHA.")*

Alcott joined XMHA in 1938. The anti–Japanese journalism for which he was already known at the *China Press* provoked numerous conflicts, physical and otherwise, with the Japanese, and he would undoubtedly have met his demise had he not been in Washington, en route to joining the news staff of WLW, when the Japanese occupied Shanghai's International Settlement immediately after Pearl Harbor. "I was not just a nuisance," he said in his book, *My War with Japan.* "I was an anti–Japanese institution and they treated me as such."[168] XMHA was an NBC affiliate by the time the Japanese took it over. Before then the station taunted the Axis with such programs as "The Free French Speak to You" and "Uncensored News From Norway."[169]

Back in America, in August, W2XAF went to 100 kw., becoming the most powerful of the stateside shortwave broadcasters. Said one South American listener, "Station W2XAF is considered a semi-official news bureau here.... When we do not hear it, we ignore the news, particularly the foreign news."[170]

General Electric was more interested in the technical side of shortwave, and thus relied increasingly on NBC for program content. The NBC programs were generally superior to all but W1XAL's. Among the comments received from NBC overseas listeners were these:

A listener in the Belgian Congo finds: "Reception is very clear, without fading or static."

* * *

A Frenchman at Provins, in tune with the French hour from New York, reports reception from America "excellent, a veritable treat and delight."

* * *

On Mauritius Island, described as "a very small dot of land, lost in the Indian Ocean," a listener comments on reception from New York as "really astounding and very distinct."

* * *

"Right at this moment," writes a Brazilian, "I am enjoying very much fine music being played by an orchestra in Chicago."

* * *

A Mexican ... continues his applause for American broadcasts as "actually making a motherland of the whole world — a motherland of exquisite culture, and such culture is invariably the patrimony of great peoples spiritually."[171]

But there was still a place for small stations. W4XB was said to put in a "fabulous signal" nightly on 6040 kc.

In May, the FCC announced new rules designed to regularize American shortwave broadcasting and make it more competitive with the shortwave services of other countries. Regular four-letter calls replaced the experimental "X" callsigns, and, effective July 1, 1940 (extended first to January 1, 1941, then to July 1, 1941), a minimum power of 50 kw., together with directional antennas, would be required. Frequency utilization was made more flexible (a single license would now cover all facilities and frequencies at a given location), and, effective June 1, 1939, the ban on commercial advertising was reversed.

Elimination of the advertising ban was intended to encourage shortwave broadcasting in general and the production of special international programming in particular, as well as promote commerce in American products. The broadcasters had long argued in favor of commercials as a means of recouping the costs of their shortwave efforts, but the rule change was a surprise and it took the broadcasters some time to ramp up for it. And there were still limits. The stations could only mention individual companies and the general nature of their products, which had to be available in the target area.

Lining up sponsors would take place in earnest in 1940. NBC and Crosley enlisted United

Fruit, Pepsi-Cola, Standard Oil, Firestone, Kleenex, Alka-Seltzer, Planters Peanuts, American Export Airlines, and others. United Fruit paid $25,000 for 15 minutes every night. The Standard Oil-sponsored transmission of the Louis-Godoy heavyweight championship fight in February 1940 brought a huge response from Latin America. Some sponsors were new to broadcast advertising, while others were existing network customers. NBC also sold blocks of air time.[172] Advertised programs were usually specially prepared for foreign audiences, and in foreign languages, most often Spanish or Portuguese.

GE was more interested in programming than profit. Its sponsors, such as Tidewater Oil and Gillette Razor, either paid only for production costs or produced their own ads, which were broadcast at

FRED A. MUSCHENHEIM
President

R. K. CHRISTENBERRY
Vice President and General Manager

HOTEL ASTOR
Times Square, New York
Telephone, Circle 6-8000

September 20, 1940

Mr. Lunsford P. Yandell, Director
International Commercial Broadcasting
National Broadcasting Company
30 Rockefeller Plaza
New York City, N. Y.

Dear Mr. Yandell:-

In renewing our contract for NBC's direct broadcasting service to Latin America, I have certain observations to make that I think will help and encourage your company to further expand this worthwhile service.

First, our own reaction to the results accomplished by our first thirteen weeks of broadcasting in Spanish are obviously favorable, or we would not be renewing our contract. The facts are that the response to this broadcast has indicated that our programs are heard and appreciated in parts of Latin America which we are sure could not be reached through any other medium. This response indicates an extraordinarily wide coverage. In addition to response in the form of letters, the program has produced tangible results by bringing to us as guests Latin Americans whose interest in this hotel and its entertainment facilities was aroused directly by our broadcasts.

Second, I want you to know that we heartily subscribe to the belief that at this time no important channel of communication with the people of Latin America should be neglected. You are offering a new and, apparently, a most effective channel of communication. Through it, we are glad to be participating with other leading organizations in creating closer ties with the twenty Latin American Republics by presenting our part of the broad picture of what democracy gives to the people of this country. We feel that the presentation of such a picture has a definite and important place in solving the vital and growing problem of national defense.

Finally, may I say that it has been a pleasure to work with you and your associates and that your staff has spared neither time nor effort to give our programs maximum quality and effectiveness.

Very truly yours,

R.K. CHRISTENBERRY
Vice President and
General Manager

NBC promoted sponsorship of its shortwave broadcasting to Latin America with a stylish brochure containing endorsements like this, as well as a letter from Secretary of State Cordell Hull.

no charge. The Westinghouse stations carried Westinghouse ads only (and a limited number of those). CBS commercialization came later. WRUL remained non-commercial.

The considerable attempts at making commercialization pay notwithstanding (including the establishment in 1940–41 of Latin American networks by NBC, CBS and Crosley), advertising on shortwave was never a success. Although Latin America was a natural American market, and many American products were already being advertised on local stations there, the effectiveness of shortwave ads directed toward Latin America was difficult to prove to potential advertisers[173] (and advertising toward Europe was completely out of the question). As a result, most transmitter time remained unsponsored, and advertising never covered more than a quarter of the stations' operating expenses, a major factor in the softening of the broadcasters' attitude toward an eventual government takeover. (The NBC advertising rates to Latin America in 1940–41 were: Spanish, 1600–1715 EST, $225 per hour; 1900–2200, $300; 2300–2400, $150; Portuguese, 1715–1900, $180; English, 2200–2300, $300.)[174]

The changes in call signs, which were effective September 1, 1939, were as follows (asterisked callsigns were assigned temporarily and were soon replaced by the indicated permanent callsigns)[175]:

Callsign Changes, 1939

Station	New Call Letters	Power	Frequencies
W1XAL, Boston, MA (World Wide Broadcasting Corp.)	WRUL (*WSLA)	20 kw.	6040, 11730, 11790, 15130, 15250, 21460
W1XAR, Boston, MA (World Wide Broadcasting Corp.)	WRUW (*WSLR)	20 kw.	11730, 15130, 25600
W1XK, Boston (Millis), MA (Westinghouse)	WBOS	10 kw.	9570
W2XE, Wayne, NJ (CBS)	WCBX	10 kw.	6120, 6170, 9650, 11830, 15270, 17830, 21570
W2XAD, Schenectady, NY (GE)	WGEA	25 kw.	9550, 15330, 21500
W2XAF, Schenectady, NY (GE)	WGEO (*WGEU)	100 kw.	6190, 9530, 21590
W3XAL, Bound Brook, NJ (NBC)	WRCA	35 kw.	9670, 21630
W3XL, Bound Brook, NJ (NBC)	WNBI	35 kw.	6100, 177780
W3XAU, Philadelphia, PA (WCAU)	WCAB (*WCAI)	10 kw.	6060, 9590, 15270, 21520, 25725
W4XB, Miami, FL (Isle of Dreams Broadcasting Corp.)	WDJM (*WBKM)	5 kw.	6040
W6XBE, San Francisco, CA (GE)	KGEI	20 kw.	6190, 9530, 15330
W8XAL, Cincinnati (Mason), OH (Crosley)	WLWO (*WLWU)	10 kw.	6060, 9950, 11870, 15270, 17760, 21650
W8XK, Saxonburg, PA (Westinghouse)	WPIT	40 kw.	6140, 9570, 11870, 15210, 17780, 21540
W9XAA, Downers Grove, IL (Chicago Federation of Labor)	WCBI	500 watts	6080, 11830, 17780

Notwithstanding the authorization of new call letters, **W9XAA**, which had been off the air since around 1937, did not return. Attempts to transfer its license to the religious group Pillar of Fire, Zarapeth, New Jersey, or to KSL in Salt Lake City, Utah, were unsuccessful.

In general the broadcasters welcomed the FCC changes, save for one: a requirement that a station "render only an international service which will reflect the culture of this country and which will promote international goodwill, understanding and cooperation"—the so-called culture rule. Despite expressions of benign intent from the FCC, opposition to the culture rule on the grounds that it represented a form of government censorship came quickly from the stations, the press, and members of Congress. As a result, the rule was suspended.[176]

Attitudes toward the culture rule would change over time. The reinstatement of the rule in 1955 (which involved little more than the elimination of a footnote by which the rule had been suspended) went largely unnoticed.[177] It remains in effect.[178]

When war arrived, NBC shortwave canceled its popular thrice-weekly German-language mailbag program where listeners were often acknowledged by name. The reason was the Führer's decree, effective September 1, 1939, making listening to foreign broadcasts punishable by hard labor or prison and confiscation of the receiver. The spreading of news received from foreign broadcasts was punishable by hard labor or death, and possible imprisonment awaited mere complicity in illegal listening, such as not ending one's listening when the nature of the program is or should have been discovered.

At year's end, **WLWO** was on its way to increasing power to 50 kw. On the broadcast band, although 500 kw. **WLW** had been required to return to 50 kw. daytime operation on March 1, its superpower transmitter was still authorized for nighttime experimental work, which typically took place between midnight and 0230 sign off. WLW continued to seek FCC reauthorization for 500 kw. daytime operation, but to no avail. Its efforts included, following the start of the war, an offer to return to 500 kw. daytime in order "to provide news flashes to rural and remote listeners." But the FCC declined.[179]

The promise of "staticless" FM broadcasting became a reality. The results of various FM experiments were impressive. By mid-year at least two stations were in regular operation— Edwin H. Armstrong's **W2XMN**, in Alpine, New Jersey (42.8 mc., 35 kw.), and **W1XOJ**, Paxton, Massachusetts (43.0 mc., 2 kw.). Five others followed suit during 1939, and a dozen more in 1940.[180] FM receivers began to appear.

Because FM required a 200 kc. bandwidth, the FCC began seeking a home for this new service in the relatively uncluttered "apex" range, where all but a few stations were operating in AM mode. The FCC encouraged FM by requiring its use by new apex stations, and requiring existing stations to convert, which nearly all of them did by the time the apex experiment ended in 1941. The 11 meter band remained available for international broadcasting, however. All told, about a hundred broadcasting stations had operated in the apex band. These channels were also home to some facsimile stations, which were often operated by newspaper-owned broadcast band stations. The short-lived popularity of "home facsimile" reception peaked in 1939.[181]

In Calgary, Alberta, **VE9CA** became **CFVP**. In Winnipeg, Manitoba, **CJRO** and **CJRX**, 6150 and 11720 kc. respectively, were carrying a DX program at 0100 Sundays. It featured a review of the week's reception, listener letters, etc. And in San Juan, Puerto Rico, two broadcast band stations obtained special FCC permission to rebroadcast some of the programs heard on American shortwave. WKAQ carried programs from **WCAB** and **WCBX**; WNEL took some shows from **WRCA** and **WNBI**. The prohibition against the rebroadcasting of American shortwave broadcast programming by U.S. standard broadcasters would be lifted in 1940.

And Newfoundland was now heard on shortwave by way of 300-watt station **VONG** (subsequently redesignated **VONH**), St. John's, operated by the **Broadcasting Corporation of Newfoundland** and relaying mediumwave station VONF. The schedule was 0730–1230 on 9475 kc. and 1630–2030 (and often later) on 5970 (Newfoundland time was a half-hour ahead of EST). VONH also sometimes relayed the BBC. Newfoundland was a separate dominion within the British Commonwealth from 1907 to 1949, when it became a province of Canada. It was ruled directly from London starting in 1934. VONF was a private station from 1932 to 1939, when it became state owned.

The development of shortwave tended to follow the pace of national development in other fields. and so it is no surprise that the growth of the medium was still comparatively slow in Africa and the Middle East. The 250-watt transmitter of **OQ2AA**, **Radio Leo**, Leopoldville,

Belgian Congo, added two new frequencies, 9525 and 15170 kc. **CR7AA** in Mozambique was now identifying as **Radio Club de Mozambique,** and the station would have a great influence on the programming style adopted by local South African broadcasters. On shortwave, despite its low power, west coast listeners were sometimes able to hear the station's 25 meter outlet, **CR7BH,** 11718 kc., when it opened at 0930 EST. East coast reception, though possible at 1600 sign off, was less reliable. However, at year's end, another channel, **CR7BE,** 9640 kc., was putting "an amazing signal" into the United States. The station also utilized **CR7BB,** 15240 kc. Advised one reporter, "This is a fine chance to log yet another rare country."

In Ethiopia, **EIAR**-related station **I2AA** was operating from Addis Ababa on 9650 kc. with 5 kw. It was broadcasting at 0355–0405, 0415–0445, 1100–1200 and 1300–1500. **Poste Algerien,** the Algerian PTT station, now offered broadcast programming as **Radio Alger** on the first and third Tuesdays of the month at 1600–1700 EST on 8960 kc. The 12120 kc. channel was also heard occasionally with broadcasting. And Iran came on shortwave, with test broadcasts from Tehran over four 20 kw. channels: **EPB** on 15100 kc., **EQB** on 6155, **EQA** on 8950, and **EQC** on 9680.

Although not reported heard in the U.S., King Faisal Ghazi of Iraq was reported to be transmitting broadcast programming over what appeared to be his ham station, **YI5KG,** on 7150 kc. The power was 1 kw., and the schedule was 0730–1500 EST. The broadcasts ended after the king's death in an automobile accident in April. The transmitters, which were said to be seven in number, were located in the Royal Palace in Baghdad, and were actually registered in the name of Faisal's son, who became King of Iraq upon his father's death. There were also reports of broadcast programming from a 5 kw. Iraqi PTT station operating on 6188 kc. (HNE), 9683 (HNF), 11724 (HNG), 15145 (HNH), and 17815 (HNI). There was some suggestion that some of the YI5KG transmissions were being carried over the PTT transmitters.

There was much activity in Asia. After the loss of Nanking to the Japanese and the relocation of the Chinese government to Chungking, the **Central Broadcasting Administration** opened a shortwave service using two transmitters, one operating at 4 kw., the other at 7.5 kw. These were **XGOX** and **XGOY,** the **Chinese International Broadcasting Station,** commonly referred to as the **Voice of China,** or **XGOY.** XGOX operated (depending on the season) on 15200 and 17805 kc., XGOY on 9500 and 11900. XGOX was used for broadcasts to North America (2100–2300 EST), while XGOY beamed to Asia (0530–0930 and 1400–1620) and Europe (1630–1820). The transmitters were built into mountain caves, which shielded them from Japanese air attack. Power was soon increased to 35 kw., giving the station a broader reach (it was easily heard on the west coast). XGOY was sometimes relayed over **XPSA, Kweichow Broadcasting Station,** Kweiyang, 6970 kc., which was also part of the Central Broadcasting Administration.

XGRV, late of Nanking, was now operating from Chungking on 11540 kc. It was on the air at 2130–2330 EST. News in Japanese and Chinese was at 0100–0135, and French and English at 0800–0835.

From Canton, in the Japanese-occupied part of China, was heard **XGOK,** 11650 kc. (later 11810), carrying the 780 kc. mediumwave program. It was on the air twice daily at 0800 and 2300, and could be heard on the west coast with English news from Japan's Domei News Agency. The transmissions ended whenever the announcer ran out of news items (which was usually 30 to 40 minutes into the broadcast.)

CQN in Macao, a Portuguese colony located about 35 miles from Hong Kong, had closed down in 1937 but was now heard again, this time on 6080 kc. using the call letters **CRY9.** It was on the air on Mondays and Wednesdays circa 0830–1000 EST, and identified often in English. In 1941 the call letters changed again, to **CR8AA.**

In July, a second radiotelephone outlet of the **Manchuria Telephone & Telegraph Company** joined **JDY** in presenting broadcast programming from Manchuria. It was **MTCY,** the

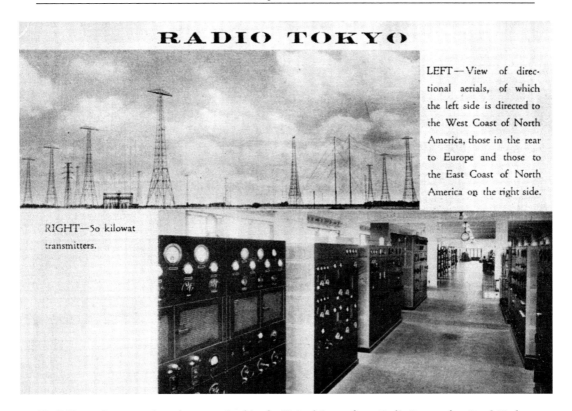

RADIO TOKYO

LEFT—View of directional aerials, of which the left side is directed to the West Coast of North America, those in the rear to Europe and those to the East Coast of North America on the right side.

RIGHT—5o kilowat transmitters.

No QSLs are known to have been received in the United States from Radio Japan after Pearl Harbor. This one is from 1939.

Hsinking Central Broadcasting Station, Hsinking, operating with 20 kw. It was heard in the mornings on 10060 kc., later on 11775. All announcements were in English. Soon it had beams to North America and Hawaii at 0130–0230 EST; to Mongolia and Soviet Russia at 0830–0930; to China, Australia and the Pacific at 0950–1050; and to Europe at 1600–1650. It queried its listeners in a questionnaire: "At what time of day do you listen most to short wave broadcasts? Which Far Eastern short wave station do you like best, and why? What is the quality of the programs from MTCY on the whole? What short wave stations in the Far East come in stronger than MTCY?"

Letters and reception reports for **NHK's** overseas broadcasts had increased since its commencement of shortwave broadcasting in 1935, but were now showing signs of decline. The numbers were reported to be: in 1935 (seven months), 974; 1936, 1,726; 1937, 12,728; 1938, 19,540; 1939 (six months), 6,778.

On the Malayan Peninsula, the **British Malaya Broadcasting Corporation** closed down its 49 meter band outlet, ZHO. ZHP on 9690 (and ZHL mediumwave) remained on the air. Siam became Thailand. The **Bangkok Short Wave Station**, the Thai experimental broadcaster, had obtained permanent status in October 1938. It was now operating over **HS4PJ**, 6125 kc., **HS8PJ**, 9510, and **HS6PJ**, 19020, all 5 kw. (*"This is Bangkok calling through the Thai National Broadcasting Station, HS6PJ."*) A 2.5 kw. PTT transmitter, **HSPP**, was also in use for broadcasting purposes. It operated on 6005 and 6150 kc. And a new 10 kw. station opened in Burma. The PTT-run **Burma State Broadcasting Service** operated on 3488 kc. (**XZZ**) and 6007 (**XYZ**) at 0630–1000 and 2100–2300 EST. Soon it would add a third channel, 6056 kc.

There was renewed activity in French Indochina. In April, **Radio Saigon** reopened. Oper-

This card from Radio Saigon, verifying reception in 1939, contained no mention of Vietnam because, at the time, Vietnam, Cambodia and Laos had been subsumed into French Indochina, of which Hanoi was the capital.

ated by a private company, **Société Indochinois de Radiodiffusion,** the "Voice of France in the Far East" broadcast in French, English and Chinese on 6116 and 11780 kc., 12 kw., and was well heard. English was at 0600–0645 EST. Listener mail was acknowledged in the Tuesday "Listeners' Courier" program. Said one happy listener, "This station is one of the best Asiatics on the 25 meter band." (*"Radio Saigon calling. We want you to write us to help us perfect our English program. You will hear from us at 12:15 noon and 8:30 night, Saigon time."*)

And there were now several shortwave stations in Manila, the Philippines. **KZRM, Radio Manila,** was still on 9570 kc., power 5 kw., sometimes relaying Manila mediumwaver KZEG. **KZRF, Radio Filipinas,** was on 6140 kc., broadcasting "from the Royal Room on the eighth floor of the Marco Polo Hotel, overlooking beautiful Manila." Both KZRM and KZRF were now owned by the Far East Broadcasting Corporation, which later became the Philippine Broadcasting Corporation (Far East Broadcasting Corp. was no relation to the Far East Broadcasting Company, the religious broadcaster which would commence operation from the Philippines in 1949.) KZRH was on 6100 and 9635 kc. It sometimes announced as *"the Voice of the Philippines in Manila, under the American flag."* KZRH soon added a low-power, 10-watt shortwave transmitter at Cebu, **KZRC,** which operated on 6105 kc. as the "Voice of Cebu." And another station, **KZIB,** operated on 6040 and 9500 kc. with 1 kw. It was owned and operated by Beck's Department Store, with studios located atop the Crystal Arcade Building in Manila, with transmitter at Novaliches.

There were a number of new voices from Latin America. New from Cuba was **COHI,** Santa Clara, on 6450 kc., 5 kw., relaying CMHI; and **COCE, La Voz del Transporte,** Havana, on 12230 kc., relaying mediumwave station CMC. Two new Mexican stations opened. One was **XEWQ, Radio Panamericana,** Mexico City, 6080 kc. (later **XEQQ,** 9680), relaying medi-

Some stations produced elaborate QSLs, such as this one from Radio Hucke in Santiago, Chile. The American government was concerned over the German and Italian connections of several stations in Chile, including this one.

umwaver XEQ. *("Ladies and gentlemen, this is XEQ and XEWQ in Mexico City. We are now closing until 9:00 A.M. tomorrow morning. Good night.")* Reception was reported good after **Radio Nacional del Peru** signed off 6082 at 2200 EST. XEWQ closed at 2330. The other Mexican was **XEKW, El Eco de Michoacan**, Morelia, 6030 kc., 500 watts, relaying XEQW.

One Central American station began experimenting with a very low shortwave frequency; **Radiodifusora Nacional** in Guatemala added its third shortwave channel, **TGWC**, on 2320 kc.

Two new radio countries were heard. **FG8AH, Radio Guadeloupe**, Pointe-a-Pitre, was reported on 7445 kc. at approximately 1800–1900 EST. The station identified in English every 15 minutes and soon it was a common logging. And new in April was **ZNS**, in Nassau, Bahamas, relaying mediumwave 790 kc. over 6090 kc. shortwave, 200 watts. It was owned by the Telecommunications Department of the Bahamas government, and sometimes identified as the Isles of June Broadcasting Station. ZNS was on the air at 1330–1400 and 2000–2100. It relayed the BBC at 1820–2000 nightly.

In South America, a station that would be known by decades of DXers commenced operation. It was **CP12, Radio Fides**, La Paz, Bolivia, on 6150 kc. with 250 watts. Also new from Bolivia was **CP22, Radio Internacional de Potosí**, on 6140 kc. New from Chile was **CB1174, Radio Hucke**, operated by Orlandini & Raggio Ltda., Santiago, on 11740 kc. (Its sign off melody was "Marching Through Georgia.") And **CB960, Radio Difusora "Pilot,"** Santiago, Chile, had become **Radio La Americana,** still on 9600 kc. and operating until 2300 EST.

From Uruguay, **SODRE** was heard over CXA4, 6125 kc., and CXA6, 9620. The power was 20 kw. Under construction were 11895 kc. (**CXA10**) and 15300 kc. (**CXA18**). Television experiments were being conducted on 26500 kc. (**CXA21**) and 29500 (**CXA22**).

Central and South American stations produced numerous harmonics. Regulars included **HJ3ABD, Emisora Nueva Granada,** Colombia, 9680 (harmonic of 4840); **HJ3CAF, La Voz de Bogota,** Colombia, 9700 (4850); and many in the 12 mc. range, e.g. **HJ3ABX, La Voz de Colombia,** 11980 (5990); **COCO,** Cuba, 12020 (6010); **HIN, La Voz del Partido Dominicano,** Dominican Republic, 12480 (6240); **COCW, La Voz de las Antillas,** Cuba, 12640 (6320); **TIPG, La Voz de la Victor,** Costa Rica, 12820 (6410). It was not only the Latin Americans that produced harmonics. The 6040 kc. channel of **W1XAL** in Boston was regularly heard on 12080, while **W1XK's** 9570 kc. transmitter could be heard on 19140.

The biggest news from South America was the mass relocation of Colombian and Venezuelan shortwave stations to the still largely unused 60 meter tropical band. The Colombian stations were supposed to move by July 1, and most did. In addition, four-letter calls now replaced the typical six-character letter-and-number calls for all Colombian shortwave stations. A few Colombians remained on 31 and 49 meters. Most Colombian stations operated with between 250 and 1,000 watts; a small number boasted 5 kw. transmitters.

Many stations in Venezuela also moved to 60 meters, and some received new call letters (within the letter-and-number convention that was still used in Venezuela). The Colombian and Venezuelan stations were often 5 kc. apart, with the Venezuelans occupying channels ending in multiples of 10, the Colombians on frequencies ending in 5. It all made for chaotic DXing, as listeners tried to determine which stations were on which channels.

The 60 meter Colombian stations and their new call letters were as follows:

        4745 HJCX, La Voz de Colombia, Bogota
        4755 HJEH, La Voz del Pacifico, Buenaventura
        4765 HJFB, Radio Manizales, Manizales
        4775 HJGB, Radio Santander, Bucaramanga
        4785 HJAB, La Voz de Barranquilla, Barranquilla
        4795 HJFI, Ecos del Combeima, Ibague
        4805 HJDU, Emisora Universidad de Antioquia, Medellin
        4815 HJBB, La Voz de Cúcuta, Cúcuta
        4825 HJED, La Voz del Valle, Cali
        4835 HJAE, La Voz de los Laboratorios Fuentes, Cartagena
        4845 HJCD, Emisora Nueva Granada, Bogota
        4855 HJCF, La Voz de Bogota, Bogota
        4865 HJBJ, La Voz de Santa Marta, Santa Marta
        4875 HJFH, La Voz de Armenia, Armenia
        4895 HJCH, La Voz de la Victor, Bogota
        4905 HJAG, Emisora Atlantico, Barranquilla
        4915 HJFC, La Voz de Pereira, Pereira
        4925 HJAP, Radio Cartagena, Cartagena

The Venezuelan stations were:

        4770 YV1RT, La Voz de la Fe, Maracaibo
        4780 YV1RO, Radio Trujillo, Trujillo
        4790 YV5RY, La Voz de la Esfera, Caracas
        4800 YV1RV, Ecos del Zulia, Maracaibo
        4810 YV1RU, Radiodifusora Maracaibo, Maracaibo
        4820 YV3RN, Radio Barquisimeto, Barquisimeto
        4830 YV5RH, Ondas Populares, Caracas
        4840 YV4RX, La Voz de Aragua, Maracay
        4850 YV1RZ, Radio Valera, Valera
        4860 YV1RL, Radio Popular, Maracibo
        4870 YV2RN, La Voz del Tachira, San Cristóbal
        4880 YV6RU, Ecos del Orinoco, Ciudad Bolivar
        4890 YV1RX, Ondas del Lago, Maracaibo
        4900 YV6RT, Radio Bolivar, Ciudad Bolivar

4910 YV1RY, Radio Coro, Coro
4920 YV5RU, Estudios Universo, Caracas
4930 YV4RP, Radio Valencia, Valencia
4940 YV5RO, La Voz de Venezuela, Caracas
4950 YV4RO, La Voz de Carabobo, Valencia
4960 YV5RS, La Voz de Philco, Caracas
4970 YV1RJ, Radio Falcón, Coro
4990 YV3RX, La Voz de Lara, Barquisimeto
5010 YV5RM, Radiodifusora Venezuela, Caracas
5020 YV4RQ, Radio Puerto Cabello, Puerto Cabello
5040 YV5RN, Radio Caracas, Caracas

In addition, three Venezuelan stations would now call the largely-vacant 90 meter band home (at the time 90 meters was 3300–3500 kc.). These were **YV5RW, Radio Turmerito**, Caracas, on 3400 kc.; **YV3RF, La Voz del Llano**, Acariqua, 3490; and **YV5RV, Emisora Vargas**, La Guaira, 3500.

One observer noted that more than 30 Venezuelan and Colombian stations could now be heard at night on 60 meters. Notwithstanding these moves, however, there were still more shortwave broadcasting stations operating on out-of-band channels between the 49 and the 31 meter bands than there were using 60 meters.

In Australia, the war in Europe, together with heightened Japanese aggression in Asia, led to the expansion and consolidation of the country's shortwave broadcasting efforts into an external service known as "**Australia Calling.**" This was the predecessor of **Radio Australia**. A joint effort of the Broadcasting Division of the wartime Department of Information (DOI), the Australian Broadcasting Commission and the Postmaster General, but with primary control in DOI, it commenced operation on December 20, 1939 using the Postmaster General's 2 kw. station, **VLR**, in Lyndhurst (near Melbourne), plus two 10 kw. transmitters, denominated **VLQ** and **VLQ2** ("V for Victory, L for Loyalty, Q for Quality"), at the large AWA transmitter base in Pennant Hills (near Sydney). Lyndhurst directed its signal to the Dutch East Indies, Pennant Hills to Europe. Call letters of the Australian stations were typically given with an added numeral to designate the specific frequency, e.g. VLR3, VLQ4, etc. AWA ceased its own shortwave broadcasting, and the "ME" broadcasting stations passed into history. Struggle for control of the government's overseas service would go on for years, with the DOI remaining the principal controlling agency until 1950, when the service became part of the ABC.[182]

Also in 1939, the ABC co-located a 2 kw. shortwave transmitter, **VLW**, with a mediumwave unit in Wanneroo, near Perth, in Western Australia. Together the two were intended for local and regional coverage. VLW shortwave operated on 6130, 9560 and 11830 kc. During U.S. mornings, 6130 kc. suffered QRM from **CHNX**. Consistent with the closure of the other "ME's," the AWA station in Perth, **VK6ME**, was reassigned from broadcast to utility work. Among the clubs, the International Short Wave Club started a postage bureau to sell postcard-value mint stamps for inclusion with members' reception reports. Sample rates included: Argentina, 6¢; Canada, 3¢; Haiti, 5¢; Sweden, 7¢; England, 4¢.

To celebrate its tenth anniversary, the ISWC arranged special programs from Turkey and Italy. Programs were broadcast for the IDA by **Zeesen**, **Radio Internacional** (Peru), **TGWA** and **TGWB** (Guatemala), and **W6XKG**, a Los Angeles apex station that billed itself as "The Pioneer Short Wave Station of the West." The Universal Radio DX Club arranged for a special program from **ZP14**, Villarica, Paraguay, and **Zeesen** broadcast a special for the NNRC.

TG2, Radio Morse, Guatemala, and **YNDG**, Leon, Nicaragua, presented programs for multiple clubs and even offered some announcements and short programs in SIRELA, an oddball "international radio language" that was being promoted by its inventor, Prof. Carlo

OFFICIAL VERIFICATION OF RECEPTION

VLQ 5 30.99m 9.680mcys at 6:25am C.S.T. 1/10/40
Mr. J. Allen 1123 Hunnell, Wichita, Kansas.

VLQ

AUSTRALIA

Sydney

General Manager

AUSTRALIAN BROADCASTING COMMISSION

The Australian shortwave service, "Australia Calling," came on the air in December 1939 and was soon operating a North American service. The 10 kw. transmitter, VLQ, was located in Pennant Hills, near Sydney.

Spatari.[183] TG2 awarded weekly prizes for the most complete and the most distant reception reports, and reportedly offered SIRELA QSLs for SIRELA-language reports.

The war would have a huge impact on the clubs. "As we go to press," wrote the ISWC in October, "the armies of England, France, Germany and the Soviet Republics are at war and others are preparing for war. Such a condition creates a feeling of despair in us, for in these countries are many of our friends. It is almost inconceivable that these friends who were so warm and friendly to each other should now be forced to try to destroy each other. We make no attempt to place the blame for the situation on any person or persons, but we do say with whole-hearted sincerity that we hope each and every friend will go through the catastrophe unharmed."[184] The ISWC, IDA and other clubs, would soon experience major declines in membership from the areas rent by hostilities.

The use of shortwave to bring speeches by European leaders to American audiences, both via direct-to-listener broadcasts and shortwave relays that serviced domestic broadcast band stations, usually with translation, commentary and the like, kept shortwave within the consciousness of American listeners. For shortwave listeners overseas, the American stations stepped up their news coverage, particularly to countries where free news coverage was not available.

The shortwave industry emphasized the utility of shortwave rather than its novelty. "Ten Years Ago Short Wave was News ... Today it Supplies News," read the banner in NBC's full-page advertisement in *Broadcasting* magazine. "NBC Short Wave Pick-ups Write History in the Skies!"

ADVENTURE ... in 1937, one of the history-making NBC short wave pick-ups came from the distant South Seas. NBC sent Announcer George Hicks, Engineers Walter R. Brown and Marvin

Adams 7000 miles to Canton Island, where in the tropic heat they painted a vivid 15-minute word picture of the longest total eclipse in 1200 years.

THRILLS ... last year one of NBC's 556 short wave pick-ups brought the thrill of exploration to millions of listeners in the United States, when, for the first time Dragomen, Arabs and Egyptologists broadcast from the base of the Gizeh Pyramid in Egypt — and from within the tomb of Cheops.

NEWS ... one of the greatest public services performed by NBC occurred in 1938 when Europe, nearly torn asunder by threats of war, tottered on the brink of world-wide catastrophe. And via short wave, NBC brought America's millions the news as it happened, through eye-witness, first-hand accounts — keeping the radio listeners of this country better informed about conditions "over there" than the Europeans themselves.

ENTERTAINMENT ... only recently a short wave "stunt" was performed with such accuracy and smoothness that millions who heard it were not aware of it. Charles Laughton and Elsa Lanchester ... stars of Paramount's "The Beachcomber" ... were separated by the Atlantic Ocean. But with one in NBC's New York studios and the other in London — they enacted scenes from their picture — without a flaw![185]

By year's end, some familiar voices had been silenced. Reprising the year's shortwave events, *The New York Times* observed:

Polish short-wave stations kept going until the night of Sept. 6. Then, like the Ethiopian wave, like those in Shanghai and Canton, like Vienna's beam, like Madrid's government transmitter and Albania's station; like the Prague short-wave outfit, the Polish waves slid out of the picture.[186]

Propagandizing on shortwave was intense, but still far from its crescendo. The state of shortwave propaganda at the end of 1939 was summarized by the Subcommittee on Programs of the Interdepartmental Committee to Study International Broadcasting:

[T]he German propaganda [favorable publicity for Germany, unfavorable publicity or silence as to rivals, and biased news] is so violent and so lacking in plausibility as largely to defeat its own purposes. Italian propaganda is apparently more direct in its nature but it is recently reported to have become less aggressive in its anti-democratic content. Italy's news broadcasts have become relatively impartial. The propaganda from the Soviet Union is also more direct, distinctly anti-democratic, frequently opposed to the United States. It is said to be stale and obvious. Programs from Great Britain and the United States contain little, if any, political propaganda.[187]

Both press and government had decided that the shortwave output of the major parties to the developing world conflict was worth listening to. CBS and NBC set up listening posts to ferret out news and obtain material for rebroadcast. The CBS facility was located on Long Island, while the NBC post was at Radio City (it was later moved to Bellmore, Long Island).[188] The CBS installation consisted of five persons operating in what was called "hermitlike isolation" in a wooded area of the town of Roosevelt, where several antennas had been erected. The property was owned by Jack Norton, who worked in CBS master control.[189]

As the war heated up, the networks kept engineers and translators on all-day duty to monitor foreign broadcasts and transmit them to the network newsroom for recording, evaluation and translation. Some stations, such as London and Zeesen, were monitored on a regular schedule, while others were checked in the course of ongoing band searches. While urgent news was always delivered immediately, the networks placed high value on minimizing the interruption of regular programs, and so news was usually presented during station breaks. Contact with network correspondents was generally accomplished through RCA's Radio Central.

The Princeton University School of Public and International Affairs, using Rockefeller Foundation money, set up the Princeton Listening Center to analyze Axis broadcasts. It would close in 1941, but its work led to the formation of the government's own listening branch, the Foreign Broadcast Information Service (originally called the Foreign Broadcast Monitoring Service, later the Foreign Broadcast Intelligence Service). And in England, the BBC Monitoring Service was established. Station information published by FBIS and BBCMS would be highly valued by the DX community for many years. The Axis countries maintained similar listening posts.[190]

The "war on the shortwaves" would soon supply the fundamental rationale for over a half century of high-power shortwave broadcasting.

4

1940–1945

Today every nation in Europe displays a keen appreciation of the importance of short-wave transmission in inter-country mass communication. The short wave knows no borders and passes freely from one country to the other. Some nations are using this method to spread their particular ideologies and their pet brands of war propaganda, it is true; but the day will come when short waves will find their rightful use as bonds of international understanding and appreciation. ¶England links the vast British Empire with such a short-wave bond. The United States has for a number of years been making its South American neighbors better acquainted with it by means of short-wave broadcasts. ¶And while we are prophesying, who knows but that the day may come when the short wave will bring forth a new and better understanding between the great nations of the earth.—*Frank Conrad, 1940*[1]

1940

Denmark and Norway came under German control in April, Holland, Belgium and Luxembourg in May, Norway in June. By year's end, Rumania and Hungary, although not occupied, were firmly in the Axis orbit, and the puppet state of Slovakia was a Reich protectorate. Paris fell on June 14, and the country was divided into occupied France in the north and west, and a then-unoccupied southern, or "free," zone, administered from Vichy by the collaborationist government of Marshal Philippe Pétain. All of the French shortwave broadcast transmitter sites were in the German-occupied area.

In June, Soviet-friendly governments were installed in Lithuania, Latvia and Estonia. Soviet troops followed, and all three countries were annexed to the Soviet Union the following month. During the second half of the year the Battle of Britain raged in the skies over London and other English cities.

Shortwave broadcasting by the major European powers now became a major political weapon, and mirrored the fighting on the ground and the geopolitical changes brought on by the war.

Protagonists on both sides of the Channel sent word volleys whizzing through space. A Lord Haw Haw led off for the Germans. England countered with sly quips.... From the Far North, on the Russo-Finnish fronts, were reports from Helsinki and Stockholm of the exploits of crack Finnish ski troops operating near the Arctic Circle. Moscow's radio worked night and day in an attempt to counter reported Finn successes.... ¶ With the first Nazi stroke the wireless lanes of both Denmark and Norway were silenced.... ¶The well-known Dutch announcer, Edward Startz, vanished from the air on May 11. That was shortly after Germany had parachuted into Holland.... ¶A day or so later the Brussels short-wave station blinked out.... ¶With the concentrated German drive on Flanders, wireless stations in Paris began to work overtime. ¶The French broadcasting spurt was short-lived.[2]

On January 12, a bomb put the **Finnish Broadcasting Corporation** in Lahti off the air, but soon it was back in service. **Radio Denmark** and **Norsk Rikskringkasting** in Oslo went silent with the German invasion of Denmark and Norway on April 9. Both soon returned to the air under German control. Holland was invaded in May. The staff disabled the transmitters and attempted unsuccessfully to blow up the antennas, but the installation was reconstructed by the Germans. Eddie Startz held forth right up until the end. "Don't worry about Holland," he said. "She will look out for herself." As England and Germany traded radio barrages, Startz was his cheerful self. "'Eddie' may be playing 'I'm Forever Blowing Bubbles' or remarking on the fresh supply of tulips now poking through the sod," noted one observer.[3]

The French shortwave transmitters at **Pontoise** went silent. For a short time a substitute station operated from **Bordeaux** on 9520 and 15240 kc., but in a week it too disappeared.[4] Soon the **Paris Mondial** channels were occupied by the Nazis, who were believed also to be using the **Allouis** transmitter site. TPC5, 15240 kc., could be heard at 1200–1515 EST with Nazi programming in French and English. The 15240 kc. channel and several others— 9520, 11845 — were particular mysteries. Sometimes they identified, both over the air and in program schedules, simply as "**Station Y.**" Although the French colonies followed the Vichy line at the outset, this changed as a result of local decisions and the success of Free French Forces. Soon French Equatorial Africa, Tahiti and New Caledonia joined the Free French. Many French military forces in North Africa did likewise when the Allies invaded in 1942; Guadeloupe, Martinique and others abandoned Vichy in 1943. French Indochina, under direct threat of Japan, stayed Vichy.

Germany and England were now the two major players on the shortwave bands, with Italy right behind. **Zeesen** was on 24 frequencies, the BBC 21. Said *The New York Times*:

> Listeners have no difficulty in spotting the chief protagonists on the dial. Summer static is dropping out of sight; the European waves are clear. One doesn't necessarily have to bother with megacycle figures any more. It is just a matter of tuning the loudest meter band (evenings now, the 25 and 31 meter spots are best), and turning the knob until London, Rome and Berlin shout into the room.[5]

As Germany occupied a country it took over its broadcasting. After a period of silence, many of the stations resumed broadcasting their own shortwave programming — now under German control — on a reduced basis, while putting their transmitters at the disposal of Germany for Reich programs at other times. As a result, it was common to hear **Zeesen** programming over transmitters located in France, Holland, etc. Some frequencies appeared to be shared by more than one transmitter site. At least when broadcasting Reich programming, many transmitters in the occupied countries utilized new "DX" callsigns, e.g. **DXD, DXQ,** etc. **Prague** (**Podebrady**) received new callsigns—**DHE2A, DHE3C** in place of **OLR2A, OLR3C,** etc.—but at times also announced the new DX callsigns.[6]

It was noted in the industry magazine *Broadcasting* that "[p]rograms are heard from stations with familiar calls but operating on different waves and in such a way as to lead some listeners to the belief that practically all of Europe has been hooked up into a single German-controlled network." Even the professionals could get fooled. After hearing German over a Japanese station, **Press Wireless** monitors concluded that the German network had now been extended to Japan. Actually, both countries were using 15160 kc., and Germany had closed without identification just as Japan's JZK was signing on.[7]

German programs included "The Enemy Listens," "Sketches from Berlin Life," "The

College Hour" (hosted by former Hunter College assistant professor turned German propagandist Dr. Otto Koischwitz), and "Listen and Judge for Yourself" (about the comparative merits of German and English war broadcasts). Lighter fare included "Fritz and Fred," "Through a Woman's Eyes," "Jim and Johnny," "Hot Off the Wire," and "The Schmidt Family." Germany also broadcast dictation-speed news (news transmitted slowly enough to be written down).

Italy's propaganda at this time was fairly benign. "In the programs aimed at America, were it not for short propaganda chats and news in English, a listener would get no clue from the broadcasts that Italy is at war, so similar is the pattern of the current programs to those of the pre-war days."[8]

American-born Englishman William Joyce was the face of Germany's English-language propagandizing, first against England, later the United States. The *London Daily Press* had dubbed him Lord Haw-Haw soon after he took over a colleague's propaganda broadcasts which had begun in April 1939. The name stuck, and soon started appearing in **Zeesen** program schedules. It was estimated that half the radios in England were tuned to Lord Haw-Haw at least once a day. Listeners in England could hear him over various German-controlled European mediumwave and longwave transmitters, but his sophisticated, usually-friendly voice was also heard on Zeesen's international shortwave broadcasts. Joyce also played a key role in the **New British Broadcasting Station** and the other English-language "clandestine" stations run by the German Büro Concordia.

Haw-Haw's line changed depending on the circumstances, but his focus was on class warfare and the sowing of fear and panic over German strength. He sought to raise doubt in British minds about the true motives of the nation's government, eventually urging open revolt and the replacement of the country's "war mongering" political leadership. Haw-Haw offered a different view of the political reality of the day, and alternative solutions to problems, with a style that ranged from humor to cool reasoning to name-calling and ridicule. The characters of Joyce's humorous skits reflected the stereotypes at the heart of German propaganda.[9]

While Lord Haw-Haw was never taken all that seriously by the British public, his audience was sizeable, not least because of the drabness of the BBC's own fare. His presence had an unmistakable influence on the shape of the BBC's programming. Listenership increased as German military advances mounted up, but declined once England had sobered on Germany's ambitions and capabilities, and its plans for the country. Lord Haw-Haw would be heard throughout the war, and his comments were often noted in the English and American press.

There were numerous other English-language propagandists who broadcast from Berlin, many of them American. These included, among others, Fred Kaltenbach (who came to be known as Lord Hee-Haw), Edward Delaney ("E. D. Ward"), Robert H. Best, Douglas Chandler, Koischwitz ("Mr. O.K."), Constance Drexel, Jane Anderson, and Mildred Gillars ("Axis Sally").[10] They added spice to the study of broadcast propaganda that developed during the war and after. All, together with Ezra Pound broadcasting from Italy, would eventually be indicted. Joyce was tried and convicted in 1945 and executed on January 3, 1946. He was 39 years old.

The propaganda of the radio traitors that was thought most effective was predictions of enemy military actions that turned out to be accurate and broadcasts reflecting detailed knowledge of Allied conditions, plans, and personnel that appeared to have been gathered from behind-the-lines sources. However, review of Axis broadcasts after the war revealed that there had actually been little such programming, and that the rumor, gossip and anxiety that propaganda broadcasts caused in the civilian and military communities was based less on what people actually heard than on what they thought they had heard.[11]

Propaganda broadcasts were not aimed solely at Britain and the United States. The Middle East was a major target. It was the Bari broadcasts from Italy that were largely responsible for the establishment of the BBC Arabic service. More widely listened to were the Arabic programs from Zeesen, which promoted anti–Semitism, appealed to Arab nationalism and Moslem religious feelings, and lambasted western scheming against the Arabs.

Radio Tokyo promoted the notion of a closer identity of the Middle East with the rest of Asia than with Europe, and Japan as the leader of "Asia for the Asians." However, Radio Tokyo programs were poorly produced and not well heard.[12] Before the war, Japanese shortwave broadcasting was as stodgy as the BBC. In 1940, one NHK employee was sent to the United States and another to Australia, New Zealand and Southeast Asia to evaluate reception and audience potential, and both reported the need for an improvement in the Japanese on-air style. Adoption of a less formal but more propagandistic tone paralleled Japanese military successes and the increased use of shortwave as a psychological warfare weapon by all sides.

At the BBC, the complement of transmitters at **Daventry** was increased from nine in February 1939 to 11 in June 1940. Early in the year a 100 kw. mediumwave transmitter at **Start Point** was converted to dual mediumwave-shortwave use and put into action on 41 and 49 meters, and in September a 15 kw. mediumwave transmitter at **Clevedon** was similarly converted to shortwave and used on 25 and 41 meters for broadcasts to Europe. The BBC sometimes identified as "This is London, the last outpost of free democracy in Western Europe." Both Germany and Britain dropped on-air references to specific frequencies in favor of giving only the meter bands. Although jamming was still relatively light, it was growing, and the use of multiple frequencies for any given broadcast was increasing.

The **BBC's** external broadcasting, commonly referred to as the Overseas Services, was now made up of four parts. The main one was the Empire Service, which broadcast mainly in English but in some other languages as well. The Empire Service was itself subdivided into four subsidiary services: Pacific, Eastern, African and North American. The other three parts of the overseas broadcasts were the European service (foreign languages), which would long have a distinct identity; the Latin American service (Spanish and Portuguese); and the Near Eastern service (Arabic, Turkish and "Iranian").

Until now there had been no North American service as such, although North American listeners were encouraged to tune in to some Empire Service broadcasts that were specifically geared to them, and to real-time relays or rebroadcasts of BBC programs— particularly Britain's premier news program, "Radio News Reel," which began in July — over the **CBC** in Canada and CBS, NBC and the Mutual Broadcasting System in the United States. The new service was slightly different from other BBC services in that the bulk of the listeners were not Britishers, and the programming and the general broadcast technique took this into account — news bulletins were shorter, entertainment programs tended to follow American patterns, etc.

The European Service moved from Broadcasting House to Bush House in 1940. (Broadcasting House was hit by aerial bombs several times during the year.) Later the European Service would be joined by many other elements of the BBC's international broadcasting structure, and Bush House would become synonymous with the World Service of later years. It was a distinctly uncomfortable place during the war years, one where even the regularly scheduled European broadcasts could fairly be said to emanate from "the underground."[13] (The World Service departed Bush House in 2012.)

Programs from London now included such titles as "Britain Speaks (intended mainly for the U.S.)," "Our Island Fortress," "Under the Shadow of the Swastika," "Atlantic Patrol," "Go to It" (about accelerating work in industrial and munitions factories), "The Land We Defend," and "An American Looks at Britain" (presented by American newsman Warren Irvin).

By the end of the year the BBC was broadcasting 145 hours of foreign-language programming each week, more than three times the number at the start of the war. Thirty-two languages were in use. News was the jewel in the BBC crown, with 78 bulletins broadcast daily. In February a "Programme for the Forces" was inaugurated to serve the British military at home and in continental Europe. It was on the air at 0130–0300 and 0530–1800, on mediumwave and also on 7230 kc. shortwave. Starting at the end of the year, the BBC also included in the Empire Service occasional special programs for the forces. There was a weekly program directed to India, and others intended for troops in Iceland, Tobruk, Malta, and Palestine, Royal Air Force trainees in Canada, etc. And the BBC Home Service, which was mainly on mediumwave, was carried on one shortwave channel, 6075 kc., at 0200–1920 EST.

Through it all, both the good and the bad of BBC culture, earned or suffered over many years, was largely preserved. Said one knowledgeable observer: "Most of the people I have talked to agree that, allowing for war-time conditions, the BBC is as truthful as could be expected. The universal complaint is that its method of presentation is dull."[14]

The governments in exile of Poland, Czechoslovakia, Norway, Belgium and Holland, and the Free French Forces, were now headquartered in London, and during the next few years time was allotted them on the BBC to address their peoples in their respective languages. These programs were called by various names, e.g. "Radio Polskie," "Radio Belgique," etc. There were two French broadcasts, "Ici la France," and a five-minute Free French program which came to be known by its opening words, "Honneur et Patrie." On June 18, General de Gaulle made his famous first broadcast from London, urging his countrymen to fight on. (The General had to repeat the speech because it had not been recorded.) Six weeks later the Dutch created "Radio Oranje," a daily 20-minute program which was transmitted over the BBC. Radio Oranje was a regular source of communication with the Dutch populace, focusing at first on morale building, then, in 1942 and 1943, resistance, and finally, in 1944, invasion instructions and post-war planning. In 1941, the regular BBC Greek service would start its transmission with the cow-and-goat-bells and shepherd's-flute tuning melody of **Athens Radio**, a recording of which had been presented to the BBC for safe keeping by the Greek minister in London.

It was the year that clandestine broadcasting began in earnest, with the German Propaganda Ministry's clandestine broadcasting office, the Büro Concordia — so named for its original location in Berlin's Villa Concordia — first off the mark.[15] Although there were many such stations, not all could be heard in the United States. One that could was the **New British Broadcasting Station**, which began operating in February. Purported to be located in England, its line was pacifist — Germany was winning the war and Britain might as well stop fighting. Frequencies at first were 11945 and 5925 kc., but soon it was operating at 1530–1600 and 1630–1700 EST on three parallel channels— 7305, 9750 and 11960 kc. The 11960 outlet was heard on the American east coast with good strength, but modulation was reportedly poor. The New British Broadcasting Station was on the air for more than five years.

Another German clandestine of the day — on the air even before the New British Broadcasting Station — was **La Voix de la Pais** (the **Voice of Peace**), also called **Poste du Réveil de la France** (Radio of the French Awakening). Speaking in both French and English, it railed against the French government, stressing the superiority of German military force and the

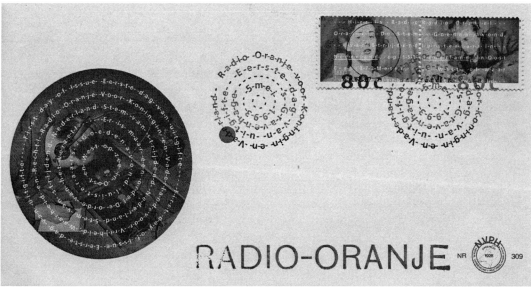

Top: France capitulated on June 17, 1940, and the next day, on the BBC, a little-known General Charles de Gaulle, who had fled to England a few days earlier, made his famous appeal to the French to fight on. A similar speech was made four days later. The stamp on this first day cover commemorates the June 18 broadcast. *Bottom:* In 1993 the Netherlands issued two postage stamps commemorating Radio Oranje, one depicting a singer who performed on the station, the other a clandestine listening scene. The text printed on the stamps is taken from the station's opening announcement.

need for peace. It signed off with "La Marseillaise" and shouts of "Vive la France." Frequencies were 6040, 6270 and 7210 kc., plus (later) mediumwave and longwave.

Among the other shortwave developments in Europe, **Radio Sofia**, Bulgaria was heard on 10310 kc. Sweden was now broadcasting nightly to North America at 2000–2100 on 9535 kc. (**SBU**) and 11705 (**SBP**), with SBU usually providing the better reception.

At the start of the year the station in Hungary began identifying as **Radio Budapest**. A North American service was transmitted at 1835–2000 EST over **HAT5**, 9625 kc., and a transmission to South America was heard at 1700–1820 on **HAD3**, 11850 kc. The low-power HAD experimental transmissions that were first noted in 1939 were still heard occasionally, but the transmitter was soon upgraded to 10 kw. Although now allied with Germany, much of the programming from Hungary remained unchanged.

ZAA, Radio Tirana, Albania, having dropped 6084 kc., was now broadcasting on 7850 only, at 0620–0830 and 1220–1700 EST. It broadcast a special transmission for North and Central America on May 14 at 2100–2200 EST, and listeners who sent reception reports were rewarded with QSLs as well as magazines, pamphlets, postcards, maps, and other souvenirs.

Radio Centre, Moscow, was heard testing on many new frequencies. The locations that were known were: Moscow, **RAN**, 9600, 10490 and 16300 kc., 20 kw.; Moscow, **RKI**, 7520, 7540, 15040 and 15080 kc., 25 kw.; Moscow, **RNE**, 6000 and 12000 kc., 20 kw.; Moscow, **RW96**, 6030, 9520, 9685, 15180, 15270 and 15410 kc., 100 kw.; Irkutsk, **RW59**, 6050 kc., 20 kw.; Khabarovsk, **RV15**, 4270 kc., 20 kw.; and Tashkent, **RIA**, 11700 and 15120 kc., 20 kw. The locations of many other channels were unknown.

Radio Nations continued its broadcasts from Geneva. The rebuilt **Swiss Broadcasting Corporation** facility at Schwarzenburg took to the air again in April, preceded for a few months by tests over a 250-watt transmitter, **HEC**, on Monday and Wednesday at 1945–2115 to South America on 11865 kc., 2145–2315 to North America on 9535. Following the tests, the **Swiss Shortwave Service**, as it was known, took over, adopting the same twice-weekly schedule. The beams to North and South America on 9535 and 11865 kc. continued, with programs offered in English, Spanish and Portuguese, in addition to the French, German and Italian that are spoken in Switzerland. The transmissions would become daily in 1941.

The United States took the first wartime-readiness steps that would culminate in a government takeover of shortwave broadcasting. In August, President Roosevelt set up the Office for Coordination of Commercial and Cultural Relations Between the American Republics. Among its other duties, the office provided the private shortwave broadcasters with research on Latin America. More important was the establishment, in the following month, of the Defense Communications Board, later renamed the Board of War Communications. Its mission was to develop a plan for radio and other communications during periods of national defense, including control of non-military communications that might be needed in time of war. Westinghouse, Crosley, NBC, CBS, GE and WRUL were all represented on the Board's International Broadcasting Committee and gave the Board full cooperation. For now, however, American shortwave remained under private control.

Major changes were afoot at Westinghouse. In July, **WBOS** in Massachusetts closed down temporarily while relocating from Millis to Hull, south of Boston, and increasing power to 50 kw. The station returned to the air in November. Henceforth, Hull would be the locus of all Westinghouse shortwave efforts. (Millis became an FCC monitoring site.) In December, the Westinghouse transmitter site at Saxonburg, near Pittsburgh, from which **WPIT** and its predecessor, **W8XK**, had broadcast since 1932, was closed and the WPIT transmitter moved to Hull, where it continued to operate for a time as WPIT. WPIT and WBOS staff operated out of space adjacent to the WBZ offices in Boston. With the retirement of the WPIT call letters on January 1, 1941, the station would be fully integrated into WBOS operations and the era of Pittsburgh as headquarters of the company's pioneering development of shortwave broadcasting came to an end.

To comply with the FCC's 50 kw. power requirement, Crosley station **WLWO** inaugurated a new 50 kw. transmitter on October 12. It was badly damaged in a fire eight days later, but temporary repairs brought it back into operation the next day. In November it increased power to 75 kw. **WRUL** increased power on one of its two transmitters to 50 kw. The American shortwave industry claimed that the 50 kw. requirement would cost the stations $2 million in new equipment, and that an additional $1 million annually would be spent on increased operating costs and new programming. It was too much for the 5 kw. "Wonderful Isle of Dreams" station in Miami, **WDJM**, which closed down and sold its equipment to WRUL.

American shortwave programming was still highly eclectic. GE offered its "Promotion of Safety" series, produced in cooperation with the Inter-American Safety Council and Rotary International, over **WGEA** and **WGEO**. It also broadcast the "French Hour," and **WCBX** carried the opening ceremonies of the Italian Art Exhibit at New York's Museum of Art. Most of the NBC shortwave broadcasting day was taken up with programs specially designed for foreign audiences. **WLWO** was transmitting some 21 hours a day to Latin America, some in Spanish and Portuguese but most still simulcast from WLW domestic programs. French and German were added later, as were various foreign-language programs produced by CBS and GE.

Notwithstanding events in Europe, Latin America remained an important target of American shortwave broadcasting. Virtually all the stations were beaming programs to the area. The Department of Commerce, in conjunction with the State Department and the Radio Manufacturers Association, sought wider publication and distribution of the stations' schedules through the Latin American press (not always easily accomplished on a non-paying basis). The stations reported broadcasting some 449 hours a week collectively to the area, including over 13 hours of news daily, and receiving nearly 10,000 letters a month.[16] They took pride in observing that their foreign news transmissions, which appeared to be the most popular programming, met the same standards of truthfulness as regular domestic news broadcasts.[17]

It was in 1940 that the notion of extending the reach of American shortwave signals to Latin America through local rebroadcasting networks took form. NBC announced that it was setting up the **Pan-American Network** ("Cadena Panamericana"), which would become the largest of the several networks, eventually growing to 124 affiliates in 20 countries. (NBC credited itself with a ten-year history of Latin American shortwave broadcasting.[18]) CBS, which believed in the efficacy of local advertising of rebroadcast programs rather than direct advertising over long-distance shortwave, followed in 1941 with the **Network of the Americas** ("La Cadena de las Americas"), which also covered 20 countries and had 76 affiliates (later 97). Crosley created the **Inter-American Radio Network** ("Cadena Radio Inter-Americana") in 1941, with 28 affiliates in Mexico, Central America, the Caribbean, Colombia and Venezuela. The **Mutual Broadcasting System**, although not operating a shortwave station of its own, sought to arrange program exchanges with Latin America, beaming its programs over **WRUL** and receiving Latin American programs in return via the **Press Wireless** station at Hicksville. Later, Press Wireless was used for transmitting as well. Announcements of these network plans invariably followed well-publicized trips to Latin America by industry executives who would, upon their return, extol the virtues of our neighbors to the south and the efficacy of the new broadcasting arrangements.[19]

The Latin American affiliates received U.S. programming by shortwave or by transcription, and retransmitted it over local channels, typically in the broadcast band but also over the many shortwave simulcasts that were in operation. However, unlike the domestic American chains, these networks were fairly informal affairs. Generally they were not exclusive, so stations could sign up with more than one American provider. And while CBS network members were supposed to carry at least one hour of CBS programming a day, local operators, whose interests did not always align with those of the American network, made the decisions.

In any event, the Latin American networks did not much help the bottom line of the American shortwave broadcasters, which continued to operate at a loss.[20]

Specific programs that were designed for wartime Europe were still comparatively few. **WRUL** broadcast the nightly "Atlantic Friendship Bridge" to help buoy British spirits. The program included greetings from British children who had been evacuated to the U.S. and Canada by parents and friends in order to ensure their safety during the Blitz. The **BBC** had a parallel program where the parents spoke to the children. Although much of WRUL's standard educational programming continued during the year (readings from Chinese poets, technical courses on radio, "The Geography of Literature"), it was supplemented by activities in clear support of Nazi victims. Late in 1940, special broadcasts were arranged for Yugoslavia from WRUL. Soon after Holland was overrun the station also commenced broadcasts in Dutch. These were organized by Walter Lemmon's well-known author-journalist

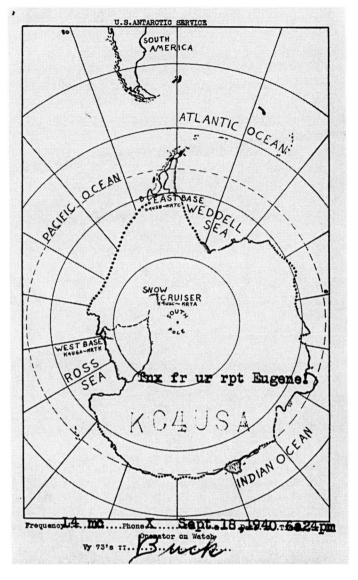

This QSL is from the 1940 Byrd Antarctic expedition. It bears the postmark of the USS *Bear* in "Little America." The *Bear* was one of two vessels that made the trip.

neighbor and shortwave aficionado, Hendrik Willem Van Loon, whose article, "A Short-Wave Journey of Discovery," had graced an RCA promotional booklet of the same name in 1937.

Perhaps WRUL's greatest contribution to the European war effort was in 1940 after Norway fell to the Germans. Every hour, the voice of the Norwegian ambassador to the United States was heard over the station, advising the 900 ships of the Norwegian merchant fleet to put in to neutral ports and ignore Nazi instructions to return home. All the ships were saved. Norway had been sponsoring Norwegian-language programs over **W1XAL** (including English lessons) since 1935.[21]

Notwithstanding the medium's newfound propaganda side, shortwave's ability to still stir the embers had not diminished. **KGEI** invited relatives and friends of missionaries to send greetings through its Sunday program, "Missionary Mail Bag," on the air at 0800–0900 EST on 9530 kc. The Westinghouse Far North broadcasts were still in operation; a new series of the long-running Saturday night feature began on October 5. It was not unusual for the Christmas and New Year's Far North broadcasts to last four or five hours.

And 1940 saw another Byrd Antarctic adventure. In 1939, at the Admiral's urging, Congress had established the U.S. Antarctic Service in order to expand the U.S. presence in the southern region in the face of increased exploration and land claims by other countries. The first expedition undertaken by Byrd under the new agency established two bases in January. In addition to an extensive internal and external communication system operated by the navy, and amateur radio operations (**KC4USA, KC4USB, KC4USC**), the expedition sent broadcast material to CBS and NBC using the expedition's commercial callsigns, **KRTC, KRTK** and **KRTA** (the latter transmitter located aboard the expedition's "snow cruiser").[22]

Starting on February 2, a special series of entertainment programs was beamed to "Little America" over **WGEO** in Schenectady and **KGEI** in San Francisco. Originating in the studios of **WEAF**, they were transmitted every other Friday night at 2330–2400 EST, each broadcast sponsored by one of a group of well-known newspapers. Eventually they turned into two-way exchanges, with keen listeners able to hear both the domestic and the KRTC sides (11060 kc. was one KRTC frequency). This program was immediately followed by another containing messages from friends and relatives. Both programs were also carried domestically on the NBC Red Network. Byrd returned to North America early in 1941. WGEO received a Peabody Award for its programs to the expedition. (The receivers of choice on the Byrd expedition were the Hammarlund "Super-Pro" and the 12-tube HQ-120.)

"Letters" from Home

The unrest in the Orient and the evacuation of American women and children from the Far East have increased interest in the Missionary Mail Bag programs of KGEI, a powerful short-wave broadcasting station in San Francisco.

Each Sunday morning from 5 to 6 o'clock, P.S.T., KGEI broadcasts messages from loved ones at home to missionaries in the Far East and Africa. Occasionally the sender broadcasts his own letter. Among the places to which oral "mail" has been "sent" are Borneo, Sumatra, Java, Shanghai, French Indo-China, Siam, Malaya, the Philippines, New Guinea, Angola and India.

"You are a God-send for lonely husbands of all of us who have had to evacuate from the Orient and we thank you," wrote one woman in submitting a "letter" to be sent to her husband at St. John's University, Shanghai.

* * *

The messages are simple but mean much to the receiver: "All are well here and we hope everything is going well with you;" "The kiddies are in school and settling in nicely;" "Everyone is wonderfully kind to us but we miss you and are counting on seeing you before very long;" "I have been too busy to be homesick but I do wish you were here," are typical.

The joy of a distant listener is expressed in the following letter received at KGEI from Mrs. J. G. McPherson in Shanghai: "We were thrilled with joy beyond description. It was just so wonderful to hear Jim's voice and all of his news. Radio is just wonderful, isn't it? We always will be indebted to you for giving us such joy as we experienced last night. I am sure everyone in foreign lands who hears you over the radio feels the same way about you."

"KGEI Shortwaves Letters to Americans in Orient"
Radio & Television, May 1941[23]

An interesting excursion of 1940 was the Fahnestock expedition to the south seas, headed by brothers Bruce and Sheridan Fahnestock, sailing aboard the schooner *Director II*. They were experienced expeditioners, having traveled to the China coast in 1934–37. The *Director II* took to the ocean in February with the goal of recording local music and collecting bird specimens. Aboard was a 1 kw. shortwave transmitter, **KFAH**, which was often heard in contact with NBC. The trip met an unplanned end in October when the *Director II* sank. Another Fahnestock expedition followed in 1941.

On November 6, **WWV** in Beltsville, Maryland was destroyed by fire. A transmitter of 1 kw. was pressed into temporary service, operating on 5 mc., 1000–2400 EST, CW only, no voice announcements. The transmissions were later extended to 24 hours and a second channel, 15 mc.

Several regulatory actions impacted American shortwave. On April 13, the FCC ordered that the rebroadcast by U.S. AM stations of non-commercial programs of the U.S. international shortwave stations, heretofore prohibited, would now be permitted. On June 4, the FCC directed that U.S. amateurs not make on-air contact with foreign amateurs. And in October the agency adopted a rule that U.S. international shortwave stations record all programs electronically and preserve the recordings, together with program manuscripts, transcripts and translations, for two years, with all of the material subject to FCC inspection. This was a relaxation of a plan that all programs be pre-scripted, a requirement that was dropped after industry objections that it would inhibit on-air spontaneity. The whole matter was born of concern that station operators often could not be certain of exactly what foreign-language speakers were saying on the air, and thus might inadvertently facilitate the broadcasting of Axis propaganda. Over time, the recording requirement was deemed too burdensome, and on December 22, 1942 it was suspended.

There was considerable TV experimentation (technical standardization of the new medium was still in the future). The big domestic broadcast news for 1940 came in May when commercial FM broadcasting got the go ahead. Effective January 1, 1941, FM would be allocated 40 frequencies in the 42–50 mc. band. By the end of 1940 there more than 15 companies manufacturing FM receivers, including Hallicrafters, which introduced the 15-tube S-27, a communications set covering 27–145 mc, AM, FM and CW. Soon there were 7,000 FM receivers in the New York area, 12,000 in other east coast cities. In December the NNRC club program over **WOR** apex station **W2XJI**, which had ceased when the apex outlet closed down, resumed on Saturdays at 1630 EST over WOR's new FM outlet, **W2XOR**, 43.4 mc. But it would be nearly 20 years before FM began achieving wide popularity.

In Africa in July, Italian forces, operating from Ethiopia (which it called Abyssinia), crossed the border into Sudan. In August, Italy pushed the British out of British Somaliland, and began threatening Kenya. Soon Italian and British forces were engaging in the area of the Libyan-Egyptian border. In September, British and Free French forces under General de Gaulle failed in a joint effort to capture Dakar in French West Africa, which was under Vichy control. Six weeks later, French Equatorial Africa was brought over to the Free French after a battle at Libreville, Gabon.

Shortwave broadcasting in Africa was about to expand. In October, following some September tests, **Radio Brazzaville**, the international voice of the Free French, commenced regular broadcasting from what was then known as the Middle Congo region of French Equatorial Africa. (Middle Congo is now the Republic of the Congo.) A modest 350 watts at first, it soon grew to 5 kw. utilizing an old telegraph transmitter, and eventually (in 1943) 50 kw. The station was on 11970 kc. and was heard at 0100–0130 and 1530–1615 EST. (*"This is Radio Brazzaville at Brazzaville, Free French Africa, calling on 25.06 meters."*) The voice of General de

Gaulle was heard often, and distant listeners thrilled to the frequent identification, "Ici Radio Brazzaville," which would be heard for decades to come. Although the station was fully French, "God Save the King" and the "Star-Spangled Banner" were often played after programs intended for the U.S. and Britain, and the station broadcast in many other languages as well. Commented one listener, "This is the strongest signal ever heard from Africa."[24]

Getting the station in operation was no small feat.

> It might have been fairly easy [to assemble a staff] in Paris or London or New York, but not 300 miles up the Congo River. Yet somehow, somewhere, they collected one of the strangest assortments of human beings anywhere on the globe. One used to teach English in French schools; another taught law in Singapore; another was a Parisian bank clerk; another a civil engineer. Still another was a gentle little man who used to sell antiques. An American girl chucked a job in Washington and came. A French girl from South Africa ... escaped from Alsace and found her way here.
>
> One of the [station's] smartest tricks is to broadcast messages from free Frenchmen to their relatives back in France. Homefolk risk anything to listen in, hoping to find out what happened to sons, fathers, husbands who followed the Cross of Lorraine.
>
> Unless Vichy already knows that the sender of the message is with DeGaulle, the messages are usually disguised like this one: "To Susanne and Yvette, who used to live near the Black Mill in Rouen. Pierre is in Syria, in good health. He asks for news from you."[25]

Brazzaville became an important radio center. In October 1941, RCA established a New York-Brazzaville radiotelegraph circuit, and when NBC set up its shortwave listening post in Bellmore, Long Island in 1941, one antenna was devoted exclusively to reception from Brazzaville. The success of Radio Brazzaville was not lost on the Germans. For a time they operated their own program (from Paris), which they called **Brazzaville II**, on the Brazzaville wavelengths, to counteract the Brazzaville station's message.

Radio Brazzaville's roots may lie in another station which was known as **Radio Club**, a broadcasting effort begun in Brazzaville in April 1936 by local Europeans who pooled their money to establish a station. Little is known about it except that it operated under the direction of the station's founder, a Dr. Bizien, until it was taken over by the Free French Forces in mid–1940, the same time that Radio Brazzaville was under construction.[26] First reports in mid–1941, mainly from outside the U.S., placed it on 8500 and 12000 kc. at approximately 0530–0700 and 1300–1430 EST. Soon, however, it was being reported on numerous other channels (8330, 9040, 9945, 12270, 17300, 17650), with broadcasts typically 20 to 90 minutes long occurring during the hours 0100–0900 and 1300–1700 EST. Some of the broadcasts were said to be Radio Brazzaville relays. In late 1941 the station informed one listener in America that it was "not powerful enough" to be heard there but that it expected to have a stronger transmitter operating circa mid–1942, perhaps a reference to the planned 50 kw. upgrade of Radio Brazzaville that occurred in 1943, or a Radio Club upgrade associated with the new station. Although by early 1943 there had been a number of receptions of Radio Club in the United States, the near-total closedown of the shortwave press later that year left the fate of the station unknown. As late as 1945, however, the Foreign Broadcast Intelligence Service reported it as active on 5858, 7035, 8500 and 9980 kc.

Also in October, regular albeit limited French-language broadcasting began from **Radio Congo Belge** in Leopoldville, the Belgian Congo, located directly across the Congo River from Brazzaville. Transmissions were via the commercial utility station in Leopoldville, which had long been heard sending occasional music programs. Transmissions were at 0600–0715 EST over **OPL**, 20040 kc. and 1400–1445 over **OPM**, 10140. Included in the program lineup was French-language news from the BBC. In addition, **OQ2AA, Radio Leo**, Leopoldville, heretofore not audible in the United States, was now heard on 15175 kc. relaying the OPL-

OPM broadcasts. Other channels for Radio Leo included 6010, 9550 and 11730 kc. The power was variously put at 50 to 200 watts.

By year's end, **FGA, Radio Dakar**, under Vichy control, was operating on 9410 kc., parallel to 6435, at around 1515–1630 EST, not coincidentally the same time as the Brazzaville afternoon broadcast, although with a much weaker signal. The station's trademark was a bugle call at the opening of transmission. Most programming was in French, but there was English on Tuesdays and Fridays at 1600–1615. Radio Dakar was also reported on the air at 0715 EST on 6435 and 13355 kc.

New on shortwave was **Radio Tunis**, Tunisia, heard on 15650 kc. in French. Broadcast programming from **CNR, Radio Maroc**, Rabat, French Morocco, reappeared after a long absence. The PTT-based transmissions were heard at 1430–1730 EST on 11940 kc. (and sometimes 12830), and the power was 12 kw. These two stations, together with the **Poste Algerien** shortwave broadcasts of **Radio Alger**, composed an informal "Saharan Network" of Vichy stations.

And regular if limited broadcasting began from Egypt in the form of the new **Egyptian State Broadcasting**. SUR, 6784 kc., and SUX, 7865, transmitted in parallel at 1330–1530 EST from the country's PTT plant at Abu Zaabal. The power was 20 kw., and programs were in Arabic with an English sign off announcement. (*"For the past two hours you have been listening to the Egyptian State Broadcasting on the following two frequencies, 7865 kc. and 6784 kc. We would appreciate reports, which should be sent to the Inspector General, Egyptian State Broadcasting, Cairo, Egypt, and please mention which of the two frequencies is heard the best. Thank you."*)

Angola had a new station, **CR6RB, Radio Clube de Benguela**, operating on two channels, 9605 and 10953 kc. And **Radio Clube de Angola** opened a second shortwave channel, paralleling 11790 kc. (CR6RC). It was CR6RA, 9470 kc., well heard on east coast late afternoons. Preparatory to the start of regular shortwave broadcasting, experimental transmissions were said to be in progress from **ZD4AA**, Accra, Ghana, 7050 kc., a 10-watt amateur station that carried programs of the **Gold Coast Relay System, ZOY**, a wired broadcasting (rediffusion) system. And a 60-watt government PTT station, **Radio St. Denis**, was reported to be carrying broadcast programming irregularly on 9600 kc. from the island of Reunion, east of Madagascar. It was not heard in the U.S., however.

The **SABC** in South Africa was expanding its shortwave service but it was still low powered and difficult to hear. In 1940 it opened several new channels: in Johannesburg, ZRI, 4955 kc., and ZTJ, 9909 (both 5 kw.); in Durban, ZTD, 4878 kc., and ZTE, 11800 (both 300 watts), and ZRO, 9755 (500 watts); in Klipheuvel, ZRL, 9606 (5 kw.); and in Pretoria, ZRG, 9523 (5 kw.). It also increased the power of ZRD, Durban, 6147 kc., from 10 to 300 watts. Call signs were not announced, but transmitter locations were.

In the Middle East, Baghdad was now heard regularly over 5 kw. HNH, 15145 kc. And testing since December 1939, **Radio Tehran** began official broadcasting on April 24, 1940, with the following schedule: 0845–1200 EST over EQC, 9680 kc., 1200–1500 on EQB, 6155, and 1500–1630 on EPB, 15100.

In what would later become Israel but in 1940 was the British Mandate for Palestine, regular broadcasting had begun in 1936 with the establishment of the **Palestine Broadcasting Service**. PBS operated only on mediumwave, however. Shortwave arrived in March 1940 when the Jewish resistance group Haganah started transmitting on about 7000 kc. The PBS Hebrew program was known as **Kol Jerusalem** (the Voice of Jerusalem). The Haganah called its broadcasts **Kol Israel**, which would become the post-independence name of the Israeli national radio. The Haganah tuning signal — a melody from Hatikvah, Israel's future national

RÁDIO CLUBE DE ANGOLA

LUANDA
(ANGOLA)
AFRICA OCIDENTAL PORTUGUESA

Recebida a vossa *Carta* em *21-2-42* ás .... h .... GMT

QRKr .... QRM .... QRN .... QSA .... QSB ....

RCVR ....

CR6RC

XMTR *Collins 30 J-250* watts

PSE QSL OM   Best 73,S

A distant and exotic place, Angola exemplified the romance of shortwave. The country was always a sought-after DX target, never more so than in the early days of broadcasting when Africa boasted few shortwave stations. Radio Clube de Angola signed on in 1938.

anthem — was the same as would be used for decades by the post-independence Kol Israel. The Haganah closed down Kol Israel after three months in favor of cooperation with the British during the war years.[27]

In Asia, **Station Boy-Landry** in Saigon appeared to have closed, with its transmitter now being used by **Radio Saigon** for low-power broadcasts on 6210 kc. (In September, the Vichy government was forced to agree to Japanese demands to place 6,000 troops in French Indochina in order to block aid from reaching China. Nine months later this permission was expanded to include bases.) The evening **NHK** broadcast from Japan to North America was heard at 2000–2100 on 11815 and 15105 kc. English news was at 2015. (*"Hello friends in America. This is Tokyo calling."*) And listeners in the Far East were hearing transmissions from a 50 watt station in Kuching, Sarawak, **VQF**, 6985 kc., which sent an hour of news and music programs on Fridays at 1910 EST.

Shanghai was the center of radio development in China. Almost all the activity was on mediumwave, however.[28] The main shortwave stations were the American station **XMHA**, the German station **XGRS**, and the French station **FFZ**.

At first Germany had served the sizeable Shanghai German community by renting another station, **XHHB**. This lasted until 1939, when **XGRS** came on the air. Operating from the Kaiser Wilhelm School, it was at first on mediumwave only, adding shortwave late in 1940. Calling itself the **Far Eastern Broadcasting Station**, the frequency was announced as 11880 kc., but reception was actually on 11920. Broadcasts, which were in German and English, were heard around 0530–0900 EST, and there was some commercial advertising. A reception report would bring a prompt QSL, plus International Reply Coupons to prepay further reports. The station hoped that listeners would write in repeatedly in order to obtain the full series of six

QSL-cards which the station offered. XGRS was under the Foreign Ministry, not the Propaganda Ministry, and a number of German Americans and expatriates of several other nations worked at the station. It was decidedly anti–British, and even had its own Lord Haw-Haws, two German-born Chinese brothers who boasted excellent English.

The French station, **FFZ, Station Radiophonique Francaise,** was first on 12050 kc., later on 12090. The power was 400 watts, and the schedule was 1900–1930, 2300–0100 and 0330–1100 EST, with English news at 0800. (*"This is station FFZ in Shanghai, operating on mediumwave 214 meters or 1400 kc., and experimentally on shortwave on a frequency of 12050 kc. or 24.8 meters. At the sound of the gong it will be exactly one minute past nine. And here is the news."*)

THE VOICE OF EUROPE

SHANGHAI, October 14th, 1941.
3 GREAT WESTERN ROAD, APT. 5
TELEPHONE: 20025

Mr. Roger Legge,Jr.
20 Beethoven Street,
Binghamton, New York,
U. S. A.

Dear Mr. Legge:

We acknowledge receipt of your letter dated September 7th and herewith enclose our Verification-Card No.1.

We thank you for the excellent programme reports of our broadcasts on September 3rd, 4th and 6th, which we have checked with our log book and found to be correct.

Please note that we are at present broadcasting a special test programme for the U.S.A. at 2 p.m. Shanghai Standard Time, which is equal to 1 a.m. Eastern Standard Time. We should appreciate it very much to hear from you, how these test programmes are received by you and if so, whether you think them interesting. Enclosed please find 3 International Reply Coupons.

From the Heading of your letter we notice that you are the editor of a magazine devoted to reception on the amateur bands. We are very much interested in receiving one or several such publications, and beg you to kindly let us have the current issue of your"Ama-Touring" with your rate for a year's subscription. If you should consider it advisable for us to also subscribe to some other magazines, we would thank you for giving us the names and adresses of the best publications available in your country.

Thanking you in anticipation, we remain,

yours very truly,
THE FAR EASTERN BROADCASTING STATION
SHANGHAI
A.G.Goldau
Manager.

AGG/HM.

Shanghai was home to several shortwave stations which were tied in one way or another to their home countries. The German station was XGRS, the "Far Eastern Broadcasting Station." As this letter indicates, it reflected the same interest in listener relations as its "Zeesen" cousin.

The communists were destined for eventual victory over the nationalists in China, but in 1940 they had suffered significant military defeats in the southeast and had regrouped in the northwest. They were in need of a radio voice, and in December inaugurated **XNCR,** the **Yenan Xinhua [New China] Radio Station,** in Shaanxi Province, a center of communist activity following the Long March of 1934–35, which had ended in Yenan. It was a primitive setup, with power generated by a car motor, but it managed to transmit for one hour, twice daily, until 1943 when it went into hiatus for almost two years for want of a tube.[29]

New shortwave stations continued to appear in Central and South America and the Caribbean, but at a reduced pace. In November 1939, Jamaican amateur John Grinan, **VP5PZ,** had begun some impromptu broadcasting. Now he arranged for the government to use his transmitter for broadcasting purposes, and **ZQI**, Kingston, was born. It operated on 4750 kc. At first the 200-watt station was on the air for only one hour a week, but soon it assumed a daily schedule of 1730–1830 EST.

A widely heard Cuban station that came on during the year was **COK**, "OK Batista," owned by Fulgencio Batista, who would be elected president of Cuba in October. It was on 11570 kc., and was a good verifier, sending listeners postcards of Cuba along with QSLs. English programming was broadcast at 1930–2330 EST. Also new from Havana was **COCY**, 9205 kc. (later 11735), relaying mediumwave CMBX (which had been relayed by shortwaver **COBX**, now off the air). The station identified in Spanish on the quarter hour and English on the half hour.

A new station in Ciudad Trujillo, the Dominican Republic, was government-owned **Broadcasting Nacional**. It operated with 750 watts on 6240 kc. (**HI1N**) and 250 watts on 6310 kc. (**HI1Z**). Also now broadcasting from the capital was 100-watt **HI6H**, **La Voz del Pueblo**, on 6115 kc.

In Central America, Costa Rica was now on 6035 kc. in the person of **TI7RVN**, **La Voz de Guanacaste**, Juntas de Abangares. The El Salvador PTT, **Dirección General de Telégrafos, Teléfonos y Radio Nacionales** in San Salvador, began some broadcast program tests over its transmitter **YUB** operating on various frequencies including 5560 and 7292 kc. And five new Nicaraguan stations took to the air: **YNJAT**, **La Voz del Aire**, Leon, on 5758 kc.; **YN2FT**, **La Voz de la Sultana**, Granada, on 7193 kc.; **YNLAT**, **La Voz del Mombacho**, Granada, 7260; **YNOW**, **La Voz de la America Central**, Managua, on 8240; and **YNCM**, **Ecos del Caribe**, Bluefields, on 9660, 100 watts.

An official list showed 23 active Colombian shortwave stations. New from Bogota on 9630 kc., the former frequency of **Radio Bucaramanga**, was government station **HJCT**, **Radiodifusora Nacional**. Operated by the Ministerio de Educación, it relayed mediumwave station HJCR and was heard requesting reports. Also new was **HJCW**, **Emisora Suramerica**, Bogota, on 4940 kc., and **HJFK**, **La Voz Amiga**, Pereira, on 4865 kc. (later 9730). More Colombian stations were showing up on 31 meters, including **HJAB**, **La Voz de Barranquilla**, 9570 kc., and **HJFH**, **La Voz de Armenia**, 9750.

It was another year of frequency change for 60 meter Venezuelan stations. A dozen or so moved to new channels in the 60 meter band, while others moved to 90 meters and were joined there by several stations new to shortwave. In addition to the three Venezuelan stations already on 90 meters, the band now hosted **YV1RO**, **Radio Trujillo**, 3340 kc.; **YV1RT**, **La Voz de la Fe**, Maracaibo, 3360; **YV5RY**, **Radio Continente** (formerly La Voz de la Esfera), Caracas, 3380; **YV3RY**, **Radio America**, Caracas, 3390; **YV6RZ**, **La Voz de Anzoategui**, Barcelona, 3450; and **YV4RQ**, **Radio Puerto Cabello**, 3480. Ninety meters was becoming a busy place.

HCJB increased power to 10 kw. The official inauguration of the new transmitter was on March 24. The frequency was 12460 kc. (later adjusted to 12455), and the schedule was 2000–2300 EST daily except Mondays, when equipment tests were carried out. The lower-power parallel frequency was 4107 kc. Signals on 12460 were strong but modulation was poor at first. Programs included "The Friendship Hour" and "Ecuadorean Echoes" (the latter would be well-known to decades of HCJB listeners). In November the station began a series of Spanish language lessons for English speakers. (Other stations with language lessons included **Zeesen, Rome, Tokyo** and **WRUL**.) A listener in England said that, other than the American stations, the 12460 outlet was the shortwave station best heard in his country. Soon it was identifying itself as "the pioneer missionary broadcasting station of the world."

Also in Ecuador, **Radio Quito** came on the air on both mediumwave and shortwave.

The shortwave channel, **HCQRX**, was 5970 kc. The station is remembered for its 1949 Martian-landing drama which produced results similar to those of the CBS "War of the Worlds" broadcast in 1938.[30]

Elsewhere in the Andes, **Radio Nacional del Peru** in Lima added a third frequency, **OAX4R**, 15150 kc., which was used for an English broadcast to North America on Saturdays at 1715–1750 EST. **Radio Nacional de Bolivia**, a private rather than a government effort, was heard for the first time. It operated with 5 kw. on two frequencies simultaneously, 6110 kc. (**CP2**) and 9505 (**CP38**), at 1100–1400 and 1630–2400 EST. At times it also used 15165 kc. (**CP43**). Reports were wanted.

Shortwave continued to advance in Australia. Although using transmitters of only 10 and 2 kw., **"Australia Calling"** pursued an ambitious agenda of foreign-language broadcasts, with beams to all parts of the world and broadcasts in English, German, Dutch, French, Spanish and Afrikaans. The station broadcast to Eastern North America at 0725–0800 EST over **VLQ5**, 9680 kc. and 1810–1900 over **VLQ3**, 15315 kc., and to Western North America at 1025–1100 on 9680 and 0055–0145 on **VLQ8**, 17800, all with 10 kw. The mailbag program to North America on Sundays at 0745 was already a hit and would remain so for 40 years. On April 7, **VLW** in Perth, a 2 kw. station that had gone into domestic service in 1939, joined the "Australia Calling" network for certain beams. Although it would leave international service in 1945, ABC regional shortwave from Perth would remain on the air until 1994.

Honolulu telephone transmitters **HKQ** and **HKE** on 14900 and 17950 kc. respectively carried the programming of mediumwave KGMB on Saturdays at 2020 EST. A 100-watt **Radio Pacifique** was reported operating from New Caledonia on 7280 kc. (soon changed to 6480), but at hours that made North American reception impossible. And **Java Wireless Station PLA**, 19500 kc., was heard transmitting broadcast programming at 0215–0815 and 1100–1200 EST, mainly in Dutch but with English at 0715–0800, including news at 0745. *("This is Netherlands East Indies calling over PLA at Batavia.")*

The war made shortwave listening more popular, particularly the casual, living room tuning of the larger stations like **Zeesen** and the **BBC**. Although shortwave was not included on new ordinary home receivers to the extent that it had been in earlier years, Charles J. Rolo, who at the time worked at the Princeton Listening Center (and would later serve as literary editor of *The Atlantic Monthly*), reported that about 30 percent of the 30 million radios in the United States could pick up European stations under favourable conditions.[31]

On the receiver front for the serious DXer, Hallicrafters introduced the SX-28 for $159.50, which included tubes and crystal, speaker extra. It would see extensive wartime use and become one of the classic shortwave receivers of the century. The 12-tube, 10-band National NC-200 also made its first appearance. The price, with tubes, crystal filter and 10-inch speaker, was $147.50. Also new in 1940 was the 11-tube RME-99, promoted by its manufacturer as "a precision communications instrument having the tuning convenience of an ordinary shortwave receiver." The cost was $137.40, with tubes and speaker.

With increasing hostilities overseas, and with the growing popularity of regular AM broadcasting, shortwave club membership saw a decline. The International Shortwave Club, which claimed the largest foreign membership, reported but three new memberships over a three month period. The International DXers Alliance likewise reported greatly-reduced receipts. But shortwave was still to be reckoned with. In the summer, the IDA bulletin dropped its mediumwave coverage, which was once the heart of the club, replacing it with "Ama-Touring," theretofore a separate newsletter available to those interested in DXing amateur radio stations. It was edited by well-known DXer Roger Legge.

Special broadcasts were fewer. An English-language special was broadcast for the ISWC over **HP5G, Emisora Ron Dalley**, Panama City, on 11780 kc. **PSH**, Rio de Janeiro, had one on 10220 kc. An IDA special from **I2AA**, Addis Ababa, Ethiopia, was broadcast in January at 1700–1730 on 9950 kc. The weekly special broadcasts from **TG2, Radio Morse**, Guatemala, continued on Sunday mornings at 0200–0230, 6195 kc. And on November 14 at 0100–0200 EST, a special was transmitted for the National Radio Club from **Radio Nacional de Bolivia** on all three of its shortwave channels.

1941

Bulgaria came under German control in January. In April, Germany, aided by Italy, invaded Greece and Yugoslavia and within a month both countries were overrun.

On June 22, Hitler attacked the Soviet Union in Operation Barbarossa and soon there was fighting from Murmansk to the Crimea. By July 11 the Germans were outside Kiev, and the next day Moscow was bombed. Kiev fell on September 19. Although the Germans would control large areas of the western Soviet Union, and would reach the Moscow suburbs, they were unable to take the city.

In North Africa, the year began with the surrender of the Italian garrison at Tobruk in Libya. The Italians were in general retreat from the British, but the situation reversed itself in February on the arrival of Rommel's troops. The British took Mogadishu from the Italians and began their move into Ethiopia. On April 1 they took Asmara, capital of Eritrea. Addis Ababa fell five days later, and by year's end the British were in control of Ethiopia, and Italy's East African empire had come to an end.

In the Middle East, an April coup in Iraq was led by elements unfriendly to the British (who had controlled Iraq under a League of Nations mandate until 1932), and by June German planes were arriving in Syria, which was still under a French mandate, and Vichy control. British forces reversed the coup in Iraq, took Baghdad and confirmed their right to station troops there. British and Free French forces attacked Syria in June and were in control by July. In August, concerned about increasing German influence in Iran and the safety of Iranian oil supplies, the British and the Soviets moved into that country and took control.

Japan attacked Pearl Harbor on December 7. Guam, Wake and Midway, U.S. possessions since the turn of the century, were attacked the same day, and the first two islands soon fell. On December 8 the U.S. and Britain declared war on Japan. The Japanese began offensive operations against Malaya, Thailand, Hong Kong and the Philippines (an American possession since 1898, a commonwealth since 1935). In the runup to these actions, several coded messages to Japanese diplomatic personnel concerning the start of the war and the burning of documents were inserted into NHK shortwave broadcasts.

Burma was soon under attack. Bangkok was occupied in one day, the same day the Japanese occupied Tarawa, capital of the Gilbert and Ellice Islands (British). Landings in the Philippines increased steadily. Hong Kong fell on Christmas day; the British withdrew from Kuching, Sarawak. On December 11, Germany and Italy declared war on the U.S. and the U.S. reciprocated.

How would the global situation reshape shortwave broadcasting in the United States? America's shortwave effort was still in private hands; the government had no shortwave broadcast stations of its own. Given shortwave's international reach, increased official interest in the medium was not unexpected, and as the likelihood of war grew, the American broadcasters realized that better planning and coordination, and a more unified voice, were needed. In April they appointed their own "Coordinator of International Broadcasting" in the person of former AP correspondent and ambassadorial assistant Stanley P. Richardson. Richardson would serve as the stations' principal liaison to the government, and much of the work of the government agencies involved in international broadcasting would be done through him. Relationships with Richardson were not always smooth, especially when he took it upon himself to reject government program content. Richardson was also named to the International Broadcasting Committee of the Defense Communications Board. The timing of Richardson's appointment was good, for governmental reorganizations would soon take place that would have a direct effect on the stations.[32]

On July 11, Col. William Donovan (reserve rank) was appointed to the new position of Coordinator of Information, the office to which the Central Intelligence Agency traces its roots. The COI was to be the government's principal intelligence official. Under Donovan was the Foreign Information Service (FIS), which was headed by playwright Robert E. Sherwood. Its considerable efforts in responding to Axis propaganda included preparing news releases and other program content for use by the shortwave broadcasters as they saw fit — releases were headed, "The following from the Coordinator of Information is for your use if desired" — as well as working with the broadcasters to improve the effectiveness of American shortwave. The stations were still producing most of their own programs, but, at least at the outset, welcomed Sherwood's help, which emanated from the COI's "international city room" on Madison Avenue. The stations also benefitted from the COI's ability to provide material in foreign languages. The COI skirted civil service rules against the employment of aliens by setting up a government-funded corporation known as Short Wave Research, Inc. to find translators and foreign-language writers. Although of questionable legality, the arrangement was worthy in its objective and produced programming in some 16 languages, most of which were well beyond the stations' own capabilities.[33]

In October the COI arranged for all the American shortwave stations (except **KGEI**) to be connected by telephone lines. This was the so-called Bronze Network, and it permitted the networking of programs, as well as the monitoring of station output by COI, which was, especially after Pearl Harbor, concerned about news that might inadvertently serve enemy purposes.[34]

On July 30, President Roosevelt transformed the Office for Coordination of Commercial and Cultural Relations Between the American Republics into the office of the Coordinator of Inter-American Affairs (CIAA), and appointed Nelson Rockefeller its first head. The CIAA was active on many media fronts. Its mission on shortwave included making programming suggestions to the stations, preparing news scripts, and supporting the production of a wide variety of specific programs, especially by NBC and CBS, which had the strongest capabilities. The CIAA leased studio facilities, employed network personnel for writing and production, promoted Latin American advertising by American companies, and even paid for unsold advertising time. It underwrote the production of news at CBS and NBC to the tune of nearly a half-million dollars, and provided considerable funding to WRUL, which, notwithstanding its many successes, was in dire financial straits and probably would not have survived without this help and a $40,000 loan from the U.S. Reconstruction Finance Agency.[35]

The CIAA also published and distributed consolidated shortwave program schedules, paid for their inclusion in Latin American newspapers, and helped establish the Latin American rebroadcasting networks, including supplying the Latin stations with such limited equipment as was available. The CIAA English programs, which were mainly U.S. domestic fare plus armed forces programs, comprised what was called the United Network. The CIAA also kept a black list of pro-Axis persons and stations in Latin America.

For the American stations it was a year of continued growth and changing mission. In less than 20 years shortwave had developed from the realm of technical experimentation into a fledgling international commercial medium (although by the end of the year, NBC, Westinghouse, GE and Crosley together had only 15 paying sponsors, including RCA and Westinghouse, and four non-paying).[36] Now it was entering the world of international relations—and war.[37]

By mid–1941, **WRUL** was on the air five hours daily using almost two dozen languages at one time or another, adding them as political and military events dictated. The station moved from an educational to a wartime footing, and much of its programming was decidedly anti–Axis. Many European refugees worked at WRUL, which became a big morale builder in Europe and environs. Some of its programs were picked up and rebroadcast by the **BBC** and by **Radio Brazzaville.**

The WRUL story was told often in both the public and the professional press, invariably positively.[38] But after the war the station would be dogged by the allegation that it had been infiltrated by, and become a pawn of, British intelligence. The full truth of the charge, which Walter Lemmon has denied, has never been firmly established. What is true is that the British, operating silently through a variety of intermediary exile groups, provided the station with extensive assistance in the form of both personnel and content. But the British were well connected with the newly-developing American intelligence community, including both Donovan and FBI Director J. Edgar Hoover, and one wonders if Lemmon or the United States government knew of the situation, and, if they did, whether they would have been moved to do anything about it. Given the general congruence of British and American intelligence interests, and the exigencies of the time, perhaps both sides saw the British effort as a useful resource at a time when the American intelligence service was just taking root, and the still relatively weak American shortwave broadcasting structure was in need of good content that was supportive of Allied interests. The post-war telling of the tale—which includes a parallel venture with **KGEI** and **KWID**, a west coast shortwave station that came on the air in 1942 (see below)—was mostly by the British, who would have had an interest in painting the events as an intelligence success.[39]

In March, NBC stations **WRCA** and **WNBI** at Bound Brook, New Jersey, went to 50 kw. WRCA operated at 0800–1600 EST on 17780 kc. and 1600–2400 on 9670, and WNBI was on at 1100–1545 on 11890 and 1600–2000 on 17780. NBC also conducted the popular "International Mail Bag" on Mondays, Thursdays and Fridays at 1230 EST. By midyear, NBC had nearly doubled its European broadcasts and sometimes operated 24 hours a day. The international division grew from 60 to 100 people.[40]

On June 9, **KGEI** closed down its 20 kw. transmitter in San Francisco and reopened a week later with 50 kw. at its new home adjacent to the **KPO** transmitter in Belmont. The new transmitter was inaugurated on September 4 and the KGEI studios removed to the Fairmont Hotel on Nob Hill in San Francisco. KGEI now broadcast daily at 0030–0400 and 0715–1215 on 9670 kc. and 1900–2400 on 15330. To increase the station's reach, some KGEI programming was relayed on point-to-point transmitters. By the end of the year the station was broadcasting in nine languages. It was the recipient of much positive publicity, and was regarded as a major morale builder for American troops in the Pacific.[41]

A big part of that morale building was journalist William Winter, whose wartime broadcasts over KGEI would earn him great acclaim. Winter says that in mid–1941 he was recruited to provide more balanced news analysis for the station, which by then was being widely heard in the Pacific. Winter's service was apparently approved in advance by high-level American officials, but the initial approach had come from a British security operative inveighing against what he said was an isolationist slant in KGEI's news broadcasts that was undermining Amer-

RCA Mfg. Co., Inc., Camden, N.J., U.S.A.
RADIO HEADQUARTERS

RCA BUILDING—New York City
BROADCASTING HEADQUARTERS

RCA VICTOR SHORT-WAVE STATION

WRCA

NATIONAL BROADCASTING COMPANY

13.8 METERS   21,630 KILOCYCLES
31.02 METERS   9,670 KILOCYCLES

TAKES PLEASURE IN EXTENDING VERIFICATION
OF RECEPTION TO Roger Legge Jr.

In 1939, the FCC substituted regular four-letter calls for the old shortwave broadcast "X" calls. WRCA was the new callsign for W3XAL, the RCA-NBC station set up in Bound Brook, New Jersey, in 1930.

ican support of anti–Japanese efforts in the Far East. The British viewed the station as being anti–British, and suspected that the enemy was using KGEI Chinese broadcasts, whose production was largely unsupervised, to send coded messages. (Winter has observed that the news problem was, at least in part, due to the absence of a news director at KGEI, and the station's practice of using the news from the Hearst news service — which, according to Winter, had a well-known isolationist slant — on a "rip and read" basis.) The British claim to have effectively "won control" of KGEI during this period, "arranged" for the construction of KWID, and recruited staff for both, all with the help of Donovan, with whom British security had established a working relationship. Whatever may have been the exact scope of Britain's involvement, Winter's broadcasts over KGEI began on September 14, 1941.[42]

On June 30, **WBOS** inaugurated a European beam. By the end of the year the station was broadcasting five hours a day to Europe and seven to Latin America. It also carried NBC network programming for the benefit of U.S. troops.

In September, CBS moved its 10 kw. Wayne, New Jersey station, **WCBX** (ex-W2XE), to a new shortwave facility in Brentwood, Long Island. The new installation was located on the grounds of the **Mackay Radio & Telegraph Company** transmitting plant. On New Year's eve, a new 50 kw. transmitter for WCBX went into operation with a special program for Latin America. A second transmitter of like power was also now available (**WCRC**), and a new 10 kw. unit, **WCDA**, was in use at times as well. CBS also constructed four new studios in New York that were devoted exclusively to international programming, which was sent to Brentwood via an FM link.[43] On December 31, CBS closed **WCAB** in Philadelphia (the former W3XAU).

While American shortwave programming became much more war-oriented, it also served other, incidental purposes. The English broadcasts became popular among foreign listeners who wished to learn or improve their English, while the foreign-language broadcasts found favor with foreign-language teachers. On February 14, as part of its "Let's Get Acquainted" program, **Zeesen** invited listeners in the United States to cable them collect (up to 25 words, cable address "Ameradio") about how they were being received and what kind of programming they would like to hear. Many people accepted the offer but were not always polite, suggesting a broadcast of Hitler's funeral, requesting the playing of Irving Berlin's "When That Man Is Dead and Gone," etc. Some telegraph companies refused to send cables that used language they considered inappropriate unless the recipient approved it in advance (which it did). The offer was canceled after a week.[44]

More important to DXers that month was the FCC's establishment of the Foreign Broadcast Monitoring Service (FBMS) to supplant the work of the Princeton Listening Center, which closed in March. Former *Public Opinion Quarterly* editor Lloyd A. Free became director, and Harold N. Graves, director of the Princeton center, became senior administrator. (Free had also worked with the center.) Monitoring and translating was done from listening posts in Maryland, Texas, Oregon and Puerto Rico, all of which were connected with Washington by wire.[45] Over the next few years the monitoring posts in Texas and Puerto Rico were closed, and new posts were added in Guam, Hawaii, and Hayward, California. Personnel soon reached almost 350, 450 by the end of 1942, including several posted to London for coordination with the BBC Monitoring Service. A close relationship of U.S. and British monitoring personnel developed and would continue for many decades.

The role of the monitoring service in the war effort was articulated by the FCC as follows:

> The importance of listening in on foreign transmissions is attested in the fact that propaganda instigated abroad almost invariably follows the example set in short-wave broadcasts, but follows it with a lag. Almost every political, diplomatic, or military move is presaged by shifts in propaganda treatment. Consequently, through study of the short wave "model" it is often possible to predict such moves. A new course in policy can be reflected in broadcasts long before it is announced officially or rumored in the press. For example, the altered tone of certain foreign broadcasts gave the first indication that Japan intended to occupy Indo-China.[46]

The monitoring service was a colorful agency, once described by a journalist as "the greatest collection of individualists, international rolling stones, and slightly batty geniuses ever gathered together in one organization." Its output included "spot bulletins, daily reports with over-all content and analysis, weekly summaries of propaganda methods on the long-range basis, and special reports and analyses."[47] Soon its services were in high demand by the civilian and military officials who received its reports, all of which were, at that time, confidential. But relations with Congress were rocky. Several employees were (unfairly) charged with being subversives; a Congressional investigation which led nowhere occupied much of the agency's time; and budgetary limitations restricted FBMS efforts.[48]

There were also some other new international monitoring efforts. NBC moved its east coast shortwave listening post from Radio City to the former WEAF transmitter site in Bellmore, Long Island, where it was dedicated on July 23. Twenty-four engineering, monitoring and translating personnel supported eight receivers.[49] A west coast NBC post began operating from North Hollywood on August 14. Provision by NBC of listening post reports to newspapers and news agencies was soon dropped, however, when the news agencies set up their own facilities.[50] CBS had set up a monitoring station in San Francisco in August 1939 to supplement its New York monitoring. (The San Francisco operation would be taken over by the Foreign Broadcast Monitoring Service — by then renamed the Foreign Broadcast Intelligence Service — in 1942 when CBS indicated that it wished to close the site.) Associated Press set up a listening post, mainly for news agency transmissions in code, in Northcastle, New York

(Westchester County).[51] And the CBC operated a modest listening post in Britannia Heights, outside Ottawa, for worldwide monitoring and for pickup of BBC signals from **Daventry** for rebroadcast in Canada.[52] Other shortwave broadcasters also had monitoring capacities.

The Japanese attack on Pearl Harbor did not immediately change the organization of American shortwave broadcasting, but it changed operations greatly. There was more supervision of network-produced programming, including news, and heightened output of government-produced programs. The stations agreed to broadcast no news originating from sources other than FIS, CIAA or the major press associations without first checking with FIS. The stations were generally cooperative, and bore the costs of increased broadcast hours, but over time they developed the view that the government programming was sometimes unsuitable in various ways. For its part, the government was unhappy with what it viewed as inadequate transmitter coordination among the broadcasters and the disjointed appearance of American foreign policy that resulted when the stations rewrote government material.[53]

Others felt that network programming itself left much to be desired. Ted Church, radio director of the Republican National Committee and formerly with NBC and CBS, railed against "the stupid broadcasting that is now being done" over American stations—identifications that were insufficient and too infrequent, the still-considerable amount of American domestic programming that was carried on shortwave and that was largely unsuitable for foreign audiences, on-air language that sometimes reinforced unflattering stereotypes of foreigners, etc.[54] Others felt that the quality of reception of American stations in Europe simply was not very good, or wondered just what the content and the efficacy of American shortwave broadcasting was supposed to be, or were concerned about whether the broadcasts were truly reflective of American foreign policy.

American author, journalist and broadcaster Dorothy Thompson, in her syndicated column in the *New York Post,* said:

"There is, inevitably, some conflict between the business mind and any larger political policy.... Shortwave programs have been, and as far as I know, still are, sponsored by American corporations, so that news and comment on them is heard through the courtesy of fruit, or oil, or fountain pens, or what not. The sponsor inevitably has his own interests to preserve, and our South American friends must inevitably obtain the impression that commercial pressures and political analysis go close together. In a world where the Axis powers continually attack us as 'money-loving commercialists,' this is deplorable. * * * ¶The men in charge have the best intentions in the world, but they are not men in close touch with the State Department. They must find persons who speak foreign languages, and who possibly have names known abroad. This is all right, but it is unfortunate that men are sometimes selected to speak who are wholly discredited in the nations whose language they command, and others present themselves to speak who have personal foreign political interests at stake."[55]

The shortwave rubber met the road with Pearl Harbor. NBC described its shortwave activity after the attack as follows:

President Roosevelt's 10-minute address to the Congress, demanding a declaration of war against Japan, starting at 12:30 P.M., December 8, 1941, was broadcast to all Europe, and was beamed point-to-point to a dozen Latin American stations for rebroadcast in English, Spanish and Portuguese. Although the text of the Chief Executive's speech was received only about ten minutes before he began speaking from the House Chamber, the Spanish version went on the air immediately after he finished speaking. The Portuguese version immediately followed the Spanish. Ten hours after Mr. Roosevelt had finished his historic address, his words were still going forth in many languages by transcription and translation. ¶The President's war address, starting at 10:00 P.M., December 9, 1941, was broadcast to the world as he spoke, and was beamed point-to-point to London, Manila, Honolulu, Australia, Batavia, and in a Spanish version to radio stations in 11 Latin American countries, and in Portuguese to Brazil. In addition, the address was [rebroadcast 29 times in nine languages].[56]

"Paris, Helsinki, Berlin, London." In order to obtain the latest news from the war's hot spots, newspapers and domestic radio networks established their own listening posts. This NBC facility relied on the venerable National HRO receiver.

As NBC put it, "When war came to the U.S., the *Fourth Front* was ready and at battle stations."[57]

The NBC and CBS stations were soon "operating on a round-the-clock schedule beaming news reports to Europe and Latin America as they have been pouring in from the fighting fronts." NBC was running three eight-hour shifts, broadcasting in eight languages besides English. CBS transmitted in 10 languages. The private broadcasters continued to operate their stations for almost a year with a mix of government and private programming prepared under tighter government supervision (but without the inroads into domestic broadcasting that the radio industry had long feared). The networks were still producing most of the on-air material, but under guidance from the government.

Pearl Harbor had other impacts on the shortwave world.[58] Amateur radio operations were immediately suspended.[59] Some hams would receive special authority to operate (in bands far above shortwave) as part of the new War Emergency Radio Service.[60] The Attorney General ordered that Japanese, German and Italian aliens surrender their short wave receivers (as well as cameras and guns). And the FCC's Radio Intelligence Division, devoted to monitoring the domestic ether, now became the agency's top priority. Numerous domestic monitoring facilities were established.[61]

C.B.C.

STATION............CBFY..............

Transmitter LOCATION......Vercheres,..Que......

POWER........7500............................WATTS

FREQUENCY........11,705...........KC.

REMARKS..Reception..date:June..29-41
Studio..Location:..Montreal,..Que.:...
Hours..of..operation:..8:00..a.m...to
midnight..E.D.S.T.................

THANK YOU FOR YOUR INTEREST

CANADIAN BROADCASTING CORPORATION

TRANSMISSION & DEVELOPMENT DEPT.
ENGINEERING DIVISION
C. B C.

PER *W. V. Richardson*

The CBC was transmitting on shortwave four years before the inauguration of its international service in 1945. Located in Verchères, near Montreal, the 7.5 kw. station broadcast mainly in French. It remained on the air until 1953.

All U.S. shortwave broadcasters were supposed to go to 50 kw. and begin utilizing directional antennas by July 1. A few were granted brief extensions. In August, the FCC relaxed existing shortwave frequency management restrictions by authorizing licensees to use more than one frequency in a given band so they could switch channels if interference warranted it. American stations did not "own" their frequencies, however. They were often shared, the same frequency being used by different American stations at complementary times. American shortwave broadcasters could not use more than one band simultaneously, however, a restriction that would be lifted in December 1942.

The year saw several shortwave developments in Canada. In 1937, a new 50 kw. CBC French-language mediumwave station, CBF, had begun operating in Montreal. Now, in February 1941, from nearby Verchères, a 7.5 kw. shortwave station with an omnidirectional antenna came into service. It was on the air at 0630–2300, usually on two of four channels: 6160 kc. (CBFW, soon moved to 6090),[62] 9630 (CBFX), 11705 (CBFY), and 15190 (CBFZ). The station identified as "Ici Radio Canada" and signed off with "God Save the King" and "O Canada." Intended mainly to serve French-speakers outside the range of Canadian mediumwave stations, most of the time it relayed CBF. However, one of the Verchères channels was sometimes devoted to either NBC programming or CBC English programs. The project was nominally the start of a broader vision for the 50 kw. shortwave service that would become a reality four years later.

CKFX in Vancouver, British Columbia, which relayed mediumwaver CKWX, had by now moved from 6070 to on 6080 kc., a frequency it would continue to use for over 50 years. And new from Vancouver was CBC station CBRX, 6160 kc., the "Voice of British Columbia," a

150-watt station that relayed CBR from 0900 to 0300 EST. *("This is the Canadian Broadcasting Corporation, station CBR and shortwave CBRX, Vancouver, British Columbia.")* It is still on the air as **CKZU**.

Shortwave in the Morning

"A run down the morning shortwave field finds the following stations standing out loudest between 6:30 and 7:30 A.M.: London, 16 meters; Berlin, 19 meters; Rabat, 23 meters; "Voice of the Andes," 24 meters; Australia, 31 meters; Hong Kong and a Manila station, though not so loud as the other stations mentioned above, are coming in with fair volume on 31 meters. Lord Haw Haw, on Germany's Asiatic wave of 15.11 megacycles, was holding forth with gusto even before the sun came up."

The New York Times
February 16, 1941[63]

In Europe the shortwave story was mostly about propaganda. The Foreign Policy Association, a non-profit research and education organization in New York, published a monograph by Harold Graves analyzing the Axis propaganda that had been monitored by the Princeton Listening Center.[64] Graves identified several threads in Nazi propaganda.

Before moving against France, **Zeesen's** broadcasts sought to destabilize French society and warn the government not to join Britain. After the German attack, Frenchmen were urged to reconcile themselves to German domination and pursue German virtues.

Germany's main radio assault was on Britain, with Lord Haw-Haw fanning English discontent by emphasizing class differences and urging the country to turn out Britain's leaders and resign themselves to inevitable capitulation. (Haw-Haw also gave the names and prison addresses of British POWs and urged British listeners to write to them.) In broadcasts to the United States, German-American friendship and the need for American neutrality in the face of British efforts to draw the country into the war were stressed. Soon, however, Germany's programs for America developed a sharper edge.

Italy was the junior partner in the Axis propaganda effort. At first its broadcasts were mild and largely non-political. This changed following Germany's military successes in Scandinavia. Italian broadcasts sought to foster defeatism in America. The rantings of one of Italy's shortwave personalities, American-born poet Ezra Pound, who had been living outside the U.S for many years, were, as Graves put it, "a world of fanciful ideas."

Radio Centre, Moscow, although very active on shortwave, was not a major player in war propaganda at this time.

Shortwave broadcasting was dangerous business in England. On January 1, Nazi bombing of Broadcasting House cost seven employees their lives. During the year the number of languages used by the **BBC** grew from 32 to 40, and the number of weekly broadcast hours from 145 to 231. There was much rebroadcasting of the BBC by local stations throughout the British empire (which was one reason put forth by the BBC for its longstanding policy of not verifying reception reports—it could never be entirely certain of the origin of a particular signal). And it was on January 14, 1941, that the four-note "V" (for "Victory") tuning signal came into use in European broadcasts. The "V" sign started appearing on walls and posters throughout occupied Europe and soon became an important symbol of resistance.[65] Sometimes Germany used a barrage of rapidly coded "V" signals to jam the BBC.

The development of the North American service, transmitted at 1710–2345 EST on 9580 kc. (**GSC**) and 11750 (**GSD**), continued. Ted Church was helping the BBC better conform its programming to North American tastes.[66] A Sunday "Answering You" program replied to questions about Britain sent to the company's Fifth Avenue address. (The **Voice of America** inaugurated a reciprocal program of the same name in October 1942.) And in an effort to reach American listeners who had standard broadcast radios with some limited shortwave coverage above the broadcast band, the BBC began testing on 2915 kc. The channel was surprisingly well heard in the United States all evening long during the DX season.

For internal purposes, the BBC now structured its services, in slightly changed form, into "networks," coded by color. The English broadcasts of the Empire Service, together with most of its foreign-language broadcasts, became the Red Network; the European Service was the Blue Network; the Near East Service, plus a smorgasbord of foreign-language broadcasts outside Europe, constituted the Green Network; and broadcasts to Latin America and to three special zones— Spain and Portugal, Scandinavia, and the Balkans—were the Yellow Network. In 1942, the broadcasts to Latin America and to the Near East were put into a new Brown Network, and a new BBC forces service (see below) became part of the Green Network.

Although at first glance this arrangement didn't mean much to the listener, its practical effect was that studios, transmitters and other technical resources were now assigned by network. This had the important benefit of permitting the timing of broadcasts so as to serve secondary audiences outside the main target area for all or part of a transmission period, or during a particular season. For example, the Pacific Service could also serve listeners in areas west of the Pacific and, during the summer, the west coast of North America.

Britain's shortwave broadcasting was greatly aided by the opening, in February, of a new transmitter site at **Rampisham**, county of Dorset, in the south of England. (Dorset and Hampshire counties were the departure points of most of the D-Day invasion troops.) The new facility had four 100 kw. transmitters and 29 aerials. And in November, a 100 kw. shortwave transmitter was installed at **Lisnagarvey**, Northern Ireland. It operated on 6140 kc. for four and a half years. The BBC also expanded its human resources. Program personnel in the overseas services now numbered 1,472, up from 103 two years earlier.

The BBC started the "Listening Post" program, a five-minute discussion of enemy propaganda broadcasts based on information gathered by the BBC Monitoring Service. Berlin's response was a similar program, called "Listen and Judge for Yourself." And each Saturday night at 2100 EST the BBC visited London's American Eagle Club, a popular establishment run by the American Field Service for American and other Allied servicemen in England. The program featured messages home from soldiers at the club.

Britain entered the world of clandestine broadcasting in a big way. Firmly in charge was journalist and, most recently, colorful BBC German-language commentator Sefton Delmer. Delmer had lived in Germany, knew the language and the culture, and had even enjoyed some contact with the Nazi leadership during their ascendancy. He would become the almost-mythic grandmaster of wartime black broadcasting, the brains behind nearly 50 British-run clandestine stations, or "research units" (RUs), as they were called. These were stations that pretended to be indigenous to their target countries but were actually operating from England.

Delmer's stations broadcast to a multitude of European target areas, including Germany, France, Italy, Norway, Denmark, Czechoslovakia, Belgium, Yugoslavia, Holland, Austria, Bulgaria, Poland, Rumania and Hungary.[67] There was also a small (1.5 kw.) RU on Mauritius, **France Libre d'Outre Mer**, which feigned a Madagascar location in its 41 meter broadcasts to that island after the fall of France.[68]

In May, what would become one of the most professional of all Delmer's creations, **Gustav Siegfried Eins**, took to the air. **GS1**, as it was called, broadcast for seven minutes before the hour during American afternoons and evenings on 9545 kc. from a 7.5 kw. transmitter plant at Potsgrove, near Woburn Abbey, home to much of Britain's wartime propaganda activity. (Potsgrove was identical to another transmitting facility located in Gawcott.) GS1 would move to other 31 meter channels in 1942, i.e. 9480, 9545, 9605, 9635. Its broadcasts began with some fake code messages, followed by the voice of "Der Chef," who was actually former-Berliner Peter Seckelmann ("Paul Sanders"), a writer of detective stories. The broadcasts were recorded daily, and the same broadcast was used during all transmissions for the day. Because the station's purpose was to sow discontent between the Nazi party and the military, GS1 often broadcast fictitious "inside" information about German leaders, including detailed and highly unflattering descriptions of their alleged sexual deviances.[69] The station's tuning signal was the second line of the melody whose first line was used by the Reich station.

In February, the **Norwegian Freedom Station**, an anti–Nazi clandestine purporting to broadcast from Norway, was heard on 10070 kc. circa 1430 EST with a strong signal. In 1942 it moved to 15060 kc. and could be heard at 1430–1440 and 1745–1755. March brought American listeners a seemingly clandestine Italian station, **Radio Libertà**, on 11505 kc. (soon changed to 11915). It broadcast half-hour programs at various afternoon and early evening hours. Also heard in North America was **Sender der Europäischen Revolution**, the European Revolutionary Station. Run by a group of German Marxists in England, the 15-minute broadcasts were transmitted five times a day on 9650 kc. *("Achtung! Achtung! Hier ist der Sender der Europäischen Revolution.")* All of these stations were Delmer productions.

A **Radio Denmark** freedom station could be heard on 9710 kc. around noon. The Danish national anthem was played, followed by the announcer saying "Long live the King. Long live Denmark." The station, later known as **Frihedssenderen,** was another British clandestine.[70] And a French-language clandestine station, **Radio Inconnue** ("Unknown"), was heard on 9750 kc. at 1430–1500. Radio Inconnue was also a British black clandestine, as was the French-language station **Radio Travail.**

The **Christian Peace Movement** station was run by the Germans. It broadcast in English on 9445 kc. *("This is the Christian Peace Movement station, which is on the air daily at 8:45 P.M. and 11 A.M., British Summer Time, on 31.76 metres.")* Claiming to be run by an organization called the British Peace Movement, its 15-minute programs were a mix of hymns, Bible readings, and low-key exhortations to peace and pacifism. Another German production, supposedly an arm of the "Scottish Peace Front," was **Radio Caledonia**. Directed to Scotland, it used 7010 kc. and was on for two years starting in mid–1940. Transmissions ended with the playing of "Auld Lang Syne."

At mid-year the **Zeesen** evening broadcasts to North America were at 1650–2300 on 9570 kc. (**DXZ**, Warsaw), 9520 ("**Station Y**"), 10540 (**DZD**), 11770 (**DJD**), and 15200 (**DJB**). Frequencies changed often, however, and transmissions beamed to other areas could also be heard in the United States. Program schedules became less available when the government shuttered the German Library of Information in New York, the main distribution point. The year also saw the introduction of two new 75 kw. transmitters at **Ismaning**, near Munich.

Although France was again heard identifying as **Paris Mondial**, the Vichy government inaugurated a new service called **Voice of France**. It could be heard at 2330–0015 and 0030–0130 on 11850 kc., as well as other times and frequencies. Some of the channels being used by the **Swiss Shortwave Service** would remain familiar to shortwave listeners for decades, including 6165 kc. (**HER3**), 9535 (**HER4**), 15305 (**HER6**), and 21520 (**HER8**). *("This is Switzerland calling in the overseas service of the Swiss Broadcasting Corporation.")* Other frequencies included 6055 kc. (**HER2**), 17785 (**HER7**), and 25640 (**HER9**). And the **Finnish Broadcasting Corporation** now transmitted a service in English to North America several times a day at 0825–0840, 1550–1605, 1810–1825 and 1955–2030 EST over 9495, 11785 and 15190 kc. American listeners were asked to send their reception reports to the Finnish Legation in Washington.

Radio Centre, Moscow, broadcast to North America in English at 1000–1052 on 15180 kc. (**RV96**) and at 1815–1900 and 1930–2000 on 15180 and 12000 (**RNE**). There was also German at 1900–1930 and Italian at 2000–2030, both beamed to North America on the same frequencies. Many other channels came and went, e.g. 9550, 9620, 11740, 11780, 11920, 15210. (*"This is Radio Centre, Moscow, calling on 19.12 and 28.14 meters."*)

Greece came on shortwave before it was

Radio Éireann came on shortwave in 1939. Plans to open a North American service and increase power to 100 kw. were discussed for years, but the station never got beyond intermittent broadcasting on a 1.5 kw. transmitter. It left shortwave a few years after the war.

attacked. It carried English to Britain at 1430–1500 EST over **SVM**, 9935 kc., and **SVJ**, 7075. (*"This is Athens calling, the Voice of Greece at war."*) Broadcasts opened with the station's call letters in Morse followed by the Greek national anthem, and ended with "God Save the King." Many other frequencies were tried as well. In March a North American service was begun at 1800–1845 EST, with English at 1800, followed by Greek. It closed with the "Star-Spangled Banner." Soon, however, both the country and the station were under German control.

The **Belgrade Short-Wave Station** in Yugoslavia went silent after the German invasion. From Slovakia, a client state of Germany, **Radio Bratislava** was heard. It broadcast in English and Slovak to North America on Monday and Friday at 1800–1900 EST on 9525 kc. Broadcasts were soon extended to Wednesday and Saturday as well. Reports were requested to the Slovak Broadcasting Corporation, Bratislava.

Some smaller broadcasters were in the DX news. Listeners in England reported hearing a new station in Spain, **EAJ3, Radio Mediterraneo**, in Valencia, on 7037 kc. The Spanish station, **EAJ9, Radio Malaga**, which had been heard throughout the Spanish Civil War, was still on the air, 7140 and 14440 kc. It was heard in the U.S. until 1730 EST sign off. And **Radio Andorra** was heard testing on 11670 kc. It would try many channels in and around the 25 and 49 meter bands.

In Africa, **ZOY**, Accra, Ghana, came on shortwave. Broadcasting daily at 1130–1500 EST, the frequency was 4910 kc. An additional channel of 6002 kc. was soon added. (*"You have been listening to the government broadcasting station, ZOY, at Accra in the Gold Coast. We are* *now closing down. Goodnight, everyone.")* **ZQP**, the **Northern Rhodesia Broadcasting Station**, in Lusaka, Northern Rhodesia, was heard in Africa on 7200 kc. And **Egyptian State Broadcasting** was now sending a nightly half-hour in English to the United States at 1915–1945 over **SUX**, 7865 kc.

"Viva Franco! Arriba España!" would be heard long after the end of the Spanish Civil War at the sign off of broadcasts from Spain and its African territories.

In the north of Africa, a dearth of advertisers gave the once well-known **EAJ43** in the Canary Islands a much reduced presence. But an early voice was heard from what in later years would become an active broadcasting center. **Radio Falange del Exterior** in Tangier was reported operating at 1500–1700 EST on 7090 kc. And Portuguese-language broadcast programming was now heard from the Azores. **Emissor Regional dos Açores**, Ponta Delgada, was a local outlet of Portugal's **Emissora Nacional**. It was heard at 1500–1600 EST on 7290 kc. and 1700–1900 on 4020. In 1942 it moved to 14680 kc., then to 11090. Its 60 meter band outlet (4845 kc., later 4865) would, for decades after it came into use in 1947, be one of the best-heard 60 meter stations on east coast afternoons.

A **Radio Cameroun** on approximately 10710 kc. was reported heard with news at 1530 EST. From Libreville, Gabon in French Equatorial Africa, broadcast programming was reported heard over the French commercial station **FHK**. It was on 9320 kc. and operated irregularly around 1600–1830. There were a number of other French commercial stations operating in French West Africa (Guinea, Tchad, Dahomey, Senegal and the Ivory Coast), and in Oubangui-Chari (today's Central African Republic) in French Equatorial Africa. They were the predecessors to the chain of shortwave broadcasting stations that would develop in French Africa in the 1950s and 1960s.

FXE, Radio Levant, Beirut, Lebanon, was on the air. A half-hour broadcast in French, opening with "La Marseillaise," could be heard at midnight EST on the station's out-of-band frequency, 8036 kc. *("Ici Radio Levant.")* The 3 kw. station also broadcast in English and Arabic. Lebanon was part of the French Mandate for Syria and the Lebanon, formed by the League of Nations after World War I (the two countries were often referred to jointly as the Levant).

A second, 500-watt station, **Radio Damascus**, was on 7090 kc. During early 1941 the Levant was under the control of Vichy, which had given Germany and Italy certain air rights. By mid-year British and Free French Forces had taken over and the identification heard on FXE was *"Fighting French station, Radio Levant."*

Also now on the air was **ZNR** in the British colony of Aden. It was on 12115 kc., broadcasting news in English, Arabic, Italian, French and Somali at 1130–1245 EST. (*"You are listening to shortwave station ZNR, Aden, Arabia, operating on 24.76 meters."*) The power was 250 watts.

NHK opened a new high-power HF transmitting plant at **Yamata**. At year's end all ears were tuned to Tokyo, which was then broadcasting to Eastern North America at 1800–2130 EST on 11800 kc. (**JZJ**) and 15105 (**JLG4**). English was at 1800–1830 and 2100–2130, with other languages at other times. The Western North America beam was at 2225–0125 EST on 11800 and 15160 (**JZK**). Radio Tokyo was now broadcasting in 16 languages, 34 hours a day.

In September the Japanese installed a 10 kw. broadcast station, **JRAK**, at Parao, Palau, in the Caroline Islands, which the Japanese had inherited from Germany in 1919 under the Treaty of Versailles. The station operated on two channels, 9565 and 11740 kc., both of which could be heard in North America (at times 9565 was used for the North American beam).

New in the Philippines, although not reported heard in the U.S., was **KZND**, Manila, which was operated by the Civil Emergency Administration of the Department of National Defense. The station was on the air daily except Sundays at 0630–0730 EST on shortwave only—3790 and 8777 kc. (and also reported on 9515). It began operating on April 30 using a 1 kw. transmitter that had been confiscated from a suspected enemy alien. Its brief life was ended with the Japanese invasion. KZND was the first government-owned station in the Philippines.[71]

Perhaps the most interesting DX targets in the orient were the numerous Chinese stations. Using only call letters, which were difficult to decipher over the air, their exact provenance was often uncertain even to DXers operating at closer range than the U.S. One that was fairly well known was **XCDN**, the British-run, subscription-supported station of the *North China Daily News* in Shanghai. It moved around among many 25 meter channels (11620, 11830, 11920). The schedule was 0230–0630 EST in Chinese, 0630–0700 in other languages, 0700–1000 in English, 1730–1800 in Chinese, and 2210–0030 in English (with foreign-language news). The 1 kw. station had many pickups from the **BBC**, and sometimes rebroadcast **KGEI**. Headquarters was the Cathay Hotel in Shanghai. (*"This is station XCDN in Shanghai, the Voice of Democracy."*)

Among the other well-known Chinese stations were the already-mentioned **XGOY** and **XGOX**, **XGRS**, **XMHA**, **XPSA** and **FFZ**. But there were numerous lesser-known "X" stations as well, including **XGOK**, Radio Canton, 11650 kc., a 1 kw. station controlled by the Japanese; **XGOL**, Fukien, 10000; **XHHB**, Shanghai, 7970; **XIRS**, an Italian-run station in Shanghai on 11980 kc.; and 10 kw. **XOJD**, Hankow, on 6015 kc.

Notwithstanding the by now well known difficulty of extracting QSLs from Latin American stations, they were a welcome island of indigenous programming in a world that was becoming more and more dominated by high-power propaganda stations. A new station in Mexico was 100-watt **XEAR, Radiodifusora Oaxaquena**, in Oaxaca, on 6035 kc. New in Port-au-Prince, Haiti was **HHBM**, the **Magloire Broadcasting Circuit** (named after owner Frank C. Magloire). It also operated with 100 watts. The frequency was 9660 kc. and it could be heard opening at 0700 EST. And the Dominican Republic had a new station—**HI9T, Broadcasting Tropical**, Puerto Plata, first on 6555 kc., then on 6170.

Stations were learning how to attract listeners. **COK** in Havana held a contest. At 1930 each night from July 20 to August 2 it broadcast a special 15-minute program about tourist and sports subjects. The names of listeners reporting at least six of these broadcasts were entered in a drawing and two winners received a free trip to Cuba. And listeners hearing **HCJB's** new program, "Morning in the Mountains," were offered an album for photos of Ecuadorean mountains. The photos were available one at a time for reports received on a monthly basis. An additional ten cents would bring the station's monthly souvenir.

And not all HCJB programming was religious. The station was one of several South American outlets which, under the sponsorship of the Gillette Safety Razor Company, carried the Joe Louis–Lou Nova heavyweight championship on September 29, picking up the Spanish-language ringside announcing beamed south over **WGEO**.

Ecuador also had a new station. It was **HC2AK, Compañía Radiodifusora del Ecuador,** Guayaquil, on 9285 kc., relaying mediumwaver HC2AJ. The closing announcement was in English as well as Spanish. (*"You have been listening to station HC2AJ long wave and HC2AK shortwave in Guayaquil, Ecuador. We would very much like to hear from listeners as to their reception of this station, and please send your reports to Compañía Radiodifusora del Ecuador, P.O. Box 412. We will now close with our national song. Goodnight."*)

New from Venezuela was **YV2RC, La Voz de la Sierra**, Merida, on 3420 kc. There were three new stations in Peru: **OAX3A, Radio Huanuco**, on 6205 kc.; **OAX4G, Radio Lima**, on 6190 (400 watts, later 6343); and **OAX6D, Radio Continental**, Arequipa, on 9500 kc. Several new Brazilians appeared. In the low bands, listeners were hearing **PRC5, Radio Clube do Pará**, Belem, Pará, on 4865 kc. Higher in frequency were **PRF3, Radio Difusora Sao Paulo**, on 6095 and 11765 kc., 25 kw., and **PRE9, Ceará Radio Club**, Fortaleza, on 6105 and 15165.

In the Pacific, **VPD2**, Fiji, was still being heard well on 9540 kc. around midnight. Soon it conducted tests on 11895 and 15160 kc. as well, and it also carried programs in support of the Free French Forces. In June, the Lyndhurst transmissions of "**Australia Calling**" were transferred from 2 kw. **VLR** to a new 10 kw. station in Lyndhurst called **VLG**, and this greatly improved reception. (VLR was upgraded to 10 kw. in 1956 and remained in Australia's domestic shortwave service until 1987.) The main VLG frequency was 9580 kc. As with VLR, the VLG frequencies were identified by number, e.g. VLG5 (11880), VLG6 (15230), and the channels were sometimes shared with other transmitters. By now the foreign-language lineup of "Australia Calling" had been drastically reduced to just French and Dutch. However, wartime exigencies would soon dictate the addition of Japanese, Mandarin, Malay and Thai. The basic mission of "Australia Calling" was to conduct psychological warfare against the Japanese, and to sustain morale and urge resistance in occupied countries. North American listeners were advised that they could send their reports to the Australian News and Information Bureau on Fifth Avenue.

In other shortwave developments, notwithstanding the decreased availability of receivers as industrial production was diverted to wartime needs, Buick brought out the "Super Sonomatic" car radio with both AM and shortwave coverage. Both bands used the same antenna.

On January 1, **HI1X** in Ciudad Trujillo, Dominican Republic, carried a special program for the NNRC on 6333 kc. as well as over HIX, 800 kc. The same month saw specials from **HCJB** and from **HC2AK**. **PRE9** in Brazil conducted one for the National Radio Club in October. But special broadcasts were in decline. On December 12, mail service from the U.S. to Germany, Italy and all countries under their control (including occupied France) was suspended.

Frank Conrad, the man who more than any other could call himself the father of shortwave broadcasting, died on December 11 in Miami, where he had gone to spend the winter. At his death he was the holder of more than 200 patents.

1942

In November, German troops occupied Vichy France, which then came under direct German rule.

In North Africa, Rommel made extensive advances in Libya, recapturing Benghazi and recovering ground lost to the British at the end of 1941. Tobruk surrendered on June 20 and the Germans and Italians pushed into Egypt. But the British were victorious at El Alamein in November and drove Rommel back.

In the Far East, Japan occupied Manila on January 2 and began attacking American forces withdrawing to Bataan. On February 22, MacArthur was ordered to turn over command to General Wainwright and leave the Philippines for Australia. (His famous "I shall return" declaration was made on March 20.) On March 2 the Japanese landed on Mindanao to the south, and on April 9 U.S. forces on Luzon surrendered. Wainwright surrendered Corregidor on May 6, whereupon control of the Philippines passed to Japan. This victory notwithstanding, a month later Japan was defeated at Midway, signaling a major change in the country's military fortunes.

Weak resistance to Japan's invasion of Thailand at the end of 1941 led to a military alliance between the two countries, and soon Japanese bases in Thailand became operational and contributed to Japanese moves against Burma and Malaya. Kuala Lumpur was captured on January 11. At the end of the month, the British and Australian forces in Malaya withdrew to Singapore, which surrendered on February 15. It was the biggest single defeat in British history. Rangoon fell on March 7, Mandalay on May 1.

The end of 1941 and the beginning of 1942 saw Japan occupy Sarawak and Sabah, British possessions in the north of Borneo. Japan also began landings in the Dutch East Indies, and soon controlled Kendari, Menado, Makassar and Banjermasin. There followed landings at Palembang (on Sumatra) and Bali, and on Portuguese Timor, as well as Sorong and Hollandia in Dutch New Guinea. Japanese activity on Java led to the fall of Batavia (today's Jakarta) on March 5, and complete Japanese control of the island soon thereafter.

In January, Japanese forces landed on Rabaul (New Britain) and soon were in control. Additional landings followed at Balikpapan (on Borneo, which was part of the Dutch East Indies — today's Indonesia — save for the British areas in the north), Kavieng (New Ireland), and Bougainville. Port Moresby in Papua New Guinea (the southeastern part of the island) was bombarded in January, Darwin in February. Japan was prevented from landing at Port Moresby in May in the Battle of the Coral Sea, which was a major check on Japanese advances. But in July Japanese troops landed in more northerly areas of New Guinea and continued building up their forces and advancing against Australian troops there. And on August 7, in response to Japanese construction of an airbase on Guadalcanal, U.S. forces invaded the island. Six months of ferocious fighting ensued.

On the home front in February, year-round Daylight Savings Time was adopted throughout the United States. It had not been in effect nationwide since 1919. Now called "Eastern War Time," it lasted until September 30, 1945. (Times shown hereafter are in EWT.)

It was an important year in American shortwave broadcasting. In June, the office of the Coordinator of Information was split into the Office of Strategic Services, led by Col. Donovan, and the Office of War Information (OWI), headed by author, journalist and well-known radio commentator Elmer Davis. The OWI's responsibilities were wide ranging, and mainly domestic, but they also included overseas information functions, including shortwave broadcasting. The Foreign Information Service, whose radio production division was by now headed by noted producer, director and author John Houseman (who gained fame many years later as Professor Charles Kingsfield in "The Paper Chase"), became the OWI Overseas Branch.[72] The OWI and the CIAA, with some overall policy guidance from the State Department, now had greater control over shortwave program content. (Later the State Department would check scripts to ensure compatibility with Department policies.) However, programs were still presented as network productions, e.g. "CBS presents," or "NBC presents."[73]

As early as 1941 there had been rumors that the government was going to "take over" shortwave broadcasting, and after his appointment as COI in July of that year Donovan was often heard to deny this. But by early 1942, well before the bifurcation of the COI's office, Donovan had concluded that the informal relationships that had grown up among the stations and FIS were inadequate and that something more had to be done. American shortwave was still too uncoordinated and underpowered.

In addition, it was felt necessary to match Britain's now-considerable shortwave activities. The **BBC** felt that its influence was wide and its on-air credibility beyond reproach. As a letter from a French village put it, "Out of 150 households there are 110 wireless sets. Out of the 110 owners of these sets, 105 at least listen to the BBC regularly."[74] According to R. W. Foot, co-Director General of the BBC at the time, "[t]here may be 45 languages, but there is only one BBC. Its news bulletins are heard throughout the whole world and wherever they are heard they are trusted. They tell the truth. That, to the Axis, is more deadly than steel."[75] But even though the shortwave service which the BBC had so haltingly inaugurated a mere ten years earlier had become the world's best, and the corporation's greatest strength, history dictated that some in conquered Europe would distrust Britain. America's voice would enjoy more credence and less suspicion. America's motives in fighting the European war were not suspect, and its national accomplishments were held in high regard.[76]

Various plans started circulating. The CIAA favored the creation of a separate agency or company structured along the lines of the BBC. CBS was pushing the consolidation of shortwave broadcasting into two private companies, an approach which it said would retain a modicum of competition. The approach that was eventually adopted called for the government to lease all the air time of the American shortwave broadcasters at a cost of about $1 million a year, two-thirds to be paid by OWI, one-third by CIAA. The resulting system would be run as a single unit. To the government this was not a takeover but a partnership with the station operators. **WLWO** had since March been voluntarily operating under a similar arrangement, with all programming done by COI (which inaugurated the playing of "Yankee Doodle" as the opening tune). And **KWID** (see below) had been programmed by the government from the start.

The stations were agreeable to most anything, having learned by now that shortwave broadcasting was distinctly unprofitable. Moreover, in January, as the spotlight on shortwave grew brighter, the stations' Coordinator of International Broadcasting, Stanley P. Richardson, had left his post to join the government's new Office of Censorship (from which, in September, he moved on to become manager of NBC's London office). If there was to be a change, this was a good time.

The government plan took effect on November 1. Under the new arrangement, the station owners continued to operate the facilities and be reimbursed on a non-profit basis, but the government was fully in charge. The OWI Overseas Branch would, among other things, be responsible for managing the foreign broadcasting effort except for transmissions to Latin America, which would be the responsibility of Rockefeller's CIAA. Transmitting hours would be divided two-thirds, one-third between OWI and CIAA. The best programs of NBC and CBS would be retained and would be supplemented by new OWI and CIAA material, much of it, especially the CIAA material, actually produced by NBC and CBS under contract with the government (an arrangement that would continue until 1948). OWI originated programs from its east coast studios in New York and also used two KGEI studios in San Francisco. Much OWI-CIAA programming was produced in the well-equipped studios of the Radio Section of the Department of the Interior.

With the CIAA it was not all shortwave, however. The agency was cognizant of the difficulties sometimes encountered in shortwave reception in the target areas, and facilitated local rebroadcasting by supporting local Latin American program producers and supplying programming to Latin American stations by way of transcription.

Only **WRUL**— which had just opened an office in New York — balked at the plan, insisting that it be able to program its own material for four hours a day in order to retain some of its unique character as a non-commercial, educational endeavor. The government felt the station was just holding out for more money, and took it over on November 5. This was just in time for the landing of American and other Allied troops in Morocco and Algeria on November 7, an event whose coverage by the new American shortwave structure — including a message in French from President Roosevelt and extensive special broadcasts to the affected areas over several days— earned it much credit. *("Attention! Attention! Stand by for an important announcement from the United States of America.")* "All transmitters were constantly alive with news of the invasion. In the moments available the strains of 'La Marseillaise' and 'The Star Spangled Banner' filled the air. OWI radio broadcasts also interpreted the invasion for overseas audiences."[77] "It was a tremendous radio operation," editorialized *Broadcasting* magazine.[78]

America's new shortwave structure was off to a good start. All stations increased both their English and foreign-language news broadcasts, and news flashes were frequent. Latin America was still an important priority, and soon the stations were transmitting 54 hours of programming a day to the area, including 15 hours of news programs. Although two knowledgeable observers of the international broadcasting scene at the time expressed the view that in the "history of radio in international politics up to the outbreak of [World War II] the United States deserves very little attention,"[79] that it was catching up quickly was evidenced by a Peabody Award given in 1942 to Stanley Richardson and the American shortwave broadcasters collectively for "their initiative and their influence" and their innovation in broadcasting to Europe.[80] And even though the quaint American notion that "propaganda" was something that only totalitarian governments did had by now been interred, the American shortwave broadcasting effort sought to anchor itself in the same commitment to truth and credibility that was serving the BBC well, even in wartime.[81]

It was the post–Pearl Harbor stepup in OWI program production activity that was midwife to the birth of the **Voice of America**. It is still uncertain exactly when in 1942 the Voice of America label came into use, but it was well before government control began in November. For many years the VOA itself proclaimed its birthdate to be February 24, 1942. A voluminous 1970 study of the early development of the VOA put it at February 25.[82] The *War Report of the OSS,* prepared by the War Department in 1947, gave the date as February 5.[83] The most recent research, in 2009, suggests that it was February 1,[84] a date that has now been adopted by the VOA itself.[85] From the start, the BBC assisted the VOA by recording VOA programs off shortwave and relaying them to Europe on mediumwave. By January 1943 they were being relayed direct, without recording. At the end of 1943 there were 107 15-minute relays per week, a number that would soon double.

Whichever of the February dates is correct, it is clear that, at the start, the Voice of America was not an organizational entity so much as an on-air marquee intended to bring some unity to an American shortwave broadcasting effort that was still disjointed after Pearl

Harbor. Initially it was used for programming produced by or at the behest of OWI (but not CIAA or the broadcast companies themselves). The broader use of the VOA name, on air and in writing, developed over some months, and for a long time it was not used on an exclusive basis. When the government took over in November, station announcements still included call letters and corporate parentage.[86]

The first mention of the Voice of America in the DX press appears to have been in July 1942, when the IDA reported a VOA identification heard during a broadcast carried over a **Press Wireless** point-to-point channel in Hicksville, Long Island, **WJQ**, 10010 kc. The reception was roughly four months after the initial "Voice of America" broadcasts in February.[87] That it was not noted sooner by short-wave hobbyists, whose finely tuned ears could have been expected to quickly pick up a new name for America's shortwave broadcasting effort, may have been due to the continued use of station-specific call letters, and to not recognizing the VOA label as referring to a distinct new service. In any event, soon the VOA identification was being heard on a variety of American shortwave channels.[88]

As early as March 1942, the VOA had a basic schedule of three "services" or "patterns"— Pattern A, 6¼ hours daily in English, German, French and Italian; Pattern B, Spanish, Portuguese, and Scandinavian and Slavic languages; and Pattern C, all others. By the end of the year broadcasts in the European anchor languages—English, German, French and Italian — were being sent out virtually around the clock, roughly a quarter-hour in each language, each hour.

It was also in 1942 that radio service directed to the military took root. In March, the American shortwave stations began carrying the new hour-long program, "Command Performance," whose production was supervised by the Radio Branch of the Bureau of Public Relations of the War Department's Morale Service Division. Consisting of popular music, comedy and sports by top-drawer artists and personalities, the hugely popular program was intended solely for American armed forces abroad. It was distributed by

This QSL is believed to be the first that was specifically designed for the VOA.

way of the American shortwave broadcasters as well as the BBC (reception was often best on BBC mediumwave channels), and it was also available via transcription. It was followed in April by the weekly "Army Hour," which was carried on NBC domestic stations as well as American shortwave outlets. "Army Hour" was produced directly by the Radio Branch.

Notwithstanding the shortage of military receivers on which to listen — a major problem — other broadcasters got into the act. Before long NBC was recording and sending American programs — many commercially sponsored — to the armed forces overseas via **WRCA, WNBI** and **WBOS**. These shows included *Fibber McGee & Molly, National Barn Dance, Kraft Music Hall*, Burns and Allen, Jack Benny, and others. General Electric produced the weekly "Men In Service," a half-hour program sponsored by various newspapers and consisting of entertainment and greetings to servicemen. It was broadcast over **WGEO, WGEA** and **KGEI**. CBS shortwaved 17 programs to the troops. The OWI produced "News from Home," which was broadcast over **WBOS, WRUL** and several **Press Wireless** channels. There were countless other military programs. And it was not only American soldiers who benefitted from the interest in the military. General Electric broadcast the "ANZAC Hour" over WGEO. It included messages home by Australian and New Zealand flyers in New York.

To bring some order to this hodgepodge, in mid year the **Armed Forces Radio Service** was formed.[89] Headquartered in Los Angeles, AFRS was to produce and distribute news, entertainment and sports for the troops. It had expected to rely on shortwave, but early experience led to a change in plans. U.S. signals were not particularly strong, and, more importantly, soldiers in the field seldom had access to receivers capable of reliable shortwave reception, notwithstanding the distribution to military units of large numbers of "B" ("Buddy") kits which included a basic AC-DC, AM-shortwave radio receiver[90] (along with a hand wound turntable, records, books, and seven harmonicas). Well over 200,000 "B" kits and standalone receivers were distributed to the troops during the war.

As a result, the main strategy for reaching the troops switched from shortwave to the establishment of large numbers of low-power (typically 50-watt), standard broadcast "American Expeditionary Stations" such as those that had been set up at the initiative of troops in Alaska in December 1941. AFRS supplied them — and other outlets that carried AFRS material — with most programming via transcription. Time sensitive material was sent by shortwave, which also served remote areas that lacked stations of their own. But AFRS was largely at the mercy of OWI and CIAA for shortwave transmitter time, which was at a premium. This would be a persistent problem for over a year, and as a result AFRS did not achieve effective shortwave operation until well into 1943.

AFRS also arranged for time on private or government stations in places where troops were stationed. Most of these stations operated on mediumwave, but those with shortwave outlets, including **ZFY** (British Guiana), **AVROS, TGW, Radio CUROM**, and others, also put AFRS programs on their shortwave channels. Both **Radio Brazzaville** and **Radio Congo Belge** carried AFRS programming.

A conservative count indicated that at one time or another between 1942 and 1946 at least 274 AFRS stations were operating worldwide, together with 392 wired sound systems and 179 government or commercial stations that carried AFRS programs.[91]

In order to expand the nation's Pacific shortwave capability, and in the face of the reluctance of the big companies to spend more on shortwave broadcasting, the government had, in October 1941, arranged for Associated Broadcasters, Inc., owners of San Francisco station KFSO, to apply to build a new shortwave station, whose call letters would be **KWID**. The project was approved in a week, and provision of construction materials was given top priority. It was planned that the station would broadcast in many languages besides English. To obvi-

The call letters of San Francisco's KWID reflected the name of Wesley I. Dumm, head of the station's operating company, Associated Broadcasters, Inc.

ate difficulties in obtaining a transmitter, the COI bought the 100 kw. WGEO transmitter for $150,000 and shipped it to KWID (a replacement was on the air at WGEO by September 1942).

KWID began testing on May 4, and was widely heard during transmissions to the Far East at 2100–0300 on 15290 kc. Soon a South American transmission at 1800–2100 was added, transmission hours were expanded, and a 9570 kc. channel opened. The KWID studios, co-located with those of KFSO, were in the Hotel Mark Hopkins, with most programming provided directly to the station through a new OWI office in San Francisco. The station's accelerated construction may have been in part the result of a report by an American news correspondent in Chungking that "an Axis propaganda blitz in the Far East had caught the United States flatfooted."[92]

Although international broadcasting was a high priority, the construction of additional new stations was delayed by the unavailability of many materials. As a result, the FCC granted special authorization to certain point-to-point stations—whose domestic activities the FCC had, in May, restricted as a wartime measure—to operate in the international broadcast service. It was the COI who, around June, first leased the facilities for this purpose, starting with **Press Wireless** and AT&T.[93] The transmitters generally operated with relatively low power, usually in the 10–20 kw. range.

The point-to-point experiment was not without problems. The stations operated on out-of-band channels that were less likely to be known to listeners, and the beams were narrow.[94] But it was all that was available, and American broadcast programming intended for direct-to-listener reception was soon heard over many of these stations. The Press Wireless transmitters in **Los Angeles** used some 19 channels (e.g. **KJE8**, 9390 kc., **KJE9**, 10750, **KJN8**, 18560), as did **Hicksville**, Long Island (e.g. **WCX**, 7850, **WCB**, 15580, **WDM**, 19470). (The two sites shared some frequencies.) *("This is station KJE8, Press Wireless, Inc., Los Angeles, California, USA, testing program channel service on a carrier frequency of 9390 kc.")* The RCA facility at **Bolinas**, California used some 28 call letters and out-of-band frequencies, such as

KEE (7715 kc.), **KEZ** (10400), and **KKW** (13780), along with four-letter stations **KRCA** and **KRCQ**. Broadcast programming was also heard from the RCA facility in **Kahuku**, Hawaii, and the AT&T stations at **Dixon**, California and **Ocean Gate** and **Lawrenceville**, New Jersey. (The VOA would open a station in Dixon in late 1944.) These stations were the source of much confusion among shortwave listeners.

Schedules of American Shortwave Broadcast Stations
circa January–June 1942

Associated Broadcasters	*San Francisco, California* **KWID** 1700-2115 on 15290; 2130-0045 & 0100-0615 on 9570; and 0629-1315 on 7230
CBS	*Brentwood (LI), New York* **WCBX** 0600-1645 & 1650-1945 on 15270; 1950-2330 on 9490; and 2345-0200 on 9650 **WCRC** 0600-1715 & 1720-1915 on 17830; and 1930-2400 on 6060 **WCDA** 0600-1845 on 11830; and 1930-0200 on 6060
Crosley	*Mason, Ohio* **WLWO** 0015-0600 on 6080; 1000-1300 on 17800; 1315-1715 on 11710; 1730-1900 on 15250; and 1915-2400 on 9590
General Electric	*Schenectady, New York* **WGEO** 0500-0800 on 9650; 0815-1530 on 15330; and 1545-1715 & 1730-2400 on 9530 **WGEA** 0800-1715 on 11847; 1730-1945 on 15330; and 2000-2400 on 7000 *Belmont, California* **KGEI** 1700-2245 on 11730; and 2300-0045 & 0058-1205 on 7250
NBC	*Bound Brook, New Jersey* **WRCA** 0900-1415 on 17780; 0500-0845, 1430-1645 and 1700-2330 on 11893 **WNBI** 0700-1700 on 15150; and 1715-0200 on 9670
Westinghouse	*Hull, Massachusetts* **WBOS** 0430-0600 on 6140; 0615-0800 on 11870; 0815-1245 on 15210; and 1300-1715 & 1730-2400 on 11870
World Wide Broadcasting	*Scituate, Massachusetts* **WRUL** 1330-0300 on 11790 **WRUW** 0200-0430 on 6040; 0430-0600 & 1430-0200 on 9700; 0600-0800, 1100-1300 & 1330-1430 on 15350; and 1100-1300 on 17750

Much of the new west coast point-to-point capability was devoted to the relay of **KGEI**, which often suffered intentional interference and on-air tricks. Its transmissions were sometimes interrupted by other stations cutting-in on the frequency mid-broadcast to present simulated news bulletins. These appeared to be Japanese stations, one of which gave "news" of a fictitious Japanese air attack on San Francisco.[95] KGEI was a thorn in the side of the Japanese. In February, **Radio Tokyo** began a program called "Answering to KGEI," disputing various statements made over the station.

In April, Lloyd Free left the director's post at the Foreign Broadcast Monitoring Service to enter Army intelligence. His replacement was Dr. Robert D. Leigh, who had served as the first president of Bennington College from 1928 to 1941. In July, at Leigh's urging, the name of the agency was changed to the Foreign Broadcast Intelligence Service. By this time it was functioning basically as a war agency, handling over a million and a half broadcast words daily.[96]

Radio equipment was in short supply. Government agencies scrounging for receivers and transmitters began inquiring of the ARRL, which set up an apparatus bureau where members could list factory-made equipment they were willing to sell to the government. Notwithstanding that amateur radio operation had been forbidden, in June the government required all amateurs to register their transmitters with the FCC.[97] By December the FCC was allowing U.S. shortwave broadcasters to transmit a program stream on more than one band simultaneously, something that had not been permitted before. It also suspended some of the other rules applicable to shortwave broadcasting so that the plan for government leasing of all the shortwave broadcast time could be implemented.

Bataan Touch
Yanks Get Real Attack with Radio Version

Realistic gunfire coincided with simulated gunfire to add a dramatic touch to one listener's reception of a *March of Time* broadcast.

According to a letter received by General Electric from Lt. Col. James E. Macklin on Bataan Peninsula, he was tuned one evening to KGEI, GE's shortwave station in San Francisco, listening to the *March of Time*. The continuity of the program purported to depict an incident in the front lines of Bataan. There was a sound effect of gunfire and a character shouted, "Here they come!" At that very instant an actual flight of Jap dive bombers roared down on Lt. Col. Macklin's position and the salvo of anti-aircraft fire combined to drown out the radio version.

Yankee complacency and coolness is echoed in Lt. Col. Macklin's simple notation — "There was a gang around the set at the time and we were all much amused at the unusual coincidence."

Broadcasting
April 20, 1942[98]

After years of call letter changes, the shortwave situation in Canada was stabilizing, often on frequencies that would remain familiar to shortwave listeners for decades. At the start of the year the country's shortwave lineup was as follows:

CBC stations

CBFW	Verchères	6090	7.5 kw.	Canadian Broadcasting Corp.
CBFX	Verchères	9630	7.5 kw.	Canadian Broadcasting Corp.
CBFY	Verchères	11705	7.5 kw.	Canadian Broadcasting Corp
CBFZ	Verchères	15190	7.5 kw.	Canadian Broadcasting Corp
CBRX	Vancouver	6160	150 watts	Canadian Broadcasting Corp.

Private stations

CFCX	Montreal	6005	75 watts	Canadian Marconi Co.
CFRX	Toronto	6070	1.0 kw.	Rogers Radio Broadcasting Co. Ltd.

CFVP	Calgary	6030	100 watts	Voice of the Prairies Ltd.
CHNX	Halifax	6130	500 watts	Maritime Broadcasting Co. Ltd.
CJCX	Sydney	6010	1.0 kw.	Eastern Broadcasters Ltd.
CJRO	Winnipeg	6150	2.0 kw.	Transcanada Communications Ltd.
CJRX	Winnipeg	11720	2.0 kw.	Transcanada Communications Ltd.
CKFX	Vancouver	6080	10 watts	Standard Broadcasting Co. Ltd.

The **BBC** dropped the shortwave transmission of its "Programme for the Forces" (it was still available on mediumwave), introducing in its place, as part of the Empire Service, the Service for British Forces Overseas, a daily service intended for British servicemen in the Near and Middle East and North and West Africa. Initially a four-hour service set up in June, it was formalized and expanded to seven hours in November. It was this service that would become the General Overseas Service.

On May 22 and May 29, the BBC ran a series of six special test programs called "Lend Us Your Ears" over stations GSC and GSD, 9580 and 11750 kc. respectively, seeking information on U.S. reception of different kinds of audio content on shortwave — voice, music, machine guns firing, wind blowing, water bubbling, babies crying, etc. Reports were to go to the BBC's North American office on Fifth Avenue.

The **Reichs-Rundfunk Gesellschaft** in Germany installed two 100 kw. transmitters at **Ismaning** and three at **Öbisfelde**. (The Öbisfelde complex would grow to 11 transmitters by 1944.) "**Zeesen**" was now broadcasting five zonal services, and programming had reached a high level of professionalism. To the end that instinctively negative reactions to Nazi programming might be counteracted, a friendly, natural style, with a good deal of informal, seemingly-spontaneous banter among announcers, was utilized. German-language broadcasts often contained greetings to any German troops that might be listening.

An interesting station was **Radio Metropole**, which could be heard on 9480 kc. An Axis station, it was run by the German Foreign Ministry rather than the Büro Concordia. Early on it operated at 1230–1805, originally in a few languages of the eastern front, i.e. Russian, Ukrainian, Georgian and Tatar. Soon it added French, English, Polish, Persian, and Uzbek. The hour-long French and English broadcasts were transmitted three times daily, and two other channels were added, 6100 and 11925 kc. The transmitter was located in Zemun, Croatia, near Belgrade, and was part of the Foreign Ministry's purchase of **Radio Belgrade** in 1941. The professionalism and the quality of the programming of Radio Metropole made it very popular, and it drew many listeners. It was on the air from March 1942 to August 1944.

The anti–Nazi **Deutscher Volksender (German Workers' Station)** was heard on 15080 kc. at 1000–1020 in German. It was directed to German intellectuals. And listeners reported numerous "freedom stations." The **Rumanian Freedom Station** was heard on 11600 kc. at 1615–1625; the **Yugoslav Freedom Station** on approximately 11010 at 1445–1500 in Serbo-Croat; the **Croatian Freedom Station**, 11350 kc., at 1430–1440. **Suomen Vapaus Radio**, a Finnish freedom station, appeared with good signals at 0730–0745 on 11590 kc. It was also reportedly on the air at 1505–1520 on 6125. It is likely that most of these stations were British efforts. **Wehrmachtsender Nord**, intended for German forces in Norway and Finland, was definitely British, and was heard in east coast afternoons and early evenings on 10040 kc.[99] Its life was short, however — just a few weeks.

The English-language "clandestine" broadcaster, **Radio Debunk**— it would "debunk" Allied war propaganda — was heard with strong signals on 7200 kc. (later 10350) nightly circa 2030–2100 EWT, feigning location in the American midwest. (*"This is the voice of America, Radio Debunk, bringing you the news from inside America."*) No one was fooled that it was anything other than a transmission from Germany. It was not a Büro Concordia station, however, but rather an undertaking of Zeeseen's North American section. Its purpose was to encourage the belief that underground sabotage movements were already active in the United States.

The Vichy station **Voice of France** was now operating worldwide on 9520, 11845, 15240, 17765 and 17850 kc., with several 45- to 60-minute broadcasts each day to North America, South America, Africa and Indochina. The North American beam was at 0730–0815 on 17850 kc., 1600–1645 on 11845, and 1900–1945 and 2315–0030 on 9520 kc. **Paris Mondial** was still being heard at other times and on other frequencies.

Rome's broadcasts to North America were at 0900–1200 EWT on 9630 (**2RO3**) and 11810 kc. (**2RO4**), 1300–1430 on 15300 (**2RO6**), and 2030–2400 on 9630, 11810 and 11950 (**2RO22**). **Radio Bucharest**, now on 9260 kc., was transmitting at 1500–1805 EWT in English, French and Italian. ("*This is the Rumanian shortwave station at Bucharest operating on 32.4 meters.*") **Radio Norway** was broadcasting to North America at 2100–2200 EWT on 9645 kc. (**LLH**). ("*Hello America, here is Oslo, operating on 31.1 meters. In one minute you will hear a special program for Norwegians in North America.*") And the old **EAQ**, now announcing as **Radio Nacional de España**, broadcast to Britain at 1400–1500 EWT and to North America at 2000–2100 on its old frequency of 9860 kc. English was at 1415–1430 and 2000–2015.

In the Soviet Union, **Radio Sverdlovsk** was heard, seemingly using its own transmitters on 12225 and 14920 kc. at 0700–0800, and relayed from Moscow on 12060 and 15080 kc. The station was heard at other times and on other frequencies as well. ("*This is Sverdlovsk calling.*") Similar was **Radio Kuibishev**, with a fairly extensive broadcasting schedule in Russian and English: 0015–0100 EWT on 7135 kc.; 0000–0030, 0100–0330 and 0700–1050 on 10040 (English at 0100, 0850 and 0930); 0850–0915 in English on 14400; 1100–1830 on 8050 (English at 1600); 1400–1700 on 7205 (English at 1600); and 1300–1600 on 6940. ("*This is Kuibishev calling.*") **Radio Komsomolsk** was also heard on many channels, in most cases relaying **Radio Centre**, Moscow. As would always be the case with international broadcasting from the Soviet Union, a program that originated in one place was often broadcast over a transmitter located in another.

For a few weeks in May, **Radio Congo Belge** was heard testing on 17770 kc. at 1430–1630, where it provided excellent reception, in parallel with 11720 and 15175 kc. The station carried an NBC French program at 1545–1630, followed by 15 minutes of French news which it picked up from **WLWO**.

Radio Addis Ababa, now operating with the help of the British pursuant to an agreement with Emperor Haile Selassie, was reported heard in Australia at 1015–1130 EWT on 9625 kc. Broadcasts were in English, French and Italian. ("*This is Radio Addis Ababa. We are now closing down till our evening transmission.*") **ZNB**, Bechuanaland, was still on the air and could be heard at 0030 EWT on 5890 kc., opening with the "V for Victory" sign in Morse. **EAJ43** in the Canary Islands was now on 7275 kc., operating at 0830–1000 and 1430–1900. And **EA9AA**, 7090 kc., variously reported to be operating from Ceuta, Tetuan, or Melilla in Spanish Morocco, at times relayed **EAJ21, Radio Melilla,** circa 1800–1900.

Radio Dakar was on 15345 kc., where it was heard at good strength at 1315–1340 with news in French, and later as well. This was a new 12 kw. transmitter. Said one NNRCer, "Radio Dakar, Senegal, has the strongest signal on this band at 4 P.M." It was also heard on 9410 kc. to 1805 close. Two new stations were reportedly operating from French West Africa: **Niamey**, Niger, on 9375 or 9977 kc., and **Cotonou**, Dahomey, on 9740.

Radio Maroc, Rabat, which had utilized 8030 and 11940 kc., 15 and 25 kw. respectively, was now being heard on 8030 only, at 0100–0200, 0300–0400, 0630–1030, 1230–1300 and 2015–2045. English was on Monday, Wednesday and Saturday at 0700–0730. In November,

Operation Torch successfully landed a force of 100,000 troops, nearly all Americans, at Casablanca and Oran in Morocco, and Algiers in Algeria. With the landings came an American presence on the airwaves of both countries. U.S. programming, in English for the troops and in French for the residents, was soon heard over Radio Maroc and **Radio Algiers**, both of which theretofore had been Vichy controlled. Algiers was particularly active and became a major base for Allied communications of all kinds.

On December 26, Manila had been declared an open city, and the people awaited the arrival of the Japanese. The main broadcasting stations left the air, supposedly having been dismantled or destroyed in anticipation of the enemy's arrival. However, **KZRH** was soon heard again, now under Japanese control and identifying as "the voice of the new Philippines." The frequencies were 6145, 9640 and 11890 kc. Several minutes of chimes were sounded before the broadcasts began at 1800 EWT. The Axis programming included greetings to and music for American troops on Bataan.

Within a month of the start of the new year several other stations were no longer heard, including **Radio Saigon; ZBW, Radio Hong Kong**; and **ZHJ**, Penang, and **ZHP**, the **Malaya Broadcasting Corporation**, Singapore (called the **British Malaya Broadcasting Corporation** until 1941). The **Thai National Broadcasting Station** was heard irregularly. Singapore returned in the middle of May on 12200 kc. (later 12000), identifying as **Radio Shonan**, the Japanese name for Singapore. It could be heard at 0700–1240 EWT, with English news circa 0915. Included in its programs were messages from Indian nationals in Malaya to relatives back home. Singapore would play a major part in the Japanese shortwave broadcasting effort, and Radio Shonan would broadcast to various parts of Asia and the Pacific, as well as relay Tokyo's broadcasts to Europe.

Later in the year **Penang** also returned, on 6095 kc., as did **Hong Kong**, now under Japanese control, and **Radio Saigon**, which remained fairly non-strident notwithstanding Japan's dominant military presence in the country, which was agreed to by the Vichy government. Radio Saigon broadcast in many languages on one or both of its two channels, 6185 and 11780 kc., with Japan renting blocks of transmitter time. For about a week in early March, at Japan's direction, Radio Saigon, pretending to be **Radio Bandoeng** in Java and using the latter's frequency of 10260 kc., broadcast propaganda programs in Dutch and Malay (the language of the Dutch East Indies) which were coordinated with Japanese troop movements around Bandoeng.[100] The Battle of Java ended with the surrender of the Dutch at Bandoeng on March 8, and other Allied forces a few days later. All Bandoeng stations were off the air after the occupation of Java. Stations in Dutch New Guinea that were still under Dutch control remained on the air.

Broadcasts in English to North America from **Radio Tokyo** were now, to the west coast, at 2325–0230, and to the east coast at 1855–2300, both on 11800 kc. (**JZJ**) and 15160 (**JZK**). English news from Tokyo was heard many times throughout the day on many frequencies. Early in the year, Radio Tokyo began including prisoner of war messages at the end of the English news broadcasts to North America, opening and closing the segment with "My Bonnie Lies Over the Ocean." At times announcements giving only the name, rank, age, address, and place of capture of the POWs replaced the personal messages.[101] In its German service the **BBC** also broadcast the names of prisoners, and would, in 1943, commence a nightly 15-minute program of recorded prisoner messages.

Japanese shortwave propaganda increased in parallel with the country's military advance. The targets were the Asian countries that were under Japanese occupation or in the cross hairs. In Asia, reception of Radio Tokyo was much stronger than Allied stations, and this gave Japan a major advantage. Radio Tokyo took care to tailor its broadcasts to the culture and history of the target area. Overall, however, the message was a racial one — an anti-western, anti-imperialist, pro-nationalist line, bottomed on local resentment of the countries whose colonial policies had long shaped the geopolitical map of Asia. The British were particularly vulnerable to attack. Other targets of radio propaganda were the "overseas Chinese," who had a commercial presence throughout Asia, and Chiang Kai-shek, for his cooperation with both the Americans and the communists. Different themes, but still basically racial, featured in the propaganda broadcasts to and about the United States: American immigration laws, which were not friendly to Asians; the internment of Japanese-Americans; and the discrimination against African Americans. African Americans, both in and out of the military, were a specific target of Japanese propaganda.[102]

Until Burma succumbed, the **Burma State Broadcasting Service** was heard on 3488 kc. (**XZZ**) and 6007 kc. (**XYZ**), opening with chimes and six clock strikes at 0730 EWT. *("Rangoon calling. This is the Burma State Broadcasting Corporation on 6.007 and 3.48 mc.")* It signed off at around 1020 with "God Save the King." In March the station was heard on 6007 circa 0900 with messages from those in Burma to their relatives and friends. Soon it was reported destroyed by Japanese bombers. However, in September it was rebuilt and resumed operation, now with 10 kw.

Starting in March, the anti–British clandestine, **Voice of Free India**, also known as **Free India Radio** and **Azad Hind Radio**, was heard at 1000–1200 on 9395 and 11470 kc., and at 2130–2330 on 9395. English news was at 1110 and 2300, and the station also used 15220 kc., which was believed to be the Huizen transmitter. Over its lifetime the station appears to have broadcast from several Axis locations, including Germany, occupied Holland, Podebrady, Tokyo, Saigon, Singapore,[103] and perhaps Shanghai. The 9395 kc. channel soon switched to 9590, where two other Indian clandestines, **Azad Moslem Radio (Free Moslem Radio)** and **National Congress Radio**, broadcast at 0930–0945 and 1215–1255 respectively. All three stations were nominally part of the Büro Concordia, but they functioned autonomously under the guidance of Indian nationalist Subhas Chandra Bose, who had escaped confinement in Calcutta and who, on a visit to Berlin, found his goals of an independent India in at least temporary alignment with the Axis strategy of destabilizing and sowing discontent in the subcontinent. (In 1943, Axis stations were broadcasting over 15 hours daily in Indian languages.)

The facilities of **All India Radio** were put to use to support Allied troop morale. On Tuesdays and Wednesdays, a special forces program was broadcast from Delhi at 1215 EWT over **VUD2**, 3495 kc., and **VUD4**, 9590, with programs such as "Your Broadway and Mine," "Downbeat," and "Yank Swing Session." Similar programming was broadcast on Mondays at 0330–0400 EWT using the Calcutta transmitter, **VUC2**, 7210 kc., and every third week the program was designed especially for the Americans. Signing on with the "Stars and Stripes Forever," the announcement was, *"This is the Voice of the United States broadcasting to the east from Delhi."* And **All India Radio** was now testing from **Dacca**, East Bengal, on 6072 kc. The call letters were **VUY**.

XGOX and **XGOY**, the **Voice of China**, was still on the air, 11 hours a day, 0600–1200 and 1500–2000 EWT, in 11 languages, plus a special program for Allied forces on Sundays at 1200–1230 EWT on 6135 kc. The station's criticism of the Japanese was surprisingly subtle and dispassionate. Its chief engineer had been trained in Schenectady by General Electric, and many of the station's personnel were students returned from abroad.[104]

In order to facilitate detailed news reporting about China in the U.S., Ventura, California dentist and ham operator Charles E. Stuart, **W6GRL**, was commissioned by the Chinese News Service of New York to record and transcribe all the English-language broadcasts of

XGOY and XGOX, which the agency then supplied to other news outlets. Many were published in *China At War,* a monthly English-language magazine which it printed and distributed on behalf of the China Information Committee in Chungking (and which carried XGOY schedules). At the end of 1941 a direct point-to-point circuit had been established between Chungking and the RCA and Mackay stations in San Francisco, and much material came via that route. (Numerous *China At War* articles were marked, "By shortwave radio from Chungking.")[105]

In December 1941 the Japanese occupied the International Settlement in Shanghai, taking over all American and British radio transmitters and shutting down various foreign magazines. Included in the transfer were **XMHA** and **XCDN**. In March 1942, XMHA was heard on 11860 kc. with greetings home from Australian POWs. (Japan urged Australia to allow families to broadcast messages to Australian POWs in the Dutch East Indies, which it promised to deliver.) And new from China was Tokyo-run **XGAP**, the **Peiping Central Broadcasting Station**, on 6100 kc. at 0500–1150 EWT, with an English hour featuring news and American dance music at 0900. The power was 10 kw., and sometimes the station relayed **Radio Tokyo**. **MTCY**, the **Hsinking Central Broadcasting Station**, Manchukuo, was still on the air. Its North American program was broadcast at 0130–0300 on 10065 and 11775 kc. (sometimes 11790). In June, at the end of each of the five daily English-language news broadcasts, MTCY started carrying personal messages and greetings from westerners interned in Manchukuo.

Closer to home, the modest pace of shortwave startups in the Caribbean and Latin America continued. The stations of this region still offered some of the most interesting DX possibilities for those willing to work at it.

There were numerous shortwave stations operating in Mexico, about which little more was known than call letters, frequencies, and (sometimes) locations. These included **XEJG**, Guadalajara, on 4820 kc. (relaying XEJB); 50-watt **XECC**, Puebla, 6190; **XETT**, Mexico City, 9555; and **XERQ, Radio Continental**, Mexico City, on 9615.

New on 7050 kc. (soon moved to 7205) in Cuba was **CMZ1, La Voz de la Democracia**, located at Havana's Presidential Palace. The 1 kw. station relayed mediumwave CMZ. Another new one, **COBQ, Radiodifusora de Publicidad**, Havana, was on 9220 kc., and relayed mediumwaver CMBQ.

From the British West Indies, **Radio Antigua**, operated by the government Publicity Office, could be heard daily in French at 1900–1915 on 7063 kc. and on Sundays with an English half hour at 1700–1745, followed by 15 minutes in French. **Radio CUROM** in Curacao, now identifying as **Radio Princesa Juliana**, had a new 3 kw. transmitter which it was testing in the evenings on 5936, 7230 and 9105 kc. Programs were in Dutch, French and English, and reports were requested.

A new Costa Rican station, **TIJMP, Sistema Nacional de Radioemisoras**, San Jose, was heard on 11900 kc. It identified as **Radio Tribuna**, and took relays from two Costa Rican mediumwave stations, Radio America Latina and Radio Libertad.

A new Venezuelan was **YV4RK, Radio Maracay**, on 3390 kc. During the year many Venezuelan stations made frequency changes, usually from 60 meter channels to frequencies in the 49 meter band. And Colombia had two new shortwave outlets: **HJCA, Radio Cristal**, Bogota, on 4855 kc., 1 kw. (with English lessons at 2245–2300), and **HJEX, Radio Pacifico**, Cali, on 4865.

Radio Nacional del Peru carried an English program, "Peru Calls You," on Mondays at 2330–2350 EWT over **OAX4Z**, 6082 kc. New from Quito was **HC1BF, Radio Commercial**, 7266 kc., relaying mediumwaver HC1BD. And **HCJB** obtained a new 1 kw. transmitter which it used on a new frequency of 9960 kc. The 1 kw. 4107 kc. channel continued in use, but the

10 kw., 12455 kc. frequency was still the main one for foreign listeners. The schedule was 0745–0945, 1330–1530 and 1800–2245 (0745–2245 continuously on Sundays). The station began a four-day-a-week transmission for Europe at 1830 EWT using a different language each day: Swedish on Tuesday, French on Wednesday, Czech on Thursday, Russian on Saturday. In addition to religious fare, HCJB carried a program called "Service Stripes" for Allied servicemen. The station also announced that it was seeking one person from each U.S. state to serve as a volunteer HCJB monitor (a communications receiver was a requirement).

AVROS in Dutch Guiana (Surinam) was now using 5946 kc. (PZX1) and 9600 (PZX3), 100 and 450 watts respectively. The schedule was weekdays at 1740–1940, Sundays 0810–1040 (Saturdays also at 1655–1724). The Sunday broadcast included a religious service by the chaplain of the U.S. forces that had been sent to the country to protect the bauxite mines (bauxite being the principal source of aluminum).

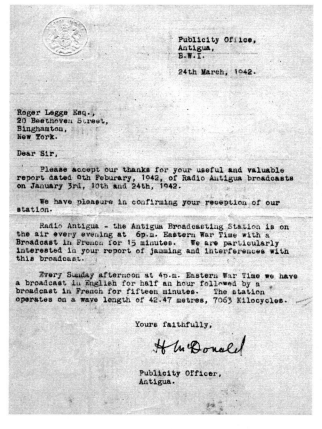

It was a small station, but for a time in the early 1940s Radio Antigua put the island on the shortwave map. Antigua would not return to shortwave until the BBC and Deutsche Welle jointly constructed a relay station there in 1976.

ZPA2, Radiodifusora de la Teleco Paraguaya, Asuncion, 11721 kc., was now carrying the programs of mediumwaver ZP10, Radio Guarani. The power of ZPA2 was 5 kw. And a new station, ZPA6, Radio Panamerica, Encarnación, was widely heard during evening tests on 15165 kc. and also on several 31 meter channels, including 9800 and 9930 kc.

"Australia Calling" was now sending to North America as follows: to the west coast at 0055–0140 EWT on 11710 kc. (VLG3) and 11870 (VLQ2), and 1025–1110 on 9580 (VLQ6); and to the east coast at 0725–0810 on 9540 (VLG2) and 7250 (VLQ9). However, times and frequencies changed often. Australia's "Americans Calling Home" program included messages from the American soldiers who started arriving in large numbers in March. The messages were grouped according to the soldiers' home town. They were monitored by NBC, which transcribed them and sent them to the appropriate regional broadcast band stations and also made individual recordings for the soldier's family.

It was not a good year for the growth of organized shortwave listening. Most men were in the service, and everyone else was working overtime in the war effort. Paper was in short supply, and receivers were very hard to find (Hallicrafters went over entirely to the manufacture of war equipment). And there were many fewer special shortwave broadcasts.

In the slimmer-than-usual January issue of *International Short Wave Radio*, ISWC editor Arthur J. Green noted the obstacles facing the club. "Just what effect [the] war will have on a publication of the character of this one is something only time can tell. At one time this organization had as many members living overseas as we had in the U.S.A. Today those memberships are gone. Today America calls for the conservation of materials that go into making radio receivers and transmitters, these to be used in making war materials. Today America asks us to conserve paper. The whole thing adds up to the fact that we must move carefully for the time being. Later on the magazine may be increased in size."[106] But that was not to be. Contributions from overseas reporters had dwindled, and receiver manufacturers, swamped with defense work, were unwilling to advertise receivers they could not deliver. The May bulletin was the club's last, at least in its American incarnation. The ISWC would be reinvented in 1946 by long-time member Arthur E. Bear of the U.K., where the club would be headquartered until its closedown 33 years later.

Other DX publications would suffer similar fates. *RADEX* looked good right up to the end, but disappeared after the February issue (which promised many interesting features in future issues). And there was no NNRC summer picnic-convention in 1942. The picnics would not return until 1947.

Although funds were a continuing problem, and the breaking news "Stop Press Sheet" bulletin supplement was discontinued in August, the International DXers Alliance appeared still to be functioning well in 1942. Local chapters were active, DX information was flowing, and bulletin content seemed at an all time high. Several times in 1941, club president Charles A. Morrison had advised members that he had been to New York and Washington, and hinted at some contacts with government officials as to how the club might help as the international conflict deepened. After Pearl Harbor he put the club on a war footing, urging members to eschew casual listening, organize their time at the dials, and submit the kind of shortwave information that would be valuable to defense agencies, e.g. new stations, changes in time and frequency, times of newscasts, etc. To this end, in February 1942 the IDA established a system of regional monitor-members who could commit to bandscanning several hours a day.

Morrison offered to compile all of the available information and send it on to unnamed government agencies. This he apparently did. For several years starting in late 1941, Morrison was under a confidential contract with the Foreign Broadcast Monitoring Service to provide them weekly reports, for which he received $25 a day (up to $100 per month). Several other hobbyists had similar arrangements, and a few, such as Roger Legge, became full-time employees. Legge was described as "living, breathing, and eating shortwave every day,"[107] a description with which those in the shortwave community who knew him would agree. From 1943 to 1946, one of Legge's duties was the production of a bi-weekly DX news bulletin, "Short Wave Schedule and Reception Notes," for a small number of experienced DXers who submitted monitoring reports to FBIS.

The agency was highly complimentary of shortwave hobbyists. Said an historian who worked for the agency during the war: "These individuals, many of them teenaged youths with a goodly sprinkling of physically handicapped, were familiar with the vibrant activity of the air waves. Next to the FCC engineers, they probably knew more about what was being broadcast for American ears than did any other group in the United States."[108]

1943

In February, on Europe's Eastern Front, the surrender of the Germans at the Battle of Stalingrad — a bloody clash that had lasted over five months — was a defeat from which German forces would never fully recover. Russian advances west gained pace. In North Africa, the Americans took Tripoli in January and reached Tunis by May, accepting the surrender of German troops there. On July 10, the Allies landed in Sicily and a month later the battle for the island was over. Italy surrendered on September 3, but German troops quickly moved in and continued to fight the advancing Allied armies.

In the Solomon Islands, fighting on Guadalcanal ended in February with the Americans victorious. The Japanese had been cleared from Papua New Guinea in January. The U.S. occupied areas around Morobe, and Sixth Army headquarters was set up at Milne Bay. There were heavy Allied attacks against Japanese forces at Wewak, farther north, and at Rabaul, on nearby New Britain island, and Australian troops moved against Japanese forces at Lae, taking the town on September 16. Fighting began on Bougainville after U.S. troops landed there on November 1, and continued for most of the war but with the Americans gaining the upper hand early in 1944. After a costly battle, Tarawa was taken on November 23.

The war caught up with the ten year-old International DXers Alliance. Before the war the club had members in over 60 countries, and as late as January 1941 membership stood at 1,960. Now foreign memberships were few, and many U.S. members were in the service. To save money the club went to bi-monthly publication, but the July-August issue of *The Globe Circler* was the last. The IDA's fate was emblematic of the state of shortwave listening in 1943. Notwithstanding the shortwave radio war and its unparalleled opportunities for dramatic listening, shortwave clubs were very hard to maintain. The war's demands were near total.

As the year began, there were 13 American shortwave transmitters in operation (see table below). It had been projected that this number would be enlarged by 22 additional transmitters and related antennas and equipment upgrades.[109] Four new units were delivered in 1943; **KWID** in San Francisco and Crosley in Mason, Ohio, each received one (**KWIX** and **WLWK** respectively), and **WRUL** received two (**WRUA** and **WRUS**). These were all 50 kw., the standard power of most U.S. shortwave transmitters at the time. (Transmitters were sometimes used in tandem to produce more powerful signals.) The new transmitters were constructed and operated under the supervision of the usual corporate licensees, who had the option to buy them after the war.

A new utility transmitter brought into broadcast service on the west coast by **Press Wireless** was **KROJ**. It would be joined in mid–1945 by a sister station, **KROU**, and both are believed to have been off the air by the end of 1945. These were either 15 or 50 kw. units. While the evidence on their location — Los Angeles, or the **Mackay Radio & Telegraph Company** facility in Palo Alto, near San Francisco — is conflicting, it appears that Los Angeles is more likely correct.

KGEI was the recipient of one of the first Alfred I. DuPont awards "for its outstanding and meritorious public service in encouraging, fostering, promoting and developing American ideals of freedom, and for loyal and devoted service to the nation and to the community it serves."[110] In October, the station broadcast the world series live to the troops.

As America stepped up its shortwave broadcasting effort, people began wondering who exactly was listening. France was said to rank high in listenership of U.S. shortwave, which provided much of the material for underground newspapers. Listeners were fewer in Spain, and it was difficult to gauge listenership in Germany and Italy, as well as places like Sweden, where propagation was difficult, and Eastern Europe, where information could not be readily obtained. Swiss newspapers, which entered Axis-controlled countries, carried the schedules of the U.S. stations.

Program content to Latin America was said to have improved, although that view was

Engineer and innovator Jack Poppele, who was in radio before KDKA and would be widely known and admired in the industry for over half a century, was also an early and active member of the Newark News Radio Club. He served as director of the Voice of America from 1953 to 1956.

not unanimous. In 1944, a CIAA advisor from Brazil characterized American shortwave programming as still being addressed to "12-year-old morons." Others disagreed.[111] On July 1, 1943, transmissions to Latin America were reorganized, with CBS and NBC alternating responsibility for programming on an hour-by-hour basis. CIAA also paired the CBS and NBC transmitters so that the same programming would often be broadcast simultaneously over the transmitters of both networks. There was great demand for OWI programming from many quarters.

After considerable negotiation with OWI and CIAA, effective September 1 the **Armed Forces Radio Service** was for the first time able to schedule regular air time over the now government-leased shortwave transmitters. This led to a more regularized on-air presence and much improved frequency management. It also facilitated relay of AFRS shortwave programs by the **BBC** on two 50 kw. shortwave channels which were received and rebroadcast further by AFRS mediumwave stations in the China-Burma-India theater. AFRS also became the sole agency responsible for military-related government program production and for relations with private program producers. AFRS news would now be supplied by the Army News Service, and military newspapers and magazines regularly carried AFRS program schedules.

Later AFRS would carry slow-speed news broadcasts so that personnel at distant AFRS stations could copy down the text for re-reading over the local station and for inclusion in local military news publications.

A military broadcasting event in 1943 Europe that is worth noting is the establishment of the **American Forces Network**. AFN was designed to provide news and entertainment to the American soldiers then arriving in droves in England. It was a large system of mostly low-powered transmitters and wired systems, originally established in England with the sometimes-hesitant cooperation of the BBC and other British agencies, and expanding to France, Germany, Austria and other parts of the continent as they were liberated. The first AFN broadcast from England was on Sunday, July 4, 1943.

The AFN transmitters, under supervision of OWI engineers, were almost entirely broadcast band, with some 70 operating in Britain by the war's end. AFN continental stations were often more powerful, and some (Munich, Frankfurt, Stuttgart) became major operations, a few even adding shortwave. AFN was part of the AFRS system and received much of its programming from AFRS, but it operated autonomously and produced a good deal of its own content. It was popular with the local people.

Coincidentally, July 4 was also the start of the BBC's "English by Radio" program. Offered at first for Europe in two daily five-minute broadcasts presented twice a day at early hours, the programs were hugely popular. By 1945, "English by Radio" had grown to four new 15-minute segments a week, presented for two hours daily and at peak listening times.

In a temporary status since the 1940 fire, **WWV** resumed permanent operations in September. Still in Beltsville, Maryland, the upgraded 10 kw. round-the-clock service operated on 5, 10 and 15 mc., offering time markers every second and standard radio and audio frequencies. Call letters were given in Morse every five minutes, and a voice announcement was heard on the hour and half hour.[112] "Many a veteran navigator of an airplane or ocean vessel nostalgically recalls the welcome sound of the monotonous format of WWV broadcasts which helped him guide his vessel through the trackless and hostile foreign territories."[113] Time announcements in code would be added in 1945.

In domestic broadcasting, antitrust concerns led to the breakup of the RCA-owned NBC radio networks by the FCC. In October the Blue Network was sold, and eventually became the American Broadcasting Company (ABC). The Red Network retained the NBC name and was called the NBC Radio Network. In other FCC action, November saw the old letter-number combinations in use by American FM stations replaced by permanent four-letter calls.

In Canada, on October 1, the call letters of the 2 kw. stations in Winnipeg, **CJRO** and **CJRX**, operating on 6150 and 11720 kc. respectively, were changed to **CKRO** and **CKRX**.

On June 13, the **BBC** made major changes in the organization of its shortwave broadcasts. The notion of two major components of Britain's foreign broadcasting effort would be preserved: the European Service and the Overseas Services. The European broadcasts were directed to three target areas: central and western Europe (network designation blue), southern Europe (yellow), and northern Europe and Spain and Portugal (grey). Within the Overseas Services, the Empire Service was retired as such, although its component parts were retained and expanded (below). Most importantly, in January 1943 the Service for British Forces Overseas, founded in 1942, became the "Overseas Forces Programme," and, in June, the General Overseas Service (GOS, color designation green). Between June and November, the General Overseas Service, a worldwide, all-English service, expanded from 13 to 21 hours a day. Although the military was still an important part of the target audience, the GOS was now the BBC's new anchor service for English-language external broadcasting.

**American Shortwave Broadcast Transmitters in Operation on December 31, 1942, and
Transmitters Added in 1943, 1944 and 1945**

	Transmitters Operating on December 31, 1942	*Added in 1943*	*Added in 1944*	*Added in 1945*
Associated	*San Francisco, California* KWID (100 kw.)	*San Francisco* KWIX (50 kw.)		
CBS	*Brentwood (LI), New York* WCBX (50 kw.) WCRC (50 kw.) WCDA (10 kw.)*		*Brentwood* WCBN (50 kw.) *Wayne, New Jersey* WOOC (50 kw.) WOOW (50 kw.) *Delano, California* KCBA (50 kw.) KCBF (50 kw.)	*Delano* KCBR (200 kw.)
Crosley	*Mason, Ohio* WLWO (75 kw.)	*Mason* WLWK (50 kw.)	*Bethany, Ohio* WLWL (200 kw.) WLWR (200 kw.) WLWS (200 kw.)	
General Electric	*Schenectady, New York* WGEO (100 kw.) WGEA (50 kw.) *Belmont, California* KGEI (50 kw.)		*Belmont* KGEX (100 kw.)	
NBC	*Bound Brook, New Jersey* WRCA (50 kw.) WNBI (50 kw.)		*Bound Brook* WNRA (50 kw.) WNRI (50 kw.) WNRX (50 kw.)	*Bound Brook* WNRE (50 kw.) *Dixon, California*** KNBA (50 kw.) KNBC (50 kw.) KNBI (50 kw.) KNBX (50 kw.)
Westinghouse	*Hull, Massachusetts* WBOS (50 kw.)			
World Wide	*Scituate, Massachusetts* WRUL (50 kw.) WRUW (20 kw.)	*Scituate* WRUA (50 kw.) WRUS (50 kw.)		

*Replaced by WCBN on May 1, 1944, and later used for Morse code communication. Cincinnati, Schenectady and Scituate were also equipped with Morse code transmitters.
**Commenced limited operation at the end of 1944.

The balance of the Overseas Services were the Pacific, African and North American services, which were carried over from the old Empire Service; the Eastern Service, also an Empire Service holdover (main target India); and the remaining two parts of the old overseas services, the Near Eastern Service, and the Latin American Service, which was now divided into separate transmissions in Portuguese and Spanish. These services carried programs in both English and relevant foreign languages. Within the Eastern Service, programming to China doubled, and in July broadcasts to Japan commenced (even though the Japanese public, and listeners throughout Japanese-occupied Asia, had long been prohibited from owning short-wave receivers).

This reorganization coincided with the opening of two new BBC transmitter plants. The first was on a 750-acre site in **Skelton**, in the north of England. Comprising twelve 100 kw. senders and 51 aerials (actually two stations on one site), it was said to be the largest short-wave broadcasting facility in the world. Its transmitters began testing in March and were in full operation by the end of April. Skelton was used for nearly all BBC broadcasting to Europe, and also for transmissions to the Americas, the Middle East and the Pacific.[114]

Skelton was followed by a 180-acre installation in the west at **Woofferton**. The six 50 kw. transmitters and 26 aerials went into service in October and November and were soon operating 24 hours a day.[115]

Germany also enlarged its shortwave facilities, installing two 50 kw. units at **Elmshorn**.

At the start of the year the North American broadcasts from **EIAR**, Rome, were as follows: to eastern North America at 1945–2400 EWT on 9630 kc. (**2RO3**), 11810 (**2RO4**), and 11950 (**2RO22**); and to western North America at 0030–0130 on 9630, 11810 and 15300 kc. (**2RO6**). Rome's English news broadcasts were offered many times throughout the day. Italy's radio belligerence declined following Mussolini's resignation on July 25, and the **Prato Smeraldo** shortwave transmitters went silent on September 9. Some of the equipment was spirited out, and soon limited shortwave broadcasting was resumed on 8560 kc. from a facility of a "new EIAR" located at **Busto Arsizio** in the northern "Italian Social Republic," a German puppet state set up nominally under Mussolini in an area not yet under Allied control. (Mussolini had been rescued from jail by the Germans after his arrest on orders of King Victor Emmanuel.) The republic, and the station, lasted about 19 months.[116]

The Lahti station of the **Finnish Broadcasting Corporation** now transmitted to Europe at 0615–0645 and 1300–1400, and to North America at 0915–0950, 2025–2110 and 2305–2350. The frequencies, and the new call letters, were 9495 kc. (**OIX2**), 11785 (**OIX3**), and 15190 (**OIX4**). TFJ, Iceland no longer carried broadcast programming. However, it could be heard on 12235 kc. transmitting correspondents' reports to the NBC network every other Tuesday at 1645–1700 EWT and Tuesdays or Thursdays at 1900–1930. And **Emissora Nacional** in Portugal now broadcast its home service program all day on 5735 kc. Broadcasts ended at 2000 EWT with 12 clock strikes and the playing of "A Portuguesa," the Portuguese national anthem which, in later years, would become well known to American east coast DXers on late afternoon searches for stations in Portugal's African colonies.

Radio Éireann in Athlone, Ireland was still on the air. Broadcasts were at 0830–0930 and 1330–1415 on 17840 kc., 1430–1700 on 15129, and 1710–1800 on 9595. The 17840 kc. channel was the best, and power was still 1.5 kw. And several low-power stations in Spain could still be heard. These included **EAJ9, Radio Malaga**, on 7143 kc. (also on 14435); **FET22, Radio Falange**, Oviedo on 7135; **FET15, Radio Córdoba** on 7040; and **EAJ47, Radio Falange**, Valladolid on 7006. **EAJ3, Radio Mediterraneo**, Valencia, was still on 7037 kc. When conditions were good these stations could be heard on the east coast circa 1700–1900 EWT.

Gustav Siegfried Eins left the air in October. Earlier in the year, in February, another British clandestine, **Deutscher Kurzwellensender Atlantik**, also known as **Radio Atlantik**, took to the air on 6210, 9545 and 9760 kc., as well as other channels, via the same Potsgrove transmitter that had been used for GS1. Masquerading as a German forces station, its broadcasts were mainly news and music. The station had wide credibility within Germany, especially after it was placed on a 100 kw. transmitter, the signal from which could be heard in the U.S. nightly around 1800. Between Atlantiksender and its highly successful, 600 kw. Crowborough mediumwave twin, **Soldatensender Calais**, which came into operation in October (and was renamed **Soldatensender West** soon after Normandy),[117] the two stations would eventually be on the air 24 hours a day. They would continue to broadcast until April 30, 1945. Unlike all other British clandestines, Deutscher Kurzwellensender Atlantik and Soldatensender Calais broadcast, at least in part, live.

TPZ, the French PTT station in Algiers, continued to operate on its usual frequencies of 8960 and 12120 kc. In addition, the 10 kw. CBS shortwave transmitter, **WCBX**, was moved to Algiers. It had been in Wayne, New Jersey before the Wayne plant was moved to Brentwood, Long Island and the WCBX unit replaced by a new 10 kw. unit. It and the TPZ transmitters were upgraded to 50 kw., making Algiers, which also had a mediumwave capability, a powerful transmitting base that could provide both local and international service. Broadcast programming was heard on 12120 kc. at 0200–0400, 0700–0900, 1300–1730 and 1745–1815 EWT. Usually it was in French, identifying as **Radio France**. However, English programming was heard as well. The station identified in English as **Allied Force Headquarters** (AFHQ), "the radio service for American fighting men and their allies." The song "Over There" was often used as the tuning signal. The 8960 kc. channel, plus others (15980, 16035), were devoted to reports of news correspondents to their American networks, military press releases, voice contact with OWI, and other utility-style transmissions. Algiers was the first to broadcast General Eisenhower's proclamation of the armistice with Italy after the latter's surrender in September.

Two officials of **Radiodiffusion Nationale Belge**, the **Belgian National Broadcasting Service**, who had escaped to London when the Nazis took over, were given the task of setting up a radio station in the Belgian Congo to give the Belgian government in exile a powerful voice that would serve both home and international audiences and help the war effort. The result was **OTC**, the "International Goodwill Station," which went on the air early in the year from Leopoldville using an American-supplied 50 kw. RCA transmitter. The schedule of the new transmissions was 1515–1715 and 2345–0130 EWT on 11670 kc., and 0615–0800 and 1230–1515 on 17770, with a special broadcast to Allied forces in the Middle East at 0800–0830 EWT. During the war much of the program material for OTC was shortwaved to Leopoldville from the BBC, OWI and NBC. Programs in Dutch, French and English were followed by other languages. The Leopoldville utility transmitters, **OPL** and **OPM**, also sometimes carried OTC programming. Reports for the Leopoldville signals were requested to be sent to the BNBS office at 247 Park Avenue, New York. **Radio Congo Belge** carried on as a lower-powered (10 kw.) domestic service on 6280, 9380 and 11720 kc.

In May, **Radio Brazzaville** increased power to 50 kw. The new transmitter, also of RCA manufacture and supplied with the cooperation of the U.S. government, was formally inaugurated with a speech by General de Gaulle on June 18, the anniversary of his famous broadcast from London three years before. The station could be heard during much of the day, from 1300 to 2045 EWT, with broadcasts for North, Central and South America. The test transmissions from the new RCA transmitter requested that reception reports be sent to the "Fighting French Delegation," 626 Fifth Avenue. Observed one DXer, "They are received like a local station during the entire emission and verify 100 percent." OTC and Radio Brazzaville became two of the world's best-known and best-heard stations.

In other African activity, **ZOY**, Ghana, added a new channel, 7300 kc. In March it conducted tests on 15428 kc. which produced excellent reception in the U.S. **VQ7LO** in Kenya was also being heard on a new, high frequency, 10730 kc., which provided good reception toward the end of its 1330–1500 transmission. **Radio Cameroun** operated at 0645–0730 and 1445–1510 on 6926 and 8000 kc., and 1515–1545 on 8000 and 12704 kc., the latter channel being the best. The tuning signal sounded like a bugle call on a penny whistle. Programming was mainly news.

Radio Maroc, Rabat, was now operating at 0230–0250 on 9082 kc., 0700–0900 on 12830 or 13965, 1100–1130 on 11940, and 1400–1845 on 8035 or 9082. Now under the control of Allied forces, the station broadcast a program called "Radio America" on Saturday afternoon at 1600 EWT on 8035. For a time this program was also carried over **Radio Tehran** on 6155 kc., daily except Thursdays at 1245–1800 EWT. The program was prepared by the Persian Gulf Service Command, an American unit in Iran whose principle mission was to facilitate lend lease shipments to the Soviet Union.

Britain's **Forces Broadcasting Service** opened a mediumwave station in Cairo, JCPA, which also operated on 7190 kc. This was followed by a 7.5 kw. shortwave outlet in Palestine, JCKW, on 7220. ("*This is your Forces Broadcasting Service, Jerusalem.*") In the early life of FBS, the Jerusalem station was a major operation. JCKW would move to Malta in 1948 as part of Britain's withdrawal from the Middle East mainland.

The **Radio Tokyo** broadcasts to eastern North America were now at 0800–0915 EWT on 9535 kc. (JZI) and 15105 (JLG4), and 1900–2245 on 9535 and 11800 kc. (JZJ). The western North America beam was 0130–0400 on 9535 and 11800 kc., and 1230–1445 on 9505 (JLG2) and 9535. The 20-minute "Zero Hour" was introduced in March 1943. By November it had grown to 75 minutes, and it stayed on the air for the balance of the war. Opening with the Boston Pops playing "Strike Up the Band," it was a disc jockey-style program aimed at enemy troops in the Pacific, staffed in part by captured prisoners with radio experience who broadcast the Japanese line (just how voluntarily has long been a matter of debate). Soon the program introduced women announcers, who attempted to undermine enemy morale by wondering on air about the fidelity of wives and girlfriends back home. From the standpoint of music and humor, however, "Zero Hour" was the best English-language program that Radio Tokyo had. ("*This is the Zero Hour calling in the Pacific, and for the next 75 minutes we're going to take you through music as you like it, sweet and hot and otherwise, music from all over the world, and a thought for the day, sometimes even two thoughts for the day. First, let's have the fighting news for the fighting men.*")[118]

The program was the home of the on-air hostess whom American GIs called Tokyo Rose. Although the name Tokyo Rose was a generic one encompassing all the female announcers—it was never used on the air—eventually it attached to Iva Toguri, a Japanese American who, at the time of Pearl Harbor, was in Japan somewhat reluctantly, visiting a relative at the direction of her father, and in the process of trying to return home. Whatever may be the truth about the scope and volition of her announcing over Radio Tokyo, she had started there as a part-time typist. After the war she was convicted on one of eight treason charges, and spent more than eight years in jail. She was pardoned in 1977.

Tokyo Rose may have done the troops less harm than good. In a 1968 study of 94 servicemen who had listened to "Zero Hour" during the war, 89 percent recognized the program as propaganda, but even more felt that they were not demoralized by the program, and 50 percent did not even consider it insulting to the troops. Eighty-four percent listened because they thought "Zero Hour" was good entertainment.[119] Observed one GI, "Lots of us thought she was on our side all along."[120]

In Radio Tokyo's English section, wide use was made of POWs with broadcasting experience. Chief among them was Australian Major Charles Cousens, who, before the war, had been an announcer on Sydney's highly regarded 2GB. Over a two-year period starting in July 1942, he wrote hundreds of scripts, voiced many programs, and also handled POW broadcasts. He, along with "Voice of Freedom" veterans Capt. Wallace Ince, who was an American, and Filipino Lt. Norman Reyes (who in April 1942 had read the announcement of Bataan's fall over the "Voice of Freedom," see below, 1944), plus a POW radio "staff" that reached 27 in number, as well as numerous non-POW Radio Tokyo staff, did the day-to-day work of the "Zero Hour" broadcasts and other spinoff programs. Throughout, the Cousens group maintained high levels of broadcast professionalism, a circumstance that no doubt contributed to Cousens being charged with treason after the war. He claimed that he and his associates were acting entirely under compulsion and actually subverted the programs in various ways. Cousens lost his military commission, but the case was otherwise dropped. Neither Ince nor Reyes was ever charged.[121]

A new station was reported operating in the inner Mongolia area of north China. It was 10 kw. **XGCA**, the **Kalgan Central Broadcasting Station**, on 9625 kc. at 0700–0900 EWT. PMC, Batavia, Java, now under Japanese control, was on 18135 kc. It had English news at 0700, 0800, 0900, 1015, 1800, 2200 and 2300, and there was a special broadcast to North America at 0055–0200 EWT. This channel also carried the **Voice of Free India** program. And the **Colombo Broadcasting Service**, last heard on shortwave in 1938, was now transmitting a program for servicemen over **ZOH**, 4902 kc. *("This is Colombo calling.")*

The challenge in tuning Latin American stations was always the absence of English-language programming and DXers' relative unfamiliarity with Spanish. English programming picked up a bit during the war. **TGWB, Radiodifusora Nacional**, Guatemala City, now on 6520 kc., had English news Tuesdays through Fridays at 2130–2145, and **HC2ET, El Telégrafo**, Guayaquil, Ecuador, had the same at 2000 on 4600 kc. There were other English programs as well, e.g. "Your American Hour," week nights at 2100–2200 on **XERQ**, 9615, and OWI's "You Can't Do Business With Hitler," Sundays at 1300 over **HP5G, Emisora Ron Dalley**, Panama City, on 11780. HP5G had English news at 1245, 1330, 1415 and 2015. Other stations with English news included **HP5A, Radio-Teatro Estrella de Panama**, 11700 kc.; **HP5K, La Voz de la Victor**, Colón, Panama, at 2300 on 6005 kc.; and **COK**, Havana, at 1200, 1530, 1800 and 2100. COK also carried its own foreign service, "The Voice of Liberty," at 1900.

Starting in February, **Cable & Wireless (West Indies) Ltd.**, Bermuda, carried some broadcast programming on Thursdays at 2000–2045 over its station **ZFA2**, 6122 kc., 3 kw. This transmission was intended for local reception only.

Two new stations in the Dominican Republic were **HI1R**, San Cristóbal, 6425 kc., and **HI2T, La Voz del Yuna**, Ciudad Trujillo. The latter would go on to become one of the country's best known and most innovative stations under the new name that it would adopt in 1949, **La Voz Dominicana**. The 7.5 kw. **HI2T** operated on 7275 and 11900 kc., as well as on mediumwave. A new Cuban government station, **COX**, operated by the Ministry of Education, began transmitting on 9640 kc., relaying **CMZ1**. **COBF, Radio Universal**, Havana, 6040 kc., was also new (it relayed CMBF).

On January 1, 1943, a powerful new station went on the air in Brazil. It was **Radio Nacional**, Rio de Janeiro, on 11720 kc. (**PRL8**). Other frequencies used at times were 9520 kc. (**PRL7**) and 17850 (**PRL9**). The 50 kw. RCA transmitter was the most powerful shortwave broadcasting unit in South America. There were eight antennas in all, three non-directional plus two directional to the U.S., two to Europe and one to Asia. In addition to relays of its mediumwave outlet, PRE8, the station broadcast a foreign service at 1500–1600 to Portugal, 1600–1740 to Europe generally (with English to the U.K. at 1630–1740), 1740–2200 to Latin America, and 2200–2310 to North America (in English). The inaugural program was hosted by Walter Winchell, then in Brazil in his capacity as a lieutenant commander in the naval reserve.

In July, **AVROS** in Dutch Guiana moved **PZX3** to 11755 kc. and began identifying as

Above and facing: The source of these promotional advertisements placed in *Selecciones del Reader's Digest,* a Latin American version of the magazine, in 1943 and 1944, was the office of the Coordinator of Inter-American Affairs.

Free Netherlands Radio. Companhia Radio Internacional do Brazil (Radio Bras) often relayed CBS Portuguese-language programs over **PPQ**, 11670 kc. Chile was now using the prefix CE rather than CB in its shortwave call letters. And mediumwave station LR3, Radio Belgrano, in Buenos Aires, was relayed on shortwave from Argentina (**LRY, Radio El Mundo,** 9640 kc.), Paraguay (**ZPA5, Radio Encarnación,** 11950), and Uruguay (**Radio Real de San Carlos,** Colonia, 6053 kc., **CXA8,** and 11840, **CXA14**).

PARA LOS RADIOESCUCHAS DE

ONDA CORTA

"Las Emisoras de los Estados Unidos"

★   ★   ★

Las emisoras internacionales de onda corta de los EE. UU. se han unido por el término de la guerra para que cada programa pueda captarse en mayor número de frecuencias.

HORA DE GUERRA DE NUEVA YORK (NOCHE)

7:30 10:45	5:30 8:15	5:30 8:15	5:30 12:00	5:30 12:00	7:30 11:30	7:30 11:15	7:30 2:00	11:30 2:00	5:30 12:00	8:30 12:00	5:30 12:00	8:30 12:00	11:00 2:00	12:00 2:00
W	W	W	W	W	W	W	W	W	W	W	W	W	W	
R	N	L	B	L	C	R	R	R	C	N	G	L	R	C
U	B	W	O	W	D	U	U	U	R	B	E	W	U	D
W	I	O	S	K	A	L	S	L	C	I	O	O	W	A

| MGS: 17.75 | 17.78 | 17.8 | 15.21 | 15.25 | 15.27 | 15.35 | 11.145 | 11.73 | 11.83 | 11.87 | 9.53 | 9.59 | 9.7 | 9.75 |

Metros 16M: 19M: 25M: 31M:

DE LAS FRECUENCIAS ARRIBA ILUSTRADAS SELECCIONE LA QUE UD. OIGA CON MÁS CLARIDAD

Todas las emisoras transmitirán el mismo programa simultáneamente. Las grandes cadenas internacionales seguirán ofreciéndole sus programas sobresalientes.

Dirija sus comentarios a su emisora favorita de onda corta. *Sintonice esta noche—*

"LAS EMISORAS DE LOS ESTADOS UNIDOS"

New from the Andes were **OAX4H, Radio Mundial**, Lima, on 6370 kc.; powerful **Radio America**, Lima, on 5935 (OAX4V) and 9410 (OAX4W); and three Ecuadorean stations: **HC1BS, Radio Teatro Bolivar**, "Voz de la Victoria," Quito, on 9355; **HC2AX, Radiodifusora Municipal**, Vinces, on 7150; and **HC2AN, Radiodifusora Cenit**, Guayaquil, on 7350 kc.

But numerous stations were no longer heard. **FG8AH, Radio Guadeloupe**, 7445 kc., left the air, as did **Radio Martinique**, 9705 kc. Martinique, which had been under Vichy control and had carried Vichy news, closed its shortwave outlet at the end of 1942 at the request of the U.S. State Department. It continued on mediumwave. Other stations missing included Cuban **COCQ**; Dominican Republic stations **HI1L** and **HI6H**; **TIEP, TIJMP** and **TIPG** in Costa Rica; **YN1GG** in Nicaragua; **HJCA, HJDU** and **HJGB**, Colombia; and the usually well-heard **HC2JSB** in Guayaquil, Ecuador.

In the Pacific, **FO8AA**, Tahiti, was now on 6980 kc., and was still audible in the U.S. around midnight. And in Australia in February, the **VLQ** callsign was transferred from AWA in Pennant Hills to a new ABC 10 kw. shortwave transmitter in Brisbane, from which short-wave broadcasts under the callsigns VLQ and **VLM** would be heard by generations of short-wave listeners until the site closed in 1993.

Prisoner of war messages were now being transmitted on a regular basis. **Zeesen** broadcast them to North America at 2105, 2305, 0005 and 0105 EWT. A Saturday program, "Calling Back Home," featured letters from prisoners. Until Italy fell, the English news broadcasts from **EIAR** were generally followed by POW messages. Prisoner reports were also given in both the east coast and west coast beams of **Radio Tokyo**, and reports on American, British and Australian prisoners were heard during the broadcasts of **PMC** in Batavia, Java.

More people were listening for POW messages and reporting them by letter and post-card to prisoners' families. An organization, SWAM, the Short-Wave Amateur Monitors Club, was formed to support these efforts, notwithstanding government discouragement of such message handling as support of Axis propaganda efforts. There were reports of some listeners charging for this service. The extent of such abuse, if any, is unknown but does not appear to have been significant.[122] The content of the messages was not always predictable. At least one American POW voicing a message urged his mother to buy a War Bond.[123]

The War Department adopted a rule prohibiting prisoners from giving such messages, but obviously this had little effect on those already interned.[124] The U.S. was not completely innocent on the matter of POW messages. The Special Warfare Branch of the Office of Naval Intelligence prepared a program called "Prisoner of War Mail" which contained news and messages from German and Italian POWs, and this program was carried over OWI transmitters.[125]

As the war progressed, some stations played the "Star-Spangled Banner" as part of their sign off sequence or during their programs. Among them were the North American broadcasts of **"Australia Calling"**; **CHNX**, Halifax, Nova Scotia; **ZQI**, Jamaica; **HH2S**, Haiti; **FK8AA**, New Caledonia; and **Radio Tananarive**, Madagascar.

1944

The Allies landed at Anzio on January 22. They reached Rome on June 5 and continued to advance. By October a foothold was established in Greece and the government in exile returned home. The following month, Allied troops reached Antwerp and the Albanian resistance occupied Tirana. On the Eastern Front, the Soviets retook extensive territory and many cities. They reached Rumania in August, and Hungary, Bulgaria and Yugoslavia soon after. However, fighting continued in many of these areas.

On April 30, the **American Broadcasting Station in Europe** (ABSIE), began operating. Its objectives were to facilitate the defeat of Germany and keep people in occupied areas informed. ABSIE was an OWI project, but relied on the BBC for most of its transmitters, both mediumwave and shortwave (some were supplied by the U.S.). It operated for eight hours a day, beaming to northern and western Europe — Germany, France, Holland, Belgium,

Denmark and Norway. It used many channels in the 25, 31, 41 and 49 meter bands. (*"This is the American Broadcasting Station in Europe. We Americans are here to join with the BBC in telling the truth of the war to our friends in Europe, and also to our enemies."*)

ABSIE's programs included some Voice of America and BBC material, together with straight news, military communiques (the "Voice of SHAEF"[126]), and special programs, such as multi-lingual coverage of the 1944 American presidential election. ABSIE's production capability was considerable, thanks in part to a 250-person staff, half of whom were Americans, half local. ABSIE also broadcast what is said to have been coded messages to the underground, and instructions to the peoples of the occupied countries, preparing them for the arrival of Allied forces. Music was also featured, one of its most listened-to programs for Germany being "Music for the Wehrmacht." Most of the programming was in languages other than English, but with English identification every 15 minutes. As Allied victory became inevitable, ABSIE became more strident, presenting testimony of Allied strength and casting doubt on Nazi propaganda. There were interviews with German prisoners and talks by well-known Germans living in Allied countries.[127]

On June 1, a coded message, part of a poem by French poet Paul Verlaine, "Chanson d'Automne" ("Autumn Song"), was sent to the French resistance in the French program of the BBC, which had been broadcasting such messages since 1940. The message meant that the invasion of the continent — Operation Overlord — would take place within two weeks. A second message, containing another passage from the same poem, was sent on June 5. It signified that hostilities would commence within 48 hours and that planned sabotage missions within France, particularly against railroads, should begin. Under torture, an underground leader had earlier revealed to the Germans that such messages would precede the invasion. Although their precise meaning was unclear, German intelligence alerted the military, but headquarters of the Normandy forces felt that the idea of an invasion alert sent by way of the BBC was preposterous and considered the messages disinformation. Thus the German troops at Normandy were not alerted, and the landings took place the next day, June 6, D-Day.[128] By month's end, Cherbourg, an important Allied objective, had been taken. Paris and the cities of southern France were liberated in August.

The OWI was ready for D-Day.

At 3:34 A.M., two minutes after the official Allied announcement of the invasion, the internal teletype system linking all radio and cable desks of the Overseas Branch in New York sent a bulletin reading: "First Allied landings in Western Europe have started." ¶At 3:37 A.M., five minutes after receipt of the news, the OWI shortwave transmitters in New York sent out the first flash — in French. At 3:42 A.M. the flash was cabled to Chungking, Algiers and Naples for rebroadcast and two minutes later the text of the first communique was sent to Bombay, Stockholm, Beirut, Istanbul, Moscow, Cairo and Naples. Five minutes later it was broadcast in Italian and one minute later direct contact was made with London.

* * *

OWI broadcasts operated on a 24-hour basis via 21 transmitters. At the invasion hour, Allied radio stations, including those in the United States, England, North Africa and Italy, were coordinated for a propaganda campaign directed at Germany and occupied countries.[129]

Not shortwave, but worth noting, was the **Allied Expeditionary Forces Programme**, which went on the air over a British mediumwave transmitter (1050 kc.) on June 7, the day after D-Day.[130] Within two weeks it was broadcasting 17 hours a day. General Eisenhower intended AEFP to be a common morale builder among British, Canadian and American troops, but it fell short of its goal, largely because of a clash of broadcasting styles — the high-energy informality of the Americans and the more measured approach of the British. All three countries contributed to the programming, but American soldiers did not warm to the British programs, and the insistence of the British to identify the program on air as the "Allied Expeditionary Forces Programme of the BBC" rankled American officialdom. All participants muddled through, however. AEFP programming was often rebroadcast over U.S. military field stations, and the station stayed on the air until July 28, 1945.

In the Pacific, the Americans landed on Kwajalein on January 31 and were soon in control. Successful attacks on Eniwetok and Truk followed. American attacks against Saipan, Tinian and Guam commenced in June, Palau in July. All were sites of fierce fighting. Tinian was taken in August, and the islands of Palau were effectively under American control by October.

There was fighting on Wake Island and Okinawa, and, in October, the first American landings at Leyte in the Philippines took place. Attacks against Luzon followed, and Formosa likewise came under Allied air attack. General MacArthur's famous "I have returned" speech to the Philippine people and the world took place at Leyte Gulf on October 20. It was intended to be carried over **WVLC**, the 10 kw. shortwave transmitter located aboard the USS *Apache*, a vessel of MacArthur's 600-ship invasion force which had been newly outfitted as a radio ship for the exclusive use of radio reporters traveling with MacArthur. A radio truck had been dispatched in advance to capture MacArthur's proclamation after he waded ashore, and send it to the *Apache* (whether direct or via an intermediate ship is unclear). However, the *Apache's* transmitter failed at the critical moment, and the historic message had to be read later in the day from the USS *Nashville*, MacArthur's headquarters ship, from whence it was picked up by the *Apache* and sent forth. The speech was rebroadcast around the world by numerous other stations.[131]

The next day, broadcasts from the *Apache* began identifying as the **Voice of Freedom**, the name of the station that had begun life with the U.S. military on Corregidor in January 1942, and had broadcast until early May when Corregidor fell. The original Voice of Freedom had been a shoe-string operation, constructed from **KZRH** equipment smuggled out of Manila just before it was occupied by the Japanese.[132] The first voice on the new Voice of Freedom was that of General Carlos P. Romulo, a well-known Manila journalist. (Romulo would serve in many important governmental positions, including foreign secretary, in the post-war Philippines.) Most often heard in the U.S. on 7795 kc. circa 0800–1000, WVLC also carried some VOA and AFRS programs. Other frequencies used included 7500, 9295, and 18600 kc. News was preceded by the playing of "Anchors Aweigh" and the "Marines' Hymn."[133]

Lorengau on the island of Manus, off New Guinea, was taken in March, followed by Hollandia, in Dutch New Guinea, in April, and Biak, also in Dutch New Guinea, in May. Although fighting would continue for months, New Guinea was now effectively under Allied control.

In the United States, expansion of America's shortwave broadcasting capabilities at government expense began in earnest. On the east coast, CBS brought its Wayne, New Jersey site, formerly home to **WCBX**, back into shortwave use with two new 50 kw. transmitters, **WOOC** and **WOOW**; and it installed another new 50 kw. unit, **WCBN**, at the Brentwood, Long Island facility. And on the air in the summer were three new 50 kw. senders at the NBC site at Bound Brook, New Jersey: **WNRA, WNRI** and **WNRX**.

Crosley opened a new transmitter plant in Bethany, Ohio, a mile west of the Mason site that housed **WLWO** and **WLWK**. Bethany was equipped with three new 200 kw. transmitters—**WLWL, WLWR** and **WLWS**— making them the most powerful in worldwide shortwave broadcasting at the time. The first low-power tests were heard on July 1, and by September 23 the station was in full operation with a powerful signal. The land and equipment were owned by the government but the station would be operated by Crosley until 1963 when it was turned over to the **VOA** (by then part of the United States Information Agency). Later, the Bethany plant would also be home to an OWI-supported school that ran two-week courses for OWI engineers who were subject to short-notice dispatch to transmitter sites worldwide when needed.

In the west, **KGEI** received a second transmitter, **KGEX**, a 100 kw. unit, twice the power of KGEI's then-50 kw. sender. In addition, a new CBS transmitter site was opened in Delano, California. It housed two 50 kw. RCA transmitters, **KCBA** and **KCBF**, which began testing in November, just six months after breaking ground, and went into full-time service on December 18.[134]

The **United Network**, the CIAA English-language service based in San Francisco, was still operating. It broadcast at 1100–1300 over **KWIX**, 15290 kc., 1300–2100 over **KWID**, same frequency, 1700–0045 on **KGEI**, 11790, and 2000–2400 on **KWIX**, 9570. Also active on the west coast was Press Wireless transmitter **KROJ**, which now carried AFRS programming on a scheduled basis to the Far East at 0000–0345 and 1200–1445 on 9897.5 kc., and 1700–2045 on 15190; and to Australia at 0400–0900 on 6100 kc., 1500–1645 on 9897.5, and 2100–2345 on 17760. KROJ stood somewhat apart from the other point-to-point broadcasters, having developed its own reputation for popular programming. In Australia, it was one of the best heard American stations.

UNITED STATES ARMY
GENERAL HEADQUARTERS SWPA
PUBLIC RELATIONS OFFICE
RADIO SECTION

January 29, 1945

Mr. Arthur T. Cushen
105 Princes Street
Invercargill, New Zealand
Dear Mr. Cushen:

Receipt is acknowledged of your report of reception of WVLC. Our transmission log verifies your report as in good order and correct on specified frequencies.

We are unable to forward a verification card at this time, due to lack of same.

We regret that we cannot give details regarding equipment used or specify operating schedules other than for the "Voice of Freedom" broadcast which takes place on 7.79mc with 5kw radiated power output. Other schedules transmitted are for restricted point to point use only and we can therefore furnish no information regarding transmission schedules or frequencies.

We wish to thank you for this valuable report of reception.

A. W. Borgia

1st Lt. Signal Corps
Transmission Engineer
WVLC

First Lt. Anthony W. Borgia, the signer of this QSL from WVLC to New Zealand DXer Arthur T. Cushen, served on the *Apache* during the time of its service at Leyte and beyond (courtesy Hocken Collections, Uare Taoka o Hakena, University of Otago, Dunedin, New Zealand).

Although other channels were assigned on a "non-interference basis," by FCC rule the frequencies that were being assigned to American shortwave broadcast stations on a non-exclusive basis were now as follows:[135]

49 m.	*31 m.*	*25 m.*	*19 m.*	*16 m.*	*13 m.*
6040	9530	11710	15130	17750	21460
6060	9550	11730	15150	17760	21500
6080	9570	11790	15210	17780	21520
6100	9590	11820	15250	17800	21540
6120	9650	11830	15270	17830	21570
6140	9670	11870	15330		21590

Date   October 1, 1945

Dear Listener:

Thank you for your reception report of our station. It has been checked and found to be correct.

We appreciate your interest and urge you to continue to listen and send us further reports, both on quality of reception and on the programs themselves.

Cordially yours,

KROJ

Please address all future messages to this station

c/o OFFICE OF WAR INFORMATION
111 Sutter Street
San Francisco, California

During the war the U.S. government pressed many point-to-point transmitters into shortwave broadcast service. One was west coast Press Wireless station KROJ. This was the standard QSL used by the Office of War Information.

49 m.	31 m.	25 m.	19 m.	16 m.	13 m.
6170		11890	15350		21610
6190					21630
					21650

While the emphasis was on English, French, German, Italian and Japanese, by mid–1944 the VOA was broadcasting 119 hours of programming daily in some 48 languages or dialects. The BBC broadcast 94 hours per day, Moscow about 65. The number of program hours continued to grow for all the broadcasters.

Quiet prognosticating about the post-war future of shortwave broadcasting was already underway. A variety of alternatives were proposed, among them a restriction on the number of stations in each country, with U.S. stations run by private operators who would lease or donate time to the government as necessary; an international agreement allocating each country a single frequency on which it could operate a powerful shortwave station; and use of American point-to-point stations to place programs on local standard broadcast stations in other countries. The government's Interdepartmental Radio Advisory Committee, which was making recommendations regarding post-war frequency utilization, favored the point-to-point plan, suggesting that direct shortwave broadcasting by U.S. stations be eliminated for reasons of spectrum economy. This was opposed by the broadcasters, OWI and the State Department. One thing on which there was widespread agreement was that, if shortwave broadcasting was to continue, the content of pre-war days had to be upgraded.

Also, better receivers and better shortwave signals would be necessary components of any effective shortwave strategy.[136] *Broadcasting* magazine editorialized in favor of a continuation of the leasing of private facilities, as opposed to government ownership, should government shortwave operations continue and be placed under the State Department, as was expected.[137]

While it would not formally go on the air until February 25, 1945, the new International Service of the **Canadian Broadcasting Corporation**, headquartered in Montreal and broadcasting over two 50 kw. RCA transmitters recently installed in Sackville, New Brunswick, began testing on December 16. On December 25, still operating in test mode, five hours of programming in English and French were beamed to Canadian troops in Europe. When regular programming commenced in February it was in English, French, German and Czech. Additional languages followed. By mid–July 1945 the CBC International Service would be operating 12 hours a day. The call letters and frequencies of the new Canadian shortwave transmitters were:

CKOB, 6090	CHAC, 6160
CKLO, 9630	CHLS, 9610
CKXA, 11705	CHMD, 9640
CKCX, 15190	CHOL, 11720
CKNC, 17820	CHTA, 15220
	CHLA, 21710

Also new from Canada was **VE9AI** in Edmonton, Alberta. Although nominally an experimental station, the 200-watter relayed its mediumwave parent, CJCA, just as did the other private Canadian shortwavers, all of which now sported regular four-letter "C" calls. VE9AI operated on 9540 kc. at 0530–2400 and on 6005 (the same channel as **CFCX**) at 0000–0200.

The General Overseas Service of the **BBC** was now on the air 22¼ hours a day. In February, nearly the entire GOS became available on mediumwave to U.K. home listeners as the "General Forces Programme" (replacing the former "Programme for the Forces"). And use of the shortwave transmitter at **Start Point** ended.

In August, the **Woofferton** transmitter site was closed down and its transmitters relocated in an ill-fated attempt to use them to jam German V-2 rockets. Although the transmitters were returned in 1945, they had not been well treated during the interim and the station never fully recovered from this episode.

After the invasion, Radio Oranje, still broadcasting over the BBC, warned the Dutch population against premature nationwide acts of resistance, and advised them to keep fishing vessels in port in order to maintain a clear field for invasion forces. The populace was also asked to familiarize itself with details of the local terrain in order to assist Allied forces. Overall, however, the BBC regained some of its pre-war footing as regards the special broadcasts of the London-based "free governments" of occupied Europe. Local broadcasting on the continent was reestablished as fighting permitted, and by year's end the BBC broadcasts to France, Belgium, and Greece returned to more traditional formats, as would other European services in 1945. As postal service with liberated areas resumed, letters from grateful wartime listeners poured in.[138]

After D-Day, the BBC's North American service was on the air around the clock save for the hours 0130–0500 EWT. The 2915 kc. channel had now been adjusted to 2880 (**GRC**) and was used all evening during the winter as a supplement to other channels. Thanks to the work of its new field War Reporting Unit, the BBC broadcast 15-minute "invasion broadcasts" — eyewitness or "actuality" reports from the front — six times a day.

Prisoner of war messages were still heard several times a night from **Zeesen**, including news of wounded American pilots "shot down over the Reich and occupied territories." Zeesen also broadcast the "Japanese Quarter Hour" at 2200, with news from Asia, including prisoner of war messages from Japan. Zeesen could be heard not only at night but during the day as well, especially in the African Service at 1115–1730, which was partly in English. This service, of six hours-plus, was transmitted over **DJL**, 15110 kc., and from around 1500 over **DJD**, 11770. The prisoner of war messages in the African Service shifted to prisoners from South Africa who were interned in Germany.

THANKS FOR THE PLUG, ROMMEL

...early in 1941 I was transferred to Tunis where I have remained until the present. During all these times your receiver gave me the best of service and enabled me to follow broadcasts from the United States as well as Europe.

Unfortunately, during the German occupation of Tunisia after our landing in North Africa, my house in Tunis was occupied by the German Commander-in-Chief who apparently found your receiver as much to his liking as I had. In any event, upon my return to Tunis after the recapture of that city, I found it missing together with the greater part of my furniture and household effects.

It would be appreciated if you would again provide me with the present equivalent of the set which I possessed.

(Excerpt from a letter we received from a member of the State Department)

NATIONAL COMPANY, INC.

MALDEN 〰️ MASS, U. S. A.

NATIONAL RECEIVERS ARE IN SERVICE THROUGHOUT THE WORLD

October, 1944   79

In 1944 it appeared that the Nazis and the U.S. State Department were in agreement as to the merits of National receivers (*Radio News*).

Germany made it a point to collect radio sets in the countries it invaded, but it was no easy matter and deadlines for turning in equipment were often extended multiple times. "The Nazis complain that in Rotterdam, the people use every conceivable hiding place for their radios, concealing them under hay and straw in barns, in rabbit hutches and attics, under floors and beds, in laundry baskets, upholstered furniture and stoves, in empty garden ponds, arbors and unused vehicles, under coal or potatoes in cellars, in chimneys, or behind partitions in built-in cupboards."[139]

Morris Pierce, in civilian life the engineering supervisor at WGAR in Cleveland and now OWI's top engineer in Europe, had been celebrated for having facilitated the surrender of the Italian fleet in 1943 through an improvised, crash modification of a key Algiers mediumwave transmitter to operate on the international distress frequency of 500 kc. This permitted the transmission of surrender terms to the Italian fleet just before Italy's capitulation and before the fleet could come under German control.

Now Pierce received a commendation for his initiative in safely bringing about the seizure and preservation of **Radio Luxembourg's** super-power longwave transmitter at Junglinster in September when the American army entered the country. The station, one of

RADIO-LUXEMBOURG
Les Studios

Although best known for its postwar role in bringing commercial broadcasting to Europe, Radio Luxembourg became a key Allied voice after its capture from the Germans in 1944.

the few in Europe that had operated commercially, had been in German hands for most of the previous five years, and its capture — a mix of luck and ingenuity — was no small feat since it was slated for destruction by German forces still in the area. After it was captured it was feared that the station would be lost in a December counteroffensive by the Germans, which was, however, ultimately unsuccessful.

The 7.5 kw. Luxembourg shortwave installation returned to the air in December on 15105 kc., later also 6020 and 7265. Luxembourg was also relayed on shortwave by other stations. However, it was Radio Luxembourg's longwave operation that was the most important prize for the Allies, for, located right on Germany's border, it could be heard far and wide in Germany. It carried the "Voice of SHAEF," and it broadcast numerous special instructions from SHAEF to both the civilian population and the German military, as well as to Allied forces. Very well informed on local events, it had a multi-lingual capability. It was one of the most authoritative sources of news in Europe, and also broadcast a wide variety of high-quality entertainment programs, both live and recorded, along with programs from the BBC, VOA and ABSIE. It also originated some programming for the Voice of America and the BBC.[140] And it was home to Operation Annie, the parent of **Radio 1212**, an American middle-of-the-night black clandestine that masqueraded as a pro-Nazi military station.[141] Although Sefton Delmer would call it second rate,[142] the station gained credibility with its target audience, the German military, through its accurate news reporting, but ultimately fooled them with false information on Allied troop movements that led to the ambush of German troops and Allied victory in the Rhineland.[143]

In February, **Radio Fighting France**, a pro-Nazi station, was heard on 7575 kc., signing on at 1715. It was believed to be via Rome, which was occupied by the Germans at the time, because it was also heard on two Rome mediumwave frequencies. Programs were mainly in French, German and Italian, but on Mondays, Wednesdays and Fridays the station had English "for the boys" at 1730. Another German-run station was **Jerry's Front Radio**, which broadcast in English at 1715–1800 on 9555 and 10615 kc., and on Rome mediumwave. The station was actually run by EIAR, former employer of Jerry's Front Radio's lead on-air personality, Rita Zucca (an Italian twin of sorts to Germany's Axis Sally). Jerry's Front Radio opened with "It's a Long Way to Tipperary," but the signal was poor in the U.S. Leaflets dropped on Allied soldiers invited them to tune in, and turn themselves in.[144]

Deutscher Kurzwellensender Atlantik was still heard, using three frequencies—7420, 9760 and 9930 kc.—until 1900, then 7420 until 2115. Observed one Ohio listener, "[i]t can be heard practically all afternoon and evening with pretty good signal strength on 9.76 mcs." Occasionally it also used a channel around 6220 kc. By November, the British-run station was reportedly featuring a tune called "When Jerry Comes Marching Home."

Sweden, now operating as **Sveriges Radiotjänst**, offered a variety of programs throughout the day—general programs, special programs for Swedes abroad, war news, etc. The frequencies heard best in the United States were SBU, 9535 kc., SBP, 11705, and SBT, 15155. By year's end, Switzerland was broadcasting nightly to North America at 2130–2300 on 7380 (HEK3), 9185 (HEF4), and 9540 kc. (HEI4). **Radio Andorra** had settled on 5985 kc., a channel that put in an excellent signal around 1800. TFJ, Iceland, on 12235 kc. could be heard with news and music at 2200–2230. Soon it was being heard regularly on Sundays at 1000–1030. And from farther afield, **Radio Komsomolsk** presented news in English at 1845 on 15110 and 15230 kc.

Africa was heard more often. **Allied Force Headquarters** in Algiers was testing on 11880 kc. at 1830, in parallel with the usual 8960, which was slightly better. Other channels included 6025, 6040, 9535, and 9610 kc. The station sometimes relayed the programming of **Allied Press Headquarters**, Rome, which also had its own transmitter. Another American station in Italy, **ICA**, was on 13250 kc. (later 10650), relaying the Allied Press Headquarters broadcasts to American networks. Algiers also carried BBC and American programming.

Radio Maroc, Rabat, was on 8085 kc. at 1530–1820, carrying programs from French stations in Algiers, Beirut, Dakar, etc., including every 15 minutes the identifications of the stations being relayed. It announced as Radio Maroc only after 1730. **Radio Douala**, Cameroun, was now on shortwave, 1415–1515 in French on 11535 kc.; and **Radio Dakar** had moved to 11415 and put in a good signal daily from around 1500 to 1700 close.

Radio Brazzaville had the best afternoon and evening signal of any African station. It was now heard on many channels besides 11970 kc., including 9440, 9550, 9705, 9780, 15560, and 17530 kc. In August the station's announcers promised listeners that before long they would be speaking from Paris (which was liberated that month). From the other side of the Congo River, at mid-year **OTC** in the Belgian Congo began relaying the North American service of the BBC at 2130–0045 on 9783 kc. The domestic Congo service, **Radio Congo Belge**, was heard after midnight on 9385 kc.

OTC carried a wide variety of programming. An interesting example was a series originating at WTAG, a local station in Worcester, Massachusetts. It was part of the city's "Worcester and the World" initiative in which, each week for six months starting on October 1, the information, entertainment and educational resources of the city were devoted to increasing understanding of one of the "United Nations," as the Allied countries were often referred to. The Office of War Information packaged the programs, and those for "Belgium Week" were broadcast over OTC. Other stations carried the programs featuring their countries. WTAG won a number of awards for the initiative.[145]

From other parts of Africa, **CR6RA, Radio Clube de Angola**, was still heard well on 9470 kc. until sign off at 1630. **Radio Clube de Mozambique** was audible in the afternoons over **CR7BE**, 9863 kc., where it opened at 1225. Programs were announced in both Portuguese and English until 1315, then Portuguese only until sign off at 1630. And **VQ7LO** in Kenya was still being heard on 10730 kc. until 1500 close. It was also operating on the new channel of 6114 kc.

In addition to Britain's **Forces Broadcasting Service** station in Jerusalem, JCKW, Palestine was represented on shortwave by **Sharq al Adna**, the **Near East Arab Broadcasting Station**. It operated on 3320 (ZJM3), 6135 (ZJM4), 6710 (ZJM5), 6790 (ZJM6), 9650 (ZJM8), and 11720 kc. (ZJM7). The power was 7.5 kw. With an office in Jerusalem and studios and transmitters in Jaffa and Beit Jala respectively (JCKW also transmitted from Beit Jala), the station's commercial appearance belied the fact that it had been run by Britain's wartime intelligence agency, the Special Operations Executive (SOE), since it first came on the air several years earlier. In 1943 it was placed under the jurisdiction of the Political Warfare Executive, an outgrowth of SOE. Sharq al Adna's Arabic-language programs were very popular; they had high production values, and they were much lighter fare than usually heard in the area. Sharq al Adna eventually moved to Cyprus and became the **BBC East Mediterranean Relay**.[146]

An offshoot of Sharq al Adna was the **British Mediterranean Station**. It too transmitted from Beit Jala, sharing some of the Sharq frequencies. It carried English and other non-Arabic programming, including special programs for soldiers from Africa, India and Ceylon, some British-produced clandestine programs intended for the Balkans, and, at 1315, "United Nations Radio," Allied-produced programs which were also heard from Cairo and Algiers. English, French, German, Dutch, Spanish and Hebrew news was heard starting at 0100.

ZNR, Aden, was still on the air, and with a much-improved signal. It was heard on 12115 kc., with American music at 1200–1215, followed by English identification and a multi-lingual program. Soon it would begin using a second channel in parallel, 6760 kc. And an **Allied Expeditionary Station** was operating in Tehran, Iran, and could be heard in America during the latter part of the afternoon on 9560 kc. It relayed BBC, NBC and OWI programming.

George Grim, Mutual Broadcasting System correspondent in Chungking, who broadcast over XGOY, characterized the Asian shortwave ether at mid-year as "the strangest radio lineup in the world."

> Every 15 minutes somewhere on the shortwave dial you hear a recorded trumpet fanfare followed by the words in English, or some other tongue, "This is the Broadcasting Corp. of Japan." I cannot report on what Tojo's broadcasters do in other languages but I have heard plenty of English, and such English. ¶Take the girl who calls herself Little Orphan Annie. Every afternoon at 4 she comes on the air with a program for Americans interned in Jap prison camps or for any American listening in the far east. Annie, who also calls herself "Your best enemy," has a brassy voice that talks about home sick sergeants, lovesick corporals. ¶Between semi-classical numbers she taunts the boys about what they're missing at home. Annie's program is interrupted once by a too-smooth English speaking announcer who gives what he calls "News from the American home front." It is a collection of strikes, floods, crimes and trouble.
>
> That blows over around 4:30 and is replaced by a loud Benny Goodman record of "I Know That You Know" which introduces the *Zero Hour*. The smooth-toned gentleman who m.c.'s the shows talks glibly about the records. He can talk quite intelligently about swing but all his records are pre–Pearl Harbor. Nonetheless, his *Zero Hour* does make pretty decent listening except when he interrupts it to bring you another dose of news from the American home front — the same bag of troubles you heard a half-hour earlier.
>
> * * *
>
> There is a German station in Shanghai [XGRS] which features Herbert Moi, an American-born

Chinese whose voice seems never to stop. Introduced by a typical brass band German fanfare, Moi has a delivery that features a steady sneer. His news sources seem to be the same as those of Radio Tokyo but this German station plays hours of classical music every afternoon.

Most annoying enemy radio broadcaster I ever heard is a Mrs. Henry Topping. She has a midwestern, motherly, folksy sort of voice. She talks on Radio Hsinking [MTCY] and tells of her visits to Americans in prison camps—how the Americans tell her there's no use fighting anybody so delightful as the Japanese. It's the most dangerous corn I've ever heard. But, perhaps, nobody takes Mrs. Topping seriously. She sounds more like somebody making fun of your mother and you resent it.

* * *

The recent landings in France have the French Radio Saigon buffaloed. They don't seem to know exactly which side of the fence they're on. Meantime, their news broadcasts sound like two different stations on the same wave.

* * *

Another enemy station that drops into my loudspeaker here in Chungking is a station that calls itself the Voice of Free India. When it speaks English I'm afraid that English sounds like Hindustani. It's only after listening very closely that you discover that the announcer thinks he is speaking English. I have yet to understand what he's driving at except that he doesn't like things the way they are in India. It's like Donald Duck with a Hindustani accent.[147]

THE BRITISH MEDITERRANEAN STATION

PALESTINE

13th December, 1944.

Paul Kary, Esq.,
153, Suppes Ave.,
Johnstown, Pa.,
U.S.A.

Dear Sir,

The transmissions mentioned in your letter of 10th October, 1944 were evidently from this station on 11720 kcs. and on 9665 kcs.

We are most grateful for your letter. Such reports help a lot when preparing new schedules.

Good listening,

(A.W. Dean)

Chief Engineer,
B.M.S.

AWD/rb

Sharq al Adna and the British Mediterranean Station were related. A. W. Dean was chief engineer for both.

By 1944, **Radio Tokyo** had 15 distinct transmissions to all parts of the world except Africa—24 languages and some 90½ transmitter hours a day. Tokyo changed frequencies often. Among those heard with strong signals in North America were 9535 kc. (JZI), 11725 (JVW3), 11800 (JZJ), 11897 (JVU3), 15160 (JZK), and 15325 (JLP2). The "Hinomaru Hour," a daily "Zero Hour"-like program intended for listeners on the American west coast, had begun in December 1943 and was now heard at 0000–0030 on 11897 (JVU3), 15160 (JZK), and 15225 kc. (JLT3). It soon expanded to include half-hour dramas. Its name was later "Americanized" to "Humanity Calls" (Hinomaru was a reference to the Japanese flag), and sometimes it included the voices of American prisoners.

Another program, "Postman Calls," which was devoted to reading POW letters, was begun in September.

JPHA, Hong Kong, was on 9470 kc., with English at 0700–0800, other languages after that. **Radio Shonan** in Singapore—upgraded to 50 kw. in December 1943—was well heard on 9548 kc., not quite so good on 11850, with news in English at 0600, followed by 10 minutes

RADIO TOKYO TRANSMISSION

BROADCAST SCHEDULE OF RADIO TOKYO BEAMED TO THIS HEMISPHERE. COMPILED THROUGH THE COURTESY OF D. BUCHAN OF THE BBC, NEW YORK OFFICE.

MEGACYCLES	CALL	TIME (EWT)	BEAMED TO:
9.535	JZI	9:00 a.m.—10:45 a.m.	E. North America and Brazil
		11:00 a.m.— 2:40 p.m.	W. North America
9.565	JRAK (Paulau)	7:00 p.m.— 8:00 p.m.	E. North America and Brazil
11.725	JVW3	7:15 a.m.— 8:15 a.m.	Latin America
		9:00 a.m.—10:45 a.m.	E. North America and Brazil
		11:00 a.m.— 2:40 p.m.	W. North America
11.80	JZJ	6:15 p.m.— 8:15 p.m.	E. North America and Brazil
		8:30 p.m.— 9:30 p.m.	Latin America
		11:00 p.m.— 4:00 a.m.	W. North America and Latin America
11.897	JVU3	6:15 p.m.— 8:15 p.m.	E. North America and Brazil
		11:00 p.m.— 4:00 a.m.	W. North America and Latin America
15.160	JZK	6:15 p.m.— 8:15 p.m.	E. North America
		11:00 p.m.— 4:00 a.m.	W. North America and Latin America
15.225	JLT3	7:15 a.m.— 8:15 a.m.	Latin America
		8:30 p.m.— 9:30 p.m.	Latin America
		11:00 p.m.— 4:00 a.m.	W. North America and Latin America
15.325	JLP2	8:30 p.m.— 9:30 p.m.	Latin America

Newscasts from Radio Tokyo are read on the hour, and are followed during all news-periods (mornings and evenings) by messages from American prisoners of war.

If you didn't see this schedule of Radio Tokyo in the July 1944 issue of *Radio News,* you could check *The New York Times,* which often printed the times and frequencies of wartime shortwave broadcasts "From Enemy Sources" (Berlin, Rome, Tokyo).

of messages from Australian prisoners of war at 0620, war commentary, and more prisoner messages at 0945–1000. **Radio Saigon** on 11780 kc. broadcast in English daily at 0715. The names of war prisoners were given at 0730.

From the Philippines, the former **KZRH, Voice of the Philippines,** had new call letters under the Japanese. From October 1943, it was— at least on mediumwave —PIAM, and it was heard in the morning hours on 6100 and 9640 kc. (It is unclear whether another set of call letters, **PIRN,** was assigned to KZRH when operating on shortwave, or to **KZRM,** which had also been operating on shortwave.) Most of the KZRH programming was in Tagalog, and many American recordings were played. News in English was at 0830.

From Japanese-controlled Batavia, Java, the station on 12270 kc., known as **JANX,** was heard at 0600–0900 during its broadcast to Australia. It was also transmitted on 18135 kc. News from Tokyo was broadcast at 0805. **Radio Makassar** was on 9952 kc. and broadcast chiefly in Dutch and Japanese until sign off at 0700.

In February, **All India Radio** began broadcasting a special program, the "All Forces Hour," to Allied troops in Assam and Burma. It was on the air daily at 0900–1000 EWT over **VUD3** in Delhi, 7290 kc., and featured programs for both British and American troops, including, especially for the latter, Jack Benny, Charlie McCarthy, Tommy Dorsey, Harry James and similar stars. Field units were requested to send reception reports to GHQ, New Delhi. It was in 1944 that AIR obtained its first 100 kw. transmitters. Of General Electric manufacture, they were installed at Kingsway in Delhi, together with two 7.5 kw. units. In eastern North America at 0800 EWT, Delhi on 6085 kc. was said to have the best signal on the 49 meter band.

In October, **Radio SEAC,** voice of the South East Asia Command, which was under British Lord Louis Mountbatten and headquartered in Kandy, Ceylon, began testing its own station from that country. *("Here is Kandy, Ceylon.")* The tests were on 11810 and 15275 kc. using a 7.5 kw. transmitter, call letters ZOJ, whose location is believed to have been the Welikada Wireless Station, east of Colombo, which was home to the Colombo Broadcasting Service. Soon Radio SEAC was on the air for four hours a day.[148] Some of the programming was announced as "United Nations Radio."

Broadcasts intended mainly for military personnel were listened to by many others, giving a much broader international audience its first taste of American culture and entertainment, and offering the potential for expanded opportunities for American commerce in the future. South Asia was an example. By 1945, both British and American programs were available to military personnel of those two countries serving in the area. A survey of the British forces indicated that nearly all who listened preferred the American programs. Many non-military personnel were listening as well, probably with similar preferences.[149]

From Chungking, China, Central Broadcasting Administration station **XGOY** was now transmitting as follows: on 11900 kc. to Allied Forces in the Far East at 2000–2100 EWT; to Asia, Australia and New Zealand at 0600–0630; to East Russia at 0630–0700; and to Japan at 0700–0730; and on 7171 and 9646 kc. to East Asia and the South Seas at 0735–0940; to North America at 0945–1140; to Europe at 1145–1230; and to East Asia and the South Seas at 1230–1345. XGOY also rebroadcast material originating with OWI. (In 1943, the State Department declined XGOY's request that **KWID** relay a planned XGOY South American service.)

XGOY was still operating from its rock-hewn caverns, where old equipment was kept operating long after its useful life thanks to the skill and imagination of the station's engineers. XGOY was one of the few sources of free news in China. The absence of reliable telephone lines led to the creation of the XGOY-run "Free China Network," an informal setup whereby a nearby station would pick up the XGOY signal off-air, amplify it, and pass it on to the next closest station, which would do the same. Since Pearl Harbor, the Saturday night "Mailbag Hour" had broadcast a multitude of 50-word messages from people in China to the outside world. They announced births, deaths, marriages, acknowledged receipt of letters, requested food and photographs, and transmitted all manner of personal communications (except requests for money). XGOY also carried much American-produced programming for U.S. troops in China.[150]

There was not much new shortwave broadcast activity in Latin America or the Caribbean. **Radio Martinique** returned to the air in January, still on 9705 kc. Administration of the island had been transferred to the Free French in July 1943 after a military coup. The station now identified as the "Voice of Fighting France in the West Indies," and had English on Tuesdays and Saturdays at 1915–1930. **HI8Z, Radio Santiago**, in the Dominican Republic, took to the air. Its frequency was 7225 kc. **HI3X**, earlier on 15260 kc., was now on 11805. New from Cuba was **COCL**, 7050 kc., heard all evening simulcasting CMCL and announcing in English as the "Voice of Democracy." Also heard was **COBL** Havana, formerly **COCM**, now called **Radio Cadena Suaritos** and operating on 9830 kc.

ZQI, Kingston, Jamaica, 4700 kc., was on the air at 1730–1930, mainly in English but with some programming for Chinese listeners as well. AFRS transcriptions were broadcast regularly. From the same island, **Cable & Wireless** was sending out some BBC and American broadcast programming in the afternoons over **VRR6**, Stony Hill, on 15620 kc. And the Cable & Wireless station in Bridgetown, Barbados could be heard occasionally with broadcast material over **VPO**, 11475 kc. The target area was the United Kingdom, but the station was heard in North America circa 1800 with an excellent signal.

In South America, **ZFY**, Georgetown, British Guiana, was on 6000 kc., and could be heard until 1945 sign off. The transmitter was capable of 1 kw., but the actual power used depended on the season. (*"This is ZFY, the Voice of Guiana in the 49 meter band."* When carrying OWI or AFRS programs, the announcement was, *"This is ZFY, the Voice of Guiana, a shortwave broadcasting station in the service of the United Nations."*) Preliminary plans for a BBC relay station in the country were scrapped due to cost. **AVROS** in Surinam was now on 15405 kc. (**PZX5**), well heard at 0800. Another channel, 5748 kc., was also in use. And religious broadcaster **HCJB** was relaying United Network programming from **KWID** at 1900 on 9958 and 12455 kc.

On May 1, the first transmitter began operating from the **Australian Broadcasting Commission's** newly-constructed, 600-acre high power shortwave base in **Shepparton**, said to have been conceived in part as a backup capability for the BBC's Empire service should wartime events have required it. (At least one writer suggests that a similar rationale was behind international shortwave broadcasting from Canada.[151]) This was a 50 kw. unit, **VLC**, obtained from the United States under Lend Lease. At first it carried not Australian material but American programming beamed to the Philippines. For about six months it identified as being from General MacArthur's headquarters in Australia, or as "the American Broadcasting Station in Australia." The Shepparton broadcasts to the Philippines—particularly the "Philippine Hour"—were very popular among Philippine listeners. They lasted until May 1945, by which time VLC had been supplanted by MacArthur's own station, the similarly-named **WVLC**, which continued broadcasting the "Philippine Hour."

In August, VLC also began transmitting "**Australia Calling**," and several months later the Pennant Hills transmissions of "Australia Calling" came to an end. Two 100 kw. senders, **VLA** and **VLB**, would come on air from Shepparton in August 1945.

As in Australia, amateurs had conducted some early shortwave broadcasting in New Zealand. By the mid twenties at least two stations, **2AZ** in Taihape and **3AU** in Rangiora, had operated in the area of 30–35 meters. In 1929, a new standard broadcast station in Christchurch, **3ZC**, was transmitting a separate shortwave program three days a week over 46.3 meters (circa 6480 kc.), and, for over a year starting in 1931, broadcaster **2ZW** in Wellington relayed its programs over its shortwave transmitter, **2ZX**. A bona fide shortwave broadcast service had long been planned, but for now country hunters had to settle for a bit of programming from the country's PTT station, **ZLT**, which was often heard on shortwave, 6715 kc., 5 kw., relaying news from **2YA** in Wellington at 0515–0545. (*"It is now 9:30 P.M. This is station 2YA of the New Zealand Broadcasting Service. We are now being joined by the Post & Telegraph Station ZLT7 for the Pacific news for our troops and other friends overseas."*)

FK8AA, Noumea, New Caledonia, was on 6135 kc. and could be heard around 0600 EWT. There was a relay of English news from **ZLT7** on Mondays. And **VPD2**, Suva, Fiji, was now testing on 6130 and 11880 kc. The mediumwave call letters, **ZJV**, were heard during the shortwave broadcasts, which for a time were confined to Sundays only at 0200–0430, but then made daily.

In 1935, towers had been erected at Lualualei, Oahu, a naval facility near Pearl Harbor, for naval communications throughout the eastern Pacific. On December 26, 1944, the towers went into service as part of the new 100 kw. VOA Hawaiian relay station, **KRHO**, which beamed west to Asia. Among the KRHO frequencies were 6110, 6120, and 17800 kc. Coincident with the opening of KRHO, a new 50 kw. mediumwave station, **KSAI**, was brought into use on Saipan, which the Americans had taken from Japan after a hard-fought battle in July. The purpose of KSAI was to reach Japan on the standard broadcast band. It got most of its content off the air from KRHO or from San Francisco. Both stations were jammed within a half-hour of sign on. KSAI provided a valuable homing signal for crippled B-29 bombers returning to base on Saipan, and sometimes operated 24 hours a day for that purpose.[152] The station closed down after the war. Today the KRHO site is used by the navy for VLF submarine communications.[153]

Several **AFRS American Expeditionary Stations** came on the air. The transmitters of the so-called **Mosquito Network** were in Noumea, New Caledonia (**WVUS**); Guadalcanal; Bougainville; Munda, New Georgia (Solomon Islands); Espiritu Santo (New Hebrides); Tutuila (Samoa); and Auckland, New Zealand. Noumea was the first on the air, starting informal transmissions under the auspices of the Red Cross in September 1943 and regular broadcasts as part of AFRS on February 1, 1944. Programming of these stations consisted mainly of transcriptions, supplemented by material received by shortwave from San Francisco, plus locally-produced material.[154] All operated on mediumwave (although at least one verification exists for reception of the Noumea station — nominal headquarters of the network — on 15460 kc.). Soon other Pacific islands boasted AFRS mediumwave stations, including the Gilbert Islands (Tarawa, Makin), the Marshalls (Kwajalein, Eniwetok), Okinawa. the Marianas (Saipan, Guam), and others. These stations comprised the **Pacific Ocean Network**. And New Guinea, part of the South West Pacific Area Command, was served by numerous AFRS mediumwavers known collectively as the **Jungle Network**. Although the stations obviously shared similar problems, they were not networks in the usual sense save for having common commands. Each station operated on its own.

New receivers were still virtually impossible to come by (the Allied Radio catalog went unpublished in 1944 and 1945). However, the DX news began flowing again, albeit slowly, thanks to a new column in *Radio News*. "International Short-Wave" first appeared in the June 1944 issue. The editor was Kenneth R. Boord of Morgantown, West Virginia, who would become one of the most prolific sources of shortwave news for almost two decades.

1945

By January 17, Russian forces had cleared Warsaw of all German resistance. The Russians reached Vienna in early April, the Allies Leipzig on April 19 and Nuremberg and Stuttgart the next day. At the end of the month, Russian forces entered Berlin. On April 28, as he attempted to escape to Switzerland, Mussolini was captured by partisans and shot. Two days later Hitler committed suicide, and on May 7 Germany surrendered unconditionally. May 8 was "V-E" (Victory in Europe) Day.[155]

The Charter of the United Nations was drafted at an international meeting in San Francisco between April and June. On June 26 it was signed by representatives of 50 countries.

Fighting in Asia continued. By January, the bombing of Japanese cities was well underway and was being continually stepped up. The Japanese naval base at Camranh Bay, as well as other targets in Indochina, were attacked by air. The Americans encountered no resistance to their landings on Iwo Jima on February 19, but fierce fighting erupted and it was over a month before the U.S. was victorious.

On March 3, the last Japanese resistance in Manila was overcome. American landings throughout the country followed, and fighting continued until the end of June. U.S. forces landed on Okinawa on April 1, and three months of bloody fighting followed before Japanese resistance was brought to an end. The Australians met little opposition when they landed in Borneo on May 1, but it took more than two months to bring the area under control. The Japanese had been in retreat in Burma for months, and gave no resistance to the British capture of Rangoon on May 3.

On August 9 the Soviets moved against Japan's Kwantung Army in Manchuria, overwhelming it. Truman had become President on April 12 after Roosevelt suffered a fatal cerebral hemorrhage. Truman's decision to drop the atomic bomb on Hiroshima and Nagasaki on August 6 and 9 respectively, together with the Soviet attacks in Manchuria, brought Japan's capitulation, which was announced on August 15. The surrender was finalized on September 2 — "V-J" Day in the United States — aboard the battleship *Missouri*.

Worth noting in connection with the end of the war were the **Voice of America** Japanese-language broadcasts by U.S. Navy Captain (later Admiral) Ellis M. Zacharias, who had studied Japan, knew the language, and had high-level contacts in the country, including many in the Japanese military. Zacharias was a cruiser and battleship commander in the Pacific. On his return to the U.S. he convinced OWI, the Secretary of the Navy and others that broadcasts directed to the Japanese leadership by an official U.S. spokesman who knew the Japanese and understood their culture might make the high command more receptive to cessation of hostilities and convince them that unconditional surrender would not include violent punishment of the Japanese people. His weekly broadcasts were transmitted over **KRHO** and **KSAI** from May 8 to August 5 — the day before Hiroshima — and actually led to a series of on-air replies by a Japanese spokesman. The Japanese monitoring agency transcribed and distributed these detailed exchanges to some 500 persons. It was a unique communications channel at a time when Japan knew that the war was lost. There was also extensive bombing of Japanese cities and a huge OWI leafleting campaign at the same time. What effect a continuation of the Zacharias broadcasts might have had if the atomic bomb had not been dropped cannot be known.[156]

The Voice of America domestic transmitter capacity continued to expand. Most of the action was on the west coast. At the end of 1944 and the beginning of 1945 a transmitter base was opened in Dixon, California, near Sacramento. It was operated by NBC and equipped with four 50 kw. RCA transmitters which operated under the call signs **KNBA, KNBC, KNBI** and **KNBX**. *("This is the United States of America, stations KNBA, 7.805, and KNBC, 9.70 mc.")* In addition, another 50 kw. transmitter, **WNRE**, was added to the NBC facility in Bound Brook, New Jersey; and a new 200 kw. unit, **KCBR**, began operation on June 15 from the CBS site in Delano, California. (The U.S. practice of assigning separate callsigns for each transmitter would end in 1951, when individual transmitters were designated by number, e.g. WLWO1, WLWO2, etc.)

At the start of the year, the VOA was transmitting 168 daily program hours, compared with 105 for the BBC, 80 for Germany, 73 for Moscow, 48 for Japan and 14 for France.[157] However, the VOA remained second to the BBC in overall listenership. OWI started including short German-language news broadcasts in transmissions of all languages in order to avoid heightened jamming of its regular German broadcasts. As more territory in Europe was liberated, VOA programming transitioned from mainly news to more music, entertainment and features, and it began tailoring its broadcasts more specifically to particular geographical areas. The VOA developed a rudimentary research capability, from which it learned that it was the English broadcasts that were most often listened to by direct shortwave, with other languages more often tuned through local mediumwave relays, no doubt in part because of the greater availability of mediumwave receivers.

As fighting in Europe came to an end and the result of the Pacific war became certain, the tableau of American shortwave broadcasting changed rapidly. Languages were dropped and personnel were cut, and while there was general agreement on the need to continue international broadcasting after the war, old issues on how it could best be delivered resurfaced. NBC urged a private but government-subsidized shortwave service; CBS wanted two parallel systems, one government, one private; and Crosley and the other shortwave broadcasters

MEET YOUR NEW NEIGHBOR...

Holland is a tiny nation, proud and independent. In time of peace, it was thought of as a land of dikes and windmills, of tulip beds and pleasant, industrious people.... But, there will be much to learn about Holland, its love for freedom and its implacable fight against tyranny and oppression ... There will be much to learn about every nation of our world, important things for understanding and tolerance that will mean a better peace.... One of the finest means of studying our World Neighbors is shortwave radio. With it, you can reach any nation almost instantaneously to know the history and politics of that nation even while they are happening.... Look to Hallicrafters, when Peace is won, for the world's best short wave receivers —the results of over fifty million dollars worth of war research and developments in Radio.

hallicrafters RADIO

HALLICRAFTERS RADIOS are the Radioman's Radio. Designed and built for experts, they are the world's finest shortwave receivers. Victorious Allied Armies all over the world will attest to their excellence. THE HALLICRAFTERS COMPANY, CHICAGO 16, U.S.A.

BUY A WAR BOND TODAY!

With the war's end in sight, Hallicrafters promoted the role of shortwave radio in expanding knowledge of other countries in a newly peaceful world. This advertisement is from the August 1944 issue of *Radio News*.

wanted things entirely private.[158] By now, however, the lesson of shortwave's limited economic potential had caused the broadcasters to lose much of their initial interest in the medium.

The U.S. began returning to a peacetime footing. OWI and CIAA closed down, and on August 31 their international broadcasting functions were transferred to a new State Department office, the Interim International Information Service, which was itself set to close on December 31, 1945. Although President Truman acknowledged the likely need for a continuing international information capability, and the State Department supported the continuation of VOA, it had little institutional experience with shortwave broadcasting. By the end of 1945, VOA was broadcasting in 18 languages—less than half the number used during the war—and little breaking news was broadcast. It was Assistant Secretary of State for Public Affairs William Benton who probably saved VOA from an early demise and gave it a new home—the International Broadcasting Division (IBD) of a new State Department office called the Office of International Information and Cultural Affairs (renamed the Office of International Information and Educational Exchange in 1947).

On July 4, its mission over, **ABSIE** ceased operation. Many **AFRS** programs ended as production personnel returned to civilian life. Some of the point-to-point transmitters that were used for broadcasting were kept on the air for hours at a time with non-stop music so as to be immediately available should war developments warrant it. Eventually, however, "point-to-point broadcasting" was cancelled.

On June 27, after much study, the FCC announced that FM would move to the 88–108 mc. range. On August 21, U.S. amateurs were allowed to return to the air on the 112–115.5 mc. VHF band. Other bands reopened later, and various changes were made in the frequencies allotted to the amateur service. In October, **WWV**, then operating on 2.5, 5, 10 and 15 mc., began giving time announcements in code every five minutes (voice announcements would be added in 1950).

In Europe, during the period leading up to V-E day, broadcasts from Germany became increasingly intermittent, finally ceasing altogether on April 24. Lord Haw-haw made his final broadcast. Also in April, British clandestines **Deutscher Kurzwellensender Atlantik** and **Soldatensender West** closed down. And in November, **Radio Luxembourg** was returned to its private owners. It would resume commercial operation in January 1946.

On May 1, in recognition of the progress of the fighting in the Far East, the **BBC** separated its Chinese, Japanese, Burmese, Siamese and Malay programs from the Eastern Service (whose main target had always been India anyway) and placed them in a new Far Eastern Service. English was specifically omitted for fear that listeners might be endangered if they were found to be listening to English broadcasts. In June, the 15 kw. BBC shortwave transmitter at **Clevedon** returned to mediumwave operation. In July, BBC mediumwave dropped the "General Forces Programme" (the General Overseas Service) from its home schedule. And the year saw the end of all broadcasts from London by the former exile governments of continental Europe.

Upon the liberation of the south of Holland in 1944, Hendrik van den Broek, head of Radio Oranje, had set up a station called **Herrijzend Nederland** at the Philips plant in Eindhoven. When the rest of the country was freed in May 1945, he moved the station to Hilversum and arranged for the programs to be transmitted on shortwave by the BBC. **PCJ** returned to shortwave via its own 35 kw. transmitter on October 13. The frequencies were familiar—9590 and 15220 kc.—as was the announcer: Eddie Startz.

Radio Moscow was still called **Radio Centre**. In August it was broadcasting in English at 0700–0740 on 11830 and 15750 kc.; 0740–0820 on 6070, 9560, 10440 and 11630; 0820–0845 and 1200–1230 on 11830 and 15750; 1847–1925 (to North America) on 7030, 11830 and 15750;

and 2000–2200 on 7030, 9460 and 11950 kc. The 6070 kc. channel was said to be from **Petropavlovsk**. Transmissions were also heard from various other Soviet locations besides Moscow: **Leningrad** in the afternoons on 5960 kc. and in the evenings on 7430 and 9715, and **Komsomolsk** in the evenings on 15230. **Tiflis (Tbilisi)**, Georgia, was on 7490 and 11960 kc.

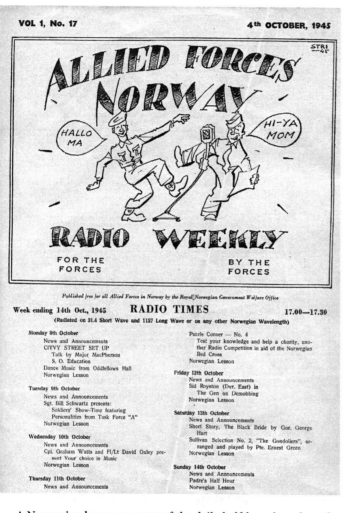

A Norwegian lesson was part of the daily half-hour broadcast for Allied troops stationed in Norway after the war.

By year's end the new French broadcasting agency, **Radiodiffusion Francaise**, a state monopoly, had inaugurated an ambitious shortwave service to North America, Europe, North Africa, the Middle East, Asia, and the Pacific, using 20 languages. The North American program, "French Radio Calling North America," was on the air at 1955–2245 on 9520, 9620 and 11845 kc.

The station in Hungary was now called **Hungarian Nations Radio**, and could be heard on 9835 and 11635 kc. **Radio Norway** shortwave was on the air on a limited basis, with a 5 kw. transmitter on 9540 kc. at 0100–0115, 0420–0700 and 1000–1600. Programming was in Norwegian, save for a half hour devoted to English for Allied forces in Norway. From Spain, **EDV10, Radio SEU**, Madrid, was heard on 7105 kc., and **EAJ9, Radio Malaga**, was on 7030. Both were heard circa 1700. The venerable EAJ43 in the Canary Islands, its pivotal role in the Spanish Civil War now largely forgotten, was still on the air, transmitting on 7570 kc. And **Radio Nacional de España** opened a new 40 kw. transmitter plant at Arganda del Rey, near Madrid.

Radio Andorra was heard on 5995 kc. at 1730. And construction began on another commercial venture that would become well known to international listeners—**Radio Monte Carlo**, Monaco. Its plans included 120 kw. on mediumwave and two 25 kw. shortwave transmitters. Transmissions on shortwave began on 6130 kc., 300 watts, and increased to 25 kw. in 1946.

After V-E day, **Radio Club Português**, off the air for years, returned to shortwave and was heard well at 1500 on 12400 kc. Also from Portugal, **CS2WD, Radio Renascença**, was active on 6155 kc. in the late afternoon. And **Radio Vienna** was now heard at 0000–0200 and 1330–2030 on three channels— 7160, 9832 and 12125 kc. (12125 was best).

EDV10, Radio SEU, was one of a number of small, non–RNE stations that remained on shortwave from Spain after the war. The last one, Radio Mediterraneo in Valencia, left shortwave around 1960.

Many programs formerly heard over **Radio Brazzaville** were now broadcast from Paris. OTC in the Belgian Congo still had a nightly program to the United States called "Belgium Speaks to America." It was at 2015 EWT on 9783 kHz. (Local broadcasting had resumed in Belgium.) After the war the **VOA**, broadcasting from **Algiers**, was heard in the morning on 11765 kc., in the early afternoon on 9610, and in the late afternoon (until 1815 close) on 6040. The Algiers identification as "United Nations Radio" had ceased by year's end, but **Radio France** was still heard via Algiers on 12120 kc. And AFRS programs could be heard over **Radio Club de Mozambique, CR7BE**, 9710 kc., until 1635 closed own.

"50 kw. Diathermy"

Back in New York last week en route to the Pacific area, Paul von Kunitz, formerly chief engineer of WINS New York, now with the OWI, told how he used the OWI's 50,000 watt transmitter in Algiers to give himself and two U.S. Army men diathermy treatment to hasten recovery from internal injuries received a year ago during the construction of another station in Africa. Mr. Kunitz wired two tin plates, attached to plywood panels, to the end of the rhomboid antenna used for the station. "Each plate was held to my chest and back by an Italian prisoner of war," he explained, "and during each treatment I could hear clearly the OWI psychological warfare programs beamed to Germany and Italy going out over the transmitter."

Broadcasting
February 19, 1945[159]

Also after the war, the **Sudan Broadcasting Service** in Khartoum, Sudan, then known as the Anglo-Egyptian Sudan, was on 9220 kc. and could be heard at 1700 EWT close down, identifying as **Radio Omdurman**. Reception was difficult, however. **Radio Dakar**, on a new channel of 7210 kc., was audible until 1715 sign off. **Radio Tananarive**, Madagascar, was heard in the morning circa 0700–0930, with French news at 0850. The frequency was 12127 kc. And while it wasn't heard in the U.S., a new station, **Radio Somali**, in Hargeisa, British Somaliland, was reported by Australian DXers on 7125 kc.

On 9465 kc., **Radio Ankara**, Turkey broadcast its "Postbag" program on Sundays at 1630–1645. Reception reports were read and listeners were promised one of the station's new QSL-cards.

Delhi was the main transmission site for **All India Radio**. Its transmitter complement now included two of 100 kw. (**VUD5, VUD7**); three of 10 kw. (**VUD2, VUD4, VUD6**); two of 7.5 kw. (**VUD8, VUD9**); and one of 5 kw. (**VUD3**). There were also 10 kw. transmitters in **Bombay** (**VUB2**), **Calcutta** (**VUC2**) and **Madras** (**VUM**). One of the best-heard channels from India was VUD5, Delhi, 7275 kc., audible from around 0730 to 1000, and also heard with a good signal in the east at 1600 and the west at 2100. AIR expanded its transmissions to Allied forces. To its British Forces Programme, which was broadcast at 2130–2300 EWT on VUD5, 11790 kc., and 0330–0500 on VUD6, 9635, it added another transmission, at 1030–1330 on VUD7, 6190. This corresponded to the peak evening listening time.

On May 25, following Germany's surrender, the German station in Shanghai, **XGRS**, was taken over by the Japanese, who operated it as **XGOO**.[160] After Japan's surrender, the station passed to the control of China's Central Broadcasting Administration, which changed the call letters to **XORA**. At that time it was operating with 5 kw. **XMHA**, also in Shanghai, was heard on 11860 kc. at 0800 with English. After the war the station came under U.S. military administration for a time (GI journalist Jack Anderson broadcast the English news for several months).[161] AFRS stations were said to be operating on shortwave in Calcutta, India (**VU2ZZ**, 14983 kc.), and, from China, Chungking (**XUSA**, 4759), Kunming (**XMEW**, 8690 kc.), and Nanking (**XMAG**, 4275). But there was little information about them. In both countries there were numerous small AFRS mediumwave outlets on the air during the 1944–46 period.

XGOY was heard signing on at 2000 on 11905 kc. (*"This is the American Hour from Chungking."*) XGOY also functioned as a utility station for the transmission of correspondents' reports to their home networks. One of them reported the station to be "a rabbit warren, the administration of which would turn an American radio executive grey with horror.... The electricity often fails, employees don't show up and a broadcast there is a thing of high nervous tension. * * * Its power plant is 15 miles away on the Chialing River. The generator is run on coal which comes down the river in barges and must be toted up a steep bank by coolie gangs. If the coolies decline to make the climb — as they sometimes do — the power fades or goes off completely."[162] It is no wonder that the XGOY signal was identifiable by a characteristic hum.

Until the Japanese surrender in mid–August, **Radio Shonan** continued to transmit to Eastern North America at 1800–1930 and to Western North America at 2000–2040, both on a drifting frequency around 15450 kc. (announced as 15360). It also relayed Philippine station **PIRN** at times.

On April 25, in Ceylon, **Radio SEAC's** test phase ended and the station commenced regular broadcasts by way of a 7.5 kw. transmitter at Ekala, north of Colombo The following year, Ekala would become home to a much stronger, 100 kw. transmitter for Radio SEAC. (Radio SEAC would leave the air in 1949 and transfer the Ekala transmitters to the new **Radio Ceylon**.)

Late in 1945, Radio SEAC supplemented its Ekala transmissions with some modest broadcasting from its new headquarters in Singapore utilizing 7.5 kw. transmitters at Jurong, a transmitter base on which construction by Britain had begun in 1939 and later completed by the Japanese and used for Radio Shonan. Jurong would soon become the transmitter site for the **British Far Eastern Broadcasting Service**, and later the **BBC Far Eastern Station**.

In March, Japan's control of Vietnam, theretofore conducted mainly through the French administration there, became complete as Japanese forces effected the surrender of the French. The Japanese kept **Radio Saigon** on the air during the six months

During the war, All India Radio provided valuable shortwave services in support of the Allied forces in Asia.

before they turned it over to the communist nationalists, the Viet Minh, at the war's end. But the Viet Minh showed no interest in it, and soon the old staff were back at the helm. In April 1946 the station was almost completely burned down in a two day-long explosion of a nearby military arsenal, and soon it was under government control. It continued to operate until December 1949 when it was replaced by **Radio France-Asie**.

On September 2, following successful Viet Minh military advances in the north, Ho Chi Minh declared the existence of the Democratic Republic of Vietnam. Several Viet Minh stations in the north combined to form **La Voix du Vietnam**, which began broadcasting from Hanoi in support of Ho. Although **Radio Tokyo** was brought under U.S. control on August 30, the station's various international services continued to operate through September, closing down soon thereafter.

Many of the usual NHK shortwave channels were now used for network correspondents' reports to the U.S., and sometimes AFRS programs. These included **JLP** on 9605 kc., **JZK** on 15160, and **JLP3** on 17835. The Japanese Home Service was also on shortwave, e.g. 6015 kc.

(JLR), 6190 (JLT), 7260 (JVW), and 7285 (JLG), and some of these channels were well heard in the United States until they signed off circa 0830.

Early in the year, with much of the Jungle Network's broadcasting now taking place in the Philippines and its headquarters moved to Manila, the network was renamed the **Far Eastern Network**. On September 23 the name was changed again, to **Far East Network (FEN)**, coincident with the commencement of broadcasting from what would become the AFRS headquarters station in Tokyo, **WVTR**, the wartime JOAK.[163] (It appears that there was some impromptu AFRS broadcasting from Japan before this date.) WVTR (it would soon become known simply as FEN) broadcast on both mediumwave and shortwave. FEN would be a reliable signal on shortwave until it dropped its HF channels in 1988. (It became **American Forces Radio** in 1997.) Numerous mediumwave outlets immediately came under AFRS control, and several in Korea soon followed.

The *Apache,* and its by now well-known station WVLC, moved to Tokyo in September. The following month its communications duties were transferred to a newly equipped radio ship, *Spindle Eye.* Early in 1946 the *Apache* became a recreational vessel, taking troops on weekend cruises in Tokyo Bay.

It was around this time that **VOA** began broadcasting from a station in Manila known as **KZFM**. KZFM had been put together by the Americans from a group of AFRS stations that had remained in the Philippines after most stations had been relocated to Japan. It was named after American newsman Frederic Marquardt, a friend of MacArthur's who had been with him at Leyte. KZFM operated with 5 kw. on both mediumwave and shortwave, and it carried VOA programs until a new VOA Philippine relay station was established.

After V-J Day, **Radio Rangoon** was heard on 11860 kc. at 0830–1000, with English news at 0930–1000. It also broadcast in local languages at 0645–0815 on 6040 kc. **ZHP**, Singapore, known as the **Malaya Broadcasting Corporation** before the war, returned as **BMA Radio (British Military Administration)**. It was on 9555 kc. **XPSA**, the **Kweichow Broadcasting Station** in Kweiyang, China, was still on the air, 7010 kc.

An oft-heard station was **KU5Q** on Guam, which became a major American communications hub. KU5Q used many channels, including 7405, 9275, 12250, 15850, and 17820 kc., and was equipped with five 3 kw. transmitters and one of 10 kw. It was heard carrying correspondents' reports and network programs from the Pacific and the Far East to the U.S., as well as working ships and other stations. After the Japanese surrender it was heard on 17810 kc., relaying the programs of **KU1M**, an American Forces station aboard the USS *Iowa* in Tokyo Bay. KU5Q was co-located with AFRS station **WXLI**. After the war it was involved in relaying reports on Operation Crossroads, the Bikini nuclear tests.

In Latin America, the war had put a brake on new station startups. However, there was always a small array of new DX targets to chase. New from Mexico City were **XENN, Radio Mundial**, which was heard in the evenings on 11780 kc.; and **XEHH, Sal de Uvas Picot**, 11880 kc., heard testing in the evening with relays of mediumwaver XERH. **XEBR, Radiodifusora de Sonora**, Hermosillo, Mexico, was still on 11820 kc., putting in a fair to good signal at 1000 sign on.

HI2A, La Voz de Trujillo, located in the Café del Yaque in Santiago, Dominican Republic, came on the air on 7215 kc. It also identified as **La Voz de la Reelección**. **HI3U, La Voz del Comercio**, Santiago, was now on 6015 kc. And **Radio Guadeloupe** was back on the air.

Heard from Guatemala from 1800 to past midnight on 10600 kc. was **TGN, La Voz Libertad**. And there were several new stations in Nicaragua: **YNBO, La Voz de Boaco**, was on 7018 kc.; **YNFM, Radio Masaya**, was on 7095, signing off at 2310 with the "Stars and Stripes Forever"; and **YNFP, La Voz del Tropico**, Managua, broadcast on 7140.

Further south, **HJCX, La Voz de Colombia,** was on 6018 kc., and **HJCD, Emisora Nueva Granada,** was on 6160. HCJB began testing on a frequency that would become a familiar HCJB channel to decades of shortwave listeners—15115 kc. This was a 1 kw. transmitter, operating at 0600–0900 and 1430–1900 daily. Reports were requested to be addressed to a name that would long be synonymous with the religious station—Clayton T. Howard.

A new station in Peru that is still well-known in the DX community was **OAX4Q, Radio Victoria,** Lima, operating with 2 kw. on 6010 kc. and relaying OAX4K mediumwave. And from very far south, **CE1227, Radio Ejercito,** at Punta Arenas, Chile, was on 12270 kc. It was heard in the evenings around 2200, and gave clear identification every 15 minutes. It was the most southerly station in the western hemisphere. Later it would move to 9200 kc.

KRHO in Hawaii was operating in various Asian languages on 17800 kc. at 1900–0245, and on 6120 at 0300–1115, with English news on the hour. And **VPD2,** Suva, Fiji, on 6130 kc., now had a 10 kw. transmitter. But it was operating with much less power, and just a few hours a day, relaying mediumwave ZJV.

In August, two 100 kw. transmitters, **VLA** and **VLB,** came into use at Australia's Shepparton site, which for a year had been carrying "**Australia Calling**" over 50 kw. **VLC.** Among the new 100 kw. channels were 7280, 9680, 11770 and 15320 kc. High-power HF broadcasting from Shepparton continues to this day. VLA and VLB were not put into immediate use for transmissions to North America. As of October 1, "Australia Calling" broadcasts to North America were as follows: 0010–0045 on 11710 (**VLG3**) and 11840 kc. (**VLC7**); 0800–0845 on 9540 (**VLC5**); 1100–1145 on 9615 (**VLC6**) and 11840 (**VLG4**); and 2045–2145 on 15315 (**VLC4**). (VLG was Lyndhurst, 10 kw.) In November, "Australia Calling" became **Radio Australia.**

The **National Broadcasting Service** of New Zealand had long been planning an international shortwave station to operate first at 7.5 kw., later 100 kw. The frequencies would be 6080 (**ZL1**), 9540 (**ZL2**), 11780 (**ZL3**), 15280 (**ZL4**), and 17770 (**ZL5**). Toward the end of the year, listeners reported tests on some of these channels, as well as others (e.g. 9896, 15500). However, these were from transmitters of the New Zealand PTT, which was making propagation studies for the new service. The **New Zealand Broadcasting Service** would not start regular broadcasting until September 1948 (almost a year after initial tests).

Of interest to shortwave listeners, the BBC adopted a reporting code for use by its official monitors. It was called RAISO, and it was an abbreviated version of a more comprehensive code. RAISO appears to be the source of the SINPO code that would soon come into common use among listeners. The full code was as follows ("SINPO" would translate into the parallel "RISAO"):

R	*Carrier strength*
A	*Fading (depth)*
F	Fading (frequency)
I	*Interference*
S	*Static*
B	Background noise
E	Transmitted noise
M	Modulation (degree)
C	Modulation (quality)
O	*Overall rating*

After the War[164]

VOA operating contracts with NBC, CBS and the other transmitter owners were extended beyond their end date of June 30, 1946. Notwithstanding Assistant Secretary Benton's championing of VOA, its time in the Office of International Information and Cultural Affairs was a period of instability, low morale, and modest appreciation by others. Personnel dropped from a high of over 3,000 in the OWI years to 226 at the end of December 1947, at which time about 75 percent of VOA programs were still being produced by NBC and CBS. About a year later, VOA cut its ties with the networks and assumed full program production responsibility (personnel were increased to 490).[165]

There was no specific Congressional authorization for U.S. international broadcasting until early in 1948, when the U.S. Information and Cultural Exchange Act of 1948 (the Smith-Mundt Act) authorized radio as one of the State Department's international information functions (but it referred specifically to shortwave broadcasting in only one particular — the government would have no monopoly). Smith-Mundt was in part a response to a failed attempt by the State Department to urge Congress to create a public corporation, the International Broadcasting Foundation of the United States, to manage shortwave broadcasting. In 1953, the VOA became part of the then-new U.S. Information Agency, formed under the authority of Smith-Mundt. Although by this time the Cold War had insured permanence for the VOA, relations with Congress would always be complicated.

The VOA transmissions from Algiers ended on May 31, 1947. A powerful new VOA transmitter at Malolos, in the Philippines, was opened on September 11, 1947. In 1948, the BBC Woofferton site was leased to the VOA, which became its prime user for many years.

WRUL had managed to continue to broadcast its own nightly 15-minute "Friendship Bridge" program even after the government takeover in 1942. Other private programming would return to the station in part in 1947, in full in 1953.

The Foreign Broadcast Intelligence Service closed operations in December 1945 and was transferred to the War Department's Military Intelligence Division the following month. In November 1946 it was transferred to the government's Central Intelligence Group (CIG), first as the Foreign Broadcast Information Service, then as the Foreign Broadcast Information Branch. It became part of the CIA — once again with the name Foreign Broadcast Information Service — when the CIA was created out of the CIG in 1947.

The BBC began broadcasting in Russian in 1946, the VOA in 1947 (including a relay from the 85 kw. Munich transmitter). Also in 1947, the CBC began carrying a daily half-hour Russian-language program from the U.N. Russian jamming began in earnest in 1948–49.

In 1946 the Swiss Shortwave Service increased power at the Schwarzenburg transmitter site to 100 kw. In Holland, a new international broadcasting service, Stichting Radio Nederland Wereldomroep, a private, non-profit foundation, was created on April 15, 1947 and would preserve for little Holland a leading seat at the international shortwave table for over a half-century.

Notwithstanding ever-increasing allied bombing, Germany's domestic broadcasting system had continued to operate from the same regional hubs and on the same mediumwave frequencies throughout the war. This structure was largely preserved by the Allies. Soon some of the stations were also being heard on shortwave. These included, from the American zone, **Radio Munich** (6190 kc.) and **Radio Stuttgart** (6180); from the French zone, **Südwestfunk**, Baden-Baden (6320); and from the British zone, **Nordwestdeutscher Rundfunk**, Hamburg (6115). (It was shortwave broadcasts from Nordwestdeutscher Rundfunk that would eventually lead to the creation of **Deutsche Welle**.) The British also set up their own **British Forces Network** in the British occupation zone. In the Soviet zone, the Leipzig transmitter on 9730 kc. carried the programs of **Mitteldeutscher Rundfunk**.

In addition, the **American Forces Network** relayed **Radio Frankfurt** on 6080 kc. over a powerful 50 kw. transmitter. In February 1946, **RIAS, Radio in the American Sector** (of

REGERINGS VOORLICHTINGS DIENST AFD. GROTE OOST

Government Information Service, East-Indonesia dep.

RADIO MAKASSAR.

Makassar, *6th of June* 19*47*
Celebes.

In answer to your report of .. *March. 15* ...... 19*47* we
have the honour to confirm herewith the correctness of your letter.
We appreciate very much that you took the trouble to inform us about the
reception of our station.
Shortage of materials prevents that it is brought up to its normal strength
of 10 K.W.
Also owing to printing difficulties we are unable to send you a verification
card, we hope that this letter can take its place.
We should be very obliged when you will keep us informed from time to time
about the reception of our station.

Yours truly,

RVD. afd. Gr. Oost

Dep. Radio Makassar.

Mrs Willemse Jeroms.

This 1947 QSL from Makassar, Indonesia, suggests some of the handicaps facing stations during the years of fighting in the archipelago.

Berlin), began operation as a wired broadcasting system, but soon moved to mediumwave and FM, adding the 6005 kc. shortwave outlet in 1951. It would serve as a major news source, at first for the American zone of Berlin, then for East Berlin and all of East Germany. In December 1946, several high-power (circa 85 kw.) Reichspost shortwave transmitters in **Ismaning**, near Munich, went into service for the VOA as the **VOA Munich Relay Station**.

In Asia, the Communist Chinese station **XNCR** would become the **Central People's Broadcasting Station**. It had become important toward the end of World War II for its exhortation of communist forces to take over from the departing Japanese, and for preserving contact with communist elements in the ensuing battles with the Nationalists. In 1946–47, the Communist Chinese and the Nationalists were locked in fighting, part of the civil war and the battle for power that followed Japan's defeat and its departure from the northern and central parts of China, much of which it had controlled for many years. XNCR, the **Yenan Xinhua Radio Station**, moved several times and changed its name to the **Northern Shaanxi Xinhua Broadcasting Station**. In September 1947, as part of an effort to obtain support from the English-speaking community both inside and outside China, XNCR began broadcasting an English-language program called the "Voice of Red China." It could be heard on approximately 7500 kc. By this time the communists had some 16 stations in operation, and at least two that broadcast on shortwave carried the program —XCHT on 6096 kc. and XCNR on 8660. In March 1949, XNCR moved to Peiping (soon renamed Peking) as the **Peking Xinhua Broadcasting Station**. Following the October 1 proclamation of the People's Republic of China, with Peking as its capital, the station became the **Central People's Broadcasting Station**.[166]

In the Dutch East Indies, the end of the war meant both freedom from Japanese occupation and the revival of a long simmering freedom movement. On August 17, two days after Japan's surrender, Sukarno (it is common in Java to have only one name), who was a national figure and the leader of the campaign for independence, proclaimed the establishment of the Republic of Indonesia, and became its first President. There followed more than four years of fighting and negotiation among Republican forces, Dutch troops that had returned to reassert Dutch control, and Allied occupation forces, mostly British, under Mountbatten. During this time various parts of the country were subject to a multitude of governmental and military authorities, including various branches of the Republican movement itself, which was united only in its opposition to the Dutch. It all came to a head in December 1949 when the Dutch, facing the rising cost of occupation and increased international political and economic pressure, finally recognized Indonesia's independence. (West New Guinea, or West Irian, remained separate until 1969.)

During the period 1945–49, the Dutch tried to impose a federal structure on the archipelago that would permit them to remain in some fashion. The radio structure was called **Radio Indonesia**. However, upon the declaration of independence in 1945, a group of eight Javan broadcasters formed an organization called **Radio Republik Indonesia (RRI)**, which soon became part of the Republic's Ministry of Information. Over the next four years, depending on who was in charge in their locale at any particular time, individual stations, of which there were many, flew under the banner of either the official Dutch administration, or the Republic's **Radio National Indonesia**, the name under which RRI at first operated. After 1949 the Radio National Indonesia umbrella extended its reach. The name **Radio Republik Indonesia** came into general use circa 1950–51. Through it all, the stations largely retained their local identity, calling themselves Radio Medan, Radio Pontianak, etc. To the international shortwave community, the country's political, military and administrative circumstances, together with the low power with which most of the stations operated — 3 kw. or less, often much less — made the Indonesian shortwave scene one of confusion if not mystery. It would became better known after a 100 kw. transmitter was brought on line in Jakarta in 1950 and more listeners were able to tune in to this exotic land.

Conclusion

Radio waves are something we ride to see where they take us—both in the world and in our minds' eye.—Susan J. Douglas, Listening In[1]

Shortwave was discovered when a proposition that had long been thought settled—that long-distance required long wavelengths (low frequencies)—turned out to be wrong. Huge sums had been spent on massive commercial longwave transmitting stations based on this misconception.

The root concept of broadcasting—transmitting by radio to a broad, general audience—was itself only a few years old when reaching distant places by shortwave first became feasible. Although there had been some earlier experimentation by Marconi, the shortwave work of Westinghouse engineer Frank Conrad began in 1920, about the same time as the inauguration of the company's pioneer broadcast station, KDKA. Shortwave trials by Conrad and others continued during the next few years, and in 1923 regular broadcasting over KDKA shortwave transmitter 8XS began. It was also at this time that RCA's Radio Central started taking a closer look at shortwave's potential. Practically overnight, shortwave changed the fundamentals of long distance radio communication.

The next few years saw a few other American broadcasters join in shortwave testing. In 1927, PCJ in Holland, the first shortwave broadcasting service with a purpose broader than experimentation, signed on. Exploratory work in England, Australia and elsewhere followed, and by the end of the decade rudimentary shortwave broadcasting was a recognized, if still tiny, corner of the broadcasting world. It was a dramatic advance of human experience to be able to hear voice and music direct, with no intermediary, from places with which one could have theretofore connected only through books and pictures. The worldwide reach of shortwave radio was truly a technological, and a cultural, wonder.

In the United States, shortwave was never viewed as an alternative to domestic direct-to-listener AM broadcasting, but as a means, first, for relaying programs from one city, or one country, to another for rebroadcast on local wavelengths, and later, for direct-to-listener international broadcasting. There had been constant improvement in ordinary AM receivers, which were easy to operate, and there was an entrenched AM broadcasting industry and a government committed to protecting it. The main body of shortwave activity was point-to-point. Thus, in the U.S., shortwave broadcast listening was a niche sport from the start. The things that DXers liked most about it—the technical challenge and the exotic side of long distance reception—were of no interest to ordinary listeners.

This was not equally true everywhere. Even though the operation of shortwave receivers was more demanding than broadcast band sets, in countries where there was limited local broadcasting, or where geography made shortwave's long reach important, or where tropical conditions degraded mediumwave reception, shortwave gained some domestic acceptance. But it was in international broadcasting that it flourished.

Shortwave's expansion was mainly the product of conflict. The first major test of broadcasting in wartime was the Spanish Civil War. While much of the action was on mediumwave, shortwave also played a part and had an important impact on both the warring sides and the general populace. And it influenced people in other countries.

It was months from the end of that war to the start of World War II, the conflict that would define the medium. Most of the secrets of shortwave communication were by then well known, and they were quickly put to work in the war. No nation did this better than Germany, which created a shortwave broadcasting system that was, at the time, the most highly developed in the world. England followed hesitatingly, conscious of the medium's differences from the traditional writ of the BBC, but compelled to not yield this new battlefield to the enemy. America, first in shortwave development, was the last of the big powers to create an effective shortwave broadcasting capability, acting only when forced to by the exigencies of war and the limitations of private industry alternatives.

With shortwave, every country could now articulate its own line, whether peaceful or hostile, over long distances, direct to the individual listener, and in his or her own language. Broadcasts could bolster friends and counter enemies, inject hope or instill fear, offer truth or falsehood or something in between, and leave it to the listener to sort out. Germany could undermine an Englishman's confidence in his country's leadership and extol the virtues of national socialism. London could urge conquered peoples to fight on. America could promise that the Axis would be vanquished. The art of persuasion, with all its subtleties and varied objectives, could now be practiced on a grand scale.

Other related wartime purposes were also served. The military built morale by providing troops with news and entertainment. Clandestine stations, feigning their parentage, said things their sponsors could not, and even where the provenance of the broadcasts was known, they could still sow doubt. So important was the new medium that governments set up monitoring services in the belief that shortwave broadcasts presaged the political and military plans of the enemy.

On the civilian side, churches and other religious organizations could now preach far and wide (a shortwave application that would gain wide use in future decades). And smaller stations that simulcast their broadcast band signals on shortwave could serve a larger area. In Latin America, where broadcasting followed the private American model, stations could improve their bottom line by promising advertisers bigger audiences. However, it was the propaganda function that was shortwave broadcasting's *raison d'être*.

At the war's end, American shortwave broadcasting was an orphan that would be saved by yet another conflict — the Cold War. It is hard to predict what would have happened under different circumstances, but what followed was a broad, decades-long expansion of international shortwave broadcasting. It was led by the big powers but joined in by practically every other country. No one wished to be left out of this new international conversation.

International shortwave broadcasting did poorly in the competition for the ear of the ordinary American radio listener. AM radio was ubiquitous and growing. Shortwave was low visibility, and not without its difficulties: inferior reception; the need for specialized receivers (all-wave receivers had proven inadequate); the requirement of "appointment listening" (most international broadcasts were at set times and of comparatively brief duration); the absence of commercial production values. But as a worldwide forum of national voices serving geopolitical ends or just plain national pride, short-wave broadcasting would remain intact, and grow, for decades.

Things changed with the fall of the Berlin Wall, when Cold War imperatives disappeared, national monopolies gave way to new non-governmental broadcasting structures, and alternative media flourished. Suddenly shortwave broadcasters were under the microscope, having to justify their work in the context of harsh new budget realities. Often the stations lacked knowledgeable supporters in high places, where shortwave was poorly understood and appeared increasingly anachronistic in a digital age. Smaller stations suffered a like fate. They were particularly vulnerable to problems of aging equipment and shortage of knowledgeable technical staff. And as international shortwave broadcasting declined, so did the availability of shortwave receivers that would nourish local shortwave listening and sustain local shortwave broadcasting.

Today, save for some broadcasts to undeveloped areas where other media are unavailable, or to places where suppression of media freedom makes outside news sources essential, shortwave is more and more visible mainly in the rear-view mirror. Many shortwave broadcasters have reduced their services or left the air entirely, opting for local FM relays, internet broadcasting, or

No shortwave personality had a longer on-air history than Eddie Startz, who joined PCJ in 1928 and, save for the war years, remained a star of Dutch shortwave until his retirement 41 years later.

leased time arrangements with other shortwave transmitter operators seeking to preserve the financial viability of their plants. Some view this turn as short sighted, arguing that the strength of shortwave lies in its usefulness under crisis conditions, where other media often fail, and its resistance to the political interdiction to which other forms of broadcasting are more susceptible. Others view it as the natural byproduct of advancing technology.

Whatever may be the epitaph of shortwave broadcasting, its greatest lesson was probably political rather than technological. It seems naive today, but many believed that this newfound capability to reach huge populations worldwide would change international relations in a fundamental way. Now that countries could put themselves on stage via this new medium, and learn about other peoples the same way, world peace and understanding would be enhanced and conflict reduced. In fact, the strongest voices on the shortwave bands usually were those in the service of conflict. Even in today's world of leased-time shortwave, it is the new generation of opposition, or "target," broadcasters that has gravitated to the medium.

To the avid shortwave enthusiast, of course, the purpose and the politics of shortwave broadcasting, and its small domestic footprint, meant little. Even in World War II, with its unprecedented opportunities for unique program listening, most shortwave listeners were mainly interested in DX, not content — in the magic of the medium, not the message. For them, at war's end, the organized shortwave listening community was in shambles.

Equipment and information are the two most important things to dedicated shortwave listeners, and on both fronts the picture was bleak. New receivers had been virtually impossible to obtain during the war. Thereafter, new models appeared only slowly, and without the technological advances that manufacturers had been hinting at during the war. On the club scene, neither of the two main American shortwave clubs, the International Short Wave Club and the International DXers Alliance, had survived. The Newark News Radio Club, the Universal Radio DX Club and the National Radio Club had managed to limp through the war, but they were in need of rejuvenation. (The National Radio Club had dropped its shortwave coverage during the war.)

Nor were there any popular magazines serving the shortwave community. The likes of *Short Wave Craft, All-Wave Radio* and *RADEX* were gone. A trickle of DX news began flowing in June 1944 when a new column, "International Short-Wave," appeared in *Radio News,* which had last covered shortwave broadcasting in 1939. The editor of the new column was Kenneth R. Boord of Morgantown, West Virginia, who, after a shaky start — the column went unpublished for five months in 1945 — would go on to become one of the most prolific sources of shortwave news for almost two decades.

Eventually, better receivers became available, clubs rebounded, and shortwave news found many outlets. A turning point was the founding of the *World Radio Handbook* in 1947. The annual compendium of the times, frequencies and addresses of the world's shortwave broadcasters provided a critical mass of information that greatly facilitated shortwave broadcast listening (as it still does today). The medium may have been unknown in most households, but the "WRH" was bringing it into the open.

It is difficult to overstate shortwave's early impact. Spanning the oceans by radio, with comparative simplicity and relatively low cost, was no small thing in the twenties and the thirties. It fundamentally changed the nature of international radio communication and the countless activities related to it. And it was a boon to the DX enthusiasts who had grown up in the early twenties when broadcast band DXing was popular. As AM radio expanded, the thrill of DXing had waned. Shortwave brought it back, with the new seduction of hitherto unachievable distance.

Recounting in 1931 the first rebroadcasts of KDKA shortwave by the BBC at the end of 1923, Westinghouse Vice-President Harry P. Davis said this:

> Here occurred an epoch in human history, for man had truly conquered space. The world's boundaries had been shifted. A human voice was heard simultaneously in North America and Europe — a greeting to millions of people spanning Nature's barriers, with no connecting media except the invisible and the unknown.... [P]robably in all the years of history no greater feat of science had been recorded.[2]

Three-quarters of a century later, the experience of today's shortwave listeners bears him out.

Appendix: Nations and Stations

This appendix serves as an index to finding where each station is discussed. Stations are identified by call letters, name or slogan, or both, as usage and clarity dictate. Within each country, stations identified only by call letters usually appear after stations identified by name or slogan. The year of discussion in the main chapters follows the station name. Clandestine and maritime stations follow the country listings. **Bold = illustration.**

Abbreviations: Cl. = Club, Clube; Em. = Emisora, Emissora; Intl. = Internacional, International; Nacl., Natl. = Nacional, National, Nationale; R. = Radio; Rdf. = Radiodifusão, Radiodifusion, Radiodifusora, Radio Difusora.

Nations

Aden. R. Aden, ZNR 1941, 1944.

Albania. R. Tirana, ZAA 1939, 1940.

Algeria. Allied Force Headquarters 1943, 1944; Poste Algerien, TPZ 1937, 1939, 1940, 1943; R. Alger, R. Algiers 1937, 1939, 1940, 1942; R. France 1943, 1945; "United Nations Radio" 1945.

Andorra. R. Andorra 1939, 1941, 1944, 1945.

Angola. R. Cl. de Lobito, Estação Rdf. CR6AA 1934, 1937; R. Cl. de Angola, CR6RA, CR6RC 1938, 1940, **1940**, 1944; R. Cl. de Benguela, CR6RB 1940.

Antarctica. KC4USA, KC4USB, KC4USC 1940, **1940**; KRTA, KRTC, KRTK 1940.

Antigua. R. Antigua 1942, **1942**.

Argentina. Compañia Internacional de Radio, LSN 1934; R. Belgrano, LR3 1937, 1943; R. El Mundo, LRY 1943; R. del Estado, LRA 1938; R. El Mundo, LR1 1935; R. Prieto, LS2 1937; R. Splendid, LS4 1934; Transradio Internacional, LSX 1930, **1930**, 1934, 1935; LOZ 1924; LRU 1935; LRX 1935.

Australia. "Australia Calling" 1939, 1940, 1941, 1942, 1943, 1945; R. Australia 1939, 1945; VK2ME Sydney 1927, 1929, 1930, **1930**, 1931, 1932, 1933, 1934, 1937; VK3LR, VK3XX Lyndhurst 1934, 1937, 1938; VK3ME Melbourne 1927, 1928, 1929, 1930, 1931, 1932, 1934, 1935, 1937; VK6ME Perth 1937, 1939; VK8SC, Australian Aerial Medical Svc. 1937; VLA, VLB, VLC Shepparton 1944, 1945; VLG Lyndhurst 1941, 1942, 1945; VLM Brisbane 1943; VLQ Pennant Hills, Brisbane 1928, 1939, **1939**, 1940, 1942, 1943; VLR Lyndhurst 1938, 1939, 1941; VLW Perth 1939, 1940; 2BL 1926, 1927, **1927**; 2FC 1927; 2GB 1943; 2SB 1927; 2YG 1927; 3AR 1927; 3LO 1927, **1927**, 1928, 1929; 3LR 1928; 6WF 1927; 7BL 1931; 9MI, M/V *Kanimbla* 1936, **1936**.

Austria. American Forces Network 1943; R. Wien, OER2, OER3 1930, 1934, 1937, 1938, 1945; Reichsender Wien 1938.

Azores. Em. Regional dos Açores 1941; CT2AJ 1935.

Bahamas. ZNS 1939.

Balearic Islands. EA6AF 1936; EDR4, Majorca 1937.

Barbados. Cable & Wireless (West Indies) Ltd. 1935, 1944; VP6YB 1935.

Bechuanaland. ZNB 1937, 1942.

Belgian Congo. R. Congo Belge 1940, 1942, 1943, 1944; R. Leo, OQ2AA 1938, 1939, 1940; OPL, OPM 1935, 1938, 1940, 1943; OTC 1938, 1943, 1944, 1945.

Belgium. R. Belgique 1940; R. Natl. Belge (Belgian Natl. Broadcasting Svc., BNBS) 1943; R. Ruysselede 1934, **1934**.

Bermuda. Cable & Wireless (West Indies) Ltd. 1943; VPN 1934; ZFS 1934.

Bolivia. Compañia Radio Boliviana, R. Illimani 1933, 1934; R. Chuquisaca 1937; R. Fides 1939; R. Intl. de Potosí 1939; R. Nacl. de Bolivia 1940.

Brazil. Ceará Radio Club, PRE9 1941; Companhia Radio Internacional do Brazil, R. Bras, PRF5 1934; Companhia Radio Internacional do Brazil, R. Bras, PPM, PPQ et al. 1933, 1934, 1937, 1940, 1943; R. Cl. do Brasil, PRA3 1933, **1933**; R. Cl. do Pará, PRC5 1941; R. Cl. de Pernambuco, PRA8 1935; R. Nacional, PRE8, PRL7, PRL8, PRL9 1943; Rdf. Sao Paulo, PRF3 1941; R. Journal do Brasil, PRF4 1937.

British Guiana. Br. Guiana Broadcasting Co., VP3MR 1935, 1937, 1938; Br. Guiana United Broadcasting Co. Ltd., VP3BG, ZFY 1938, 1942, 1944; Crystal Broadcasting Co., VP3BG 1936, **1936**, 1937, 1938; VP3THE 1937; VRY 1928, 1930.

British Honduras. ZIK2 1937.

British Somaliland. R. Somali 1945.

Bulgaria. R. Sofia 1936, 1940.

Burma. Burma State Broadcasting Svc. 1939, 1942; Mingaladon Radio 1937, **1937**; R. Rangoon 1945.

Cameroun. R. Cameroun 1941, 1943; R. Douala 1944.

Canada, shortwave broadcast: Canadian Broadcasting Corp. (CBC) 1940, 1941, 1944, 1945; CBFW 1941, 1942; CBFX 1941, 1942; CBFY 1941, **1941**, 1942; CBFZ 1941, 1942; CBRX 1941, 1942; CFCX 1931, 1936, 1937, 1942, 1944; CFRX 1937, 1942; CFVP 1939, 1942; CHAC 1944; CHLA 1944; CHLS 1944; CHMD 1944; CHNX 1930, 1938, 1939, 1942, 1943; CHOL 1944; CHTA 1944; CJCX 1937, 1942; CJRO 1934, 1937, 1939, 1942, 1943; CJRX 1928, **1928**, 1929, 1931, 1934, 1937, 1939, 1942, 1943; CKCX 1944; CKFX 1936, 1941, 1942; CKOB 1944; CKLO 1944; CKNC 1944; CKRO 1943; CKRX 1943; CKXA 1944; CKZU 1941; CRCX 1935, 1937, 1938; VE9AI 1944; VE9AS 1935; VE9BJ 1932; VE9BY 1931; VE9CA 1935, 1937, 1939; VE9CF 1930; VE9CL 1928, 1931, 1933, 1934; VE9CS 1931, 1935, **1935**, 1936, 1937; VE9DN 1933, 1937; VE9DR 1931, **1931**, 1933, 1936; VE9GW 1930, 1931, 1932, 1933, 1935, 1938; VE9HX 1930, 1933, 1937, 1938; VE9JR 1931, 1933, 1934.

_____, **standard broadcast:** CBF 1941; CBO 1937; CBR 1941; CFCA 1928; CFCF 1931; CFCN 1935; CFRB 1937; CHNS 1930, 1938; CJCA 1944; CJCB 1937; CJRC 1934; CJRM 1928; CJRW 1928; CKFC 1935; CKGW 1930; CKWX 1941.

_____, **utility:** "CF" 1927, 1928.

Canary Islands. R. Cl. Tenerife, EAR58, EA8AB, EAJ43 1933, 1934, 1936, 1937, **1937**, 1938, 1941, 1942, 1945; EA8AE 1937; EA8AK 1937; EA8AS 1937; EA8AT 1937.

Ceylon. Colombo Broadcasting Svc. 1936, 1943; R. Ceylon 1945; R. SEAC 1944, 1945.

Chile. Em. Otto Becker 1937; R. La Americana **1937**, 1939; R. Cooperativa Vitalicia 1938; R. Ejercito 1945; R. Hucke 1939, **1939**; R. El Mercurio 1938; R. Service 1937; R. Sociedad Nacl. de Agricultura 1938; R. Sur 1937; Rdf. "Pilot" 1936, 1939.

China. Central Broadcasting Admin. 1936, 1939; Central People's Broadcasting Stn. 1945; FFZ, Station Radiophonique Francaise 1940, 1941; XBX 1937; XCDN 1941, 1942; XCNR 1945; XCHT 1945; XGAP, Peiping Central Broadcasting Stn. 1942; XGCA, Kalgan Central Broadcasting Stn. 1943; XGOA 1936, 1937; XGOK, R. Canton 1939; XGOL 1941; XGOO 1945; XGOW 1938; XGOX, Voice of China 1936, **1936**, 1937, 1939, 1941, 1942; XGOY, Voice of China 1939, 1941, 1942, 1944, 1945; XGRS, Far Eastern Broadcasting Stn. 1940, **1940**, 1941, 1944, 1945; XGRV 1939; XGRX 1937; XGW 1934; XGX 1938; XHHB 1940, 1941; XIRS 1941; XMAG 1945; XMEW 1945; XMHA 1939, 1940, 1941, 1942, 1945; XNCR, Northern Shaanxi Xinhua Broadcasting Stn. 1945; XNCR, Peking Xinhua Broadcasting Stn. 1945; XNCR, Yenan Xinhua Radio Stn. 1940, 1945; XOJD 1938, 1941; XORA 1945; XPSA, Kweichow Broadcasting Stn. 1938, 1939, 1941, 1945; XTF 1937; XTJ 1937, 1938, **1938**, 1939; XTR 1937; XUSA 1945.

Colombia. Colombia Broadcasting 1932, 1933; Colombian Radio & Electric Co. 1931; Ecos del Combeima 1935, 1938, 1939; Ecos de la Montana 1935; Ecos de Occidente 1935; Em. Atlantico 1935, 1938, 1939; Em. Claridad 1936, 1938; Em. Nueva Granada 1937, 1938, 1939, 1945; Em. Philco 1936; Em. Suramerica 1940; Em. Universidad de Antioquia 1938, 1939, 1943; Estación del Barrio Noreste de Bogota 1932; La Voz Amiga 1940; La Voz de Antioquia 1935; La Voz de Armenia 1936, 1938, 1939, 1940; La Voz de Barranquilla 1933, 1934, 1938, 1939, 1940; La Voz de Bogota 1933, 1938, 1939; La Voz de Caldas 1933; La Voz de Catia 1935; La Voz del Choco 1935; La Voz de Ciénaga 1935; La Voz de Colombia 1934, 1936, 1939, 1945; La Voz de Cúcuta 1936, 1938, 1939; La Voz de los Laboratorios Fuentes 1934, **1934**, 1935, 1938, 1939; La Voz del Pacifico 1936, 1939; La Voz del Pais-Ecos de Bocaya 1933; La Voz de Pereira 1935, 1939; La Voz de Santa Marta 1935, 1938, 1939; La Voz del Valle 1934, 1938, 1939; La Voz de la Victor 1934, 1937, 1938, 1939;

Ondas de la Heroica 1934, 1935; R. Bucaramanga 1935, 1938, 1940; R. Cartagena 1939; R. Cristal 1942, 1943; R. Manizales 1932, 1939; R. Pacifico 1942; R. Santander 1938, 1939, 1943; Rdf. Cartagena 1936, **1936**; Rdf. de Medellin 1933, 1935; Rdf. Nacional 1940; Universal Broadcasting Co. 1930; HJCR 1940; HKA 1931; HKD 1931; HKE 1931; HKF 1931; HKM 1931; HJ2ABG 1934; HJ3ABI 1934; HJ5ABH 1934.

Costa Rica. "Alma Tica" 1935; Broadcasting Stn. "Para Ti" 1938; Costa Rica Radio and Broadcasting Stns. 1932; Ecos del Pacifico 1936; Estacion Cultura 1938; La Reina del Aire 1934; La Voz de Guanacaste 1940; La Voz de San Ramon 1936; La Voz del Tropico 1934, **1934**, 1943; La Voz de la Victor 1935, 1936, 1938, 1939, 1943; Ondas del Caribe 1936; R. America Latina 1942; R. El Mundo 1938; R Libertad 1942; Radioemisora Athenea 1937; Radioemisora Católica Costarricense 1935, 1936; Sistema Nacl. de Radioemisoras-R. Tribuna 1942, 1943; Voz Radio Pilot-La Voz de la Republica 1938; TIXGP3 1934; TI1EP 1934; TI2PG 1935; TI4NRH 1928, 1930, 1932, 1933, 1934, 1935, 1936, 1938, **1938**.

Cuba, shortwave broadcast: Ecos del Valle del Yumuri, COGF 1937; El Progreso Cubano, COBC 1937; International Broadcasting Co., CMCI 1931, 1932; Laboratorio Radio-eléctrico Grau y Caminero, CO9GC 1935; La Voz de las Antillas, COCW 1937, 1939; La Voz de la Democracia, CMZ1 1942; La Voz del Radio Philco, COCX 1936; La Voz del Aire, COCD 1935; Observatorio Nacional, CLX 1937; R. Alvarez, COBX 1937; R. Cadena Suaritos, COBL, COCM 1944; R. Salas, COBZ 1937; R. Universal, COBF 1943; R. Zenith, COJK 1937; Rdf. de Publicidad, COBQ 1942; Transradio Columbia, COCM 1937; CMZI 1943; COBX 1940; COC, COCO 1934, 1935, 1939; COCA 1937; COCE 1939; COCL 1944; COCO 1935, 1939; COCQ 1936, 1943; COCY 1940; COH, COCH 1934, 1935, 1936; COHI 1939; COK 1940, 1941, 1943; COKG 1935; COX 1943; CO9JQ 1935; CO9WR, COHB 1935, 1937; CO9XX 1937.

_____, **standard broadcast:** CMBC 1937; CMBF 1943; CMBQ 1942; CMBX 1937, 1940; CMBZ 1937; CMC 1939; CMCA 1937; CMCD 1935; CMCL 1944; CMCM 1937; CMCY 1934; CMGF 1937; CMHB 1935, 1937; CMHI 1939; CMJK 1937; CMX 1936; CMZ 1942; 6KW 1927, 1937.

Curaçao. R. CUROM (R. Princesa Juliana) 1937, **1937**, 1942.

Cyprus. BBC East Mediterranean Relay 1944.

Czechoslovakia. R. Podebrady 1930; R. Journal, OLR 1930, 1936, 1940, 1942; R. Prague, OLR 1934, 1937, 1938, 1939, 1940.

Dahomey. Cotonou 1942.

Denmark. Copenhagen 1937; Kalundborg 1937; R. Denmark, Statsradiofonien, OZF 1928, 1937, 1940; OXY 1929, 1931, 1935; OZ7MK, The Midnight Sun 1928; OZ7RL 1928.

Dominican Republic. "Broadcasting Hotel Mercedes" 1936; Broadcasting Nacional 1940; Broadcasting Tropical 1941; Ecos de Isabel de Torres 1938; Em. "Diario del Comercio" 1937; Estación Perifonica HI3U-La Voz del Comercio 1936; "FA-DOC" (Fabríca Dominicana de Calzado) 1936; La Voz del Almacén Dominicano 1936; La Voz de la Asociación Católica 1936; La Voz del Comercio 1945; La Voz Dominicana 1943; La Voz de la Feria 1934; La Voz del Higuamo 1934, 1935; La Voz de la Hispaniola 1936; La Voz de la Marina 1936; La Voz de Moca 1937; La Voz de los Muchachos 1933, 1935, 1936; La Voz del Partido Dominicano 1936, 1939; La Voz de la Philco 1936; La Voz de la Provincia 1938; La Voz del Pueblo 1940, 1943; La Voz de Quisqueya 1934; La Voz de la RCA Victor 1936; La Voz de Trujillo-La Voz de la Reelección 1945; La Voz del Yaque 1933; La Voz del Yuna 1943; R. "La Opinión" 1936; R. Santiago 1944; Radioemisora Nacl. "El Diario" 1938, 1943; Rdf. HIL 1936; Rdf. HI1J 1936; HIX, HI1X, HI2X, HI3X 1933, 1937, 1941, 1944; HI1R 1943; HI5G 1937.

Dutch East Indies. Nederlands-Indische Radio Omroep Maatschappij (NIROM) 1934, 1935, 1936, 1938; R. Indonesia 1945; R. National Indonesia 1945; R. Republik Indonesia (RRI) 1945; Bandoeng 1928, 1934, **1934**, 1936, 1937, 1938, 1942; Banjermasin 1935; Batavia (Jakarta) 1934, 1936, 1940, 1943, 1944; Jember 1935; Jogjakarta 1935; Makassar 1934, **1935**, 1944; Malabar 1928, **1928**, 1931; Malang 1935; Medan 1928, 1934, 1936, 1938; Menado 1934; Semarang 1934, 1935; Soerabaya 1936, 1937, 1938; Surakarta (Solo) 1935, 1938, 1938; Tanjung Priok 1934; JANX 1944; PK1WK 1934; PK6XX, PO6ZA 1938, **1938**.

Dutch Guiana (Surinam). Algemeene Vereeniging Radio Omroep Surinam (AVROS), Free Netherlands Radio 1935, 1942, 1943, 1944; PZ1AA 1936.

Ecuador. Compañia Rdf. del Ecuador 1941; Diario Hablado 1938; Ecuador Radio 1932, 1936, 1943; "El PRADO" 1934; El Telégrafo 1935, 1938, 1943; Em. "El Condor" 1937; Estación El Palomar 1936; HCJB 1931, 1932, 1933, 1934, 1936, 1937, 1938, 1940, 1941, 1942, 1944, 1945; La Voz del Alma 1937; La Voz del Diablo 1938; La Voz de Manabí 1938; La Voz del Tungurahua-"R. Ambato" 1936; Ondas del Pacifico 1935, 1936; "Quinta Piedad" 1933, 1934, 1936; R. Comercial 1942; R. Quito 1940; R. Teatro Bolivar 1943; Rdf. Cenit 1943; Rdf. del Estado 1936; Rdf. Municipal 1943; Teatro Bolivar 1935; HC1BD 1942; HC1DR 1930, 1931; HC1JB 1937; HC1SC 1931; HC2AJ 1941; HC2AT 1935, **1935**.

Egypt. Egyptian State Broadcasting 1940, 1941; JCPA (FBS) 1943.

El Salvador. Dirección General de Telégrafos, Teléfonos y Radio Nacionales, 1940; La Voz de Cuscutlan, 1938; YSS et al. 1937.

Ethiopia. Imperial Ethiopian Broadcasting Stn. 1935, 1936; R. Addis Ababa 1938, 1942; I2AA 1939, 1940; PTT 1945.

Fiji. Amalgamated Wireless (Australasia) Ltd., VPD, VPD2 1935, 1936, 1941, 1944, 1945; Fiji Broadcasting Co., ZJV 1935, 1944.

Finland. Finnish Broadcasting Corp. (Oy Suomen Yleisradio Ab) 1938, **1938**, 1940, 1941, 1943.

France. American Forces Network 1943; "Ici la France" 1940; "Honneur et Patrie" 1940; Paris Mondial, Paris Ondes Courtes 1938, 1939, 1940, 1941, 1942; Paris Radio Experimental 1928; R. Coloniale 1931, 1934, 1936; R. "LL" 1928; R. Paris 1928; R. Vitus 1928; Rdf. Francaise 1945; Voice of France 1941, 1942; Allouis 1939, 1940; Bordeaux 1940; Essarts-le-Roi 1938; Pontoise 1936, 1938, 1940; St. Assisse 1934; F8AB 1923.

French Equatorial Africa. R. Brazzaville 1940, 1941, 1942, 1943, 1944, 1945; R. Club 1940; FHK Libreville 1941.

French Indochina. La Voix du Vietnam 1945; Philco Radio 1936, **1936**; Radio-Club de l'Indochine du Nord 1936; R. France-Asie 1945; R. Hai Phong 1938; R. Hanoi 1938; R. "Michel Robert" 1936; R. Saigon 1928, 1930, 1932, 1936, 1939, **1939**, 1940, 1942, 1944, 1945; Station Boy-Landry 1936, 1940.

French West Africa. R. Dakar, FGA 1940, 1942, 1944, 1945.

Germany. American Forces Network 1943, 1945; British Forces Network 1945; Deutsche Welle 1945; Elmshorn 1943; Ismaning 1941, 1942, 1945; Mitteldeutscher Rundfunk 1945; Munich 1941; Nauen 1925, 1929, 1934; Nordwestdeutscher Rundfunk 1945; POZ 1925; Radio In the American Sector (RIAS) 1945; R. Berlin Intl. 1925; R. Frankfurt 1945; R. Munich 1945; R. Stuttgart 1945; Südwestfunk 1945; VOA Munich Relay Station 1945; "Zeesen" (Reichs-Rundfunk Gesellschaft, Deutscher Kurzwellensender) 1929, **1929**, 1930, 1932, 1933, 1934, 1935, 1936, **1936**, 1938, 1939, 1940, 1941, 1942, 1943, 1944.

Ghana. Gold Coast Relay Sys., ZOY 1940, 1941, 1943; ZD4AA 1940.

Greece. Athens Radio 1940; Voice of Greece, SVJ, SVM 1941.

Guadeloupe. R. Guadeloupe 1939, 1943, 1945.

Guam. KU5Q 1945; WXLI 1945.

Guatemala. Dirección de la Policía Nacional, 1935; La Voz Libertad 1945; La Voz de Quetzaltenango 1938; Ministerio de Fomento 1935; R. Morse 1937, 1939, 1940; Rdf. Nacional, TGW 1931, 1935, 1937, 1938, 1939, 1942, 1943; TGCA 1931; TGX 1931, 1932.

Haiti. Magloire Broadcasting Circuit, HHBM 1941; Société Haitienne de Automobile, HH2R 1935; Société Haitienne de Rdf. (West Indian Broadcasting Co.), HH2S 1935, 1938, 1943; HHK 1935; HH2W 1935; HH3W (R. Haiti) 1935.

Hawaii. HKE, HKQ 1940; KGMB 1940; KGU 1929; KRHO 1944, 1945.

Honduras. El Eco de Honduras 1935; La Voz de Honduras 1935, 1938; Tropical Radio-Voice of the Tropics 1930, 1931; Voz de Atlantida 1936.

Hong Kong. JPHA 1944; ZBW, ZCK 1935, **1935**, 1936, 1942.

Hungary. Hungarian Nations Radio 1945; R. Budapest 1939, 1940; Royal Hungarian Post, Radiolabor, HAS, HAT 1934; HA1K 1939.

Iceland. Ríkisútvarpid (Iceland State Broadcasting Svc.) 1935, 1943.

India. All India Radio 1938, **1938**, 1942, 1944, 1945; Indian Broadcasting Co. 1930; Indian Broadcasting Svc. 1930, 1938; Kingsway 1944; VUB Bombay 1930, 1934, 1938, **1938**, 1945; VUC Calcutta 1930, 1933, 1938, 1942, 1945; VUD Delhi 1938, 1942, 1944, 1945; VUM Madras 1930, 1938, 1945; VUY Dacca 1942; VU2ZZ 1945; VU7MC 1937; 2GR, 7BY, 7CA 1930.

Indonesia. See Dutch East Indies.

Iran. Allied Expeditionary Stn. 1944; R. Tehran 1939, 1940, 1943.

Iraq. HNE et al. 1939, 1940; YI5KG 1939.

Ireland. R. Éireann 1939, **1941**, 1943.

Italian Somaliland. R. Mogadiscio 1938.

Italy. Allied Press Headquarters 1944; Busto Arsizio 1943; EIAR (I2RO, I3RO, etc.) 1930, 1932, 1934, **1935**, 1936, 1937, 1938, 1939, 1942, 1943, 1944; ICA 1944; Italo Radio 1934, 1938; Prato Smeraldo 1934, 1937, 1938, 1943; R. Bari 1934, 1938.

Jamaica. Cable & Wireless (West Indies) Ltd. 1944; VP5PZ 1940; VRR6 1944; ZQI 1940, 1943, 1944.

Japan. Far East(ern) Network (FEN), American Forces Radio 1945; Intl. Wireless Tel. Co. of Japan,

Ltd. 1934, 1935, 1936, 1937; Nippon Hoso Kyokai (NHK) 1928, 1935, 1936, 1939, 1940, 1941; R. Tokyo 1935, **1939**, 1941, 1942, 1943, 1944, **1944**, 1945; Yamata 1941; JOAK 1928, 1930, 1932, 1934, 1945; J1AA 1930, 1932; KU1M 1945; WVLC [see also Philippines] **1944**, 1945; WVTR 1945.

Kenya. VQ7LO 1928, 1932, 1934, 1937, **1937**, 1943, 1944.

Lebanon. R. Levant, FXE 1941.

Libya. IQN 1938.

Lithuania. LYR 1939.

Luxembourg. R. Luxembourg 1938, 1939, 1944, **1944**, 1945.

Macao. CQN, CRY9, CR8AA 1936, 1939.

Madagascar. R. Tananarive 1931, 1937, 1943, 1945.

Madeira. CT3AQ 1933.

Malaya (incl. Singapore). BBC Far Eastern Stn. 1938, 1945; BMA Radio (British Military Admin.) 1945; British Far Eastern Broadcasting Svc. 1938, 1945; British Malaya Broadcasting Corp., ZHL 1938, 1939, 1942; Malaya Broadcasting Corp., ZHP 1942, 1945; Malayan Amateur Radio Society, ZGE 1933, 1934, 1938; Penang Wireless Society, ZHJ 1934, **1934**, 1936, 1938, 1942; Radio Svc. Co., ZHI 1934, 1936, 1938; R. Shonan 1942, 1944, 1945; VS1AB 1934; VS1AD 1934.

Manchuria. Hsinking Central Broadcasting Stn. (MTCY) 1939, 1942, 1944; JDY-Voice of Manchukuo 1937; JQAK 1937, **1937**.

Martinique. R. Fort-de-France 1937; R. Martinique 1937, 1938, 1943, 1944.

Mexico, shortwave broadcast: Cadena Radio Nacional, XEUZ 1937; Cadena Rdf. "DAPP," XEXA 1936; El Buen Tono, XEBT 1934; El Eco de Michoacan, XEKW 1939; El Eco de Sotavento, XEUW 1935; El Pregonero del Pacifico, XEBM 1937; Empresa de Teléfones Ericsson, XETE 1933, **1933**; Estación Radio Cultural, XEVI 1935; La Voz del Aguila Azteca, XEJW 1937; La Voz de la America Latina, XEWW 1931, 1937; La Voz del Pacifico, XEBQ 1937; La Voz de Tampico, XETW 1937; La Voz de Veracruz, XEFT 1935; La Voz de Yucatan, XEME 1936; R. Cultural, XEWB 1937; R. Mundial, XENN 1945; R. Panamericana, XEWQ 1939; Rdf. Oaxaquena, XEAR 1941; Rdf. del Pueblo, XEDQ 1935; Rdf. de Sonora, XEBR 1945; Sal de Uvas Picot, XEHH 1945; Trans-Mexican News Agency, XDA 1931; Universidad Nacional, XEYU 1937; XBJQ 1935; XEAW 1937; XEBF 1937; XEBR 1937; XECC 1942; XECR 1935, 1936; XECU 1937; XECW 1935; XEJG 1942; XEQQ 1939; XERQ 1942, 1943; XETA 1937; XETF 1935; XETM 1937; XETT 1942; XEW 1935; XEWI 1936; X26A 1931.

_____, **standard broadcast:** XEAL 1933; XEB 1934; XEBH 1937; XEBL 1937; XED 1935; XEFC 1936; XEFO 1937; XEJB 1942; XEP 1931; XEPW 1937; XEQ 1939; XERH 1945; XET 1937; XEU 1935.

_____, **utility:** XDC 1934.

Monaco. R. Monte Carlo 1945.

Morocco. Radio Maroc 1928, 1931, 1933, 1934, 1940, 1942, 1943, 1944.

Mozambique. Grêmio dos Radiofilos da Colonia de Mozambique, CR7AA 1934, 1937; R. Cl. de Mozambique 1939, 1944, 1945.

Netherlands. Herrijzend Nederland 1945; Kootwijk, Voice of Holland 1931, 1936; PCGG 1926; PCJJ, PCJ 1926, 1927, **1927**, 1928, 1929, 1931, 1932, 1934, 1937, **1937**, 1945; PCLL 1928, 1919; PHI (PHOHI) 1927, **1927**, 1928, 1929, 1930, 1932, 1934, 1935, 1936; R. Oranje 1940.

New Caledonia. R. Noumea 1938, 1943, 1944; R. Pacifique 1940; WVUS 1944.

New Zealand. National Broadcasting Svc. 1945; New Zealand Broadcasting Svc. 1945; ZLT 1944; ZMBJ TSS *Awatea* 1937; 2AZ 1944; 2YA 1930, 1944; 2ZW, 2ZX, 3AU, 3ZC 1944; 4YA 1930.

Newfoundland. VONF, VONG, VONH 1939.

Nicaragua. "Alma Nica" 1937; Ecos del Caribe 1940; La Voz del Aire 1940; La Voz de la America Central 1940; La Voz de Boaca 1945; La Voz de los Lagos 1935, 1943; La Voz del Mombacho 1940; La Voz de Nicaragua 1934, **1934**; La Voz del Pacifico 1936; La Voz de la Sultana 1940; La Voz del Tropico 1945; R. Masaya 1945; Radioemisora Rubén Dario 1935; Radiotransmisora de la Casa Presidencial 1936; Rdf. "Bayer" 1935; Rdf. YN3DG, YNDG 1938, 1939.

Niger. Niamey 1942.

Norway. R. Norway, Norsk Riksringkasting 1939, **1939**, 1940, 1942, 1945; LKJ1 Jeløy 1934, 1938, 1939, **1939**; LLS Trømso 1939.

Palau. JRAK 1941

Palestine. British Mediterranean Stn. 1944, **1944**; Kol Israel 1940; Kol Jerusalem 1940; Palestine Broadcasting Svc. 1940; Sharq al Adna (Near East Arab Broadcasting Station) 1944; JCKW (FBS) 1943, 1944.

Panama. Em. Ron Dalley 1938, 1940, 1943; Estación Rdf. Miramar 1935; Las Ondas del Baru 1937;

La Voz de Colón 1935, 1936; La Voz del Interior 1937; La Voz de Panama 1935, **1935**; La Voz de la Victor 1936, 1943; Radio-Teatro Estrella de Panama 1935, 1938, 1943; Rdf. Panamericana 1937.

Paraguay. R. Cultura 1937, 1939; R. Encarnación 1943; R. Guarani 1942; R. Nacional 1937, 1938; R. Panamerica 1942; Rdf. de la Teleco Paraguaya 1937, 1942.

Peru. R. America 1943; R. Arequipa 1936; R. Colcochea 1936, 1937, 1945; R. Continental 1941; R. Cuzco 1936; R. Delcar 1937; R. Dusa, Difusora Universal-La Voz del Peru 1934, 1937; R. Grellaud 1937; R. Huancayo 1936; R. Huanuco 1941; R. Internacional 1935, 1937, 1939; R. Lima 1941; R. Mundial 1943; R. Nacional del Peru 1937, 1939, 1940, 1942; R. Rancho Grande de la Hacienda Chiclin 1938; R. Record 1937; R. Universal 1936, 1937; R. Victoria 1945; OAX1A 1937; OAX4B 1935; OAX4G 1935.

Philippines. KA1XR 1929, 1930; KAZ 1936; KBD 1936; KZEG 1939; KZFM 1945; KZIB 1939; KZND 1941; KZRC 1939; KZRF, R. Filipinas 1939; KZRH, Voice of the Philippines 1939, 1942, 1944; KZRM, R. Manila 1929, 1936, 1937, 1939, 1944; PIAM 1944; PIRN 1944, 1945; VOA Malolos 1945; "Voice of Freedom" 1943, 1944; WVLC [see also Japan] 1944, **1944**.

Pitcairn Is. "PITC," VR6A, VR6AY 1938, **1938**.

Poland. Polskie Radio Warsaw 1931, 1935; R. Polskie 1940; SPW, SP19 et al. 1935, 1937, **1937**.

Portugal. Em. Nacional 1935, 1936, 1937, 1938, **1938**, 1941, 1943; R. Colonial 1931, 1932, 1933, 1934, 1935, 1937; R. Cl. Português 1934, 1935, **1935**, 1936, 1937, 1945; R. Renascença-Em. Catolica Portuguesa 1937, 1945.

Reunion. R. St. Denis 1940; FR8VX 1937.

Rhodesia, No. No. Rhodesian Broadcasting Stn., ZQP 1941.

Rhodesia, So. Bulawayo 1935; Salisbury 1935.

Rumania. Bucharest Polytechnic School 1939; Electro-Technical Inst. 1930; R. Bucharest 1939, 1942, 3324; R. Experimental 1939.

St. Kitts. Caribbean Broadcasting Svc. 1938; ICA Radio Sales & Svc. Laboratories 1938; VP2LO, ZIZ 1938.

Saipan. KSAI 1944, 1945.

Sarawak. VQF 1940.

Singapore. See Malaya.

South Africa. African Broadcasting Co. Ltd. 1931, 1934; So. African Broadcasting Corp. (SABC) 1937; SABC Durban 1937, 1940; SABC Johannesburg 1940; SABC Klipheuvel 1937, 1940; SABC Maraisburg 1937; SABC Pretoria 1940; SABC Roberts Heights 1937, **1937**; "JB" 1925.

Spain. EAN 1931; EAQ, Transradio Española 1931, 1932, 1934, 1935, 1936, 1937; EAQ No. 2, EAR, Voice of Republican Spain, La Voz de Libertad, la Voz de Madrid, La Voz de España; 1937, **1937**, 1942; EAR 1929; EARR 1937; EAR110, Madrid 1933; ECN1 1937; EHZ 1936; FET1, Valladolid 1937, 1938; FET5, Burgos 1938; FET15, R. Córdoba 1943; FET22, R. Falange 1943; Barcelona Radio Club, EAJ25 1933; Falange Española Tradicional 1936; Gobierno Civil de Malaga **1938**; PSU1 (Partit Socialista Unifacat de Cataluña) 1937; R. España 1938; R. España, Bilbao 1938; R. Falange, EAJ47 1943; R. Guardia Civil 1936; R. Malaga, EAJ9 1938, 1941, **1941**, 1945; R. Mediterraneo, EAJ3 1941, 1943; R. Nacional "AZ" 1938; R. Nacional de España 1936, 1937, 1938, 1939, 1942, 1945; "R. POUM," ECP2 (Partido Obrero de Unificación Marxista) 1937; R. Requeté 1936, 1937; R. Requeté, Bilbao, EAJ8 1937; R. Requeté de Guipuzcoa, San Sebastian, EAJ8 1937, 1938; R. Requeté, Malaga 1937; R. Requeté, Santander 1937; R. Requeté, Vitoria, RR6 1938; R. SEU, EDV10 1945, **1945**; Rdf. Ibero-Americana 1932; Union Radio, EAJ1 1937.

Spanish Morocco. R. Tetuan 1936; EA9AA 1942; EA9AH 1936, **1937**; EA9AI **1936**; EA9BJ 1937.

Sudan, Anglo-Egyptian. Sudan Broadcasting Svc., R. Omdurman 1945.

Sweden. Motala, Motala Rundsradiostation 1929, 1937; SM5SX, Royal Tech. Univ. 1936, **1936**, 1937; Sveriges Radiotjänst 1944.

Switzerland. Radio Nations (League of Nations) 1929, 1932, 1934, 1935, 1938, 1940; Radio-Suisse 1932, 1939; Schweizerische Rundspruch-Gesellschaft, Swiss Broadcasting Corp. 1935, 1937, 1939, 1940; Schweizerische Telegraph Verwaltung 1938; Swiss Shortwave Svc. 1940, 1941, 1945; Prangins 1939; Schwarzenburg 1939.

Syria. Damascus 1941.

Tahiti. R. Océania 1936, 1943; R. Tahiti 1936.

Taiwan. Taihoku (Taipei) 1936; JFAK 1937; JIB 1937.

Tangier. R. Falange del Exterior 1941.

Thailand. Bangkok Broadcasting Stn. 1939; Experimental Radio Broadcasting Stn. HS8PJ 1936, **1936**, 1938; Radio Bangkok 1932; Thai Natl. Broadcasting Stn. 1942; HSP 1936; HSPP 1939; HS1BJ 1938; HS1PJ, HS2PJ, HS4PJ 1929, 1936.

Trinidad. VP4TC 1935.

Tunisia. R. Tunis 1940.

Turkey. Turkish Broadcasting Sys., R. Ankara 1938, 1945.

United Kingdom. American Broadcasting Station in Europe (ABSIE) 1944, 1945; American Forces Network 1943; BBC 1923, 1924, 1925, 1926, 1927, 1928, 1929, 1932, **1932**, 1933, 1934, 1935, 1936, 1937, 1938, 1939, 1940, 1941, 1942, 1943, 1944, 1945; Chelmsford 1925, 1926, 1927, 1932; Clevedon 1940, 1945; Daventry 1926, 1927, 1932, 1936, 1937, 1940; Forces Broadcasting Svc. (FBS) 1943, 1944; G2NM 1927, **1927**; G5SW 1927, 1928, 1929, 1930, 1931, 1932, 1935; G6RX 1934; "Honneur et Patrie" 1940; "Ici la France" 1940; International Broadcasting Co. 1932; Lisnagarvey 1941; R. Belgique 1940; R. Oranje 1940; R. Polskie 1940; Rampisham 1941; Rugby Radio 1934, 1937; Skelton 1943; Start Point 1940, 1944; Woofferton 1943, 1944, 1945; 2AC 1923, 1924; 2LO 1925, **1925,** 1927, **1927**; 2MT, 2WP, 2ZY, 1927; 5XX 1925, **1925,** 1926.

United States, shortwave broadcast: American Forces Network (AFN) 1943; Armed Forces Radio Svc. (AFRS) 1943, 1944, 1945; Mackay Radio & Telegraph Co. 1941, 1942, 1943; Voice of America (VOA) 1927, 1941, 1942, **1942,** 1944, 1945; KCBA 1943, 1944; KCBF 1943, 1944; KCBR 1943, 1945; KDPM 1923, **1923**; KFKX 1923, **1923,** 1924, 1925, 1926, 1927; KGEI 1939, 1940, 1941, 1942, 1943, 1944; KGEX 1943, 1944; KNBA 1943, 1945; KNBC 1943, 1945; KNBI 1943, 1945; KNBX 1943, 1945; KWID 1941, 1942, **1942,** 1943, 1944; KWIX 1943, 1944; WBKM 1939; WBOS 1939, 1940, 1941, 1942; WCAB 1939, 1941; WCAI 1939; WCBI 1939; WCBN 1943, 1944; WCBX 1939, 1940, 1941, 1942, 1943, 1944; WCDA 1941, 1943; WCRC 1941, 1942, 1943; WCDA 1942; WDJM 1939, 1940; WGEA 1939, 1940, 1942, 1943; WGEO 1939, 1940, 1941, 1942, 1943; WGEU 1939; WLWK 1943, 1943, 1944; WLWL 1943, 1944; WLWO 1939, 1940, 1942, 1943, 1944, 1945; WLWR 1943, 1944; WLWS 1943, 1944; WLWU 1939; WNBI 1939, 1941, 1942, 1943; WNRA 1943, 1944; WNRE 1943, 1945; WNRI 1943, 1944; WNRX 1943, 1944; WOOC 1943, 1944; WOOW 1943, 1944; WPIT 1939, 1940; WRCA 1939, 1941, **1941,** 1942, 1943; WRUA 1943; WRUL 1927, 1936, 1939, 1940, 1941, 1942, 1943, 1945; WRUS 1943; WRUW 1939, 1942; WSLA 1939; WSLR 1939; W1XAL 1931, 1933, 1934, **1934,** 1935, 1936, 1937, 1938, 1939, 1940; W1XAR 1939; W1XAZ 1924, 1925, 1930, 1932, **1932,** 1933, 1934, 1935; W1XK 1935, 1936, 1937, 1939; W2XAD & W2XAF et al. 1924, 1925, 1926, 1927, 1928, **1928,** 1929, 1930, **1930,** 1931, 1932, **1932,** 1933, 1934, 1935, 1936, 1937, 1938, 1939; W2XAL 1927, 1929, **1929,** 1930, 1931; W2XE 1928, 1929, 1930, 1932, 1933, 1934, 1935, 1936, 1937, 1938, 1939, 1941; W2XHI 1935; W3XAL 1931, 1933, 1935, 1936, 1937, 1938, 1939; W3XAU (CBS) 1930, **1930,** 1933, 1935, 1936, 1937, 1938, 1939, 1941; W3XL (NBC) 1927, 1931, 1933, 1935, 1936, 1938, 1939; W4XB 1932, 1935, 1936, 1938, 1939; W6XBE 1939; W6XN 1929, **1929;** W8XAL 1924, 1927, 1928, 1929, 1930, 1931, 1932, 1934, 1935, 1936, 1939; W8XK 1923, 1924, 1927, 1928, 1929, 1930, 1931, 1932, 1933, 1934, 1936, 1937, 1939, 1940; W9XA 1930; W9XAA 1929, 1930, 1931, 1933, 1935, 1936, 1939; W9XBS 1935; W9XF 1929, 1930, 1932, 1933, 1935, 1936, 1938; 2XAR 1925; 2XBA 1927; 2XI 1924; 3XM 1928; 8XAA 1924; 8XAO 1927; 8XS 1923, 1924; 9XU 1927.

_____, **amateur:** W2AG 1934; W2USA 193; W6GRL 1942; W9USA 1934; 1HX 1923; 1MO 1923; 1RD 1923; 1XA 1923;; 1XAM 1923, 1925; 1XAO 1925, **1925;** 1XM 1923; 8ZZ 1923; 9ZN 1923; 9ZT 1923.

_____ **apex, ultra-high:** W1XEH 1936; W1XER 1938; W1XKA 1936; W1XKB 1938; W2XDV 1935; W2XJI 1938, 1940; W3XES 1937; W3XEY 1936; W3XKA 1936, **1936;** W4XBW 1937; W4XCA 1936; W5XAU 1937; W6XKG 1936, 1937, 1939; W6XRE 1938; W8XAI 1936; W8XH 1934; W8XKA 1936; W8XNU 1938; W8XWJ 1936, 1937, 1938; W9XAZ 1935, **1935,** 1937; W9XJL 1937; W9XOK 1936, 1937; W9XPD 1935; W9XUP 1938.

_____ **FM:** W1XOJ 1939; W2XF 1934; W2XMN 1934, 1939; W2XOR 1940.

_____ **high fidelity:** KPMC 1934; KXBY 1934; WBRY 1934; WQXR 1934; W1XBS 1934; W2XR 1934; W6XAI 1934; W9XBY 1934.

_____ **military:** NAA 1923, 1929, 1930, 1931; NERK 1924; NKF 1923; NRRL 1923; NSS 1930, 1931; WMEF 1937; W10XDA 1934.

_____ **standard broadcast:** KDKA 1923, **1923,** 1924, **1924,** 1925, 1926, 1927, 1928, 1929, 1930, 1931, 1932, 1934, 1936; KFI 1925, 1927, 1938; KFSO 1942; KGFJ 1936, 1938; KGO 1923, 1924, 1929, 1930, 1939; KMA 1925; KOA 1925, 1930; KOIL 1927, 1928; KPO 1939, 1941; KSTP 1938; KYW 1923, 1924, 1925, 1927, 1936; WAAM 1927, 1929 n.121; WABC 1928, 1929, 1930, 1931, 1932; WAHG 1928; WARC 1927; WBEN 1934; WBZ 1923, 1924, 1925, 1930, 1934, 1936, 1940; WBZA 1924, 1925, 1930, 1934, 1938; WCFL 1929, 1930; WEAF 1923, 1928, 1930, 1931, 1933, 1940, 1941; WEEI 1931; WENR 1929; WEW 1936; WFBR 1936; WGAR 1944; WGY 1924, 1925, 1926, 1927, 1928, 1929, 1931, 1932; WHAM 1936; WHAZ 1925; WHK 1927; WIOD 1932; WJAZ 1925; WJR 1927; WJZ 1923, 1924, 1925, 1926, 1928, 1930, 1931, 1937; WKAQ 1939; WLW 1924, 1927, 1928, 1929, 1934, 1938, 1939, 1940; WMC 1936; WMH 1924; WNAC 1923, 1938; WNEL 1939; WNYC 1936; WOC 1925; WOR 1930, 1935, 1938, 1940; WOWO 1927, 1928; WQXR 1934; WRAH 1927; WRNY

1927, 1929; WSAI 1928; WSLA 1939; WSLR 1939; WTAG 1944; WTIC 1936; WTMJ 1935; WWJ 1927, 1936; W8XO 1934.

_____ **television:** W1XAU 1931; W1XAV 1931.

_____ **utility:** AT&T, Dixon, CA 1934, 1942; AT&T, Hialeah, FL 1934; AT&T, Lawrenceville, NJ 1934, 1942; AT&T, Ocean Gate, NJ 1934, 1942; Press Wireless 1935, 1940, 1942, 1943; RCA, Bolinas, CA 1934, 1939, 1942; RCA, Kahuku, HI 1934, 1935, 1938, 1942; RCA, Koko Head, HI 1934; RCA, New Brunswick, NJ 1934; RCA, Point Reyes, CA 1934; RCA, Rocky Point (LI), NY 1934, 1936, 1939; KEE 1942; KEZ 1942; KFY 1934; KFZ 1934, 1935; KILS 1934; KJE8, KJE9, KJN8 1942; KJTY 1934, 1935; KKW 1942; KNRA 1934; KRCA 1942; KRCQ 1942; KROJ 1943, 1944, **1944**; KROU 1943; WAP 1925; WCB 1942; WCX 1942; WDM 1942; WEF 1936; WHEW 1934; WJQ 1942; WJS 1924; WNP 1925; WWV 1923, 1931, 1932, 1935, 1940, 1943, 1945; W2XBJ 1936; W2XGB 1935; W9XAM 1931; W10XEP 1937; W10XFH 1935; W10XFN 1935; 1XAO 1925; 2WE 1923; 2WM 1923, 2XAO 1928; 6XBM 1923; 9XN 1925.

Uruguay. El Espectador 1938; R. Continental 1937; R. Real de San Carlos 1937, 1943; R. Sport 1938; Servicio Oficial de Difusión Radio Eléctrica (SODRE) 1938, 1939.

U.S.S.R. Alma Ata 1934; Khabarovsk 1928, 1930, 1932, 1935, **1935**, 1937, 1939; Komsomolsk 1942, 1944, 1945; Kuibishev 1942; Leningrad 1932, 1945; Minsk 1932; Moscow 1932, 1934, 1935, 1939, 1940, 1941, 1942, 1945; Petropavlovsk 1945; Sverdlovsk 1942; Tashkent 1934; Tiflis (Tbilisi) 1945.

Vatican. Vatican Radio 1931, 1937.

Venezuela. Broadcasting Caracas 1931, **1931**, 1934, 1935; Broadcasting Nacional 1931; Ecos del Avila 1935; Ecos del Caribe 1934, 1936; Ecos del Llano 1936; Ecos del Orinoco 1936, 1937, 1938, 1939; Ecos del Zulia 1936, 1937, 1939; Em. Vargas 1939; Em. 24 de Julio 1936; Estudios Universo 1938, 1939; La Voz de Anzoategui 1940; La Voz de Aragua 1936, 1937, 1939; La Voz de Carabobo 1934, **1934**, 1937, 1939; La Voz de la Esfera 1937, 1939, 1940; La Voz de la Fe 1939, 1940; La Voz de Lara 1935, 1936, 1937, 1938, 1939; La Voz del Lago 1932; La Voz del Llano 1939; La Voz de la Philco 1936, 1937, 1939; La Voz de la Sierra 1941; La Voz del Tachira 1935, 1936, 1937, 1938, 1939; La Voz de Venezuela 1939; Ondas del Lago 1936, 1937, 1939; Ondas Populares 1937, 1939; R. America 1940; R. Barquisimeto 1938, 1939; R. Bolivar 1937, 1939; R. Caracas 1935, 1937, 1939; R. Continente 1940; R. Coro 1937, 1939; R. Falcón 1939; R. Maracaibo 1938; R. Maracay 1942; R. Popular 1937, 1939; R. Puerto Cabello 1938, 1939, 1940; R. Trujillo 1939, 1940; R. Turmerito 1939; R. Valencia 1936, 1937, 1939; R. Valera 1936, 1937, 1939; Rdf. Maracaibo 1936, 1937, 1939; Rdf. Venezuela 1933, 1937, 1938, 1939; Sociedad Anónima de Radio 1934; YVQ 1934, 1936.

Yugoslavia. Belgrade Short-Wave Stn. 1936, 1939, 1941; R. Belgrade 1942; R. Bratislava 1941.

Clandestine

Azad Moslem Radio (Free Moslem Radio) 1942; Brazzaville II 1940; Christian Peace Movement 1941; Croatian Freedom Stn. 1942; Deutscher Freiheitsender 1937; Deutscher Kurzwellensender Atlantik (R. Atlantik) 1943, 1944, 1945; Deutscher Volksender 1942; France Libre d'Outre Mer 1941; Frihedssenderen 1941; Gustav Siegfried Eins 1941, 1943; Jerry's Front Radio 1944; La Voix de la Pais 1940; National Congress Radio 1942; New British Broadcasting Stn. 1940; Norwegian Freedom Stn. 1941; Poste du Réveil de la France 1940; R. Caledonia 1941; R. Debunk 1942; R. Denmark 1941; R. España Independiente 1936; R. Fighting France 1944; R. Inconnue 1941; R. Libertà 1941; R. Metropole 1942; R. 1212 1944; R. Travail 1941; Rumanian Freedom Stn. 1942; Sender der Deutschen Freiheitspartei 1938; Sender der Europäischen Revolution 1941; Soldatensender Calais, Soldatensender West 1943, 1945; Suomen Vapaus Radio 1942; Voice of Free India, Free India Radio, Azad Hind Radio 1942, 1943, 1944; Wehrmachtsender Nord 1942; Worker's Challenge 1939; Yugoslav Freedom Stn. 1942.

Maritime

FNSK SS *Normandie* 1935; KFAH *Director II* 1940; GBTT *Queen Mary* 1936; VDM *Arctic* 1924.

Chapter Notes

Chapter 1

1. "Radio Currents" [editorial], *Radio Broadcast*, May 1922, p. 1.

2. These first one-way "broadcasts" from Brant Rock, Massachusetts, consisted of holiday greetings, vocalizing, and instrumental music, and were intended for anyone who might pick them up. Fessenden telegraphed advance notice of his plans to radio operators of U.S. Navy vessels and United Fruit Company ships that possessed suitable receiving equipment. He had done similar voice-and-music experimental transmissions, albeit on a point-to-point basis, as early as 1900. These are referenced in early literature, and in events memorialized by physical markers. One such transmission, made just a few days before Christmas Eve 1906, was confirmed by witnesses.

While the Christmas and New Year's Eve events have become an accepted part of radio history, the earlier transmissions are seldom mentioned. Most would consider them close enough to "broadcasting" to confirm Fessenden's place as "first" voice broadcaster in any event. However, respected radio historians have been unable to find a single reference to the Christmas and New Year's broadcasts in any literature (including Fessenden's own considerable writings), or in relevant archives, prior to 1928, a full 22 years after the events. Even then they received but perfunctory mention in a history of early broadcasting. Fessenden mentioned the broadcasts in a letter written four years later, and a few other references in various publications followed. The "Eves" story gained wide acceptance only after publication of Mrs. Fessenden's 1940 biography of her husband, which quotes a detailed but otherwise unidentified description of the events that was said to have been written by him. Donna L. Halper and Christopher H. Sterling, "Fessenden's Christmas Eve Broadcast: Reconsidering an Historic Event," *AWA Review,* Vol. 19 (2006), p. 119; James E. O'Neal, "Fessenden: World's First Broadcaster?" *Radio World,* October 25, 2006, http://www.rwonline.com/article/258; Donna L. Halper, "In Search of the Truth About Fessenden," *Radio World,* February 14, 2007, http://www.rwonline.com/article/922; and James E. O'Neal, "Fessenden — The Next Chapter," *Radio World,* December 23, 2008, http://www.rwonline.com/article/72046. See also Helen M. Fessenden, *Fessenden — Builder of Tomorrows* (New York, NY: Coward-McCann, 1940), pp. 151–155.

3. For opposing views, see *(pro)* Bartholomew Lee, "Marconi's Transatlantic Triumph — A Skip Into History," *AWA Review,* Vol. 13 (2000), p. 81; Bartholemew Lee, Joe Craig and Keith Matthew, "The Marconi Beacon Experiment of 2006–07," *AWA Review,* Vol. 21 (2008), p. 1; Crawford MacKeand, "A Mountain of Water," *AWA Review,* Vol. 21 (2008), p. 23; and Steve Nichols, "GB3SSS — Marconi's Transatlantic Leap Revisited," *QST,* December 2007, p. 40; and *(con)* Peter R. Jensen, *In Marconi's Footsteps, 1894 to 1920: Early Radio* (Kenthurst, NSW, Australia: Kangaroo Press, 1994), pp. 40–43 ("Marconi hearing any signal at all has to be seen as either remarkably good fortune and the result of freakish behaviour of the ionosphere, or an exercise in self-deception or deliberate fraud"); John S. Belrose, "Fessenden and Marconi: Their Differing Technologies and Transatlantic Experiments During the First Decade of this Century" (1995), http://www.ieee.ca/millennium/radio/radio_differences. html; John S. Belrose, "A Radioscientist's Reaction to Marconi's First Transatlantic Wireless Experiment — Revisited" (2001), http://www.radiocom.net/Fessenden/Marconi_Reprint.pdf; and John S. Belrose, "Marconi's First Transatlantic Experiment," *QST,* March 2008, p. 53 ("Technical Correspondence").

4. The claims that Nathan B. Stubblefield of Murray, Kentucky, "invented radio" in 1892 are commonly dismissed because, while he was able to transmit voice and music without wires over distances of probably less than three miles, his was an induction system that did not produce the continuous waves needed for reliable long range communication. Elliot N. Sivowitch, "A Technological Survey of Broadcasting's 'Pre-History,' 1876–1920," *Journal of Broadcasting,* Vol. XV, No. 1 (Winter 1970–71), p. 1; Thomas W. Hoffer, "Nathan B. Stubblefield and His Wireless Telephone," *Journal of Broadcasting,* Vol. XV, No. 3 (Summer 1971), p. 317. For the full story, including how the Stubblefield legend developed, see Bob Lochte, *Kentucky Farmer Invents Wireless Telephone! But Was It Radio?* (Murray, KY: All About Wireless, 2001).

5. But Massachusetts amateur Irving Vermilya made a convincing claim to the title. See "Who's Who in Amateur Wireless," *QST,* February 1920, p. 25; "1HAA, Marion, Mass.," *QST,* October 1920, p. 35; "Amateur Number One," Part I, *QST,* February 1917, p. 8; Part II, *QST,* March 1917, p. 10; and Paul W. Stiles, "No. 1 Ham," *Radio News,* May 1938, p. 31.

6. Clinton B. DeSoto, *200 Meters and Down: The Story of Amateur Radio* (West Hartford, CT: American Radio Relay League, 1936), p. 2.

7. The early activities of the Department of Commerce in the radio field are described in J. H. Dellinger, "The Radio Work of the Department of Commerce," *QST,* June 1921, p. 18. Much of the Department's early work was decentralized and in the hands of a cadre of regional radio inspectors. To stations of all kinds, the radio inspectors were important and powerful people. See Howard S. Pyle, "Shake Hands With the 'R.I.,'" *Radio Broadcast,* December 1924, p. 289.

8. The special authorizations were the so-called Special

Amateur stations, or "Z" calls, e.g. 1ZE, generally available only to more experienced operators.

9. The history of amateur radio licensing is described in Neil D. Friedman, "83 Years of U.S. Amateur Licensing," *AWA Review,* Vol. 9 (1995), p. 225. The ins and outs of amateur frequency allocations, and mandatory quiet hours, in 1923 are described in "Amateur Regulations" [editorial], *QST,* June 1923, p. 35; "The Status of the Amateur" [editorial], *QST,* July 1923, p. 35; and "The New Amateur Regulations," *QST,* August 1923, p. 13.

10. Pierre H. Boucheron, "Two Hundred Meters and What it Means," *Radio Amateur News,* April 1920, p. 548.

11. A Bureau of Standards study of two broadcast stations undertaken during a seven-month period in 1922–23 found that, on average, about a third of the obstacles to reception were from interference from other broadcast stations, a third from fading and static, and only 6% from amateurs. "Concerning Amateur Interference With Broadcast Reception," *QST,* June 1923, p. 33.

12. Hams had already used "quiet hours" to facilitate amateur DXing. See "Quiet Hours for Listening for DX," *QST,* August 1921, p. 18.

13. "What the Department of Commerce Thinks of Our A.R.R.L. Voluntary Lid," *QST,* March 1923, p. 19. See also *supra* note 9.

14. Although there was at least one claimed reception, later disproved, of a New York station heard in Scotland in October 1920, and, around the same time, a well-regarded ham's claimed reception of his New York station aboard one ship 3,200 miles distant (Gibraltar) and another off Pernambuco, Brazil, the first confirmed transatlantic reception was in December 1921 (U.S. stations heard in Great Britain). A highly-structured, well-planned event, it is described in detail in three articles in the February 1922 issue of *QST:* "The Story of the Transatlantics," p. 7; Paul F. Godley, "The Official Report of the Second Transatlantic Tests," p. 14; and George E. Burghard, "Station 1BCG," p. 29; and also in Robert C. Higgy, "The Successful Transatlantic Stations," *QST,* March 1922, p. 11; Philip R. Coursey, "Report on Receptions By British Amateurs in the Transatlantic Tests, December, 1921," *QST,* May 1922, p. 23; and *The Story of the First Trans-Atlantic Short Wave Message — Proceedings of the Radio Club of America, Inc.—1BCG Commemorative Issue* (New York: Radio Club of America, October 1950). The reference to shortwave is to 200 meters, or 1500 kc., not to the short-wave range as it is known today (3–30 mc.). The Scotland story is related in "2QR Heard in Scotland?" *QST,* December 1920, p. 21, and followed up in *QST,* June 1921, p. 55, and "2QR's Transatlantic Claim Disproved," *QST,* January 1922, p. 8. For the Gibraltar story, see "2RK, Brooklyn," *QST,* February 1921, p. 42, followed up in *QST,* June 1921, p. 44 (2RK closed due to operating illegalities), and "Who's Who In Amateur Wireless," *QST,* September 1921, p. 40.

15. "Trans-Pacific Amateur Reception," *QST,* January 1923, p. 24; "Pacific Completely Bridged By Amateur Sigs.," *QST,* February 1923, p. 27; "Across the Pacific Again," *QST,* March 1923, p. 11; "The Passing of the Pacific," *QST,* August 1923, p. 7.

16. Page 31.

17. Albert Hoyt Taylor, *Radio Reminiscences: A Half Century* (Washington, DC: Naval Research Laboratory, 1948 [reprinted in 1960]), Ch. IX, pp. 157–161.

18. "The New York Radio Central Station," *QST,* August 1920, p. 14; Pierre Boucheron, "President Harding Opens the World's Largest and Most Powerful Radio Station," *Radio News,* December 1921, p. 480; Pierre Boucheron, "Radio Central," *QST,* June 1922, p. 26; Carl Dreher, "What Goes On at a Transatlantic Station," *Radio Broadcast,* April 1923, p. 464; Fred J. Turner, "'Radio Central—Conqueror of Time and Distance," *Radio Broadcast,* November 1925, p. 41; "QST Visits Riverhead and Rocky Point," *QST,* September 1940, p. 8; Christopher Bacon, "Commemorating the 75th Anniversary of Radio Central," *AWA Review,* Vol. 10 (1996), p. 151.

19. Edgar H. Felix, "How New York Talks to London," *Radio Broadcast,* June 1926, p. 111. For a 1968 and 1973 interview with Beverage and H. O. Peterson about River Head and other topics of radio history, see "Oral History: Harold H. Beverage and H. O. Peterson," http://www.ieeeghn.org/wiki/index.php/Oral-History:Harold_H._Beverage_and_H._O._Peterson.

20. Robert Hertzberg, "A Visit to 'Radio Central,'" *Radio News,* August 1928, p. 104.

21. "Behind the Scenes of a S.-W. Rebroadcast from Europe," *Short Wave & Television,* May 1938, p. 10.

22. Bacon, *supra* note 18 at p. 180. Riverhead was closed in 1975, and the last message from Rocky Point was sent in 1978. Equipment and antennas were transferred or demolished. The site would be heavily vandalized and eventually bulldozed. It is now owned by the State of New York.

23. Although today "broadcasting" commonly means wireless transmission, there was substantial progress in "wired broadcasting" long before the arrival of wireless. It never caught on in the United States, but its history in Europe can be traced as far back as 1880. David L. Woods, "Semantics Versus the 'First' Broadcasting Station," *Journal of Broadcasting,* Vol. XI, No. 3 (Summer 1967), p. 199; Elliott Sivowitch, "Musical Broadcasting in the 19th Century," *Audio,* June 1967, p. 19. See also "The 19th Century iPhone," about the Electrophone, http://news.bbc.co.uk/2/hi/technology/8668311.stm.

24. Eric P. Wenaas, *Radiola: The Golden Age of RCA, 1919–1929* (Chandler, AZ: Sonoran, 2007), pp. 68–71 ("[I]t is much more probable that Conrad actually used phonograph records to test his radio designs throughout much of the war." P. 71)

25. Charles Gilbert, "Earlier Days in Radiophone Broadcasting," *Radio News,* October 1922, p. 621.

26. The early days of San Francisco broadcasting are chronicled in John F. Schneider, "Early Broadcasting in the San Francisco Bay Area—Stations That Didn't Survive, 1920–25," http://www.theradiohistorian.org/early.htm. See also "The California Theatre Radio Station," *Radio News,* June 1921, p. 857.

27. Of the seven "radiophone" stations listed in the first of the "With Our Radiophone Listeners" columns in *QST* (December 1921), only three—KDKA, WBZ and WJZ—were licensed broadcasters. The rest were experimental stations—1XE in Medford Hillside, Massachusetts, 6XC and 6XG in San Francisco, and 6XAK in Los Angeles.

28. Louise Benjamin, "In Search of the Sarnoff 'Radio Music Box' Memo: Separating Myth From Reality," *Journal of Broadcasting and Electronic Media,* Vol. 38, No. 3 (Summer 1993), p. 325; Louise Benjamin, "In Search of the Sarnoff 'Radio Music Box' Memo: Nally's Reply," *Journal of Radio Studies,* Vol. 9, No. 1 (2002), p. 97.

29. *Radio Service Bulletin,* No. 69, January 2, 1923, p. 8; *QST,* March 1923, p. 58.

30. Credo Fitch Harris, *Microphone Memoirs* (Indianapolis, IN: Bobbs-Merrill, 1937), pp. 24–25.

31. For some powerful images from the early days of listening and transmitting, see James E. O'Neal, "A Portal into Radio's Past: Francis A. Hart and His Radio Log" [1906–1909], *AWA Review,* Vol. 20 (2007), p. 169; Daniel C. McCoy, "Amateur Radio in the New York City Area Pre-WW I" [1906–1915], *AWA Review,* Vol. 6 (1991), p. 115; and Lloyd Espenschied, "An Early Chapter in Radio-Electronics" [1907], *Old Timer's Bulletin,* May 1990, p. 12. Other reminiscences include Irving Vermilya, "Amateur Number One," *supra* note 5; Paul Oard, "The Passing of the 'Old Days,'" *QST,* April 1917, p. 30; Austin C. Lescarboura, "Pioneer Days in Radio Telephony," *Radio Amateur News,* May 1920, p. 632; George E. Burghard, "Eighteen Years of Amateur Radio," *Radio Broadcast,* August 1923, p. 290; "Fans of Yesterday," *Radio News,* March 1924, p. 1228; "Jes' Reminiscing," *QST,* December 1923, p. 47; Robert H. Marriott, "'As It Was in the Beginning,'" *Radio Broadcast,* May 1924, p. 51; Charles

Magee Adams, "'Sure, Them Was the Happy Days,'" *Radio News*, July 1928, p. 8; E. T. Jones, "Back in the Days of Crashing Spark-Gaps," *Radio & Television*, October 1938, p. 330; and Dwight A. Myer, "Up from a Bread-Board — KDKA's Tale," *Broadcasting*, November 24, 1941, p. 24.

32. "The Radiotrola" [editorial], *Radio News*, December 1921, p. 479.

33. "Radio Currents," *supra* note 1 at pp. 1–2.

34. Page 81.

35. Alfred N. Goldsmith and Austin C. Lescarboura, *This Thing Called Broadcasting* (New York: Henry Holt, 1930), pp. 309–311; see also "Broadcast Receivers: The First 10 Years," *The Old Timer's Bulletin*, December 1975, p. 16.

36. Susan J. Douglas, *Listening In: Radio and the American Imagination* (Minneapolis: University of Minnesota Press, 2004), pp. 55–82.

37. Goldsmith and Lescarboura, *supra* note 35 at pp. 309–310.

38. "The Transatlantic Broadcasting Tests and What They Proved," *Radio Broadcast*, January 1924, p. 183; "Who Heard England?" *Radio Broadcast*, February 1924, p. 341; George E. Oliver, "The Trans-Atlantic Broadcast Tests," *Radio News*, March 1924, p. 1225; Arthur H. Lynch and Willis K. Wing, "The International Radio Broadcast Test of 1924," *Radio Broadcast*, February 1925, p. 676; Willis K. Wing, "The 1926 International Radio Broadcasting Tests," *Radio Broadcast*, February 1926, p. 462; Willis K. Wing, "What Happened During the 1926 International Tests," *Radio Broadcast*, April 1926, p. 647.

39. Armstrong Perry, "The ITCH for Distance," *Radio News*, April 1923, p. 1777.

CHAPTER 2

1. Guglielmo Marconi, "Will 'Beam' Stations Revolutionize Radio?" *Radio Broadcast*, July 1925, p. 323, 330–331.

2. The technical details of 8XK are described in "8XK, Pittsburgh, PA.," *QST*, September 1920, p. 32.

3. See comments in "History of KDKA, Pittsburgh," http://jeff560.tripod.com/kdka.html.

4. "Radio Concerts" [editorial], *Radio News*, September 1920, p. 133. Gernsback was one of the leading publishers on radio, and an early commentator on the medium. See Paul O'Neil, "Barnum of the Space Age," *Life*, July 26, 1963, p. 62; "Hugo Gernsback, Founder," *Radio-Electronics*, October 1979, p. 62; Robert A. W. Lowndes, "Hugo Gernsback: A Man with Vision+," *Radio-Electronics*, August 1984, p. 73; Daniel Stashower, "A Dreamer Who Made Us Fall in Love with the Future," *Smithsonian*, August 1990, p. 44; Gil McElroy, "Remembering Hugo Gernsback," *QST*, February 1995, p. 37; Keith Massie and Stephen D. Perry, "Hugo Gernsback and Radio Magazines: An Influential Intersection in Broadcast History," *Journal of Radio Studies*, Vol. 9, No. 2 (2002), p. 264. The text of what appears to be Gernsback's autobiography, written in the 1950s, was found in 2002 and subsequently published. See Larry Steckler, ed., *Hugo Gernsback — A Man Well Ahead of His Time* (Marana, AZ: Poptronix, 2007).

5. *The Reminiscences of Donald G. Little* (New York: Oral History Research Office, Columbia University, 1984 [microfiche]), pp. 14–15.

6. S. Kruse, "Exploring 100 Meters," *QST*, March 1923, p. 12; S. Kruse, "Getting the Transmitter Down to 100 Meters," *QST*, April 1923, p. 24; "Calls Heard," *QST*, May 1923, p. 75; S. Kruse, "Getting Away From 200 Meters," *QST*, September 1923, p. 19.

7. S. Kruse, "The Bureau of Standards-ARRL Tests of Short Wave Radio Signal Fading," *QST*, November 1920, p. 5; followed up in *QST*, December 1920, p. 13; January 1921, p. 12; May 1921, p. 14; June 1921, p. 55; and August 1923, p . 29 (Part I) and September 1923, p. 23 (Part II).

8. Francis W. Dunmore, "Bureau of Standards Explores Short-Wave Region," *QST*, July 1923, p. 77.

9. Robert F. Gowan, "9ZN," *Radio News*, July 1920, p. 26; "9ZN, Chicago, Ill.," *QST*, February 1923, p. 60. Matthews co-owned the Chicago Radio Laboratory (CRL), whose popular radio receivers would be sold by Zenith Radio Corp., which was founded for that purpose in 1923 by Eugene F. McDonald, Jr., by then a CRL partner and the company's general manager. Zenith, and McDonald, would become leaders in the radio industry.

10. Francis W. Dunmore and Francis H. Engel, "Short Wave Directive Radio Transmission," *Radio News*, August 1923, p. 128.

11. "International Amateur Radio—New Zealanders Turning to Short Waves," *QST*, November 1923, p. 61.

12. "Radio Communications by the Amateurs—French Work on 45 Meters," *QST*, October 1923, p. 30.

13. Frank Conrad, "The Story of Short Waves," *Science* (New Series), Vol. 91, No. 2534 (February 9, 1940), p. 131, 132.

14. "Polarizing Radio— A Double Barreled Scheme" [editorial], *Radio News*, December 1922, p. 1049.

15. W. W. Rodgers, "Is Short-Wave Relaying a Step Toward National Broadcasting Stations?" *Radio Broadcast*, June 1923, p. 119.

16. Actually this was the date that AT&T toll broadcasting began over the company's New York City station, WBAY. Because WBAY gave poor coverage, it was closed down and its equipment moved to WEAF, a station licensed to Western Electric Co., an AT&T subsidiary, which began operating on August 16.

17. See Ludwell A. Sibley, "Program Transmission and the Early Radio Networks," *AWA Review*, Vol. 3 (1988), p. 34.

18. The WEAF stations became the NBC Red Network and the WJZ stations formed the NBC Blue Network. The Blue Network eventually became ABC, and the Red Network became the NBC Radio Network.

19. Gleason L. Archer, *Big Business and Radio* (New York: American Historical, 1939), p. 96; Eugene Lyons, *David Sarnoff* (New York: Harper and Row, 1966), p. 122; Elmer E. Bucher, *Shortwave Radio and David Sarnoff*, 1953, Pt. 25 of the 56-volume typescript, Bucher, *Radio and David Sarnoff* (Princeton, NJ: David Sarnoff Library, approx. 1942–1957), pp. 3441–3443.

20. *Big Business and Radio*, *supra* note 19 at pp. 51–52.

21. Marconi, *supra* note 1 at pp. 323–329; W. J. Baker, *A History of the Marconi Company* (New York: St. Martin's, 1971), pp. 216–225; "Marconi, With New Device, Guides Radio in Chosen Direction," *The New York Times*, June 21, 1922, p. 1.

22. According to D. G. Little and F. Falknor, "Radio KFKX, Repeating Station at Hastings," *Radio Journal*, March 1924, p. 111, tests began in September 1922. Frank Conrad says the date was October 27, 1922; see Frank Conrad, "Short-Wave Radio Broadcasting," *Proceedings of the Institute of Radio Engineers*, Vol. 12, No. 6 (December 1924), p. 723, 728. In his Ph.D. dissertation, Sidel gives the date as March 4, 1923, a date supported by a seemingly authoritative albeit anonymous and undated paper about Westinghouse shortwave. Michael Kent Sidel, *A Historical Analysis of American Short Wave Broadcasting, 1916–1942*, Ph.D. dissertation (Evanston, IL: Northwestern University, Speech, 1976), p. 71. The Westinghouse paper is *History of Short Wave Broadcasting*, p. 4; see bibliography for details.

23. Conrad, "Short-Wave Radio Broadcasting," *supra* note 22 at pp. 736–737.

24. The KFKX transmitting and receiving apparatus is described in detail in Conrad, "Short-Wave Radio Broadcasting," and in Little and Falknor, both *supra* note 22, as well as in "Westinghouse Radio Station KFKX — Pioneer Repeating Station of the World" and "Radio Station KFKX — Empress of the Air," early publications (undated) of KFKX. However, the descriptions are not entirely consistent.

25. "The Value of High Frequencies," *Radio News*, October 1924, p. 617.

26. "Pittsburgh is Heard Clearly in England," *The New York Times,* January 2, 1924, p. 19.

27. W. W. Rodgers, "Broadcasting Complete American Programs to All England," *Radio Broadcast,* March 1924, p. 359, 364.

28. "Making Europe Part of U.S. Radio Audience," *Radio News,* March 1924, p. 1354, 1355.

29. Conrad, "Short-Wave Radio Broadcasting," *supra* note 22 at p. 735.

30. W. J. Brown, "The Inside Story of the British Broadcasting Experiments," *Radio Broadcast,* June 1924, p. 116.

31. William H. Easton, "'Out-of-the-Studio' Broadcasting," *Radio Broadcast,* March 1923, p. 364.

32. "Reporting News by Radio," *Radio News,* October 1920, p. 202.

33. *The Reminiscences of Donald G. Little, supra* note 5 at pp. 34–35.

34. "Radio Bells to Welcome the New Year," *The New York Times,* December 30, 1923, p. X8.

35. "Navy's Short Waves Span Continent and Reach Brazil," *Radio News,* November 1924, p. 856; A. Hoyt Taylor, "The Navy's Work on Short Waves," *QST,* May 1924, p. 9. For a highly readable account of the navy's early work with shortwave, see Albert Hoyt Taylor, *Radio Reminiscences: A Half Century* (Washington, DC: Naval Research Laboratory, 1948 [reprinted in 1960]), Ch. X and XI, pp. 173–248.

36. "Navy Picks Schnell for Tests," *QST,* April 1925, p. 17; F. E. Handy, "NRRL-ARRL Contact," *QST,* June 1925, p. 28; A. Hoyt Taylor, "NRRL In Action," *QST,* July 1925, p. 31; A. L. Budlong, "NRRL Homeward Bound," *QST,* August 1925, p. 28; F. H. Schnell, "The Cruise of NRRL Aboard the USS Seattle," *QST,* January 26, 1926, p. 9.

37. "Transatlantic Amateur Communication Accomplished!" *QST,* January 1924, p. 9; Laurence S. Lees, "Another Historic Event in Amateur Radio," *Radio News,* March 1924, p. 1236.

38. Rexmond C. Cochrane, *Measures for Progress: A History of the National Bureau of Standards* (Washington, DC: U.S. Dept. of Commerce, 1966), pp. 289–291; Marvin R. Bensman, *The Beginning of Broadcast Regulation in the Twentieth Century* (Jefferson, NC: McFarland, 2000), pp. 88–91; M. Adaire Garmhausen, "WWV At Home," *QST,* March 1924, p. 25; Hoy J. Walls, "The Standard-Frequency Set at WWV," *QST,* October 1924, p. 9; "History of WWV," http://www.nist.gov/pml/div688/grp40/wwv-history.cfm.

39. But see Robert Champeix, "Who Invented the Superheterodyne?" *AWA Review,* Vol. 6 (1991), p. 97.

40. Also known as the Radiola Super-Heterodyne Second Harmonic. See *The Old Timer's Bulletin,* June 1971, p. 21.

41. Harold S. Fraine, "What Radio Equipment Does the American Fan Use?" *Radio Broadcast,* April 1, 1925, p. 1115.

42. Marconi, "Beam System," *supra* note 1; Guglielmo Marconi, "Radio Communication," *Proceedings of the Institute of Radio Engineers,* Vol. 16, No. 1 (January 1928), p. 40; Baker, *supra* note 21; Chetwode Crawley, "Marconi's Radio Beam Transmitter," *Radio News,* March 1925, p. 1624.

43. *Radio Service Bulletin,* No. 67, November 1, 1922, p. 13; *Radio Service Bulletin,* No. 74, June 1, 1923, p. 18.

44. See Marconi, "Beam System," *supra* note 1; Kenneth B. Humphrey, "Linking Continents With Twenty Kilowatts," *Radio Broadcast,* February 1927, p. 351; A. Dinsdale, "First Link in English Radio Beam System," *Radio News,* March 1927, p. 1090; Marconi, "Radio Communication," *supra* note 42; "The Marconi Short Wave Beam System," Pamphlet No. 242 (Marconi's Wireless Telegraph Co. Ltd., 1928), http://www.marconicalling.com/museum/html/objccts/cphcmcra-/objects-i=808.001-t=2-n=0.html.

45. "Pittsburgh Programs Relayed to England on Short Waves," *The New York Times,* April 20, 1924, p. XX18; J. A. Fleming, "Radio Broadcasting in Great Britain," *Radio News,* June 1924, p. 1724.

46. "Radio Relay Makes World Wide Broadcasting Possible," *Radio News,* June 1924, p. 1728, 1804; "Sextet of Stations Broadcast Over A Span of 7,000 Miles," *The New York Times,* March 16, 1924, p. XX16; Gleason L. Archer, *History of Radio to 1926* (New York: American Historical Society, 1938), p. 355; Sidel, *supra* note 22 at p. 74. Accounts differ slightly. Frank Conrad said that KFKX was rebroadcasting the signal on its regular frequency, 1050 kc., rather than shortwave, and that KGO picked it up there. Conrad, "Short-Wave Radio Broadcasting," *supra* note 22 at pp. 737–738. Bucher says that KGO picked up the KDKA shortwave signal. Bucher, *supra* note 19 at p. 3449. The *New York Times* story indicated that KFKX was operating on both its regular channel and on shortwave, and that KGO picked up the latter.

47. Sidel, *supra* note 22 at pp. 81–83.

48. John English, "Radio In South America," *Radio News,* October 1924, p. 479 [quote], and November 1924, p. 686.

49. "Special Broadcast Received at Great Distance," *Radio News,* January 1925, p. 1313.

50. "Short Waves to Link 62 Banquets," *The New York Times,* October 5, 1924, p. XX18; "10,000 Diners in 62 Cities Hear Same Speakers by Radio," *Radio News,* January 1925, p. 1314.

51. (Read) "Reception of KDKA in Africa Attributed to Novel Antenna," *The New York Times,* January 25, 1925, p. XX16. (Retransmitted) Harry P. Davis, "The Early History of Broadcasting in the United States," in *The Radio Industry: The Story of its Development* (Chicago: A. W. Shaw, 1928), p. 217; Conrad, "The Story of Short Waves," supra note 13 at pp. 131–132.

52. The facility is described in "KDKA's Powerful Short Wave Station," *Radio News,* September 1924, p. 292. See also "Station KDKA Has New Home on Outskirts of Pittsburgh," *The New York Times,* May 3, 1925, p. XX18.

53. *The Reminiscences of Donald G. Little, supra* note 5 at p. 86.

54. In 1942 the date was put at 1921. "CBC Arctic Broadcasts for Far North Resumed," *Broadcasting,* November 16, 1942, p. 45.

55. C. P. Edwards, "The 'Arctic' Sails," *QST,* July 1924, p. 12; "KDKA to Broadcast for Polar Ship 'Arctic' Now on Way North," *Radio News,* October 1924, p. 481; Fred James, "Radio Adventuring in the 'Arctic,'" *Radio Broadcast,* November 1924, p. 56; William Choat, "The 1924 Trip of the C.G.S. 'Arctic,'" *QST,* December 1924, p. 38; "KDKA Signals Heard Near the North Pole," *Radio News,* January 1925, p. 1318.

56. *The Reminiscences of Donald G. Little, supra* note 5 at pp. 83–85.

57. *RADEX,* October 1931, p. 19.

58. "Eskimos Hear Bishop of Hudson Bay Speaking Their Native Tongue from KDKA," Westinghouse promotional brochure, c. 1927.

59. *The Reminiscences of Donald G. Little, supra* note 5 at pp. 33–34, 54–55 and 85–86, and pp. 98–100 [the latter an address by Frank Conrad, 1940]; Conrad, "The Story of Short Waves," *supra* note 13 at pp. 131–132 [slight variation of the same address]; "International Broadcasting," *Radio Broadcast,* September 1924, p. 402; Bucher, *supra* note 19 at pp. 3465–3467; Frank Conrad, "Short Wave Broadcasting — as a Pioneer Sees It," *Short Wave & Television,* August 1938, p. 197; T. R. Kennedy, Jr., "An Early Short-Wave Episode Is Recalled," *The New York Times,* December 21, 1941, p. X12.

60. M. Harvey Gernsback, "18 Years of S.W. Broadcasting!" *Short Wave & Television,* August 1938, p. 200.

61. Sidel, *supra* note 22 at pp. 89–90; W. J. Purcell, "The Rebroadcasting Set at WGY," *Radio Broadcast,* September 1924, p. 387.

62. "Two American Radio Stations Send Short Waves to England," *The New York Times,* May 18, 1924, p. XX17.

63. "Begins Broadcasting on 15.85 Meter Wave," *The New York Times,* July 25, 1924, p. 15.

64. Myra May, "The Story of Powel Crosley," *Radio Broadcast,* November 1924, p. 63.

65. Sidel, *supra* note 22 at p. 111; Lawrence W. Lichty, "The

Nation's Station," *A History of Radio Station WLW*, Ph.D. dissertation (Columbus: Ohio State University, Speech, 1964), Vol. 1, pp. 26–91; Dick Perry, *Not Just A Sound: The Story of WLW* (Englewood Cliffs, NJ: Prentice-Hall, 1981), pp. 1–35; and Charles J. Stinger, "The Eminent Years of Powel Crosley Jr., His Transmitters, Receivers, Products, and Broadcast Station WLW, 1921–1940," *AWA Review*, Vol. 16 (2003), p. 7.

66. "Tests Reveal Short Wave Possibilities," *The New York Times*, October 12, 1924, p. XX16; "The Value of High Frequencies," *Radio News*, October 1924, p. 617; "Will Short-Wave Transmission Solve Problems of Static and Interference?" *Radio News*, November 1924, p. 756; "What Is Happening on Short Waves," *Radio Broadcast*, January 1925, p. 476.

67. The exact frequencies, as later clarified by the Department of Commerce, were 3500–4000, 7000–8000 and 14000–16000 kc., and 56–64 mc. *Radio Service Bulletin*, No. 93, January 2, 1925, p. 11.

68. Clinton B. DeSoto, *200 Meters and Down: The Story of Amateur Radio* (West Hartford, CT: ARRL, 1936), pp. 147–159.

69. "The Radio-Telegraphy of the Hamilton Rice Expedition, 1924–25," *The Geographical Journal*, Vol. 67, No. 6 (June 1926), p. 536, 542; see also T. S. McCaleb, "Radio With the Rice Amazon Expedition," *Radio News*, November 1925, p. 588; John W. Swanson, "Radio: The Jungleman's Newspaper," *Radio Broadcast*, February 1926, p. 427. As to earlier Rice expeditions, see A. Hamilton Rice, "Notes on the Rio Negro (Amazonas)," *The Geographical Journal*, Vol. 52, No. 4 (October 1918), p. 205; and John W. Swanson, "The Wireless Receiving Equipment of the Hamilton Rice Expedition, 1919–20," *The Geographical Journal*, Vol. 60, No. 3 (September 1922), p. 205.

70. *QST*, May 1925, p. 63.

71. "Radio-Telegraphy," *supra* note 69 at p. 539

72. See Ralph M. Heintz, "KFUH — Somewhere East of Suez," *QST*, November 1925, p. 15; P. J. Townsend, "KFUH's Receiver," *QST*, November 1925, p. 19; Capt. H. J. Adams and F. C., Ryan, "Short-Wave Radio on the Pacific," *Radio News*, April 1926, p. 1402. Its transmitter, KFUH, had been installed by Heintz & Kohlmoos, one of whose principals, Ralph Heintz, was an early shortwave experimenter who would, later in the 1920s, also provide equipment to Commander Byrd for his Arctic and Antarctic expeditions. Heintz & Kohlmoos became Heintz & Kaufman. They were highly regarded for their innovative radio designs, and they were instrumental in building Globe Wireless Ltd., a company spun off from private communications company Dollaradio, a branch of the Dollar Line, in 1930. Globe later became part of Mackay Radio.

73. The *Shenandoah* was the first rigid airship built in the United States. It is the same craft that NNRC patron Jack Poppele helped guide to safety from the ground during a storm on January 16, 1924. See Jerome S. Berg, *Listening on the Short Waves, 1945 to Today* (Jefferson, NC: McFarland, 2008), p. 53.

74. *Recommendations for Regulation of Radio Adopted by the Third National Radio Conference Called by Herbert Hoover, Secretary of Commerce, October 6–10, 1924* (Washington, DC: Government Printing Office, 1924).

75. "World-Wide Radio Soon to Be a Fact," *The New York Times*, April 14, 1924, p. 15.

76. Hugo Gernsback, "For Better Radio" [editorial], *Radio News*, November 1924, p. 655.

77. Louis Frank, "Super-Power in Radio Broadcasting," *Radio News*, January 1925, p. 1136.

78. "Radio Voices Here Reach Australia," *The New York Times*, January 28, 1925, p. 18; Davis, "The Early History of Broadcasting in the United States," *supra* note 51 at p. 217; Frank Conrad, "The Story of Short Waves," *supra* note 13 at pp. 131–132.

79. S. McClatchie, "KDKA Rebroadcast in Germany on a Single Tube," *Radio News*, September 1925, p. 272.

80. Sidel, *supra* note 22 at p. 86; *Radio News*, April 1925, p. 2011; R. F. Durant, "Short-Wave Work in 'Iraq [Mesopotamia]," *Radio News*, March 1926, p. 1271, 1340.

81. "Program Tomorrow for Prince of Wales," *The New York Times*, June 21, 1925, p. XX16.

82. *Radio News*, February 1926, p. 1134.

83. "The CGS 'Arctic' Sails Again," *QST*, July 1925, p. 65; "WBZ to Use Short Waves in Experiments," *Boston Daily Globe*, July 11, 1925, p. A13.

84. *Radio News*, February 1929, p. 750.

85. "Short Waves Successful in National Relay Tieup," *Boston Daily Globe*, November 17, 1925, p. A29.

86. "America to Hear British Waves Relayed Nightly Next Winter," *The New York Times*, March 22, 1925, p. 156.

87. "The Progress of International Broadcasting," *Radio Broadcast*, June 1925, p. 204.

88. http://www.state.me.us/newsletter/dec2003/radio_free_belfast_maine.htm. See "England Entertains America," *World Wide Wireless*, c. 1925–26, p. 22; "Belfast Now Transoceanic Radio Center," *The Republican Journal* [Maine], May 5, 1927, p. 1; Dave Piszcz, "Radio Archaeology," *The Republican Journal*, June 5, 2003, p. 1; Harold E. Nelson, "Radio Free Belfast (Maine)," *Maine IS Technology*, Vol. 6, Issue 12 (December 2003), p. 6, http://www.state.me.us/newsletter/dec2003/BIS-December.pdf. Belfast was said to be the first application of crystal control of transmitter frequency on shortwave. Bucher, *supra* note 19 at pp. 3464–3465.

89. H. E. Hallborg, L. A. Briggs and C. W. Hansell, "Short-Wave Commercial Long-Distance Communication," *Proceedings of the Institute of Radio Engineers*, Vol. 15, No. 6 (July 1927), p. 467.

90. "IARU News," *QST*, July 1925, p. 46; List of stations, *QST*, September 1925, p. 44 (correcting a list that had been published in the August 1925 issue at p. 43).

91. "*Nauen Sendet!— Nauen Is Broadcasting!*" Commemorative Publication of Nauen Station's Presentation, April 25, 1997 (Deutsche Telekom/Telefunken/Thomcast/Deutsche Welle, Germany).

92. The trip, with particular emphasis on the role of radio, is chronicled in detail in John H. Bryant and Harold N. Cones, *Dangerous Crossings* (Annapolis, MD: Naval Institute, 2000). See also Donald B. MacMillan, "The MacMillan Arctic Expedition Returns," *National Geographic*, November 1925, p. 478, and Richard E. Byrd, "Flying Over the Arctic," *National Geographic*, November 1925, p. 519. The navy had placed Lt. Commander Richard E. Byrd, Jr. in charge of the aircraft. It was his first polar trip. See also John L. Reinartz, "Radio Goes to the North Pole," *Radio News*, July 1925, p. 16.

93. "Radio Sends News to Arctic Expedition," *The New York Times*, January 27, 1924, p. X9; Donald B. MacMillan, "The 'Bowdoin' in North Greenland," *National Geographic*, June 1925, p. 677.

94. Donald H. Mix, "My Radio Experience in the Far North," *QST*, November 1924, p. 17.

95. John L. Reinartz, "The Reflection of Short Waves," *QST*, April 1925, p. 9; John L. Reinartz, "A Year's Work Below Forty Meters," *Radio News*, April 1925, p. 1894; A. Hoyt Taylor and E. O. Hulburt, "Wave Propagation at High Frequencies," *QST*, October 1925, p. 12; A. Hoyt Taylor, "Navy Investigates Ultra Frequencies," *Radio News*, January 1926, p. 954; A. Hoyt Taylor, "Radio Communication With Short Waves," *The Scientific Monthly*, Vol. 22, No. 4 (April 1926), p. 356; Taylor, *supra* note 35 at pp. 187–192.

96. Orrin E. Dunlap, Jr., "Further Radio Developments Expected to Come With 1926," *The New York Times*, December 27, 1925, p. XX12 (Dunlap); "Experts Review Radio Growth and Forecast New Trends," *The New York Times*, December 27, 1925, p. XX14 (Dellinger).

97. "Australia Hears Concert Over KDKA," *The New York Times*, October 8, 1926, p. 3.

98. "London Chimes on Radio in America New Year's

Day," *The New York Times*, December 27, 1925, p. XX13; "Londoners Dance to Radio from Here," *The New York Times*, January 1, 1926, p. 4.

99. A. Dinsdale, "Britain's New Superpower Broadcast Station," *Radio News*, December 1925, p. 770; Alfred N. Goldsmith and Austin C. Lescarboura, *This Thing Called Broadcasting* (New York: Henry Holt, 1930), pp. 181–182.

100. Not involved were a 50 kw. standard broadcast transmitter (2XAG), which occasionally took the place of the 5 kw. unit, and a longwave unit, 2XAH, 192 kc., 40 kw.

101. C. J. Young, "The South Schenectady Tests," *QST*, April 1926, p. 38; "South Schenectady and the April Tests," *QST*, June 1926, p. 33; M. K. Prescott, "General Electric Short-Wave Test Results," *QST*, November 1926, p. 9; "WGY Making Low Wave Tests," *The New York Times*, March 21, 1926, p. XX19; "World-Wide Survey Reveals Peculiarities of Short-Wave," *The New York Times*, November 14, 1926, p. XX15.

102. "Short Waves Skip and Jump Over World-Wide Distances," *The New York Times*, May 9, 1926, p. XX18.

103. "The Grebe Short Wave Receiver," *Short Wave Craft*, August-September 1930, p. 146; "Grebe Low-Wave Receiver," *The Old Timer's Bulletin*, March 1976, p. 17; Bruce Kelley, "The Grebe 18 Shortwave Receiver," *The Old Timer's Bulletin*, February 1995, p. 11; G. J. Gray, "The Grebe Radio Story," *The Old Timer's Bulletin*, June 1992, p. 14.

104. Details of the contest can be found in the following 1926 issues of *Radio Broadcast:* February, p. 444; April, p. 657; May, p. 46; June, p. 128; August, p. 332; September, p. 384.

105. "'P.C.J.—Holland—Speaking," *Short Wave Craft*, August-September 1931, p. 89.

106. *BBC Handbook*, 1928, pp. 297–298.

107. "British Formulate Project for Broadcasting Culture," *The New York Times*, August 1, 1926, p. X18.

108. "Broadcasters Plan Overseas Programs," *The New York Times*, October 19, 1927, p. 30; "Special Short Wave Stations to Relay Concerts Between United States and British Isles for Rebroadcasts Over WEAF and 2LO," *The New York Times*, October 23, 1927, p. XX14; "Seeks Wave Bands for British Tie-Up," *The New York Times*, November 2, 1927, p. 23; "Urges Radio Need of Waves to Europe," *The New York Times*, November 9, 1927, p. 34; "Giant Central Broadcaster is Visualized For Future," *The New York Times*, November 27, 1927, p. XX18.

109. *Radio News*, March 1929, p. 844.

110. John Clarricoats, *World at Their Fingertips* (London: RSGB, 1967), pp. 130–132.

111. "Australian Radio 1922–2012—Amateur Radio DJs Lead the Way," http://www.radioheritage.net/Story255.asp.

112. *From Sea to Sea, infra* note 113 at p. 3.

113. *From Sea to Sea: A Mari Usque Ad Mare*, Canada's Jubilee Radio Broadcast, July 1, 1927, 63 pages [date, author and publisher unspecified]; "Radio Satisfactory In Eastern Cities," *The New York Times*, July 12, 1927, p. 28.

114. *World-Radio*, June 3, 1927, p. 547; July 1, 1927, p. 9; July 15, 1927, p. 57.

115. Alan Pennington, "Königs-Wusterhausen, 'Birthplace of German Radio,'" *Communication* [British DX Club], August 2012, p. 14.

116. See *The BBC Engineering Measurement and Receiving Station at Tatsfield* (BBC, Engineering Information Dept., March 1961), http://www.bbceng.info/Operations/Receivers/Tatsfield/BBC_Tatsfield_March%201961.pdf.

117. "Tourists 8,500 Miles Away Hear Home Radio," *The New York Times*, March 7, 1927, p. 1.

118. *Radio News*, October 1927, pp. 362, 395.

119. "Short Wave Tests Heard in Antipodes," *The New York Times*, July 15, 1927, p. 14.

120. "Short Waves to Link Crosley Factories," *The New York Times*, August 29, 1926, p. X14. WARC had operated as WGI from February 1922 to February 1925, and had carried some broadcasting programming, as well as other transmis-

sions, from as early as 1916, when it had operated as 1XE. See Alice Brannigan, "Radio of Yesteryear," *Popular Communications*, September 1989, p. 16; Donna Halper, "The Rise and Fall of WGI, Boston's Pioneer Station," *Popular Communications*, June 1999, p. 36.

121. WAAM had a 1:00 A.M. program that rebroadcast in real time the DX listening experiences of amateur Paul F. Godley, whose receiver was connected to the station by landline. Godley was the American amateur who had been sent to England in 1921 and been the first to hear transatlantic amateur signals. *Radio Broadcast*, April 1928, p. 430. See references in Chapter 1, note 14.

122. "Radiophone Starts Today with Scores Calling Up London," *The New York Times*, January 7, 1927, p. 1; "Phones to Link More Countries," *The New York Times*, January 13, 1929, p. 130; *Short-Wave Transatlantic Radio-Telephony*, Bell Laboratories, 1929 (reprinted from "Bell Laboratories Record"); D. K. deNeuf, "History of Wireless In Public Telephone Service," *The Old Timer's Bulletin*, September 1979, p. 16.

123. Carl H. Butman, "The New Short Wave Field Is Opening," *RADEX*, November 1927, p. 4; Keith Henney, "Why Not Try the Short Waves?" *Radio Broadcast*, September 1927, p. 290.

124. Lt. H. F. Breckel, "In the Future—Intermediate- or Short-Wave Broadcasting?" *Radio News*, November 1927, p. 460; "Why Short Waves Should Not Be Opened to Broadcasting," *Radio Broadcast*, February 1927, p. 356.

125. "World-Wide Audience Listens to Australian Broadcasts," *The New York Times*, May 27, 1928, p. 132.

126. Rose D. Meyer, "Listening In Across Canada," *Radio News*, August 1925, p. 144.

127. See Amando Céspedes Marín, "How I Operate My Little Station 'NRH,'" *Short Wave Craft*, July 1933, p. 136. For a review of the book by Amando Céspedes Marín, "Me and Little Radio NRH," visit http://www.ontheshortwaves.com/reviews.html. Don Amando had a long friendship with Eugene McDonald, head of Zenith; see Harold Cones and John Bryant, "Amando Cespedes Marin and Commander Eugene F. McDonald, Jr.—A Unique Friendship," *Monitoring Times*, December 2007, p. 10.

128. "British 'Radio Echo' to Be Re-Broadcast," *The New York Times*, February 21, 1928, p. 34; "WGY Broadcasts English Radio Talk," *The New York Times*, February 22, 1928, p. 22.

129. "Radio Carried Result of Election to Africa," *The New York Times*, December 28, 1928, p. 26.

130. Francis Gow Smith, "Thanks to WGY—!" *Radio Broadcast*, April 1928, pp. 403, 404–405.

131. Don Moore, "Ice Cold Radio—Broadcasting and the Byrd Expeditions to Antarctica," *Monitoring Times*, January 2000, p. 14; "Broadcasters Will Cheer Byrd's Crew in Antarctic," *The New York Times*, October 7, 1928, p. X16; "Broadcasts Flash News Items to the Arctic and Antarctic," *The New York Times*, November 18, 1928, p. XX18; "Byrd Sends Thanks for Radio Program," *The New York Times*, December 27, 1928, p. 2; R. L. Duffus, "Covering the News of Frozen Antarctica," *The New York Times*, February 10, 1929, p. 138. The expedition's radio equipment is described in "Radio on the Byrd Expedition," *QST*, December 1928, p. 17.

132. Vol. 16, No. 11 (November 1928), p. 1575.

133. An adapter was a detector, sometimes with R.F. amplifier, that used the audio amplifier of the standard broadcast set; a converter was an oscillator that converted the incoming signal to a broadcast band frequency that was then tuned by the broadcast receiver. See Henry B. Herman, "How to Build Really Efficient Short Wave Converters," *Short Wave Craft*, August-September 1930, p. 130; George W. Walker, "Adapting Your Broadcast Receiver to Short-Wave Reception," *Radio News*, November 1930, p. 422; "Short Waves Heard on Broadcast Sets," *Radio Call Book Magazine and Technical Review*, January 1932, p. 39.

134. See Bill Fizette, "The Silver-Marshall 'Round the World Four,'" *The Old Timer's Bulletin,* June 1985, p. 10.

135. William I. Orr, "The Receiver That Started It All—The SW-2," *CQ,* October 1977, p. 18.

136. Although the "Wasp" was obsolete by 1934, devoted Wasp users learned how to modify it for improved reception. "Revamping the Old 'Super-Wasp,'" *Short Wave Radio,* June 1934, p. 27.

137. E.g. H. M. Bayer, "How to Succeed in Short-Wave Operation," *Radio News,* December 1928, p. 552.

138. "Broadcasting Below 100 Metres," *World-Radio,* June 3, 1927, p. 547.

139. *Radio News,* September 1929, p. 276.

140. *Radio Broadcast,* October 1928, p. 348.

141. *Radio Broadcast,* April 1928, p. 428.

142. *Radio News,* August 1928, p. 188.

143. Hugo Gernsback, "The Short-Wave Era" [editorial], *Radio News,* September 1928, p. 201.

144. "King of Siam Buys a Pilot 'All-Wave' Receiver," *Radio Design,* Vol. 4, No. 1 (Fall 1931), p. 45; "King of Siam Uses 14 Tube Short Wave Set," *Short Wave Craft,* August-September 1931, p. 92.

145. *Fourth Annual Report of the Federal Radio Commission (Fiscal Year 1930),* p. 67.

146. *Second Annual Report of the Federal Radio Commission (For the Year Ended June 30, 1928, with Supplemental Report for July 1, 1928-September 30, 1928),* Part III & Appendix M(1)-(4); Rules and Regulations Governing Relay Broadcasting, *Radio Service Bulletin,* No. 144, March 30, 1929, p. 16; General Orders No. 64 & 68, *Radio Service Bulletin,* No. 147, June 29, 1929, pp. 25 and 27–28.

147. Lloyd Jacquet, "The Realization of an Aviation-Radio Idea," *Radio News,* August 1929, p. 150.

148. E. H. Gager, "W9XF Short Wave Transmitter Associated with WENR," *Citizens Radio Call Book Magazine and Technical Review,* January 1931, p. 40; Adrian M. Peterson, "Shortwave Station 9XF in Chicago," *Radio World* (May 7, 2012), http://www.radioworld.com/article/shortwave-station-xf-in-chicago/213309.

149. The full story of WCFL is told in Nathan Godfried, "The Origins of Labor Radio: WCFL, the 'Voice of Labor,' 1925–1928," *Historical Journal of Film, Radio and Television,* Vol. 7, No. 2 (1987), p. 143; and Nathan Godfried, *WCFL, Chicago's Voice of Labor, 1926–1978* (Urbana and Chicago: University of Illinois Press, 1997). See also Maynard Marquardt, "W9XAA—The Short Wave Voice of Labor," *Short Wave Craft,* February–March 1931, p. 346.

150. Orrin E. Dunlap, *Advertising by Radio* (New York: Ronald, 1929), pp. 164–165.

151. "Inauguration Has World Broadcast," *The New York Times,* March 5, 1929, p. 8.

152. "Byrd Greetings Are Broadcast," *The New York Times,* March 10, 1929, p. 164.

153. "Byrd Offers Radio New Opportunity," *The New York Times,* April 14, 1929, p. 159.

154. *BBC Year-Book,* 1930, p. 134.

155. *Radio News* printed the address. See Guglielmo Marconi, "A Radio Dream Come True," *Radio News,* March 1930, p. 784.

156. "Radio Unites World In Christmas Fete; 4 Nations Broadcast," *The New York Times,* December 26, 1929, p. 1.

157. Stuart C. Mahanay, "Current Comment," *Radio News,* March 1930, pp. 786, 787.

158. "Voices Across the Sea," *Scientific American,* May 1930, p. 356.

159. D. K. deNeuf, "1944 Carrier Pigeon," *The Old Timer's Bulletin,* June 1976, p. 30; D. K. deNeuf, "A History of Press Wireless, Inc.," *The Old Timer's Bulletin,* June 1978, p. 12; Don DeNeuf, "More History of Press Wireless, Inc.," *The Old Timer's Bulletin,* November 1989, p. 29; Alice Brannigan, "Radio: The Press Wireless Era," *Popular Communications,* April 1995, p. 18.

160. For detailed history of Cable & Wireless Ltd., see K.

C. Baglehole, *A Century of Service* (London: Cable and Wireless, 1969); Hugh Barty-King, *Girdle Round the Earth* (London: Heinemann, 1979); Charles Graves, *The Thin Red Lines* (London: Standard Art, undated).

CHAPTER 3

1. Arthur H. Lynch, "Current Comment," *Radio News,* June 1930, pp. 1088, 1089.

2. "KDKA Wire Sprays Music Into Space," *The New York Times,* January 26, 1930, p. 120; "New KDKA Antenna System for Spray Transmission on Both Long and Short Wave," *Short Wave Craft,* October-November 1930, p. 189.

3. "Commercial Stations as Frequency Markers," *QST,* January 1931, p. 26.

4. Arthur J. Green, "Results of International Short Wave Test," *Short Wave Craft,* June-July 1931, p. 22.

5. "Easter Service Goes Over World By Radio," *The New York Times,* April 20, 1930, p. 18.

6. "100,000,000 Listen to Parley On Radio," *The New York Times,* January 22, 1930, p. 3; see also *BBC Year-Book,* 1931, pp. 121–123.

7. Orrin E. Dunlap, Jr., "All the World Eavesdrops On The London Conclave," *The New York Times,* January 26, 1930, p. 120; "The King's Voice Traveled Afar," *The New York Times,* March 9, 1930, p. 155.

8. "Byrd's Voice Leaps Over 10,000 Miles From New Zealand," *The New York Times,* March 12, 1930, p. 1; Orrin E. Dunlap, Jr., "Byrd's Voice Flies Back to America On Radio's Wings," *The New York Times,* March 16, 1930, p. X16.

9. "The Listeners' Paradise," *The New York Times,* July 6, 1930, p. 110; see also "Ellsworth's Operator Calls Bottom of the Earth 'Paradise' for Listening In," *The New York Times,* September 2, 1934, p. XX11.

10. The first North American reception of shortwave broadcast signals from the islands—a major event within the shortwave listening community—was in 1958.

11. The facility is described in U.S. Department of Commerce, *Radio Activities of the Department of Commerce* (Washington, D.C.: U.S. Government Printing Office, July 1, 1931), p. 6.

12. Hugo Gernsback, "Short-Wave Opportunities" [editorial], *Short Wave Craft,* August-September 1930, p. 101; see also James Millen and Robert S. Kruse, "An Analysis of A.C. Operated Short-Wave Receiver Design," *Radio News,* June 1930, p. 1101.

13. The device is explained in detail in W. H. Hoffman and D. H. Mix, "Revolutionary High-Frequency Tuner Design," *QST,* February 1930, p. 9.

14. *Short Wave Craft* became *Short Wave & Television* in January 1937, *Radio & Television* in October 1938. It was absorbed by *Radio Craft* in 1941.

15. "Radio Historians Begin to List 1930's Advances in Broadcasting," *The New York Times,* December 21, 1930, p. 122; Orrin E. Dunlap, Jr., "A Look Back and Then Ahead," *The New York Times,* December 28, 1930, p. XX8.

16. Michael Kent Sidel, *A Historical Analysis of American Short Wave Broadcasting, 1916–1942,* Ph.D. dissertation (Evanston, IL: Northwestern University, Speech, 1976), p. 103.

17. The W2XAF transmitter capability is described in Guy Bartlett, "W2XAF Can Send Code, Voice and Photos Simultaneously," *Short Wave Craft,* February-March 1931, p. 344.

18. "Tolls for International Programs Are Not Justified, Says Examiner Yost," *The New York Times,* March 22, 1931, p. X16.

19. "World Fliers Talk to the Australians," *The New York Times,* July 19, 1931, p. 13.

20. "Radio Girdles Globe to Honor Marconi for His Invention," *The New York Times,* December 13, 1931, p. 1.

21. "Dickey Off on Trip to Explore the Orinoco," *The*

New York Times, April 2, 1931, p. 27; "Amateurs Will Tune for Dickey on Orinoco," *The New York Times,* April 5, 1931, p. 133; "Dr. Dickey Reaches First Orinoco Base," *The New York Times,* May 8, 1931, p. 10; "Orinoco Is Traced to Source by Dickey," *The New York Times,* July 29, 1931, p. 1; "Radio Helped Explorers on Trek Up the Orinoco," *The New York Times,* September 20, 1931, p. XX9.

22. Guglielmo Marconi, "'HVJ' Rome—Italy Heard Around the World," *Short Wave Craft,* April-May 1931, p. 425; "Pope Pius to Speak Over Radio Feb. 12," *The New York Times,* February 4, 1931, p. 10; "All the World to Hear Vatican City Station," *The New York Times,* February 8, 1931, p. 120; "Pope Pius Decides to Speak Over Radio," *The New York Times,* February 10, 1931, p. 11; "Pope to Dedicate Radio Tomorrow," *The New York Times,* February 11, 1931, p. 24; "World Will Hear Pope Pius on Radio Today; He Will Speak in Both Latin and Italian," *The New York Times,* February 12, 1931, p. 1; "Station Here [W2XAD] Helps London to Hear Pope," *The New York Times,* February 13, 1931, p. 14; "150 Stations Carry Program to Nation," *The New York Times,* February 13, p. 15.

23. *Radio Design,* Vol. 3, No. 4 (First 1931 Issue), p. 27.

24. *Radio Design,* Vol. 4, No. 1 (Fall 1931), p. 10.

25. "YV2RC—The S-W Voice from Caracas, Venezuela," *Short Wave Craft,* October 1934, p. 326. The station's history is outlined in "Short-Wave Stars From Caracas," *Official Short Wave Listener,* February-March 1935, p. 6.

26. The history of HCJB, told from a missionary perspective, is recounted in Clarence W. Jones, *Radio, the New Missionary* (Chicago: Moody, 1946); Frank S. Cook, *Seeds in the Wind* (Miami, FL: World Radio Missionary Fellowship, 1961); Lois Neely, *Come Up to This Mountain* (Wheaton, IL: Tyndale House, 1980); Marilee Dufendach, ed., *Catch The Vision* (Opa Locka, FL: World Radio Missionary Fellowship, 1989); Janet Benge and Geoff Benge, *Clarence Jones: Mr. Radio* (Seattle, WA: YWAM, 2006); and *Vision to Reach the World* (Colorado Springs, CO: HCJB Global, 2006). For other relevant tellings of the HCJB story, see Timothy H. B. Stoneman, *Capturing Believers: American International Radio, Religion, and Reception, 1931–1970,* Ph.D. dissertation (Atlanta: Georgia Institute of Technology, School of History, Technology and Society, 2006); and Kenneth D. MacHarg, "HCJB 1931–1991: A Celebration of Beginnings," *Monitoring Times,* November 1991, p. 18. (MacHarg is a minister and was a well-known shortwave personality when he worked at HCJB.)

27. "VK2ME—The Short-Wave Voice of Australia," *Short Wave Craft,* January 1934, p. 520; George Lilley, "VK2ME-VK3ME (Famous S.W. Broadcasters)," *Radio News,* June 1934, p. 729; "VK2ME, VK3ME—Voices of Australia," *Short Wave Radio,* October 1934, p. 6.

28. *Radio News,* July 1931, p. 8 [advertisement].

29. Edward Pawley, *BBC Engineering, 1922–1972* (London: BBC, 1972), pp. 126–133; "A World-Wide Voice," *The New York Times,* July 31, 1932, p. X7; "The Development of the British Broadcasting Corp.," *Short Wave Radio,* August 1934, p. 44.

30. *Radio Design, supra* note 23.

31. The facility is described in "The New Daventry Station," *Short Wave Craft,* April 1933, p. 714; and "Daventry, England ... Short-Wave Hub of the Empire," *Short Wave Craft,* December 1933, p. 457.

32. *BBC Year-Book,* 1934, pp. 243–273, 373–383; Norman Tomalin, *Daventry Calling the World* (Whitby, North Yorkshire, England: Caedmon of Whitby, 1998), pp. 29–33, and on line at http://www.bbceng.info/Books/dx-world/dx-calling-the-world-2008a.pdf.

33. "The Story of 'EAQ,'" *Short Wave Craft,* August 1933, p. 202.

34. Donald R. Browne, "Radio Normandie and the IBC Challenge to the BBC Monopoly," *Historical Journal of Film, Radio, and Television,* Vol. 5, No. 1 (1985), p. 3. IBC activities are covered at length in Seán Street, *Crossing the Ether: British Public Service Radio and Commercial Competition 1922–1945* (Eastleigh, England: John Libbey, 2006), and Keith

Wallis, *And the World Listened: The Biography of Captain Leonard F. Plugge, a Pioneer of Commercial Radio* (Tiverton, Devon, England: Kelly, 2008).

35. "When Holland Broadcasts via 'PHI,'" *Short Wave Craft,* June 1934, p. 70.

36. Page Taylor, "This Summer on the Short Waves," *RADEX,* Midsummer Ed. 1933, p. 19.

37. The technical details of the station are outlined in Constance Drexel, "League of Nations Station at Geneva," *Short Wave Craft,* June 1933, p. 71, and R. H. Tomlinson, "HBL-HBP—'Radio-Nations' (League of Nations Stations)," *Radio News,* June 1936, p. 712.

38. "W2XE—The Short-Wave Voice of the Columbia Broadcasting System," *Short-Wave Craft,* April 1934, p. 712.

39. "Barks at His Echo Around World; Terrier Cuts In on Radio Test," *The New York Times,* April 6, 1932, p. 1; "Short Wave Snapshots," *Short Wave Craft,* February-March 1931, p. 342.

40. The company made it easy to get the receiver in your hands. "Tear out part of this page [a coupon]—pin a $5 bill to it with your name and address, and the 727SW will be shipped balance C.O.D. Play with it for 10 days—give it every operating test. And if it is not the best receiver you ever tuned, return it and your money will be promptly refunded." *QST,* June 1932, p. 95.

41. Orrin E. Dunlap, Jr., "Echoes of a Year on the Air," *The New York Times,* December 31, 1933, p. X11.

42. "Kremlin Bell on Radio," *The New York Times,* February 9, 1933, p. 23.

43. The Zeesen facility is described and pictured in Karl Tetzner, "Zeesen—Germany's Short Wave Voice," *Short Wave Craft,* July 1934, p. 134, and W. W. Diefenbach, "The German Short-Wave Transmissions," *Radio News,* October 1934, p. 232. The installation included an airfield, anti-aircraft guns and barbed wire protection. Charles J. Rolo, *Radio Goes to War* (New York: Putnam, 1942), pp. 40–41.

44. "Radio Will Carry Event to World," *The New York Times,* March 4, 1933, p. 4; "World-Wide Radio Centres in Capital," *The New York Times,* March 5, 1933, p. 5.

45. Lloyd Roberts, "Voice Over the Arctic," *Maclean's Magazine,* January 15, 1937, p. 25.

46. "The Empire Station—Reports of Reception," *World-Radio,* November 17, 1933, p. 645.

47. *Short Wave Craft,* December 1933, inside front cover [advertisement].

48. *QST,* December 1933, p. 91 [advertisement].

49. *Short Wave Craft,* March 1933, outside back cover [advertisement]; "Commercial Type S-W Super," *Radio News,* Pt. I, April 1933, p. 610; Pt. II, May 1933, p. 676; "The Lincoln R-9," *Short Wave Craft,* April 1933, p. 729.

50. *Radio News,* January 1933, outside back cover [advertisement].

51. *Short Wave Craft,* November 1933, inside front cover [advertisement].

52. *Radio News,* October 1933, p. 247 [advertisement].

53. *QST,* January 1934, p. 70 [advertisement].

54. Raymond S. Moore, *Communications Receivers, The Vacuum Tube Era: 1932–1981* (Key Largo, FL: RSM Communications, 4th ed. 1997), p. 4.

55. In 1934, both were embarrassed by their public misidentification of what was thought to be the rare 500-watt station, CQN, in Macao, the Portuguese colony in south China. They had actually been hearing HIX in the Dominican Republic.

56. E.g. Orrin E. Dunlap, Jr., "Antarctic Explorers to Test Short-Wave Broadcasting," *The New York Times,* October 15, 1933, p. X9; "Byrd Expedition Gets Under Way," *QST,* November 1933, p. 26; Samuel Kaufman, "The South Pole Calling!" *Radio News,* January 1934, p. 394; H. Winfield Secor, "When Little America Speaks," *Short Wave Craft,* January 1934, p. 518; "Authorized Call Letters and Operating Frequencies of the Byrd Expedition," *Short Wave Radio,* February 1934, p. 12; H. Winfield Secor, "Short-Waving with

Byrd in the Antarctic," *Short Wave Craft,* March 1934, p. 648; "Byrd 'Mailbag' Delivered Regularly," *Short Wave Radio,* August 1934, p. 9; Don Moore, "Ice Cold Radio—Broadcasting and the Byrd Expeditions to Antarctica," *Monitoring Times,* January 2000, p. 14.

57. The facilities at Riverhead in 1934 are described in "A Forest of Aerials," *Short Wave Radio,* April 1934, p. 4.

58. Page 4.

59. "Around-the-World S.W. Broadcasts," *Short Wave Radio,* April 1934, p. 7; *Aboard the Seth Parker* (Dayton, OH: 1934, Frigidaire). Frigidaire provided refrigeration equipment for the ship.

60. Lewis Winner, "With Bob Bartlett in the Uncharted Arctic Regions," *Short Wave Radio,* March 1934, p. 8; Robert Moe, "W10XDA Back From the North," *QST,* December 1934, p. 10; Clifton Foss, "CQ de W10XDA," *QST,* July 1938, p. 23.

61. Creation of the Foundation was a precondition for Rockefeller support that lasted for a decade. The Rockefellers were interested in educational broadcasting, but Rockefeller funding eventually dried up due to the station's limited success and Lemmon's administrative weaknesses. William J. Buxton, Rockefeller Family Support for W1XAL/WRUL, 'Boston's Vest-pocket BBC,'" http://www.rockarch.org/publications/resrep/buxton2.pdf (cited with permission).

62. "All the World Invited to Pick Up One Program," *The New York Times,* March 11, 1934, p. X11; "Unique 1-Hour Program Covers World," *Short Wave Radio,* June 1934, p. 5.

63. "All the World Invited to Pick Up One Program," *The New York Times,* March 11, 1934, p. X11.

64. Ralph Stranger, "You Can Join in Round-The-World Research," *Short Wave Craft,* August 1935, p. 248.

65. "Radio Colonial, the French Empire Station," *Short Wave Craft,* December 1934, p. 456.

66. Callum A. MacDonald, "Radio Bari: Italian Wireless Propaganda in the Middle East and British Countermeasures, 1934–38," *Middle East Studies,* Vol. XIII (May 1977), p. 195.

67. Orrin E. Dunlap, Jr., "Yuletide 'Round the Earth," *The New York Times,* December 23, 1934, p. X13; "Along Short-Wave Trails," *The New York Times,* December 30, 1934, p. XX15.

68. *International Short Wave Radio* [ISWC], March 1934, p. 10.

69. *International Short Wave Radio* [ISWC], April 1934, p. 16.

70. *International Short Wave Radio* [ISWC], November 1934, p. 20.

71. Drew O. McDaniel, "Broadcasting in the Malay World" (Norwood, NJ: Ablex, 1994), pp. 38–41.

72. J. A. Gracie, "Rugby Radio Station," *Post Office Electrical Engineers' Journal* [U.K.], April 1939, p. 16.

73. Orrin E. Dunlap, Jr., "Hopes of Radio's Industry," *The New York Times,* April 22, 1934, p. X9.

74. *International Short Wave Radio* [ISWC], May 1934, p. 10.

75. Page X11.

76. The roles of others in the invention of FM have only recently received attention. Christopher H. Sterling and Michael C. Keith, *Sounds of Change: A History of FM Broadcasting in America* (Chapel Hill: University of North Carolina Press, 2008); Gary L. Frost, *Early FM Radio: Incremental Technology in Twentieth-Century America* (Baltimore: John Hopkins University Press, 2010).

77. The Madrid Telegraph and Radiotelegraph Conferences of 1932 had approved the range 25600–26600 kc. for shortwave broadcasting, but the FCC did not approve use of the band in the United States until 1937.

78. For a discussion of the development of the apex band, see John Schneider, "Ultra Shortwave—America's Apex Broadcast Stations of the 1930s," *Monitoring Times,* December 2010, p. 8; and Everett L. Dillard, "The High Frequency Broadcasting Station—10 Meters and Down!" *Short Wave &*

Television, September 1938, p. 261. See also Orrin E. Dunlap, Jr., "On High Perches," *The New York Times,* February 16, 1936, p. X15.

79. For a time line of the 500 kw. operation, and much related information, see "Jim Hawkins' WLW Transmitter Page," http://hawkins.pair.com/wlw.shtml.

80. "Broadcasts Go on Though King Dies," *The New York Times,* October 14, 1934, p. E3.

81. "The Editor's Mill" [editorial], *QST,* January 1935, p. 7.

82. "Stratosphere Flight Broadcast by NBC," *Radio Broadcast,* November 15, 1935, p. 61. Full details of the radio side of the flight are contained in G. S. Granger, "The Stratosphere Flight," *All-Wave Radio,* December 1935, p. 103.

83. George C. Sholin, "Radio in the Soviet Union," *All-Wave Radio,* November 1936, p. 490.

84. "Britain Prevents Relay from Italy," *Radio Broadcast,* October 15, 1935, p. 61.

85. "Capt. Hall's Short-Wave Page," *Radio News,* March 1935, p. 546.

86. Data Sheet No. 3, May 8, 1935, p. 5.

87. George S. Kanahele, ed., *Hawaiian Music and Musicians: An Illustrated History* (Honolulu: University Press of Hawaii, 1979), pp. 109–114; Susan Smulyan, "Hawaii Calls: Transnational Radio in the Pacific World," in *Radio in the World: Papers From the 2005 Melbourne Radio Conference* (Melbourne, Australia: RMIT, 2005), pp. 267–275.

88. Hugo Gernsback, "All-Wave Sets" [editorial], *Short Wave Craft,* June 1935, p. 69.

89. "To Aid Shortwave Fans," *The New York Times,* December 16, 1935, p. 41; "Detroit Has New Station," *The New York Times,* February 2, 1936, p. X13; "Short-Wave Radio Sped Hitler's Ultimatum Over Here Before All in Reichstag Heard It," *The New York Times,* March 16, 1936, p. 11; "A New Market Is Foreseen," *The New York Times,* June 28, 1936, p. X10; "FCC Defers Curb On Foreign Radio," *The New York Times,* July 3, 1936, p. 2; Sidel, *supra* note 16 at p. 131; and the author's correspondence with Schuette biographer James Castellan.

90. "Forecasts for the Year 1936," *Radio News,* February 1936, p. 460, 461.

91. "American Short-Wavers Picked-Up in Australia," *The New York Times,* May 24, 1936, p. X10.

92. Sol Taishoff, "FCC Paves Way for New Broadcast Services" [with Text of Revised FCC Rules], *Broadcasting,* June 1, 1936, p. 7; Jerry Ray Redding, *American Private International Broadcasting: What Went Wrong and Why,* Ph.D. dissertation (Columbus: Ohio State University, Mass Communication, 1977), pp. 108–113; Sidel, *supra* note 16 at pp. 141–143.

93. W. H. Moffat, "W2XDV—Pioneer H-F Broadcaster Reaches Europe," *Short Wave & Television,* August 1938, p. 205; C. H. Wesser, "W8XWJ—WWJ's High Stepper," *All-Wave Radio,* May 1936, p. 206.

94. *RADEX,* November 1936, p. 12.

95. Orrin E. Dunlap, Jr., "George V Was First British Ruler Known By Voice in Dominions Beyond the Sea," *The New York Times,* January 26, 1936, p. X15.

96. "Radio's 1936 Finale," *The New York Times,* December 13, 1936, p. X14.

97. "Hess Broadcasts to World Germans," *The New York Times,* December 25, 1936, p. 14.

98. For a history of Czech shortwave broadcasting, see "History of Radio Prague," http://www.radio.cz/en/static/history-of-radio-prague.

99. T. E. Gooteé, "Radio's Role in the Spanish War," *Radio News,* January 1937, p. 394. Radio and the Spanish Civil War is covered in O. W. Riegel, "Press, Radio, and the Spanish Civil War," *Public Opinion Quarterly,* Vol. 1, No. 1 (January 1937), p. 131; Thomas E. Gooteé, "Radio and the Spanish War," *Radio News,* May 1938, p. 29; Alan Davies, "The First Radio War: Broadcasting in the Spanish Civil War," *Historical Journal of Film, Radio and Television,* Vol. 19, No. 4

(1999), p. 473; Col. José Luis Goberna Caride, "Broadcasting in the Spanish Civil War (Military Engineers Work In the Conflict)," in *Telecommunications Conference (HISTEL-CON), 2010 Second IEEE Region 8 Conference on the History of Telecommunications (Madrid, Spain)* (Institute of Electrical and Electronics Engineers [IEEE], November 2010), p. 131.

100. "Radio in Spain," *QST,* September 1937, pp. 67, 68.

101. QSL letter from Paul C. Brown, Chief Engineer, Philco Radio, Saigon, to William Sparks, 1936.

102. C. L. Pujitha-Gunawardana, *This Is Colombo Calling: 1924–1949 (Reminiscences)* (Nugegoda, Sri Lanka: Peralia, 1990), pp. 35, 46–50, 62.

103. Michael B. Salwen, "The Origins of CMQ: Pre-Castro Cuba's Leading Radio Network," *Historical Journal of Film, Radio and Television,* Vol. 13, No. 3 (1993), p. 315.

104. G. Wallington, "Short Waves Growing in Popularity," *Radio News,* August 1936, p. 103.

105. Page 73.

106. The transmitting equipment is described in "CBS Station W2XE In Action!" *Short Wave & Television,* March 1938, p. 630.

107. A. E. Kennelly, "The URSI Programs of Short-Wave Station W1XAL," *Science,* Vol. 85, No. 2209 (April 30, 1937), p. 419.

108. Chester T. Crowell, "Dogfight on the Air Waves," *The Saturday Evening Post,* May 31, 1938, p. 23; J. S. Wilson, "Short Wave War in Latin America," *Radio News,* September 1938, p. 10; John W. White, "Propaganda War on U.S. Launched," *The New York Times,* December 4, 1938, p. 52.

109. Lewie V. Gilpin, "Bills for Government Stations Wither From Lack of Support," *Broadcasting,* June 1, 1938, p. 19.

110. Sidel, *supra* note 16 at pp. 148–154; Redding, *supra* note 92 at pp. 143–160; Fred Allan Fejes, *Imperialism, Media, and the Good Neighbor: New Deal Foreign Policy and United States Shortwave Broadcasting to Latin America,* Ph. D. dissertation (Urbana-Champaign: University of Illinois, 1982 [also Norwood, NJ: Ablex, 1986]), pp. 99–119.

111. "American Short Wave Broadcasting—What's Wrong with It?" *Short Wave & Television,* September 1938, p. 264, 265.

112. Boyd W. Bullock, "An Outline of Future Plans and Progress in International Broadcasting," *All-Wave Radio,* September 1937, p. 502. The president of CBS had expressed similar views in 1930. William S. Paley, "International Broadcasting: Now and in the Future," *Annals of the American Academy of Political and Social Science,* Vol. 150 (Economics of World Peace), July 1930, p. 40.

113. "W8XWJ Broadcasts on 7.3 Meters—With 14 Hour Daily Program," *Short Wave & Television,* September 1938, p. 271.

114. Pages 39–40.

115. For examples of civil war-era QSL cards, see Ronald G. Shelley, "A Guide to the Postal History of the Spanish Civil War, 1936–1939," Pts. 2.19 (Republican) and 3.15 (Nationalist).

116. "Red Radio Station Heard in Germany," *The New York Times,"* March 21, 1937, p. 11; "Secret Red Station Heard," *The New York Times,* March 28, 1937, p. 168; "Anti-Nazi Station Grim Reality!" *Radio and Hobbies* [Australia], November 1939, p. 4; "Anti-Nazi Station Heard in Australia," *Radio and Hobbies* [Australia], November 1939, p. 52.

117. The station was the subject of a monograph by its "representative in Great Britain." "The Representative in Great Britain of the Freedom Station," *Freedom Calling! The Story of the Secret German Radio* (London: Frederick Muller Ltd., 2d ed. 1939). Deutscher Freiheitsender featured poetry specially written for the station by Bertolt Brecht. Michael Minden, "Satire as Propaganda: Brecht's 'Deutsche Satiren' for the Deutscher Freiheitsender," in Ronald Speirs, ed., *Brecht's Poetry of Political Exile* (Cambridge, England: Cambridge University Press, 2000), p. 100.

118. "Broadcast Rites Heard by Millions," *The New York Times,* May 13, 1937, p. 19.

119. H. W. Secor, "When PCJ and Eddie Startz 'Tell the World,'" *Short Wave & Television,* May 1938, p. 6.

120. "PCJ, Holland's New Revolving Beam Antenna," *Short Wave & Television,* January 1938, p. 472.

121. "Radio's Short Waves," *The New York Times,* October 24, 1937, p. 174.

122. ZNB moved to Gaborone as Radio Bechuanaland in 1965 and became Radio Botswana the following year. The station's history is recounted in James J. Zaffiro, *From Police Network to Station of the Nation: A Political History of Broadcasting in Botswana, 1927–1991* (Gaborone, Botswana: Botswana Society, 1991).

123. For a capsule view of broadcasting in China in mid-1937, see Robert H. Berkov, "China's Millions Twist the Dials," *Modern Mechanix,* June 1937, p. 76.

124. QSL letter from JDY/JQAK to William Sparks, September 25, 1937.

125. Philip L. Barbour, "Short-Wave Broadcasting and Latin America," *Bulletin of the Pan American Union,* Vol. 7, No. 10 (October 1937), pp. 739, 749.

126. See Richard A. Bartlett, *The World of Ham Radio, 1901–1950* (Jefferson, NC: McFarland, 2007), pp. 114–115; and "Radio in Guiana Jungle," *RADEX,* May 1938, p. 35.

127. "Short Waves Say —," *The New York Times,* November 21, 1937, p. 186.

128. Ric Gillespie, *Finding Amelia: The True Story of the Earhart Disappearance* (Annapolis, MD: Naval Institute, 2006). Gillespie's research on the Earhart incident is summarized in Eric Beheim, "The Enduring Amelia Earhart Mystery: Could Unidentified Radio Signals Provide New Clues?" *Monitoring Times,* October 2009, p. 10.

129. "The Earhart Project—Betty's Notebook," http://tighar.org/Projects/Earhart/Archives/Documents/Notebook/notebook.html, and "The Earhart Project—Harmony and Power: Could Betty Have Heard Amelia Earhart on a Harmonic?" http://tighar.org/Projects/Earhart/Archives/Research/Bulletins/30_BettyHarmonic/30_Bettyharmonic.html. A higher quality image of the notebook pages is contained on the CD that accompanies the Gillespie book; see note 128 *supra.*

130. Alvin Webster, "Communications Type Receivers Serve the Whole Family," *Short Wave & Television,"* July 1938, p. 170.

131. *General Radio Communication Regulations et al., International Telecommunication Convention Revision of Cairo, 1938* (London, England: H. M. Stationery Office, 1938), Art. 7, §7 & 8, ¶130–148; Francis Colt de Wolf, "The Cairo Telecommunication Conferences," *American Journal of International Law,* Vol. 32, No. 3 (July 1938), pp. 562–568; Howard S. LeRoy, "Treaty Regulation of International Radio and Short Wave Broadcasting," *American Journal of International Law,* Vol. 32, No. 4 (October 1938), pp. 719–737; "The Cairo Conference Report," *RADEX,* September 1938, p. 38. For a brief history of international radio regulation, a description of the international conference process, and an explanation of the Cairo conference from an amateur radio point of view, see A. L. Budlong, "Cairo," *QST,* Pt. I, January 1938, p. 11; Pt. II, February 1938, p. 32; and Kenneth B. Warner and Paul M. Segal, "The Battle of Cairo," *QST,* July 1938, p. 9.

132. "NBC's Foreign Response Shows 20-Fold Increase," *Broadcasting,* May 1, 1939, p. 46.

133. Raymond F. Guy, "An International Broadcasting System," *RCA Review,* July 1938, p. 27; "American Short Wave Broadcasting," *supra* note 111 at p. 264.

134. "Behind the Scenes of a S.-W. Rebroadcast from Europe," *Short Wave & Television,* May 1938, p. 10.

135. "Making Latin America Listen," *Business Week,* April 23, 1938, p. 42; Chris Mathisen, "Propaganda in Latin America," *Radio News,* August 1938, p. 19.

136. "W1XAL's Modern Radio Course," *Radio News,* November 1938, p. 30.

137. "American Short Wave Broadcasting," *supra* note 111 at p. 264.

138. Howard S. LeRoy, "Treaty Regulation of International Radio and Short Wave Broadcasting," *American Journal of International Law,* Vol. 32, No. 4 (October 1938), pp. 719–737. The considerable governmental machinations surrounding the Pan American frequencies are described in Redding, *supra* note 92 at pp. 114–142. The 16 half-hour Pan American programs broadcast over W1XAL were funded by a $12,800 grant from the Rockefeller Foundation, and were also made available to domestic Latin American stations by transcription. This W1XAL-Rockefeller connection is described in Gisela Cramer, "The Rockefeller Foundation and Pan American Radio," in William J. Buxton, ed., *Patronizing the Public: American Philanthropy's Transformation of Culture, Communication, and the Humanities* (Lanham, MD: Lexington, 2009), p. 77.

139. Sidel, *supra* note 16 at pp. 158–160.

140. "Daily Short-Wave Time Table," *The New York Times,* January 16, 1938, p. 160.

141. "Listening-In on Distance," *The New York Times,* March 26, 1939, p. 142.

142. "Wooing the Americas," *The New York Times,* February 20, 1938, p. 158.

143. Nevill Barbour, "Broadcasting to the Arab World: Arabic Transmissions from the B.B.C. and Other Non-Arab Stations," *Middle East Journal,* Vol. 5 (Winter 1951), p. 57; Beresford Clark, "The BBC's External Services." *International Affairs* [Royal Institute of International Affairs], Vol. 35, No. 2 (April 1959), p. 170; MacDonald, *supra* note 66; Philip M. Taylor, *The Projection of Britain—British Overseas Publicity and Propaganda, 1919–1939* (Cambridge, England: Cambridge University Press, 1981), pp. 181–215; Donald R. Browne, "Going International: How BBC Began Foreign Language Broadcasting," *Journalism Quarterly,* Vol. 60, No. 3 (Autumn 1983), p. 423; Peter Partner, *Arab Voices: The BBC Arabic Service, 1938–1988* (London: BBC External Services, 1988), pp. 1–32; Manuela A. Williams, *Mussolini's Propaganda Abroad: Subversion in the Mediterranean and the Middle East, 1935–1940* (New York: Routledge, 2006), pp. 82–89, 156–158.

144. D. Cameron Watt, "The Sender der Deutschen Freiheitspartei: A First Step in the British Radio War Against Nazi Germany?" *Intelligence and National Security,* Vol. 6, No. 3 (1991), p. 621.

145. Chester T. Crowell, "Dogfight on the Air Waves," *The Saturday Evening Post,* May 21, 1938, p. 23.

146. "When 2RO—Rome—Goes on the Air," *Short Wave & Television,* January 1938, p. 473.

147. "'Ici Paris Mondial'—'This Is Paris World Wide,'" *Short Wave & Television,* August 1938, p. 207.

148. Nicholas Pronay and Philip M. Taylor, "'An Improper Use of Broadcasting ...': The British Government and Clandestine Radio Propaganda Operations Against Germany During the Munich Crisis and After," *Journal of Contemporary History,* Vol. 19, No. 3 (July 1984), p. 357.

149. "Short-Wave Broadcasting In India," *Short Wave & Television,* April 1938, p. 668.

150. Alan Eurich, "CQ PITC," *QST,* August 1937, p. 9; "CQ PITC," *QST,* September 1937, p. 56; "More on PITC," *QST,* October 1937, p. 30; Lew Bellem, "The New PITC," *QST,* January 1938, p. 19; Lew Bellem, "A New Voice for 'PITC'—Pitcairn Island," *All-Wave Radio,* February 1938, p. 72; "Pitcairn Island Gets Station, NBC Plans Shortwave Series," *Broadcasting,* February 15, 1938, p. 111; Dorothy Hall, "The Story of VR6AY," *The T. & R.* [Transmitting & Receiving] *Bulletin* [Radio Society of Great Britain], December 1938, p. 334; Bartlett, *supra* note 126 at pp. 133–135; Raymond A. Dillon, "CQ-'PITC,'" *Radio News,* May 1941, p. 6. A number of issues of "Wavescan," the Adventist World Radio DX program written by radio historian Dr. Adrian M. Peterson, have covered various aspects of the Pitcairn saga in detail: July 5, 2009 (NWS 19); July 12, 2009 (NWS 20); De-

cember 13, 2009 (NWS 42); December 20, 2009 (NWS 43); and "Reminiscing with a Radio—Radio to the Rescue (III): On the Rocks—The Voice of PITC, Adamstown, Pitcairn Island, 1938" (December 2005). The scripts of these programs are available at http://www.ontheshortwaves.com ("Specialized Resources").

151. Andy Robins, "Conquistador of Science," http://andyrobinsradio.com/writing.

152. Script courtesy of Adrian M. Peterson and used with his permission.

153. "A Decade of Shortwave Broadcasting—TI4NRH Celebrates," *RADEX,* May 1938, p. 2.

154. *Short Wave Reporter* [Quixote Radio Club], January 1938, pp. 4–5.

155. "Short-Wave Pick-Ups," *The New York Times,* January 1, 1939, p. 104.

156. For an analysis of Germany's subsequent Arabic propaganda campaign in the Middle East, see Jeffrey Herf, *Nazi Propaganda for the Arab World* (New Haven, CT: Yale University Press, 2009).

157. W. T. Arms, "Listening-In on the Waves of '39," *The New York Times,* December 31, 1939, p. 94.

158. Orrin E. Dunlap, Jr., "Spinning the Dial to Europe," *The New York Times,* September 17, 1939, p. 144.

159. Nelson Costa Ribeiro, *BBC Broadcasts to Portugal in World War II* (Lewiston, ME: Edwin Mellen, 2011), pp. 220–226.

160. J. C. Furnas, "The War of Lies and Laughs—The Story of Radio's 24-Hour-a-Day Word Battle," *The Saturday Evening Post,* February 3, 1940, pp. 16, 69.

161. *International Short Wave Radio* [ISWC], January 1939, p. 19.

162. Arthur H. Lynch, "W2USA—DeLuxe Ham Station," *Radio & Television,* April 1940, p. 714; and these further Lynch articles in *Radio & Television:* "W2USA—World's Fair, New York," May 1940, p. 8; "W2USA at World's Fair," June 1940, p. 90; and "World's Fair Station W2USA," July 1940, p. 158.

163. For a concise history of the station, with photos, see "International Broadcast Station KGEI: 1939–1994," http://www.theradiohistorian.org/kgei.htm. For more photos, go to "FEBC International—Photo/Document Archive," http://www.febinfo.com/photo/photosummary.php, and search for "KGEI."

164. Sidel, *supra* note 16 at p. 189.

165. Michael A. Krysko, *American Radio in China* (New York: Palgrave Macmillan, 2011), pp. 90–125; Michael A. Krysko, "Homeward Bound: Shortwave Broadcasting and American Mass Media in East Asia on the Eve of the Pacific War," *Pacific Historical Review,* Vol. 74, No. 4 (November 2005), p. 511; Michael Alexander Krysko, *China Tuned Out: American Radio in East Asia, 1919–1941,* Ph.D. dissertation (Stony Brook: State University of New York, History, 2001), pp. 267–348.

166. "Short-Wave Lullaby Finds Infant Lost in China," *Radio & Hobbies* [Australia], February 1941, p. 57.

167. Krysko, *American Radio in China, supra* note 165 at p. 160.

168. Krysko, at p. 174, and Carroll Alcott, *My War with Japan* (New York: Henry Holt, 1943), p. 18.

169. Rolo, *supra* note 43 at p. 210.

170. "Big Bertha," *Time,* July 17, 1939, p. 47; see also "Radio 'Big Bertha' Challenges Axis," *The New York Times,* July 5, 1939, p. 5; "Powerful Tube Gives 'Big Bertha' Voice to Shout Around the Earth," *The New York Times,* July 16, 1939, p. 114.

171. "Foreign Targets," *The New York Times,* August 13, 1939, p. 10.

172. "Foreign Time Sold by NBC; Westinghouse Names Nelson," *Broadcasting,* November 15, 1939, p. 30; "Adams Hats to Use NBC's Shortwave," *Broadcasting,* June 1, 1940, p. 30; "WLWO Starts Service to Latin America with Four Sponsors Already Secured," *Broadcasting,* September 1, 1940, p. 36;

"Commercial Series for Latin Nations Viewed as Aid to Hemisphere Relations," *Broadcasting,* October 15, 1940, p. 26.

173. J. J. Clarey, Jr., "Radio Advertising in Latin America," *Broadcasting,* September 29, 1941, p. 30.

174. "Second Rate Card of NBC Shortwave," *Broadcasting,* October 27, 1941, p. 38. The story of commercial American shortwave during this period is explored in Lenore Emily Franz, *Short-Wave Communications to Latin America,* Master's thesis (Madison: University of Wisconsin, Speech, 1947), pp. 135–137; Douglas A. Boyd, "The Pre-History of the Voice of America." *Public Telecommunications Review,* Vol. 2, No. 6 (December 1974), p. 38; Robert A. Rabe, "Selling the Shortwaves: Commercial Shortwave Broadcasting to Latin America and the Limits of the 'American System,'" *American Journalism,* Vol. 24, No. 4 (Winter 2007), pp. 127, 136–139; Sidel, *supra* note 16 at pp. 173–179; Fejes, *supra* note 110 at pp. 132–138.

175. "Wavescan," NWS184, September 2, 2012, http://www.ontheshortwaves.com/Wavescan/wavescan120902.html.

176. Sol Taishoff, "Centralized Federal Radio Activity Seen," *Broadcasting,* May 15, 1939, p. 9; "New Ruling Is a Puzzle," *The New York Times,* May 28, 1939, p. X10; "Censorship Seen in International Ruling," *Broadcasting,* June 1, 1939, p. 13; "FCC Rule Fought By Broadcasters," *The New York Times,* June 6, 1939, p. 24; "A Storm of Protest," *The New York Times,* June 11, 1939, p. X10; "FCC Disclaims Censor's Role," July 23, 1939, p. X10; "Radio Men Hit 'Good-Will' Rule," *The New York Times,* July 16, 1939, p. 27; "FCC Quietly Inters International Rule as a Result of Disturbed World Scene," *Broadcasting,* October 1, 1939, p. 11.

177. Douglas A. Boyd, "The Pre-History of the Voice of America," *Public Telecommunications Review,* Vol. 2, No. 6 (December 1974), pp. 38, 45 n. 26.

178. "A licensee of an international broadcast station shall render only an international broadcast service which will reflect the culture of this country and which will promote international goodwill, understanding, and cooperation. Any program solely intended for and directed to an audience in the continental United States does not meet the requirements for this service." Code of Federal Regulations, Title 47, Chapter I, Sec. 73.788, http://edocket.access.gpo.gov/cfr_2004/octqtr/47cfr73.788.htm.

179. Lawrence W. Lichty, *"The Nation's Station," A History of Radio Station WLW,* Ph.D. dissertation (Columbus: Ohio State University, Speech, 1964), Vol. 1, pp. 361–367. At the government's request, the station conducted some tests at 750 kw. in 1943.

180. Sterling and Keith, *supra* note 76 at pp. 23–30; "Earliest FM Stations," http://jeff560.tripod.com/fmfirst.html.

181. John Schneider, "The Newspaper of the Air: Early Experiments with Radio Facsimile," *Monitoring Times,* February 2011, p. 12.

182. Ian K. Mackay, *Broadcasting in Australia* (Melbourne, Australia: Melbourne University Press, 1957), pp. 104–107; Alan Thomas, *Broadcast and Be Damned: The ABC's First Two Decades* (Melbourne, Australia: Melbourne University Press, 1980), pp. 113–121, 162–164.

183. E. Stanton Brown, "'SIRELA'—A Universal Radio Language," *Radio News,* Pt. I, November 1938, p. 34; Pt. II, January 1939, p. 31; Pt. III, February 1939, p. 38; Pt. IV, March 1939, p. 38.

184. *International Short Wave Radio* [ISWC], October 1939, p. 6.

185. *Broadcasting,* February 1, 1939, p. 35 [advertisement].

186. Arms, *supra* note 157.

187. Subcommittee on Programs, *Report of the Interdepartmental Committee to Study International Broadcasting* (Washington, DC: December 15, 1939), pp. 2–3.

188. The operation of these installations is described briefly in Rolo, *supra* note 43 at pp. 264–266.

189. Furnas, *supra* note 160, p. 68.

190. Jerome S. Berg, *On the Short Waves, 1923–1945* (Jefferson, NC: McFarland, 1999), pp. 208–212 and sources cited therein; Jerome S. Berg, *Listening On the Short Waves, 1945 to Today* (Jefferson, NC: McFarland, 2008), pp. 139–143 and sources cited therein; Alice Brannigan, "Memories of Radio," *Popular Communications,* August 1993, p. 18; Bartholomew Lee, "Radio Spies: Episodes in the Ether Wars," *AWA Review,* Vol. 15 (2002), pp. 7, 69–78; Hideharu Torii, "A Short History of Japan's Monitoring Services," *Popular Communications,* October 2002, p. 10.

CHAPTER 4

1. Frank Conrad, "The Story of Short Waves," *Science* (New Series), Vol. 91, No. 2534 (February 9, 1940), pp. 131–132, 132.

2. W. T. Arms, "The Changing Radio Map," *The New York Times,* July 7, 1940, p. X7.

3. "Short-Wave Pickups," *The New York Times,* April 28, 1940, p. 126.

4. "'City of Light' Signs Off," *The New York Times,* June 23, 1940, p. XX10; "Listening-In on Europe," *The New York Times,* June 30, 1940, p. 110. The end of independent French shortwave broadcasting is recounted in Charles J. Rolo, *Radio Goes to War* (New York: Putnam, 1942), pp. 81–93.

5. W. T. Arms, "Short-Wave Pickups," *The New York Times,* September 1, 1940, p. X8.

6. "Nazis Take More Stations," *The New York Times,* May 26, 1940, p. X10; "Huge Nazi Radio Net Hinted by Pick-Ups," *The New York Times,* July 6, 1940, p. 2.

7. "Network Commentators in Paris Safe; German Shortwave Operations Confuse," *Broadcasting,* July 15, 1940, p. 73.

8. W. T. Arms, "Listening-In On Europe," *The New York Times,* July 21, 1940, p. X8.

9. James B. Reston, "'Lord Haw Haw,'" *The New York Times,* February 25, 1940, p. 95; Harold N. Graves, Jr., "Lord Haw-Haw of Hamburg: The Campaign Against Britain," *The Public Opinion Quarterly,* Vol. 4, No. 3 (September 1940), p. 429; Henry Durant and Ruth Durant, "Lord Haw-Haw of Hamburg: His British Audience," *The Public Opinion Quarterly,* Vol. 4, No. 3 (September 1940), p. 443; "Lord Haw-Haw's Impact on the British," *Broadcasting,* October 1, 1940, p. 38. Many authors have traced William Joyce's life and broadcasts, e.g. J. A. Cole, *Lord Haw-Haw & William Joyce* (New York: Farrar, Straus and Giroux, 1965); Francis Selwyn, *Hitler's Englishman: The Crime of Lord Haw-Haw* (London: Penguin, 1993); M. A. Doherty, *Nazi Wireless Propaganda: Lord Haw-Haw and British Public Opinion in the Second World War* (Edinburgh, Scotland: Edinburgh University Press, 2000); Peter Martland, *Lord Haw Haw: The English Voice of Nazi Germany* (Lanham, MD: Scarecrow, 2003); Mary Kenny, *Germany Calling: A Biography of William Joyce, Lord Haw-Haw* (Dublin, Ireland: New Island, 2004); Nigel Farndale, *Haw-Haw: The Tragedy of William and Margaret Joyce* (London: Macmillan, 2005). Haw-Haw was also the subject of a novel of the time, as well as an English spoof of his broadcasts. Brett Rutledge, *The Death of Lord Haw Haw* (New York: Random House, 1940); Jonah Barrington, *Lord Haw-Haw of Zeesen* (London: Hutchinson, 1939).

10. Rolo, *supra* note 4 at pp. 94–109; John Carver Edwards, *Berlin Calling: American Broadcasters in Service to the Third Reich* (New York: Praeger, 1991); M. Williams Fuller, *Axis Sally* (Santa Barbara, CA: Paradise West, 2004); Frank Rybicki *The Rhetorical Dimensions of Radio Propaganda in Nazi Germany, 1933–1945,* Ph.D. dissertation (Pittsburgh, PA: Duquesne University, Communication, 2004), pp. 199–243; Judith Keene, *Treason on the Airwaves: Three Allied Broadcasters on Axis Radio During World War II* (Westport, CT: Praeger, 2008); Richard Lucas, *Axis Sally—The American Voice of Nazi Germany* (Philadelphia, PA: Casemate, 2010). See also John K. Hutchens, "In the Camp of the

Enemy," *The New York Times,* May 17, 1942, p. X10; and John W. Gerber, "Berlin Signs Off," *The New York Times,* May 6, 1945, p. X5.

11. Ann Elizabeth Pfau and David Hochfelder, "'Her Voice a Bullet': Imaginary Propaganda and the Legendary Broadcasters of World War II," in Susan Strasser and David Suisman, eds., *Sound In the Age of Mechanical Reproduction* (Philadelphia: University of Pennsylvania Press, 2010), p. 47.

12. Seth Arsenian, "Wartime Propaganda in the Middle East," *The Middle East Journal,* Vol. 2, No. 4 (October 1948), p. 417.

13. William D. Bayles, "London Calling—Goebbels Jamming," *The Saturday Evening Post,* April 11, 1942, p. 9; see also David Boyle, "The Real Origins of Bush House," http://davidboyle.blogspot.com/2012/07/real-origins-of-bush-house.html.

14. Charles J. Rolo, "America's Ears," *The Spectator,* March 22, 1940, p. 407.

15. World War II clandestine broadcasting is documented in Lawrence C. Soley and John S. Nichols, *Clandestine Radio Broadcasting: A Study of Revolutionary and Counterrevolutionary Electronic Communication* (New York: Praeger, 1987), pp. 25–50; and Lawrence C. Soley, *Radio Warfare: OSS and CIA Subversive Propaganda* (New York: Praeger, 1989). For a finely grained look at British clandestine broadcasting operations, see Geoffrey Pidgeon, *The Secret Wireless War* (London: UPSO, 2003), pp. 129–148, 255–262. An interesting description of the European clandestine radio scene, written in 1942, is in Rolo, *supra* note 4 at pp. 222–233.

16. For excerpts from letters received by NBC, see T. R. Kennedy, Jr., "Radio's Newest Tide of Mail," *The New York Times,* January 26, 1941, p. X12; and Earl Sparling, *America Calling All Peoples* (New York: NBC, 1941).

17. "Broadcasters Plan Powerful Beams to Roll Music and News Down to Rio," *The New York Times,* July 28, 1940, p. 102; Guy C. Hickok, "America Dominates the Latin Waves," *Broadcasting,* October 1, 1940, p. 30; "Radio Service Expansion to South America Expected in 1941 as the Facilities Improve," *The New York Times,* January 2, 1941, p. 40; "More American Radio Sought By Latins, Francisco Claims," *Broadcasting,* March 17, 1941, p. 18. It was reported in 1941 that BBC news broadcasts were favored in Brazil, while American news was preferred in Argentina. "Argentina Favors U.S. Shortwave," *Broadcasting,* July 7, 1941, p. 40.

18. "Ten Years of Latin Programs," *Broadcasting,* April 7, 1941, p. 46.

19. E.g. "MBS to Exchange with Latin Nations; Dickers with AP for Sponsored News," *Broadcasting,* November 15, 1940, p. 26-B; "NBC to Start Regular Pickups by Stations in Latin America," *Broadcasting,* December 1, 1940, p. 28; "Shouse to Tour Latin Countries," *Broadcasting,* January 27, 1941, p. 15; "CBS Latin Hookup to Start Sept. 1," *Broadcasting,* March 3, 1941, p. 18; "Networks Differ in Methods of Reaching Nations to South," *Broadcasting,* March 24, 1941, p. 18; William Paley, "Radio Turns South," *Fortune,* April 1941, p. 77; "Royal Leaves on Latin-American Tour to Promote NBC Activities to the South," *Broadcasting,* July 21, 1941, p. 37; "Press Wireless Granted FCC Authority to Handle MBS Latin Program Service," *Broadcasting,* October 27, 1941, p. 22.

20. Lenore Emily Franz, *Short-Wave Communications to Latin America,* Master's thesis (Madison: University of Wisconsin, Speech, 1947), pp. 133–134; E. Roderick Deihl, "South of the Border: The NBC and CBS Radio Networks and the Latin American Venture, 1930–1942," *Communication Quarterly,* Vol. 25, No. 4 (Fall 1977), pp. 2–12; Fred Allan Fejes, *Imperialism, Media, and the Good Neighbor: New Deal Foreign Policy and United States Shortwave Broadcasting to Latin America,* Ph. D. dissertation (Urbana-Champaign: University of Illinois, 1982 [also Norwood, NJ: Ablex, 1986]), pp. 145–147; Michael B. Salwen, "Broadcasting to Latin America: Reconciling Industry-Government Functions in the Pre-Voice of America Era," *Historical Journal of Film, Radio and Television,* Vol. 17, No. 1 (1997), pp. 67–89, 75–79.

21. Andre J. E. Mostert, Jr., *A History of WRUL: The Walter S. Lemmon Years, 1931–1960,* Master's thesis (Salt Lake City, UT: Brigham Young University, Communications, 1969), pp. 40–41, 59–63.

22. Clinton B. DeSoto, "Byrd Antarctic Expedition to Use Amateur Radio," *QST,* December 1939, p. 11.

23. DeSoto, p. 6.

24. Often Radio Brazzaville was associated with the call letters FZI. However, FZI appears to have been the call of the commercial telegraph station in Brazzaville.

25. Gordon Gaskill, "Voice of Victory," *The American Magazine,* December 1942, pp. 35, 106.

26. Virginia Thompson and Richard Adloff, *The Emerging States of French Equatorial Africa* (Stanford, CA: Stanford University Press, 1960), p. 315; *These You Can Hear* (London: Amalgamated Short Wave, 1947) p. 10.

27. Douglas A. Boyd, "Hebrew-Language Clandestine Radio Broadcasting During the British Palestine Mandate," *Journal of Radio Studies,* Vol. 6, No. 1 (1999), pp. 101–115. For further information on clandestine broadcasting in connection with the birth of Israel, see John Zimmerman, "Radio Propaganda in the Arab-Israeli War 1948," *The Wiener Library Bulletin,* Vol. 27, No. 1 (Winter 1973–74), p. 2; Douglas R. Browne, "The Voices of Palestine: A Broadcasting House Divided," *The Middle East Journal,* Vol. 29, No. 2 (Spring 1975), p. 133; and "From the Archives—A Brief History of Radio in the Country," http://www.israelradio.org/history/history.html.

28. "Shanghai Radio Dial 1941," http://www.radioheritage.net/Story129.asp.

29. Won Ho Chang, *Mass Media in China* (Ames: Iowa State University Press, 1989), pp. 151–154; Shuying Xie, *People's Republic of China's International Broadcasting: History, Structure, Policy and Politics,* Master's thesis (Houston, TX: University of Houston, 1992), pp. 11–14.

30. Don Moore, "The Day the Martians Landed—Or Stories They Never Tell on HCJB," *Monitoring Times,* October 1992, p. 26, and http://donmoore.tripod.com/south/ecuador/martians.html.

31. Charles J. Rolo, "America's Ears," *supra* note 14 at p. 407.

32. "Short Wave Coordinated," *The New York Times,* April 14, 1941, p. 13; "Overseas Radio Is Mobilized," *The New York Times,* April 20, 1941, p. X12; War Department (History Project, Strategic Services Unit, Office of the Asst. Secretary of War), *War Report of the OSS (Office of Strategic Services)* (New York: Walker, 1976) [prepared in 1947], pp. 41–42.

33. Robert William Pirsein, *The Voice of America: A History of the International Broadcasting Activities of the United States Government, 1940–1962,* Ph. D. dissertation (Evanston, IL: Northwestern University, 1970 [also New York: Arno, 1979]), pp. 45–46.

34. "Program Lines Tie Shortwave Stations, Permitting Combined Use of Facilities," *Broadcasting,* October 27, 1941, p. 51; "Short Waves on 24-Hour Basis," *Broadcasting,* December 15, 1941, p. 18. Among the important advantages of the network was the capability of the government, in 1942, to broadcast multi-lingual warnings of coming bombardments to those living in occupied France. "Shortwave Warnings," *Broadcasting,* October 12, 1942, p. 12.

35. Michael Kent Sidel, *A Historical Analysis of American Short Wave Broadcasting, 1916–1942,* Ph.D. dissertation (Evanston, IL: Northwestern University, Speech, 1976), pp. 197–200; "$40,000 RFC Loan Is Granted WRUL," *Broadcasting,* June 30, 1941, p. 39; "U.S. Cultural Group to Buy $200,000 Time on World-Wide," *Broadcasting,* July 14, 1941, p. 20.

36. Fejes, *supra* note 20 at p. 162.

37. For a summary of the development of shortwave broadcasting to 1941–42, see Charles J. Rolo and R. Strausz-Hupé, "U.S. International Broadcasting," *Harper's Magazine,* August 1941, p. 301; Douglas A. Boyd, "The Pre-History of the Voice of America," *Public Telecommunications Review,* Vol. 2, No. 6 (December 1974), p. 38; and John Schneider,

"Wartime Voices— Early Shortwave Broadcasting on the West Coast," *Monitoring Times,* July 2011, p. 11.

38. E.g. Hendrik Van Loon, "WRUL— This Unique Short Wave Radio Station Sells Nothing and Builds International Good Will," *Current History,* May 1941, p. 22; Webb Waldron, "Democracy on the Short Waves," *Reader's Digest,* September 1941, p. 40 (condensed from *The Living Age*); Robert J. Clements, "Foreign Language Broadcasting of 'Radio Boston,'" *The Modern Language Journal,* Vol. 27, No. 3 (March 1943), p. 175.

39. H. Montgomery Hyde, *Room 3603* (New York: Lyons, 2001 [copyright 1962]), pp. 157–160 (WRUL), 160–163 (KGEI, KWID); Mostert, *supra* note 21 at pp. 59–70; Donald R. Browne, *International Radio Broadcasting: The Limits of the Limitless Medium* (New York: Praeger, 1982), pp. 151–152; Bradley F. Smith, *The Shadow Warriors* (New York: Basic, 1983), pp. 85–86; Nicholas John Cull, *Selling War: The British Propaganda Campaign Against American "Neutrality" in World War II* (New York: Oxford University Press, 1995), p. 133; British Security Coordination, *The Secret History of British Intelligence in the Americas, 1940–45* (London: St. Ermin's, 1998), pp. 59–65; David Garnett, *The Secret History of PWE: The Political Warfare Executive 1939–1945* (London: St. Ermin's, 2002), pp. 136–137; Tim Brooks, *British Propaganda to France, 1940–1944: Machinery, Method and Message* (Edinburgh, Scotland: Edinburgh University Press, 2007), pp. 33–34, 153.

40. The WRCA-WNBI operation is described in detail in Raymond F. Guy, "NBC's International Broadcasting System," *RCA Review,* July 1941, p. 12, and Raymond F. Guy, "International Beams," *Scientific American,* November 1941, p. 268.

41. Lawrence E. Davies, "Coast Radio Wars On Tokyo By Air," *The New York Times,* February 1, 1942, p. E4; "Over Radio to Bataan Traveled A Song of 'Old Doug MacArthur Just Fightin' Along,'" *The New York Times,* February 22, 1942, p. 2; Lawrence E. Davies, "KGEI Tells Them," *The New York Times,* July 19, 1942, p. 8X; Frank J. Taylor, "He Bombs Tokyo Every Day," *The Saturday Evening Post,* July 25, 1942, p. 9.

42. Schneider, *supra* note 37; William Winter, *Voice from America: A Broadcaster's Diary 1941–1944* (Pasig, Metro Manila, Philippines: Anvil, 1994), pp. 1–50; British Security Coordination, *supra* note 39 at pp. 96–101.

43. For details of the Brentwood facility, see A. B. Chamberlain, "CBS International Broadcast Facilities," *Proceedings of the I.R.E.,* Vol. 30, No. 3 (March 1942), pp. 118–129; see also "CBS Builds Special Facilities for New Shortwave Operation," *Broadcasting,* April 14, 1941, p. 18.

44. "Nazi Radio Offers to Pay Cable Tolls from America," *The New York Times,* February 15, 1941, p. 3; "Cable At Nazis' Expense Urges Funeral of Hitler," *The New York Times,* February 16, 1941, p. 23; "Nazis Quit Under Radio Barrage; Stop Paying for U.S. Messages," *The New York Times,* February 21, 1941, p. 8; "Hitler Messages Go On," *The New York Times,* February 22, 1941, p. 17; "America Speaks, Germany Pays," *Broadcasting,* February 24, 1941, p. 51.

45. The operation of the Silver Hill, Maryland monitoring station in 1944 is described in some detail in Oliver Read, "Hams in the FBIS," *QST,* January 1945, p. 34.

46. *Seventh Annual Report of the Federal Radio Commission (Fiscal Year 1941),* p. 4; see also "Short-Wave Ears Get Big News Tips," *The New York Times,* August 26, 1941, p. 17.

47. Helena Huntington Smith, "It Pays to Listen," *Collier's,* January 30, 1943, pp. 42, 44.

48. Stephen C. Mercado, "FBIS Against the Axis, 1941– 1945," https://www.cia.gov/library/center-for-the-study-of-intelligence/csi-publications/csi-studies/studies/fall_winter_2001/article04.html#_ftn10; Joseph E. Roop, *Foreign Broadcast Information Service— History, Pt. I: 1941–1947* (Washington, DC: CIA, 1969), https://www.cia.gov/library-/center-for-the-study-of-intelligence/csi-publications/books-and-monographs/foreign-broadcast-information-service/

index.html; T. R. Kennedy, Jr., "Sleuths of the Air," *The New York Times,* April 27, 1941, p. X12; Cabell Phillips, "War of the Air Waves," *The New York Times,* December 28, 1941, p. SM12; "U.S. Ears for Axis Voices," *Broadcasting,* April 13, 1942, p. 24.

49. "Listening Station Dedicated by NBC," *The New York Times,* July 24, 1941, p. 14; "New NBC Station to Pick Up Foreign Programs Opened," *Broadcasting,* July 28, 1941, p. 14.

50. "NBC's Shortwave Post Dropped for Economy," *Broadcasting,* March 9, 1942, p. 13.

51. "AP Listening Post Set Up in New York," *Broadcasting,* August 4, 1941, p. 26.

52. "Canada Shortwave Post Busy Production Center," *Broadcasting,* November 24, 1941, p. 53; "Canada Hears the Homeland," *The New York Times,* April 5, 1942, p. X10.

53. Sidel, *supra* note 35 at pp. 163–164.

54. Ted Church, "A Long-Range Look at the Shortwaves," *Broadcasting,* May 18, 1942, p. 52.

55. "Foreign Broadcast Office in State Dept. Urged in Column by Dorothy Thompson," *Broadcasting,* May 12, 1941, p. 118. From March to September 1942, CBS shortwave carried a series of broadcasts to Germany by Thompson, who had considerable experience in Germany, from which she had been expelled by Hitler in 1934. In the broadcasts she explored German thinking and the many issues of the war. The broadcasts, together with related material by her, were published in Dorothy Thompson, *Listen, Hans* (Cambridge, MA: Riverside, 1942). It appears that Thompson was subject to the same kind of clandestine British influence as was WRUL. See British Security Coordination, *supra* note 39 at pp. 69–71; Smith, *supra* note 39 at pp. 84–86.

56. Addenda to Earl Sparling, *America Calling All Peoples* (New York: NBC), 1942 addenda [undated]).

57. Ibid.

58. For a recounting of domestic radio reporting of the events surrounding the Pearl Harbor attack, see Eric Beheim, "Air Raid on Pearl Harbor," *Monitoring Times,* December 2009, p. 13.

59. "War Comes!" *QST,* January 1942, p. 99.

60. "The War Emergency Radio Service," *QST,* July 1942, p. 11.

61. Cabell Phillips, "G-Men of the Airwaves," *The New York Times,* September 14, 1941, p. SM9; Oliver Read, "Hams in the RID," *QST,* October 1944, p. 18.

62. Some authorities of the time put the power of CBFW at 200 watts.

63. W. T. Arms, "Pick-Ups from Overseas," *The New York Times,* February 16, 1941, p. X10.

64. Harold N. Graves, Jr., *War on the Short Wave* (New York: Foreign Policy Association, 1941).

65. Rolo, *supra* note 4 at pp. 172–181.

66. Rolo, at pp. 184–189; "Ted Church Instructing BBC Newscasting Staff," *Broadcasting,* March 9, 1941, p. 41.

67. For a full list, see Garnett, *supra* note 39 at pp. 210–211.

68. Garnett, at p. 233.

69. Pidgeon, *supra* note 15 at pp. 134–137.

70. Jeremy Bennett, *British Broadcasting and the Danish Resistance Movement 1940–1945: A Study of the Wartime Broadcasts of the B.B.C. Danish Service* (Cambridge, England: Cambridge University Press, 1966), pp. 217–243.

71. Elizabeth L. Enriquez, *Appropriation of Colonial Broadcasting: A History of Early Radio in the Philippines, 1922–1946* (Quezon City: University of the Philippines Press, 2008), pp. 93, 96, 131, 180.

72. Houseman served from December 1941 to June 1943. His contributions to the founding of the Voice of America are discussed in Holly Cowan Shulman, "John Houseman and the Voice of America: American Foreign Propaganda on the Air," *American Studies,* Vol. 28, No. 2 (Fall 1987), p. 23.

73. Salwen, *supra* note 20 at p. 81.

74. *BBC Year Book,* 1943, p. 104.

75. *BBC Year Book,* 1943, at p. 6. Not everyone agreed. From the standpoint of swashbuckling black propagandist

Sefton Delmer, the wartime BBC was "spinsterish," "plod[ding] along in ... dreariness and pious unrealism...." Sefton Delmer, *Black Boomerang* (New York: Viking, 1962), p. 263. The process for the daily preparation and broadcasting of the news around this time was described in detail in Frank Singleton, *London Calling the World* ["Britain Advances"] (London: Longmans Green, 1943).

76. Martin Codel, "How to Wage War on the Shortwave Front," *Broadcasting*, October 5, 1942, p. 12. For excerpts of letters to NBC from "Voice of America" listeners in France, see Fernand Auberjonois, "Letters from France," *The New York Times*, May 3, 1942, p. SM12.

77. Allan M. Winkler, *The Politics of Propaganda: The Office of War Information, 1942–1945* (New Haven, CT: Yale University Press, 1978), pp. 121–122.

78. "Untold Saga" [editorial], *Broadcasting*, November 16, 1942, p. 36. But it was not all bouquets for OWI, which in July 1943 was upbraided by the press and the State Department for repeating the words of a *New York Post* columnist who had called Italy's King Victor Emmanuel III "a moronic little king," and Marshal Pietro Badoglio, Prime Minister of Italy in the country's last days of Fascism, a "leading fascist." These were arguably correct reflections of existing American policy, but they came at a time when the president wished to take a less strident line but had not changed official policy. The revelation that OWI sometimes spoke over the air through an imaginary political commentator, "John Durfee," did not help matters. Winkler, *supra* note 77 at pp. 89–101; "State Dept. Is Seen Advising the OWI," *Broadcasting*, August 2, 1943, p. 54.

79. John B. Whitton and John H. Herz, "Radio in International Politics," in Harwood L. Childs and John B. Whitton, eds., *Propaganda by Shortwave* (Princeton, NJ: Princeton University Press, 1942), pp. 1, 44.

80. "Peabody Awards Focus on Program Merit," *Broadcasting*, April 13, 1942, p. 8.

81. Harold Callender, "The Voice of America Echoes Widely," *The New York Times*, November 15, 1942, p. SM10.

82. Pirsein, *supra* note 33 at pp. 52–58.

83. *War Report of the OSS, supra* note 32 at p. 37.

84. Walter R. Roberts, "The Voice of America — Origins and Recollections," *American Diplomacy*, http://www.unc.edu/depts/diplomat/item/2009/1012/fsl/roberts_voice.html; see also Chris Kern, "A Belated Correction: The *Real* First Broadcast of the Voice of America," http://www.chriskern.net/essay/voaFirstBroadcast.html.

85. "The Beginning: An American Voice Greets the World," http://www.insidevoa.com/content/a-13-34-beginning-of-an-american-voice-111602684/177526.html.

86. "Government to Assume Control of All Short Wave Radio Tonight," *The New York Times*, October 31, 1942, p. 1. Worthy sources on the birth of the Voice of America and the years preceding it include: Leonard Carlton, "Voice of America: The Overseas Radio Bureau," *The Public Opinion Quarterly*, Vol. 7, No. 1 (Spring 1943), p. 46; *History of the Office of the Coordinator of Inter-American Affairs: Historical Reports on War Administration* (Washington, DC: U.S. Government Printing Office, 1948); Pirsein, *supra* note 33; Roberts, *supra* note 84; Charles A. H. Thomson, *Overseas Information Service of the United States Government* (Washington, DC: Brookings Institution, 1948); *War Report of the OSS, supra* note 32.

87. W. T. Arms, the regular *New York Times* shortwave reporter, had noted the broadcast about a month earlier. W. T. Arms, "From All Directions," *The New York Times*, June 7, 1942, p. X10.

88. Walter Lemmon is reported to have said that in 1940, well before the "Voice of America," an editorial writer in a Washington, D.C., newspaper once referred to WRUL as "the voice of America," and that when the government took over shortwave broadcasting in November 1942, OWI Director Elmer Davis asked Lemmon if he would be willing to let the government use the name, to which Lemmon responded in the affirmative. Thus, station identification over WRUL is said to have taken the form of "*This is the Voice of America, reaching you over station WRUL, World Wide Broadcasting Corporation, Boston, the United States of America.*" Mostert, *supra* note 21 at p. 60.

89. For background on the development of AFRS, see Edward M. Kirby and Jack W. Harris, *Star-Spangled Radio* (Chicago, IL: Ziff-Davis, 1948); Theodore Stuart DeLay, Jr., *An Historical Study of the Armed Forces Radio Service to 1946*, Ph.D. dissertation (Los Angeles: University of Southern California, 1951); Trent Christman, *Brass Button Broadcasters* (Paducah, KY: Turner, 1992); *History of AFRTS: The First 50 Years* (Ann Arbor: University of Michigan Library, 1993 [Michigan Digitization Project], http://afrts.dodmedia.osd.mil/heritage/page.asp?pg=50-years; and Donald R. Browne, "The World in the Pentagon's Shadow," *Educational Broadcasting Review*, Vol. 5, No. 2 (April 1971), p. 31.

90. Hallicrafters designed a receiver specifically for this purpose. It was the seven-tube RE-1 Sky Courier, which covered standard broadcast and 2.8–19 mc. in three bands. C. T. Read, "Radio for Morale," *Radio News*, May 1945, p. 30.

91. DeLay, *supra* note 89 at p. 500.

92. "Government Buys GE Transmitter," *Broadcasting*, December 22, 1941, p. 55.

93. "FCC Places Bans on Radiotelegraph," *Broadcasting*, June 1, 1942, p. 10; "Radio Drive Waits Naming of Board," *Broadcasting*, June 15, 1942, p. 11; *Ninth Annual Report of the Federal Radio Commission (Fiscal Year 1943)*, pp. 57–58.

94. "'Make Maximum Use of Existing Air Facilities First,' OWI Is Told," *Variety*, September 30, 1942, p. 28.

95. "Japanese Cut-Ins Interrupting KGEI," *Broadcasting*, January 5, 1942, p. 21.

96. The work of FBIS is detailed in *Ninth Annual Report of the Federal Radio Commission (Fiscal Year 1943)*, pp. 9–12, and *Eleventh Annual Report of the Federal Radio Commission (Fiscal Year 1945)*, pp. 89–90.

97. "Happenings of the Month," *QST*, April 1942, p. 16; "Happenings of the Month," *QST*, August 1942, p. 29.

98. Page 48.

99. Stefan J. Rundt, "Headaches for the Doctor," *The New York Times*, January 3, 1943, p. X10. One *Times* reader properly observed that most of the "clandestine" stations were surely run by either the Nazis or the British. "The Readers Write," *The New York Times*, January 17, 1943, p. X10 [letter from Leslie Ingersoll]. See also "Radio Mailbag: By Way of Reply," *The New York Times*, January 24, 1943, p. X10 [reply from Rundt].

100. Jane Robbins, *Tokyo Calling: Japanese Overseas Radio Broadcasting, 1937–1945* (Firenze, Italy: European Press Academic, 2001), pp. 92–93; Isao Ugusa, *Broadcasting Stations of Vietnam* (Kobe, Japan: DX Front Line, 1985), pp. 9–10.

101. "Tokyo Uses Prisoners as Bait," *The New York Times*, January 17, 1942, p. 3; Lisa L. Spahr, *World War II Radio Heroes: Letters of Compassion* (Pittsburgh, PA: Spahr Consulting, 2008); Jerome S. Berg, *World War II Radio Heroes: Letters of Compassion* (book review) and sources cited therein, http://www.ontheshortwaves.com/Reviews/World_WarII_Radio_Heroes.pdf; "Honoring Those Who Listened," http://www.usmm.org/duffyhonoring.html; Roop, *supra* note 48 at pp. 108–115; "DX History, POW Monitoring," http://www.ontheshortwaves.com.

102. Selden C. Menefee, "Japan's Psychological War," *Social Forces*, Vol. 21, No. 4 (May 1943), p. 425; Sato Masaharu and Barak Kushner, "'Negro Propaganda Operations': Japan's Short-wave Radio Broadcasts for World War II Black Americans," *Historical Journal of Film, Radio and Television*, Vol. 19, No. 1 (1999), p. 5. The content of Japanese wartime shortwave broadcasts is described in detail in Robbins, *supra* note 100.

103. Soley and Nichols, *supra* note 15 at p. 38.

104. Rolo, *supra* note 4 at pp. 211–215; "China's Broadcasts Stir Wide Interest," *The New York Times*, November 22, 1942, p. 35.

105. "New Wireless Routes From China," *China At War*,

February 1942, pp. 45–46; "An American Ear for China," *Broadcasting*, March 9, 1942, p. 45; "W6GRL Is China's U.S. Listening Post," *QST*, May 1942, p. 53.

106. *International Short Wave Radio* [ISWC], January 1942, p. 4.

107. Roop, *supra* note 48 at pp. 105–108.

108. Roop, at p. 105.

109. "22 New Shortwave Outlets Projected," *Broadcasting*, August 24, 1942, p. 62; Sol Taishoff, "Radio Steps Into Leading Wartime Role," *Broadcasting*, October 12, 1942, p. 7.

110. "DuPont Prizes to KGEI, Fulton Lewis," *Broadcasting*, March 8, 1943, p. 9.

111. Benjamin Fine, "Good-Neighbor Aim Declared In Peril," *The New York Times*, June 10, 1944, p. 9; "Latin Americans Hail U.S. Ties; Deny Charges of Deterioration," *The New York Times*, June 11, 1944, p. 20.

112. "New Standard-Frequency Service of the Bureau of Standards," *QST*, October 1943, p. 53.

113. "WWV 50th Anniversary," *The Old Timer's Bulletin*, March 1974, p. 24.

114. Ken Davies, *Skelton, Penrith and the World, 1943–1993* (Carlise, Cumbria, England: Cumbria County Council, 1995); G. P. Lowery, "Skelton Transmitting Station, 1942 to 1998 — Over Half a Century of Short Wave Broadcasting," http://www.bbceng.info/Operations/transmitter_ops/Reminiscences/skelton/sk1.htm.

115. Jeff Cant, *Fifty Years of Transmitting at BBC Woofferton, 1943–1993: A Social and Technical History of a Short Wave Station* (2006), http://www.bbceng.info/Operations/transmitter_ops/Reminiscences/Woofferton/woof50y-v2.pdf.

116. "A Short-Lived Station in a Short-Lived Country," *Communication* [British DX Club], October 2010, p. 6.

117. An upgrade of a 500 kw. RCA sender that had originally been built for New Jersey station WJZ, which was unable to get FCC approval for its use, the transmitter was known as "the biggest Aspidistra in the world." It remained in use by the BBC until 19[...]. ...tensender Calais also used a 500-watt mobile transmitter located directly across the English Channel from Calais.

118. K. R. M. Short, Namikawa Ryo and Frans Nieuwenhow, "World War II Broadcasting in the Pacific," *Historical Journal of Film, Radio and Television*, Vol. 3, No. 1 (1983), p. 51, 54. NHK has said that "Zero Hour" began in April 1942. *The History of Broadcasting in Japan* (Tokyo: Radio and TV Culture Research Institute, NHK, 1967), p. 108; *50 Years of Japanese Broadcasting* (Tokyo: Radio and TV Culture Research Institute, NHK, 1977), p. 100.

119. Rosa Maria Fazio, *The Effects of the Broadcasts of "Tokyo Rose" During World War II*, Master's thesis (University Park: Pennsylvania State University, Speech, 1968).

120. Fazio, at p. 26, citing Lee Clark, *One Last Look Around* (New York: Duell, Sloan and Pearce, 1947), p. 90.

121. Judith Keene, "Japanese Overseas Broadcasting and Allied Prisoners of War During WW II," in Sianan Healy, Bruce Berryman and David Goodman, eds., *Radio in the World: Papers from the 2005 Melbourne Radio Conference* (Melbourne, Australia: RMIT, 2005), p. 276; Robbins, *supra* note 100 at pp. 141–164.

122. Jack Gould, "One Thing and Another," *The New York Times*, March 12, 1944, p. X7; "Army Warns Public to Discount War-Captive Tales on Axis Radio," *The New York Times*, October 23, 1944, p. 5.

123. "War Prisoner in Reich Asks Mother to Buy Bond," *The New York Times*, June 14, 1944, p. 4.

124. "Army Forbids Soldiers from Broadcasting on Enemy Radio Stations," *Broadcasting*, March 15, 1943, p. 36.

125. Soley, *supra* note 15 at p. 97.

126. Supreme Headquarters, Allied Expeditionary Forces. Notwithstanding the broadcast of military directives and the like, the Voice of SHAEF was intended to influence mainly the civilian population.

127. "Allied Radio Preparing Final Coup," *Broadcasting*, December 25, 1944, p. 22; Pirsein, *supra* note 33 at pp. 81–84.

128. Russell Hart, "With Unbelieving Eyes," in Jane Penrose, ed., *The D-Day Companion* (New Orleans, LA: Osprey, 2004), p. 225. Only the forces at the Pas de Calais, which the Germans mistakenly believed to be the planned invasion point, went on alert.

129. "OWI Tells Story of Invasion to the World in 28 Tongues," *Broadcasting*, June 12, 1944, p. 62.

130. For an interesting hour-by-hour account of D-Day reporting at home over the CBS radio network, see Eric Beheim, "D-Day (June 6, 1944) as Reported by Radio," *Monitoring Times*, June 2009, p. 12.

131. Sanford T. Terry, *The Apache Project: How News of General MacArthur's Victories Reached America* (unpublished manuscript, 1989), pp. 69–72; and Capt. L. A. Pierce, "The Story of the Apache," p. 4, an unpublished account accompanying the Terry manuscript.

132. Enriquez, *supra* note 71 at pp. 132–134, 146–147, 154–157; "Voice of Freedom" [editorial], *The New York Times*, October 21, 1944, p. 16.

133. The activities of the *Apache* are described in detail in Allen J. Raymond, "The Ship with the Singing Masts," *The Saturday Evening Post*, May 12, 1945, p. 20; Lt. Anthony W. Borgia, "Those Singing Masts," *QST*, September 1945, p. 39; Edward M. Kirby and Jack W. Harris, *Star-Spangled Radio* (Chicago: Ziff-Davis, 1948), pp. 90–106; William J. Dunn, *Pacific Microphone* (College Station: Texas A&M University Press, 1988), pp. 236–243; and Terry, *supra* note 131.

134. A detailed description of the development of the Bethany and Delano sites is contained in James E. O'Neal, "The United States Enters International Broadcasting: A Tale of Two Unusual Radio Stations," *AWA Review*, Vol. 21 (2008), p. 233. The Delano story is told in James E. O'Neal, "Last of VOA's Wartime Transmitting Stations Goes Dark," http://www.rwonline.com/article/last-of-voas-wartime-transmitting-stations-goes-dark/20235. The technical side of the Bethany installation is addressed in R. J. Rockwell, "OWI 200 kw. H.F. Transmitters at Bethany, Ohio," *RCA Communications*, November and December 1944.

135. Eleven 11 meter channels, 25 kc. apart in the 25600–25850 kc. band, were also available but seldom used.

136. Bill Bailey, "Fight Looms for Postwar Shortwaves," *Broadcasting*, July 10, 1944, p. 11; "Back 'Short Wave' for Foreign Use," *The New York Times*, August 12, 1944, p. 11; "Planners Omit International Shortwave," *Broadcasting*, August 14, 1944, p. 11; "Room for Internationals Seen Before Allocation Is Finished," *Broadcasting*, August 21, 1944, p. 18; Jack Gould, "Radio and the Peace," *The New York Times*, August 27, 1944, p. X5; "Urge World Radio as Post-War Need," *The New York Times*, October 6, 1944, p. 9.

137. "Tomorrow — The World" [editorial], *Broadcasting*, December 11, 1944, p. 40.

138. *BBC Year Book*, 1945, pp. 109–128.

139. "Hidden Radios Keep Dutch Informed," *Broadcasting*, February 14, 1944, p. 68.

140. "Pierce, Italian Navy Capturer, Conquers Radio Luxembourg," *Broadcasting*, October 23, 1944, p. 16; "Pierce Leaves OWI After Two Years," *Broadcasting*, November 20, 1944, p. 61; Robert T. Colwell, "Radio Luxembourg," *Life*, March 5, 1945, p. 17; "SHAEF Radio Drive Against Germany," *Broadcasting*, November 12, 1945, p. 60; Helen House, "Luxembourg Shortwave Radio Tribulations Told by Mueller," *Broadcasting*, January 29, 1945, p. 28; William Harlan Hale, "Big Noise in Little Luxembourg," *Harper's Magazine*, April 1946, p. 377; *The Psychological Warfare Division (PWD), Supreme Headquarters, Allied Expeditionary Force (SHAEF)— An Account of Its Operations in the Western European Campaign, 1944–1945* (1951), pp. 27–30.

141. Did "1212" mean 1212 kc. mediumwave; or 1212 meters, corresponding to 247 kc. longwave; or something else? **1212 kc.:** Erik Barnouw, "Propaganda at Radio Luxembourg: 1944–1945," in K. R. M. Short, ed., *Film & Radio Propaganda in World War II* (Knoxville: University of Tennessee Press, 1983), pp. 192, 195; Tom Kneitel, "The Strange Case of Op-

eration Annie," *Popular Communications,* April 1983, p. 16 [Kneitel calls the station Voice of the Rhineland]). **1212 meters:** Soley, *supra* note 15 at pp. 1, 140. The station was under the Psychological Warfare Branch of the 12th Army Group.

142. Delmer, *supra* note 75 at p. 265.

143. H. H. Burger, "Operation Annie: Now It Can Be Told," *The New York Times,* February 17, 1946, p. SM12; Jack Althouse, "The Short, Treacherous Life of Radio 1212," *Electronics Illustrated,* September 1968, p. 95; Alice Brannigan, "The Mysterious Radio 1212," *Popular Communications,* December 1998, p. 12; Berrin A. Beasley, "Hier Ist 1212: Operation Annie, World War II Allied Psychological Warfare, and the Capture of the Rhineland," *Journal of Radio Studies,* Vol. 8, No. 1 (2001), p. 104 (Berrin is mistaken in his reference to Radio 1212 as a shortwave operation); Soley, *supra* note 15 at pp. 138–145; Soley and Nichols, *supra* note 15 at pp. 42–45.

144. Herbert A. Friedman, "Radio Leaflets During Wartime," http://www.psywarrior.com/RadioLeaflet.html.

145. "Worcester Will Celebrate United Nations Weeks," *Nashua Telegraph* [Nashua, New Hampshire], September 25, 1944, p. 9; "David H. Harris, "WTAG Plan for World Harmony," *Broadcasting,* October 2, 1944, p. 44; "This Is the Belgian Congo ... Calling WTAG, Worcester," *Broadcasting,* November 13, 1944, p. 4 [advertisement].

146. Douglas A. Boyd, "Sharq al-Adna/The Voice of Britain," *Gazette: The International Journal for Communication Studies,* Vol. 65, No. 6 (2003), p. 443; Peter Partner, *Arab Voices: The BBC Arabic Service, 1938–1988* (London: BBC External Services, 1988), pp. 50–54; Garnett, *supra* note 39 at pp. 156–159.

147. George Grim, "Fighting the Air War in the Orient," *Broadcasting,* July 17, 1944, p. 22.

148. The history of Radio SEAC is told in detail by Eric Hitchcock, who was involved in setting up the 100 kw. transmitter that commenced operation in 1946. See Eric Hitchcock, *Radio SEAC's Transmitters* (South Croydon, Surrey, UK: 2007 [draft]), and Eric Hitchcock, "Radio SEAC's Transmitters," *Short Wave Magazine* [UK], October 2000, p. 45. See also C. L. Pujitha-Gunawardana, *This Is Colombo Calling: 1924–1949 (Reminiscences)* (Nugegoda, Sri Lanka: Peralia, 1990), pp. 142–144.

149. Fred Henry, "Good Future for Shortwave Is Seen," *Broadcasting,* June 11, 1945, p. 24; see also "U.S. Programs Rebroadcast for G.I.'s Create Possible Markets in Australia," *Broadcasting,* June 11, 1945, p. 28.

150. Harrison Forman, "The Voice of China," *Collier's,* June 17, 1944, p. 14.

151. Ian McFarland, "Radio Canada International: Canada's Underrated Ambassador," *Broadcast Technology* [Canada], September 1994, p. 36.

152. "Feature of the Week," *Broadcasting,* September 10, 1945, p. 10.

153. For two interesting illustrated articles about KRHO, see "Radio History — KRHO Honolulu 1944," http://www.radioheritage.net/Story109.asp, and "Radio History: OWI Central Pacific Operations," http://www.radioheritage.net/Story103.asp.

154. Martin Hadlow, "The Mosquito Network: American Military Radio in the Solomon Islands During World War II," *Journal of Radio Studies,* Vol. 11, No. 1 (2004), p. 73; Sgt. Bob LeMond, "'This Is the AES Mosquito Network,'"

Broadcasting, May 8, 1944, p. 20. The Hadlow article, with illustrations, also appears in three parts on the Radio Heritage Foundation website, specifically at http://www.radioheritage.net/Story137.asp (Pt. 1); http://www.radioheritage.net/Story138.asp (Pt. 2); and http://www.radioheritage.net/Story139.asp (Pt. 3). An updated version of the article is Martin Hadlow, "The Mosquito Network: American Military Broadcasting in the South-West Pacific 1944–46," in Peter Dennis and Jeffrey Grey, *The Military and the Media: The 2008 Chief of Army Military History Conference* (Loftus, NSW, Australia: Australian Military History, 2008), p. 74. The Mosquito Network became more professional as time went on. Spencer M. Allen, "Mosquito Net Finds Home Methods Best," *Broadcasting,* April 30, 1945, p. 20.

155. T. R. Kennedy, Jr., "V-E Day on the Radio," *The New York Times,* May 13, 1945, p. X5.

156. Winkler, *supra* note 77 at pp. 143–148; Robbins, *supra* note 100 at pp. 188–193. The ins and outs of the broadcasts are described by Zacharias himself in E. M. Zacharias, "Eighteen Words That Bagged Japan," *Saturday Evening Post,* November 17, 1945, p. 17, and Ellis M. Zacharias, *Secret Missions: The Story of an Intelligence Officer* (New York: Putnam's, 1946), pp. 285–389 [transcripts of the broadcasts at pp. 399–424]. See also Bill Davidson, "He Talked to Japan," *Collier's,* October 13, 1945, p. 15.

157. Pirsein, *supra* note 33 at pp. 94–95.

158. "State Dept. Studies Shortwave Future," *Broadcasting,* December 31, 1945, p. 63.

159. Page 48.

160. Bernard Wasserstein, "Secret War in Shanghai" (New York: Houghton Mifflin, 1998), pp. 66–69, 173–180, 261–263; *Radio News,* July 1946, pp. 90, 112.

161. Jack Anderson, *Peace, War, and Politics* (New York: Tom Doherty, 1999), pp. 51–52.

162. "Feature of the Week," *Broadcasting,* May 7, 1945, p. 10.

163. DeLay, *supra* note 89 at pp. 467–483. For stories about AFRS and WVTR, see "AFRS Japan," http://www.radioheritage.net/Story57.asp; "WVTR's Sea Monster," http://www.radioheritage.net/Story32.asp;"WVTR Memories," http://www.radioheritage.net/Story33.asp; "WVTR Tokyo Xmas 1945," http://www.radioheritage.net/Story34.asp.

164. The history of shortwave broadcasting and shortwave listening from 1945 to 2008 are covered in two McFarland books by Jerome S. Berg: *Broadcasting on the Short Waves: 1945 to Today* (2008) and *Listening on the Short Waves: 1945 to Today* (2008).

165. Pirsein, *supra* note 33 at pp. 90, 122, 132, 145–146.

166. Won Ho Chang, *supra* note 29; Shuying Xie, *supra* note 29 at pp. 11–14, 30–31.

CONCLUSION

1. Susan J. Douglas, *Listening In* (Minneapolis: University of Minnesota Press, 2004), p. 346.

2. H. P. Davis, "Short-Wave Broadcast Pioneering," *Radio-Craft,* March 1931, pp. 543, 565.

Bibliography

Books and Other Major Works

Adams, Mike. *Lee de Forest: King of Radio, Television, and Film.* New York: Springer, 2012.

Ahmad, Nihal. *A History of Radio Pakistan.* Oxford, England: Oxford University Press, 2005.

Aitken, Hugh G. J. *The Continuous Wave: Technology and American Radio, 1900–1932.* New York: Wiley, 1976.

_____. *Syntony and Spark: The Origins of Radio.* Princeton, NJ: Princeton University Press, 1985.

Alcott, Carroll. *My War with Japan.* New York: Henry Holt, 1943.

Anduaga, Aitor. *Wireless and Empire: Geopolitics, Radio Industry and Ionosphere in the British Empire, 1918–1939.* Oxford, England: Oxford University Press, 2009.

Aniceto, Ben. *Stay Tuned: The Golden Years of Philippine Radio.* Marikina City, Philippines: Stay Tuned, 2007.

Anthony, Ian A. *Radio Wizard: Edward Samuel Rogers and the Revolution of Communications.* Toronto, ON: Gage Educational, 2000.

Archer, Gleason L. *Big Business and Radio.* New York: American Historical, 1939.

_____. *History of Radio to 1926.* New York: American Historical Society, 1938.

Awasthy, G. C. *Broadcasting in India.* Bombay, India: Allied, 1965.

Badenoch, Alexander. *Voices in Ruins: West German Radio Across the 1945 Divide.* Basingstoke, Hampshire, England: Palgrave Macmillan, 2008.

Baglehole, K. C. *A Century of Service: A Brief History of Cable and Wireless Ltd., 1868–1968.* London, England: Cable and Wireless Ltd., 3d ed. 1978.

Baker, Jill, Frank Sulek and Peter Kanze. *The Airwaves of New York.* Jefferson, NC: McFarland, 1998.

Baker, W. J. *A History of the Marconi Company.* New York: St. Martin's, 1971.

Banning, William Peck. *Commercial Broadcasting Pioneer: The WEAF Experiment, 1922–1926.* Cambridge, MA: Harvard University Press, 1946.

Barfield, Ray. *Listening to Radio, 1920–1950.* Westport, CT: Praeger, 1996.

Barnouw, Erik. *The Golden Web: A History of Broadcasting in the United States 1933–1953.* New York: Oxford University Press, 1968.

_____. *A Tower in Babel: A History of Broadcasting in the United States to 1933.* New York: Oxford University Press, 1966.

Bartlett, Richard A. *The World of Ham Radio, 1901–1950.* Jefferson, NC: McFarland, 2007.

Barty-King, Hugh. *Girdle Round the Earth: The Story of Cable and Wireless.* London, England: Heinemann, 1979.

Baruah, U. L. *This Is All India Radio.* New Delhi, India: Ministry of Information and Broadcasting, 1983.

Bennett, Jeremy. *British Broadcasting and the Danish Resistance Movement 1940–1945: A Study of the Wartime Broadcasts of the BBC Danish Service.* Cambridge, England: Cambridge University Press, 1966.

Bensman, Marvin R. *The Beginning of Broadcast Regulation in the Twentieth Century.* Jefferson, NC: McFarland, 2000.

Berg, Jerome S. *Broadcasting on the Short Waves, 1945 to Today.* Jefferson, NC: McFarland, 2008.

_____. *Listening on the Short Waves, 1945 to Today.* Jefferson, NC: McFarland, 2008.

_____. *On the Short Waves, 1923–1945: Broadcast Listening in the Pioneer Days of Radio.* Jefferson, NC: McFarland, 1999.

Bergmeier, J.P., and Rainer E. Lotz. *Hitler's Airwaves: The Inside Story of Nazi Radio Broadcasting and Propaganda Swing.* New Haven, CT: Yale University Press, 1997.

Boyd, Douglas A. *Broadcasting in the Arab World: A Survey of the Electronic Media in the Middle East.* Ames: Iowa State University Press, 1993.

_____. *Egyptian Radio: Tool of Political and National Development* [Journalism Monographs, No. 48]. Lexington, KY: Association for Education in Journalism, February 1977.

Briggs, Asa. *The BBC: The First Fifty Years.* Oxford, England: Oxford University Press, 1985.

_____. *The History of Broadcasting in the United Kingdom.* London, England: Oxford University Press, Vol. I, *The Birth of Broadcasting* (1961); Vol. II, *The Golden Age of Wireless* (1965); Vol. III, *The War of Words* (1970).

British Security Coordination. *The Secret History of British Intelligence in the Americas, 1940–45.* London, England: St. Ermin's, 1998.

Broadcasting and the Australian Post Office 1923–1973. Melbourne, Vic: Australian Post Office, 1973.

Broadcasting House. London, England: BBC, 1932.

Broadcasting in Japan: Twentieth Century Journey from Radio to Multimedia. Tokyo: NHK, 2002.

Broadcasting Stations of the World. Washington, DC: Foreign Broadcast Intelligence Service, August 1, 1945.

311

Brooks, Tim. *British Propaganda to France, 1940–1944: Machinery, Method and Message.* Edinburgh, Scotland: Edinburgh University Press, 2007.

Brown, Robert J. *Manipulating the Ether: The Power of Broadcast Radio in Thirties America.* Jefferson, NC: McFarland, 1998.

Browne, Donald R. *International Radio Broadcasting: The Limits of the Limitless Medium.* New York: Praeger, 1982.

_____. *The Voice of America: Policies and Problems* [Journalism Monographs, No. 43]. Lexington, KY: Association for Education in Journalism, February 1976.

Bryant, John H., and Harold N. Cones. *Dangerous Crossings.* Annapolis, MD: Naval Institute, 2000.

Bucher, Elmer E. *Shortwave Radio and David Sarnoff,* 1953, Pt. 25 of the 56-volume typescript, Bucher, *Radio and David Sarnoff.* Princeton, NJ: David Sarnoff Library, approx. 1942–1957.

Bumpus, Bernard, and Barbara Skelt. *Seventy Years of International Broadcasting.* Paris, France: UNESCO, 1984.

Bussey, Gordon. *Wireless, the Crucial Decade: History of the British Wireless Industry 1924–34.* London: Peter Peregrinus, 1990.

Cain, John. *The BBC: 70 Years of Broadcasting.* London: BBC Information Services, 1992.

Cant, Jeff. *50 Years of Transmitting At BBC Woofferton, 1943–1993: A Social and Technical History of a Short Wave Station* (2006). http://www.bbceng.info/Operations/transmitter_ops/Reminiscences/Reminiscences.htm.

Chang, Won Ho. *Mass Media in China.* Ames: Iowa State University Press, 1989.

Chapman, Ivan. *Tokyo Calling: The Charles Cousens Case.* Sydney, NSW, Australia: Hale and Iremonger, 1990.

Childs, Harwood L., and John B. Whitton, eds. *Propaganda by Shortwave.* Princeton, NJ: Princeton University Press, 1942.

Christman, Trent. *Brass Button Broadcasters.* Paducah, KY: Turner, 1992.

Clarricoats, John. *World at Their Fingertips.* London: Radio Society of Great Britain, 1967.

Claxton, Robert Howard. *From Parsifal to Perón: Early Radio in Argentina, 1920–1944.* Gainesville: University of Florida, 2007.

Coase, R. H. *British Broadcasting: A Study in Monopoly.* London: London School of Economics and Political Science, 1950.

Cochrane, Rexmond C. *Measures for Progress: A History of the National Bureau of Standards.* Washington, DC: U.S. Department of Commerce, 1966.

Codding, George A., Jr. *Broadcasting Without Barriers.* Paris, France: UNESCO, 1959.

_____. *The International Telecommunication Union: An Experiment in International Cooperation.* Leiden, Netherlands: E. J. Brill, 1952.

Cole, J. A. *Lord Haw-Haw and William Joyce.* New York: Farrar, Straus and Giroux, 1965.

Cones, Harold N., and John H. Bryant. *Zenith Radio: The Early Years: 1919–1935.* Atglen, PA: Schiffer, 1997.

The Constant Voice. Melbourne, Vic: Australian Broadcasting Corp. and Radio Australia, 1st ed. 1964; 2d ed. 1969.

Cruickshank, Charles. *The Fourth Arm: Psychological Warfare 1938–1945.* Oxford, England: Oxford University Press, 1981.

Curran, Charles J. *Broadcasting from West of Suez.* London: Lunch-Time Lectures, 7th Series, No. 2, BBC, 1968.

Cushen, Arthur. *Radio Listeners Guide.* Invercargill, New Zealand: Arthur Cushen, 2d ed. 1990.

Cushen, Arthur T. *The World In My Ears.* Invercargill, New Zealand: Arthur T. Cushen, 1979.

Dachis, Chuck. *Radios by Hallicrafters.* Atglen, PA: Schiffer, 2d. ed. 1999.

Daugherty, William E., and Morris Janowitz. *A Psychological Warfare Casebook.* Baltimore, MD: John Hopkins Press, 1958.

Davidson, Randall. *9XM Talking: WHA Radio and the Wisconsin Idea.* Madison: University of Wisconsin Press, 2006.

Davies, Ken. *Skelton, Penrith and the World, 1943–1993.* Carlisle, Cumbria, England: Cumbria County Council, 1995.

Davis, H. P. "The Early History of Broadcasting in the United States," in *The Radio Industry: The Story of Its Development.* Chicago: A. W. Shaw, 1928.

Davis, Stephen. *The Law of Radio Communication.* New York: McGraw-Hill, 1927.

DeLay, Theodore Stuart, Jr. *An Historical Study of the Armed Forces Radio Service to 1946,* Ph.D. dissertation. Los Angeles: University of Southern California, 1951.

Delmer, Sefton. *Black Boomerang.* New York: Viking, 1962.

De Mendelssohn, Peter. *Japan's Political Warfare.* London: George Allen and Unwin, 1944 [1972 reprint, Arno].

DeSoto, Clinton B. *200 Meters and Down: The Story of Amateur Radio.* West Hartford, CT: American Radio Relay League, 1936.

Doherty, M. A. *Nazi Wireless Propaganda: Lord Haw-Haw and British Public Opinion in the Second World War.* Edinburgh, Scotland: Edinburgh University Press, 2000.

Douglas, Alan. *Radio Manufacturers of the 1920s* [three volumes]. Vestal, NY: Vestal, 1988.

Douglas, George H. *The Early Days of Radio Broadcasting.* Jefferson, NC: McFarland, 1987.

Douglas, Susan J. *Inventing American Broadcasting 1899–1922.* Baltimore, MD: Johns Hopkins University Press, 1987.

_____. *Listening In: Radio and the American Imagination.* Minneapolis: University of Minnesota Press, 2004.

Downes, Peter, and Peter Harcourt. *Voices in the Air.* Wellington, New Zealand: Methuen, 1976.

Dunlap, Orrin E., Jr. *Dunlap's Radio & Television Almanac.* New York: Harper and Bros., 1951.

_____. *The Story of Radio.* New York: Dial, 1927, 1935.

Duus, Masayo. *Tokyo Rose: Orphan of the Pacific.* Tokyo: Kodansha, 1979.

DX Almanac. Worcester, MA: Victory Radio Club, 1944.

Edwards, John Carver. *Berlin Calling: American Broadcasters in Service to the Third Reich.* New York: Praeger, 1991.

Emery, Walter B. *National and International Systems of Broadcasting: Their History, Operation and Control.* East Lansing: Michigan State University Press, 1969.

The Empire Broadcasting Service. London: BBC, 1936.

Enriquez, Elizabeth L. *Appropriation of Colonial Broadcasting: A History of Early Radio in the Philippines, 1922–1946.* Quezon City: University of the Philippines Press, 2008.

Ettlinger, Harold. *The Axis On the Air.* Indianapolis, IN: Bobbs-Merrill, 1943.

Farndale, Nigel. *Haw-Haw: The Tragedy of William and Margaret Joyce.* London: Macmillan, 2005.

Fazio, Rosa Maria. *The Effects of the Broadcasts of "Tokyo*

Rose" *During World War II*, Master's thesis. University Park: Pennsylvania State University, Speech, 1968.

FBIS in Retrospect: 30 Years of the Foreign Broadcast Information Service, 1941–1971. Washington, DC: Foreign Broadcast Information Service, 1971.

Fejes, Fred Allan. *Imperialism, Media, and the Good Neighbor: New Deal Foreign Policy and United States Shortwave Broadcasting to Latin America*, Ph. D. dissertation. Urbana-Champaign: University of Illinois, 1982; and Norwood, NJ: Ablex, 1986.

Fessenden, Helen M. *Fessenden: Builder of Tomorrows*. New York: Coward-McCann, 1940.

Fifty Years of A.R.R.L. Newington, CT: American Radio Relay League, 1965.

50 Years of Japanese Broadcasting. Tokyo: History Compilation Room, Radio and TV Culture Research Institute, NHK, 1977.

Finnie, Andrew K. *Radio Canada International, 1945–1995*. Montreal, QC: Radio Canada International, 1996.

Fox, Elizabeth. *Latin American Broadcasting: From Tango to Telenovela*. Luton, England: John Libbey, 1997.

Franz, Lenore Emily. *Short-Wave Communications to Latin America*, Master's thesis. Madison: University of Wisconsin, Speech, 1947.

Frost, Gary L. *Early FM Radio*. Baltimore, MD: Johns Hopkins University Press, 2010.

Fuller, M. Williams. *Axis Sally*. Santa Barbara, CA: Paradise West, 2004.

Galgay, Frank, Michael McCarthy and Jack OKeefe. *The Voice of Generations: A History of Communications in Newfoundland*. St. John's, NL: Robinson Blackmore, 1994.

Garnett, David. *The Secret History of PWE: The Political Warfare Executive 1939–1945*. London: St. Ermin's, 2002.

Gebhard, Louis A. *Evolution of Naval Radio-Electronics and Contributions of the Naval Research Laboratory*. Washington, DC: Naval Research Laboratory, 1979.

Geeves, Philip. *The Dawn of Australia's Radio Broadcasting*. Alexandria, NSW: Electronics Australia/Federal, 1993.

Giblin, Helen L. *The BBC External Services: National Priorities and the Development of the Language Services 1932–1946*, Master's thesis. Houston, TX: University of Houston, Communication, 1994.

Goldsmith, Alfred N., and Austin C. Lescarboura. *This Thing Called Broadcasting*. New York: Henry Holt, 1930.

Gorham, Maurice. *Forty Years of Irish Broadcasting*. Dublin, Ireland: Talbot, 1967.

_____. *Sound and Fury: Twenty-One Years in the BBC*. London: Percival Marshall, 1948.

Grace, Alan. *The Link with Home: Sixty Years of Forces Radio*. London: SSVC [Services Sound and Vision Corp.], 2003.

_____. *"This Is the British Forces Network...": The Story of Forces Broadcasting in Germany*. Stroud, Glouc., England: Alan Sutton, 1996.

Grandin, Thomas. *The Political Use of the Radio*. New York: Arno and The New York Times, 1971 [reprinted from *Geneva Studies*, Vol. X, No. 3, August 1939].

Graves, Charles. *The Thin Red Lines*. London: Standard Art, undated [c. 1945].

Graves, Harold N., Jr. *War on the Short Wave*. New York: Foreign Policy Association, 1941.

Greb, Gordon, and Mike Adams. *Charles Herrold, Inventor of Radio Broadcasting*. Jefferson, NC: McFarland, 2003.

Guback, Thomas, and Steven P. Hill. *The Beginnings of Soviet Broadcasting and the Role of V. I. Lenin* [Journalism Monographs, No. 26]. Lexington, KY: Association for Education in Journalism, December 1972.

Hale, Julian. *Radio Power: Propaganda and International Broadcasting*. Philadelphia, PA: Temple University Press, 1975.

Hall, James L. *Radio Canada International: Voice of A Middle Power*. East Lansing: Michigan State University Press, 1997.

Harris, Credo Fitch. *Microphone Memoirs*. Indianapolis, IN: Bobbs-Merrill, 1937.

Harris, William Gibson. *Radio Propaganda in Latin America: A Study of Modern Propagandas in the Region of their Fiercest Competition*, Senior thesis. Princeton, NJ: Princeton University, Politics, 1939.

Hart, Justin W. *Empire of Ideas: Mass Communications and the Transformation of U.S. Foreign Relations, 1936–1953*, Ph.D. dissertation. New Brunswick, NJ: Rutgers University, 2004.

Haslach, Robert D. *Netherlands World Broadcasting*. Media, PA: Lawrence Miller, 1983.

Haslett, A. W. *Radio Round the World*. New York, NY: Macmillan, 1934.

Head, Sydney W., ed. *Broadcasting In Africa*. Philadelphia, PA: Temple University Press, 1974.

Headrick, Daniel R. *The Invisible Weapon: Telecommunications and International Politics, 1851–1945*. New York: Oxford University Press, 1991.

_____. *The Tentacles of Progress: Technology Transfer in the Age of Imperialism, 1850–1940*. New York: Oxford University Press, 1988.

Heil, Alan L., Jr. *Voice of America: A History*. New York: Columbia University Press, 2003.

de Henseler, Max. *The Hallicrafters Story, 1933–1975*. Charleston, WV: Antique Radio Club of America, 1991.

Herf, Jeffrey. *Nazi Propaganda for the Arab World*. New Haven, CT: Yale University Press, New Preface ed. 2010.

Hines, Mark *The Story of Broadcasting House: Home of the BBC*. London, England: Merrell, 2007.

History of AFRTS: The First 50 Years. Ann Arbor: University of Michigan Library [Michigan Digitization Project], 1993; and http://afrts.dodmedia.osd.mil/heritage/page.asp?pg=50-years.

The History of Broadcasting in Japan. Tokyo: History Compilation Room, Radio & TV Culture Research Institute, NHK, 1967.

History of Short Wave Broadcasting, an undated 41-page paper prepared circa 1952–53, author unidentified. The paper focuses on the history of Westinghouse shortwave broadcasting, and appears to be based on a review of documents, interviews with company employees, and personal knowledge, the author seemingly being a long-term employee who had worked for the company since the early 1920s. The paper is in the files of the Library of American Broadcasting, University of Maryland, College Park.

History of the Office of the Coordinator of Inter-American Affairs: Historical Reports on War Administration. Washington, DC: U.S. Government Printing Office, 1948.

Hitchcock, Eric. *Making Waves: Admiral Mountbatten's Radio SEAC 1945–49*. Solihull, UK: Helion, 2013.

Hobbs, Marvin. *E. H. Scott.... The Dean of DX*. Chicago: North Frontier, 1st ed. 1985; Mendon, NY: Radio Daze, 2d ed. 2002.

Hodge, Errol. *Radio Wars: Truth, Propaganda and the Struggle for Radio Australia.* Cambridge, England: Cambridge University Press, 1995.

Hook, Taffy. *The Pitcairn Islands Radio Station and Its Postal History.* Little Current, ON: Pitcairn Islands Study Group, 1992.

Horten, Gerd. *Radio Goes to War: the Cultural Politics of Propaganda During World War II.* Berkeley: University of California, 2003.

Houseman, John. *Front and Center.* New York: Simon and Schuster, 1979.

Howe, Ellic. *The Black Game: British Subversive Operations Against the Germans During the Second World War.* London: Queen Anne/Futura, 1988.

Howe, Russell Warren. *The Hunt for Tokyo Rose.* Lanham, MD: Madison, 1990.

Howeth, Capt. L. S. *History of Communications: Electronics in the United States Navy.* Washington, DC: U.S. Government Printing Office, 1963.

Huth, Arno. *Radio Today: The Present State of Broadcasting.* New York: Arno and *The New York Times,* 1971 [reprinted from *Geneva Studies,* Vol. XII, No. 6, July 1942].

Hyde, H. Montgomery. *Room 3603.* New York: Lyons, 2001 [copyright 1962].

Jensen, Peter R. *In Marconi's Footsteps, 1894 to 1920: Early Radio.* Kenthurst, NSW, Australia: Kangaroo, 1994.

Johansen, O. Lund. *Kørtbolge-Haandbog.* Copenhagen, Denmark: O. Lund Johansen, 1945.

_____. *World Radio Handbook for Listeners.* Copenhagen, Denmark: O. Lund Johansen, 1947.

Jones, Clarence W. *Radio, The New Missionary.* Chicago: Moody, 1946.

Keene, Judith. *Treason on the Airwaves: Three Allied Broadcasters on Axis Radio During World War II.* Westport, CT: Praeger, 2008.

Kenny, Mary. *Germany Calling: A Biography of William Joyce, Lord Haw-Haw.* Dublin, Ireland: New Island, 2004.

Kirby, Edward M., and Jack W. Harris. *Star-Spangled Radio.* Chicago: Ziff-Davis, 1948.

Kneitel, Tom. *Radio Station Treasury 1900–1946.* Commack, NY: CRB Research, 1986.

Kraeuter, David W. *A Bibliography of Frank Conrad.* Pittsburgh, PA: Pittsburgh Antique Radio Society Monograph 1, Pittsburgh Antique Radio Society, 3d ed. 2007.

Krugler, David F. *The Voice of America and the Domestic Propaganda Battles, 1945–1953.* Columbia: University of Missouri Press, 2000.

Krugler, David Franklin. *The Voice of America and the Republican Cold War, 1945 to 1953,* Ph.D. dissertation. Urbana: University of Illinois, History, 1997.

Krysko, Michael A. *American Radio in China.* New York: Palgrave Macmillan, 2011.

Krysko, Michael Alexander. *China Tuned Out: American Radio in East Asia, 1919–1941,* Ph.D. dissertation. Stony Brook: State University of New York, History, 2001.

Kuhn, Raymond. *The Media in France.* London: Routledge, 1995.

Landry, Robert J. *Who, What, Why Is Radio?* New York: George W. Stewart, 1942.

Lavine, Harold and James Wechsler. *War Propaganda and the United States.* New Haven, CT: Yale University Press, 1940.

Lean, E. Tangye. *Voices in the Darkness: The Story of the European Radio War.* London: Secker and Warburg, 1943.

Lent, John A., ed. *Broadcasting in Asia and the Pacific.* Philadelphia, PA: Temple University Press, 1978.

Lerner, Daniel. *Psychological Warfare Against Nazi Germany: The Sykewar Campaign, D-Day to VE-Day.* Cambridge, MA: The M.I.T. Press, 1971 (original ed., New York: George W. Stewart, 1949).

Lewis, C. A. *Broadcasting from Within.* London: George Newnes, undated (1924).

Lewis, Tom. *Empire of the Air: The Men Who Made Radio.* New York: HarperCollins, 1991.

Lichty, Lawrence W. *"The Nation's Station," A History of Radio Station WLW,* Ph.D. dissertation [three volumes]. Columbus: Ohio State University, Speech, 1964.

Lin, Pai-ting. *The Historical Development of the Republic of China's Domestic and International Broadcasting and Its Political Role,* Master's thesis. Houston, TX: University of Houston, 1996.

Listening in on the World ... New York: NBC, 1941.

Lowery, G. P. *Skelton Transmitting Station 1942 to 1998: Over Half a Century of Shortwave Broadcasting.* Written in 1990, later supplemented. http://www.bbceng.info/Operations/transmitter_ops/Reminiscences/skelton/sk1.htm.

Lucas, Richard. *Axis Sally: The American Voice of Nazi Germany.* Havertown, PA: Casemate, 2010.

Luis, William. *Culture and Customs of Cuba* (Ch. 5, "Broadcasting and Print Media"). Westport, CT: Greenwood, 2001.

Mackay, Ian K. *Broadcasting in Australia.* Melbourne, Vic., Australia: Melbourne University Press, 1957.

_____. *Broadcasting in Nigeria.* Ibadan, Nigeria: Ibadan University Press, 1964.

_____. *Broadcasting in Papua New Guinea.* Melbourne, Vic., Australia: Melbourne University Press, 1976.

Maclaurin, W. Rupert. *Invention and Innovation in the Radio Industry.* New York: Macmillan, 1949.

MacLeod, Mary K. *Whisper in the Air: Marconi, The Canada Years, 1902–1946.* Hantsport, NS: Lancelot, 1992.

Mansell, Gerard. *Let Truth Be Told: 50 Years of BBC External Broadcasting.* London: Weidenfeld and Nicolson, 1982.

The Marconi Short Wave Beam System. Pamphlet No. 242. Marconi's Wireless Telegraph, 1928. http://www.marconicalling.com/museum/html/objects/ephemera-/objects-i=808.001-t=2-n=0.html.

Marín, Amando Céspedes. *Me and Little Radio NRH.* Heredia, Costa Rica: Amando Céspedes Marín, 1931.

Martland, Peter. *Lord Haw Haw: The English Voice of Nazi Germany.* Lanham, MD: Scarecrow, 2003.

Maxwell, Allen Brewster. *Evoking Latin American Collaboration In the Second World War: A Study of the Office of the Coordinator of Inter-American Affairs (1940–1946),* Ph.D. dissertation. Medford, MA: Tufts University, Fletcher School, 1971.

Mayes, Thorn L. *Wireless Communication in the United States: The Early Development of American Radio Operating Companies.* Greenwich, RI: New England Wireless and Steam Museum, 1989.

McClure, Rusty, with David Stern and Michael A. Banks. *Crosley: Two Brothers and a Business Empire that Transformed the Nation.* Cincinnati, OH: Clerisy, 2006.

McDaniel, Drew O. *Broadcasting in the Malay World.* Norwood, NJ: Ablex, 1994.

McNeil, Bill, and Morris Wolfe. *The Birth of Radio in Canada: Signing On.* Toronto, ON: Doubleday, 1982.

Meo, L. D. *Japan's Radio War on Australia, 1941–1945.* Melbourne, Vic., Australia: Melbourne University Press, 1968.

Moore, Raymond S. *Communications Receivers, The Vacuum Tube Era: 1932–1981.* La Belle, FL: RSM Communications, 4th ed., 1997.

Morley, Patrick. *"This Is the American Forces Network."* Westport, CT: Praeger, 2001.

Morrisey, John W., ed. *The Legacies of Edwin Howard Armstrong.* Proceedings of the Radio Club of America, Vol. 64, No. 3, November 1990.

Mostert, Andre J. E., Jr. *A History of WRUL: The Walter S. Lemmon Years, 1931–1960,* Master's thesis. Salt Lake City, UT: Brigham Young University, Communications, 1969.

Murray, Jacqui. *Watching the Sun Rise: Australian Reporting of Japan, 1931 to the Fall of Singapore.* Lanham, MD: Lexington, 2004.

Murray, Robert P., ed. *The Early Development of Radio in Canada, 1901–1930.* Chandler, AZ: Sonoran, 2005.

"Nauen Sendet!— Nauen Is Broadcasting!" Commemorative Publication of Nauen Station's Presentation, April 25, 1977. Deutsche Telekom/Telefunken/Thomcast/Deutsche Welle, Germany.

Newcourt-Nowodworski, Stanley. *Black Propaganda in the Second World War.* Stroud, England: Sutton, 2005.

Nichols, Richard. *Radio Luxembourg: The Station of the Stars.* London: W. H. Allen, 1983.

O'Donoghue, David. *Hitler's Irish Voices: The Story of German Radio's Wartime Irish Service.* Belfast, Ireland: Beyond the Pale, 1998.

Orlick, Peter Blythe. *The South African Broadcasting Corporation: An Historical Survey and Contemporary Analysis,* Ph.D. dissertation. Detroit, MI: Wayne State University, 1968.

Osterman, Fred. *Shortwave Receivers Past and Present: Communications Receivers, 1942–1997.* Reynoldsburg, OH: Universal Radio Research, 3d ed. 1998.

OTC Leopoldville — Belgium Calling the World. Brussels: Radiodiffusion Nationale Belge, c. 1947.

Otero, Gustavo Docampo. *La Radio Antigua.* Barcelona, Spain: Marcombo, 2000.

Panfilov, A. *Broadcasting Pirates.* Moscow, USSR: Progress, 1981.

Parker, Everett L. *"Calling Pitcairn...": The Picairn Island Expedition of 1938 and Its Postal History.* Greenville, ME: Moosehead, 2008.

Partner, Peter. *Arab Voices: The BBC Arabic Service, 1938–1988.* London: BBC External Services, 1988.

Paulu, Burton. *Factors in the Attempts to Establish a Permanent Instrumentality for the Administration of the International Broadcasting Services of the United States,* Ph.D. dissertation. New York: New York University, Education, 1949.

Pawley, Edward. *BBC Engineering, 1922–1972.* London: BBC Publications, 1972.

Pedrick, Gale. *Battlefield Broadcasters.* London: British Forces Broadcasting Service, 1964.

_____. *Battlefield Broadcasters.* A program marking the twenty-first anniversary of the British Forces Broadcasting Service (CD, 1964).

Peterson, Adrian M. *Voice of America Relay Bases.* Box Hill, Vic.: Australian Radio DX Club, 1977 [with Updater]; also serialized in the February-June 1977, August-September 1977, and May 1978 issues of *SPEEDX.*

Pidgeon, Geoffrey. *The Secret Wireless War* (Chap. 18, "Black Propaganda," and Chap. 29, "Phil Luck, Operating with Black Propaganda"). London: UPSO, 2003.

Pirsein, Robert William. *The Voice of America: A History*

of the International Broadcasting Activities of the United States Government, 1940–1962, Ph. D. dissertation. Evanston, IL: Northwestern University, 1970; and New York: Arno, 1979.

Playfair, Giles. *Singapore Goes Off the Air.* New York: Dutton, 1943.

Potter, Simon J. *Broadcasting Empire: The BBC and the British World, 1922–1970.* Oxford, England: Oxford University Press, 2012.

Presenting A New Ambassador to Latin America to Meet a New National Need. New York: NBC, 1940.

The Psychological Warfare Division (PWD), Supreme Headquarters, Allied Expeditionary Force (SHAEF), An Account of Its Operations in the Western European Campaign, 1944–1945 (1951).

Raby, Ormond. *Radio's First Voice: The Story of Reginald Fessenden.* Toronto, ON: Macmillan, 1970.

Rankin, Nicholas. *Churchill's Wizards: The British Genius for Deception, 1914–1945.* London: Faber and Faber, 2008.

Redding, Jerry Ray. *American Private International Broadcasting: What Went Wrong and Why,* Ph.D. dissertation. Columbus: Ohio State University, Mass Communication, 1977.

Reid, Colin. *Action Stations: A History of Broadcasting House.* London: Robson, 1987.

Reith, J. C. W. *Broadcast Over Britain.* London: Hodder and Stoughton, 1924.

_____. *Into the Wind.* London, England: Hodder and Stoughton, 1949.

The Reminiscences of Donald G. Little. New York: Oral History Research Office, Columbia University, 1984 [microfiche]), including three appendices: a Westinghouse publicity release about Dr. Frank Conrad, a Westinghouse history of radio broadcasting and KDKA, and "The Story of Short Waves," an address delivered by Conrad in 1940. The Conrad address can also be found in *Science,* New Series, Vol. 91, No. 2354, February 9, 1940, pp. 131–132.

Renier, Olive, and Vladimir Rubenstein. *Assigned to Listen: The Evesham Experience 1939–43.* London: BBC External Services, 1986.

"The Representative in Great Britain of the Freedom Station." *Freedom Calling! The Story of the Secret German Radio.* London: Frederick Muller Ltd., 2d ed. 1939.

Ribeiro, Nelson Costa. *BBC Broadcasts to Portugal in World War II.* Lewiston, ME: Edwin Mellen, 2011.

Rigby, C. A. *The War on the Short Waves.* London: Lloyd Cole, 1944.

Robbins, Jane. *Tokyo Calling: Japanese Overseas Radio Broadcasting, 1937–1945.* Firenze, Italy: European Press Academic, 2001.

Roberts, Beth Alene. *United States Propaganda Warfare in Latin America, 1938–1942,* Ph. D. dissertation. Los Angeles: University of Southern California, Political Science, 1943.

Rolo, Charles J. *Radio Goes to War.* New York: Putnam, 1942.

The Romance of Short Waves and Television. Boston, MA: Shortwave and Television Corp., 3rd ed. 1931.

Roop, Joseph E., *Foreign Broadcast Information Service: History, Pt. I: 1941–1947.* Washington, DC: CIA, 1969 [released 2009], https://www.cia.gov/library/center-for-the-study-of-intelligence/csi-publications/books-and-monographs/foreign-broadcast-information-service/index.html.

Rosenthal, Eric. *You Have Been Listening....* Cape Town, South Africa: Purnell, 1974.

Rudel, Anthony. *Hello, Everybody! The Dawn of American Radio*. Orlando, FL: Harcourt, 2008.

Rybicki, Frank. *The Rhetorical Dimensions of Radio Propaganda in Nazi Germany, 1933–1945*, Ph.D. dissertation. Pittsburgh, PA: Duquesne University, Communication, 2004.

Saerchinger, César. *Hello America!* Boston: Houghton Mifflin, 1938; published in England as César Saerchinger, *Voice of Europe* (London: Victor Gollancz, 1938).

Salwen, Michael B. *Radio and Television in Cuba: The Pre-Castro Era*. Ames: Iowa State University Press, 1994.

Schmeckebier, Laurence F. *The Federal Radio Commission: Its History, Activities and Organization*. Washington, DC: Brookings Institution, 1932.

Schofield, William G. *Treason Trail*. Chicago: Rand McNally, 1964.

Schubert, Paul. *The Electric Word: The Rise of Radio*. New York: Macmillan, 1928.

Schwoch, James. *The American Radio Industry and Its Latin American Activities, 1900–1939*. Urbana and Chicago: University of Illinois Press, 1990.

Selwyn, Francis. *Hitler's Englishman: The Crime of Lord Haw-Haw*. London, England: Penguin, 1993.

Shacklady, Norman, and Martin Ellen. *On Air: A History of BBC Transmission*. Orpington, Kent, England: Wavechange, 2003.

Short, K. R. M., ed. *Film and Radio Propaganda in World War II*. Knoxville: University of Tennessee Press, 1983.

Short-Wave Transatlantic Radio-Telephony. Reprinted from Bell Laboratories Record, October 1929.

Shulman, Holly Cowan. *The Voice of America: Propaganda and Democracy, 1941–1945*. Madison: University of Wisconsin Press, 1990.

_____. *The Voice of Victory: The Development of American Propaganda and the Voice of America, 1920–1942*, Ph.D. dissertation. College Park: University of Maryland, 1984.

Shurick, E. P. J. *The First Quarter Century of American Broadcasting*. Kansas City, MO: Midland, 1946.

Sidel, Michael Kent. *A Historical Analysis of American Short Wave Broadcasting, 1916–1942*, Ph.D. dissertation. Evanston, IL: Northwestern University, Speech, 1976.

Siegel, Arthur. *Radio Canada International: History and Development*. Oakville, ON: Mosaic, 1996.

Siepmann, Charles. *Radio In Wartime* [No. 26, "America In A World At War"]. New York: Oxford University Press, 1942.

Simhi, Kohava. *The Historical Development of Kol Israel As An International Broadcaster*, Master's thesis. Houston, Texas: University of Houston, Communication, 1993.

Singleton, Frank. *London Calling the World* ["Britain Advances"]. London: Longmans Green, 1943.

Sington, Derrick, and Arthur Weidenfeld. *The Goebbels Experiment: A Study of the Nazi Propaganda Machine*. New Haven, CT: Yale University Press, 1943.

Slotten, Hugh R. *Radio and Television Regulation: Broadcast Technology in the United States, 1920–1960*. Baltimore, MD: John Hopkins University Press, 2000.

Smulyan, Susan. *Selling Radio: The Commercialization of American Broadcasting, 1920–1934*. Washington, DC: Smithsonian Institution, 1994.

Soley, Lawrence. *Free Radio: Electronic Civil Disobediance*. Boulder, CO: Westview, 1999.

_____. *Radio Warfare: OSS and CIA Subversive Propaganda*. New York: Praeger, 1989.

_____, and John S. Nichols. *Clandestine Radio Broadcasting: A Study of Revolutionary and Counterrevolutionary Electronic Communication*. New York: Praeger, 1987.

Sorenson, Thomas C. *The Word War: The Story of American Propaganda*. New York: Harper and Row, 1968.

Spahr, Lisa L. *World War II Radio Heroes: Letters of Compassion*. Pittsburgh, PA: Spahr Consulting, 2008.

Sparling, Earl. *America Calling All People*. New York: NBC, 1941 (with 1942 addenda [undated]).

Steckler, Larry. *Hugo Gernsback: A Man Well Ahead of His Time*. Marana, AZ: Poptronix, 2007.

Sterling, Christopher H., and John Michael Kittross. *Stay Tuned: A History of American Broadcasting*. Mahwah, NJ: Erlbaum, 3d ed. 2002.

Sterling, Christopher H., and Michael C. Keith. *Sounds of Change: A History of FM Broadcasting in America*. Chapel Hill: University of North Carolina Press, 2008.

Stoneman, Timothy H. B. *Capturing Believers: American International Radio, Religion, and Reception, 1931–1970*, Ph.D. dissertation. Atlanta: Georgia Institute of Technology, School of History, Technology and Society, 2006.

The Story of the First Trans-Atlantic Short Wave Message: Proceedings of the Radio Club of America, Inc.—1BCG Commemorative Issue. New York: Radio Club of America, October 1950.

Street, Seán. *Crossing the Ether: British Public Service Radio and Commercial Competition 1922–1945*. Eastleigh, England: John Libbey, 2006.

Tarrant, D. R. *Marconi's Miracle: The Wireless Bridging of the Atlantic*. St. John's, NL: Flanker, 2001.

Taylor, Albert Hoyt. *Radio Reminiscences: A Half Century*. Washington, DC: Naval Research Laboratory, 1948 (reprinted 1960).

Taylor, Doreen. *A Microphone and a Frequency: Forty Years of Forces Broadcasting*. London: Heinemann, 1983.

Taylor, Philip M. *British Propaganda in the Twentieth Century: Selling Democracy*. Edinburgh, Scotland: Edinburgh University Press, 1999.

_____. *The Projection of Britain: British Overseas Publicity and Propaganda, 1919–1939*. Cambridge, England: Cambridge University Press, 1981.

Terry, Sanford T. *The Apache Project: How News of General MacArthur's Victories Reached America*. Unpublished, 1989.

These You Can Hear. London: Amalgamated Short Wave 1947.

Thompson, Dorothy. *Listen, Hans*. Cambridge, MA: Riverside, 1942.

Thomson, Charles A. H. *Overseas Information Service of the United States Government*. Washington, DC: Brookings Institution, 1948.

Thomson, Malcolm M. *The Beginning of the Long Dash: A History of Timekeeping in Canada*. Toronto, ON: University of Toronto Press, 1978.

Tidy, Roger. *Hitler's Radio War*. London: Robert Hale, 2011.

Tomalin, Norman. *Daventry Calling the World*. Whitby, North Yorkshire, England: Caedmon of Whitby Publishers, 1998; and at http://www.bbceng.info/Books-/dx-world/dx-calling-the-world-2008a.pdf.

Tomlinson, John D. *International Control of Radiocommunications*. New York: Arno, 1979 [reprint of Ann Arbor, MI: J. W. Edwards, 1945].

Toubia, Nebil B. *A Descriptive History of International Broadcasting From Its Origins to 1932*, Master's thesis. Bowling Green, KY: Bowling Green State University, 1982.

Ugusa, Isao. *Broadcasting Stations of Vietnam.* Kobe, Japan: DX Front Line, 1985.

Usher, Len, and Hugh Leonard. *This Is Radio Fiji: Twenty-Five Years of Service, 1954–1979.* Suva, Fiji: Information Services South Pacific (for Fiji Broadcasting Commission), 1979.

Vaughan, David. *Battle for the Airwaves: Radio and the 1938 Munich Crisis.* Prague, Czechoslovakia: Radioservis and Cook, 2008.

Vipond, Mary. *Listening In: The First Decade of Canadian Broadcasting, 1922–1932.* Montreal, QC: McGill-Queen's University Press, 1992.

Walker, Andrew. *A Skyful of Freedom: 60 Years of the BBC World Service.* London: Broadside, 1992.

Wallis, Keith. *And the World Listened: The Biography of Captain Leonard F. Plugge, A Pioneer of Commercial Radio.* Tiverton, Devon, England: Kelly, 2008.

Wander, Tim. *2MT Writtle: The Birth of British Broadcasting.* Sandy, Bedfordshire, England: Authors Online, 2010.

War Department (History Project, Strategic Services Unit, Office of the Asst. Secretary of War). *War Report of the OSS (Office of Strategic Services).* New York: Walker, 1976 [report prepared in 1947].

Wasburn, Philo C. *Broadcasting Propaganda: International Radio Broadcasting and the Construction of Political Reality.* Westport, CT: Praeger, 1992.

Wasserstein, Bernard. *Secret War In Shanghai.* Boston: Houghton Mifflin, 1999.

Webb, Jeff A. *The Voice of Newfoundland.* Toronto, ON: University of Toronto Press, 2008.

Weightman, Gavin. *Signor Marconi's Magic Box.* Cambridge, MA: Da Capo, 2003.

Weir, E. Austin. *The Struggle for National Broadcasting in Canada.* Toronto, ON: McClelland and Stewart, 1965.

Wenaas, Eric P. *Radiola: The Golden Age of RCA, 1919–1929.* Chandler, AZ: Sonoran, 2007.

West, W. J. *Truth Betrayed.* London: Duckworth, 1987.

Williams, Manuela A. *Mussolini's Propaganda Abroad: Subversion in the Mediterranean and the Middle East, 1935–1940.* New York: Routledge, 2006.

Williamson, Tom. *Across Time — And Space: Listening for Sixty Years From Four Continents.* Hamilton, ON: Tom Williamson, 1998 [distributed by Ontario DX Association].

Winkler, Allan M. *The Politics of Propaganda: The Office of War Information, 1942–1945.* New Haven, CT: Yale University Press, 1978.

Winter, William. *Voice from America: A Broadcaster's Diary 1941–1944.* Pasig, Metro Manila, Philippines: Anvil, 1994.

Wood, James. *History of International Broadcasting.* Stevenage, Herts., England: Peter Peregrinus, 1992.

_____. *History of International Broadcasting, Vol. 2.* Stevenage, Herts., England: Institution of Electrical Engineers, 2000.

Xie, Shuying. *People's Republic of China's International Broadcasting: History, Structure, Policy and Politics,* Master's thesis. Houston, TX: University of Houston, 1992.

Yang, Daqing. *Technology of Empire: Telecommunications and Japanese Expansion in Asia, 1883–1945.* Cambridge, MA: Harvard University Asia Center, 2010.

Articles

Adams, Mike. "The Race for Radiotelephone: 1900–1920." *AWA Review,* Vol. 10 (1996), p. 79.

Aitken, Hugh G. J. "Allocating the Spectrum: The Origins of Radio Regulation." *Technology and Culture,* Vol. 35, No. 4 (October 1994), p. 686.

Alisky, Marvin. "Early Mexican Broadcasting." *The Hispanic American Historical Review,* Vol. 34, No. 4 (November 1954), p. 513.

"American Short Wave Broadcasting: What's Wrong with It?" *Short Wave and Television,* September 1938, p. 265.

Armour, Charles. "The BBC and the Development of Broadcasting in British Colonial Africa 1946–1956." *African Affairs,* Vol. 83, No. 332 (July 1984), p. 359.

Arms, W. T. "Short-Wave Review" [1942]. *The New York Times,* December 27, 1942, p. X12.

_____. "The Short-Wave Year in Review" [1941]. *The New York Times,* January 4, 1942, p. X12.

Arsenian, Seth. "Wartime Propaganda in the Middle East." *The Middle East Journal,* Vol. 2, No. 4 (October 1948), p. 417.

Auberjonois, Fernand. "Letters from France." *The New York Times,* May 3, 1942, p. SM12.

Bacon, Christopher. "Commemorating the 75th Anniversary of Radio Central." *AWA Review,* Vol. 10 (1996), p. 151.

Bale, B. J. "The BBC Shortwave Station Daventry," in J. M. Frost, ed., *1976 World Radio TV Handbook.* Hvidovre, Denmark: Billboard, 1976, p. 16 ("Listen to the World").

Barbour, Nevill, "Broadcasting to the Arab World: Arabic Transmissions from the B.B.C. and Other Non-Arab Stations," *Middle East Journal,* Vol. 5 (Winter 1951), p. 57.

Barbour, Philip L. "International Radio in the Three Americas." *The Inter-American Quarterly,* Vol. 2, No. 1 (January 1940), p. 32.

_____. "Open Questions in Inter-American Broadcasting." *Annals of the American Academy of Political and Social Science,* Vol. 213, "New Horizons in Radio" (January 1941), p. 116.

_____. "Short-Wave Broadcasting and Latin America." *Bulletin of the Pan American Union,* Vol. 7, No. 10 (October 1937), p. 739.

Baudino, Joseph E., and John M. Kittross. "Broadcasting's Oldest Stations: An Examination of Four Claimants." *Journal of Broadcasting,* Vol. 21, No. 1 (Winter 1977), p. 61.

Bayles, William D. "London Calling — Goebbels Jamming." *The Saturday Evening Post,* April 11, 1942, p. 9.

Becker, Howard. "The Nature and Consequences of Black Propaganda." *American Sociological Review,* Vol. 14, No. 2 (April 1949), p. 221.

Benjmain, Louise. "Working It Out Together: Radio Policy from Hoover to the Radio Act of 1927." *Journal of Broadcasting and Electronic Media,* Vol. 42, No. 2 (Spring 1998), p. 221.

Bent, Silas. "International Broadcasting." *The Public Opinion Quarterly,* Vol. 1, No. 3 (July 1937), p. 117.

Benton, William. "Self-Portrait — By Uncle Sam." *The New York Times,* December 2, 1945, p. SM7.

Berkov, Robert H. "China's Millions Twist the Dials." *Modern Mechanix,* June 1937, p. 76.

Boyd, Douglas A. "Hebrew-Language Clandestine Radio Broadcasting During the British Palestine Mandate." *Journal of Radio Studies,* Vol. 6, No. 1 (1999), p. 101.

_____. "The Pre-History of the Voice of America." *Public Telecommunications Review,* Vol. 2, No. 6 (December 1974), p. 38.

_____. "Sharq al-Adna/The Voice of Britain." *Gazette: The International Journal for Communication Studies,* Vol. 65, No. 6 (2003), p. 443.

Brannigan, Alice. "Broadcasting From the Outlaw Empire" [Manchuria]. *Popular Communications,* April 2000, p. 16.

_____. "KFKX: A Most Historic Broadcast Station." *Popular Communications,* October 1998, p. 14.

_____. "World's First Major Shortwave Broadcaster" [PCJ]. *Popular Communications,* November 1997, p. 16.

Brown, F. J. "The Story of Broadcasting in England." *Radio Broadcast,* June 1925, p. 175.

Brown, W. J. "The Inside Story of the British Broadcasting Experiments." *Radio Broadcast,* June 1924, p. 115.

Browne, Donald R. "Going International: How BBC Began Foreign Language Broadcasting." *Journalism Quarterly,* Vol. 60, No. 3 (Autumn 1983), p. 423.

_____. "International Commercial Radio Broadcasting: Nation Shall Speak Profit Unto Nation." *Journal of Broadcasting and Electronic Media,* Vol. 30, No. 2 (Spring 1986), p. 195.

_____. "Radio Normandie and the IBC Challenge to the BBC Monopoly." *Historical Journal of Film, Radio and Television,* Vol. 5, No. 1 (1985), p. 3.

_____. "The World in the Pentagon's Shadow." *Educational Broadcasting Review,* Vol. 5, No. 2 (April 1971), p. 31.

Burton, John. "Short-Wave Radio and the Postwar World," in *Writers' Congress* [Proceedings of the conference held on October 1943 under the sponsorship of the Hollywood Writers' Mobilization and the University of California]. Berkeley: University of California Press, 1944, p. 188.

Callender, Harold. "The Voice of America Echoes Widely." *The New York Times,* November 15, 1942, p. SM10.

Caride, Col. José Luis Goberna. "Broadcasting in the Spanish Civil War (Military Engineers Work in the Conflict)," in *Telecommunications Conference (HISTELCON), 2010 Second IEEE Region 8 Conference on the History of Telecommunications (Madrid, Spain).* Institute of Electrical and Electronics Engineers (IEEE), November 2010, p. 131.

Carlton, Leonard. "Voice of America: The Overseas Radio Bureau." *The Public Opinion Quarterly,* Vol. 7, No. 1 (Spring 1943), p. 46.

Cary, William H., Jr. "England's Venture Into Broadcasting." *Radio Broadcast,* July 1924, p. 191.

Cawte, Mary. "Making Radio into a Tool for War." http://www.bmartin.cc/pubs/peace/96Cawte.pdf.

Chamberlain, A. B. "CBS International Broadcast Facilities." *Proceedings of the I.R.E.,* Vol. 30, No. 3 (March 1942), p. 118.

Church, George F. "Short Waves and Propaganda." *The Public Opinion Quarterly,* Vol. 3, No. 2 (April 1939), p. 209.

Clark, Beresford. "The BBC's External Services." *International Affairs* [Royal Institute of International Affairs], Vol. 35, No. 2 (April 1959), p. 170.

Clements, Robert J. "Foreign Language Broadcasting of 'Radio Boston.'" *The Modern Language Journal,* Vol. 27, No. 3 (March 1943), p. 175.

Codel, Martin. "How to Wage War on the Shortwave Front." *Broadcasting,* October 5, 1942, p. 12.

Colton, F. Barrows. "Winged Words—New Weapon of War." *National Geographic Magazine,* Vol. LXXXII, No. 5 (November 1942), p. 662.

Cones, Harold, and John Bryant. "How Zenith and SW Transformed the Arctic and Amateur Radio!" *Monitoring Times,* December 2006, p. 13.

Conrad, Frank. "Short-Wave Radio Broadcasting." *Proceedings of the Institute of Radio Engineers,* Vol. 12, No. 6 (December 1924), p. 723.

Cramer, Gisela. "The Office of Inter-American Affairs and the Latin American Mass Media, 1940–1946." *Research Reports from the Rockefeller Archive Center,* Pt. I, Fall/Winter 2001, p. 14; Pt. II, Fall 2002, p. 14.

_____. "The Rockefeller Foundation and Pan American Radio," in William J. Buxton, ed., *Patronizing the Public: American Philanthropy's Transformation of Culture, Communication, and the Humanities.* Lanham, MD: Lexington, 2009, p. 77.

Crossman, R. H. S. "Psychological Warfare." *The Journal of the Royal United Service Institution* [U.K.], Vol. XCVII, No. 587 (August 1952), p. 319.

Crowell, Chester T. "Dogfight on the Air Waves." *The Saturday Evening Post,* May 21, 1938, p. 23.

Davies, Alan. "The First Radio War: Broadcasting in the Spanish Civil War." *Historical Journal of Film, Radio and Television,* Vol. 19, No. 4 (1999), p. 473.

Davis, H. P. "The Early History of Broadcasting in the United States," in *The Radio Industry: The Story of Its Development.* Chicago: A. W. Shaw, 1928, p. 189.

Deihl, E. Roderick. "South of the Border: The NBC and CBS Radio Networks and the Latin American Venture, 1930–1942." *Communication Quarterly,* Vol. 25, No. 4 (Fall 1977), p. 2.

DeWald, Erich. "Taking to the Waves: Vietnamese Society Around the Radio in the 1930s." *Modern Asian Studies,* Vol. 46, Special Issue 1 (January 2012), p. 143, http://www.viet-studies.info/VN_Radio_1930. PDF.

de Wolf, Francis Colt. "The Cairo Telecommunication Conferences." *American Journal of International Law,"* Vol. 32, No. 3 (July 1938), p. 562.

_____. "Telecommunications in the New World." *Yale Law Journal,* Vol. 55, No. 5 (August 1946), p. 1281.

Doherty, Martin. "Black Propaganda by Radio: The German Concordia Broadcasts to Britain, 1940–1941." *Historical Journal of Film, Radio and Television,* Vol. 14, No. 2 (1994), p. 167.

Dreher, Carl. "How the Wasteland Began: The Early Days of Radio." *The Atlantic Monthly,* February 1966, p. 53.

Dunlap, Orrin E., Jr. "Broadcasts of Good-Will." *The New York Times,* November 29, 1936, p. X12.

_____. "From Garage to Skyscraper" [KDKA]. *The New York Times,* November 5, 1933, p. X11.

_____. "Singing Down to Rio." *The New York Times,* December 11, 1938, p. 200.

Durant, Henry, and Ruth Durant. "Lord Haw-Haw of Hamburg: His British Audience." *The Public Opinion Quarterly,* Vol. 4, No. 3 (September 1940), p. 443.

Forman, Harrison. "The Voice of China." *Collier's,* June 17, 1944, p. 14.

Furnas, J. C. "The War of Lies and Laughs—The Story of Radio's 24-Hour-A-Day Word Battle." *The Saturday Evening Post,* February 3, 1940, p. 16.

Gaskill, Gordon. "Voice of Victory." *The American Magazine,* December 1942, p. 35.

"Government to Assume Control of All Short Wave Radio Tonight." *The New York Times,* October 31, 1942, p. 1.

Graves, Harold N., Jr. "European Radio and the War." *Annals of the American Academy of Political and Social Science*, Vol. 213 ["New Horizons in Radio"] (January 1941), p. 75.

_____. "Lord Haw-Haw of Hamburg: The Campaign Against Britain." *The Public Opinion Quarterly*, Vol. 4, No. 3 (September 1940), p. 429.

Greb, Gordon B. "The Golden Anniversary of Broadcasting." *Journal of Broadcasting*, Vol. 3, No. 1 (Winter 1958–59), p. 3.

Green, Arthur J. "Getting the Most Out of the Short Waves." *Radio News*, September 1933, p. 142.

Griset, Pascal. "Innovation and Radio Industry in Europe During the Interwar Period," in François Caron, Paul Erker and Wolfram Fischer, *Innovations in the European Economy Between the Wars*. Berlin, Germany: Walter de Gruyter, 1995.

Guha, Manosij. "Egmore to Aligarh: Indian Radio's 78 Years," in Lawrence Magne, ed., *Passport to World Band Radio*. Penn's Park, PA: International Broadcasting Services, 2002, p. 12.

_____. "'This Is All India Radio,'" in Lawrence Magne, ed., *Passport to World Band Radio*. Penn's Park, PA: International Broadcasting Services, 2002, p. 26.

Guy, Raymond F. "International Beams." *Scientific American*, November 1941, p. 268.

_____. "An International Broadcasting System." *RCA Review*, July 1938, p. 20.

_____. "NBC's International Broadcasting System." *RCA Review*, July 1941, p. 12.

Hadlow, Martin. "The Mosquito Network: American Military Broadcasting in the South-West Pacific 1944–46," in Peter Dennis and Jeffrey Grey, *The Military and the Media: The 2008 Chief of Army Military History Conference*. Loftus, NSW, Australia: Australian Military History, 2008, p. 74.

_____. "The Mosquito Network: American Military Radio in the Solomon Islands During World War II." *Journal of Radio Studies*, Vol. 11, No. 1 (2004), p. 73.

Hajkowski, Thomas. "The BBC, the Empire, and the Second World War." *Historical Journal of Film, Radio & Television*, Vol. 22, No. 2 (2002), p. 135.

Hale, William Harlan. "Big Noise in Little Luxembourg." *Harper's Magazine*, April 1946, p. 377.

Hallborg, H. E., L. A. Briggs and C. W. Hansell. "Short-Wave Commercial Long-Distance Communication." *Proceedings of the Institute of Radio Engineers*, Vol. 15, No. 6 (July 1927), p. 467.

Halper, Donna L., and Christopher H. Sterling. "Fessenden's Christmas Eve Broadcast: Reconsidering an Historic Event." *AWA Review*, Vol. 19 (2006), p. 119.

Harbord, James G. "Radio and the Americas." *Bulletin of the Pan American Union*, Vol. 74 (September 1940), p. 626.

Harris, E. T. Buck. "Short-Wave Broadcasting in the Pacific Basin," in *Writers' Congress* [Proceedings of the Conference held on October 1943 under the sponsorship of the Hollywood Writers' Mobilization and the University of California]. Berkeley: University of California Press, 1944, p. 175.

Headrick, Daniel R. "Shortwave Radio and Its Impact on International Telecommunications Between the Wars." *History and Technology*, Vol. 11 (1994), p. 21.

Herman, Steven L. "The Evolution of U.S. Government-Funded External Broadcasting: From the Dawn of Broadcasting to 1948." February 2011. http://www.academia.edu/542000/The_Evolution_of_U.S._-

Government-Funded_External_Broadcasting_From_the_dawn_of_broadcasting_to_1948.

Hitchcock, Eric. "Radio SEAC's Transmitters." *Short Wave Magazine* [UK], October 2000, p. 45.

Hulten, Charles M. "How the OWI Operates Its Overseas Propaganda Machine." *Journalism Quarterly*, Vol, 19, No. 4 (December 1942), p. 349.

Hutchens, John K. "'This Is America Speaking —.'" *The New York Times*, May 10, 1942, p. SM10.

Jensen, Don. "Lord Haw Haw's Secret Nazi Stations." *Popular Communications*, December 1983, p. 50.

_____. "South Pole Calling!" *Popular Communications*, January 1985, p. 37.

_____. "Tom Delmer and Britain's 'Black' Radio." *Popular Communications*, May 1984, p. 42.

Jolly, Stephen. "Ungentlemanly Warfare: A Reassessment of British Black Propaganda Operations 1941–1945." *Falling Leaf: The Journal of the Psywar Society*, Pt. I, No. 171 (Winter 2001), p. 148; Pt. II, No. 172 (Spring 2001), p. 23.

Kaempffert, Waldemar. "Electric Fingers that Span the World." *The New York Times*, August 6, 1933, p. SM6

Keene, Judith. "Japanese Overseas Broadcasting and Allied Prisoners of War During WW II," in Sianan Healy, Bruce Berryman and David Goodman, eds., *Radio in the World: Papers from the 2005 Melbourne Radio Conference*. Melbourne, Australia: RMIT, 2005, p. 276.

Kenyon, Mark. "Black Propaganda." *After the Battle*, No. 75 (1992), p. 8.

Kranz, Henry B. "War on the Short Wave." *Nation*, February 3, 1940, p. 123.

Kruse, S. "Exploring 100 Meters." *QST*, March 1923, p. 12.

Krysko, Michael A. "Homeward Bound: Shortwave Broadcasting and American Mass Media in East Asia on the Eve of the Pacific War." *Pacific Historical Review*, Vol. 74, No. 4 (November 2005), p. 511.

Landry, Robert J. "The Impact of OWI on Broadcasting." *The Public Opinion Quarterly*, Vol. 7, No. 1 (Spring 1943), p. 111.

Lee, Bartholomew. "Marconi's Transatlantic Triumph — A Skip Into History." *AWA Review*, Vol. 13 (2000), p. 81.

_____. "Radio Spies: Episodes in the Ether Wars." *AWA Review*, Vol. 15 (2002), pp. 7.

_____, Joe Craig and Keith Matthew. "The Marconi Beacon Experiment of 2006–07." *AWA Review*, Vol. 21 (2008), p. 1–22.

LeRoy, Howard S. "Treaty Regulation of International Radio and Short Wave Broadcasting." *American Journal of International Law*, Vol. 32, No. 4 (October 1938), p. 719.

Lewis, Christopher. "The Voice of America." *The New Republic*, June 25, 1945, p. 864.

Lilley, George. "VK2ME–VK3ME." *Radio News*, June 1934, p. 729.

Lin, Chua Ai. "'The Modern Magic Carpet': Wireless Radio in Interwar Colonial Singapore." *Modern Asian Studies*, Vol. 46, Special Issue 1 (January 2012), p. 167.

Little, D. G., and F. Falknor. "Radio KFKX, Repeating Station at Hastings." *Radio Journal*, March 1924, p. 111.

MacDonald, Callum A. "Radio Bari: Italian Wireless Propaganda in the Middle East and British Countermeasures, 1934–38." *Middle East Studies*, Vol. XIII (May 1977), p. 195.

Marconi, Guglielmo. "Radio Communication." *Proceedings of the Institute of Radio Engineers*, Vol. 16, No. 1 (January 1928), p. 40.

_____. "Will 'Beam' Stations Revolutionize Radio?" *Radio Broadcast*, July 1925, p. 323.

Margry, Karel. "The Capture of William Joyce." *After the Battle,* No. 136 (2007), p. 3.

Masaharu, Sato, and Barak Kushner. "'Negro Propaganda Operations': Japan's Short-Wave Radio Broadcasts for World War II Black Americans." *Historical Journal of Film, Radio and Television,* Vol. 19, No. 1 (1999), p. 5.

Menefee, Selden C. "Japan's Psychological War." *Social Forces,* Vol. 21, No. 4 (May 1943), p. 425.

Mercado, Stephen C. "FBIS Against the Axis, 1941–1945." https://www.cia.gov/library/center-for-the-study-of-intelligence/csi-publications/csi-studies/studies/fall_winter_2001/article04.html#_ftn10.

Minden, Michael. "Satire as Propaganda: Brecht's 'Deutsche Satiren' for the Deutscher Freiheitsender," in Ronald Speirs, ed., *Brecht's Poetry of Political Exile.* Cambridge, England: Cambridge University Press, 2000, p. 100.

Moore, Don, "Ice Cold Radio: Broadcasting and the Byrd Expeditions to Antarctica." *Monitoring Times,* January 2000, p. 14.

_____. "The Unique Story of TI4NRH." *Monitoring Times,* March 1993, p. 18.

Ogilvie, John W. G. "Inter-American Short-Wave Radio." *World Affairs,* Vol. 108, No. 2 (June 1945), p. 107.

_____. "The Potentialities of Inter-American Radio." *Public Opinion Quarterly,* Vol. 9, No. 1 (Spring 1945), p. 19.

O'Neal, James E. "The United States Enters International Broadcasting: A Tale of Two Unusual Radio Stations" [Bethany and Delano]. *AWA Review,* Vol. 21 (2008), p. 233.

Paley, William S. "International Broadcasting: Now and in the Future." *Annals of the American Academy of Political and Social Science,* Vol. 150 (Economies of World Peace, July 1930), p. 40.

_____. "Radio Turns South." *Fortune,* April 1941, p. 77.

Perkins, Capt. O. D., and A. David Middleton. "Signal Corps Radio Relay in North Africa." *QST,* September 1945, p. 11.

Peterson, Adrian. "O Canada!— Independent Shortwave Broadcasting in Canada." *Monitoring Times,* Pt. I, April 1995, p. 20; Pt. II, May 1995, p. 24.

Pfau, Ann Elizabeth. *Miss Yourlovin* (Chap. 5, "The Legend of Tokyo Rose"). http://www.gutenberg-e.org/pfau/index.html.

_____, and David Hochfelder. "'Her Voice a Bullet': Imaginary Propaganda and the Legendary Broadcasters of World War II," in Susan Strasser and David Suisman, eds., *Sound In the Age of Mechanical Reproduction.* Philadelphia: University of Pennsylvania Press, 2010, p. 47.

Phillips, Cabell. "G-Men of the Airwaves." *The New York Times,* September 14, 1941, p. SM9.

_____. "War of the Air Waves." *The New York Times,* December 28, 1941, p. SM12.

Phipps, Steven P. "The Commercial Development of Short Wave Radio in the United States, 1920–1926." *Historical Journal of Film, Radio and Television,* Vol. 11, No. 3 (1991), p. 215.

Pirsein, Robert W. "An International Radio History ... the VOA." *Foreign Service Journal,* Vol. 44 (February 1967), p. 23.

Price, Clair. "Europe Wages a War of Electric Words." *The New York Times,* September 10, 1933, p. SM6.

Pronay, Nicholas, and Philip M. Taylor. "'An Improper Use of Broadcasting ...'— The British Government and Clandestine Radio Propaganda Operations Against Germany During the Munich Crisis and After." *Jour-nal of Contemporary History,* Vol. 19, No. 3 (July 1984), p. 357.

Rabe, Robert A. "Selling the Shortwaves: Commercial Shortwave Broadcasting to Latin America and the Limits of the 'American System.'" *American Journalism,* Vol. 24, No. 4 (Winter 2007), p. 127. (Rabe presented a predecessor paper of like title at the 86th Annual Conference of the Association for Education in Journalism and Mass Communication in 2003.)

Read, Oliver. "Foreign Broadcast Intelligence Service." *Radio News,* January 1945, p. 25.

_____. "Hams in the FBIS." *QST,* January 1945, p. 34.

Reeks, W. H. "Short-Wave DX Reception." *Radio News,* Pt. I, March 1933, p. 523; Pt. II, May 1933, p. 664.

Rhine, Larry. "Bridge of Words," in *Writers' Congress* [Proceedings of the conference held in October 1943 under the sponsorship of the Hollywood Writers' Mobilization and the University of California]. Berkeley, CA: University of California Press, 1944, p. 182.

Robbins, Jane. "Presenting Japan: The Role of Overseas Broadcasting by Japan During the Manchurian Incident, 1931–7." *Japan Forum,* Vol. 13, No. 1 (2001), p. 41.

Roberts, Walter R. "The Voice of America — Origins and Recollections." *American Diplomacy,* http://www.unc.edu/depts/diplomat/item/2009/1012/fsl/roberts_voice.html.

Robertson, E. D. "British Broadcasting for Asia." *Asian Affairs,* Vol. 2, Issue 1 (1971), p. 34.

Rodgers, W. W. "Broadcasting Complete American Programs to All England." *Radio Broadcast,* March 1924, p. 359.

_____. "Is Short-Wave Relaying a Step Toward National Broadcasting Stations?" *Radio Broadcast,* June 1923, p. 119.

Rolo, Charles J. "America's Ears." *The Spectator,* March 22, 1940, p. 407.

_____, and R. Strausz-Hupé. "U.S. International Broadcasting." *Harper's Magazine,* August 1941, p. 301.

Saerchinger, Cesar. "Propaganda Poisons the European Air." *Broadcasting,* April 15, 1938, p. 20.

Salwen, Michael B. "Broadcasting to Latin America: Reconciling Industry-Government Functions in the Pre-Voice of America Era." *Historical Journal of Film, Radio and Television,* Vol. 17, No. 1 (1997), p. 67.

_____. "The Origins of CMQ: Pre-Castro Cuba's Leading Radio Network." *Historical Journal of Film, Radio and Television,* Vol. 13, No. 3 (1993), p. 315.

Sarnoff, David. "A Modern Pioneer" [Frank Conrad]. *Science,* New Series, Vol. 91, No. 2354 (February 9, 1940), p. 129.

Schneider, John. "The Newspaper of the Air: Early Experiments with Radio Facsimile." *Monitoring Times,* February 2011, p. 12.

_____. "Ultra Shortwave — America's Apex Broadcast Stations of the 1930s." *Monitoring Times,* December 2010, p. 8.

_____. "Wartime Voices— Early Shortwave Broadcasting on the West Coast." *Monitoring Times,* July 2011, p. 11.

Short, K. R. M., Namikawa Ryo and Frans Nieuwenhow. "World War II Broadcasting in the Pacific." *Historical Journal of Film, Radio and Television,* Vol. 3, No. 1 (1983), p. 51.

Shulman, Holly Cowan. "John Houseman and the Voice of America: American Foreign Propaganda on the Air." *American Studies,* Vol. 28, No. 2 (Fall 1987), p. 23.

_____. "The Voice of America, U.S. Propaganda and the Holocaust: 'I would have remembered.'" *Historical*

Journal of Film, Radio and Television, Vol. 17, No. 1 (1997), p. 91.

Sibley, Ludwell A. "Program Transmission and the Early Radio Networks." *AWA Review,* Vol. 3 (1988), p. 34.

Sivowitch, Elliot N. "A Technological Survey of Broadcasting's 'Pre-History,' 1876–1920." *Journal of Broadcasting,* Vol. XV, No. 1 (Winter 1970–71), p. 1.

Slattery, J. F. "'Oskar Zuversichtlich': A German's Response to British Radio Propaganda During World War II." *Historical Journal of Film, Radio and Television,* Vol. 12, No. 1 (1992), p. 69.

Smith, Helena Huntington. "It Pays to Listen." *Collier's,* January 30, 1943, p. 42.

Soley, Lawrence. "Radio: Clandestine Broadcasting, 1948–1967." *Journal of Communications,* Vol. 32 (Winter 1982), p. 165.

Sowersby, P. C. "Progress of the Short-Wave Art." *Short Wave Radio,* July 1934, p. 6.

Spencer, Len. "Early Canadian Radio Broadcasting." *Broadcast Engineering* [Canada], Vol. 10, No. 4 (April 1968), p. 58.

Sterling, Christopher H. "CBQ Review Essay (Part One), Overall Histories of International Radio Propaganda," and "CBQ Review Essay (Part Two), International Radio Propaganda in World War II," both in *Communication Booknotes Quarterly,* Vol. 35, No. 3 (Summer 2004), pp. 151 and 166 respectively.

Stewart, Irvin. "The International Radiotelegraph Conference of Washington." *American Journal of International Law,* Vol. 22, No. 1 (January 1928), p. 28.

_____, and Harvey B. Otterman. "Some Administrative Aspects of International Broadcasting." *Proceedings of the American Society of International Law at Its Annual Meeting (1921–1969),* Vol. 32 (April 28–30, 1938), p. 62.

Stinger, Charles J. "The Eminent Years of Powel Crosley, Jr., His Transmitters, Receivers, Products, and Broadcast Station WLW, 1921–1940." *AWA Review,* Vol. 16 (2003), p. 7.

Taishoff, Sol. "FCC Paves Way for New Broadcast Services" [with "Text of Revised FCC Rules"]. *Broadcasting,* June 1, 1936, p. 7.

Tallents, Sir Stephen. "British Broadcasting and the War." *The Atlantic Monthly,* March 1940, p. 361.

Taylor, A. Hoyt. "Radio Communication with Short Waves." *The Scientific Monthly,* Vol. 22, No. 4 (April 1926), p. 356.

Taylor, Frank J. "He Bombs Tokyo Every Day." *The Saturday Evening Post,* July 25, 1942, p. 9.

Trethowan, Sir Ian. "The BBC and International Broadcasting." A speech given by the director-general, BBC, to the Royal Overseas League, London, February 2, 1981.

"The U.S. Short Wave," *Time,* November 3, 1941, p. 54.

Van Loon, Hendrik. "WRUL — This Unique Short Wave Radio Station Sells Nothing and Builds International Good Will." *Current History,* May 1941, p. 22.

Waldron, Webb. "Democracy on the Short Waves." *Reader's Digest,* September 1941, p. 40 (condensed from *The Living Age*).

Webb, Jeff A. "VOUS — Voice of the United States: The Armed Forces Radio Service in Newfoundland." *Journal of Radio Studies,* Vol. 11, No. 1 (2004), p. 87.

Weldon, J. O. "The Early History of U.S. International Broadcasting From the Start of World War II." *IEEE Transactions on Broadcasting,* Vol. 34, No. 2 (June 1988), p. 82.

White, John W. "Propaganda War on U.S. Launched." *The New York Times,* December 4, 1938, p. 52.

Whitton, John B. "War by Radio." *Foreign Affairs,* Vol. 19, No. 3 (April 1941), p. 584.

Williams, Barry C. "Pages from the Past." Pt. I (Asia and Africa), *NNRC Bulletin,* August 1971, p. SWC-8; Pt. II (Europe and the Americas), *NNRC Bulletin,* January 1972, p. SWC-4; Pt. III (Dutch East Indies), supplied by Mr. Williams.

Wittels, David G. "Hitler's Short-Wave Rumor Factory." *The Saturday Evening Post,* November 21, 1942, p. 12.

Wolters, Larry. "The Menace of Short Wave Propaganda." *Radio News,* May 1938, p. 14.

Wulff, Fred. "A Brief, Technical History of the VOA Network." *The Old Timer's Bulletin,* November 1995, p. 28 ("The Early Years, 1940 to 1945"), p. 29 ("The Relay Station Network").

Yeang, Chen-Pang. "Scientific Fact or Engineering Specification? The U.S. Navy's Experiments on Wireless Telegraphy circa 1910." *Technology and Culture,* Vol. 45, No. 1 (January 2004), p. 1.

_____. "The Study of Long-Distance Radio-Wave Propagation, 1900–1919." *Historical Studies in the Physical and Biological Sciences,* Vol. 33, No. 2 (2003), p. 369.

_____. "When Hobbyists Were Experts: The U.S. Radio Amateurs' Long-Range Short-Wave Experiments Circa 1920." Working Paper No. 37, Program in Science, Technology and Society, MIT (Cambridge, MA: 2003), http://web.mit.edu/sts/pubs/pdfs/MIT_STS_WorkingPaper_37_Yeang.pdf.

Websites

AmericanRadioHistory.com: http://www.americanradiohistory.com

Armed Forces Network, Europe: http://www.usarmygermany.com/Sont.htm?http&&&www.usarmygermany.com/units/afneurope/usareur_afneurope.htm

BBCeng.info: http://www.bbceng.info

History of American Broadcasting: http://jeff560.tripod.com/broadcasting.html

The History of Shortwave Radio In Australia: http://bpadula.tripod.com/australiashortwave/

International Broadcast Station KGEI: 1939–1994: http://www.theradiohistorian.org/kgei.htm

Marconi Calling: http://www.marconicalling.com/

ontheshortwaves.com: http://www.ontheshortwaves.com

Patepluma Radio: http://www.patepiumaradio.com/index.html

Radio Heritage Foundation: http://www.radioheritage.net/

United States Early Radio History: http://earlyradiohistory.us/

Western Historic Radio Museum: http://www.radioblvd.com/

Periodicals

CLUB PUBLICATIONS

AWA Journal [formerly *The Old Timer's Bulletin*] (Antique Wireless Association)

The Globe Circler (International DXers Alliance)

International Short Wave Radio (International Short Wave Club)

NNRC Bulletin (Newark News Radio Club)
Short Wave Reporter (Quixote Radio Club)

OTHER RADIO AND DX PUBLICATIONS

All-Wave Radio
Broadcasting
Keller's Radio Call Book and Log
Monitoring Times
Official Short Wave Radio Magazine
Popular Communications
QST
RADEX (Radio Index)
Radio & Hobbies [Australia]
Radio Broadcast
Radio Design
Radio Guide, Movie-Radio Guide
Radio News
Short Wave Craft
Short Wave and Television
Short Wave Radio
Stevenson's Radio Bulletin
White's Radio Log
World-Radio [BBC]

Other Materials

Allied Radio, Concord Radio and Lafayette Radio catalogs
Annual Reports, Federal Communications Commission (1935–1945)
Annual Reports, Federal Radio Commission (1927–1933)
BBC Handbook [Called the *BBC Handbook* in 1928–1929; *BBC Year-Book*, 1930–1934; *BBC Annual*, 1935–1937; *BBC Handbook*, 1938–1942; *BBC Year Book*, 1943–1952; *BBC Handbook*, 1955–1987. It was not published in 1953 and 1954. The 1987 edition was the last.]
The New York Times
Radio Service Bulletins (Department of Commerce, 1915–1932)
Scott News and other E. H. Scott publications
Wavescan scripts et al. written by Dr. Adrian M. Peterson (http://www.ontheshortwaves.com/Wavescan/wavescan.html)

Index

Numbers in **bold italics** indicate pages with photographs.